Anti-Jewish Violence in Pola

Widespread anti-Jewish pogroms accompanied rebirth of Polish state-hood out of World War I and the Polish-Soviet war. William W. Hagen offers the pogroms' first scholarly account, revealing how they served as brutal stagings by ordinary people of scenarios dramatizing popular anti-Jewish fears and resentments. While scholarship on modern antisemit-ism has stressed its ideological inspiration ("print-antisemitism"), this study shows that anti-Jewish violence by perpetrators among civilians and soldiers expressed magic-infused anxieties and longings for redemp-tion from present threats and suffering ("folk-antisemitism"). Illustrated with contemporary photographs and constructed from extensive newly discovered archival sources from three continents, this is an innovative interpretation of central and eastern European history. Using extensive first-person testimonies, this work reveals gaps – but also correspon-dences – between popular attitudes and those of the political elites. The pogroms raged against the conscious will of new Poland's gover-nors, while Christians high and low sometimes sought, even success-fully, to block them.

William W. Hagen is Professor Emeritus of History at the University of California, Davis. He has published extensively, including *German History in Modern Times* (2012), which was selected as an "outstanding academic work" by the American Library Association's journal, *Choice*.

Frontispiece I. The Old Synagogue in Przemyśl (Yiddish: Pshemishl), an important Galician city on the Polish-Ukrainian ethnographic boundary, as photographed in 1905. Market sellers and buyers mingle with passers-by. The synagogue, dating to the late sixteenth century, possessed a fortress-like quality often found in the premodern Polish Commonwealth's eastern borderlands, where interconfessional wars and Cossack rebellions raged sporadically. In 1746, Jesuit academy students plundered it, destroying Torah scrolls and other sacred furnishings. Such riots, inspired or tolerated by the Catholic Church, scarred the Commonwealth's final centuries. In November 1918, anti-Jewish violence of a different character exploded.

Source: Imagno. Getty Images, 53312817.

Frontispiece II. Rzeszów (Yiddish: Raysha), a provincial city in West Galicia. This undated early twentieth-century photograph displays the Renaissance-era town hall and central square. Among the public are Austro-Hungarian military officers, traditionally clad Jews, and civilians in proletarian and bourgeois attire – or, as was often said of acculturated Jews, in "European dress." Here, in May 1919, a pogrom wave in Rzeszów's rural hinterland engulfed the city.
Source: Imagno. Getty Images, 92327429.

Anti-Jewish Violence in Poland, 1914–1920

William W. Hagen

University of California, Davis

CAMBRIDGE
UNIVERSITY PRESS

CAMBRIDGE
UNIVERSITY PRESS

University Printing House, Cambridge CB2 8BS, United Kingdom

One Liberty Plaza, 20th Floor, New York, NY 10006, USA

477 Williamstown Road, Port Melbourne, VIC 3207, Australia

314–321, 3rd Floor, Plot 3, Splendor Forum, Jasola District Centre,
New Delhi – 110025, India

79 Anson Road, #06–04/06, Singapore 079906

Cambridge University Press is part of the University of Cambridge.

It furthers the University's mission by disseminating knowledge in the pursuit of
education, learning, and research at the highest international levels of excellence.

www.cambridge.org
Information on this title: www.cambridge.org/9780521884921
DOI: 10.1017/9781139025737

First published 2018

Printed in the United States of America by Sheridan Books, Inc.

A catalogue record for this publication is available from the British Library.

Library of Congress Cataloging-in-Publication Data
Names: Hagen, William W., 1942– author.
Title: Anti-Jewish violence in Poland, 1914–1920 / William Hagen.
Description: New York, NY : Cambridge University Press, [2018] |
Includes bibliographical references and index.
Identifiers: LCCN 2017045847 | ISBN 9780521884921
Subjects: LCSH: Antisemitism – Poland – History – 20th century. |
Jews – Poland – History – 20th century. | Poland – Ethnic relations. |
Pogroms – Poland – History – 20th century.
Classification: LCC DS146.P6 H34 2018 | DDC 305.892/4043809041–dc23
LC record available at https://lccn.loc.gov/20170458471

ISBN 978-0-521-88492-1 Hardback
ISBN 978-0-521-73818-7 Paperback

And there are secret motives of conduct. A man's most open actions have a secret side to them.

That is interesting and so unfathomable!

Razumov, in Joseph Conrad's *Under Western Eyes*
(Toronto, 2010, pp. 120–21)

Pogroms surprised not only Jews, but also Poles.

They tried therefore to make excuses not only to the world, but to themselves.

Galician-born journalist Benjamin Segal, in *Allgemeine
Zeitung des Judenthums*, no. 25 (June 20, 1919)

True, they were robbed, and they live in fear of total extermination (*zupełnej zagłady*), but this inspired in them great national feeling.

Polish army intelligence report on Volhynian Poles facing
Bolshevik domination, 1919

We didn't have any books at home. Not even children's books or fairy tales. The only "fantastic" stories came from religion class. And I took them all very literally, that God sees everything, and so I felt I was always being watched. Or that dead people were in heaven right over our village. I looked for the faces of the deceased neighbors in the clouds, and I found them, too. I was worried about them when the wind picked up or when it rained or there was thunder and lightning. Then I asked myself whether "the good Lord" was punishing them, because they had to race through the sky together with the clouds.

Novelist/Nobelist Herta Müller (b. 1953), on childhood in
a German-speaking Romanian village,
in *New York Times*, July 17, 2016

The terror of the unforeseen is what the science of history hides, turning a disaster into an epic.

Philip Roth, *The Plot Against America* (New York, 2004), 114.

For not forever will the poor man be forgotten, the hope of the lowly not lost forever.

Arise, O Lord, let not man flaunt his strength, let nations be judged in Your presence.

O Lord, put fear upon them, let the nations know they are mortal!

Book of Psalms, 9:19–21, translation Robert Alter (New York, 2007)

It would mean that the descendants of poor Poles would have to pay the descendants of those who were rich.

Jarosław Kaczyński, chairman of Poland's Law and Justice Party, rejecting
Jewish Holocaust victims' compensation claims for dispossessed property;
available at www.facebook.com/tv1polska/videos/1089260141153880/
(August 14, 2016)

Contents

Figures

Maps

Preface

This book's theater spans the multinational lands of historical Poland, much more far-flung than today's ethnographically homogeneous, post-Communist nation-state. They were Judaism's greatest exilic stronghold. The drama is that of the Polish-Jewish relationship in World War I and its tumultuous and bloody aftermath, culminating in the Polish-Soviet War of 1920, little remembered in the West but crucial for East Europe's future. At center stage are Christian Poles' actions toward the multitudinous Jews in their midst, whose voices respond in something like a Greek tragedy's chorus.

This is a book about Judeophobic deeds and their justification in words; about anti-Jewish riots and pogroms, both soldierly and civilian; and about antisemitic ideology and politics. But it is also especially about popular or grassroots ethnic violence, perpetrated independently of state authority far more often than not and mostly in defiance of it (but frequently supposing covert government approval). In this it dovetails with present-day scholarly debates on pogroms in the Russian Empire and, more broadly, on popular violence as social phenomenon and practice. It aims to contribute by emphasizing the *expressive* character of popular ethnic violence – its *enactment* of social-cultural *scripts*. Its arguments in explanation of these dark dramas, as they occurred among Christian Poles and their Jewish neighbors in the years 1914–20, will emerge in the pages that follow, but here it should be said that much of the perpetrators' violent behavior was unreflective and conventionalized, ingrained and unquestioned (though their *intent* to inflict damage is another matter).

There are valuable studies of ethnic violence as a tool of political conflict and implementation of ideological programs, most of them probing how it – as successful, premeditated action by political entrepreneurs – advanced aggressors' interests and damaged victims' possessions, bodies, and lives. Such works steer clear of interpreting ethnic violence as behavior expressive of unreflected-on, if not altogether unconscious, social and cultural beliefs, fears, and wishes. This is what these pages, in their farthest reach, undertake. If it were true that human action is *both* conscious, purposive, and in some sense rational *and also* unself-critical, culturally embedded, and often irrational, then these two approaches to understanding ethnic violence might be complementary. But this study, while assuming the sufficiently challenging task of puzzling out the messages in the mayhem's medium, will also show that ethnic violence generally damaged the "rational interests" – slippery concept – both of perpetrators and of state and society.

This is a study resting on years-long, wide-ranging research into previously unconsulted or neglected unpublished sources reposing in archives in Warsaw, Kraków, Vienna, Jerusalem, and New York. Its chapters assemble archival mosaic stones into pictures of ethnonational relations of Poles and Jews in their several respective subcultures and the violence accompanying them during six years of war and revolution. While this book supplies – in passing rather than all at once – political and social context essential to following its arguments, it should not be taken for a sustained and authoritative narrative history of politics (whether among Christians or Jews), nor of war, state, society, or even of anti-Jewish violence itself, whose full extent requires further exploration. It illuminates in passing many issues controversial among historians, leaving it to them and their readers to ponder further implications (although prospectors for triumphalist nationalism will pocket no new nuggets). It will be seen that suffering and injustice spared almost no one, though in radically varying degrees.

This book's aim is to analyze social and cultural *meanings* of ethnonational conflict and violence as *embodied* and *expressed* in participants' acts, as articulated in their *words*, and as I, their interpreter, have *inferred* them. The method results in myriad vignettes that are suggestive of many lines of analysis. Historical understanding is author's offering but also reader's response to newly excavated evidence and fresh argumentation. These pages display a gallery of hundreds of historically forgotten individuals, of whom only glimpses are seen, but from which comprehension of the culturally disparate worlds they inhabited will flow as by osmosis. Their words are these pages' most eloquent. As for scenes of cruel violence the reader will occasionally encounter, they serve as evidence for arguments this book proposes. The psyche can be morbidly or obsessively drawn to them; whole societies can be gripped with traumas of remembrance or reenactment. Of this I am well aware, so painful scenes are not lingered over.[1]

---

[1] Dominick LaCapra, *Representing the Holocaust: History, Theory, Trauma* (Ithaca, NY: Cornell University Press, 1996); Eva Hoffman, *After Such Knowledge: Memory, History, and the Legacy of the Holocaust* (London: Public Affairs Press, 2005).

These pages' rich micro-level documentation reveals something of deep importance that pales or is lost in macro-level generalizations: in violence among people, innumerable decisions are made, both for good and ill. To recognize that individual actions diminish as well as intensify strife is, if not to demonstrate the operation of ethically guided free will, to dispel the oppressive sense left in great or cruel violence's aftermath that it was but the predetermined consequence of one or another fatal human propensity. Microactions make a difference, whether they embody individual freedom or not.

As for this book's ethical standpoint, it does not depend on assumptions about universal morality but accepts that codes of values are historically evolved and inflected in varying ways. History's actors are not ourselves. We do not legislate for the past. The quest here is for insight into conscious and unconscious motives and meanings. Moral judgment and censure are subjective prerogatives, or they repose in power's hands – though the authorities (including the democratic collectivity), themselves entangled in moral ambiguities, often fail to act.

The published sources and scholarly monograph literature touching on this book's themes are mountainous and unscalable to their peak by even the most persistent and polyglot historian. The notes in the chapters, apart from identifying archival documents and other unpublished sources, confine themselves mainly to citations of scholarly works indispensable to the discussion at hand.

Some documentation in these pages will be found controversial, especially by readers accustomed to the view, justifiable in itself, that Poland's rebirth in an age of cataclysmic war and revolution was a glorious affirmation of the nation's will to live freely. But, as these pages demonstrate, and as all serious scholars of the subject know, it was, except for the privileged and well-cushioned few, an agonized, hunger-wracked, crime-ridden, fear-beset, and often bloody resurrection. Yet Poland's Jews, through their competing political leaders, invested high hopes in Poland's emergence as a democratic republic and widely, if also apprehensively, welcomed it. There was little Jewish nostalgia for Russian rule, and Habsburg Austria and Imperial Germany, though far friendlier to their Jewish subjects than the fallen tsardom, had vanished irretrievably.

A book such as this must take a stand on violence in general. Undeniably, it stalks the shadows of human life. Without it, history is imaginable only as utopia. Though it derives physiologically from *Homo sapiens'* brute origins, human violence broke free during the long process of civilization from the blind imperatives of survival and reproduction. Like the axe, it became a tool, both in individual and communal hands.

Application of its sharp edge ceased to be instinctual and became instead a matter of choice in the pursuit of conscious ends. These might be one or another form of collective or individual self-aggrandizement, as in the seizure of material goods, but violence came just as well to serve religious and moral purposes, particularly in warding off threats, imagined or real, to social and cultural existence.

Human violence also explodes unpremeditatedly or, at any rate, without prior calculations of advantage or necessity. Such volcanic events reveal the delicacy of the webs of cohesion humanity has spun for itself, and the force of repressed resentment and desire. Yet it is a rare outburst of spontaneous violence whose perpetrator is not prepared to defend it as right and just, however self-servingly. To recognize that the enabling condition of human violence is its subjectively felt *righteousness* gets to the heart of the matter. It is tempting to think that if violence were impossible to justify, it would wither like an unused bodily organ or pass into the realm of the pathologic, where certain rare behaviors still dwell.

Understanding of human violence thus derives from its positive, value-laden *meaning* in its practitioners' eyes. To those who believe that people's actions are rationally directed toward maximizing power and wealth, an emphasis on social or cultural rationales for violence may seem like exchanging substance for shadows. Yet political government and economic power manifest themselves in myriad forms, all of them historically evolved and invariably clothed in ideological and cultural dress. Like violence, wealth and political rule seldom, if ever, figure as ends in themselves, but rather their pursuit is meant to realize cultural *values*. These find expression in languages of individual or social morality descending from larger conceptions of cosmic order and human perfection or redemption.

Ethnic and cultural antagonisms are *lived* more consequentially than they are *thought*, but they must be harbored – even if unconsciously – in mind and heart to be acted on. Rarely are antagonists evenly balanced. Aggression will flow more forcefully from one side than from the other (or others). It is easier to reconstruct hostile *ideas* and suppose that minds thinking them will eventually translate them into *deeds* than to understand how people turn to violence against imagined outsiders among whom they have peacefully lived, no matter with what prejudices and resentments. One of this book's challenges is to transcend opposition of idea and action by showing how action *embodies* ideas. This will have the good effect of demonstrating, through looking at action, just *which ideas* are being enacted (for mind and heart harbor many contradictions).

One consequence of stressing *practice* over disembodied *ideas* or *ideological doctrines* is to highlight the *situationality* of such *identities* as *Pole* or *Jew* (or *Christian* or *peasant*). Recent debates among historians and social scientists on "national indifference" emphasize that ethnonational identity has often been, and today often still remains, a passive, ambivalently experienced, or even irrelevant aspect of ordinary people's quotidian lives, leaving many in doubt and disarray at moments of political crisis in which national loyalties are summoned. The pages that follow will illustrate identity's kaleidoscopic dynamics, usefully eroding the common tendency to concretize and absolutize – reify or ontologize – ethnonational and religious categories. In their light, readers will soon find that all collective judgments on the groups involved – "Poles," "Jews," and others – are false. At most, tendencies or potentialities, not necessarily expressive of majorities, come to light. Nations and peoples are abstractions, not, except in simplest demographic or citizenly sense, flesh and blood. They cannot be "naturalized," however much it continually happens in everyday discourse (and even though newly admitted American citizens are, revealingly, said to be naturalized). Few, if any, want only to be what others think them to be.[2]

Some readers may question the veracity of one or another account of violence registered in these pages. Especially in East European historiography, scarred by past ideological distortions from both left and right, factual accuracy is often fetishized, not infrequently to dismiss unwelcome argumentation. What might be called the "forensic approach" often prevails, seeking to establish individual or group agency so as to assign historical *responsibility* or *guilt*. The professional historian is sworn to empirical truth. Yet facts, once established, require interpretation, which when strong can and must bridge gaps or blind spots in the documentary record until new evidence, if discovered, requires reconceptualization.[3]

---

[2] Rogers Brubaker and Frederick Cooper, "Beyond 'Identity,'" *Theory and Society*, vol. 29 (2000), 1–47; Rogers Brubaker, *Ethnicity without Groups* (Cambridge, MA: Harvard University Press, 2004); Rogers Brubaker et al., *Nationalist Politics and Everyday Ethnicity in a Transylvanian Town* (Princeton, NJ: Princeton University Press, 2008); Tara Zahra, "Imagined Noncommunities: National Indifference as a Category of Analysis," *Slavic Review*, vol. 69, no. 1 (2010), 93–119; for nuancing of the indifference argument, emphasizing socially differentiated, politically generated, and culturally distinctive meanings of national identity within historically evolved linguistic communities, see Jakub Beneš, *Workers and Nationalism: Czech and German Social Democracy in Habsburg Austria, 1890–1918* (Oxford: Oxford University Press, 2017), 10ff, 243ff. On emergence through violence of national identity within highly diverse communities, see Max Bergholz, *Violence as a Generative Force: Identity, Nationalism, and Memory in a Balkan Community* (Ithaca, NY: Cornell University Press, 2016).

[3] On these and related points, see William W. Hagen, "A 'Potent, Devilish Mixture' of Motives: Explanatory Strategy and Assignment of Meaning in Jan Gross's *Neighbors*," *Slavic Review*, vol. 61, no. 3 (2002), 466–75.

Doubtless exaggeration occurred, and panicked misreportage, of the mayhem and injury these pages analyze. I have sought out multiple accounts so as to minimize bias. The gravest violence is well documented, but I have not disqualified plausible eyewitness testimony by lone individuals. In the end, the wide extent and destructiveness – physically, materially, and psychologically – of anti-Jewish violence in these war-torn years is as irrefutable as daily nightfall. The first challenge is to accurately reconstruct it, recognizing that very many localities escaped it and that popular participation was limited. It was almost always a minority affair, usually dependent on the presence of armed men. Greater still is the challenge to understand its social and cultural meaning, contemporary signification, and legacy to the present day – for expressive violence still inflames the horizon and perhaps always will.

Most things having to do with Central and Eastern Europe are, viewed through Western eyes, complex, unfamiliar, even exotic. As we encounter the Polish lands, home of Europe's largest Jewish population, they lay divided, bereft of once-savored sovereignty, under the rule of Austro-Hungarian, Russian, and Imperial German monarchies. Readers must accustom themselves to thinking of historic Poland and its inhabitants engulfed by the light and shadows of these mighty states. As in the course of World War I they broke free of them, Poles' and Jews' relationships to each other (and also among themselves) faced a new dawn, hopeful but also ominous amid political cataclysms and renewed warfare, culminating in 1920's Polish-Soviet War.

The Introduction following this Preface is unusual in largely foregoing a critique of previous historical scholarship, offering instead a portrait gallery of leading-role actors in this book's dramas, some individual, some collective, including scholarly writers who have influentially interpreted the Polish-Jewish relationship. It is these mentalities, existential perspectives, and world views that must be understood if interpretation and explanation are to move toward objectivity's sunlight. A minichapter follows, entitled, "Theoretical Footnote: Ethnic Violence in Social Science and Historiography," in which this book's relation to powerful analytical traditions is briefly identified and defended. Readers allergic to such scholarly pollen – enticing to many worker bees! – may choose to fly over it.

The succeeding chapters will move to and fro between cultural-psychological and social-political levels. The mythic meanings and messages projected on the first of these two planes – notably the scenarios pogroms enact – are released by upheavals on the second plane: economic and political crises, foreign or civil war. The historical setting of expressive violence must be known. It often denies itself, pretending to be mere self-defense or unapologetic rapacity when it is, in cultural-psychological reality, much more.

The stage shifts from Austrian Poland (Galicia) during and immediately after World War I to wartime Russian Poland and eastward regions. The Galician account, assembled from rich but largely neglected Austrian civil and military archives, dramatizes at ground-floor level the Habsburg monarchy's slow-motion buckling. It reveals the eruption, from small tremors, of pogrom violence that reached volcanic intensity at war's end, transforming in 1919 into rural social war targeting Jews foremost but with new Poland's officials and gentry also under fire.

After the independent state's chaotic birth in November 1918, anti-Jewish violence's terrain moved toward the 1920 war's battlegrounds in eastern ethnographic Poland and the nationally mixed Lithuanian, Belarusian, and Ukrainian borderlands beyond. Perpetrators of ethnic violence among Poles were mostly, during the world war, unarmed civilians and off-duty soldiers; in the war's immediate aftermath, they were irregular armed bands of demobilized imperial soldiers, deserters, desperados, and criminals trailed by motley civilian mobs; these pogromists were slowly superseded by soldiers in newly arisen government armed forces, whose anti-Jewish deeds likewise attracted civilians; finally, during the Polish-Soviet War, chief aggressors were Polish army soldiers and Russian-oriented irregulars allied with Poland against the Red Army.

This study's new light on wartime *Russian Poland* radiates from largely unmined German and Polish Zionist records and those too of the philanthropic American Jewish Joint Distribution Committee. The final chapters, focused on 1919–20 soldierly violence in eastern Poland and beyond, rest on Jewish-assembled eyewitness reports and long-inaccessible and never before deployed documentation lying, stamped "secret" in Polish army intelligence archives.

Multiple types of anti-Jewish violence stalk these pages, enacted according to varying scripts. Unsurprisingly, the trend, mainly because of perpetrators' advancing militarization, was toward more extreme and comprehensive violence. But soldiers were simultaneously, by socialization, civilians. They brought with them to army life their preexisting social and cultural imaginations. The war's sufferings, and the Bolshevik revolution, found reflection in shifting scenarios of violence, even while old and deep-rooted fantasies continued to cause retributive dramas to be staged, cudgels to be gripped and fists to ball.

The aim is not to construct would-be authoritative macro-political narratives, whether triumphalist or debunking, but rather to summon up, in first-person testimony, the dilemmas and delusions driving perpetrators' hostile or violent actions, the reactions of those under attack, and how aggression was, in participants' and contemporary observers' minds, interpreted. Anti-Jewish violence commonly assumed symbolical, collectively enacted, theatricalized form. Few of the many worthy scholarly studies cited in pages below sought to solve the riddles such behavior posed, and none that contemplate this book's historical subject matter. The tradition of emphasizing ethnic violence's political and sociological dimensions has dominated interpretation to the neglect of deep-rooted cultural expressiveness.

In the end, readers will have confronted, in its many masks, the cruel face of collectively staged rituals of plunder, humiliation, imagined revenge, and murder. But it will also be seen that when society and civilization, at the grassroots level, totter on destruction's brink, individuals commonly attempt to prevent, limit, or halt its plunge. History, in these pages, is a never decisively settled duel of life and death, both in the streets and in the human head and heart.

I have engaged with this book's themes for many years. Colleagues who have aided my quest for evidence and insight are too numerous to name. I thank Cambridge University Press's anonymous referees, who helped pull the first draft down to earth. Among other things, these pages reap the harvest of long engagement in the interdisciplinary, graduate-level Center for History, Society, and Culture at the University of California, Davis. Perhaps surprisingly, the greatest challenge has been to peer through Poles' eyes, for their multifarious world views and historical vantage points differ in important ways from those farther west. Among many others, let me recall five departed scholarly eminences whose company taught me a great deal about Poland – Jerzy Topolski, of Poznań, and Stefan Kieniewicz, Antoni Mączak, Jacek Kochanowicz, and Jerzy Tomaszewski, of Warsaw. Among active historians of Poland, Alina Cała has been an insightful guide to Polish Jewish history. Jerzy Jedlicki and his seminar colleagues opened their forum to me. In the pages that follow, which address painful issues in Polish history, these scholars' spirit is present, counseling resolution of controversy through empirical objectivity, recognizing that Poland, like all countries, has suffered painful traumas that still hurt today; that facts must be interpreted, not left in futile hope that they will speak for themselves (or justify that which they depict); and that contextualization, nuance, and historicization of regrettable events are essential tools of understanding.

Poland's history, in its brilliance as in its tragedies, is one of Europe's greatest, and so too is that of Poland's Jews. I have explored Jewish history in English, German, and Polish, but not Yiddish and Hebrew. Fortunately, much work of crucial importance by writers in these two languages originally appeared in Polish, German, or English or has been translated. In this book's primary-source documentation, Jewish voices speaking in the latter three idioms have been most consequential. They gave expression also to the Yiddish-speaking multitudes on whose behalf they often spoke.

Numerous archivists aided my researches in Israel, as in Poland, Austria, and New York. Lewis Bateman, seasoned editor, supported this book from its beginning. His successor, Michael Watson, supplied sagacious counsel. It is mysterious how one synthesizes far-ranging research and experience into a book, but many other people's lives are positively and happily intertwined with it, including especially my wife Ursula's.

Note on the Cover Image

This 1920 poster cries out for aid to Polish soldiery in stemming the incoming flood of inhuman, nightmarish invaders who brandish a Soviet red star–bearing flag. A powerful image of the war's apocalyptic dimension, it will have connected with specters of demons stalking the dark side of traditional popular culture. This was a creation of eminent and prolific graphic artist Edmund Bartłomiejczyk (1885–1950). (*Source:* Muzeum Wojska Polskiego w Warszawie.)

Guide to Polish Pronunciation

Accents normally fall on the second-to-last syllable.

Vowels:	*a, e, i, o, u* uniform, as in "s*a*w," "m*e*t," "*i*t," "sh*o*w," "sh*oo*t" (*ó* = *u*).
Vowels:	*ą, ę* lightly nasalized; *ą* as in softly and rapidly pronounced English "*own*" or French *on; ę* as in softly pronounced English "*en*ter" or French "m*ain*."
Diphthongs:	*au, eu* as in "*ou*t" and "b*oy*," respectively.
Hard consonants:	(1) *b*at, *d*og, *f*ox, *g*et, *k*it, *l*et, *m*et, *n*et, *p*et, *r* (lightly rolled), *s*it, *t*ot, *z*ero.
	(2) *c*, at word's end or when followed by any letter except *i* or *z* (on which, see below): "*ts*" as in "ca*ts*."
Soft consonants:	*h* or *ch* (identical sounds) as in "*h*at"; or aspirated, as in Scottish "*loch*" (*e.g.*, "bread" (*chleb*) = *h*leb).
	j like English *y*, as in "*y*et."
	w like English *v*, as in "*v*at"; at word's end, as *f* in "sta*ff*."
Other	*ł* ("dark l"), like English *w*.
letters/sounds:	*rz, ż* (identical sound), like *s* in English "plea*s*ure."
	ź soft form of *rz, ż*.
	cz as in "*ch*at."
	sz as in "*sh*ot."
	szcz continuous double consonant, as in "ca*sh ch*ange."
	ś (or *si*) soft English *sh*, as in "*sh*e."
	ć (or *ci*) soft English *ch*, as in "tea*ch*."
	śc continuous double consonant, as in soft "fre*sh ch*eese."
	ń before consonants or at word's end, slightly nasalized, as in "o*ni*on"; before vowels, spelled as *ni* and pronounced like "*ny*et."

Map I Lands historically stamped by Polish rule and culture before the partitions (1772–95) of the centuries-old Polish Commonwealth – an elective monarchy, governed by a numerous democracy of nobles led by regionally entrenched magnate aristocrats. It was one of Europe's largest states. Stretching from near Berlin to St. Petersburg and Kiev, from the Baltic to the Black Sea, perched on the Danube basin's northern mountain frontiers, its Catholic aristocratic-republican political culture contrasted sharply with the life-worlds of Orthodox Russia, Protestant Germany, and the Muslim-ruled Turkish Ottoman Empire. On a line running roughly north and east of Białystok (northeast of Warsaw) to Przemyśl (west of Lwów), the population was mostly non-Polish-speaking and largely non-Catholic. Yet everywhere within the Commonwealth the political power holders were nearly all Polish Catholic landed nobility, many of them scions of earlier polonized and catholicized local lineages. Despite the

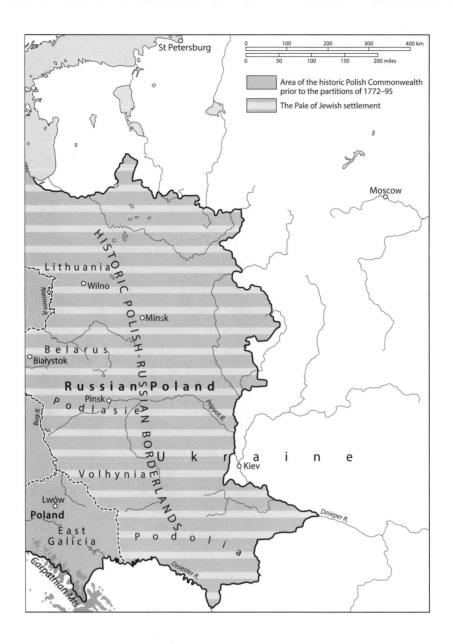

Caption for Map I   (cont.)

partitions, local Polish landowners and clergy and intelligentsia springing from their ranks retained great regional influence and even, as officeholders in the partitioning powers' administrative hierarchy, governing authority. The Commonwealth's Jewish community, the world's largest, approximated a half-million in a prepartition population of some twelve million. Polish Jews were accustomed to life in a polyglot and religiously variegated world overarched by a Polish aristocratic culture that, in ethnographic Poland's eastern borderlands, only the wars and revolutions of the twentieth century finally extinguished.

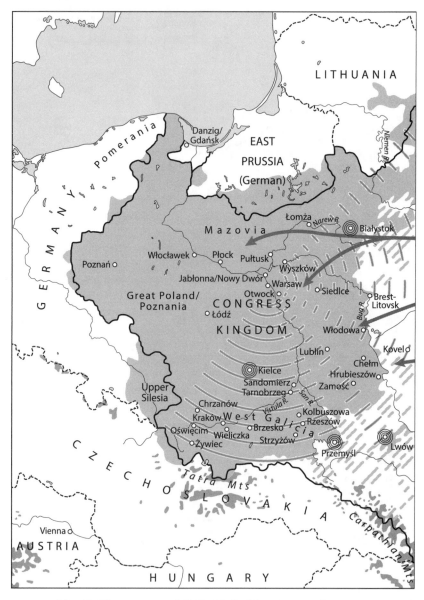

Map II The pogroms of 1918–20. Polish-perpetrated pogroms erupted first in November 1918 in West Galicia and in East Galicia's Lwów, with notable outliers in Przemyśl and Kielce. Thereafter, anti-Jewish violence accompanied the war fronts established by Polish military conquest eastward, toward Wilno, Pinsk, and Kiev, and in 1920 by the Polish-Soviet War, whose culminating battles blazed on ethnographic Polish soil. Along the Polish-Belarusian settlement frontier, the largely non-Polish Bałachowicz army perpetrated much anti-Jewish violence, some

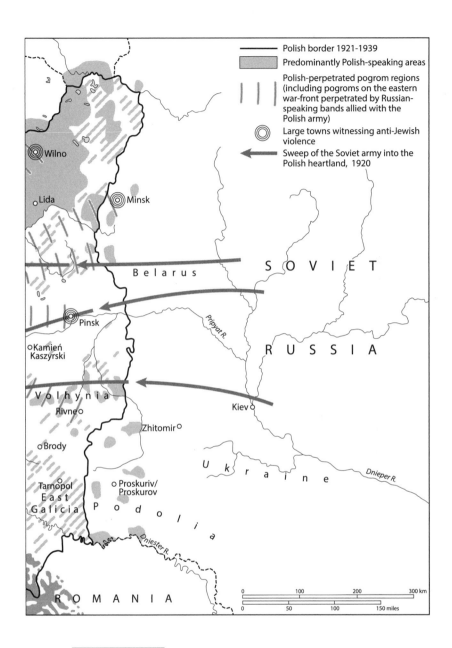

Polish border 1921-1939

Predominantly Polish-speaking areas

Polish-perpetrated pogrom regions (including pogroms on the eastern war-front perpetrated by Russian-speaking bands allied with the Polish army)

Large towns witnessing anti-Jewish violence

Sweep of the Soviet army into the Polish heartland, 1920

Wilno

Lida

Minsk

S O V I E T

Belarus

Pripyat R.

R U S S I A

Pinsk

Kamień Kaszyrski

Volhynia

Rivne

Kiev

Zhitomir

Brody

U k r a i n e

Dnieper R.

Tarnopol

Proskuriv/ Proskurov

East Galicia

P o d o l i a

Dniester R.

R O M A N I A

0   100   200   300 km

0   50   100   150 miles

Caption for Map II   (cont.)

of whose sites are included here. But the widespread pogroms in Ukraine and elsewhere in the historic Polish-Russian borderlands, instigated by Ukrainian, Russian, and other non-Polish hands, are left unidentified.

Introduction
Culture and Psychology of the Polish-Jewish Relationship

The Theoretical Footnote that follows this Introduction engages the historical and social science literature that underpins – or challenges – this book's arguments. But such matters do not rivet all readers' attention. Many will be drawn to these pages by personal ties of ancestry, religion, or nationality. Others will seek in them illumination of the conflict-beset, often-tragic history of twentieth-century Central and Eastern Europe or of the present-day world's passionate, often cruel and bloody clashes of ethnicity and culture. Crucial are the perspectives in which the Polish-Jewish relationship appeared to those enmeshed in it, whether in the early twentieth century or thereafter. This Introduction conveys dissonant voices, some scholarly, some popular, in the conviction that readers hearing them will begin to understand the human dynamics of this book's dramas and grasp the interpretational problems they pose. Notable are recent works, informed by cultural anthropology, that insightfully reframe the problem of antisemitism in historically Polish lands.

The Jewish Plight in Anna Kahan's Eyes

Anna Kahan was a girl of fourteen when World War I erupted. She lived with her family – her father a lower-middle-class, partner-swindled retail butcher – in Siedlce (Shedlets in Yiddish), in Russian Poland's east. In 1911 it was a town of some 31,000 civilians, 54 percent Jewish, the rest mainly Catholic Poles alongside some Christian Orthodox east Slavs (Belarusians, Russians, Ukrainians). In 1906, as the revolution of 1905 faded, Russian soldiers unleashed by tsarist authorities staged a military pogrom that may have claimed as many as fifty Jewish lives, with another one-hundred wounded. Anna possessed admirable maturity and intelligence, reflected in the Yiddish-language diary she kept in 1915–16. To assist her parents, she curtailed her studies to work as milliner, earning in April 1915 eight rubles monthly, woefully little but not insignificant. The war-gripped tsardom ruthlessly uprooted Jewish communities living

1

near its western front opposite the German and Austrian armies, though Siedlce initially evaded this fate. But the Russian Empire's discriminatory western Pale of (Jewish) Settlement was awash in refugees, while wartime shortages undermined Jews' precarious existence. They were filled with *tsores* (worries) about *parnose* (their livelihoods) and life itself. Anna (Figure i.1) wrote on April 15, 1915:

I walk on the street and see a suffering face. I'd like so much to read this face. So many faces are now filled with sorrow. Fear overwhelms me. What if I am one of the weak ones that cannot help anyone, not even themselves? All these people had been young once, full of ambitions and strivings, yet life had broken them, given them nothing.

I cannot understand how one can be an optimist after seeing so much poverty and injustice. Yet many of these people have preserved hope. They keep deceiving themselves: tomorrow, tomorrow things will be better.

Figure i.1 Anna Kahan (second from upper right) with her family on the eve of her 1916 departure for New York with sister Bracha (on Anna's right). This picture was taken in Siedlce's park, where Anna pondered Jewish fate with her friends. Though economically insecure, the Kahan family appears robust, self-assured, and dignified. In this and other extant pictures, Anna and her friends – some drawn to emigration to America, others through Zionism to settlement in Palestine – project a maturity, seriousness, and longing for better life characteristic of such education-keen and hopeful young people.
Source: Muzeum Walki i Męczeństwa w Treblince.

My father is a religious man. He is sure that God will help. I am not so sure now.

... My heart is breaking in me today – there is just too much suffering around me. When will mankind be redeemed?[1]

She pondered Jewish fate in ardent discussions with friends. Of Greenbaum she wrote:

Not so long ago he had tried to convince me that the Jewish people would either assimilate or perish. He saw no inner or outer forces that would rise to their defense. There is no sense in suffering meaninglessly, he said. The Jewish people ought to stop reproducing themselves. Of course, I had protested against this pessimism. I told him our nation is alive and doesn't want to die.

Later Greenbaum became a confident and optimistic Zionist.[2]

Multilingual Anna was proudly Jewish but open to its different political expressions. Though she studied Hebrew, Zionists' preferred language, she defended Yiddish, rapidly developing as modern literary language. "Yiddish has deep roots in the Jewish people, it has become sacred, for it is *Mame-loshn*, mother-tongue. But he [a friend] insists that Yiddish must perish. Whenever it encounters another language, it is vanquished, assimilated."[3]

---

[1] "The Diary of Anna Kahan. Siedlce, Poland, 1914–1916," *YIVO Annual of Jewish Social Science*, vol. XVIII (1983), 141–371, here 175*ff.* Anna Kahan was mother of Arkadius Kahan, one of the author's graduate program professors. On Siedlce, see Edward Kopówka, *The Jews in Siedlce, 1850–1945* (New York, NY: JewishGen, 2014). There is an important Jewish memoir literature encompassing the late nineteenth and early twentieth centuries. On Russian Poland, see, for example, I. J. Singer, *Of a world that is no more* (New York, NY: Vanguard, 1971 [Yiddish original: 1946]); Isaac B. Singer, *In My Father's Court* (New York, NY: Farrar, Straus and Giroux, 1966 [Yiddish original: 1963]); David Assaf, ed., *Journey to a Nineteenth-Century Shtetl: The Memoirs of Yekhetzkel Kotik* (Detroit, MI: Wayne State University Press, 2002 [Yiddish original: 1913]). On Austrian Poland, see Joachim Schoenfeld, *Shtetl Memoirs: Jewish Life in Galicia under the Austro-Hungarian Empire and in the Reborn Poland 1898–1939* (Hoboken, NJ: KTAV Publishing House, 1985).
   Critical to understanding the wartime Polish–Jewish relationship: Konrad Zieliński, *Stosunki polsko-żydowskie na ziemiach Królestwa Polskiego w czasie pierwszej wojny światowej* (Lublin: Wydawnictwo Uniwersytetu Marii Curie-Skłodowskiej, 2005). An authoritative and judicious synthesis of the vast polyglot literature is Anthony Polonsky, *The Jews in Poland and Russia*, 3 vols. (Portland, OR: Littman Library of Jewish Civilization, 2010–12), here vols. II–III (1881–1914, 1914–2008).Cf. Heiko Haumann, *Geschichte der Ostjuden* (Munich: Deutscher Taschenbuch Verlag, 1990); Jerzy Tomaszewski et al., *Najnowsze dzieje Żydów w Polsce w zarysie (do 1950 roku)* (Warsaw: Wydawnictwo Naukowe PWN, 1993); Andrzej Żbikowski, *Żydzi* (Wrocław: Wydawnictwo Dolnośląskie, 1997); Andrzej Paluch, ed., *The Jews in Poland*, 2 vols. (Cracow: Jagiellonian University Press, 1992, 1999); Israel Bartal, *The Jews of Eastern Europe, 1772–1881* (Philadelphia: University of Pennsylvania Press, 2005).
[2] Kahan, 212 (July 15, 1915).   [3] Ibid., 310 (October 3, 1915).

She viewed Jewish life's imperfections sternly: "The Jewish communal leaders who ruled and taxed without pity; the sharp distinction between rich and poor; the contempt of the learned for the ignorant; above all, the poverty of the masses." The *maskilim* – assimilation-oriented (or "integrationist") Jews, "modernized" by nineteenth-century German-born Jewish Enlightenment *(haskalah)* – deluded themselves into thinking the antisemitic tsarist government was only waiting for Jews "to acquire education and European manners" to grant them equal rights.[4]

Despite her ambivalent feelings toward Poles, she avidly read Polish literature, including the idealistically nationalist Nobelist Henryk Sienkiewicz (who fired no anti-Jewish cannons). Zionist friend Ackerman "criticizes me for reading Polish books. 'If you read Polish for six months,' he says, 'you develop assimilationist tendencies.'" She archly replied that "even specifically patriotic works in Polish would not have an adverse effect on a person who is conscious of his own nationality."[5]

In the park she discussed with friends Polish-Jewish relations, "which are not good." Yet the venerable Polish Commonwealth, before its partition among Russia, Austria, and Prussia (1772–95),

had given refuge to Jews when [in the late Middle Ages] they were expelled from other countries and Jews had been mighty patriots of Poland, defending her with their blood and possessions. Now things have changed. I don't know who started this bigotry and hatred among peoples, but the Poles certainly swallowed a big dose of it.

Of this she had personal experience. A friend told her of his hospital stay, where many wounded soldiers lay abed. They liked him, making no invidious religious distinctions. "But one single Pole in that ward kept yelling: 'Jew! Jew!' He was just sick with hatred."[6]

When in August 1915 Siedlce Jews were evacuated eastward, she sat with her family in the crowded train. A "handsome Polish lady, wearing a Red Cross armband" arrived with husband and child. A Jewish man tried to walk past her. She refused to let him through.

I never saw such a transformation in a person. She turned green, her eyes flashed, her lips grimaced, her hands shook. She spewed out invective like vomit. "The swine! The Jews! They're everywhere! They grab everything! Even the train! You can't get away from them! They dirty up everything! That dirty Jew!"

She kept on in this vein for a long time. "The Jews are usurers, the Jews are swindlers, the Jews are spies ... *Żydzi, Żydzi* [Jews, Jews]."

[4] Ibid., 333 (January 8, 1916).   [5] Ibid., 349 (March 29, 1916).
[6] Ibid., 205, 211 (June 25 and July 10, 1915).

Oh, God! The Poles themselves don't have it good, yet they're forever accusing the Jews, as if the Jews were the cause of all evil, of all trouble. Where does all this hatred come from? How can a human being absorb so much poison and go on living?[7]

Victorious advance of the Central Powers' armies brought Russian Poland's heartland (the 1815-defined, Warsaw-centered "Congress Kingdom") under German occupation, allowing the Kahans to return home. During the fighting, they heard that "Cossacks are coming!" She reflected, "What terror in the one word 'Cossacks.'" Though a small girl at the time, she remembered Siedlce's pogrom during the 1905–6 revolution:

The shooting, the fear, the soldiers knocking on the door, their hoarse cries and my father's soothing, cheerful voice. (He bought them off with money and a drink.) I remember vividly one night, all of us lying on the floor, bullets whistling through the windows across, and my mother crouching, examining my feet in fear that a bullet hit me.[8]

During 1915 fighting, a drunken Cossack was "out on the street, brandishing his sabre, shouting 'I'll kill all the Jews!' The German fired twice and finished him off with his sword. Cossacks they don't take as prisoners, but kill them off on the spot. 'I think that's barbarous,' I say."[9]

The German occupiers permitted Siedlce's Poles to celebrate their holiday – forbidden under tsarist rule – of May 3, commemorating the liberal constitution promulgated in 1791. Blue and white Zionist flags decorated houses alongside Poles' red and white. "No wonder the joy of the Polish people is great – they have waited 125 years for this holiday. I wonder whether the Jewish people will ever celebrate their own national holiday." Jews, wearing Zionist armbands and badges, marched alongside Poles. Anna found Polish girls in Cracovian costume good-looking. Warsaw-based Zionist luminary Antoni Hartglas spoke. "At the end he expresses the hope and wish for a free and friendly life for both nations, living in harmony and peace."[10]

Germans' pitiless requisitioning of war supplies embittered the Jews. Anna heard that "They'll come and take whatever they please, and you have to smile while they're robbing you." But in Siedlce, locally quartered Germans were friendly and decent (Figure i.2). "They are extremely patriotic and awfully proud. They have no regard for

---

[7] Ibid., 236 (August 8, 1915). Another train-riding obsessive antisemite among educated Poles appears in Alfred Döblin's impressive *Journey to Poland* (New York, NY: Paragon House, 1991 [German original: 1924]), 257–58.

[8] "The Diary of Anna Kahan," 370 (September 18, 1916); on the pogrom, see Kopówka, *The Jews in Siedlce, 1850–1945*, chap. 3.

[9] Kahan, 275 (September 17, 1915).   [10] Ibid., 356–57 (May 3, 1916).

Figure i.2 German soldiers, 1915, entering Mława, formerly a Russian
Polish town north of Warsaw. Jewish residents – mostly men – observe
them. This is a not untypical Jewish street in a *shtetl* or small town with
a large Jewish population (here, in 1910, lived some 15,000 souls,
45 percent Jewish, but many *shtetls* were smaller). Onlookers wear
customary everyday dress. Mutual understanding of Yiddish and
German was possible, given a will to achieve it. For German Jewish
soldiers, contact with Polish Jews was often bewildering. They tended to
sentimentalize and exoticize their eastern coreligionists, pitfalls that still
yawn today in Western countries. Polish Jews inclined toward caution in
associating themselves with Germans, despite often strong incentives to
do so. Wartime requisitions by rival armies and governmental controls
on food supplies severely injured Jewish merchant interests while
infuriating townspeople and, ruinously, stoking antisemitism.
Source: Ullstein Bild. Getty Images, 501372297.

anyone but Germany and the German people. 'Deutschland,
Deutschland über alles!' If you're not a German, you're an inferior
creature. (They hate the Cossacks most of all, and all want to kill
several.)" Yet German policy reversed tsarist prohibition of public
schooling in Polish and Jewish languages. "So the Germans do bring
culture wherever they come!"[11]

---

[11] Ibid., 294, 298, 312 (September 28 and 30 and October 3, 1915).

Figure i.3 A Warsaw street scene from 1906, centered on Jewish workers amid others in bourgeois dress. Jewish artisans and other laborers, including dairymen and butchers, were a massive presence in Poland. Many were poor, but others supported stable households, and some rose to prosperity. The more secular-minded among them were often rough and tough, strongly inclined to cooperative organizations and labor unions and drawn to leftist politics. Alongside such scenes stood the vast, ramshackle structure housing Jewish textile workers throughout the Polish lands. Technological change imposed adaptability and, often, self-exploitation. The Russian Empire's greatest industrial textile center was Łódź/Lodzh, west of Warsaw. Factory jobs were frequently barred to Jews, even when employers were Jewish, because Christian workers aimed to monopolize them and would work on Saturdays. Jews found employment as handloom weavers and tailors and in finishing or labor-intensive home labor.
Source: Ullstein Bild. Getty Images, 542350157.

Penury, even starvation, stalked Anna's gloomier thoughts. During the German advance, she wrote that "the rich have plenty of money and most of them have already sent their families deeper into Russia. But for people like us who have a few hundred rubles, the question arises: How long can a sum like this last? What then?" In winter 1915 she wrote:

Figure i.4 A Galician Jewish Passover celebration, 1915. Two Austrian soldiers are present, together with students and, seemingly, a rabbinical guest. Here depicted is the complex cultural hybrid of religiously stamped identity, including bearded patriarch; Austro-Hungarian education and citizenship; and contemporary middle-class life, including a young woman presenting herself in modern light. Nor should the photographer – a profession to which many Jews were drawn – be overlooked.
Source: Imagno. Getty Images, 53313274.

Destitution is increasing, whoever has bread today will not have it tomorrow. Riots will surely break out. Hunger compels the most law-abiding man to use force. When he'll see a bread, he'll take it, money or no money. The starving will grow wild, break into stores and warehouses. And the end will be that sooner or later we'll all die the horrible death of hunger.

In March 1916, she wrote: "Oh, these hunger riots! The roar: 'Bread!' keeps ringing in my ear."[12]

Anna Kahan sharply perceived the dilemmas and dangers facing Russian Poland's Jews. Among these, Polish anti-Jewish violence did not figure, even if Judeophobia among Poles shocked and baffled her.

[12] Ibid., 215, 326, 350 (July 22 and November 12, 1915, March 31, 1916).

Figure i.5 Unidentified Jewish family portrait, Warsaw, ca. 1910. This photograph, free of religious imagery, captures the marriage of contemporary Jewish and Christian European domesticity. Many such pictures, including prominently those of notables from the world of business, literature, and politics, testify to Jewish acculturation to the social and cultural patterns of the Polish (and Russian) intelligentsia and urban propertied classes. Embrace of a Polish cultural and political mentality sometimes accompanied the process, bringing about what

Figure i.6 Eight of the thirteen Jewish deputies elected in 1919 to the first (Constituent) Polish parliament (further discussed below). Front and center (3) is Abraham Perlmutter, Warsaw's principal rabbi and widely respected advocate of Polish-Jewish cooperation on a basis of religious and cultural equality. In their self-presentation, the deputies display varying modes of integration in secular Polish public life. Others depicted: (1) Rabbi Moshe Halpern (Agudas Israel), (2) journalist-politician Noach Prylucki (Folkist), (4) Solomon Weinzieher, (5) Itzhak Grűnbaum (Zionist leader), (6) Dr. and Rabbi Osias Thon (Zionist leader), (7) Dr. Jerzy Rosenblatt (Zionist), and (8) Dr. Ignacy Schiper (historian and leader of worker-oriented Poale Zion).
Source: YIVO Institute of Jewish Research.

Caption for Figure i.5   (cont.)

was commonly understood to be "assimilation." But from the interactive process of Jewish acculturation within contemporary Polish and Russian secular civilization there also emerged Hebrew-oriented modern-minded Jewish nationalism. Family portraits of such Zionist giants as Nahum Sokolow and David Grűn (David Ben-Gurion), both born near Warsaw, display similar or still more modern self-presentations as that depicted here.
Source: Imagno. Getty Images, 551786891.

She did not stay to witness worse things, for in September 1916 her family's and American relatives' efforts to secure her and her sister's emigration permitted their departure for New York. There she would apply her millinery skills to financing her Siedlce family's westward trek. She herself lived successfully in America into old age.

Village Farmer Jan Słomka's Views on His Jewish Neighbors

On 1914's eve, some 80 percent of Christians in Russian and Austrian Poland lived in villages or agriculturally oriented small towns. Many urban workers had rural roots. So did parish clergy, while landed nobility and lesser gentry, and the intelligentsia of education mostly born among them, were heirs too of agrarian not urban civilization. Christian Poland was a rural society within which industrialism, with its many Jewish, German, Russian, and Western European capitalists and entrepreneurs, burgeoned as an exotic and – to many – ominous urban growth. Bigger towns boasted Renaissance and Baroque glories, alongside grand ecclesiastical and magnatial palaces and the partitioning powers' imposing bureaucratic and military fortresses. But cities housed far more Jews – some rich, more poor – and more Christian artisans and laborers than Polish bourgeoisie, who were only slowly gaining strength. Midsized and small urban communities were commonly Jewish *shtetls* ("townlets" in Yiddish), where Christians might be a minority.

Among Christians, especially ordinary people, rural-born attitudes toward Jews were pervasive and widely authoritative, whether through village membership or country roots. Voicing them from Austrian Poland (Galicia), as embodied in an economically successful, modern-minded small farmer and village mayor, was Jan Słomka (1842–1929), who published his valuable ethnography-like memoirs in 1912, updating them in 1927 (Figure i.7). He was born under manorial serfdom that ended only in 1848 and grew up poor in subsequent difficult decades during which the emancipated peasantry struggled to survive as smallholding cultivators in an unaccustomed market economy, bereft of whatever threadbare patriarchal protection their former noble lords, themselves now tottering in capitalism's turbulence, had once extended.

Słomka's book – not to be mistaken for dispassionate scholarship! – depicted the Jews of West (Polish-speaking) Galicia as cynical exploiters of Christian villagers' weaknesses and ignorance. It did not harmonize with his rational and practical self-image to dwell on pervasive magical beliefs about Jews' malevolent powers and practices. Yet he remembered

Figure i.7 Jan Słomka: frontispiece from first edition of his memoir, 1912. A governmental medal, awarded for meritorious civilian service, adorns his Galician peasant robe. The image presents him as well-dressed, educated villager (peasant *inteligent*), a type both urban intelligentsia and self-modernizing peasantry strove to create in place of the "dark" (*ciemne*) and "superstitious" (*zabobonowe*) rural "masses." *Source: Pamiętniki włościanina od pańszczyzny do dni dzisiejszych* (Kraków, 1912).

from childhood how, when fire destroyed his Dzików village's manor house, the story circulated that it was "heaven-sent punishment for blasphemy perpetrated by the Jews, when they staged [the charge, which Słomka left unchallenged, was unlikely] a mock representation of the sufferings of our Lord."[13]

Słomka's Jews sometimes seemed to menace Christians' physical survival, a fear that, as we will see, ballooned after 1914. He remembered how, earlier, Jewish merchants

> would begin from harvest-time to buy up provisions from the farmers, mostly paying them with vodka: and these they would sell during the hunger-period [late winter or spring, before the new year's first harvests] at huge profit. They would set things out on market days in sacks; and around these sacks there would wander a hungry throng . . . buying grain [impoverishedly] in pots or quart measures.

Or, if Christians could not buy ahead, they would find themselves empty handed when Jews closed shops for their religious holidays (which Poles found unpredictable and mysterious).[14]

Reckless vodka drinking plagued rural Poland in the mid–nineteenth century, consequence both of reorientation of the nobility's large-estate production away from grain export and falling costs of distilling. Słomka, a teetotaler, castigated villagers for foolhardy drinking but pilloried manorial lords' tavern keepers and other Jewish merchants for self-servingly stoking village alcoholism. Similarly, he blamed them for bankrupting the emancipated peasantry with usurious credit and foreclosing on their miniscule farms (as they also did with spendthrift noblemens' large estates).[15]

> If the Jews had been willing to live and work on farms, the whole land today would belong to them, and they would be the lords of Southern Poland. Both peasant and prince would be their servants, and work for them as hired men. Instead of serfdom [pańszczyzna] we should have had for the whole of our Catholicism [note his conflation of Polishness and religion] a worse thing, viz. Jewdom [żydowszczyzna]. In Dzikov there isn't a bit of land that has not been in Jewish hands, and been bought back with a lot of toil. Elsewhere it is no better.

---

[13] Jan Słomka, *From Serfdom to Self-Government: Memoirs of a Polish Village Mayor 1842–1927* (London: Minerva, 1941), 50. This translation by Polonophile scholar William J. Rose, supplied with a foreword by the Polish government-in-exile's Interior Minister, made the point, politically sharp in 1941, that Polish common folk were capable of living in democratic freedom and deserved it. Polish version: *Pamiętniki włościanina od pańszczyzny do dni dzisiejszych* (Kraków: Towarzystwo Szkoły Ludowej, 1929). Rose's translation omits some of Słomka's detail. Cf. Polish text at www.linux.net.pl/~wkotwica /slomka/slomka.html.

[14] Słomka, *From Serfdom to Self-Government*, 46, 200.

[15] Ibid., 84–85 and chap. V, *passim*.

But the Jews have never wanted to till the soil, they have preferred to live by their wits, to profit by trading in the lands peasants have had to pay for [in compensation for receiving postemancipation freeholds]. [Jews] would only settle in the cities and towns, buying up property there from the Catholics.

Such, Słomka held, had been the fate of Tarnobrzeg, his village's chief market town, whose prestigious houses ringing the central square, once Catholic, passed after the 1860s into Jewish hands.[16]

This vision of Poland's "Judaization" was a paranoid nightmare scenario well known among Poles, seemingly deprived of self-defense against it by loss of statehood in a homeland housing the world's largest and densest Jewish population. Well-respected author Julian Ursyn Niemcewicz had in 1858 published his dystopic fantasy, *The Year 3333*, when Warsaw would bear the name *Moszkopolis* (derived from a common mocking Polish name for Jews). The danger was greater for Poles having anciently ceded dominance in retail and wholesale trade to Jews. Słomka wrote:

Peasants had nothing to do with trade, holding it to be a Jewish enterprise, for which only Jews (the saying was) were fitted. They were ashamed of it, and made fun of anyone of their number who would begin it. [Peasants sold their surpluses to Jews at the local market town.] These then did the business and got the profits. Often the peasant would pay dearly in the spring for grain he had sold the autumn before for a song ... We had no schools, and the peasant was not trained to do business – he couldn't reckon [do arithmetic] at all.[17]

Słomka was unrelenting. "In business the Jews were crooks and unreliable." They would cheat on measure, quality, price. "The level of intelligence [secular learning] among the Jews was formerly very low, mostly lower than that of Christians." Town-dwelling Jews (the vast majority) often could not speak Polish. "Others would so mutilate the language (even worse than they do now!) that they were the objects of mockery and laughter." When Austrian-imposed compulsory schooling arrived, they opposed it more stubbornly "than the most ignorant peasant."[18]

In Słomka's as in most other ambitious peasants' eyes, salvation from the Jewish exploitation they had no doubt they suffered came through the movement, from the 1880s, of peasant self-organization, especially cooperative marketing of farm produce and establishment of cooperative-organized retail stores, supplying villagers with their purchased necessities at Jewish merchants' loss. The local Catholic priesthood often greatly aided the peasant movement, as did benevolent landed gentry and

---

[16] Ibid., 88–89, 98.   [17] Ibid., 81.   [18] Ibid., 96–97.

nobility. Yet, in politics, peasant populism frequently attacked Christian elites alongside Jews.[19]

When Słomka recalled World War I, he saw Jews, "friends of Austria though they were," as draft dodgers or, when unable to evade conscription, malingerers and shirkers of frontline duty. He thought military authorities avoided billeting soldiers on town-dwelling Jews, so Christian villagers, apart from paying war's blood tax, had to bear the burden of housing and feeding troops on the march. And in newly independent postwar Poland, he saw Jews as Bolshevism's chief, if unsuccessful, fomenters.

Yet, from his 1927 vantage point, Polish-Jewish relations were improving. The rural cooperative movement had triumphed, and peasants, even if possessing but six acres of land, could make a living. Poles had proved their competence in commerce.

The new [Christian] businesses are mostly better run than the Jewish ones . . . There is absolute cleanliness and order within and without, as well as more integrity and honesty of dealing. It is not true to say that only the Jews are made for business . . . Polish firms are superior to the corresponding sort of Jewish ones, and should rouse us to even bigger efforts.

The butchering and selling of beef had remained in Jewish hands, "and the complaints are general at the lack of good meat," though finally "the Jews have begun also to take better care of their places, and keep them clean."[20]

In the countryside, "in the face of a rural unrest that was in many cases directed against them" (as Słomka understatedly wrote), Jews sold their businesses and moved to town. "Nearly all our villages were freed from the Jews" (*odżydziły się*, i.e., "dejudaized themselves"), and in independent Poland, "scores of taverns that had been dens of corruption were closed." Tarnobrzeg remained three-quarters Jewish, but Christians were regaining urban real estate, and when Jewish women converted to Christianity, there was no Jewish "counter-agitation." "In general, the

---

[19] See these solid sociopolitical analyses: Kai Struve, "Die Juden in der Sicht der polnischen Bauernparteien vom Ende des 19. Jahrhunderts bis 1939," *Zeitschrift für Ostmitteleuropa-Forschung*, vol. 48, no. 2 (1999), 184–225; Kai Struve, *Bauern und Nation in Galizien: Über Zugehörigkeit und soziale Emanzipation im 19. Jahrhundert* (Göttingen: Vandenhoeck & Ruprecht, 2005); Kai Struve, "Gentry, Jews, and Peasants: Jews as Others in the Formation of the Modern Polish Nation in Rural Galicia during the Second Half of the Nineteenth Century," in Nancy Wingfield and Pieter Judson, eds., *Creating the Other: Ethnic Conflict and Nationalism in Habsburg Central Europe* (New York, NY: Berghahn, 2003), 103–26; Keely Staudter-Halsted, *The Nation in the Village: The Genesis of Peasant National Identity in Austrian Poland, 1848–1914* (Ithaca, NY: Cornell University Press, 2001); Jan Molenda, *Chłopi, Naród, Niepodległość* (Warsaw: Instytut Historii PAN, 1999).

[20] Słomka, *From Serfdom to Self-Government*, 265.

Figure i.8 Village farmers in Russian Poland, ca. 1910, in town to buy and sell. These well-insulated people appear healthy and self-confident, an impression not always conveyed by ethnographic photographs of "the peasantry." By 1914, market-responsive family farms of the type championed by Jan Słomka and the village-based agrarian parties in all three partition zones had made great progress, which the impending world war, despite the booming demand for agricultural goods it would generate, would gravely imperil, stoking rising resentments and fears in the countryside. Those pictured here were probably relatively substantial peasant-farmers. Officials dealing with anti-Jewish violence might refer to solid senior cultivators as "serious" or "respectable" villagers, of whom it could be hoped that they would oppose rioting and law breaking by youths and "disreputable elements." Such hopes were sometimes but not always fulfilled.
Source: Ullstein Bild. Getty Images, 501372539.

Jews became more conciliatory, and sought closer relations with the Christian population, and their support."[21]

Thus did an intelligent, patriotic, pious, and benevolent villager depict his people's struggle for emancipation from Jewish influence – no less necessary and hard than their resistance to oppressive noble landlords. His account's veneer of reasonableness veiled considerable animosity and

---

[21] Ibid., 268–69. I translate from the Polish version.

Figure i.9 A Polish-language elementary school established in 1915–16 under German occupation in the town of Lida in the northeastern Polish-Lithuanian borderland. The young clergymen will have been teachers, the uniformed men, presumably, German functionaries. The children – both boys and girls – display a spectrum of age and material well-being. The priesthood's high authority in ordinary laypeople's eyes will find discussion later. Under Russian rule, the reach of elementary education was inadequate, while the language of instruction was, on paper, Russian. It corresponded with German occupation policy to favor conversion to Polish-language instruction so as to win support for a lasting German-Austrian overlordship in conquered Russian Poland. In towns and cities, sons of families of some degree of property and education had a chance to advance to the prestigious and nonobligatory university-preparatory secondary schools, notably the humanistic *gymnasium*, launching careers in the *inteligencja* of the learned professions and public service. Advancement through marriage into the lower ranks of the nobility, especially lesser gentry who had left the countryside for town life, was even possible. Secondary-level instructors, often entitled professors, were members of the middle intelligentsia and dressed as gentlemen. High politicians and intellectuals often appeared little different. The conservative landed gentry and aristocracy might on festive occasions don traditional costumes, with feathered headgear, embroidered robes, high boots, and swords, but otherwise presented themselves as urbane businessmen or tweedy country gentlemen. Upper-class Polish women

aggression, if not by himself, then by other peasants. In his memoirs, rural violence against Jews, even though it flared destructively in 1898 and especially, as we will see, in 1918–19, figured mainly as "pranks" of which he disapproved. When villagers foolishly (or sinfully) participated in anti-Jewish plunder, Słomka wished to see them – as sometimes happened – sober up and return the ill-gotten gains. The struggle against Jewish capital was a contest, in his telling, of morality, self-control, and will power, with transformative effect even on Jews themselves.

To Słomka, as to most Poles, including the higher intelligentsia, Jewish life, flowing through its religiously ordained and popularly beloved channels, was entirely foreign and opaque, unworthy of investigation or sympathy. How Jewish interactions with Christians were shaped and limited by prejudicial restrictions on them, how Jewish poverty drove exertions to gain and uphold *parnose*, even at the cost of law breaking (as in smuggling between Austrian and Russian Poland) and sometimes deceptive business practices – this was lost on Słomka and colleagues. Christians, though they might praise Jewish piety, especially of the Orthodox, white-bearded kind, also – and oftener – *feared* Judaism, showing no interest in understanding it as a free-standing cultural system coexisting in the Polish lands with their own Christianity on a massive, even intimidating scale.

Poland's Jews in Unfriendly Professorial Eyes

Born 1875 in a Galician village, Franciszek Bujak rocketed to professor rank at Kraków's venerable, prestigious Jagiellonian University as Polish culture's first modern social and economic historian, notably of the peasantry he was born among. Politically balanced between moderate agrarian populism and intelligentsia nationalism, he assisted among negotiators of Poland's rebirth at 1919's Paris Peace Conference. For this occasion, he penned a hefty pamphlet published in English as "The Jewish Question in Poland." Under a thin patina of sociological

---

Caption for Figure i.9   (cont.)

struck corresponding poses, following fashions in Vienna or Paris, though patriots among them sometimes wore unadorned black in mourning for Poland's lost independence. In post-1914 anti-Jewish tumults, schoolboys, along with secondary-level students, were, as will be seen, often embroiled.
Source: Ullstein Bild. Getty Images, 501370589.

reasonableness there shone forth from it most of the anxieties over the Jewish presence powering antisemitism among propertied and educated Poles.

Bujak displayed defensiveness toward supposed Jewish threats common among Judeophobes and evident in Słomka's outlook.

> We may speak with more truth about Jewish antipolonism than about Polish antisemitism, which is not an aggressive movement displaying itself in consequent deeds, but merely a psychic reaction against damages suffered by the Polish nation from their [Jews'] part.[22]

To Bujak's secularized mind, the injuries were largely economic, although he faulted Poland's Jews, medieval refugees from German persecution, for perversely clinging to Teutonic language in their Yiddish speech and for supposed pro-Germanism before and during the World War. Bujak thought that "their dialect, incomprehensible for the local population, ensures them in commercial relations considerable benefits," including maintaining ties with German and other Jews outside Poland.

> The Jews are typical representatives of the capitalistic spirit, i.e., of an unbounded and unrestricted covetousness for money. They busy themselves mainly in undertakings in which invention and cunning have a fairer play than capital and physical work, and render to others all sorts of services, as honourable as that of physicians, and as dishonourable as that of the white slave trade.
>
>   Being quite strange in society, they can employ so much easier all unscrupulous means of dealing in relations with the economically weaker population.[23]

Bujak credited Jews with a "sense of superiority" deriving from pride in their membership in God's chosen nation and in "their secretion from all non-Jews."

> Led by laws of their own and a different morality, prescribed by their holy books [sanctioning, as Bujak and other Poles commonly believed, double-dealings with Christians], the Jews sever themselves and do not allow the Christians to participate really in their life, hiding themselves as in ancient times in ghettos.[24]

An "insignificant part" sought assimilation, eagerly seeking, "in an intruding way," to find roles and influence in Polish society. In politics, they veered toward radicalism and revolution. "This is the consequence of their heated temperament and their inclination toward analysis and criticism." They were "overwhelming" the Polish and Russian people with the "international socialism" they had invented.[25]

As for Zionism, it aimed to create "a foreign Jewish State within the Polish State," now just emerging into independence. This contradicted

---

[22] Franciszek Bujak, *The Jewish Question in Poland* (Paris: Levé, 1919), 30.
[23] Ibid., 22–23.   [24] Ibid., 21.   [25] Ibid., 26.

the "predominating modern tendency towards widening and strengthening the sphere of activity of the State" – "a very nice reward for [the Polish people's] hospitality and tolerance shown to the Jews in the past!" Bujak extolled Polish Jews' already existing "complete autonomy in all matters connected with religion, charity, and schools," pointing to their "richly endowed charitable and cultural institutions." They already largely "foster their own culture and nationality." In politics, education, and the professions they had figured, in Austrian Poland, in proportion or more to their demographic share.[26] It was as if he were saying, what more could they reasonably want?

In May 1919, the anti-Jewish violence this book will explore was flaring in Galicia, just as it had in November 1918 following the Central Powers' collapse. Bujak addressed what he defensively saw as widespread Jewish opinion that such disorders proved Poles "incapable and unworthy of an independent state existence, because their first steps were an outbreak of racial hatred." In fact, he replied, before 1914 "there had never been any pogrom at all, or even serious riots, in Poland." By pogrom, Bujak meant "systematically organized massacres and robberies carried out with the aid of an indifferent attitude, or even of a co-ordinate action of the police authorities, as was the case in [pre-1914] Russia."

This was also the predominant view in Jewish public opinion and one the pages that follow will explore.[27] For Bujak, it was convenient because

---

[26] Ibid., 40–41, 43.

[27] The concept of pogroms as state-steered or covertly state-sanctioned events originated in tsarist Russia, but modern scholarship has considerably qualified or, in specific cases, refuted it, though the salience of military involvement in wartime violence implicates the state in pogrom incitement in a different way. The literature, oriented to Russian history, is vast, including notably John D. Klier and Shlomo Lambroza, eds., *Pogroms: Anti-Jewish Violence in Modern Russian History* (Cambridge: Cambridge University Press, 1992), emphasizing popular expression in anti-Jewish violence of social resentment over unwelcome aspects of urbanization and industrialization, with varying official responses but little instigation by civil authorities. In similar vein, see Darius Staliūnas, *Enemies for a Day: Antisemitism and Anti-Jewish Violence in Lithuania under the Tsars* (Budapest: Central European University Press, 2015). Highlighting socioeconomic tensions and ideological exhortation to anti-Jewish aggression, also popular hostility to nineteenth-century supersession of old-regime judicial practices by liberal institutions: Edward Judge, *Easter in Kishinev: Anatomy of a Pogrom* (New York, NY: New York University Press, 1992); David Engel, "What's in a Pogrom? European Jews in the Age of Violence," in Jonathan Dekel-Chen et al. eds., *Anti-Jewish Violence: Rethinking the Pogrom in East European History* (Bloomington, IN: University of Indiana Press, 2011), 19–38; see also this same volume's other essays, *passim*; Werner Bergmann, "Ethnic Riots in Situations of Loss of Control: Revolution, Civil War, and Regime Change as Opportunity Structures for Anti-Jewish Violence in Nineteenth- and Twentieth-Century Europe," in Wilhelm Heitmeyer et al., eds., *Control of Violence: Historical and International Perspectives on Violence in Modern*

it enabled him to argue, or imply, that anti-Jewish violence in Poland (which had occurred in 1881 and 1898 and again in the revolution in Russian Poland of 1905–6) was a matter not of pogroms but of criminal disorders. These the Polish authorities in prewar Austrian Galicia, and now in post-1918 emergent united Poland, aimed to suppress, not encourage. That Polish villagers and urban commoners should have staged "comparatively insignificant riots" against war-induced misery, targeting Jewish merchants, Bujak found unsurprising, if not justifiable. The indisputably destructive anti-Jewish violence in Galician Lemberg (Lwów) in November 1918 Bujak attributed not to pogromist antisemitism but to Polish-Ukrainian fighting and attendant lawlessness that engulfed Jews as well.[28]

Societies (Berlin: Springer, 2011), 487–516; John Klier, *Russians, Jews, and the Pogroms of 1881–1882* (Cambridge: Cambridge University Press, 2014). Robert Weinberg, *Blood Libel in Late Imperial Russia: The Ritual Murder Trial of Mendel Beilis* (Bloomington, IN: University of Indiana Press, 2014), broadly defines pogroms as "acts of popular violence against Jews and their property" (p. 15).

Stefan Wiese, *Pogrome im Zarenreich. Dynamiken kollektiver Gewalt* (Hamburg: HIS, 2016) refocuses interpretation by conceiving pogroms as assaults by considerable spontaneity by perpetrators on targeted groups, not only Jewish, within a field of collective interaction or situationality where outcomes are unknown (though pogromists' aggressions are indubitable). Wiese radically locates agency not in the hands of wire pullers from above or journalistic agitators but of the pogromists themselves, in the Russian case mostly urban commoners (the notorious "Black Hundreds" proving nondiscoverable). He emphasizes the importance of establishing pretexts through rumors for pogroms so as to gain support among onlookers, thus swelling participants' ranks and impeding intervention by state authorities. He holds that the targeted group possessed means of self-defense, sometimes effective, whether in the form of physical resistance or alliances with pogromists' opponents. Unlike the approach taken in this book, Wiese systematically occludes the social-cultural messages conveyed by pogroms and other anti-Jewish group violence. His work stands alongside other studies by sociologically oriented German historians that highlight inner-group dynamics among perpetrators of mass violence while bracketing questions of their ideational-psychological motives and strivings. Their aim corresponds in part with that of this book: to relocate pogrom violence within popular culture, questioning the influence on it of the antisemitic press and of presumed (or real) exhorters to anti-Jewish violence within the propertied and political classes, while resisting attribution of causal primacy in the generation of pogrom violence to macro trends in state formation, industrialization, and crises of late feudalism or capitalism.

Recent literature on anti-Jewish violence in ethnographic Poland is discussed below, but path-breaking was Frank Golczewski's formidably researched and rigorously argued *Polnisch-Jüdische Beziehungen 1881–1922: Eine Studie zur Geschichte des Antisemitismus in Osteuropa* (Wiesbaden: Steiner, 1981),which combines analysis of successive episodes of violence with the political history of Polish–Jewish relations, framed in part by Freud-derived social-psychological theory of resentment and aggression projection. Golczewski viewed ideological antisemitism as a "vehicle of an emancipatory movement" (p. 358), i.e., nationalists' efforts to mobilize the often nationally indifferent Polish popular classes in their support. Cf. Artur Markowski, "Anti-Jewish Pogroms in the Kingdom of Poland," in Dynner et al., eds., *Polin*, vol. 27 (2015), 219–56.

[28] Bujak, *Jewish Question*, 33–35, 37.

The future looked sunnier:

In peace-time the Jews will quickly make friends with a strong Polish State, where their existence will be a great deal better than in Russia, as they are in reality a sober-minded race, inclined to look at things from a practical point of view. A certain guarantee of future peaceful relationship, may be seen in the circumstance that the Poles [as Bujak imagined] did not let themselves be instigated by the inopportune and insolent attitude of the Jews, and did not lose their temper.[29]

Moreover, there would be beneficent Jewish emigration from Poland not only to the accustomed lands of the United States and England but also to Russia, "this great and rich country, so undeveloped yet and therefore affording many openings of a very profitable nature." They would leave also for Germany and "Palestine where they can begin to build up their own national state on a popular basis." Bujak anticipated the Jewish proportion in Poland's population to fall from "12–13% to 6–7% at least." Among other benefits, he declared (curiously muddling supply and demand) "the high prices charged by the middlemen in trade would fall, as the number of middlemen ... and their mutual competition would be considerably reduced." In time, "the feeling of agitation and strained relationship" between Jews and Poles would subside.[30]

In 1908 Bujak had advocated policies pressuring Jews to assimilate fully or emigrate. Ideally, the future Poland ought to be entirely free of culturally distinctive Jews, even of Judaism itself, though he pessimistically doubted the probability of this – as some called it – "asemitic" outcome. In 1919 he conceded, grudgingly, that ethnonationally distinctive Jews would continue to inhabit the Polish landscape. Like Słomka, he discerned a future in which Poles determined the terms of Jewish life, reversing what the two men resentfully and paranoically saw as recent history's opposite pattern.[31]

Diagnosis and Cure of Polish Antisemitism: Professor Jan Niecisław Baudouin de Courtenay (1845–1929)

Baudouin was pioneering linguist of world reputation, luminary both of pre-1914 Russian and Galician academic life, and politically influential icon of multiculturalism in interwar Poland. Following early education in Warsaw, he attained eminence as professor at Russian universities. His

---

[29] Ibid., 31.   [30] Ibid., 46.

[31] Franciszek Bujak, *Galicya* (Lwów: Altenberg, 1908), vol. I, 99–119 ("Kwestya żydowska"). Note that present-day scholars sometimes prefer "integration" to "assimilation," e.g., Polonsky, *The Jews of Poland and Russia*.

appointment at Kraków's Jagiellonian University in the 1890s ended with dismissal on suspicion of anti-German Slavophilism. In independent Poland he inspired supporters of his liberal conception of citizenly and national rights and advocacy of secularism in public life. In 1913 he delivered and published a far-ranging lecture entitled, "The 'Jewish Question.'" Embracing philosophical individualism and English utilitarianism, wittily lampooning the Polish National Democratic Party, which feverishly preached anti-Jewish boycott (after having suffered stinging defeat by combined Polish socialist and Jewish voters in the 1912 Warsaw election to the Fourth Russian Duma), Courtenay stepped forth as a kind of liberal Polish George Bernard Shaw.

He held that human beings were born into "unconscious, linguistically determined herd thinking" (*myślenie kolektywne [stadowe] senno-językowe*); that they were predisposed toward "brutality and lustfulness" yet also capable of logical thinking and moral self-control. This would prove easier if all suppositions of "original sin" were abandoned, whether burdening humanity as a whole or its component parts, notably women and Jews. Baudouin, self-declared freethinker, rejected both Christianity's and Judaism's prescriptions for redeeming fallen human nature, trusting in rational self-interest and benevolence instead.[32]

He diagnosed National Democrats' ("Endeks'"; see Figure i.10) strident pre-1914 antisemitism as displacement of their surging "patriotic energy" that, having encountered traumatic frustration in the failed 1905 revolution and its aftermath, turned against an antagonist weaker than tsarism – "the Jews" – this plural noun Baudouin regularly enclosed in quotation marks, along with "the Poles" and "Christians," for he denied their ontological reality as collectivities. He waxed ironical over the Endeks' persecutory, discriminatory zeal toward Jews, blind to its mirroring of Russian and Imperial German anti-Polish legislation, justified largely by the Poles' alleged "original sin" of insurrectionism and disloyalty (as in the anti-tsarist 1863 revolt, work of radicals for which all Poles under Russian rule were still paying in 1913).[33]

Baudouin conjured with the tendency in Polish political culture to self-condemnation and inferiority feelings generated by foreign rule, failed strivings for independence, and social and economic backwardness. Such oppressive thoughts encouraged scapegoating. "Despise your neighbor as you despise yourself," expressed this mentality. Thus, in the Endeks' cruel self-image, "Poland is hunchbacked by the Jew" (*Polska jest żydem garbata*). Similarly self-incriminating, "the Jew infects the air" (*Żyd zaraża*

---

[32] Jan Baudouin de Courtenay, *W "Kwestii Żydowskiej"* (Warsaw, 1913), 16–17, 65, 87.
[33] Ibid., 18–21, 48–49.

Figure i.10 Endeks. Here pictured in 1910 in St. Petersburg are Polish National Democratic deputies to the Russian Empire's Third Russian Duma (consultative quasi-parliamentary assembly). Absent is Roman Dmowski, the party's chief ideologist and iconic leader. Second from right stands Władysław Grabski, later prime minister in independent Poland, economist, and influential parliamentarian. This group portrait captures the relatively youthful and well-educated Endek leadership's self-confidence and determination to take the helm of a modernizing and Westernizing Polish nation, whether having broken into independence or having achieved self-government within the Russian Empire. Of mixed bourgeois and gentry heritage, they embodied the secular, scientifically minded nationalist intelligentsia. In rationalist terms, they understood their antagonism to the Jewish presence as necessary to the emergence of a modern Polish nation with a strong Polish-Catholic capitalist commercial-industrial class and an efficient market-integrated peasantry. But, in cultural-psychological terms, they often succumbed to paranoic Judeophobic anxieties, as Dmowski's and other Endeks' writings and speeches unselfconsciously revealed.
Source: Provenance unknown.

powietrze). Antisemites knew that, earlier, Jews had been vital to the land's structure, but now Poles were "strong enough" to stand alone and exclude Jews through social, political, and economic boycott.[34]

---

[34] Ibid., 23, 43, 58. On self-defensiveness vis-à-vis the West within Polish political culture, see Jerzy Jedlicki, "Polish Concepts of Native Culture," in Ivo Banac and

Baudouin judged this exclusionary thought futile and self-defeating. Rhetorically (but to my mind ominously), he canvassed "extermination, expulsion, starvation" (*wytępienie, wypędzenie, ogłodzenie*) as "solutions" to the "Jewish question." But Jews would not suffer physical assaults passively; Poles had no means to expel them from the partitioning states, and to immiserate them (beyond the current dire state of their under-employed proletariat) would only create a mass of antisocial desperados. As for "assimilation," it was, he believed, a strictly one-way street on the Polish map and unacceptable to the Jewish masses.[35]

Zionism Baudouin judged harshly as the Jewish equivalent to Endeks' and other aggressive nationalists' "zoological" ideology, denying individual freedom and self-definition under pressure of group conformism. Historic Judaism was no fountainhead of the Polish freethinker's liberal-rationalist values.

I recognize the "Jews' power," i.e., the power of Jewish tradition's influence on other human groups' mentality. For at the base of our thinking, our beliefs about fundamental matters, we encounter a Jewish source [the Old and New Testaments]. We are ourselves but "modified" Jews.

Principled "mercilessness," unforgivingness, readiness to exterminate, raised to ideological level – all this we imbibed from literary monuments [the Christian Bible] of Jewish descent.

Thanks to the "Judaization" of our thinking even those rush forward into wholesale attacks on Jews who dare call themselves servants of him born in Bethlehem ... those who profess Jehova, God of Israel.[36]

Evident here is the deep seriousness, the radicalism, of Baudouin's critique and the knife edge it traversed. He feared that as antisemitic strategies proved fruitless, nationalists would suffer "hang-overs" leading to "new bloody nightmares in the future." He thought he sensed violence's nearness in 1913: ritual-murder rumors in the province, the Endek press's promotion of religious antisemitism, "pogrom weather."[37]

His solution was far sunnier: "territorial solidarity." Recognizing that Russia's Jewish subjects had reason to gravitate toward the reigning imperial culture, despite its discrimination against them, rather than taking their stand with the hard-pressed and powerless Catholics of Russia's "Vistula Province," Poles needed to win Jewish backing through greater liberality than Russians would show. The aim should be equal rights in the Polish lands for every individual, whether man or women and of whatever religious persuasion. There must be recognition of the "individual's right not only to belong to no confession [*bezwyznaniowość*] but also to embrace no nationality [*beznarodowość*], or embrace multiple nationalities [*wielonarodowość*]."

The Jew, endowed with equal rights, who on Polish soil is free to remain a Jew, whom no one will scorn or persecute, whom no one will force to transform himself into a "Pole," will feel himself at home in such a land, and out of thankfulness for such freedom will, slowly and despite himself, become a "Pole," if not in an ethnic-national sense, then at least territorially. And that should be enough for us.[38]

This was Baudouin de Courtenay's formulation of what is today approvingly conceived as "citizenly" national identity. It entailed – unobjectionably to most Jews – learning of the official language and acceptance of the institutions of liberal democracy (though many pious Jews found army service problematic). Few Polish liberals, whose modernizing, rationalizing zeal had flourished after 1863, could accept Baudouin's stalwart rejection of collectivist nationalism, even as he ardently sought Polish society's improvement along Western European lines and preservation of its cultural distinctiveness. The temptations of mass-based nationalism were too great, the multifarious inner resentments over their own weaknesses and dependency among most Poles, high and low, too painful to allow adoption of the cosmopolitan – but deeply Polish – linguist's lofty individualism. Yet there were others like him.

The Caste Theory of Polish-Jewish Relations

Aleksander Hertz (1895–1983) was a Warsaw-born sociologist and public intellectual of Polonophile Jewish heritage – his father joined the 1863 rebellion – and secularized assimilated character. In 1961, in American exile, he published with the anticommunist liberal Polish émigrés in Paris a classic work, appearing in English translation in 1988 as *The Jews in Polish Culture*. It distilled Hertz's deep life experience into an analysis of historic Poland as a *caste society*, shaped by the numerous nobility who had dominated the centuries-old pre-1795 independent Polish Commonwealth. As a social formation, the Polish Jews were, as Hertz rightly emphasized, the nobility's creation, and the two groups lived down to peasant serfdom's nineteenth-century abolition, and even to World War II, in (unequal) economic symbiosis.[39]

---

[38] Ibid., 74, 91, 95, 97–99.

[39] Aleksander Hertz, *The Jews in Polish Culture* (Evanston, IL: Northwestern University Press, 1988 [Polish original: *Żydzi w kulturze polskiej*]), 59–60, 81–83. Cf. Michael Steinlauf, "Whose Poland? Returning to Aleksander Hertz," *Gal-Ed*, vol. XII

Historic Poland's castes, Hertz proposed, were nobility, peasantry, Christian burghers or town dwellers (*bourgeoisie* refers to the well-educated and propertied among them), and – chief among "native foreigners" – Jews. Castes were in principle closed and inescapable, indelibly marking their members' social-cultural attributes and demanding their self-identification with them, whether proud or abject. The nobility (*szlachta*), together with the intelligentsia sprung from their ranks and Christian clerics buttressing them, decreed that the enserfed peasantry were descendants of Noah's son Ham and thus were *chamy* (*cham* still today means "boor"). The Jew, Noah's son Shem's descendant, bore the contemptuous generic name *parch* ("scab"). The petty Christian townsman was a *łyk* ("sip," "gulp"). Each caste viewed the others – and itself – in these homely terms. "The peasant and the Jew – two groups with especially clear-cut caste traits – fully accepted the definition of *cham* and *parch*," albeit as the premodern world slowly tottered in the late nineteenth century, these names faded or became free-floating pejoratives. Indeed, the voluminous documentation underpinning the chapters that follow, mostly of grassroots provenance, uncovers not a single *parch* or *łyk*. Other epithets prevailed.[40]

It was not, Hertz believed, a matter of antisemitism, a modern ideology. "This [traditional] attitude toward Jews – contemptuous, ill disposed, derisive – was not the attitude toward enemies who are responsible for our misfortunes and who should be destroyed. There the Jew was simply an element in a larger system, which besides the 'lords' also contained the *łyks*, the *chams*, and the *parchs*." Nobles – and peasantry too – distinguished a Jew acceptable to them, or befriended by them, as *żydek* ("little Jew").[41]

(1991), 131–42; Janusz Tazbir, "Obraz Żyda w opinii polskiej XVI-XVIII w.," in Janusz Tazbir, ed., *Mity i stereotypy w dziejach Polski* (Warsaw: Interpress, 1991), 64–98. See also Polonsky, *The Jews of Poland and Russia*, vol. I; Gershon David Hundert, *Jews in Poland-Lithuania in the Eighteenth Century: A Genealogy of Modernity* (Berkeley, CA: University of California Press, 2004); Bernard Weinryb, *The Jews of Poland: A Social and Economic History of the Jewish Community in Poland from 1100 to 1800* (Philadelphia: Jewish Publication Society of America, 1973); Murray Rosman, *The Lords' Jews: Magnate-Jewish Relations in the Polish Lithuanian Commonwealth in the Eighteenth Century* (Cambridge, MA: Harvard University Press, 1990); Nancy Sinkoff, *Out of the Shtetl: Making the Jews Modern in the Polish Borderlands* (Providence, RI: Brown Judaic Studies, 2004).

[40] Hertz, *The Jews in Polish Culture*, 72.

[41] Ibid., 75, 81–83. Michał Ringel, outstanding Zionist politician and parliamentarian in interwar Poland, considered "belittlement and contempt" (*lekceważenie i pogarda*) of Jews as a "special characteristic" of Polish antisemitism, in comparison with other European varieties. From his mid-1920s vantage point, Ringel (concerned to dissuade his Jewish readers from adopting leftist-materialist interpretations) saw antisemitism not as a socioeconomic but rather as a "social-psychological" problem, rooted in "the sphere

But it was, Hertz readily conceded, a matter of racism, one of humanity's many "magical world views." Deep into the twentieth century (and beyond), Christian Polish racism converged on the consensus that "Jews were organically and by definition alien to and different from Poles." Non-antisemites, friends of Jews, Jews themselves, Hertz held, all accepted Jews' "differentness and even their alienness."[42]

Yet, except for a few explosive Cossack-peasant revolts that raged in historic Poland's eastern borderlands in the seventeenth and eighteenth centuries, in which Jews figured among the slaughtered, such racism entailed little large-scale anti-Jewish violence. Instead, as a German Nazi-era study of some 400 Polish proverbs concerning Jews revealed, derision and belittlement prevailed: "the ridiculousness of the Jews was the dominant motif." Hertz thought that self-deprecating Jewish humor – *shmontses* – was a reflection of this.[43]

The serious and sober Jewish self-image was just the opposite.

The Polish Jew felt that he was a member of a great religious community, the inheritor of rich historical and cultural traditions. But, above all, he felt that he was a member of a charismatic group, a participant in that charisma. There are not many communities in the world whose sense of collective and individual charisma is developed to the degree it is among Jews.

They were, Hertz emphasized, "the Chosen People." The Polish Jew, in his daily prayers, "thanked God for creating him a Jew." To abandon Jewry "meant to renounce the charisma." The convert to Christianity – the *meches* – was execrated (even though pride in renegades' accomplishments in the non-Jewish world was common).[44] As for the non-Jew or gentile (Hebrew: *goy*):

The Jew had a twofold view of the goy: the goy was a creature of a higher order even if he was a peasant; but he was also a stupid goy, a *cham*, a lower creature deserving of contempt. Outside the caste the first definition was obligatory, within the caste, the second.[45]

Exceptions were numerous, especially for benevolent, well-educated non-Jews, who were met with "genuine respect." It was cynical street wisdom that "all Poles are anti-Semites." Conversely, Hertz thought that

---

of feelings and attitudes," enabling, like a drug, its adherents to cope with their anxieties living in a precarious and backward country. Michał Ringel, *Antysemityzm w Polsce* (Warsaw: Wende, 1924), 3, 29, 39.

[42] Hertz, *The Jews in Polish Culture*, 15–17.

[43] Ibid., 200. Cf. Michael Steinlauf, "Mr. Geldhab and Sambo in *Peyes*: Images of the Jew on the Polish Stage, 1863–1905," *Polin*, vol .4 (1989), 98–128.

[44] Hertz, *The Jews in Polish Culture*, 93.   [45] Ibid., 65, 70–71.

while within the caste honesty was required, outside it no one expected excessive scrupulousness. "Small business in Poland was marked by the double standard, which was born of the caste system." Yet commonplace too was the "good goy," especially wise advocates of justice toward Jews.[46]

Modern antisemitism blossomed, Hertz argued (as many social scientists have), when anticaste tendencies, including religious conversion, spread among Jews. This threw doubt on the hitherto prevailing certainty that "a Jew was a Jew and that said everything about him." Hertz rightly stressed the importance of cultural-political assimilation in the crystallization of modern Jewish identities, including Zionist nationalism, for it was principally through intellectual and political acculturation in non-Jewish society that Jewish self-understandings could expand to include the secularized, scientized, nationalized modern Jewish *persona*. Hertz thought that Polish antisemitism displayed greater hostility to Yiddish-speaking movements that proclaimed Jews' right to develop as a modern nationality in the Polish lands than to Hebrew-favoring but also Polish-speaking Zionists, who aimed in principle to settle eventually in Palestine.[47]

Yet assimilation rarely was complete. Poles supposed that Jews speaking Polish would "judaize" the language, using "grammar, expressions, an accent and inflections that accorded with the accepted image of the Jew." Similarly, a Jew who "'dressed like a European' was expected to appear garish, betraying his 'Jewish taste.'" In America, Hertz discovered parallels. He was particularly struck by lower-class white American resistance to post-1945 emancipation of African-Americans from the system of segregation. He thought of American race relations also as caste system, conferring psychic advantages on poor whites, who then complained "most loudly about the arrogance of blacks, their insolence, garishness, pushiness, and so forth. These accusations are astonishingly reminiscent of those leveled at the Jews in Poland." There were "certain aggressive tendencies" in Polish Jews' and African-Americans' dress and

---

[46] Ibid., 78, 81–83.

[47] Ibid., 88, 92, 145–47, 164–65. On Jewish assimilation and its political accompaniments, see Alina Cała, *Asymilacja Żydów w Królestwie Polskim, 1864–1897: postawy, konflikty, stereotypy* (Warsaw: Państwowy Instytut Wydawniczy, 1989); and Agnieszka Jagodzińska, *Pomiędzy: Akulturacja Żydów Warszawy w drugiej połowie XIX wieku* (Wrocław: Wydawnictwo Uniwersytetu Wrocławskiego, 2008), highlighting cultural and behavioral aspects. On later years, see Celia Heller, *On the Edge of Destruction: Jews of Poland Between the Two World Wars* (New York, NY: Columbia University Press, 1977); Katrin Steffen, *Jüdische Polonität. Ethnizität und Nation im Spiegel der polnisch-sprachigen jüdischen Presse 1918–1939* (Göttingen: Vandenhoeck & Ruprecht, 2004); Anna Landau-Czajka, *Syn będzie Lech ... Asymilacja Żydów w Polsce międzywojennej* (Warsaw: Instytut Historii PAN, 2006).

behavior. "This has deep psychological roots," though Hertz left them unearthed.[48]

Thomas and Znaniecki's Portrait of Peasant Culture

Hertz's views are not canonical within Jewish scholarship, but they recall widespread early twentieth-century mutual perceptions among Polish Jews and Christians. His caste theory is imaginative and illuminating, even if it minimizes great social and cultural differences within Polish Jewry – a multimillions-strong and far-flung population – that these pages will unveil. He is silent on sexual relations across caste lines. And, though he invoked the importance of magical thinking, he did not plumb its depths, stressing only its salience especially during times of sociopolitical crisis, when supposed agents of communally suffered evil are scapegoated – a view still common, including among anthropologists of witchcraft.[49]

In *The Polish Peasant in Europe and America* (1918–20), a milestone of European ethnography, American sociologist William Thomas and Polish counterpart Florian Znaniecki limned the deep structures of Polish peasant mentality, highlighting its magical dimension. Because Jews figured crucially as an uncanny presence and force in ordinary Poles' (largely unconscious) everyday perceptions or thoughts, Thomas and Znaniecki's psychological architecture of Polish villagers is important for illuminating how this could be so.[50]

They posited four strata of religious and magical attitudes. First and oldest, indeed pre-Christian, was animism, free of notions of disembodied spirits. Natural phenomena – including animals, plants, and the Earth itself – were individualized and given consciousness such that, for example, arable fields would not yield to usurpers. There was "solidarity of life in nature" against death and decay, sickness, misery, and destruction but no "principle of evil." Pessimism and fatalism were absent, for life was "always ultimately victorious over death, thanks to the solidarity of living beings." In harmony with Słomka's views on villagers' deaths, Thomas and Znaniecki wrote that

---

[48] Landau-Czajka, *Syn będzie Lech*, 60, 187. The US–Polish comparison Hertz proposed remains unfulfilled. Support for its cogency may be found in W. J. Cash's insightful classic, *The Mind of the South* (New York, NY: Knopf, 1941).

[49] Peter Geschiere, *The Modernity of Witchcraft: Politics and the Occult in Post-Colonial Africa* (Charlottesville, VA: University of Virginia Press, 1997).

[50] William I. Thomas and Florian Znaniecki, *The Polish Peasant in Europe and America* (New York, NY: Dover, 1958), vol. I, 87–302.

the peasant is able to prepare himself calmly for his own death or for that of his dearest ones, but he grows almost insane with fear when a calamity menaces the whole community.

(Such fears abounded in post-1914 war and revolution, and again during World War II.) People dealing with death were shunned or despised. "Most of the butchers and skin-dealers are still Jews."[51]

The second, historically later stratum entailed belief in spirits, benevolent and malevolent. "The beliefs are religious, the practice is magical." Inimical, among others, were *boginki* (water sprites, menacing children and mothers), *południcy* (strangling noon sleepers in the fields), and *planetniki* (cloud beings). Six types of human souls existed, sometimes roaming the world and, in vampire form, terrorizing it. The Christian Church transformed all but the Christian soul – also known to visit the living – into the devil, but folk belief was resistant. There were, besides, many devils. "The devil is not an essentially evil being, although often malicious, harmful, or disgusting." As the saying went, "he who lives near hell, asks the devil to be his *kum*" ("chum"). The devil tempted people mainly to "do business" with him, and the sin he instigated in his followers was "break of the magical solidarity with the heavenly powers," leading to sacrilege, denial of God, and acceptance of rites of recognition of the devil's power. We may add that it is easy to see how this attitude could color or even determine peasants' dealings with Jews.[52]

To combat evil spirits, religious magic was deployed. Chief offenses against Christianity were "those against religious rites," or sacrilege. We will see how such an idea figured often, as both grievance and revenge, in anti-Jewish violence. But church rituals, including appeals to God, Jesus, Virgin Mary, and relevant saints and angels, could "destroy every sin" and maintain or reestablish "magical harmony with God in order to keep one's self and one's property safe." Malevolent magical actions were not necessarily physical in operation. The witch milked a stick in her house, and the neighbor's cow's milk was drawn into her pot. To prevent this, it was necessary "to *abolish* the magical influence, *destroy* it, by introducing some determined contrary factors." Magically conceived effects were never without their agents, whether human or spirit. Their destruction was virtuous.[53]

---

[51] Ibid., 208, 223, 231, and 208–33, *passim.* Słomka, *From Serfdom to Self-Government,* 132: "Folk would pass away without fear, and with extraordinary calm." Cf. Joanna Tomicka and Ryszard Tomicki, *Drzewo życia: ludowa wizja świata i człowieka* (Warsaw: Ludowa Spółdzielnia Wydawnicza, 1975).

[52] Thomas and Znaniecki, *The Polish Peasant,* 206, 235–36, 240–41, 245–46.

[53] Ibid., 251–54 (author's emphasis).

The Christian Host possessed very wide potency against evil menaces. Conversely, "every witch or magician tries to get hosts, church candles, consecrated earth, water, oil, or salt." Such figures felt "morally obliged to perform [sacrilege] whenever they can" so as to destroy consecrated objects' power and weaken the Christian community. Again, it is clear that Jews, conceived as Christianity's enemies, could easily be fitted into this picture. By 1920, Thomas and Znaniecki thought such attitudes had sunk to "'old women's stuff,' not disbelieved, but unworthy of a real man's occupation, [yet] it still exerts an attraction." The devil's magical importance was still great enough "to make the question of belonging to the community of God or the devil the main religious problem."[54]

Thomas and Znaniecki associated this second complex of assumptions about life with the assertion that

the peasant feels that he lacks any control of the world, [while] others have this control to an almost unlimited degree. He has no consciousness of the limitations of power of those who are his intellectual superiors and whom he does not understand, and he ascribes to somebody the responsibility for anything that happens. His only weapon in these conditions is cunning – apparent resignation to everything, universal mistrust, deriving all the benefits possible from any fact or person that happens to come under his control.[55]

Such a mentality, as we will see, offered little resistance to exhortations to aggression emanating from seemingly authoritative individuals.

The third layer of peasant perception was "purely Christian." In place of magically deployed Christianity's mechanical effects against inimical forces, here God's response to the believers' piety was "divine reward" and "conscious action of the divinity moved by human worship." But, significantly for our interests, Christian practice was collectivist, not individualized. Congregations reacted to sermons "in a determined way by gestures, sighs, sometimes even exclamations. A priest who does not know how to use the unofficial ritual can never be an influential preacher." Finally, the fourth layer led the individual to "mysticism, the tendency to self-perfection and salvation" and a "personal relation with the divinity." But this was "not very much developed among the peasants," who were much more concerned (unlike Russian peasants) to cleave to "absolute orthodoxy."[56]

Thomas and Znaniecki said of the peasant's engagement with autonomous thought and decision making that it was arduous and time-consuming: "he remembers for many years every act of reflection which he performed." Consequently, he seldom tested his conclusions against experience or otherwise criticized them. "This explains the many evident

---

[54] Ibid., 268–71.   [55] Ibid., 274–75.   [56] Ibid., 278, 284, 286–87.

absurdities and contradictory statements among the peasants . . . He may agree another opinion is right, but so too is his." His general assumption about people is that "everybody is moved only either by his egotistic interest or by solidarity with his group; if neither can be detected, then evidently the man is clever enough to keep his motives hidden." Or he is stupid.

The peasant knows the parish priest, accepting his weaknesses. He thinks the noble squire "in his heart wants return of serfdom, but otherwise can be lived with and even admired and loved." As for "the Jew," he

is classed once and forever as merchant and cheater, and no other motive than money is ascribed to him. [The peasant knows] little, if anything, about his family and religious life. [It was believed the Jew] often cheats the peasant by putting forward a smaller or pretended interest ... keeping the larger interest in the background.[57]

Urban officials and skilled artisans, also political agitators, exercised similar deceit. But recently some "few eminent men" have persuaded peasants of the sincerity of their desire to raise them up. "And when some of the city men succeeded in breaking down the peasants' mistrust and becoming political or social leaders, the confidence of the peasants in them became unlimited, absurd."[58]

Peasants' cultural interests steered toward knowledge of reality, not the city dweller's preferred "fiction, imagination, invention." If a villager turned philosopher, devouring books, he was likely to become anticlerical. Fitting him for participation in collective violence, the peasant had "a very keen sense for the picturesque, theatrical side of ceremonial groups and collective or individual performances." Popular poems were songs. There were "few, if any, among the half-educated peasants who do not try to become poets."[59]

Bohdan Baranowski's Nineteenth-Century Villagers

Thomas and Znaniecki painted on a macrocanvas, but their still-admired portrait of the postemancipation Polish peasantry finds reflection in eminent anthropologist Baranowski's 1969 study of villagers' daily life in southwestern Russian Poland. His analysis of the villagers' psychic and religious life helps frame these pages' interpretations. After emancipation, they sought to escape serfdom's humiliations by adopting the nobility's manners and discourse – investing recklessly, so far as their pinched purses allowed, in riding horses, unaccustomedly addressing one another

---

[57] Ibid., 291.   [58] Ibid., 292–93.   [59] Ibid., 300–1.

as "sir" (*pan*), and sporting new stylish wardrobes. As their earnings rose, so too did vodka drinking. But they were slow to imbibe Polish nationalism. A peasant memoirist remembered his grandfather's admonition: "children, pray God you don't live to see Poland, because in Poland we had it bad."[60]

Yet uncertainties of post-1863 existence as newborn market-dependent freeholders caused villagers' religious fervor to rise to "extreme fanaticism." Emotions exploded in church services. Unwed mothers were publicly humiliated; spectacle-rich pilgrimages undertaken. Collective illusions of miraculous events were frequent: Jesus' face was seen in a tree, the Virgin Mary appeared on a meadow.[61]

Low-grade violence was endemic. "In the peasant family rigorous discipline prevailed. Frequent beating was thought to improve children's education," and "moderate beating" of wives was widespread. Women's "lowliness" (*niższość*) and ritual uncleanliness were emphasized: they could not ride horses, nor handle seed grain. Unsociable, unloved village women were often branded witches. Losses to horse thieves triggered "complete psychic breakdown, or outbursts of terrible rage," leading – when offenders were caught – to "exceptionally atrocious punishment": burning with live coals, crippling, hanging on tree branches by the hands.[62]

At twentieth-century dawn, "the great majority of rural society lived in constant fear of 'unclean powers' threatening them." There were "charmed eyes'" spells and curses. Older people avoided looking in mirrors, whose inner sanctum dark forces stalked. Fortune telling was universal. On Christmas Eve, farmers communicated with livestock by knocking on stalls. There were vital-fluids-sucking incubi (*zmory*), ghosts (*upiory*), nightmarish aggressors (*strzygonie*), and vampires. The latter had two souls, one baptized, the other pagan (and liable to break out after death). They might have two sets of teeth.

The devil's name was avoided, in favor of speaking of "him" or "something." He could appear in any guise, including as magnanimous handsome nobleman or Jew. His helpers, Boruta or Rokita, might drag night travelers into the swamp and drown them. "Repressed sexual complexes" were externalized in imagined devilish orgies. The best defenses against unseen enemies were frequent Christian masses. The more pious

---

[60] Bohdan Baranowski, *Życie codzienne wsi między Wartą i Pilicą w XIX wieku* (Warsaw: Państwowy Instytut Wydawniczy, 1969), 13ff, 28, 142: "*Dzieci, prośta Boga, ażebyśta Polski nie dociekały, bo nam w Polsce źle było*" (p. 184). See also Bohdan Baranowski, *Kultura ludowa XVII I XVIII w. na ziemiach Polski Środkowej* (Łódź: Wydawn. Łódzkie, 1971).
[61] Baranowski, *Życie codzienne*, 71ff.   [62] Ibid., 113, 138, 157.

a community, the more seldom were the devilish visitations (about which people were embarrassed to speak).[63]

Tavern keepers were Jews and were assumed to cheat drunken peasants on drink tabs. Jews might be accused of magically diverting cholera from their settlements to the Christians' (although, conversely, the latter might burn wood from a Jewish cemetery to ward off illness). Christians stigmatized goats and their milk, consumed among poor Jews, as channels of diabolic intervention and avoided them. At christenings, it was commonly said that "they took [to the church] a pagan [or Jew or Protestant] and brought back a Christian [or Catholic]."[64]

Baranowski's villagers were susceptible to collective panic and aggression toward outsiders. Yet they were stratified by age cohort, marital status, and income and separated along the boundary line between pious and respectable and impious and disreputable. How many Jan Słomkas were among them? Baranowski, in 1969 Socialist Poland, left this question unposed.[65]

Joanna Tokarska-Bakir's "Legends of Blood"

This 2008 book, subtitled "Anthropology of Prejudice," is Polish scholarship's deepest inquiry into popular antisemitism. It takes the medieval Christian blood libel legend – that Jews stole or otherwise committed sacrilege against the Host and abducted and murdered Christians to gain blood to be mixed at Passover with matzoth (see Figure i.11) – as Polish antisemitism's fundamental mythic framework, in structural linguist and folklore analyst Vladimir Propp's sense. With her exploration of European and Polish blood-libel history, Tokarska-Bakir paired testimony of interviews she conducted among Poles who had lived alongside Jews in pre-1945 Sandomierz, an important Galician town that lay, during the partition era (1772–1918), on Russian Poland's frontier, not far from Jan Słomka's village. Catholic Church bastion, it witnessed repeated blood-libel accusations, anti-Jewish tumults, murders, trials, and executions from the sixteenth to the eighteenth century.[66]

---

[63] Ibid., 79, 81, 91–106.   [64] Ibid, 29, 111, 141, 160.

[65] There is a rich Polish scholarly tradition debunking popular prejudices and narcissistic self-delusions. See Jan Bystroń, *Megalomania narodowa* (Warsaw: Rój, 1935); Tazbir, ed., *Mity i stereotypy*; Wojciech Wrzesiński, ed., *Polskie mity polityczne XIX i XX wieku* (Wrocław: Wydawnictwo Uniwersytetu Wrocławskiego, 1994); Ludwik Stomma, *Antropologia kultury wsi polskiej XIX wieku oraz wybrane eseje* (Łódź: Piotr Dopierała, 2002).

[66] Joanna Tokarska-Bakir, *Legendy o krwi. Antropologia przesądu (z cyklu: Obraz osobliwy)* (Warsaw: Wydawnictwo WAB, 2008). Also important: Zenon Guldon and Jacek Wijaczka, "The Accusation of Ritual Murder in Poland, 1500–1800," *Polin*, vol. X (1997), 99–140, analyzing eighty-one ritual murder trials between 1547 and 1787, exogenously brought to an end by papal directives.

Figure i.11 Eighteenth-century large-scale depiction of imagined ritual murder, painted by Karol de Prevot (ca. 1670–1737), Polish artist of Italian origins, and exhibited in Sandomierz cathedral. The boy is craftily abducted, cruelly murdered, and bled, his corpse devoured by a dog. The killers appear, transhistorically, in ancient and modern, priestly and secular dress. Much controversy swirls about this image and others of its type elsewhere in Poland, particularly because they are housed in sacred quarters. In Sandomierz, the painting is shielded from public view by a curtain.
Source: Provenance unknown.

Following philosopher Paul Ricoeur, Tokarska-Bakir understands the persistence in Polish popular culture of the blood-libel myth as "petrifaction" (*skamielina*). Its contents floating unmoored from its medieval harbor, it continues to provide script and scenario housing modern prejudice and ethnic aggression. It is not a case of recurring meanings but rather of forms whose historically changing semantic content must be empirically discovered. Antisemitic myths, though they have grown "absurd" (*niedorzeczne*), persist like dreams that cannot be dispelled by rational exhortation but require psychoanalytic dissolution.[67]

[67] Tokarska-Bakir, *Legendy o krwi*, 47*ff.*

The blood-libel myth posits violation of the general prohibition of Christian-Jewish interaction. The "antagonist" commits theft of the "hero's" magical property (the Host), and/or abducts and tortures a Christian victim, and/or desecrates a holy image. Struggle ensues, in which the hero ("the Christian") defeats and unmasks the antagonist, whose condign punishment is followed by celebration. Tokarska-Bakir finds, underlying this scenario, an opposition between ego and nonego, in which Christianity's nonego, Satan, becomes the Jew, whose expulsion or destruction amounts to self-purification. The "spectral" or phantasmic history here enacted appeals to the subconscious impulse to free oneself of existential or cosmic curse or guilt. The Jews figuring in her book are entirely symbolical, "beings half from the dream-world, half from daylight, settled on the boundary of fear and theological perplexity [*bezradność*]: the traditional terrain of popular religiosity."[68]

The blood-libel myth embodied a discourse casting Jews as Christianity's collective *antagonista*, bereft of their own proper religion. Self-engendered curses on them for instigating Jesus' death drove them to repeat primal scenes, from Jesus' mocking to his crucifixion. Thirst for revenge for subsequent Jewish abuse at Christian hands also drove blood-libel offenses. Moreover, as a group, mythical Jews led a biologically weak life, deficient in blood and so in need of Christian blood's magical agency. Christians suffered, in Jews' attacks on their holy sacraments, "demonic invasion," resulting in bodily mutilation and death. Imitations of Christ occurred: victims died but underwent miraculous resurrection and salvation. The antagonist was defeated, and a commemorative chapel arose in the demolished synagogue's place. Christian joy (and dominance) triumphed.[69]

Whether Tokarska-Bakir's interpretive garment fits the collective actors in the pages that follow remains to be seen. Meanwhile, let us contemplate some of her findings about Christian attitudes and actions toward Jews in twentieth-century Sandomierz. Her informants recalled how at interwar Christian fests young men would dress as Jews and act as hawkers of wares, charging exorbitant prices to the public's amusement. Christians' sense of Jewish religious practice's uncanniness emerged in belief that the Torah scroll in its richly embroidered cover would, in the course of synagogue worship, turn into a "golden calf." Street urchins reviled elderly Jews, calling out nonsensically "*hamajehu.*" Anti-Jewish "pranks" (*wybryki*) – we will often encounter this word – were endless.

---

[68] Ibid., 54–57, 63–64, 125.
[69] Ibid., 300–1. Cf. David Biale, *Blood and Belief: The Circulation of a Symbol Between Jews and Christians* (Berkeley, CA: University of California Press, 2007).

An interviewee remembered having participated as a child in throwing a black cat down a Jewish chimney out of resentment for having been forbidden to play ball. The cat survived and raced through the house. "The Yids [*żydy*], oy yoy! how everybody ran away, they really didn't like a black cat, they were afraid of it."[70]

Other youthful "pranks" included smearing bacon fat on Jewish mouths or disassembling a Jewish droshky and remounting it on the owner's roof. Many saw Jewish girls as well groomed, "good-looking and very elegant." "To tease, we took weeds with burrs and threw them at a Jewess [*żydówka*]." A boy released a live crow in a synagogue during prayers. "They exploded with fright." Children would seize Jews and forcibly mock-baptize them, acting on the belief that "Jews fear baptism, but also want it, so that before their death they cry out 'baptism!'"[71]

Elderly interviewees charged, sometimes imitating Jewish accents, that Jews had taunted them, saying "the streets are yours, the houses ours" (*nasze kamienice, wasze ulice*) or (through money lending) "the keys to your churches will be ours." Some expressed paranoid resentment that Jews strove to be first in everything: in greeting visiting interwar ruler Józef Piłsudski or invading Bolsheviks. Communism would mean "Poles to Siberia, their properties to the Jews" (*polacy na sybir, żydzi na majątki*). "They wanted to create their own country here, a second Israel, *Judeopolonia*."[72] Widespread was belief that "every Jew has buried gold somewhere, whether in his sepulcher or in the cemetery grave" – or closer to hand. One recalled that Christian customers would address the shop-keeper as "you there, Jew, and he would bow deeply." Yet others thought Christians paid lower prices to Jews than to coreligionists. And it was a compliment to someone's reasoning powers to say "you've got a Jewish head."[73]

Tokarska-Bakir's unsophisticated informants often spoke ungrammatically of Jews in the third-person plural nonmasculine voice, as if to emphasize their womanishness or childishness. An uncomfortable question, swirling around unacknowledged Christian guilt feelings, was whether prewar Jews had harbored vengeful thoughts toward Poles. Some remembered Jews as calm and nonlitigious, untempted by drink or violence. "They never got mad, they didn't want to quarrel, they always spoke mildly." They were "peaceful" and "kept their equilibrium." Hooligan peasant boys harassed Jewish youths as they studied. They prodded them, "but they kept quiet. Do what you like, [the Jew] won't shout at you." He avoided walking the streets at night, fearing that

---

[70] Tokarska-Bakir, *Legendy o krwi*, 456–57, 461, 470, 506–7, 595.
[71] Ibid., 596–97, 615.   [72] Ibid., 583, 611.   [73] Ibid., 470–75.

a Catholic "might give him one on the head, another might kick him." Did everyone do this? "Whoever wanted to."[74]

Some said – this again a widespread view, still alive today – that "maybe they were better than Catholics . . . they were more just." They helped one another. "They had such concentrated strength in their Jewish tribe [*ród*]." An amateur ethnologist thought Poles viewed Jews with both "admiration and envy" as "shrewd merchants." Yet there was "contempt, a note of superiority in the Poles' relationship – or rather the Catholics' – to a person of another faith." Still, Tokarska-Bakir also found not inconsiderable evidence of Christian affection for Jewish neighbors and friends. Not surprisingly, the greater the mutual intimacy – however much this violated cultural codes – the greater was Christian sympathy toward Jews.[75]

As a girl, a woman witnessed a Jewish wedding. "They started to speak their gibberish and I ran away, because I was scared." Some interviewees laughed at Jewish prayer rituals or said, "there was fear in watching them. Or no, not fear, but seriousness [*powaga*] and that seriousness was terrible." They were believers; "they believed more deeply than we." Of Succoth huts, one said: "they had some kind of curses and spells in those little huts. If anything by chance went wrong, everyone grew afraid, because they had these spells." If they wanted to injure a Pole, "they did *haimr*, so-called. They went to the prayer-house and decided to destroy this or that." If Poles tried to sell flour at 40 groszy, *haimr* would decree Jews sell at 35 groszy.[76]

Were they Poles? "Yes, Poles, only of the Jewish tribe." "If the Jew was born in Poland, he was Jewish Pole [*żyd-polak*]." It was commonly understood that if a Jew assimilated, he would "somehow cut himself off from his roots." But another called them "a separate caste, they had their own laws, religion. But it wasn't hostility, absolutely not."[77]

A former Polish soldier claimed his mother had narrowly escaped being taken "for matzo" (*na macę*). As a boy, he learned antisemitic songs, sung on Sundays after mass on the square. Translated unrhymed, one proclaimed, linking fear of pollution with corresponding aggression,

> [The Jew] always watered our milk
> and, not washing his claws,
> kneaded the pastry with his feet, or whatever he wanted.
> Beat, beat, beat the Jew, beat.
> Let his blood flow.

[74] Ibid., 477–87.   [75] Ibid., 476, 482.
[76] Ibid., 484, 500–3. Probably a reference to *herem* – rabinically pronounced excommunication.
[77] Ibid., 492, 570.

Beat, beat, take a strong rod.
They must be driven away.
Don't let them deceive and swindle us.
Their blackmail has to go.
Send them now to hard labor,
that's the best thing.

Anthropologist Pawel Buszko recorded from Poland's Orthodox Christian Belarusian eastern districts a pre-1939 parody of a patriotic Polish hymn: "march, march, Goddammit, we need Hitler. He beats the Jews, may he live a hundred years!"[78]

A bad son threatened to have his mother buried not in a Catholic cemetery but in the Jewish graveyard (*kierkut*) because she had frightened him by threatening to hand him over to Jews for matzo. People thought Christians could cast spells by acquiring or being near a Jewish corpse. It was widely believed that there was competition between Jews and Christians over who, after death and burial, would be first at Last Judgment and the heavenly gates. Jews were said to be interred with walking staffs, enabling them to vault forward, or were buried seated, ready to run, with eggshells over their eyes to prevent sand from blurring their vision.[79]

Tokarska-Bakir summarized the workings of Freud's "narcissism of small differences," by which human groupings, despite underlying similarities, self-polarize. Each side was obliged to deny any kinship with the other; a code was reciprocally followed forbidding any "too close group contacts" and requiring a distancing expressed in a "categorical matrimonial taboo" (interconfessional marriages, infrequent, usually entailed conversion to Christianity and corresponding departure, or expulsion, from the natal religious community). Regardless of real relationships, "the symbolic relationship between the two social groups remained slanted, enduringly falsified."

Poles, whose only indisputable advantage was numerical preponderance, "pretended they were better, while Jews, who towered over Poles in industriousness, education, resourcefulness and practical sense, behaved as the code required, as always subordinate and worse." It was narcissism, too, unopposed by Catholic clergy, that encouraged dehumanizing and insulting anti-Jewish stereotypes (e.g., "pig's nephews"), preparing the soil in which ideologized and biologized antisemitism might take root. Anthropologist Bronisław Malinowski reminisced of his youth in Poland,

---

[78] Quoted in ibid., 498. "Marsz, marsz, cholera, trzeba nam Hitlera. Hitler Żydów bije, niech on sto lat żyje."
[79] Ibid., 508, 600.

where Jews were always present. "They smelled different – of garlic, onions, geese and goats – and they suffered from the itch. They were more untouchable that the USA's southern blacks."[80]

Tokarska-Bakir seconded Buszko's finding among Belarusians: "violence toward Jews was not seen as violence, since the position of Jews in popular culture presupposed precisely a hostile relationship to them." In their family circles, Poles sometimes fantasized giving their Mosaic neighbors orders: "you, Jew! Do this, or that!" Other Christians fell into grotesque self-deprecation, saying, "the Yids raised Poland up, where there was terrible backwardness. No one could read or write." They built mills and factories. "All that the Jews did. The Poles only had windmills." Christians cursed one another: "may you haul Jews' water."[81]

Naming Jews was deeply problematic. Among many epithets were Russian *iwrej* and the (quite rare) Polish *gudłaj* ("kike"), *pejsaty* ("ear-locked"), *mościk* (little Moses), or *icek* ("Ike"), *obrzyn* ("circumcised"), and *szlochaty* ("sobbing"). The Jews' name could substitute for "renegade, traitor, heretic" (*odszczepieniec*). "Educated Poles lower their voice in pronouncing this word, or avoid it altogether." An interviewee said, "it wasn't obvious he was a Jew, but you knew he was."[82]

People spoke in timeworn clichés: "Jewish chutzpah, arrogance, shamelessness, cockiness [*buńczuczność*]." Medieval stereotypes lived on: Jewish birth took place through the rectum, Jewish women's vaginas were horizontal, Jews slept in star formations and did not die natural deaths but were smothered by fellow Jews. It was common to avoid the correct verb "to die" in relation to departed Jews, who instead "kicked the bucket" (*kitnął*) or "croaked" (*zdechł*) or "perished" (*zginął*).[83]

Tokarska-Bakir concluded that blood-libel beliefs were European antisemitism's "secret nucleus" – notably the idea of Jewish "bloodthirstiness" (*krwiożerczość Żydów*). They underwent transformation into modern antisemitic notions of Jewish threats to the "national substance, faith, and property." But the "nucleus" lived on subconsciously to justify with powerful emotionality anti-Jewish aggression. The shocking, long-hushed-up post–World War II Polish pogroms in Kraków, Kielce, and elsewhere, which finally received postcommunist analysis (including by Tokarska-Bakir), all began, she observed, with blood libel or ritual murder charges. The "fetishistic 'obsession with innocence'" that she discovers in post-Holocaust Polish society points also to characteristics of the blood-libel myth. Its survival among her Sandomierz interviewees testified to "the unbroken presence in the Polish imagination of archaic,

---

[80] Ibid., 586, 590, 596–7.   [81] Ibid., 588, 590, 594.   [82] Ibid., 604–5.
[83] Ibid., 589–92, 596.

deeply internalized convictions," rooted in deep-structural human perception "about Jewish uncleanliness, about the stigma of Jewish birth." Still today "mention of Jewish roots" diminishes anyone's status in public life.[84]

Jolanta Żyndul, in a recent study of ritual murder accusations in nineteenth- and twentieth-century Poland, discovered 185 from 1795 to 1950, some 100 in 1880–1914, and fifty in the traumatized 1945–49 era. Almost none were seriously adjudicated, and the Polish lands witnessed nothing like the internationally sensationalized 1882–83 Hungarian Tiszaeszlár or the 1913 Russian Beilis trial. Yet accusations kept older anxieties alive. Żyndul observed long-term "laicization" of ritual-murder discourse, in which imagined victims ceased being boys, appearing instead as girls, especially young Christian servants in Jewish households. Supposed murderers, earlier commonly religious figures, increasingly become Jewish slaughterers (*shochetim*), acting from inherent antagonism toward non-Jews rather than in pursuit of religious effects. Eventually, ritual-murder controversies led to charges that Jews themselves provoked them, in absence of real victims, so as to blacken Poland's reputation in the West. "In such rationalized form, no one believed in ritual murder for blood, yet the legend lived on."[85]

Alina Cała's *Image of the Jew in Polish Popular Culture*

This path-breaking book, based on village interviews in eastern and southeastern Poland conducted in the 1970s and 1980s, covers a wider spectrum of popular attitudes toward Jewish presence than Tokarska-Bakir's. Cała concluded that in rural society, locked in the precarious annual vegetative cycle but also soaked in unsophisticated Christianity, "Jews were dangerous, but their existence was necessary." Similarly, "the Jew aroused fear, but also respect."[86] Images of Jews were numerous in Polish folk art, woodcarvings of pious Jews sometimes executed as life-size beehives alongside those carved as soldiers, priests, and other rural

---

[84] Ibid., 637–39.

[85] Jolanta Żyndul, *Kłamstwo krwi. Legenda mordu rytualnego na ziemiach polskich w XIX i XX wieku* (Warsaw: Wydawn. Cyklady, 2011), 282. Yet, in a crowd-discourse analysis, Joanna Tokarska-Bakir shows how in postwar pogroms the blood-libel myth attained powerful demotic expression, accompanying severe violence against Holocaust survivors: Joanna Tokarska-Bakir, "Cries of the Mob in the Pogroms in Rzeszów (June 1945), Cracow (August 1945) and Kielce (July 1946) as a Source for the State of Mind of the Participants," in Jan Gross, ed., *The Holocaust in Occupied Poland: New Findings and New Interpretations* (Frankfurt/M: Peter Lang, 2012), 205–230.

[86] Alina Cała, *The Image of the Jew in Polish Folk Culture* (Jerusalem: Magnes Press, 1995 [translation of *Wizerunek Żyda w polskiej kulturze ludowej*. Warsaw: Wydawnictwo Uniwersytetu Warszawskiego, 1992]), 131, 150.

types. It was usual to present such Jewish figures as solemn, even melancholy, but dignified. Happier representations of Jews could (and still can) be found on carved wooden coin banks given to children to encourage savings and as talismans of future prosperity.

Village culture saw Jesus' crucifixion, and the whole sacred past, recurring cyclically. "Every year Christ dies and is resurrected. The existence of the universe depends on this." The most essential religious rites were connected with winter solstice – end of one crop cycle, before the next began. This was the dangerous break in nature's flow. The hard winters' folk-cultural celebrations – Christmas pageants, Herod plays, and many others – were midwives to nature's rebirth in the spring, together with Jesus' resurrection. "The jocular mood and mockery of these scenes should not deceive: behind them were matters so terrifying that it would have been difficult to bear them in another form." Jews appeared in all such spectacles, especially as "carriers of features symbolizing fertility in the broad sense, prosperity, abundance, and good luck." A notable exception were pre-Easter Judas Fests, known to southern Poland (we will encounter one later in this book). Villagers, accompanied by priest and local Christian notables, might drag a Judas effigy to the river, where it was hung above the water and burned. Jews sometimes paid ransoms to avoid such performances or the tumults and plunder that might ensue.[87]

But throughout Polish lands, figurines and other representations of Jews, sold at winter and Eastertide markets, stood for good luck. It was tellingly thought propitious for bridal couples to borrow something from a Jewish lender on route to the wedding. In Christmastide folk theater, the comic Jewish characters, played by Christians, often stood for male potency. "The actors were dressed in shaggy or hairy costumes, symbolizing nature's fecundity. The Jewish character told bawdy jokes and accosted girls in the audience. His lines were full of allusions to sex and childbirth."[88]

The "calamitous [New Testament] formula, 'His blood on us and on our children,'" corresponded to a "crime of cosmic significance." It put Jews under curse and "thrust them into the embrace of devilish forces" so that they were "capable of causing a crisis of cosmic dimensions. Since they had influence on the vegetative cycle, they could stop or disturb it." And because the sacred and natural rhythms repeated themselves annually, the Jews' crime, and the dangers flowing from it, was endlessly

---

[87] Ibid., 152, 161–63, 223; Cała, *Żyd – wróg odwieczny? Antysemityzm w Polsce i jego źródła* (Warsaw: Wydawnictwo Nisza, 2012), 191.
[88] Cała, *Żyd*, 189.

renewed. In this sense, Jews, as part of the sacred order, were necessary but dangerous.

"As participants in the mythical beginnings of things, [they were] also present in ideas about the End of the World." One of Cała's informants recalled the cold winter of genocidal year 1942, when "partridges died out."

> The Jews themselves told me that this was their end. In the Talmud [they] had prophecies about their own destruction: when the partridges die out, it will mean the extermination of the Jews, but when the hares die out, it will mean the end of the Poles.[89]

The Jews were "sacred strangers" among Christian Poles. People respected Jewish piety, even if they also mocked ritual practices. The magical powers of Hasidic tsadiks or "wonder rabbis" inspired admiration. Christians were not loathe to consult them over their own concerns.[90] Few wished to provoke Jewish curses, widely considered prepotent. Disturbing synagogues or desecrating Jewish cemeteries could bring "illness, sudden death, or loss of good fortune in life, inheritable by future generations." There was, further, the ritual murder threat. Cała found the "vitality and popularity" of contemporary belief in Jewish use of Christian blood in various rituals "astonishing." She highlighted periods of danger or breakdown in things' normal course as the moment when blood-libel beliefs, otherwise "frozen" in culture, might explode in pogrom flames, funneling pent-up Christian fears into violence – "the same psychological process that makes a man take out his frustrations on his wife and children." Pogroms were, Cała pithily observed, ritual murder of Jews.[91]

Like Tokarska-Bakir, following anthropological tradition, Cała captured Christian ambivalence in dyadic pairs, whose first term expressed positive understanding, the second a dark side. Jews' "group solidarity" stood opposed to "hostile attitude toward non-Jews." Further opposites were piety versus atheism, calm self-possession versus cowardice, good neighborliness versus work-shy loafing, commercial skill versus inability to till the land, competent money management versus dishonesty and

---

[89] Cała, *Image*, 117, 184, 221.
[90] Ibid., 222, 142ff. On Hasidism, see Glenn Dynner, *Men of Silk: The Hasidic Conquest of Polish Jewish Society* (New York, NY: Oxford University Press, 2006); Marcin Wodziński, *Haskalah and Hasidism in the Kingdom of Poland: A History of Conflict* (Portland, OR: Littman, 2005 [Polish original: 2003]); Marcin Wodziński, *Hasidism and Politics: The Kingdom of Poland, 1815–1864* (Portland, OR: Littman, 2013); David Biale et al., *Cultures of the Jews: A New History* (New York, NY: Schocken, 2002), 519–72, 799–862.
[91] Cała, *Image*, 130, 142ff, 187–89, 222; Cała, *Żyd*, 195.

swindling, conciliatoriness versus quarrelsomeness, politeness and good will versus insincerity and treachery, and cleanliness versus uncleanliness.[92]

Cała contrasted traditional popular conceptions of Jews, ambivalent in their bipolarity, to modern antisemitism, in which Jews figure entirely negatively, implicitly playing the devil's role. Fascination with malevolent machinations became obsessive. "The stereotype of the Jew became detached from reality and social practice, serving to release frustration, cement artificial unity, and *to project popular feelings of powerlessness and sin*. This is the reason why anti-Semitism can still be aroused in Poland even without the physical existence of Jews there."[93]

In her 2012 political-intellectual history, *The Jew – Eternal Enemy? Antisemitism in Poland and Its Sources*, Cała stressed anti-Jewish writers' and politicians' strong susceptibility since the eighteenth-century Enlightenment, whether they stood on the right or left, to attributing socioeconomic backwardness to Jewish presence. Of partitioned Poland in 1914, she wrote that

the real affliction of the epoch was backwardness, yet antisemitic publicists poisonously attacked every manifestation of modernization [e.g., big industry, artistic modernism, class tensions, secularism], accusing Jews of its introduction. The call to boycott Jewish businesses was irrational when Jews still to a high degree played the role of the third estate [bourgeoisie]. It was also mystification, for economic rhetoric [to build a *Christian* Polish middle class] veiled purely ideological goals [ethnic "purification"] ... The propaganda of antisemitism could only change consciousness, not the social or economic status quo ... What was peculiar to Poland was *liberalism's succumbing to antisemitism*, when at the century's turn it had been a political current considered "progressive."[94]

Thus, in interpreting antisemitic *politics*, Cała navigates in scholarly tradition's mainstream, which has long held that ideological print-antisemitism served *ulterior purposes* – especially of nationalist mobilization by anti-Jewish elites battling social tensions emanating from urban industrialism's advance. Polish antisemites insisted that anti-Jewish boycotting helped create a new commercial-industrial middle class, but it was, at best, mostly only a modestly capitalized lower middle class. Cała is right in holding that economic development was not a zero-sum game but that the Jewish-owned business sector was a vital propeller of Polish society into modernity's comfortable precincts.[95]

---

[92] Cała, *Żyd*, 201–2.   [93] Cała, *Image*, 231 (author's emphasis).

[94] Cała, *Żyd*, 286 (author's emphasis).

[95] Ibid., 308–9. Cała's citation of the English-language literature on Polish antisemitism is comprehensive. See also Abram Leon, *The Jewish Question: A Marxist Interpretation* (New York, NY: Pathfinder, 1970 [French original: 1946]; Aleksander Smolar, "Jews

Cała's books, like the others highlighted here, show that while social and ideological interpretation of antisemitic politics is indispensable, antagonism to Jews and Judaism possessed its own deep, indwelling cultural-psychological rationale. As phenomenon and cause or motor of behavior, it cannot be reduced to sociology's "society" or economics' "economy" or political science's "power." It must be taken for itself, as an independent variable – a cultural-psychological realm with its own *irrational* (though not inexplicable) rationales.

Cała rejected the oft-raised apology that antisemitism in Poland was "not racist (as Hitlerism's pseudo-scientized worldview was). She showed that the blood-libel tradition of "bestialization" of Jews easily transmuted into ideological racialization. Catholic Christianity smoothed this passage. Its Polish hierarchy did not pronounce authoritatively against the ritual-murder myth, leaving it to believers' consciences "to decide." While during the world-infamous 1911–13 Beilis ritual murder trial in Kiev, the Eastern Orthodox and Protestant presses in Russian Poland forbore endorsing the proceedings or condemned them, the Catholic press thundered denunciation of the – finally and grudgingly – acquitted defendant.[96]

as a Polish Problem," *Daedalus*, Spring 1987, 31–73; Andrzej Żbikowski, *Dzieje Żydów w Polsce. Ideologia antysemicka 1848–1914* (Warsaw: Instytut, 1994); Joanna Michlic, *Poland's Threatening Other: The Image of the Jew from 1880 to the Present* (Lincoln, NB: University of Nebraska Press, 2006); Glenn Dynner et al., *Polin*, vol. 27: *Jews in the Kingdom of Poland, 1815–1918* (Portland, OR: Littman, 2015); Theodore R. Weeks, *From Assimilation to Antisemitism: The "Jewish Question" in Poland, 1850–1914* (DeKalb, IL: Northern Illinois University Press, 2006); Jerzy Jedlicki, *A Suburb of Europe: Nineteenth-Century Polish Approaches to Western Civilization* (Budapest: Central European University Press, 1999 [Polish original: 1988]); Jerzy Jedlicki, "The End of the Dialogue: Warsaw, 1907–1912," in Sławomir Kapralski, ed., *The Jews in Poland* (Cracow: Judaica Foundation, 1999), vol. II, 111–23; Brian Porter, *When Nationalism Began to Hate: Imagining Modern Politics in Nineteenth-Century Poland* (New York, NY: Oxford University Press, 2000); Grzegorz Krzywiec, *Szowinizm po polsku. Przypadek Romana Dmowskiego (1886–1905)* (Warsaw: Wydawn. "Neriton," 2009); William W. Hagen, "Before the 'Final Solution:' Toward a Comparative Analysis of Political Antisemitism in Interwar Germany and Poland." *Journal of Modern History*, vol. 68, No.2 (June 1996), 351–81. On the relationship of Jewish to Christian business enterprise, see Joseph Marcus, *Social and Political History of the Jews in Poland, 1919–1939* (Berlin: Mouton, 1983). On historical memory, see Michael Steinlauf, *Bondage to the Dead: Poland and the Memory of the Holocaust* (Syracuse, NY: Syracuse University Press, 1997); Maria Janion, *Do Europy tak, ale razem z naszymi umarłymi* (Warsaw: Wydawn. Uniwersytetu Wrocławskiego, 2000); Maria Janion, *Hero, Conspiracy, and Death: The Jewish Lectures* (Frankfurt/M: Peter Lang, 2014); Dorota Głowacka and Joanna Zylinska, eds., *Imaginary Neighbors: Mediating Polish-Jewish Relations After the Holocaust* (Lincoln, NE: University of Nebraska Press, 2010).

[96] Cala, *Żyd*, 309–10. John Connelly, *From Enemy to Brother: The Revolution in Catholic Teaching on the Jews, 1933–1965* (Cambridge, MA: Harvard University Press, 2012). See also Konrad Sadkowski, *Catholic Power and Catholicism as a Component of Modern Polish*

To this, we may add that in the historically Polish-ruled lands, the Catholic Church had not in the early modern centuries commanded all loyalties, but only those of the geographically far-flung Catholic aristocracy and gentry and the common folk in narrowly ethnographic Poland. In its political struggles with crown and nobility, the church inclined to stigmatize Jews as corrupters of the landlords they served and the Christian servants they employed and not infrequently championed legal assaults on them, including blood-libel trials. In this way, the Christian clergy formalized an anti-Jewish ideological syndrome in advance of modern antisemitism's nineteenth-century arrival and took action on it through criminal law. But Jews were not without defenses and Christian defenders. Their successes in warding off clerical onslaughts heightened the church's discontent with its imperfect command within Polish society.[97]

From the above-arrayed perspectives, the cultural complexity and emotional polytonality of Christian-Jewish relations will have come into view, and the potentialities too for coexistence and confrontation within them. Much depended on the historical stage on which they played out. War would drape it in black.

Postscript: Jedwabne

The following pages' temporal horizon is the year 1920, but many pogroms scarred Polish history beyond the end of the anti-Soviet war, sporadically in the 1930s and infamously during the Nazi occupation, especially in summer 1941, as Hitler's troops' expulsion of the Red Army from occupied Poland set the stage for brutal mass killings, civilian perpetrated, at Jedwabne and other places in northeastern Poland. At war's end, bloody pogroms exploded again, notably in Kraków and Kielce, within a nationwide setting of scattered violence cruelly directed against Holocaust survivors. In communist Poland, antisemitism rumbled within the political system, erupting in 1968's "anti-Zionist" campaign purging the government of Poles of Jewish heritage and driving

---

National Identity, 1863–1919 (Seattle, WA: University of Washington Press, 2001); Neal Pease, *Rome's Most Faithful Daughter: The Catholic Church and Independent Poland, 1914–1939* (Athens, OH: Ohio University Press, 2009); Brian Porter, *Faith and Fatherland: Catholicism, Modernity, and Poland* (New York, NY: Oxford University Press, 2011).

[97] See Magda Teter, *Jews and Heretics in Catholic Poland: A Beleaguered Church in the Post-Reformation Era* (New York, NY: Cambridge University Press, 2006); Magda Teter, *Sinners on Trial: Jews and Sacrilege after the Reformation* (Cambridge, MA: Harvard University Press, 2011).

many of them – and other similarly stigmatized nonpolitical people – into westward emigration. Nor has antisemitism ceased even now to figure in Polish political culture, chiefly on the nationalist right, where its presence is easily discerned.[98]

The murder by fire in July 1941 of many hundreds of Jews, forced into a barn by Poles in the small town of Jedwabne, became, in the light of Jan Gross's powerful 1999 book, *Sąsiedzi* (*Neighbors*), the focus of a far-ranging controversy over Polish-Jewish relations. Doubtless the ensuing discussions and new research have had intellectually and morally liberating impact, greatly raising awareness in Poland of the gravity of past anti-Jewish prejudice and violence. Among many decisive post-*Neighbors* publications, including Gross's own further contributions, journalist Anna Bikont's 2004 book, *My z Jedwabnego* (*We of Jedwabne*), translated in 2014 as *The Crime and the Silence*, is notable for giving voice to some of the witnesses of the 1941 atrocity alongside present-day inhabitants of the unfortunate town.[99]

This is not the place to analyze the Jedwabne debates, nor the other aforementioned post-1920 explosions of violence. They all arose in their time and space and cannot be extrapolated deterministically from the events and historical developments this book explores, however much these prefigure them (as they importantly do). The Jedwabne controversy

---

[98] For extensive bibliography, see Polonsky, *The Jews in Poland and Russia*, vol. 3 (2012); Cała, *Żyd* (2012); Michlic, *Poland's Threatening Other* (2006). On the 1930s, see Jolanta Żyndul, *Zajścia antyżydowskie w Polsce w latach 1935–37* (Warsaw: Fundacja im. K. Kelles-Krauza, 1994); Piotr Gontarczyk, *Pogrom? Zajścia polsko-żydowskie w Przytyku 9 marca 1936 r.* (Biała Podlaska: Oficyna Wydawnicza Rekonkwista, 2000). On the 1940s, see Tomasz Szarota, *On the Threshold of the Holocaust* (Frankfurt/M: Peter lang, 2015); Marcin Zaremba, *Wielka Trwoga. Polska 1944–1947. Ludowa reakcja na kryzys* (Kraków: Znak, 2012).

[99] The Jedwabne-inspired literature is vast. See Jan Gross, *Neighbors* (Princeton, NJ: Princeton University Press, 2001); Jan Gross, *Fear: Antisemitism in Poland after Auschwitz* (New York, NY: Random House, 2006); Jan Gross, *Golden Harvest: Events at the Periphery of the Holocaust* (New York, NY: Oxford University Press, 2012); Hagen, "A 'Potent, Devilish Mixture' of Motives"; Antony Polonsky and Joanna Michlic, *The Neighbors Respond: The Controversy over the Jedwabne Massacre in Poland* (Princeton, NJ: Princeton University Press, 2004); Anna Bikont, *The Crime and the Silence* (New York, NY: Farrar, Straus and Giroux, 2015); Andrzej Żbikowski, *U genezy Jedwabnego: Żydzi na kresach północno-wschodnich II. Rzeczypospolitej wrzesień 1939 – lipiec 1941* (Warsaw: Żydowski Instytut Historyczny, 2006); Elazar Barkan et al., eds., *Shared History, Divided Memory: Jews and Others in Soviet-Occupied Poland, 1939–1941* (Leipzig: Leipziger Universitätsverlag, 2007); Witold Mędykowski, *W cieniu gigantów: pogromy 1941 r. w byłej sowieckiej strefie okupacyjnej. Kontekst historyczny, społeczny i kulturowy* (Warsaw: Instytut Studiów Politycznych Polskiej Akademii Nauk, 2012). Useful on Gross's work and his critics is Marci Shore, "Conversing with Ghosts: Jedwabne, Żydokomuna, and Totalitarianism," in Michael David-Fox et al., eds., *The Holocaust in the East. Local Perpetrators and Soviet Responses* (Pittsburgh, PA: University of Pittsburgh Press, 2014), 5–28.

revolves, unlike my approach, overwhelmingly around what I referred to earlier as *forensic* questions of indisputable *facts* establishing unquestionable *guilt* (or *innocence*). The agonized central theme concerns *revenge*: did Jews in Stalin-occupied eastern Poland in 1939–41 "betray Poland" through pro-communist collaboration, thus *explaining*, even *justifying*, murderous *reprisals* at Polish hands? And could it not be said that Polish perpetrators were *forced* or *driven* to bloody deeds by the Nazi occupiers? The question of *causation*, or of understanding perpetrators', bystanders', and victims' *motives*, reduces to rightist nationalist ideology, religious prejudice (also seen as "ignorance" or "benightedness"), Christian self-interest, and alleged Jewish pro-communism, all distilling into terrible revenge taking. Antisemitism figures (alongside individual perpetrators' self-serving motives) as an explanation, but its *meanings* in perpetrators' minds and actions are left locked within the black box of the ideological concept itself.

By contrast, this book seek to illuminate the *cultural* and *social logics* (and *illogics*) at work, consciously and unconsciously, in the minds and actions not only of perpetrators but also of others who sought to interpret the tragic explosions. The Theoretical Footnote that now follows addresses the difficulties – but also the feasibility – of such a journey of discovery.

Theoretical Footnote
Ethnic Violence in Social Science and Historiography

> Patterns and structures can be collective, deeply emotional, and subjectively meaningful, all at the same time. Culture is patterned emotion. Emotion is culture experienced. If the social is subjective, then a meaning-centered sociologist [or historian] must learn to speak with the listening voice of the psychoanalyst, to employ the same hermeneutic method of deep interpretation, and to read structures of social feeling as imaginatively as psychotherapists read individual-feeling texts.
>
> – Jeffrey Alexander (2014)[1]

Scholarly, scientific history explodes myths and demystifies the past. It transmutes that which is essentially elusive – the mind, the heart that moves it, life itself – into rational knowledge of causes and effects. When it confronts the irrational – illusions, delusions, enigmas, nightmares – it recodes them in the language of science and logic. It illuminates and enlightens, tracing paths of (retrospectively perceived) "necessity" – or, alternatively, "unintended consequences" – that have led to the present, the only ("as it happened") possible world and even, in most eyes, the best, despite all catastrophes, including those that raged but a generation past or are raging now.

But do mysteries not linger? Does not quest for rationally satisfying – and thus psychologically reassuring – causes and outcomes all too often fail to unmask the visages whose unsettling presence provoked the inquiry? Is the tree's shining crown not something distinct from its subterranean roots?[2]

---

[1] In Lynn Chancer et al., *The Unhappy Divorce of Sociology and Psychoanalysis: Diverse Perspectives on the Psychosocial* (New York, NY: Palgrave Macmillan, 2014), xiv.

[2] On the author's philosophical–epistemological approach, see his "Master Narratives Beyond Postmodernity: Germany's 'Separate Path in Historiographical-Philosophical Light," *German Studies Review*, vol. XXX, no. 1 (February 2007), 1–32, which addresses postpositivist and constructivist questions of interpretation's relation to evidence. Cf. Patricia Waugh, ed., *Literary Theory and Criticism* (Oxford: Oxford University Press, 2006), chaps. 3, 15, 20–22. On mythical and subliminal dimensions of history and historical experience, see note 6. An important Polish contribution is Leszek Kołakowski, *The Presence of Myth* (Chicago, IL: University of Chicago Press, 1989 [Polish original: 1972]); see too his "Antysemityzm: pięć tez nienowych i przestroga," in

At this book's heart lie pogroms and other anti-Jewish aggression during World War I and its Eastern European aftermath. No one today can contemplate the inhumanity these pages depict without sensing its ominousness. Yet its memory has been overshadowed by subsequent tragedies or lost in the sunlight of triumphalist narratives of Polish recovery of independent statehood, embraced – or acquiesced in – also by others, including many then-contemporary Polish Jews.

In everyday speech, ethnic violence figures as *hatred*'s harvest or as *evil* whose mysterious origins are interwoven with cosmic fate. Social science, including scholarly history, has long favored its attribution to clash of "interests" – or even "rational interests." Individual or collective self-aggrandizement through accumulation of political, economic, and demographic power, at others' expense and by means, when opportune, of violence, is still today almost universally accepted as *natural* and, when viewed from the accumulator's viewpoint, (amorally) *rational*. Explanation of such bloodstained phenomena as pogroms, massacres, wars, and genocides as consequences or entailments of interest pursuit by actors strong enough to proceed by violence still possesses near-hegemonic persuasiveness.[3]

Leszek Kołakowski, *Światopogląd i życie codzienne* (Warsaw: Państwowy Instytut Wydawniczy, 1957), 156–73. Worth pondering still are the simultaneously published Ernst Cassirer, *An Essay on Man: An Introduction to a Philosophy of Human Culture* (New Haven, CT: Yale University Press, 1944); and Max Horkheimer and Theodor Adorno, *Dialectic of Enlightenment* (New York, NY: Herder, 1972 [German original: 1944]).

[3] Rational understanding through empirically based interpretation, such as this book seeks, differs from rational-choice or rational-actor theory, which presupposes that the world is best understood when the inquirer assumes that historical actors consciously – rationally evaluating and weighing alternatives – pursue their interests in self-aggrandizement in power, social status, and wealth. It is sometimes argued that whatever actors do is ipso facto rational in the sense that it was the one thing they chose to do, so, in retrospect, one understands how and why it was *subjectively* rational. Yet rational-actor theory, as a form of Enlightenment-tradition methodological individualism, is reluctant to concede that people in general are moved by psychologically internalized collective norms or unreflected-on irrational motives, such as those that might emanate from a group's moral economy, unspoken culture, ideological conditioning, or mass pathologies. Similarly, *individuals* are conceived of as capable of rationally weighing choices, as they see them, free of constraints of subconscious psychology or uncritically assimilated culture. While rational-actor theory illuminates some historically given situations, it is essential to this book's purpose to acknowledge that human action is, in empirically observable ways, also animated by irrational and unconscious drives, however debatable their sources. Simultaneity (though not necessarily harmony) of rational and irrational action, and of conscious and unconscious motivation, is also common to human behavior.

For empirically valuable and thought-provoking rational-actor analyses relevant to this book's theme, see Stathis N. Kalyvas, *The Logic of Violence in Civil War* (New York, NY: Cambridge University Press, 2008), important in dismantling rational-choice superficialisms concerning political violence and in arguing for the post-1944 Greek civil war's "privatizing" of politics by transmutation of personal interest clashes and antagonisms into ideological partisanship. Max Bergholz, *Violence as a Generative Force: Identity,*

Master sociologist Max Weber influentially distinguished between rationality of means or ends (*Zweckrationalität*) and value rationality (*Wertrationalität*). Action in the first category figured as rational if it employed (or *instrumentalized*) means that efficiently achieved its goal in practice. In the second category, action was rational if it conformed to preexisting, subjectively embraced values or aspirations intended to govern life in the present or future, even if defeated, or self-defeating, in practice. The distinction showed how pursuit of values was no less rational (though in a different sense) than pursuit of wealth or power.

Weber also allowed for "affectual" (emotionally driven) as well as "traditional" (habitual or automatic) behavior, though both tended to merge with one or the other form of rational motivation.[4] But, I may add, to starkly dichotomize these latter two risks obscuring the *vital point* that *ends-oriented or instrumental rationality too is driven by values*, that is, by cultural norms. For *power* is wielded to some *social purpose*. And *wealth* exists not as accumulated treasure but to realize *immaterial* aspirations, if only to stamp physical domination with a rationale for existence, however narcissistic.

Violence *also* embodies cultural intent, even when perpetrators suppose its deployment favors their political or material interests. This is one of the broad, general points this book will demonstrate. If in some corners of academia it is a comfortable thought, it cannot be said that the historical and social-science literature on ethnic or social violence finds it so, for there, emphasis on pursuit through violence of self-aggrandizing power or material advantage commonly entails treating violence's social-cultural meaning as a question of the perpetrators' *ideological self-justification*. Thus, for example, ethnic cleansing and territory-conquering genocide are explained, apart from underlying "more fundamental" motives of instrumentalist-materialist nature, by aggressors' racist doctrines. Yet deeper, unconsciously housed drives are commonly left unexplored.

Nationalism, and Memory in a Balkan Community (Ithaca, NY: Cornell University Press, 2016), highlights rationally perceived self-aggrandizement as a trigger of ethnicized violence. See also Donald L. Horowitz, *The Deadly Ethnic Riot* (Berkeley, CA: University of California Press, 2001); Paul R. Brass et al., *Riots and Pogroms* (New York, NY: New York University Press, 1996); Earl Conteh-Morgan, *Collective Political Violence. An Introduction to the Theories and Causes of Violent Conflicts* (New York, NY: Routledge, 2004); Michael Mann, *The Dark Side of Democracy: Explaining Ethnic Cleansing* (Cambridge: Cambridge University Press, 2005), a work weakened by conflation of liberal democracy and repressive populism. For friendly critique of social-science approaches, see Rogers Brubaker and David Laitin, "Ethnic and Nationalist Violence," *American Review of Sociology*, vol. 24 (1998), 423–52.

[4] Max Weber, *Economy and Society* (Berkeley, CA: University of California Press, 2013), vol. I, 24–26.

Violence's *meanings*, distinct from its perpetrators' conscious ideological disposition or instrumental motives, are not in some objectivist sense inherent or immanent in it. They are instead *empirically discoverable in it* by interpreters in search of richer understandings of life and history than are gained through invocation of ideological alibis or ostensible motives, or mechanical reduction to preconceived notions of why things happen, or – most simplistically – when it is said that violence was employed because it was, *ipso facto*, rational to do so. It explodes the concept of rationality to treat violence as nothing more than its tactical manifestation. Rational-actor analysis must admit of irrational choice.[5]

---

[5] Charles Tilly, *The Politics of Collective Violence* (New York, NY: Cambridge University Press, 2003), and Charles Tilly, *Contentious Performances* (New York, NY: Cambridge University Press, 2008), analyze political clashes' structural dynamics, largely eschewing psychological and cultural dimensions. Randall Collins, *Violence: A Micro-Sociological Theory* (Princeton, NJ: Princeton University Press, 2008) concentrates on the *process* and *group dynamics* of initiation and subsequent stages of eye-to-eye violence, including riots and military and police atrocities. He largely brackets questions of instrumental rationality and perpetrators' motives, as also of violence's social meaning. Wolfgang Sofsky, *The Order of Terror: The Concentration Camp* (Princeton, NJ: Princeton University Press,1997 [German original: 1993]) highlights tendencies toward self-absolutization of violence, beyond justificatory rationales. Relevant to the present book is Felix Schnell, *Räume des Schreckens: Gewalt und Gruppenmilitanz in der Ukraine (1905–1933)* (Hamburg: Hamburger Edition, 2012), which illuminates recent discussions in the sociology and historiography of east European violence. Schnell too emphasizes group dynamics among violence's perpetrators, eliding the social-cultural expressiveness of such acts of violence as pogroms. See also: Jörg Baberowski et al., "Gewalt: Räume und Kulturen," *Zeithistorische Forschungen*, v. 5:1 (2008). An extension of this approach is Stefan Wiese, *Pogrome im Zarenreich* (2016), whose argument is sketched in the Introduction, note 27. For historical context: Julius R. Ruff, *Violence in Early Modern Europe 1500–1800* (Cambridge: Cambridge University Press, 2001).

Above-cited Max Bergholz, *Violence as a Generative Force* (2016), usefully shows that violence may be deployed with instrumental rationality in culturally and socially diverse settings by individuals bent on self-aggrandizement, with the *result* that polarizing ethnicization and political nationalization among the groups defined by the violence follow. Yet social-cultural analysis of the scripts enacted is left unaddressed. Similarly, on medieval Christian anti-Jewish violence sustaining and defining unequal Christian–Jewish relations, see David Nirenberg, *Communities of Violence: Persecution of Minorities in the Middle Ages* (Princeton, NJ: Princeton University Press, 1996).

On collective, often ritualized violence, see E. J. Hobsbawm, *Primitive Rebels: Studies in Archaic Forms of Social Movement in the 19th and 20th Centuries* (Manchester; University of Manchester, 1959); E. J. Hobsbawm, *Bandits* (London: Weidenfeld & Nicolson 2000); E. J. Hobsbawm, with George Rudé, *Captain Swing* (New York, NY: Pantheon, 1968); George Rudé, *The Crowd in History; A Study of Popular Disturbances in France and England, 1730–1848* (London: Lawrence & Wishart, 1964); James Scott, *Weapons of the Weak: Everyday Forms of Peasant Resistance* (New Haven, CT: Yale University Press, 1985); Natalie Davis, *Society and Culture in Early Modern France* (Stanford, CA: Stanford University Press, 1975); Emmanuel Le Roy Ladurie, *Carnival in Romans* (New York, NY: Braziller, 1979); Robert Darnton, *The Great Cat Massacre* (New York, NY: Basic Books, 1984); Robert Darnton, "Reading a Riot," *New York Review of Books*, October 22, 1992; Christhard Hoffmann et al., *Exclusionary Violence: Antisemitic Riots in Modern German History* (Ann Arbor, MI: University of Michigan Press, 2002); Edward Muir,

Collective violence is frequently instrumental but also and nearly always *symbolic*, more often unconsciously than not. This book will seek out the symbolical, even theatricalized – in short, *expressive* – meaning or content of the flood of violence it contemplates, some small-scale and physically restrained, some just the opposite.[6] But through what interpretive lens should *unconscious* behavior be read? A preexisting psychological theory will tend to confirm itself, seeing what it predicts will be seen. I proceed differently, drawing from the empirical record of collective violence psychological explanations that, in my mind, plausibly account for it. The reality of unconscious behavior, if skeptics wish to doubt it, gains in plausibility by the coherence and meaningfulness of its collective enactments, as perceived by the observer. The historical record, like the

Ritual in Early Modern Europe (New York, NY: Cambridge University Press, 1997); Catherine Bell, *Ritual: Perspectives and Dimensions* (New York, NY: Oxford University Press 1997); René Girard, *Violence and the Sacred* (London: Continuum, 2005 [French original: 1972]); Philip Dray, *At the Hands of Persons Unknown: The Lynching of Black America* (New York, NY: Random House, 2002); Jack Katz, "Criminals' Passions and the Progressives' Dilemma," in Alan Wolfe, ed., *America at Century's End* (Berkeley, CA: University of California Press, 1991), 396–420.

[6] See in Hubert Cancik et al., eds., *Handbuch religionswissenschaftlicher Grundbegriffe*, 5 vols. (Stuttgart: Kohlhammer, 1988–2001), Hanna Gekle, "Aggression," vol. I, 394–406; Jürgen Ebach, "Antisemitismus," vol. I, 495–504; Hans Krippenberg, "Magie," vol. IV, 85–97; Aleida and Jan Assmann, "Mythos," vol. IV, 179–200; Hubert Seiwert, "Opfer," vol. IV, 268–84; Renate Schlesier, "Strukturalismus," vol. V, 106–23; Gerhard Bauty, "Tod," vol. V, 207–26. See also Göran Aijmer and Jon Abbink, *Meanings of Violence: A Cross-Cultural Perspective* (Oxford: Berg, 2000). Seminal but evasive about violence: Clifford Geertz, *The Interpretation of Cultures: Selected Essays* (New York, NY: Basic Books, 1973). On cultural theory and symbolic analysis generally, see (apart from works cited in note 1) Victor Turner, *The Ritual Process: Structure and Anti-Structure* (Chicago, IL: University of Chicago Press, 1969); William H. Sewell, "Geertz and History: From Synchrony to Transformation," *Representations*, vol. 59 (Summer 1997), 35–55; William H. Sewell, "The Concept(s) of Culture," in Victoria Bonnell and Lynn Hunt, eds., *Beyond the Cultural Turn: New Directions in the Study of Society and Culture* (Berkeley, CA: University of California Press, 1999), 35–61; Adam Kuper, *Culture: The Anthropologists' Account* (Cambridge, MA: Harvard University Press, 1999).

On myth, metaphor, and ideology in popular culture and behavior, see Richard Slotkin, *Gunfighter Nation: The Myth of the Frontier in Twentieth-Century America* (New York, NY: Atheneum, 1992); Michael Rogin, *Ronald Reagan, the Movie, and Other Episodes in Political Demonology* (Berkeley, CA: University of Californias Press, 1987); Orlando Patterson, *Rituals of Blood. Consequences of Slavery in Two American Centuries* (New York, NY: Basic Civitas, 1999), with keen observations on lynching rituals. Insightful about ideological saturation of society and culture is Geoff Eley, *Nazism as Fascism: Violence, Ideology, and the Ground of Consent in Germany 1930–1945* (London: Routledge, 2013). Paul Connerton, *How Societies Remember* (Cambridge: Cambridge University Press, 1989), highlights collective behavior's *performative* dimension: how social meaning is generated and sustained through *enactment* of scripts, scenarios, ideologies, and ideas whose existence in *cognition* alone is no measure of significance or efficacy; *racist ideas* linger in cultural memory but only stamp history when *acted on*. This distinction is important to this book's argument. Cf. Rogers Brubaker et al., "Ethnicity as Cognition," *Theory and Society*, vol. 33 (2004), 31–64.

larger world, does not explain itself without interpretation, nor were general theories of psychology crafted with this book's subjects in mind. It is an author's responsibility – and freedom – to interpret his findings, including in psychological terms, and his challenge to win readers' assent.[7]

[7] A path-breaking study of the social-psychological context of mass violence, calling for English translation, is above-cited Marcin Zaremba, *Wielka Trwoga, Polska 1944–1947: Ludowa reakcja na kryzys* [*The Great Fear, Poland 1944–1947: Reactions to Crisis among Ordinary People*] (2012). Employing social-psychological trauma theory, focused on the Polish population's shattering experiences under Hitlerite occupation and their witnessing (and involvement in) the Jewish genocide, Zaremba analyzes Poland's widespread post-war violence, including numerous pogroms accompanied by antisemitic ritual-murder panics. Such violence was the trauma's expression, couched both in deep-rooted fears of the Jewish presence (and absence) and anxieties about Jewish spearheading of Soviet communism. It will be seen that this book's argumentation concerning World War I and its aftermath in part harmonizes with Zaremba's approach. I have hypothesized explanations of World War II violence parallel to Zaremba's in Hagen, "A 'Potent, Devilish Mixture' of Motives." See also Marcin Zaremba, "Mit mordu rytualnego w powojennej Polsce. Archeologia i hipotezy," *Kultura i Społeczeństwo*, vol. 51, no. 2 (2007), 91–135; and Marcin Zaremba, "Trauma wielkiej wojny: Psychospołeczne konsekwencje drugiej wojny światowej," *Kultura i Społeczeństwo*, vol. 52, no. 2 (2008), 3–42. Cf. Joanna Tokarska-Bakir's aforementioned approach to ritual-murder discourse in postwar pogroms, in "Cries of the Mob."

On psychoanalytical and psychological interpretations of ethnonational conflict, anti-semitism, and social-political life generally, see Jürgen Straub and Jörn Rüsen, eds., *Dark Traces of the Past: Psychoanalysis and Historical Thinking* (New York, NY: Berghahn, 2010), especially Karola Brede, "On Social and Psychological Foundations of Anti-Semitism," 139–58. See also Ernst Simmel et al., *Anti-Semitism: A Social Disease* (New York, NY: International Universities Press, 1946); Golczewski, *Polnisch-jüdische Beziehungen 1881–1922*, which ties social-political ethnic conflict to a justificatory psychology of aggressors' resentment and self-splitting/projection; Group for the Advancement of Psychiatry, *Us and Them: The Psychology of Ethnonationalism* (New York, NY: Brunner/Mazel, 1987); Sudhir Kakar, *The Colors of Violence: Cultural Identities, Religion, and Conflict* (Chicago, IL: University of Chicago Press, 1996); Joshua Searle-White, *The Psychology of Nationalism* (New York, NY: Palgrave, 2001); Robert Bocock, *Sigmund Freud* (London: Tavistock, 2002); Anthony Elliott, *Psychoanalytic Theory: An Introduction* (Durham, NC: University of North Carolina Press, 2002); Anthony Elliott, *Social Theory since Freud: Traversing Social Imaginaries* (London: Routledge, 2004); John Duckitt, "Prejudice and Intergroup Hostility," in David O. Sears et al., *Oxford Handbook of Political Psychology* (Oxford: Oxford University Press, 2003), 559–600; Ervin Staub and Daniel Bar-Tal, "Genocide, Mass Killing, and Intractable Conflict," ibid., 710–40; Stephen Frosh, *Hate and the "Jewish Science": Anti-Semitism, Nazism and Psychoanalysis* (Basingstoke: Palgrave Macmillan, 2005); Jacques Semelin, *Purify and Destroy: The Political Uses of Massacre and Genocide* (New York, NY: Columbia University Press, 2007). Steven Pinker, *The Better Angels of Our Nature: Why Violence Has Declined* (New York, NY: Viking Press, 2011), offers a macrohistorical argument fusing Norbert Elias's history of social self-disciplining with the spread of Enlightenment liberalism that occludes or minimizes modernity's subtle and not-so-subtle forms of soft and hard violence. He holds, however, that much violence is culturally sanctioned and thus seen as admissible or necessary. Cf. Zygmunt Bauman's forceful case for assimilation of mass violence to bureaucratic rationality in *Modernity and the Holocaust* (Ithaca, NY: Cornell University Press, 1989). Judicious on consensus and coercion is Peter Wagner, *A Sociology of Modernity: Liberty and Discipline* (New York, NY: Routledge, 1994).

If social-political violence aims, as this book argues, to realize or rein-state *values*, whether alongside or in place of *interests*, how can it be said to relate to *morality*? Anthropologists Alan Fiske and Tage Rai address this question in *Virtuous Violence: Hurting and Killing to Create, Sustain, End, and Honor Social Relationships*, arguing that "across cultures and history, most violence is morally motivated to regulate relationships in a culturally prescribed manner."[8] Of these relationships, four are historically univer-sal and command behavior seeking to maintain them in their given cultural form. These are "communal sharing (unity); authority ranking (hierarchy); equality matching (equality); market pricing (proportional-ity)," amounting in practice, in the latter case, to "an eye for an eye." Perpetrators of violence, individual or collective, *aim* or *intend* to uphold or restore culturally idiosyncratic norms governing these relationships and understand the violence they inflict to this end as *virtuous*, as do also their cultural peers and fellows. Human experience refutes any moral postulate that infliction of pain and suffering is universally under-stood as *evil*. "In short, most violence is the exercise of moral rights and obligations."[9]

Persuasive though this argument may be, the analysis that follows does not require its acceptance, but only that perpetrators will commonly regard the violence they inflict, at the time they do so or thereafter, as justified and in some social-cultural sense *righteous* (though they may *also* have acquisitive ambitions and personal scores to settle). Fiske and Rai hold that violence not only redresses but also "sustains and modulates social relationships" or "simply *is* the relationship," in the sense of its practice or process.[10] This gestures toward one of this book's central points – that the violent act's performative reality frequently *displays* its social-cultural meaning and message – a dimension that Fiske and Rai leave unexplored. Nor do they invoke the concept of *moral economy*, familiar to historians as norms embedded in popular culture prescribing how relations between distinctive, usually unequal social groupings should be governed and whose violation justifies violent reprisals, usually from the weaker side. In this book, the mobilizing force of the moral economy seen, in Christian eyes, to regulate the Polish-Jewish relation-ships will emerge as vividly real.[11]

---

[8] Alan Fiske and Tage Rai, *Virtuous Violence: Hurting and Killing to Create, Sustain, End, and Honor Social Relationships* (Cambridge: Cambridge University Press, 2015), 16.

[9] Ibid., 1 and 1–21, *passim*.   [10] Ibid., 13.

[11] Edward P. Thompson, "The Moral Economy of the English Crowd in the Eighteenth Century" [1971] and "The Moral Economy Revisited," in *Customs in Common* (London: Merlin, 1991), 185–351. On the concept's application in this study and for further references, see Chapter 3. Bruce Berman et al., eds., *The Moral Economies of Ethnic and Nationalist Claims* (Vancouver: University of British Columbia Press,

Historians of Central and Eastern European ethnic relations have almost invariably preferred to peer through the lenses of interest analysis and political logic rather than the dark glass of deeply embedded, culturally contoured, self-hidden or ideologically veiled antagonism and aggression. To take a recent example, the reader of the empirically valuable essay collection, *Shatterzone of Empires: Coexistence and Violence in the German, Habsburg, Russian, and Ottoman Borderlands* (2013), will encounter but one foray in this direction, by a cultural anthropologist. In crafting the interpretive approach this book follows, I have instead followed cues given by historians of Western Europe, notably Natalie Davis, Edward Thompson, and E. J. Hobsbawm, and by the anthropological, sociological, and psychological literature.[12]

High also on this book's horizon looms political scientist Roger Petersen's *Understanding Ethnic Violence: Fear, Hatred, and Resentment in Twentieth-Century Eastern Europe* (2002), which – uniquely in current scholarship on the area – links emotion to nationality conflict and bloodshed. Petersen aims to overcome the oft-assumed emotion–reason dichotomy. Allowing that alongside self-aggrandizing interests, consciously held norms also motivate and structure political contention, he enlists "emotional mechanisms" too as "nonrational (but not necessarily irrational)" triggers or enablers of violence directed toward ethnic outsiders. Assuming that individuals "strongly and commonly desire a few basic things: safety, wealth, and status or self-esteem," Petersen sees emotions as "switches," creating "compulsions to meet one environmental demand above all others." The salient emotions are "Fear, Hatred, Rage, and Resentment." Yet, in emphasizing that "*many, but not all, emotions are instrumental,*" Petersen risks arguing that their arousal serves

---

2016), usefully charts the concept's history while applying it as an analytical tool in a series of contemporary case studies. The editors note (p. 246) that few texts "have engaged with the issue of moral economy in relation to ethnic conflict." A "rare exception," in their view, is my "The Moral Economy of Popular Violence: The Pogrom in Lwów, November 1918," in Robert Blobaum, ed., *Antisemitism and Its Opponents in Modern Poland* (Ithaca, NY: Cornell University Press, 2005), 124–47.

[12] Omer Bartov and Eric Weitz, eds., *Shatterzone of Empires: Coexistence and Violence in the German, Habsburg, Russian, and Ottoman Borderlands* (Bloomington, IN: University of Indiana Press, 2013). A historical study that interestingly explores the symbolic and expressive dimension of Balkan ethnic violence, as committed by individuals, small bands, and political authorities, is İpek Yosmaoğlu, *Blood Ties: Religion, Violence, and the Politics of Nationhood in Ottoman Macedonia, 1878–1908* (Ithaca, NY: Cornell University Press, 2014). Cf. Keith Brown, *Loyal unto Death: Trust and Terror in Revolutionary Macedonia* (Bloomington, IN: University of Indiana Press, 2014). On Davis and Hobsbawn, see note 5; on Thompson, see note 11.

only to make possible action pursuing self-protection and self-aggrandizement.[13]

Fear prompts us to seek safety, hatred to satisfaction of "historical grievance," resentment to repair of "status/self-esteem discrepancies." Rage, "emanating from frustration or a troubled personality," leads to "counterproductive actions (such as searching for scapegoats)." Status anxieties are inseparable from issues of social hierarchy and domination. "Violence and cruelty can, with swiftness and devastation, establish new status realities." Social structural displacements – e.g., shifts in class power or demography – may release them more powerfully than ideological programs.[14]

Hatred, fired by "historical grievance," finds expression in campaigns "to take back what is ours," "to settle old scores" – phrases this book often documents. The cultural-psychological schemas corresponding to Petersen's emotional-behavioral array are often deep rooted, distilled into "relatively unchanging scripts and rituals." Acts of violence and humiliation, he observes, will often "possess ritualistic qualities." Rage derives from one or more "diffuse or unconscious" sources. Unlike the other three cases, in which "information converts into beliefs which only then create the emotion," in rage, "emotion precedes cognition," so the target of aggression may be selected by "irrational psychological mechanisms." Negative images characterizing rage's objects "change to fit any current situation that requires release of internalized tensions." "There will be elements of projection and attribution," that is, of the enraged subjects' own consciously unacceptable aggressions, desires, and defects. Rage may manifest as a "minor phenomenon" within the other three emotions. It is a "judgment call" whether, in such cases, new psychologically contoured processes are created.[15]

Petersen's book and the work it builds on, notably political scientist James Scott's, encourage this book's exploration in anti-Jewish violence of unconscious but culturally deeply embedded scripts and scenarios.[16] Petersen's notion of underlying rationality in (rage-free) human behavior, channeled into action by emotion, is questionable, especially because he excludes from basic human drives the search for existential meaning, climbing even unto heaven.

---

[13] Roger Petersen, *Understanding Ethnic Violence: Fear, Hatred, and Resentment in Twentieth-Century Eastern Europe* (New York: Cambridge University Press, 2002), xii, 2–3, 19.

[14] Ibid., 19, 51.   [15] Ibid., 65, 77, 82, 84.

[16] James Scott, *Weapons of the Weak*; James Scott, *Domination and the Arts of Resistance: Hidden Transcripts* (New Haven, CT: Yale University Press, 1990). Jeffrey Alexander et al., *Social Performance: Symbolic Action, Cultural Pragmatics, and Ritual* (New York, NY: Cambridge University Press, 2006), reviews theoretical approaches to the staging of public events without illuminating the terrain of violence.

Part I

War, Hunger, Revolt
Galicia, 1914–1918

1 Peacetime Precursors, Russian Invasion, and the First Wartime Pogroms, 1914–1916

On the eve of the war that would destroy the polyglot Habsburg monarchy, Polish-Jewish relations in Galicia glowed with the heat of passions both ancient and modern. These radiated from the German-language letter Lemberg/Lwów attorney Marek Rappaport wrote in March 1914 to the Vienna office of the Alliance Israélite Universelle, Paris-based Jewish philanthropic organization. Evidently he doubted the efficacy of addressing Austrian authority directly. He protested against "the barbaric custom," still embedded in West Galician townlets, of the "Judas Fest." Christian youth constructed a figure costumed as a Hasidic Jew, with caftan (*bekesche*), fur-fringed hat (*stramel*), and prayer shawl (*tales*). On four successive pre-Easter days, they carried it through the streets, stopping "every few feet to whip it with their sticks into the air or trample it on the ground, crying out 'beat the Jew! Strike him down!'"

The town's "cultured" circles (judge, notary, mayor, apothecary, doctor, etc.), along with children and servants, celebrate this parade with such applause as if they were greeting Napoleon marching to Russia to free the Poles from tsarism's yoke.[1]

Then "the Jew" was taken up the church tower and hurled down "on the trash-heap" before being "ceremonially dragged to the river and, to the crowd's cheers, thrown in the water."

Judas' memory disquieted Rappaport, who wrote that "even if" the ritual recalled a 2,000-year-old legend, "still not confirmed by historians," of Jesus' betrayal, "the ceremony should be condemned and banned." Christian participants saw it not as "innocent historical theater" but as "beating the Jew in effigy." This was the yearly season when "fairy-

---

[1] For Rappaport's letter and resulting correspondence, see Allgemeines Verwaltungsarchiv (AVA), Vienna. Staatsarchiv des Innern und der Justiz. Ministerium des Innern. Präsidiale. Galizien (hereafter cited as AVA. MdIP-G.) Sign. 22. Fsz. 2116, No. 3271 (March 17, 1914); No. 3529 (March 30, 1914). Prefect: *Bezirkshauptmann* or, in Polish, *starosta*. See, on the "Judas Fest" and similar folk customs, previously cited works by Cała and Tokarska-Bakir.

tales of alleged ritual murder were circulated," when Jesuits during Easter missionizing gave sermons

that could serve as models for [Polish-born but Russianized antisemite] Puryszkiewicz's Black Hundreds in Russia, and when, because of the [Polish] Endeks' and other antisemitic parties' radical hate-mongering, the gulf between Christians and Jews widens every day, and [as Rappaport added, in seeming assimilationist anxiety] when Zionists are registering gains.

In these towns, half the population was Jews: "indeed, poor, dirty, often broken-down Jews, bent under misery." In the town of Osiek, "disorders" had occurred some fifteen years ago "following a [furtive Christian] simulation of ritual murder!" Perhaps such Jews were "too poor and too weak to let themselves be spurred to resist," but an "enflamed Jew, wounded in religious or national feeling," might speak insulting words "that could lead to blows and corpses, if among so many Christians there was but one hot-head – even a peasant – who would cry out 'down with the Jews!'"

Rappaport was enlightened and secular minded. Judas Fest, he thought, kept alive "wild instincts and only deepened the gulf that history, superstition, differences in occupation and lifestyle, various economic factors, lack of schooling and culture have until now, unfortunately, opened between the Christian world and Jewry." The ceremony violated "Christianity's spirit." Whatever happened in the time of "wild, fanatical Judas 2,000 years ago, in an age of barbarism," cannot today bind Christianity, which ought to honor higher ethics.

Rappaport had managed in 1912 to persuade Jasło district prefect Łąckczyński to bar the Judas Fest in two offending towns. He acted "very correctly," sending imperial police (gendarmes) at Eastertide. But in 1913 the fest was staged "very provocatively, and it was only thanks to two or three sensible Jews' personal influence that no clash occurred." Now he requested Alliance Israélite to press Habsburg officialdom in Vienna, parliamentarians, Catholic bishops, and the Galician viceroy's Lemberg office (Statthalterei) to suppress the fest altogether.

Belying its tortoise-like reputation, Austria's bureaucracy accomplished this promptly. Soon Viceroy Witold Korytowski sent Vienna's Interior Ministry the order it had requested of him, in Polish and German, to all West Galician prefects. The Polish-language version said, "these processions take place in an apparently very provocative manner, injuring the Jewish population's religious and racial feelings." Though the ceremony was banned, no publication of the present directive or the minister-ial order mandating it would occur, leaving the prefects, mostly Poles of noble heritage or intelligentsia standing, to bear responsibility. This was, evidently, a move to stifle criticism on charges of Judeophilism of the Habsburg government, mostly in German hands, and empowered to appoint the Galician viceroy unilaterally.

Rappaport's intervention, whatever its immediate efficacy, did not halt the Judas Fest's reenactment in interwar and even post-1945 years. It was one act in the centuries-old, culturally deep-rooted drama of Christian anti-Judaism as staged in the historically Polish lands, where most of Europe's Jews then lived. Rappaport did not label it antisemitism, though he rightly charged hostile political parties with stoking anti-Jewish passions. He saw that the fest was symbolic murder. He ascribed its survival into the twentieth century to Galicia's legendary poverty and benightedness, conditions afflicting Jews alongside Christians. His prescription for its suppression was modern liberalism's: enlightenment and rule of law, imposed from above by benevolent state power and educated and propertied elites.[2]

Political antisemitism's fires smoldered and flared across Galicia, as elsewhere in pre-1914 Europe. So too were its enemies on lookout. In May 1914, maverick Lemberg "independent Socialist" and anti-antisemite Ernst Breiter excitedly telegraphed Austrian Interior Minister Baron von Heinold. In the West Galician town of Mielec,

total defeat of Father Pawlikowski's clerical-antisemitic party in communal elections has enormously provoked part of the Christian population against the Jews. Jewish houses are being torched, domestic animals poisoned. Jewish citizens' lives are in danger, as during the Russian pogroms.

Breiter volunteered to travel to Mielec, "since the prefect offers no adequate protection," while "danger lurks that the antisemitic flood will engulf other towns." The Ministry instructed viceroy Korytowski to intervene.[3]

---

[2] On Galician image and reality, see Larry Wolff, *The Idea of Galicia: History and Fantasy in Habsburg Political Culture* (Stanford, CA: Stanford University Press, 2010). Economic modernizer (and non-antisemite) Stanisław Szczepanowski popularized the Galician poverty trope in *Nędza Galicyi w cyfrach* (Lwów: Gubrynowicz i Schmidt, 1888). A valuable update was Józef Tenenbaum's knowledgeable *Żydowskie problemy gospodarcze w Galicyi* (Vienna: Nakł. Dr. W. Berkelhammera, 1918). Cf. Włodzimierz Bonusiak et al., *Galicja i jej dziedzictwo*, 2 vols. (Rzeszów: Wydawnictwo Wyższej Szkoły Pedagogicznej w Rzeszowie, 1994–95); Zbigniew Fras, *Galicja* (Wrocław: Wydawnictwo Dolnośląskie, 1999); Israel Bartal and Anthony Polonsky, eds., *Focusing on Galicia: Jews, Poles, Ukrainians, 1772–1918* (*Polin*, vol. 12 [Portland, OR, Littman, 1999]). On the Habsburg monarchy, see William McCagg, *A History of Habsburg Jews, 1670–1918* (Bloomington, IN: University of Indiana Press, 1989); Helmut Rumpler, *Eine Chance für Mitteleuropa: bürgerliche Emanzipation und Staatsverfall in der Habsburgermonarchie* (Vienna: Ueberreuter, 1997); Pieter Judson, *The Habsburg Empire: A New History* (Cambridge, MA: Harvard University Press, 2016).

[3] AVA. MdIP-G. Sign. 22. Fsz. 2116, No. 6908 (May 18, 1914).

Fear that political antisemitism, frustrated at the polls, might transmute into violence is evident, however limited the 1914 damage in Mielec. Symbolic injuries also moved antisemites to mayhem, as celebrated Zionist Nahum Sokolow's 1914 speaking tour demonstrated. His inoffensive theme was substitution of Hebrew for German as instructional language at the Zionist-projected Technical University in Palestine. After his presentation in Russian-ruled Warsaw, it was rumored he had announced that "Poland is a corpse, which only needs a poke of the foot to fall to pieces." Though denied by Warsaw Zionists, this potent insult gained wide credence among Galician Polish nationalists and even among "Jewish youth belonging to the assimilation party" – sometimes self-identified as "Poles of Mosaic faith." Since Poland's partition, metaphors of national death had haunted its patriots. Taunts such as that attributed to Sokolow figured among embittered or hostile Jews' linguistic weaponry, who themselves – as Judas Fest showed – were often enough forced to witness their symbolic demise.

Sokolow's Polish and Jewish enemies halted his lecture in Kraków, West Galicia's capital. In provincial Tarnów, local Zionists honored him with a closed banquet, but when Christian "high-schoolers and artisan youth" learned of this, they broke hotel windows. Sokolow's panic-stricken Zionist hosts telegraphed Austria's Interior Ministry (commanding the gendarmerie, standing above city police):

At banquet in City Hotel Tarnów 200 lives hang in balance under siege by mob. Police stand idly by. Despite repeated urgings prefect does nothing.[4]

Eventually, local police intervened, as in Lemberg the previous day, when, after cancelation of Sokolow's public address, Zionism's youthful foes and friends clashed in the streets. The authorities hurried Sokolow out of Tarnów.

These Galician snapshots bring into focus one of this book's – and Central and Eastern European history's – weightiest problems. In what relation did popular anti-Judaism stand to ideologized antisemitism or, what I propose to call, refashioning a famous formulation, print-antisemitism?[5] We have seen how scholars Cała and Tokarska-Bakir connected Christian ritual-murder fantasies and diabolization of Jews to modern Judeophobic politics. Other influential interpretations, while acknowledging Christian anti-Judaism's legacy, have highlighted the

---

[4] AVA. MdI-P. Sign. 22. Fsz. 2116, No. 5590.
[5] Compare Benedict Anderson's concept of "print-nationalism" in his *Imagined Communities: Reflections on the Origin and Spread of Nationalism* (New York, NY: Verso, 1983).

interplay of print-antisemitism and *political power*, whether that wielded by the state or that sought by mass-based political parties challenging entrenched conservative or liberal elites. Like Rappaport, prominent writers on antisemitism have taken popular anti-Jewish *prejudice* for granted, concentrating instead on top-down enactments of *ideologies* in which antisemitism, however heartfelt among street-level adherents, figures – *functions* – as vehicle of power struggles, accompanied by multifarious class resentments and anxieties, raised to society's stormy surface by "modernization's" mighty tides. It escapes such interpreters' attention that, as these pages argue, the educated political classes' print-antisemitism was itself a rationalization, in seemingly modern and scientific dress, of historically deeper anxiety and animus.

As we saw, scholarly explorers of antisemitism – a profoundly irrational phenomenon – have influentially understood it as a tool serving adherents' "rational interests" – rational, that is, insofar as they aimed, in wielding it, to aggrandize themselves materially and politically. Yet we found, in this book's Theoretical Footnote, that instrumental rationality cannot be separated from value-saturated social-cultural intention, conscious or unconscious. To suppose that anti-Jewish violence is but the consequence of top-down propagation of antisemitic ideology in service of entrenched power elites or movements against them steered by upstart challengers, all in pursuit of objectives having little or nothing to do Judeophobes' actual relations with Jews, is to blind the eye to the violence's meaning and message in the minds, conscious or unconscious, of its perpetrators, whether the plebeian or the educated and propertied.[6]

In historically Polish-ruled lands, popular anti-Judaism was formidably present, alongside more benign, centuries-old modes of Christian-Jewish coexistence. And while political antisemitism strove to harness everyday demotic Judeophobia, this mentality led its own life. This book exposes its embeddedness not so much in antisemitic political movements as in

---

[6] See Introduction, note 27; Theoretical Footnote, note 3. Interpretation of modern antisemitism as right-wing political response to "strains of modernization" is pervasive. It accompanies the intentionalist view of the Hitlerian Holocaust, which stresses the ideologically prefigured, consciously premeditated character of the Jewish mass murder. Exemplary are Leon Poliakov, *History of Anti-Semitism*, 4 vols. (New York, NY: Vanguard, 1965–85; French orig. 1956–77); Walter Laqueur, *The Changing Face of Antisemitism: From Ancient Times to the Present Day* (New York, NY: Oxford University Press, 2006). For further discussion, see Hagen, "Before the Final Solution"; and William W. Hagen, "The Three Horsemen of the Holocaust: Antisemitism, East European Empire, Aryan Folk Community," in Helmut Walser Smith, ed., *The Oxford Handbook of Modern German History* (New York, NY: Oxford University Press, 2011), 548–72. Influential are Nirenberg, *Communities of Violence*; and David Nirenberg, *Anti-Judaism: The Western Tradition* (New York, NY: Norton, 2013), neither of which offers this book's culturalist and performative approach.

popular-cultural and social-psychological structures. It shows how, through collective enactments in crisis situations of an anti-Jewish theater of persecution and violence, deep-rooted and often subconscious socially shared visions of the world, and especially its dangers and menaces, found expression and channeled – at the cost of Jewish suffering – recuperative, even redemptive action.

This chapter deepens readers' familiarity with Galicia, scene of recurring waves of anti-Jewish mobilization that later pages will reconstruct and analyze. It offers indispensable minimum knowledge of this large European landscape's ethnoreligious composition and class-riven politics. It depicts the pogrom-violence Russian invasion and occupation in 1914–15 inflicted on East Galicia and how Galician and Austrian Jews reacted to it. This was the first stage of Habsburg civility's calamitous collapse.

Galicia's Poles, Ukrainians, Jews, and Germans

The 1910 census found that of Galicia's 8 million inhabitants, some 47 percent were, by religion, Roman Catholics, 42 percent were Greek Catholics, and 11 percent were Jewish. Linguistic statistics purporting to report subjectively felt national identity blurred rather than illumined. It suffices that throughout the crownland, Poles outnumbered Ukrainians, but not by much, and Jews tallied about 900,000.[7]

On West Galician streets and roads, the traveler heard variants of Polish, Yiddish, and German. In East Galicia, it was mainly Polish in towns, Ukrainian (Habsburg officialdom preferred "Ruthenian") in villages, Yiddish among widely settled Jews (who, like many Christians, often spoke languages other than mother tongue). Everywhere were linguistic islands and subcultures. But language did not straightforwardly signal subjective consciousness, or outwardly projected ethnicity, or cultural identity and nationality. In West Galicia, Habsburg officials distinguished between "Poles" and "Masurians," the former educated and propertied Polish speakers who had embraced the national history (and, usually, the nationalist movement), the latter villagers who spoke local Polish dialect but who viewed "Poland" as an ominous home of nobility and gentry – "Poles" who had held them centuries long, until 1848's revolution, in serfdom.

In Galicia's forested heights there were villages of farmer-pastoralists and lumbermen. Some were Catholic "mountaineers" (*górale*), sentimentally hailed as "younger brothers" by literate urban Polish nationalists.

---

[7] https://en.wikipedia.org/wiki/Kingdom_of_Galicia_and_Lodomeria#Demographics.

Others were numerically small kinship-ordered Orthodox Christian subcultures – Lemkos, Boykos, Hutsuls – claimed by Ukrainian nationalists but self-willed and insubordinate. Galician Germans, mostly Catholic, were not only Habsburg soldiers and officials but also merchants and educated professionals, gentry estate owners, and old-settled free peasant colonists.[8]

Galicia was a stronghold of Jewish Hasidism (pietism), which shared with Orthodoxy meticulous observance of Talmudic law and disapproving distance from Reform Judaism, born in Moses Mendelssohn's Enlightenment Germany. Reformism redefined the religion to encourage Jewish acculturation into European liberalism's educational and social-political life. Often its houses of worship were called "German synagogues."[9]

In East Galicia, Polish nobility and intelligentsia ruled through the system of provincial autonomy granted their crownland (including West Galicia) by the Habsburg monarchy during the 1860s' constitutional reorganization. The Lemberg-seated Galician viceroyalty and bureaucracy were theirs to wield, under the central government's indulgent eye, to their own advantage, protected – though also blocked from breakaway sovereignty – by the empire-wide ("k.k.") army.[10] Magnate aristocracy and landed gentry owned half the rich farmland and most of the forests, though upward-bound Jews had acquired many noble estates from faltering Polish lineages. Villagers were mostly Ukrainian speakers and parishioners of the Habsburg-sponsored, Vatican-subordinate version of Orthodox Christianity, commonly termed "Greek Catholic," but also known as "Uniate" (referring to 1596's Union of Brest, creating this Christian hybrid, which retained a married clergy and certain non-Catholic liturgical practices). Orthodoxy subservient to the Patriarchate of Moscow was officially banned within Habsburg borders, though nothing could prevent Greek Catholics from bowing to it in their hearts. Lemberg housed a deep-rooted Armenian commercial community with its own church hierarchy but cultivating ties with Polish aristocracy and sharing their tradition-laden patriotism.

Many Ukrainian villagers were owners of market-integrated family farms, gained as property in serfdom's post-1848 dissolution. Still more

---

[8] See, *inter alia*, Ireneusz Ihnatowicz et al., *Społeczeństwo polskie od X. do XX. wieku* (Warsaw: Książka i Wiedza, 1996).

[9] Apart from previously cited works on Hasidism and Jewish Galicia, see Börries Kuzmany, *Brody: Eine galizische Grenzstadt im langen 19. Jahrhundert* (Vienna: Böhlau, 2011); Joshua Shanes, *Diaspora Nationalism and Jewish Identity in Habsburg Galicia* (New York, NY: Cambridge University Press, 2012).

[10] *Kaiserlich und königlich*, "imperial and royal," signaling dynastic sovereignty in both the non-Hungarian and Hungarian lands.

owned but a patch of land or none and found themselves dependent on Polish (and Jewish) estate owners for rented or sharecropped land and for wage labor, imperiously needed by gentry in planting and harvesting seasons. Landlords' bailiffs or leaseholders, often minor Polish nobles but sometimes Jews, struck hard bargains with employment-hungry villagers. Nor were Jewish proprietors of village inns and small-town stores and artisan workshops or Jewish leaseholders of noble-owned taverns dispensing manor-distilled drink excessively softhearted in extending credit to penniless or debt-ridden villagers. When peasants sold crops or livestock, Jewish merchants typically bought them or collected them for debt. Yet, as Rappaport lamented of West Galician Jews, many were themselves bent under poverty.

By 1914, Ukrainian nationalism was robust. Earlier pioneered by village priests' sons, its champions multiplied through recruitment among family farmers, secondary and university students (educated in Polish- and German-speaking classrooms), and burgeoning private-sector middle class and intelligentsia (though few degree holders found government jobs). As, from 1906, universal male suffrage entered the parliamentary and electoral life of the Habsburg monarchy's "Austrian half" – including Galicia but not the multilingual, oligarchical Kingdom of Hungary – Ukrainian demands for democratization of Galician institutions grew militant: creation of a separate Ukrainian-language university and proportional representation in Galician provincial parliament and in teaching corps and other public-sector posts.

In 1908 a Ukrainian nationalist assassinated viceroy Count Andrzej Potocki. Polish backlash thwarted compromise between the two ethnicities sought by Potocki's successor Michał Bobrzyński, eminent Polish historian and Habsburg loyalist. Increasingly, Viennese officials worried that Polish intransigence – and the shadowy operations (greased by ample Muscovite ruble notes) of anti-Habsburg tsarist secret agents – were multiplying seeds among Ukrainian speakers of "Russophilism." War's outbreak smothered an unpopular government-brokered compromise of January 1914 offering Ukrainian nationalists fairer parliamentary representation and a university within four years.[11]

---

[11] On Ukraine and Ruthenian Galicia, see Paul Robert Magocsi, *A History of Ukraine: The Land and Its Peoples* (Toronto: University of Toronto Press, 2010); John-Paul Himka, *Religion and Nationality in Western Ukraine: The Greek Catholic Church and Ruthenian National Movement in Galicia, 1867–1900* (Montreal: University of Montreal Press, 1999); John-Paul Himka, "Ukrainian-Jewish Antagonism in the Galician Countryside during the Late Nineteenth Century," in Peter Potichnyj et al., eds., *Ukrainian-Jewish Relations in Historical Perspective* (Edmonton: University of Alberta, 1988), 111–58; Stella Hryniuk, *Peasants with Promise: Ukrainians in Southeastern Galicia 1880–1900* (Edmonton: University of Alberta, 1991); Ivan Rudnytsky, "The Ukrainians in Galicia

Names would prove fateful. Habsburg police, translating the Ukrainian nationalist self-descriptor as *russisch* when Ruthenian speakers said *ruskyi*, hammered into official minds specters of disloyal irredentism.[12] Russophiles culturally attached to the Moscow Patriarchate and indifferent to modern Ukrainian nationalism were largely content with Habsburg citizenship, but war with tsarism would bend or break that bond. Influential Polish nationalists also looked (discreetly) to future Russian support for Polish breakaway from Vienna's rule, notably Roman Dmowski's National Democrats (*endecja* [Endeks] or, in pejorative governmental usage, "Pan-Poles" [*Allpolen*]).

Ukrainian claims to autonomous self-rule or statehood menaced Polish interests, invested in nationalists' eyes in retention under their domination of the "borderlands" (*kresy*). These were the provinces, stretching far east of ethnographic Poland's heartland toward Kiev/Kiyiv that had once belonged to the now-vanished Polish Commonwealth, where Polish nobility, or *szlachta*, were estate owners and gentry-born Polish intelligentsia who dominated culture and politics. As for Franz Joseph's Austria, the only tolerable form of Ruthenian-Ukrainian nationalism was one that would accept loyal (*habsburgtreu*) East Galician semiautonomy. Metaphors of fragile old women were not admissible at imperial court.[13]

Peasant Explosions, 1846 and 1898

Memories of violent peasant uprisings were alive among Galician Poles and Austrian officials. In 1846, a desperate revolt among intellectuals and insurrectionary gentry in West Galician Kraków, aiming to resurrect independent Poland, fell bloodied victim to Austrian armed counterattack, sensationally reinforced by enserfed peasants' rising, centered around Tarnów, against seigneurial landlords and feudal masters. Several thousand noblemen, alongside family members, manorial officials, and pro-aristocratic priests, were murdered, some nine hundred

---

under Austrian Rule," in Andrei Markovits et al., eds., *Nationbuilding and the Politics of Nationalism: Essays on Austrian Galicia* (Cambridge, MA: Harvard University Press, 1982), 23–67.

[12] AVA. MdIP-G. Sign. 22. Fsz. 2116, No. 1224 (February 2, 1914).

[13] On Endeks, see Porter, *When Nationalism Began to Hate*; Krzywiec, *Szowinizm*; Hagen, "Before the Final Solution"; Wilhelm Feldman, *Geschichte der politischen Ideen in Polen seit dessen Teilungen (1772–1914)* (Munich: Oldenbourg, 1917). On the eastern borderlands, see Daniel Beauvois, *Trójkąt Ukraiński: szlachta, carat i lud na Wołyniu, Podolu i Kijowszczyźnie 1793–1914* (Lublin: Wydawnictwo Uniwersytetu Marii Curie-Skłodowskiej, 2011); Jacek Kolbuszewski, *Kresy* (Wrocław: Wydawnictwo Dolnośląskie, 1998).

manors pillaged. Local Austrian officials cynically encouraged this "slaughter" (*rzeż, rabacja*), driving deeper the wedge between upper-class "Polish" nationalists and antinationalist "Masurian" peasantry, among whom memories of eighteenth-century Austrian rulers Maria Theresia and Joseph II, authors of cautiously pro-peasant legislation, were loyally cultivated. Notoriously, some Austrian officials rewarded peasant rebels with ringing coin for aristocratic heads. The rising's commander, Jakub Szela, lived on as the worst of upper-class nightmares.

In 1898, West Galician villages exploded again, but now against Jews, who had escaped 1846's violence untouched. Foreshadowed during 1897 elections to the Viennese Parliament (*Reichsrat*) by lesser but myriad anti-Jewish tumults, the riots' aims were not maiming and murder but plunder and property destruction, especially of Jewish-operated taverns and households. Some four hundred villages and small towns witnessed violence; thousands were arrested, of whom 962 had been pronounced guilty by February 1899 and sentenced, on average, to one-month jail terms. During imposition of martial law to quell the tumults, Austrian soldiers killed twelve rioters.

Historian Tim Buchen insightfully interpreted 1898's violence. As serfdom vanished, small-holding villagers disadvantaged by social change – marketization, above all – came to stigmatize any and all negatively experienced phenomena as "Jewish." Instead of acceptance, as before 1848, of once-limited social roles performed by Jews – livestock dealers, tavern keepers, moneylenders – as fixtures, even if unwelcome, of the social landscape. "Jewishness" became a free-floating signifier for adversity. That which previously had been sacred – such as farmland – could now be seen (as did Jan Słomka) as having been "sold out to the Jews." In this perspective, peasant assaults on Jews and their economic operations were, after the 1846 uprising, another "performance of the old order's dissolution."[14]

Galicia from the 1880s witnessed a burgeoning agrarian populist movement – a multicornered contest between educated social radicals (Jan Stapiński), clerical organizers (Stanisław Stojałowski), and peasant tribunes (Jakub Bojko). Antagonism toward Jews, especially rural merchants, was central. Emergence of village-based parties enormously advanced antisemitism's politicization not only through electoral campaigning and inflammatory journalism but also in parliamentary debates in Vienna, especially interpellations staged by antisemite deputies, typically charging the government with inaction in the face of one or another

---

[14] Tim Buchen. *Antisemitismus in Galizien: Agitation, Gewalt und Politik gegen Juden in der Habsburgermonarchie um 1900* (Berlin: Metropol, 2012), 141–43 and *passim*.

alleged Jewish outrage. The interpellations assumed rhetorical form of modern fairy tales, mirroring the magical character of folk-cultural charges against Jews. They corresponded to the charivaris (noisy and derisive crowd demonstrations) that frequently preceded (or substituted for) grassroots anti-Jewish violence. They created, discursively, "antisemitic realities."[15]

Two things were vital: first, that in rioters' eyes, plundering of Jewish tavern keepers and other merchants was *legitimate*, given their view that Jews' accumulated capital had been immorally gained at peasant expense and on condition that plunder was directed against a village's "own Jews" and distributed fairly among its members. Interlopers from other villages had no right to rob them. Second, it was necessary that villagers felt, as they did, that plundering Jews gained them "valuable symbolic capital," demonstrating their superiority over Jews (if only of brute force) and their courage in defying authorities.

Ostensible reasons they gave for plunder – to punish Jews for (improbably) attempting to assassinate Kaiser Franz Joseph or to show support for Archduke Rudolph (who had not, they claimed, committed suicide in 1889 but was in hiding to protect himself against Jewish threats) or because the Pope authorized punishment for Jewish attacks on priests – aimed at self-vindication by appeal to higher authority and their own monarchical and Christian loyalty. "The whole Christian community presented the plunder, not as nocturnal crime, but as folk festival."[16]

In 1903, as Ruthenian peasant strikes in East Galicia erupted, populist propaganda sought to incite Polish peasant attacks on Jews, but in vain. Buchen argued that peasants were loathe to sacrifice anything of their material self-interest for populist politicians' sake, as shown by their refusal to cooperate at their own monetary loss in boycott campaigns against Jewish businesses, even while often complying with the clergy's antisemitically justified temperance movement. Nor did appeals to patriotism or nationalism move them to violence, especially not after the government had demonstrated readiness to command soldiers to fire on rioters.

In the Galician countryside, anti-Jewish politics, with sporadically accompanying violence, moved on two parallel but sometimes converging tracks: that of folk culture informing the 1898 rioting and that of populist propaganda amplifying demotic violence through villagers' interpretation of it. In 1898, the two discourses reinforced each other. In 1903, folk mentality rejected populist appeals. Future configurations were unpredictable.

[15] Ibid., 324.   [16] Ibid., 211, 215.

To Buchen's account we add that in July 1898, Galician viceroy Count Leon Pininski summed up the peasant-ignited "runaway blaze" in a report to Austrian Chancellor Count Thun-Hohenstein. Perpetrators he archly branded "immature" and "deluded." He invoked "the poorer classes' material misery" – result, he thought, of "unrestrained freedom to divide and parcelize their farmland." The "popular masses, who are able only with the greatest exertion to gain their daily bread," had been led astray by "conscienceless party leaders" seeking votes after the 1897 widening to include all adult males of the franchise in a still-undemocratic system unequally weighting votes according to electors' tax payments. "Rural folk," the Polish viceroy wrote, "attribute their impoverishment, not without reason, to their usurious exploitation by a significant number among the Jews that still goes unpunished" (despite anti-Jewish-tinged legislation against rural usury in the 1880s). Compounding tensions was "the arrogant and provocative behavior of some Jews," not to mention the previous year's bad harvest. There was, too, "Masurians' hot temper, quick to flare up."

Armed intervention and martial law quelled "excesses." The viceroy complained that oppositional Social Democrats dismissed his actions as mere "repression of antisemitism" – obviously a familiar concept in government thinking, wedded to tumult and insubordination. But he aimed to reform inheritance law to lessen tax burdens and work against subdivision of the villagers' small farms. He thought Galicia undergoverned: there had been more officials on the ground in 1867 than now. At bottom, he saw the riots' triggers as social, while demagogic politics interpreted them as religious and ethnonational. Prime Minister Thun embraced Pininski's recommendations, forwarding them immediately to Emperor Franz Joseph, who read and signed off on them. The Habsburg ruling class was of one mind – paternalist, antidemocratic, cautiously reform-ready, critical of certain Jewish social roles in upper-class antisemitic fashion.[17]

Galician Politics in Imperial Eyes: October 1914

We now take an eagle's-eye look at Galician politics to better understand how, under impact of Russian invasion and material privation, trust

---

[17] AVA. MdIP-G. Sign. 22. Fasz. 867, No. 6345 (July 21, 1898), fos. 1–16, *passim*; ibid., Pr. 30/7. Jostling these archival documents was an 1882 letter from then-viceroy Potocki to then-chancellor Taaffe, forwarding an anonymous German-language letter sent to a Kraków-based fire insurance company. It curtly warned, "Pay heed! Great fires will soon occur in Galicia and all Jewish property will be reduced to ashes. Extend no more insurance. Cancel existing obligations. Respectfully, *Comitet*." But no such fires flared. AVA. MdIP-G. Sign. 22. Fasz. 867, No. 3269 (June 20, 1882).

deteriorated, lawlessness proliferated, and the slide began toward the ethnic violence that will soon dominate these pages. In September 1914, the tsar's army engulfed East Galicia, imposing an occupation regime lasting to June 1915, when, with Imperial German help, Franz Joseph's troops recovered the ravaged land. The Russians had expelled eastward suspect communities along the front – Jews above all. Masses of Poles, Germans, and Greek Catholics fearfully fled westward or were plundered and banished to the east. The Brusilov offensive in 1916 returned Russians to East Galicia until summer 1917, when their revolution-rocked troops chaotically departed.

The physical damage these onslaughts inflicted is inestimable but huge. Psychologically, it extinguished the Galician version of belle-époque Austria, delivering the population into a thunder-skied world of danger, persecution, and widespread unnatural death. When the Russians retreated in 1915, half or more of East Galicia's Jewish settlements had been ravaged. Some 30,000 to 50,000 Jews languished in inner Russian exile, another 50,000 lived as refugees in the land, while some 200,000 had fled to Vienna and other inner Austrian shelters. Altogether, about one-half of East Galicia's 1910 Jewish population of 662,412 was uprooted.[18]

Russian invasion cast all political loyalties in doubt, even those of Galicia's Habsburg officialdom. For war's remainder, Austrian authorities strove to flush out traitors and opportunists, keeping one eye cocked on their own colleagues and subordinates. An October 1914 Interior Ministry scan of the Galician scene descried few contingents Franz Joseph could count on.[19] Among Poles, the West Galician or Kraków conservatives (*Stańczycy*), loyalist Catholics with agrarian noble and urban intelligentsia backing, were seeking mass support in the villages, raising dangerous demagogy's specter. The East Galician ultraconservatives (Podolians) scorned their Ukrainian inferiors. The Catholic clerical Center Party was still "more antisemitic, more anti-Ruthenian." After war's outbreak, many conservatives, including prewar loyalists, steered into "an ultra-Pan-Polish, non-Austrian current," joining Endek leader Count Skarbek in opposing proposed formation of a pro-Austrian Polish-led East Galician Legion meant to fight against Russia. The Interior Ministry saw that upper-class East Galician Poles aimed to maintain an

---

[18] Alexander Prusin, *Nationalizing a Borderland: War, Ethnicity, and Anti-Jewish Violence in East Galicia, 1914–1920* (Tuscaloosa, AL: University of Alabama Press, 2005), 62, 119, and *passim*.

[19] Relevant quotations here and later from AVA. MdIP-G. Sign. 22. Fsz. 2116, No. 12328 (October 31, 1914), fos. 1–10.

option to bargain with Russia over alternatives to Habsburg rule, should it buckle.

Among "democrats," the Endeks, embodying the "chauvinist-national direction," dominated Lemberg's and provincial East Galicia's intelligentsia. They followed Roman Dmowski, their Russia-based party chief, in his Pan-Slavic Russophile turn, reckoning that Polish statehood might be wrung as a concession from Moscow, if not seized from tsarist collapse. An independent Poland would need Russian backing to defy Prussian-German anti-Polonism, which Teutonophobe Dmowski assumed would be unwavering.

The unchauvinistic "Polish Democrats" (*Stronnictwo Postępowo-Demokratyczne*), led by Kraków's mayor, gathered Polish urban liberal loyalists, striving "to win Jews for Polishness." They held mayorships (thanks to the bourgeoisie-friendly urban electoral system) "in almost all larger cities of the land." Then there were the populists, foremost the Polish People's Party (*Polskie Stronnictwo Ludowe* [PSL]), congregating West and central Galician villagers under leadership of farmer's son Wincenty Witos. "Very influential" and "competent," he helped diminish the influence of antiaristocratic, anticlerical pioneer populist Jan Stapiński. Yet Witos's party lacked a "guiding spirit," while the intelligentsia held too many party posts. The rank-and-file might push them aside to follow Stapiński "or some other similarly gifted demagogic personality."[20] The Christian People's Party, earlier founded by turbulent priest Stojołowski, now bent its knee to Endeks, exploiting "antisemitism, popular here and there in the countryside."

The Social Democrats – here the intelligence agent seemingly thought both of the Polish party (*Polska Partia Socjalistyczna* [PPS]) and the Vienna-based, German-oriented Austrian Social Democrats – despite the influence Jews (also in Galicia) wield over this party, are heavily emphasizing the national issue" and so for the moment were strongly anti-Russian (for tsarism was socialism's worst enemy). Politically engaged Jews were rightly seen as largely pro-Habsburg, but not even cosmopolitan socialists among them were insensible to nationalism's kaleidoscopic temptations.

Among Ruthenians, apart from officially suspect Russophiles, there was the National Democratic (formerly Radical) Party, aiming for their Moscow-ruled brothers' and sisters' independence from Russia and union, possibly under Habsburg scepter, of Austrian Ruthenes with them. They finally settled on calling themselves "Ukrainians," a name still novel. It was, government analysts perceptively thought,

---

[20] Ibid., Sign. 22. Fsz. 2116, No. 8906 (July 29, 1914).

unclear whether the idea of national self-sufficiency has penetrated the rural population, whether leaders have a reliably like-minded following, and not a great rural popular mass behind them that might easily be diverted by social concerns from the official nationalist political program.

As for Jews, "the polonized Jews belong principally to the Polish Democratic Party. The majority comprise Orthodox Jews, who take no part in the cultural and political life of the land. They bow to every sitting government." From both Orthodox and assimilationist ranks, Zionists had emerged, but Jewish parties – except locally – wielded little influence in Galician politics.[21]

Such was Galicia's shadow-streaked political landscape, not inaccurately seen through conservative Austrian bureaucratic eyes, alert for popular – especially agrarian – radicalism, suspicious of Russophilism of any stripe (but also of upper-class Polish breakaway impulses), ambivalent toward antisemitism, complacently counting on (partly Jewish) bourgeois liberalism but dismissive of religious Jews.

Pogroms under the Russians

The scourges symbolized by the New Testament's Four Horsemen of the Apocalypse included, alongside famine and death, both war and conquest. Invading subjugators were agents of death. So it was for Eastern European Jewish settlements, beginning in those heavily Jewish East Galician *shtetls* captured in 1914–15 by the Russian army. Comprehensive statistics are lacking; not every community suffered violence, and in those that did, ferocity varied greatly. The paradigmatic pattern was Cossack-inflicted plunder, rapine, and murder, into which other Russian-commanded soldiers plunged. Local Christians looked on before many among them – having previously supplied themselves, in premonition of pogrom, with sacks and hauling carts – claimed their share of the loot, if not murder and rapine.[22]

---

[21] Shanes, *Diaspora Nationalism*, and Kuzmany, *Brody*, correct this biased view.

[22] Prusin, *Nationalizing a Borderland, passim*; Mark von Hagen, *War in a European Borderland: Occupations and Occupation Plans in Galicia and Ukraine, 1914–1918* (Seattle, WA: University of Washington Press, 2007); Piotr Wróbel, "Foreshadowing the Holocaust. The Wars of 1914–1921 and Anti-Jewish Violence in Central and Eastern Europe," in Jochen Böhler et al., eds., *Legacies of Violence: Eastern Europe's First World War* (Munich: Oldenbourg, 2014), 167–208. On World War I's crushing death toll in the Polish lands and on malnutrition and forced population movements, though with little attention to Jewish experience, see Katarzyna Sierakowska, *Śmierć, Wygnanie, Głód w dokumentach osobistych: ziemie polskie w latach Wielkiej Wojny, 1914–1918* (Warsaw: Instytut Historii PAN, 2015).

Justification of such assaults was always ethnoreligious, and Jews were almost exclusively its target. Where prosperous settlements of German Protestants existed, as among Don and Volga basin (pacifist) sectarians, deadly attacks crescendoing toward ethnic cleansing and mass murder occurred, and eventually, as wartime anarchy spread across southern Russia, Ukrainians similarly attacked Polish settlements.[23] It was understandably rare for ethnoreligious minorities to initiate violence, though efforts at self-defense occurred. But if a friendly army crossed the horizon, a besieged minority – already bloodied or not – might cooperate with it to wreck vengeance or disarm, if possible, enemies among a hostile majority. Such, after 1917, was many Jews' relationship to the Soviet Red Army.

In Slavic languages, such plunder and violence constitute a "pogrom," a word cognate with "to strike" or "blast" that spread westward from nineteenth-century Russia. Its association with anti-Jewish aggression grew so complete that, in Western eyes, all other meanings atrophied. Was any and all anti-Jewish violence of a military or mob nature a pogrom? Plundering of Jewish homes and businesses was sometimes intended, and occasionally occurred, without physical violence against persons. But tumultuous public robbery easily turned into bodily assault, particularly when resistance was attempted, as sporadically happened, and vodka flowed. Conversely, collective violence against Jews rarely occurred without plunder. Nor did orchestras of ideological antisemitism necessarily accompany the mayhem with their dissonant music.

In these pages, then-contemporary definitions and uses of the pogrom concept (or equivalents) will attract our eye. From today's perspective, crowd violence, whether by soldiers or civilians, directed against Jews or their possessions self-evidently constitutes pogrom, though "anti-Jewish riot" also serves. Losses inflicted were often tallied, both in dead and injured and money value of property lost. Such data, imperfect and disputed, offer murderous metrics useful for comparing pogroms and suggesting macrodamage, but no final balance sheet is computable. It is enough to recognize that maiming and murder, more or less massive, and attendant impoverishment and misery occurred frequently. Explanation and interpretation supersede quantification.

The impulse survives today, as we saw, to ascribe mass violence against Jews and other targeted and stigmatized minorities to organized power: state officials; army; police; social, political, or religious movements; ethnic entrepreneurs; and thuggish underlings. Pogromist mobs commonly claimed to act with sanction from above – or on behalf of higher

---

[23] Schnell, *Räume des Schreckens*, 145–378, *passim*.

authorities that, mysteriously, had failed to halt the wrongdoings rioters ascribed to their victims. Pogromists' relations to higher authority require elucidation, but more vital still is comprehension of their self-understanding. How did they interpret and justify their own violence? Earlier pages probed this question's complexities.[24] How, too, did Jewish sufferers, and their political tribunes, understand the pogroms? Our quest for answers begins by pondering previously unconsidered evidence of pogrom violence under Russian occupation in 1914–16.

In April 1916, Austria's Foreign Ministry received a survey of East Galicia's Russian conquerors' anti-Jewish "atrocities and other assaults." This was the work of Lemberg gymnasium (university-preparatory school) Professor Bernard Hausner, who had agreed to initiate emergency relief, distributing funds (probably of private provenance) while chronicling Russian crimes. The ministry sent the report to Count Duglas Thurn, its agent at Galician army headquarters, with the request that Hausner's evidence be verified prior to its inclusion in a forthcoming "Collection of Proofs" – seemingly a white paper on Russian atrocities. From Jewish committees in eighteen East Galician towns Hausner collected reports, along with petitions for emergency money grants.[25]

Russians occupied the town of Horodenko – 11,613 souls, 4,255 Jewish – in fall 1914, only to withdraw in February 1915 before returning in May. Here as elsewhere, Russians' first appearance inspired some Jewish flight, especially among the well-to-do. The pogrom occurred at their second entry. Three hundred of the Jews' 400 houses were torched. Hausner employed a bitterly ironic carnavalesque rhetoric (which we will often encounter) to describe the violence. Evidence will show that it often mirrored pogromists' actual behavior, typically roughened by liquor.

Music played as the Cossacks danced before the burning homes, and where a Jew, having remained inside, tried to save himself, he was thrown into the fire to the mocking laughter of the Ruthenian population in attendance.

A nameless refugee sought to rescue a Torah scroll from a burning prayer house but was forced back into the flames. These deaths are imaginable as consignment, both of Jews and their religion, to hellfire, the domain of fiends vividly inhabiting many Christian minds.

Cossacks seized forty Jews, cynically charging them with arson. Twenty were condemned to death, seven immediately hanged, including a father of seven, whose wife "has now gone mad with grief." From one Jew,

---

[24] On the literature, see Introduction, note 27, and Theoretical Footnote, note 5.

[25] AVA. MdIP-G. Sign. 22. Fsz. 2117, No. 14416 (April 3,1916). The text that follows draws on this unpaginated document's separate entries on the various localities it surveyed.

evidently a restauranteur, the Cossacks demanded food and drink. After they had "eaten themselves full," they shot him. They dragged another victim through the streets with a rope around his neck until he died. Having left the bodies of the executed to hang for twenty-four hours (the period within which Jewish burials must occur), the (outcast) "dog skinner" cut them down for interment. Other condemned Jews bought themselves free after three days in jail without food. Various men were dragooned to Russia. Some 300 Jews, including whole families, died of typhus, cholera, and plague (*dzuma*). The report added that 500 Horodenko Jews were active-duty Austrian soldiers. Hausner's committee was given 3,000 Kronen – roughly, monthly earnings of thirty male laborers, no large sum – to provide immediate relief.

Recent literature on Cossacks is silent on traditions of murderous abuse of conquered civilians that doubtless prefigured Horodenko's pogrom and others Hausner chronicled.[26] But the Cossacks' righteous slaughter of religious infidels – as in Bogdan Khmelnitsky's fighters' 1648 mass murder of perhaps 50,000 Poles and Jews and rebel Cossacks' 1768 slaughter of some 2,000 Poles and Jews in Uman – met with celebration, still echoed today, in nineteenth-century Ukrainian nationalist literature, especially in Taras Shevchenko's poetry and Khmelnitsky's enduring heroization.

Cossack cavalry of 1914 were a far cry from their once-independent (and anti-Muscovite) forebears. They had been disciplined by tsarist rule into ultrapatriotic defenders of Russian autocracy and orthodoxy. Yet their anti-Jewish violence will have been theatricalized – or otherwise culturally structured – enactment of deep-rooted memories of communal murder, desecrating the religion of Judaism, plundering Jews of their supposed wealth (but also pragmatically sparing lives through bribes), and sometimes suggesting, if not accomplishing, an exterminatory removal of Jewish presence generally. This typically occurred with permission of Cossacks' Russian superiors, many sharing the ruling dynasty's and military high command's widespread antisemitism, heightened by paranoid belief that Jews were, collectively, enemy powers' agents – in East Galicia, of the Austrians.[27]

---

[26] Shane O'Rourke, *The Cossacks* (Manchester: University of Manchester Press, 2007). Nor do the recent previously cited studies of Russian paramilitary formations and pogroms by Schnell and Wiese pose the question of the sociocultural specificity of Cossack violence.

[27] See Magocsi, *Ukraine*; Peter Kenez, "Pogroms and White Ideology in the Russian Civil War," in Klier et al., *Pogroms*, 293–313; Schnell, *Räume*; Oleg Budnitskii, *Russian Jews Between the Reds and the Whites, 1917–1920* (Philadelphia: University of Pennsylvania Press, 2012), a fundamental work; Orlando Figes, *A People's Tragedy: The Russian Revolution, 1917–1924* (New York, NY: Viking Press, 1997), which greatly emphasizes (without historically deriving) pervasive violence in Russian life and tradition. Isaac Babel,

Rape commonly figured in soldierly pogroms, but in these and other Jewish-sourced reports it often appears more as desecration of Jewish honor, dignity, and ritual purity than as sexualized simulation of murder, often entailing real death, though it was inescapably this too. In Jaryczów near Lemberg – 3,200 souls, half Jewish – soldiers in September 1914 "wound Hersch Reiser in his prayer shawl, strangling him with it, because he would not willingly hand over his daughter." Later, before departing in 1915, they burned the town, starting with Pinkas Felsner's house, fired by an officer's hand to whom Felsner had refused his daughter. "The soldiers went from house to house in a group, in the company of a higher clergyman, plundering everything they came across. They also made the people surrender their footwear." The Jews were left in snow-covered ruins. Austrian authorities wanted to send them to a village emptied by fleeing Moskophile Ruthenians. Priests condemned robbery from their pulpits.

In September 1914, Christians dissuaded invaders from burning the town, but robbery and rape persisted for three months. A "Ukrainian commander" then arrived "who allowed no acts of violence, but took an interest in the Jews and defended them from all denunciations and slander." He summoned seven Jews for deportation and then accepted 200 rubles to bribe superiors against it. Characteristic of Jewish reactions to pogroms was the great importance attached to the virtue of enemy commanders and other righteous Gentiles among the upper classes, seemingly the only force capable of restraining Christian common folk's cruelty and rapacity (once aroused).

In Jezierna – with 1,800 Jews, 1,600 Catholic Poles, and 3,600 Ruthenians – there were robberies but no fires or murders. For this Jews thanked the Jewish mayor, Polish and Ruthenian priests, and teachers at Baron Hirsch School.

These clergymen warned and restrained people from the pulpit against all bad deeds and violence. These gentlemen also intervened positively in giving Jews protection and sanctuary at their houses. The relationship of Jews to Christians is generally harmonious. [Austrian] authorities' behavior also is humane, so that at no time do religious differences make themselves felt. Fortunately, Jews' material circumstances are presently favorable.

"1920 Diary," in *The Complete Works of Isaac Babel* (New York, NY: Norton, 2002), 377–472, offers a view of Cossacks emphasizing (and admiring) their extraordinary group solidarity, even in plunder, murder, and rapine. Joshua Sanborn, *Imperial Apocalypse: The Great War and the Destruction of the Russian Empire* (Oxford: Oxford University Press, 2014), affirms Cossacks' primacy in Russian military violence (pp. 60–63) but also, like O'Rourke, Figes, Schnell, and Wiese, without accounting for its social-cultural roots or significance.

Though such reports may seem implausible, this was the moment to report losses, had they occurred. Doubtless Jezierna displayed ethnocultural relations as Jewish notables wished them to be.

In Rohatyn, a half-Jewish settlement of 7,200 that, before Russians torched it, had been a "rich and blooming town," the Imperial German front command "had treated those left behind very humanely," while the current Austrian frontline commander "is a soft-hearted man with a sense of justice." Russians abducted all men aged over fourteen. Three hundred people died of epidemic disease. Survivors in rags sought shelter from villagers – "Moskophile peasants. Even these otherwise such hard people show empathy for women and children stricken so heavily by fate."

In Gwóździec – 2,400 souls, two-thirds Jewish – Russian soldiers plundered Jews in fall 1914 and burned their houses in May 1915. Four women died of "dishonoring." Peasants joined in robbery, bringing horse carts "as if to county fair." "When Leib Breindel asked farmer-acquaintance Wasyl Bendziuk why he was robbing him, a Cossack, at Bendziuk's command, badly pummeled the Jew." Local Poles' relations with Jews were "not bad. Poles even helped them occasionally." Austrian front commander "Siszczowski is very friendly to Jews," as were military authorities generally. Local farmers got their harvest in "and otherwise earned a lot from the war." Yet aid for war losses was going 60 percent to Christians, while Jews lived in stalls and cellars. Eighty-four Jewish family fathers were under arms, and thirty war orphans were present.

Brody's religious institutions and cross-border trade into Russia made it East Galicia's most important Jewish town.[28] It counted 18,000 souls, including 13,000 Jews, of whom 5,000 had been "well-to-do," but a majority of these had fled. Along with Jewish houses, most of the mills and factories had burned, causing a huge 10 million Kr. loss. "Cossacks impaled [*aufgespiesst*] the girl Malka Charasz in shameful fashion." (Impalement was earlier practiced in interconfessional wars of Christians and Muslims on Ukrainian and Black Sea steppe.)

"Relations with local Ruthenians were good, even though they were almost all Moskophiles, and with Poles they were tolerable." This report's stress fell on the "burghers' and middle class's almost unbelievable contribution to alleviating the town's distress," where nine-tenths of the people were impoverished, and seventy people had died of typhus, cholera, and pox. Estate owner Schmidt – perhaps German – was now mayor; Josef Szab – perhaps Polish – was food provisioner. Christian relations with Jews were "normal, fully so since the warm engagement [in Brody's recovery] shown by His Excellency the successor to the throne." A public

[28] See Kuzmany, *Brody*.

kitchen served 400 meals daily: soup, "something solid," and a half-pound (250 grams) of bread, at a quarter Krone for those who could pay. A tearoom served 1,000 free portions daily. Such rations would later seem heavenly.

In the larger town of Kolomea – 34,000 inhabitants, nearly half Jewish – it was Jewish women – Frau Schiller and Frau Mulles – who maintained "very good order and cleanliness" in the children's home and successfully ran a public kitchen serving 500 midday meals, half free. A thousand refugees were present who could or would not go to the government-run "concentration camps" (*Konzentrationslager*) in Bohemia-Moravia.

Other towns suffered similarly. In Ottynia – 5,000 souls, 2,000 Jewish – "the first Cossack Hundreds to arrive behaved humanely, paying roughly equal value for requisitioned goods." But when Jews' supplies ran out, Mayor Bohaczenko "threatened them with murder and disaster at hands of local Catholics." Plunder "with sacks and baskets" followed, under Russian officers' eyes. In Gródek Jagielloński, Jewish middle classes and intelligentsia suffered material losses of 20,000 to 200,000 Kr. The poor were "not completely homeless," but life was now even harder than under Russians because of Austrians' tight control on merchants' internal movement. In Wielkie Mosty – 4,500 souls, one-third Jewish – Jews mostly fled in August 1914 but soon returned to find their houses bare. Christian-Jewish relations had earlier been tolerable. Local Ukrainian and Polish priests "warned their flocks to protect Jewish property." Mayor Jan Siegel caused trouble – seemingly through Russophile collaboration. Returning Austrians sentenced him to seven years' hard labor. Barracks for homeless Jews were erected.

In Bohorodczany – 4,300 souls, one-fourth Jewish – three-day pogrom accompanied Russian arrival, with rapine and four murders. "Unheard-of atrocities were committed, Torah rolls torn apart." There was "indescribable misery." In fire-ravaged Bolszowce – 4,000 souls, half Jewish – Jews lived either with farmers, "who take them in only unwillingly, even for high sums, because the population is Moskophile." Or they lived in "burnt-out chimneys." "Women have gone mad. The most respected citizens of Jewish faith were dragged off to Russia, their wives and children reduced to beggary." In Halicz on the Dniester River – 5,000 souls, one-third Jewish – where soil was fertile and grain trade brisk, Russians withdrew before they could fire the well-plundered town. "More than Russians, the town's plague was the deep-dyed Moskophile population, which [robbed Jews] under Russian patronage." In October 1914, a Russian soldier shot off his finger – seemingly seeking mustering out.

Russians held certain Jews responsible, fining them 1,000 Kr. each and imprisoning them for five months at hard labor.

Such was the picture Jews themselves painted of their suffering under Russian occupation. Cossacks brought with them "unheard-of atrocities," while Jews' Christian neighbors' depredations all too often humiliated, frightened, and beggared them. Yet Christian-Jewish solidarity manifested itself, and there was hope for protection from the Austrian emperor and Polish vassals. In the future, this would fail, and far bloodier days arrive.

Jewish Charges of Official Antisemitism under Austrian Rule, 1914–15

Despite their mixture of dark and light, Dr. Hausner's local committee reports triggered the viceroy's office's skepticism. They did not altogether "rest on truth." Soundings of the (Polish) prefects yielded an indistinct total of murders in the range of perhaps a dozen. Rapes occurred but were not widely demonstrable. Cossacks wielded knouts, and Jewish men were deported. Material damage went largely unremarked. The tone was one of superior objectivity.[29]

Meanwhile, Austrian Zionists (of the *Jüdischer National-Verein in Österreich*) charged Galician Polish complicity with Russians and anti-Jewish actions by them and postoccupation Austrian authorities. A July1915 letter accompanied submission to the Interior Ministry of dossiers on Jewish exposure to "chauvinism and racial hatred." One detailed "treachery of the ruling strata." It catalogued well-known, mostly Endek collaborators, including Stanisławów's police chief, who "allowed Jewish businesses' plunder [and] named Jews for Russians to take hostage." Former viceroy Piniński, leading Podolian conservative and alleged antisemite, welcomed the tsar at Lemberg's Hotel George, while Russia's new Galician viceroy Bobrinskyj, "apostle of all Russophiles and Austria's bitter enemy, was received [by Poles at his installation] like a ruling prince."

By contrast, East Galician Jews, whom Russia's military governor declared real or potential spies, denying them internal passports, clung to the Habsburg monarchy "with body and soul." Not one Jewish official failed in his duty (though prewar Polish discrimination had kept their numbers sparse).

Many, many thousands of Austrian war prisoners were rescued by Jews from Russian captivity at mortal risk, kept hidden and – despite Jews' own misery –

---

[29] AVA. MdIP-G. Sign. 22. Fsz. 2117, No. 14407 (September 19, 1916).

clothed and fed. In most places Poles directly incited Russians to plunder Jewish businesses and carry off Jewish hostages.[30]

Austria's return triggered "frenzy of joy" among Jews. Yet the government restored favor to such alleged collaborators as Piniński, closed down Vienna's Zionist newspaper, maintained the Russian-Polish punitive custom of public thrashings, and generally squandered Jewish loyalty, even as Imperial Germans in occupied Russian Poland successfully cultivated it.[31]

Zionists bitterly denounced Austria's currying Polish friendship at Jewish expense. At war's outbreak, Austria and Germany alike had promised Russian Jews "golden mountains – their aeroplanes dropped on the towns' proclamations in Yiddish and Hebrew announcing the hour of liberation from Russian rule's terrors had struck." Russian Jews remained cautious but "could not stop the mouths of their 'German friends,' for whose benevolence they had to pay in advance in blood and tears." Russians invaded and "completely ruined" the Jews.

"The Ruthenian peasantry received, as first installment of coming rights [under Russian rule], permission to make pogroms." Some stolen property was recovered later by Austrian gendarmes, but Jewish ownership claims were often rejected, leaving Christians in possession. Sometimes authorities maliciously demanded Jews swear oaths on Shabbat. Innumerable were harassments and humiliations. In Jędrzejów, a Polish official, seizing goods from a Jewish dealer, cried out, "I'll reduce all you Jews to beggars." In Vienna, ten Jews held in a camp were invited to join the Polish Legion – on condition of baptism. Two only accepted.[32]

Extensive evidence aimed to demonstrate Galician Polish officialdom's "systematic persecution of Jews, their exclusion, pauperization, and humiliation." In Russian-occupied Rymanów, a newly appointed Polish mayor ordered local Jews to build roads and bury corpses. Six witnesses testified to his having shouted out to policemen, "Give on my authority every Hebrew one hundred blows of the knout [*nahajka* – the Cossack-

---

[30] Central Zionist Archives, Jerusalem (hereafter CZA). CZA. L6/763. Beilage L (July 25, 1915). Signatories were Adolf Stand, Galician Zionist president; Robert Stricker, Austrian Jewish National Union president; Karl Pollack, Austrian Zionist president.

[31] CZA L6/763 (1915), doc. 1. On Imperial Germany's occupation policies, see Werner Conze, *Polnische Nation und deutsche Politik im Ersten Weltkrieg* (Köln: Böhlau, 1958); Vejas Liulevicius, *War Land on the Eastern Front: Culture, National Identity and German Occupation in World War I* (New York, NY: Cambridge University Press, 2000); Vejas Liulevicius, *The German Myth of the East: 1800 to the Present* (New York, NY: Oxford University Press, 2009).

[32] CZA, L6/763 (1915), doc. 2, assembled by Hermann Bernstein.

borne cat-o'-nine-tails]" and "thank God, Austria's gone and Russians are here. We'll settle scores with you Jews. Your end has come."

In Borysław, where a Pole replaced the Jewish mayor – who, "reviled out of office," left town – an elderly passport seeker "was simply grabbed by the beard and dragged out of the office." The jail was packed to overflow with "Jewish criminals." In Żydaczów, town clerk Bolec, promoted by Russians to policeman, arrested brothers Bienenstock, university students in hiding and Jewish communal president's kinsmen, and promised them a "gallows death." Bolec drove Jews to trench digging, "beating them terribly with the knout." Elias Nestl, seeking Bolec's permission to sell groceries, heard the answer, "unfortunately no longer uncommon in Galicia: get out, dirty Jew, you've sucked enough blood."

In Rohatyn, prefect Potocki assembled local judges, informing them from his balcony that "no Jew may be admitted to a village, because they are all traitors, thieves, and swindlers." Bursztyn's mayor bellowed to Jews: "Wait, you dogs, I'll have Cossacks slaughter you all." Russians appointed a Polish veterinarian town manager, who took bribes for travel passes. "No Jews were permitted to tread the sidewalk before his house, but had to use the street, while his children and servants uttered all manner of threats, such as 'here in Russia you have nothing more to do, soon you'll all be slaughtered.'"[33] In Gliniany, Czech-nationality front-line commandant Captain Roczik imposed public thrashing: "the condemned person is led out on the central square, his trousers are dropped, he is tied hand and foot on a bench, two soldiers deliver blows with wooden staffs and a sergeant counts them." In five instances of victims each condemned to twenty-five blows, infractions included overstaying a pass by three days, illegally selling brandy, overcharging for a loaf of self-baked bread, and dumping water improperly on a burned-out central square. Butcher Joseph Roth was guilty of this last misdeed. His old father, who subsequently died, had wanted to pay his last 50 Kr., earmarked for buying a cow, to spare his son punishment. One brandy seller vainly offered 500 Kr. to the Red Cross, another 4,000 Kr., to escape the beating. One man fainted after the twelfth blow, causing the attending lawyer to summon a military doctor.[34]

It was a measure of anti-Judaism, Zionists thought, that Polish-language warnings were issued in June 1915 against Jewish efforts to evade conscription (although these certainly occurred, especially among Hasidim). Among draft dodgers' "various tricks" were self-starvation and "simulation of madness."[35] Yet Zionist dossiers were silent on

---

[33] Ibid., Beilage A (September 3–9, 1915).   [34] Ibid., Beilage B.   [35] Ibid., Beilage N.

pogroms, seemingly assuming these were the work of Russians and their Christian followers. It was Polish- and Austrian-imposed injuries to Galician Jews' citizenly equality and to individual dignity that elicited the mostly bourgeois and Germanophone Zionist leaders' protest.

Conviction that Habsburg Jews enjoyed equal rights and civilian honor paid tribute to Jewish emancipation's success in Austria, however stormy opposition to it had become. Recitation of incidents in themselves minor, such as Polish officials' petty tyrannies in provincial towns, revealed Jewish anxieties over their dangerous implications, flaring in casual threats of mass slaughter. No one, perhaps, supposed such threats would be actualized, but their utterance, even by children and servants, hung jarringly in the air.

Austria's respect for Jewish subjects seemed doubtful to sixty-three inhabitants of Galician Bolechów, who in December 1915 protested to the Interior Ministry that, two days earlier, fifty Habsburg soldiers with officers, gendarmes, and detectives occupied their town, suspected of disloyalty. They withdrew twelve hours later, with apologies. Yet Bolechovians' "patriotic feelings were offended in highest measure." "We endured for full nine months Russian invasion, and many a burgher of our little town was rewarded for his patriotism by Cossack's knout." They rejoiced when Austrians returned, and all turned out for army muster, "except those who emigrated to America." Now town government, joined with Jewish commune, had committed itself to invest 100,000 Kr. in the empire's third war bond issue, hard as payment would be. They suffered through bad provisioning for a month without flour, which "in view of the seriousness of wartime we bore in patience and silence, without grumbling. Nevertheless [the authorities] wanted to brand our little town with the stigma of disloyalty and ordered military quartering." It was by aggregation of many thousands of such offenses and disappointments that the Habsburg monarchy's grassroots legitimacy withered, strained already at Christmas 1915 by three never to be repaid war-bond issues.[36]

Jewish grievances extended beyond Christian injustice. Vienna police investigated charges lodged by a self-described "Viennese manufacturer and exporter" doing business in East Galicia and Bukovina. His warehoused stock in Kolomea was lost when the propertied and educated fled Russian occupation, leaving behind "only those individuals who had nothing to lose morally or materially."

---

[36] AVA. MdIP-G. Sign. 22. Fsz. 2117, No. 220 (December 10, 1915).

These people exploited refugees' absence in the lowest and most criminal manner, enriching themselves by theft and sale of abandoned assets worth millions. Some have now come to Vienna and have illegally converted enormous ruble holdings into Austrian money.

He named four Jewish offenders, one a draft dodger living with false papers in Franzensbad. He cited another as saying to a third, in German-Yiddish idiom, "Listen to what I tell you, your dad deserves to be bumped off; he was informer for Mayor Bukojemski." The unsigned petitioner named fifteen Jewish refugee witnesses.[37]

In the war's first two years, anti-Jewish violence exploded like strings of dynamite in the Russian army's van. It took the form not only of murder, plunder, rapine, and expulsion but often, perhaps invariably, in Judeophobic religious desecration. It blended the print-antisemitism of educated Russian military and civil elites with the polyglot tsarist soldiers' demotic folk-antisemitism. Also acting on popular antagonisms, doubtless similar to those manifested in 1898's West Galician pogroms, East Galician Christians – Ruthenians and Poles – swooped down in the aftermath of Cossack and other soldierly assaults on Jewish communities to gather plunder's fragments.

Tsarist General Brusilov's offensive of June–September 1916 returned much of East Galicia to another year of ruinous Russian rule. Its rigors, and conquered inhabitants' loss of faith in Austria's capacity to protect the land, further corroded Habsburg legitimacy. In Austrian-held West Galicia, war's last two years worked similar dissolution. Pogrom violence, previously confined to the Russian front, crept westward, powered not by sabered horsemen but by immiseration's resentments and utopian visions of national purification.

---

[37] AVA. MdIP-G. Sign. 22. Fsz. 2117, No. 16309 (n.d.). *Hörsti wus ich will Dir derzählen, as dein Tato verdient gehærget zu werden; er ist gewesen ein Musser beim Bürgermeister Bukojemski.*

2 West Galicia's Jews, 1917–1918
Objects of Envy, Targets of Rage

In the war's last years, Galicia's economic misery and political anxieties were vengeful godfathers of pogrom violence at Polish Catholic hands. This chapter guides readers, swiftly, through crisis zones of hunger and fear for the Polish national future – precincts from which pogromists issued. We then arrive at rising plateaus of violent contention, leading into the realm of full-blown pogroms. We encounter Poles and Jews straining to comprehend the brutalities before their eyes, most revealingly perhaps in a Polish judge's confidential reflections on the long-suffering Christian common folk's mentality, but tellingly too in Jewish nationalists' pogrom emplotments. Commentators' vision encompassed some of violence's sources, but they were blind to others, whether because they denied them in themselves or could not see into the depths from which they sprang.

Food Shortages and Social Disorder, 1917

The Central Powers' decision to proclaim on November 5, 1916 a "Kingdom of Poland" in the Russian Polish lands Germany had conquered in 1915 broke the fin-de-siècle ice gripping the century-old "Polish question." The client state's new ruler, presiding over a polity where, as Berlin and Vienna hoped, aristocratic conservatives would predominate, was likely to be a junior Habsburg dynast. How would Galicia or, at any rate, Polish-speaking West Galicia relate to the new kingdom? Would there be national cohabitation or continuing separate "Russian" and "Galician" bedrooms? Could the German-dependent masters of this new Polish house sleep secure in their brocaded chambers, or would the servant class upend them from their soft mattresses? Much depended on the kitchen.[1]

---

[1] Werner Conze, *Polnische Nation und deutsche Politik, passim*; Alexander Watson, *Ring of Steel. Germany and Austria-Hungary in World War I* (New York: Basic Books, 2014), 412–14. Peter Haslinger, "Austria-Hungary," in Robert Gerwarth et al., *Empires at War, 1911–1923* (New York, NY: Oxford University Press, 2014), 73–90; Paul Latawski, ed., *The Reconstruction of Poland, 1914–23* (New York, NY: St. Martin's Press, 1992).

And to what quarters would Jews be assigned? The Habsburg monarchy's Christian subject nationalities, in making a war's-end break from the defeated "prison-house of nations," not only massively spurned the Viennese dynasty and its Austrian German servitors but also widely eyed Jews inhabiting their newborn nation-states as Habsburg orphans they were reluctant to embrace as siblings. Polish nationalists, in the war's last starvation-stalked years, were more inclined to act as if their Jewish countrymen did not exist than to welcome them into their councils.

In Galicia, 1917 brought revolutionary tremors but no conflagrations. Russia's renewed armed incursions had affected only East Galicia's eastern and southwestern periphery. In Kraków and Lemberg/Lwów, food and fuel shortages threatened internal peace, as did village farmers' resistance to military requisitions. In February, Kraków's k.k. Polizei-Direktor informed the viceroy that a crowd of some five hundred people

of the poorest working class, mostly women and children, gathered before the municipal sales depot for potatoes, bread and milk, and after they received no potatoes – for none were available – they went to city hall and raised against municipal president Excellency Dr. Leo loud protests ... while numerous children present wept from hunger.

Later – as police recorded – a red-inked graffito appeared on Kraków's iconic Renaissance cloth-hall: "*niech żyje rewolucya*" [long live revolution].[2]

In March 1917, Lemberg's food provisioning chief informed the Interior Ministry of "untenable and threatening conditions." He sketched drastic social decline. The city's "external character had quickly changed" as "broad circles fell into poverty and misery and families had no food who, on strength of social or economic position, had previously led carefree existences." Under Russian occupation, Lemberg had been abandoned by Austria-Hungary's central government, its banks, "and all who through their material circumstances had stamped the city with prosperity and helped their unfortunate fellow townspeople."

In place of earlier hope and joy in work came desperation and demoralization. In place of those who had left the city there flocked poor and desperate people from all East Galicia who, leaving behind their worldly goods, could only save their bare lives and swell the number of those here in the [crownland's] capital who depend on public charity.[3]

---

[2] AVA. MdIP-G. Sign. 22. Fsz. 2117, No. 3484 (February 26, 1917).
[3] Ibid., No. 4174 (March 8, 1917).

Bread rations had fallen to a weekly kilogram, and cooking flour was gone, along with groats, rice, and legumes. There were free kitchens for the poor, once dispensing potatoes and meat, but now dwindling. Daily potato rations fell 50 percent to a half a kilogram, inadequate in normal times ("And how!" someone wrote in the margin), and now this quantity was undeliverable. "In face of the conflagration consuming the monarchy – indeed, the whole world," sacrifices were unavoidable, but hunger was triggering spotted typhus and threatening everyone with starvation.[4]

In Kraków, which in 1910 counted some 140,000 souls (one-quarter Jewish) and at war's end was pushing toward 200,000, large-scale protests over food and coal shortages had punctuated late winter and spring 1917 and started again as winter returned. In West Galician Chrzanów, "two hundred reservists' wives" demanded, in "provocative manner," bread and potatoes at the prefect's office. Later the crowd swelled to 500 women, "whose excitement rose so high that finally around 6 o'clock in the evening windows were broken at the governor's office, at individual merchants' shops, and in the officials' co-op store." Soldiers' arrival quelled unrest. The bureaucratic record is silent on anti-Jewish actions, though some of the shattered glass will have fronted Jewish-owned businesses. Instead, crowds voiced their wrath at the state and its agents.[5]

Peasant farmers' resentment targeted soldiers requisitioning village food and livestock. In October 1917, an East Galician estate leaseholder testified that "requisitioning troops" (of Austria's separate Hungarian Honvéd army) "treat people ruthlessly, taking potatoes from producers without measuring or weighing [and] rifle-butting them, even shooting." Villagers were helpless, especially because they couldn't understand the soldiers' foreign tongue. Slovenian-speaking troops killed a Polish peasant's horse – he valued it highly at 3,000 Kr. – after he refused to surrender his wagon. They arrested and punched him and injured his pregnant wife with rifle butt to the hip. Other troops ransacked Greek Catholic Anna Wyzdryk's cottage, seizing her potato supply. She lay sick after childbirth but ran after them. "The soldier aimed his gun at me and I told him I was not afraid, He fired and I fled in terror home."[6]

A year earlier, in October 1916, gendarmes in West Galician Krościenko Niżne discovered revolutionary posters on a barn wall, even though the population's behavior, despite embitterment over food requisitions, was reportedly peaceful and unthreatening. Perpetrators were not

---

[4] Ibid., No. 20505 (October 17, 1917).
[5] Ibid., No. 5036 (March 24, 1917); No. 5125 (March 26–28, 1917); No. 5249 (March 28, 1917); No. 7924 (May 14, 1917); No. 7924 (May 14, 1917).
[6] Ibid., No. 22536 (October 25, 1917).

discovered, but villagers apologized for the provocation. The texts, in unartful demotic language, are eloquent:

Who shall it be? The lords and the Jews! On Saturday at 9:00 PM let's throw ourselves on them like lions, and on government offices, let's destroy everything, especially what's Mr. (*pan*) Neumann's. No grain for requisition! Let them go to the devil. Let's go after them, because we're perishing, we're going to die! What will we eat if they take our grain? Let's don't allow it. Let's beat them like dogs. Don't sell them anything. Let them work like the peasant. We start Saturday night at nine with the lords. Krościenko Niżne the Jews, Krościenko Wyżne the lords, Pan Neumann in Suchodół, Głowienka the government offices, Białobrzegi and Krosno the government banks.[7]

The second poster read:

Dear sisters and brothers! Peasants! Misery is heaped on us and that's this terrible war. The lords are our misery's cause! We'll soon have a second war – of hunger, for there'll be nothing to eat. It's because of the lords. Who serves in the army? Peasants. Who gives everything for this war? Peasants. Who has plenty of everything? The lords and the Jews. And what do they do with the peasant? They beat him, they exhaust him, and we're supposed to accept that. What do we do? Make revolution [*zrobić Rewulicyę*].[8]

In their fiery hatred of "the lords" – nobility, landlords, the state and its offices and agents – these words breathed 1846's spirit but expanded to encompass all the peasantry's tormentors, including "the Jews," whose fault here lies not in religion or culture but in their worldly power and privilege, granted and protected by "the lords."

Hopes and Fears for the Polish Future, 1917

Even before Russia's tsardom toppled in February 1917, rebirth of Polish statehood, adumbrated already in November 1916's German-sponsored Kingdom of Poland, blazed brighter in the stars, especially for those myriad Poles who prayed for the Central Powers' defeat. This prospect confronted East Galician Ruthenians with new fears and hopes. In Lemberg, the principal Ukrainian party, the National Democrats, heard its leader, Dr. Kostj' Lewickyj, excoriate Poland as "the Ukrainian people's eternal enemy." Present were activists and parliamentarians, but – as police reported – "the country population is practically unrepresented." A "future Polish state" was inevitable, Lewickyj conceded, but East Galicia must not be part of it. Instead, Ukrainian nationalists must strive for its union, in alliance with the Central Powers, with formerly Russian-ruled Ukraine and former Russian Poland's polyglot Chełm province, home to

---

[7] Ibid., No. 27857 (November 24, 1916).   [8] Ibid.

a large Ukrainian population but claimed too by Polish nationalists. This was Ukrainian maximalism.[9]

Among Poles, broadly supported Endeks vied with a nationalism-friendly Socialist Party (PPS) and a moderate Populist (Peasant) Party (PSL) in uninhibitedly pushing for independent statehood despite still-standing Habsburg sovereignty. Deputies both in Lemberg's Galician parliament (Sejm) and the Viennese Reichsrat gathered in Kraków in May 1917. Debate swirled around the "Tetmajer resolution," adopted in the Sejm. Rather than the Central Power's kingdom, it demanded an independent Poland encompassing all three partition zones, with access to the sea. Moderates and liberals agreed but tried to defend the German-Austrian-sponsored kingdom's "real value as political act." The prestigious conservative leader Count Adam Tarnowski urged the Reichsrat delegation (*Polenklub*) to "express its thanks [to the Austrian government] for this initiative toward formation of [a] self-sufficient and independent Poland and its wish to remain true to the tradition of western civilization [*Westkultur*]," adding some friendly words for departed Franz Joseph's young successor, Karl I. But, facing defeat, Tarnowski retreated in national solidarity's name, gaining instead the conference's public assent that "participation in rebuilding Poland will secure Austria a natural and stalwart ally."[10]

Actually, Galician politics were heatedly anti-Austrian. The Viennese *Polenklub*, hitherto long pro-government, withdrew into opposition. Charismatic socialist Ignacy Daszyński apostrophized the Russian Revolution and the United States' entry into the war:

These events give the Polish question a wholly new character, since Russia has ceased to be our mortal enemy and greatest terror, while America will have the decisive voice at the peace conference. [Austria's ally Imperial Germany had, he said, no Polish friends.] Austria has much in common with the Poles: both are Catholic, both are continental states, and both have a drive to the east [*Drang nach Osten*]. An independent Poland will support Austria's existence. But [as the police reporter wrote] the speaker warned against Byzantine incense-burning and unnecessary concessions [i.e., to Austria] that only diminish the nation's dignity.[11]

Daszyński's unapologetic invocation of Poland's eastern mission threw down the gauntlet to Ukrainians.[12]

In December 1917, women-led hunger protests erupted anew in Kraków. "They threw snow at the people peacefully watching, or just passing by." At the cloth-hall, "they overturned the food-stands and the

---

[9] AVA. MdIP-G. Sign. 22. Fsz. 2117, No. 3270 (February 6, 1917).
[10] Ibid., No. 9438 (May 9, 1917).   [11] Ibid., No. 9438 (May 30, 1917).
[12] Ibid., No. 9995 (May 26, 1917).

sales-tables" – expressions, seemingly, of resentment toward those who could afford to buy high-priced food. "Some of the demonstrators wanted to proceed to the Jewish Kazimierz district," but police intervened. Class war and pogroms were looming.[13]

In January 1918, week-long protests flared. Three thousand women gathered at central square, where "one of them spoke in agitated words over the escalating misery," whereupon they moved to Catholic Prince-Bishop Sapieha's palace. He promised relief. Simultaneously, another crowd stormed shops and restaurants, breaking windows and plundering.

Daszyński and friends ascribed the people's suffering to "Germans, because they ruthlessly stripped Galicia of food." But the viceroyalty was also guilty of failing to control the "big agriculturalists" (estate owners) and "chain-merchants" (*Kettenhändler*) – code for Jewish wholesalers and retailers reputedly driving up prices through collusion. Some of the crowd moved toward Jewish Kazimierz, but police again intervened. "The mood is embittered in highest degree, and if bread and flour shortages continue one must be prepared for very serious incidents."[14]

On January 17, the "assembled women" surrounded a conference of parliamentarians and the prince-bishop, throwing stones and breaking windows at the viceregal office. It was agreed that Austrian occupation authorities in Russian Poland should ship food to Kraków and that k.k. gendarmes should cease confiscating food gained in peripheral villages by Cracovians. "Certain indications of bolshevist ideas' impact on the lower strata are perceptible."[15] Police labeled the protests "peace action," with ten thousand present. Speakers included female "university auditor Kłuszyńska, in women's name." Patriotic songs filled an "anti-Prussian" atmosphere ascribing Austria's suffering to German annexationism. Railroad workers threatened pacifist strikes.[16]

February 1918: Explosions over Brest-Litovsk

On February 9, 1918, Germany and Austria signed, after Machiavellian negotiations in Brest-Litovsk, what many of their undernourished subjects cynically – or thankfully – termed the "bread treaty" with the new-born "Ukrainian People's Republic." This child of European nationalism emerged from the Central Powers' midwifery in revolutionized Russia's southern lands. Its proud Ukrainian parents promised delivery to the

[13] Ibid., No. 24226 (December 6, 1917).
[14] AVA. MdIP-G. Sign. 22. Fsz. 2118, No. 1719 (January 17, 1918).
[15] Ibid. (January 18, 1918).   [16] Ibid., No. 1880 (January 21, 1918).

food-starved German powers of 1 million tons of grain, in recognition of their baptism and military fostering of this first-ever Ukrainian state. Its borders were wide, encompassing lands in the mixed Polish-Ukrainian ethnic frontier zone – above all, Chełm province – universally thought among Poles to belong to them by ethnographic and historical right. No less maddening were Polish suspicions, subsequently justified, that in a secret treaty clause Austria had agreed to transform East Galicia into a separate crownland free of Polish domination.

Polish reactions were explosive. The recently established Kingdom of Poland's Polish-manned provisional government in Warsaw angrily resigned. The conservative Polish "Regency Council" that had appointed that government abjured subordination to the Central Powers. The armed Polish Legions remaining at Austria's side – others, under Józef Piłsudski, had refused further cooperation in 1917 – defected under Józef Haller's command to the Entente side. And across West Galicia, protest demonstrations erupted, locally and spontaneously at first and then well organized by the pro-independence parties on February 18 across the land. Some escalated into pogroms.

An anonymous Polish-language proclamation voiced outrage in a characteristic Endek idiom of suffering, wounded self-righteousness, national hatred, and defensiveness about foreign dismissiveness toward Poland:

Countrymen! The hour has struck to revenge ourselves on our eternal Prussian enemy. Our children, wives and mothers in their homes, our fathers, brothers, and husbands in the trenches suffer hunger, while our enemies carry off food from our land. Our enemies – the Austrian and Prussian governments – shamefully exploit and betray us. They partition Poland for the fourth time, refusing to admit Poles to the peace negotiations in Brześć [Brest]. That is a great injury to us Poles, calling to God for vengeance. Let us act, let us expel from the land the enemy who grinds us down. Shame and eternal disgrace on those Poles who fraternize and mix with them – they who scorn you, who laugh at you poor little Poles (*wyśmiewają was Polki*). Down with the scoundrels, oppressors of our nation. Act![17]

In Kraków, even before February 18's protest wave, police reported "tumultuous street excesses" especially targeting their own ranks so that fielding of a "citizens' guard composed of respected persons, and especially of university students" was necessary. Now, "in a spirit of hope," a great crownland-wide popular protest was proclaimed for February 18, with church services and public swearing of an oath against loss of Chełm province. The oath's text, somehow obtained beforehand by police, condemned, in rhetoric combining Christian tradition and Wilsonianism,

[17] Ibid., No. 6199 (n.d.).

"the separation from Poland's living body" of the bartered-off land. Addressing "all free and fair peoples," it condemned treacherous and cunning diplomacy and swore, "so long as we breathe, to fight with all means to recover a united and undiminished Poland, 'so help us God!'"[18]

The protest entailed a daytime rail strike alongside closure of schools and other public institutions. Cooperation of railroad workers, themselves state employees, was vital, though hardly in doubt, given their radical politics. News traveled fast along Habsburg rails, and locomotives linked protest movements among the various nationalities. Witnesses quoted a stationmaster's words at a closed meeting preceding the anti-Brest-Litovsk strike:

Look here, gentlemen, there's no more eagle on my cap. Out with the Austrian government ... we've had enough little Karls [Karlis] and Wilhelms. If a train comes on February 18, I'll sideline it and if soldiers try anything, you'll give them a bath in the Vistula.[19]

In Jarosław, the stationmaster abetted posting of militant posters. One, excoriating the "thieves of Chełm," cried, "To the gallows with Karl and Wilhelm." The other proclaimed that the holding of Austrian titles and distinctions "disgraces the Poles."

Away with Excellencies, with Court, Imperial, and Privy Counselors, with "Cavaliers of the Orders," with all insignias of loyalty to the robbers' government ... Every step, every deed for Poland! Struggling for independence, we throw off all signs of slavery and service to the foreigner.[20]

Kraków Police Commissioner Steinhäusl described how, earlier, protesters tore down the Austrian double eagle wherever they found it, burning it if made of wood and blacking it out if located on mailboxes. On the central square they unveiled a picture "that displayed Christ on the cross, between His k.u.k. Apostolic Majesty Kaiser Karl and His Majesty the German Kaiser. The picture was inscribed, 'Christ, Thou Wert never on the cross in the company of two such scoundrels.'"[21] Irredentist unanimity overtrumped class differences; "no one can stand aloof if he doesn't want to lose the ground under his feet."[22]

On February 18, the "mourning strike" took place in Kraków, with copies of the crucifixion picture distributed. In Lemberg, a handbill circulated mocking Austro-Polish loyalty, adorned with a caricature of the Polish eagle bearing a stereotyped Jewish face. Everywhere the strike was so finely tuned that it seemed a "dress rehearsal for a later strike,"

[18] Ibid., No. 4146 (February 16, 1918).   [19] Ibid., No. 12928 (February 16, 1918).
[20] Ibid., No. 12928 (n.d.).   [21] Ibid., No. 11092 (April 1918).
[22] Ibid., No. 4663 (February 25, 1918).

alluding seemingly to breakaway into independence. Catholic clergy plunged into agitation, exhorting people in church not to speak German, even if fluent. The intelligentsia were bombarding "uneducated Polish commoners" with masses of patriotic history while scorning all Germans as "*Prusacki*." They were working "to make the [national] movement's necessity palatable to unlettered and indifferent Polish folk."

Galicia had divided into "two great camps." Poles, including k.k. officials, wore Polish eagle insignias and red-white armbands, whereas "members of the Ukrainian nation" displayed lions and blue-gold armbands. Bookshops offered only Polish history and literature, nothing on Austria. Pictures of the two kaisers and army leaders, once common, had disappeared. Nowhere in Galicia did Steinhäusl see black-gold Habsburg banners flying. Although some or even many West Galician Jews embraced Polishness, "hatred of Jewry – apart from economic motives – is very great. They are seen as a foreign body and subservient to the central government." Who was directing the protest movement? Steinhäusl suspected the mountain resort and intelligentsia retreat of Zakopane, where there was no surveillance of Polish political leaders, ostensibly taking the cure.[23]

Viceroy Huyn drew despairing conclusions from the Chełm protest wave. He had wired Foreign Minister Czernin requesting, fruitlessly, that Brest-Litovsk's terms remain unannounced "until sufficient main force is on hand" to defend the government's Galician presence. Instead, "some shameful incidents" occurred. Undeniably, "nearly the entire bureaucratic corps have strong [Polish] national feelings," and some 80 percent were Endeks.

The February 18 demonstrations showed that the entire Polish bureaucracy, the professors, teachers, and clergy feel themselves as Poles only. The Austrian idea was nowhere to be found.[24]

Anti-Chełm Protests in the Galician Province

Anti-Jewish tumults accompanying February 18 protests were few, sporadic, and nonlethal. Their Judeophobic visage, sometimes hid itself, both in perpetrators' and in official eyes, behind hunger rioting's veil. In four localities near West Galician Tarnów, crowds of fifty to one-hundred persons, having destroyed Austrian symbols, defied gendarmes in plundering Jewish shops, though warning shots halted one such disorder. Thirty-one people were arrested for looting. In seven other West Galician towns, similar tumults occurred, entailing death in Nowy Targ of one woman by soldiers' bullets. In Strzyżów, "Pater Bolek's" speech

---

[23] Ibid., No. 11092 (April 1918).   [24] Ibid., No. 6632 (March 4, 1918).

"occasioned assaults on Jews," who, the cleric complained, held aloof from Brest-Litovsk protests and "exploited the people . . . [Consequently] we must break off connections with them, without engaging in violence." In Tarnów, crowds attacked gendarme headquarters and demonstrated against "savings bank director Kusz" for having sent "large sums to Vienna for an eventual eighth war-bond."[25]

In West Galician Żywiec, a picturesque Habsburg-favored provincial town of antisemitic complexion that – with spurious legality – had long barred Jews from residency, boisterous anti-Brest-Litovsk protests addressed by local notables ended in state symbols and portraits thrown into "filth, and in crudest way sullied." Railroaders ripped imperial crowns from their caps while announcing that in Jewish-inhabited nearby settlements on February 18 and 19 "it was permitted to plunder Jews and Germans." In Milówka, a thousand-strong crowd gathered, mainly "outsiders." School Director Koczar urged them to return home peacefully "and not be misled and incited," but they held "their threatening posture." They cried out, "First come Jews and then the gentlemen, by which were meant state officials, since these have been bought by Jews."

The crowd set to work, breaking into shops through windows or by crowbarring or axing down metal grills and sliding doors protecting Jewish businesses. Many losses resulted, topped by goods valued at 150,000 Kr. plundered from Kleinzeller's fabric shop. "Herr Gutmann's [unspecified] energetic action prevented new incursions," enabling the crowd's dispersion.

People in Milówka believed plunder resulted from incendiary speeches in Żywiec, which excitedly claimed that

The emperor has had to flee to Prussia. There is no state anymore, no prefect, no tax bureau. No need to pay taxes any longer. We'll give no more recruits. Soldiers on leave don't need to return to their companies, and shouldn't. In short: it's now a republic [*kurz es ist Republick*].

Gendarmes later recovered some stolen goods and arrested looters. No injuries were reported. This riot's anarchistic – "republican" – dynamic focused police minds, not its anti-Judaism. Yet the claim that Jews corrupted Austrian officialdom through bribery, thereby delegitimizing the state, reveals one important antisemitic rationale for lawlessness and violence, as Milówka's pogrom – the first detected in wartime West Galicia – showed.[26]

---

[25] Ibid., No. 4414 (February 1918); No. 5062 (February 22, 1918); No. 14116 (June 24, 1918). AVA. MdIP-G. Sign. 22. Fsz. 2119, No. 5222 (n.d.).

[26] AVA. MdIP-G. Sign. 22. Fsz. 2118, No. 13470 (February 25, 1918); Kriegsarchiv, Vienna. Kriegsministerium. Präsidium (hereafter KMP). 1918–19. No. 52–5/20 (February 21, 1918).

Pogrom in Kraków, April 16–21, 1918

Viceroy Huyn's reaction to the February explosions was to maintain bureaucratic imperturbability and await the tempest's end. He ordered all state symbols restored to public display. Huyn hopefully detected "sobering up" among Poles, as their leading newspapers began warning readers against provocateurs and shadowy agitators.[27] Yet, in April, Kraków's streets resounded for nearly a week with the uproar of a food riot that rocketed into a pogrom. Following Milówka's plundering and other minor provincial anti-Jewish violence accompanying the February 1918 Chełm protests, anti-Jewish resentment's tide engulfed Galicia's most liberal and culturally advanced bastion, where Jewish assimilation had flourished among the educated and propertied. It was ominous.

Among discordant official accounts, army's and gendarmerie's reports were soberest and least apologetic.[28] "The violence is said to have erupted because bread rations were reduced for three weeks, or even halted, while nevertheless flour was available on the black market for 16–18 Kr. per kilo," a jarringly high price. Similar disturbances had shaken Bielitz, where "during bread deliveries to the Polish Officials' Cooperative women plundered the shop."

On Monday, April 16, "Jews are said to have bought grain, offered for sale by farmers from Russian Poland, at exorbitant prices, thereby making Christians' purchase of bread-grain impossible." In police eyes, farmers' prices were already too high when Jewish buyers overbid them, leading to "mutual conflict and indignation against Jews." Housewives, joined by children and the "usual street-proletariat" of adolescent youth, spearheaded a gathering crowd that finally stormed into Jewish Kazimierz district, dismantling metal shop shutters and smashing windows. Rioters threw plundered goods on the street for collective seizure.

"On some trolley lines, moving cars were halted and passengers wearing Jewish costume hauled out and badly roughed up." One such traveler, cigarette-paper vendor Psachie Meller, "is said to have died of maltreatment," succumbing to stroke. Mounted military police "did not feel up to

---

[27] AVA. MdIP-G. Sign. 22. Fsz. 2118, No. 6097 (March 8, 1918).

[28] Reports by military authorities and gendarmerie in AVA. MdIP-G. Sign. 22. Fsz. 2118, No. 11092; by Kraków police, the viceroyalty, and other civilian offices in ibid., Nos. 9180, 9035, 9226, and 9518. Sources for citations in the text that follows will be found by official provenance and date in these archivally aggregated unpaginated files. Jan Małecki, "Zamieszki w Krakowie w kwietniu 1918 r. Pogrom czy rozruchy głodowe?," in Paluch, ed., *Jews in Poland*, vol. 2: 245–57, argues against categorization of the Kraków riots as "comparable to the pogroms staged in the tsarist state," as he found the prestigious Viennese *Neue Freie Presse* to have exaggeratedly proclaimed (p. 256). They were, as he reasonably holds, instead a combination of hunger protest and anti-Jewish riot inflamed by antigovernment resentments.

their task," for the two present in Kazimierz passively observed plundering before "timidly" calling for dispersal.

Next day, shops were closed and streets were patrolled by soldiers. Yet women and youth roamed about, "and it seemed the individual groups were only looking for victims." Adolescents continued to stop streetcars in search of Jews. City police observed renewed plundering, causing soldiers with them to fix bayonets. Crowds stoned two patrols, drawing gunfire that injured three and killed Elisabeth Lempert, master glazier's daughter. Forty-five arrests ensued.

On day three, police reported another shooting, of a railroader's twenty-year-old daughter, Genowefe Chrząszcz. She and other youth had taunted a military escort leading a column of army-conscripted legionnaires to barracks. The government's earlier dissolution of the Austro-Polish volunteer army still stung Galician patriots. Stroke-felled Meller, who had come from provincial Stryj to meet his soldier son, was buried amid anti-Jewish indignities. Stones were thrown at mourners from a suburban "workers' train" passing the funeral procession to the Jewish cemetery, injuring several lightly. Meller had sought refuge in Rebeka Rappoport's hotel. Dr. Ehrenpreis confirmed his death. An eye witness to the beating declined to testify, fearing "revenge or some other unpleasantness." Autopsy found no hints of internal or external abuse. That Meller died of traumatic shock seemingly escaped bureaucratic insight.

On day four, "there gathered in Szeroka Street's old Jewish temple more than one hundred young Jews who, armed with cudgels, iron rods and such-like, betook themselves to the second-hand market. There they fell upon the Christian public, physically maltreating them and lightly injuring a few." Ringleaders were arrested, weapons confiscated. A different report portrayed the Jewish band shouting against mounted gendarmes, "seize their weapons, kill them." This invoked the most common of wartime clichés justifying anti-Jewish violence, that shots were surreptitiously fired at passing policemen, a charge otherwise unregistered and subsequently ignored, as was that identifying reserve infantryman Olexy as victim of Jewish beating. Policeman Mycyk, charged with rifle butting Jews, countered that they were "armed with clubs and stones and advanced challengingly toward the Catholic population." Had he tried to restrain them, "he would have exposed himself to danger at the hands of armed Jews" – an image highly provocative and disagreeable to Judeophobic minds. Meanwhile, at city hall, all municipal councillors "condemned excesses in sharp words," demanding controls on marauding youth.

On day five, Christian street bands "made fun of passing Jews, calling out insults." Day six, Jewish Sabbath, witnessed Elisabeth Lempert's burial, accompanied by some four thousand mourners. Father Kulinowski and gymnasial teacher Simionov delivered eulogies. "In moving words they both exhorted the audience to peaceful and reasonable behavior."

In the aftermath of these anti-Jewish tumults, socialist Daszyński attributed police passivity to "authorities' hostile attitude toward Jews." Investigators gathered Jewish testimony. Dr. Löbel, having urged mounted police to intervene, met with shrugged shoulders. Dr. Goldwasser saw them gallop away. They told Salomea Franzblau, protesting a Jew's beating by street youth, that "this doesn't concern you." Merchant Kaufmann said that "police are here to protect us," but "they rode off laughing." The seasoned but indolent policemen, one a Polish-speaking Greek Catholic and the other a Roman Catholic Pole, faced unsympathetic military interrogators. They had ignored exhortations, shouted from an army command post's window, by General Staff's Major Morawski to intervene energetically. The army's dignity had been impugned by the crowd's disarming of a Jewish officer who attempted to shield the first day's riot victims.

Nor did the crownland's governor distinguish himself. In a "phonogram," Viceroy Huyn informed Austrian Chancellor von Feuchtenegg, well in the pogrom's aftermath, that "Jewish merchants' usurious prices underlay the violence, triggered by bread shortage." The policemen were "inferior material." Should the "anti-Semitic movement" break out in the countryside, he would apply "sharpest measures." Evident here is a Judeophobe's readiness to fight antisemitism – for order's sake and to protect big landowners.

The government's "Lemberg Gazette" (*Gazeta Lwowska*) declared itself authorized to put Kraków events "in a true light" – that Jewish usury triggered them, while false rumors concerning Meller's death enflamed them, leading to gunfire and two fatalities. It charged that while Viennese opinion, notably the liberal *Neue Freie Presse*, sought to give them "another character" – taboo blocked the word *pogrom* – the correct diagnosis must be "hunger riots." Steps had now been taken to improve food provisioning, which would produce "complete pacification." Later, Huyn informed the Interior Ministry that his suppression of press reports on the pogrom and Kraków's prince-bishop's pastoral letter – presumably condemning the violence, if not the perpetrators' anti-Jewish resentments – was justified "because such occurrences have had, as experience shows, unfavorable consequences for us in enemy countries." Censorship permitted later release of a softened-down episcopal missive.

Kraków's violence was many sided: a hunger riot degenerating into anti-Jewish plunder and murder, soldierly and police passivity alongside shootings by the authorities of Christian protesters, and politicization through debates over the pogrom concept's applicability, which neither Austrian authorities nor Polish nationalists countenanced. No one charged that entrepreneurs of ethnic violence stood as wire pullers in the shadows. Pogroms were shameful events, even if neither authorities nor press explained just why.

We notice that while Jewish merchants manned Galicia's mercantile trenches, and so necessarily found themselves in possession of food and other vital consumer goods, the pogromists' conviction that Jewish dealers could, if they but willed it, lower prices or bring out hidden stocks for sale signaled an irrational belief, often exhibited in this book, that Jewish possessions were vast but out of sight. They could be a cornucopia of essential goods if only they were wrenched from hostile hands and brought out into Christian daylight. This was, as Tokarska-Bakir might say, a fairy-tale, more deeply rooted than believers knew.

The Wieliczka Pogrom and Other Post-Cracovian Violence

A May 2 Kraków army report to Vienna's War Ministry found "excesses against the Jewish population everywhere discussed." Polish liberals were distressed, blaming riots on "foreign provocateurs who wanted to compromise Poles in their national strivings." Jews were "painfully stricken." Those among them who had engaged strongly for Polish interests had "sobered up considerably." Poles, preparing for their May 3 national holiday, planned to celebrate it in Sokół gymnastic clubs and church services, to avoid involving state authorities, whose Brest-Litovsk concessions and internment of legionnaires unwilling to accept regular army conscription infuriated the intelligentsia. "Radical elements," weighing ongoing food shortages and popular rage evident in Kraków's riots, were reckoning on "start of full-scale revolution" in two or three months. A Polonophone undercover agent informed the army, referring evidently to Social Democrats, of a secret organization supporting "all unrest" and pressing for unification of Habsburg subject nationalities and political parties to end the war through railroad and telegraph shutdowns, relying on the soldiers' war weariness and the lawlessness of freed prisoners of war.[29]

---

[29] AVA. MdIP-G. Sign. 22. Fsz. 2118, No. 11474 (May 2, 1918).

On April 10, such returnees "from Russian captivity," serving in an army regiment's auxiliary battalion, assaulted on Nowy Sącz's railway platform "several thousand Jews from Austria, Hungary, Germany, Kingdom of Poland and Switzerland during their annual remembrance of Rabbi Halberstam's death, praying at his grave." Some were beaten,

robbed of clothing and footwear, while many thousands of Kronen in cash were taken. The soldiers were agitated by the pilgrims' prosperous appearance, pointing to their own misery and suffering.

Two miscreants (only) were arrested. "Civilians took no part."[30] Here again we observe poor Christians' bafflement at seeming Jewish imperviousness to the ruination war was raining down on them.

In April, a railroad engineer's wife, Josefa Spero, was visiting rural Rabka, seeking a summer house rental. At the market she informed country folk "that Kraków Jews had murdered a Catholic clergyman and a girl, so that people should not sell Jews either butter or eggs." For this outburst, police ticketed her. She also faced charges of saying that "Jews didn't go to the front and couldn't fight," that Kraków Jews "had thrown themselves with nails in their hands on the Christians," and that "one shouldn't talk about Jews, or patronize them." The Viennese Justice Ministry weighed the case on October 29, days before the monarchy's fall. It thought a guilty verdict would not issue from a jury trial, whose publicity might spark "street excesses." The woman should have known, considering the "population's anti-Semitic mood," that her remarks would endanger public security. That she could imagine Jews assaulting Christians with nails in their hands sparked association with the crucifixion of Jesus, while claims of Christian children's killing were ritual murder discourse, in this case routinized into banal boycott advocacy.[31]

In May, unsigned Jewish supplicants wrote the Interior Ministry protesting growing Galician insecurity and especially Kraków's excesses, which displayed "the character of a regular pogrom." To aid victims, Jewish city councilmen and religious leaders established a legal bureau offering free representation "to the population injured by wartime occurrences."

Acts of violence, to which the Jewish population have already in many parts of Galicia fallen victim, have doubtless not yet ended, but rather new outbursts are to be feared daily and hourly. *The hardest time* [it was presciently said] *is only just beginning.*

---

[30] Ibid., No. 9591 (April 17, 1918).
[31] Ibid., No. 11792 (May 16, 1918); AVA. MdIP-G. Sign. 22. Fsz. 2119, No. 24022 (October 29, 1918).

Jew had borne war's burdens "without grumbling," but now there was "a feeling of deep embitterment and injury that a people" – *Volksstamm*, as Habsburg discourse termed groups not formally recognized as nationalities – "has been targeted for special mistreatment and robbery by unrestrained mobs." The viceroyalty compounded Jewish pain by "sending out into the world a disavowal of truths known throughout the city. Such is the only recompense offered Kraków Jewry for a four-day pogrom in the twentieth century."[32]

The Interior Ministry filed another letter from Lutcza, which in the 1880s had witnessed Christian ritual murder charges against Jewish neighbors. At a recent May 3 Polish fest, a local catechist "exhorted farmers in our village to revolt against the few Jewish residents." The five supplicants, who signed firmly in German cursive, asked for measures "to forestall the danger threatening us." It was characteristically Galician to describe anti-Jewish violence as revolt rather than riot or even pogrom.[33]

On May 16, Chairman Rosenzwejg of the Israelite Religious Commune in Wieliczka, a town near Kraków famous for artfully sculpted medieval salt mines, telegraphed Interior Minister Toggenburg, informing him of a "Jewish pogrom" (*Judenpogrom*) the previous day that had raged for six hours "without being energetically suppressed." Windows of "nearly all Jewish homes and every prayer-house" were broken. "Jews were bloodily maltreated on the street and in their homes," and numerous Jewish enterprises had been plundered. This happened under the few gendarmes' eyes, whose passivity "encouraged the rabble." The "anti-Semitic movement" threatened to engulf the whole district, against which danger Rosenzwejg pleaded for the widening of army protection that finally halted Wieliczka's pogrom.

Wieliczka's prefect informed the Interior Ministry of these "anti-Jewish excesses," rooted in food provisioning difficulties but also "provoked by the Jewish population." Losses in the plundering – blamed on women and youth, though adult men had joined in – totaled 500,000 Kr. The prefect conceded the gendarmes' passivity. Twenty-nine arrests occurred, with two exceptions of males only. In Polish prefectural eyes, the incident was regrettable but understandable, assuming congenital lack of self-control among women and youth and local police reluctance to risk strife with fellow Christians on behalf of Jews.[34]

---

[32] AVA. MdIP-G. Sign. 22. Fsz. 2118, No. 15075 (n.d.) (author's emphasis). Cf. Marsha Rozenblit, *Reconstructing a National Identity: The Jews of Habsburg Austria during World War I* (New York, NY: Oxford University Press, 2001).

[33] AVA. MdIP-G. Sign. 22. Fsz. 2119, No. 22805.

[34] AVA. MdIP-G. Sign. 22. Fsz. 2118, No. 11792 (May 16, 1918); No. 14469 (June 5, 1918).

These terse accounts of Wieliczka's explosion veiled a mass of injuries, resentment, delusions, and hatreds that surfaced after Kraków District Court opened its police-assisted inquiry. Eventually, thirty-six defendants faced trial, derailed by the November 1918 revolution, although in 1920 the public prosecutor petitioned to press charges of theft against fourteen people, with thirty-two witnesses, albeit with unknown outcome.[35] Theodor Adorno once defined antisemitism as "the rumor about the Jews."[36] To listen to plaintiffs' and defendants' voices will reveal how such rumors channeled material deprivation into violence and blinded its interpretation.

The Wieliczka County Court registered testimony from eyewitnesses Natan Gold and Markus Lipschitz. They recalled how some dozens of women and children queued for bread at the salt-mine's food dispensary. From their midst an unknown woman's voice lamented that "they had to wait hours for bread while Jews had everything beyond measure at home." This inspired plundering of Hudesa Weiss's nearby shop. The crowd swelled to a thousand, revealing, in plaintiffs' eyes, that this was "work organized against the Jewish community" that could not be justified by hunger "since both town and k.k. salt-works had the previous week baked bread, so the population was supplied with it."

The crowd then mobbed the main square, breaking Jewish windows and robbing Jewish-owned shops. "False stories of all sorts circulated, among them one that could have led to incalculable catastrophe, namely, that in Efroim Joachimsmann's house the young boy Kozubski had been murdered or was hidden, and that Joachimsmann's hands were bloody." Later the crowd moved to the Jewish Klasno district, plundering and injuring "practically fatally, elderly communal chief Salomon Tiefenbrunner and his wife with blows to the head with a bottle."

Only at 9:00 PM did army intervention halt the riot, which local police had viewed passively or joined in. But it could flare up again if ringleaders were not arrested, including women and men who had stormed Joachimsmann's house, shouting "hand over the boy, or we'll murder you all and burn the house." Joachimsmann "expressed readiness to open all rooms and the basement, but to only three people, since the charge was only a pretext for robbery." The three then attacked and wounded him. Bloodshed was impending, had not "one of the Catholic women" (not "Poles") announced that the boy was safe at his home, whereupon the crowd returned to city-center plundering. Mieczysław "L." (Lachmann)

---

[35] Archiwum Państwowy w Krakowie, Oddział IIh. Sąd Okręgowy (hereafter SOKKr): S8/II. No 10: J 819/20: Wieliczka.

[36] From *Minima Moralia*, cited in Buchen, *Antisemitismus in Galizien*, 78.

gestured violently with an axe, breaking into shops and threatening Adolf Hirsch: "Just wait, you'll be the first!" In Klasno, someone cried "Go to Perlberger, he's rich, at home he's got plenty of leather" (footwear was scarce). Gendarme Iglicki refused to act even as "legionnaire Glatz beat Dawid Silberfeld while others held him."[37]

"Capitalist" Salomon Rosenzweig, sixty-five, witnessed the crowd attacking Reicherowa's bakery. Three people carried out a meager haul of "three trays of small wheat rolls, which the crowd shared around."[38] Weiss, fifty-three, whose shop was first to be plundered – of candy and pastry – faced a "whole band" led by two men, who struck her in the head and choked her so that she fell unconscious, one of them crying, "Kill the Jewess, the bitch."[39] Jozua Perlberger, twenty-three, was a soldier on leave and vodka manufacturer in civilian life. Visiting his father, whose leather works were plundered, he was injured in a hail of rocks.[40]

Doughty merchant Joachimsmann, fifty-three, skirted mortal danger. Fearing riot, he closed his shop and remained in his upstairs dwelling. Around 4:00 PM the crowd, "shouting '*hura*,'" broke in and robbed his store. "Calling my wife for help, I expelled the crowd from the shop, and seeing gendarme Litwin, asked him to help me, but he said that with the crowd stoning him, he was powerless." The mob pressed into the court-yard "and demanded handover of some boy I had allegedly captured. Holding a hatchet in my hand I announced to the crowd: 'if one of you dog's-bloods [*psiakrew*] comes in, I'll smash your head." Three men who jumped on him punched him and injured his eye. "After searching my house it turned out that there was no boy and then some person came who informed the crowd that the lad had been found, whereupon they peace-fully departed my home."[41]

Aforementioned miner Mieczysław Lachmann, thirty-five (literate, propertyless, previously convicted for drunkenness), corroborated Joachimsmann's testimony. He had been sitting, unapologetically drunk, in a pub when he heard the ritual murder charge. "Outraged and excited by this news, I went with other people through Joachimsmann's house." He saw how the householder faced the men in his courtyard, holding an axe and saying, "come on, dog's-bloods, I'll kill you all," whereupon Lachmann jumped a fence and tore the axe from his hand. "Some Catholic woman arrived, saying the lost boy Kozubski Antoni had been found, whereupon I returned to the crowd and said we could depart in peace since Joachimsmann was not guilty." He wanted to give the axe to the police, but Joachimsmann's sister, "Rachel, commonly named 'the

---

[37] SOKKr: S8/II. No. 10: J 819/20, fos. 273–79.   [38] Ibid., fos. 155–58.
[39] Ibid., fo. 311.   [40] Ibid., fo. 218.   [41] Ibid., fo. 156.

peasant,' called him into her apartment and, pouring me plum-brandy, asked for the axe back. I drank a few brandies, how many I can't say," but he didn't return the axe. Taking it to the authorities, "someone punched me in the head and I lost consciousness," losing the axe.[42] We note the custom, followed also by Anna Kahan's father, of buying pogromists off with drink, risky though it was.

The (literate) Pole Lachmann accepted that the ritual murder charge might be true and required investigation, whereas in Jewish eyes it was but pretext for plunder. Far more nuanced and revealing were frank ruminations of Franciszek Sypowski, sixty-one, Chief Justice in Wieliczka County Court and Judicial Councillor in Kraków Court. He knew common folk's suffering intimately. "I never constrain their testimony or complaints. I have therefore long had opportunity to acquaint myself with their feelings and thoughts." He never encountered popular anger that could not be assuaged "by reasonable explanations that poverty is the general condition, touching everyone, and that it's necessary, with the citizenry's mutual support, to suffer through and endure bad times patiently."

Common people had never organized themselves for violent action. "Our population remain passive, even though they live in constant dejection and dissatisfaction, confining these feelings to their hearts' depth, long accustomed to poverty." But they were not blind and saw the causes of the present unsatisfactory food provisioning. They well knew "who buys up daily necessities, who controls them, where and by whom they are transported, and who engages most in usurious price-gouging."

They know that commissioners for grain, potatoes, fats, etc. are Israelites alone, that for example here in Wieliczka the actual salt dealers are Jews Blau, Dominitz, Licht et al., who reaped fat fortunes, that Israelites control trade in sugar, heating and cooking oil, tobacco and spirits, and can trade these goods for any foodstuffs they need, so that they are, unlike Christians, in such a favorable position that they know no shortages, so it cannot be said that war's misery has touched them.

Never was an Israelite seen queuing for food. Yet Judge Sypowski had never observed among Christian common people "expressions of dislike or hatred of Israelites, i.e., anti-Semitism."

And when you add that the Christian population is spilling its blood massively on the battlefield while Jewish common soldiers work at headquarters and in military hospitals, one must acknowledge a great moderation among Christian folk.

[42] Ibid., fos. 191–93.

The explosion would never had occurred, averred the judge, had the "Israelite population" previously shown compassion for the paupers,

and if on that day it had not transpired – a lamentable fact, deserving of punishment – that, as everyone was saying, a certain Jewess in Lwów Street, where the crowd was gathered before the salt-works' bakery, had not cried out the provocative words to a Christian woman lamenting the bread shortage and that her child was dying of hunger: "we are only waiting for you all to croak from starvation."

No wonder, he said, this mockery led the crowd to hurl themselves on the speaker's little shop. "From this spark of irony the Jewess cast out exploded a blaze of indignation, previously long suppressed by the starving poor's quiet resignation." Already in 1917 the judge had learned that miners in the salt tunnels were furtively and ashamedly feeding themselves during work with potato peels and scraps stuffed in pockets. Food had been so comprehensively requisitioned that people knew there was no more to be legally had.

The judge did not doubt that wounding words had been spoken. "But in the aftermath of the terrible and enormously regrettable riot that ensued, it would be hard to suppose that the woman who heard them and repeated them to the crowd would admit it, or that someone among the defendants would betray her." It would have taken sixty to one-hundred policemen to halt the riot, while there were only some ten present. The Jewish commune's complaints were unfair: against the mob of "outraged women and youths enflamed by excesses" only fire hoses could have prevailed. These were the violent deeds

of *irrational* people, *thoughtless*, no longer masters of their will, because hunger and poverty, including the *threat of nakedness* from lack of clothing, deprived them of self-control, *robbed them of reason*. To ascribe these acts of violence to anti-Semitism I consider an unfair provocation of our society, and moreover an attempt to elicit conflict between the two social groups and maintain it for political purposes.

The judge did not believe Wieliczka's common folk were capable of translating antisemitism into action. They had not done so before the war, when conditions might have made it likely. Twenty years ago, a German abbot had allegedly proclaimed, "Jews have not subjugated all Galicia with sharp sword, but with brandy bottle." This saying applied to Wieliczka. "Through drunkenness for some fifteen or twenty years, or maybe one hundred, the Christian population has degenerated terribly and succumbed to poverty despite continual good earnings in the salt-works." Drunkenness brought with it usury, at rates rising to 7 to 9 percent or more annually. "Nevertheless one never heard of hatred of

Jews," even though industry brought them well-being while the "degenerate Christian population cannot hold the threads of prosperity in its hands."

Sypowski did not believe the wounding words had been politically prearranged, but he found the post-riot commentaries of Jewish leaders to be "thoughtless, or the result of haughtiness and arrogance," possibly even intended to stir up antagonism to Polish society in "ruling circles or abroad." He was wounded to learn that Jewish schoolgirls, when given the opportunity to collect money for poor children, informed teachers that "this was forbidden to them, because this was not their affair." Were not Polish-language incitations to anti-Jewish violence being printed in Berlin and smuggled into Galicia? Were not "certain Israelite notables" defaming Polish society and planting the idea that it was incapable of self-rule, thereby pushing it toward acts of violence?

Here in Wieliczka, it was the poorest who participated in the riots, unpolitical people gripped by the struggle to survive. Nor had it been charged that "anyone from really well-educated spheres had encouraged or incited the population to violence" so that it was not antisemitism but lack of food provisioning that caused it, after being triggered by the unnamed Jewess's alleged "arrogant provocation." The sixty German soldiers the government had now stationed in town were unnecessary, for the people, if inflamed with anti-Judaism, could overwhelm them. They were, instead, "an advertisement for a non-existent anti-Semitism," summoned, the judge heard, "solely at the Jewish commune's demand." Local authorities were fully capable of seeking out real thieves and lawbreakers and subjecting them "to condign judicial punishment they fully deserve."[43]

Here, uttered in judicial confidentiality, were condescending and patriarchal views of a Polish notable, uncomfortably aware of antisemitism's moral defects, disappointed in common people's imperfections, and passive-aggressively willing to make "the Israelites" responsible not just for the riot (which only a few Jewish leaders sought to brand as pogrom) but also for Polish society's debilities generally. Judge Sypowski, distressed at common folks' benightedness, could not bring himself to mention ritual murder rumors, nor did he otherwise invoke religious considerations. But he himself took refuge in a rumor that no other witness mentioned, whose credibility – what Jewess would publicly wish Christians dead of starvation? – was miniscule. The thought that perhaps he was – having *himself* put such words in the woman's mouth – unconsciously projecting this wish onto "the Israelites" was beyond self-questioning's horizon. Such

---

[43] Ibid., fos. 179–85 (author's emphasis).

imagining displays the defensiveness infusing Polish Christian attitudes toward their Jewish neighbors, investing them with life-and-death powers (through their commercial position) *and* a malevolent wish that the Christians dependent on their mercy (in supplying food) should die out.

The judge betrayed paranoid awareness that disorder and backwardness evidenced in his society by popular anti-Jewish violence strengthened Poland's foreign adversaries. Blaming Germans for secretly fomenting such violence signaled his denial that antisemitic political movements in Poland were busy themselves with aggressive handiwork. His was, probably, the most common form of antisemitism among educated and propertied Poles, requiring no Western European racial or social theory. It was, for Jews, the bitter wages of a religiously outcast middleman minority imagined as powerful in a poor country bled white by war.

The Reichsrat Jewish Delegation's Antipogrom Protest

In July, Benno Straucher, seasoned anti-assimilationist champion of Jewish interests and leader of the Viennese Reichsrat's ten-member Jewish nationalist delegation, passionately indicted the government's hapless dealing with Galician anti-Jewish violence. His speech, free of censorship that often strangled wartime journalism, both reflected and constructed wider Jewish opinion. He tough-mindedly aimed to explode all apologetics and lay bare hard truth about Polish antisemitism and Vienna's collusion in it. Austrian officialdom subsumed pogroms in hunger riots while blaming Jewish trading practices for sparking them. How did Straucher and colleagues understand them? The answer seemed clear: "a mysterious, invisible hand guided the entire action, proceeding systematically to an uncommon degree." But whose hand?[44]

Straucher conjured up the Milówka pogrom erupting from anti–Brest-Litovsk protests, its perpetrators laughably ignorant and gullible bumpkins, its victims peaceable agents of civilization and prosperity:

What unholy confusion had been sown in peasants' heads that they, at a given signal, fell like a wild horde on unsuspecting people and, armed with hoes, manure forks, threshing flails, millstones and tree branches, carried out comprehensive robbery and plunder against Jews and their property, against those Jews who had acquired it over years of laborious work, living among these farmers for practically an entire generation?

---

[44] AVA. MdIP-G. Sign. 22 Fsz. 2119, No. 19867: Haus der Abgeordneten. 79. Sitzung der 22. Session am 22. Juli 1918, p. 28.

Whence this sudden upwelling of rage? . . . Whence and why this bloody Jew-hatred? As the crowd of hostile peasants, led and spurred on by so-called intelligent elements, tore down – for example – Kleinzeller's shop shutters, they cried "you have stolen Poland from us, give Poland back!" And as they made off with goods stolen from Jews, they cried "now we have Poland, now we have Poland"! Who told them they would find the Chełm province they grieve for in Jews' shops?[45]

Unwittingly, Straucher perceived the nationalist symbolism in pogromists' actions: plundering Jews, they recovered their motherland and assuaged their grief.

Already in March 1918 the Jewish Club had interpellated the government to answer for Galician antisemitic agitation. In Lemberg and elsewhere, they charged, railway stations were distribution sites for inflammatory propaganda, traceable to a new Lemberg publication entitled, "Poland's Dejudaization" (Odżydzenie Polski). The flyer in question proclaimed that "Jews shall leave Galicia immediately, also Jewish assimilators and Jewish Poles shall depart for Zion, or they will be driven out with fire and sword." Benno Straucher voiced Jewish disappointment that civilian authorities, viceroy included, were fully informed of antisemitic agitation's rising tide yet did not stem it. "Burning Jew-hatred" was deliberately stoked, leading to such "well-prepared excesses" as anti-Jewish assaults accompanying hunger protests. This elicited among Jews "deepest embitterment, righteous indignation, and boundless outrage."[46]

The Milówka pogrom, like others nearby, was "well conceived and organized." The Jewish population was small. Żywiec itself, though not its suburbs, was by earlier Habsburg privilege "free of Jews" (judenrein), as Straucher recalled. Yet Christian-Jewish relations hereabouts were "peaceful and friendly." War's mushrooming antisemitism had not burst forth. On Sunday, February 17, Żywiec district council approved Chełm protests in municipalities under its authority. Present was Felix Koczor, who, as Milówka elementary school principal and head of the farmers' cooperative (kółko rolnicze), was a local nationalist leader.

On Monday, after a tear-swelling church sermon about Chełm's loss and amid railroaders' call for revolution, the people – among whom aforementioned wild "republican" rumors were circulating that Vienna's writ no longer ran and that army requisitions could now be refused – heard Koczor's open-air speech, delivered after he had huddled

---

[45] Ibid., p.2. Citations below concerning violence in Milówka and neighborhood derive from this source, pp. 3–8.

[46] AVA. MdIP-G. Sign. 22. Fsz. 2119, No. 19867. Haus der Abgeordneten. 68. Sitzung der 22. Session am March 5, 1918, pp. 1–2.

with his counterparts from Żywiec and Kamesznica in Knopp's tavern. (As it happened, Straucher added, the tavern's speech-deprived servant later told his mother, "in sign-language," of impending plunder, but though she informed the mayor, he took no countermeasures.) Koczor's audience understood his concluding words – duplicitous admonition – as pogrom warrant: "You will not plunder, not rob, not smash windows! Long live Poland!"

"Two masked invalid soldiers" led in dismantling iron-shuttered shops. Straucher presented a long list of plundered goods, including harmonicas and dolls, whose innocence and happy associations deepened robbery's pathos. He denied looters were poor, hungry people, much less a "wild Cossack horde." Straucher seemed to wander into a *Jewish* fantasyland, exclaiming:

No, these peasants are rich farmers, whose larders are filled with plenty of food, who suffer absolutely no hunger, who have always lived in peace with the resident Jews they now plunder. And one should believe they carried out this comprehensive robbery and looting on their own impulse, yielding to some higher revelation?

Koczor's speech, Straucher said, was banal, hardly reward for villagers' time-consuming trek to town. And why did he warn against violence on "national mourning day," unless he knew it was about to erupt? Why was his speech's text nearly identical with that of his counterparts in Żywiec, whose suburb Zabłocie exploded in violence, and in pogrom-stricken Kamesznica?

Straucher designated Koczor as pogrom mastermind but named accomplices, too, including school principal Jasicki. Illustrative of the effect Jasicki's cooperative society speech elicited were the peasant's words who, "in greatest agitation, seized his head in his hands and cried, 'not tomorrow, but today and immediately we must attack the Jews.'"

Yet Żywiec county cooperative association's directors unequivocally condemned the pogroms, blaming them, in Straucher's words, on "whisperings of bad and perverse elements." They could, under wartime law, provoke stern punishment. Inciters to violence must be surrendered.

Think [as Straucher paraphrased their admonitions] of the present historic moment ... Away with the slogans 'plunder' and 'highway robbery' ... They are unworthy of the Polish farmer! They harm the Polish cause and bring advantage and pleasure to our enemies. May God spare us from the crime of harming our own homeland and dishonoring the Polish people's name!

Straucher concluded by pillorying gendarmes' inaction, local judicial officials' failure to act, and cabinet minister for Galicia, Twardowski, for calling the Galician population's behavior "exemplary" and saying "complete order and calm prevail everywhere."

The Jewish Club interpreted these largely bloodless provincial pogroms as intentional provocations of antisemitic nationalists, intent on "dejudaizing" the land. It was easy to imagine a group of small-town or village schoolteachers and farmers' cooperative managers huddled in Knopp's tavern, planning to steer popular consternation over "Chełm's loss," whipped up by men such as themselves, into anti-Jewish riots that would suggest to local Jewry that departure for Palestine or another country was health's dictate. Thus would new economic spaces open for the burgeoning but still struggling Polish Catholic middle class to expand. Such was, without recourse to violence, the National Democrats' and agrarian Populist Party's stated program.

Yet conspicuously missing from Straucher's analysis were Catholic parish clergy, often cooperative organizers and otherwise vital to Galician common folks' nationalist mobilization. Whether aligned with populists, Endeks, or conservative landlords, priests were tribunes of demotic Polish nationalism. Yet Straucher only noted a Chełm sermon's pathos, without charging its declaimer with inciting violence. Nor did Straucher's speech allow that Poles inflicting the violence – villagers and small-towners – might have had their own motives for plunder. They were not, Straucher claimed, suffering hunger. They had lived peacefully with Jews for long years. Their explosion represented release of common people's "bad and perverse" impulses and rustic gullibility and foolishness, through professional antisemites' rhetorical incitement and emotional exploitation.

Jews knew that poor and ill-educated, hyper-Catholic provincial Christians harbored bizarre and hostile ideas about themselves and Judaism. But Straucher's presentation demonstrated, as will repeatedly be seen, that Jewish interpretations of antisemitic violence preferred to emphasize its incitement from above rather than its generation from below out of popular conceptions of Jews and the Polish-Jewish relationship. In this way, it could be hoped – as lawyer Rappaport did regarding "Judas Fest" – that top-down enlightenment might dispel Judeophobic ideas among common people, exposing antisemites as immoral political gangsters and enabling liberal-democratic coexistence of Christians and Jews.

The prime weakness of the top-down pogrom concept, as then and later commonly understood, is that it ignores or obscures plunderers' and rampagers' self-generated motivation, flowing from the popular culture in which they made sense of the world. Nor can we ratify Straucher's pogrom reading, despite its plausible elements, not only because it takes no account of the Catholic clergy but also because it concedes that local Polish notables and authorities counseled against violence and retroactively condemned it.

Kraków's April 1918 pogrom wounded and outraged Jewish sensibilities more profoundly than earlier provincial violence. It would, as Straucher said, long remain "a painful memory of the world war, for it disturbed peaceful coexistence of religious confessions and undermined trust in security organs." Kraków was Jewish assimilationism's stronghold. If Jews were assaulted within its walls, they were nowhere secure in Habsburg Galicia. The attack's gravity was weightier for being not a "spontaneous act of willfulness" but – once again, as in the Żywiec tumults – "staged according to plan" and led by a "secret, unseen hand."[47]

Straucher reviewed Kraków's food riots of spring 1917 and January 1918. He thought "they had no religious character." Christians even threatened Jews with violence, he averred, if they did not join in protests against food provisioning authorities. Yet windows were smashed, and furloughed Jewish soldiers needed to be summoned to prevent the mob from spilling into Kazimierz district, "predominantly inhabited by Orthodox Jews." When the February Chełm protests grew unruly, Christian townspeople pushed police aside and restored order through an improvised citizens' militia.

The pogrom of 1918 allegedly arose from Jewish trading abuses, but Straucher claimed market tumult concerned but "a single sack of flour." And "between this incident and plundering's outbreak such short time elapsed as to make impossible a big crowd's mobilization." The mob immediately began beating and plundering, excesses breaking out simultaneously in different quarters. Prime targets were "caftan Jews," thrown from streetcars and pummeled. Even attorney and city councilman Dr. Meisels was beaten as he hurried to the municipal assembly to protest the violence. In addition to one Jewish death, the pogrom left twenty seriously wounded, a toll that would have been higher had not "Jewish youth" – organized by the Poale Zion Party – formed a self-defense unit that "bravely opposed the pogrom-heroes [*Pogromhelden* – mocking cliché]."

Among plunderers, alongside ubiquitous "half-grown lads," uniformed schoolboys, and furloughed soldiers, were "ladies wearing hats" – bourgeois symbol – and carrying sacks and handbags. "One heard repeatedly that leaders were legionnaires" – men admired as nationalist

---

[47] AVA. MdIP-G. Sign. 22. Fsz. 2119, No. 19867. Haus der Abgeordneten. 83. Sitzung der XXII. Session am July 26, 1918, pp. 27–28. Citations below on the Kraków pogrom, unless otherwise specified, are drawn from pp. 25–29.

revolution's foot soldiers. For two days, "specialists working with crowbars and lockbreakers" opened shops to looters. In high-class clothing stores they wore stolen dress over street clothes and departed. The "allegedly hungry mob" restrained itself from seizing food meant for Christian consumption, just as Christian shops, often displaying religious icons in their windows ("in Russian manner"), went untouched. Pepi Rapaport warded off blows by imploring her attackers to desist "for the sake of Christ's wounds."

On the pogrom's second day, villagers at a suburban market asked if it were true that "Jews had killed a priest." Jews "enlightened questioners' minds" – revealing phrase – "saying this rumor was planted to incite the Christian population." Many illogically blamed Jews for the protesting Christian girl's death by army bullet. The Jewish Club found Kraków police and k.k. gendarmerie guilty of total passivity, and the Polish press's initial reaction mere bald-faced denial. Perhaps to avoid incurring libel charges, the Jewish Club read into the parliamentary record press reports excoriating the Poles. The newsletter of the Stockholm-based Zionist Jewish Press Bureau fulminated, in oft-to-be-repeated indictment:

There is not the slightest doubt that Kraków's crimes were direct result of Polish chauvinism's ruthless antisemitic propaganda disseminated since the Brest-Litovsk treaty. It is highly revealing of Poles' mental state that in this moment, so decisive for their nation, they think they can demonstrate to the civilized world their readiness for independent statehood by carrying out Jewish massacres.

Straucher conceded that Galicia's Polish leaders eventually, if unheroically, condemned Kraków's violence, blaming Habsburg censorship for muzzling Bishop Sapieha's and the Reichsrat Polish Club's exhortations to law and order. His last rhetorical sally was to challenge the government to bring pogromists to justice. "For in Austria it's not open season on Jews."[48]

Jewish nationalists perhaps believed the "secret, unseen hand" belonged to the widely imagined, though nonexistent, Polish revolutionary central-planning office. But Straucher's speech was, except for one barb directed against the Peasant Party's antisemitic leanings, devoid of specific references to Polish politics. It detected in Kraków's pogrom no political rationale and viewed plunderers' self-serving motives with dismissive irony. Yet, as Straucher concluded, "the Jewish population anticipates the future with great anxiety. The [Christian] lower orders are exhausted by hunger and in a state of excitement. They have already savored campaigns of robbery on a grand scale, and observed the security

[48] Ibid., July 22, 1918, pp. 9–12.

organs' passivity." In the present preharvest months, further anti-Jewish assaults would not be lacking.[49] This was tacit, seemingly unconscious, admission that the greatest danger facing Jews was popular fury and aggression.

Voices of the Plundered

The Jewish Club submitted notarial protocols of robbed Jews' losses. These are eloquent on subjective experience. Daniel Ritterman, who with wife Rozalia owned and operated a store and restaurant in Kraków's central business district, reported heavy loss in goods and damage (108,256 Kr.) Hearing that crowds were robbing Jews, "I shut my business in the early morning and sat the whole time with my wife in the closed shop." In the late afternoon, "a huge crowd" approached. Ritterman telephoned police, who assured him – falsely – of protection. Plunderers were "soldiers, legionnaires, university students, secondary students, workers, women from [proletarian] suburbs, even elegant ladies in hats and gloves." As Rittermann sought to remove cash and keys from the shop, the mob swarmed in through broken windows, handing goods out into the street, "including drinks." His wife, "being at the critical moment in the shop, fainted. I had to rescue her, taking her into a hallway, where I stayed with her during the entire robbery," lasting two hours. Four police, two mounted, were present but refrained from intervention, as three witnesses would affirm. Finally army troops arrived and dispersed looters.[50]

Józef Wildstosser's shop selling mixed wares and drinks lost 13,342 Kr. Like other plaintiffs, he had been plundered in Kraków's January 1918 tumults, then costing him 14,908 Kr. From his private living quarters he heard in the night "whistling and shouts," including "let's get the Jew" (*chodźmy na żyda*). Neighboring Christian shops went untouched. His son ran in vain to the police. Jakób Goldstein, bar owner and tobacconist, faced a crowd shouting, "Goldstein, he's a Jew, we've got to beat and rob him."

Anna and Joachim Messer lost 16,937 Kr. The mob had begun dismantling their shop shutters when mounted policemen dispersed it. Retreating looters vowed to return, as they did after the army swept through, firing on the crowd and killing the glazier's daughter. Messer, like other plaintiffs, highlighted presence among plunderers of "three or four persons in legionnaires' caps" and "ladies with elegant hats," icons of the educated and propertied classes' involvement in the riots, otherwise

---

[49] Ibid., 26 July 1918, p. 29.   [50] Ibid., p. 18. Citations below, pp. 17–22, 45–47.

undetectable. Messer imagined the crowd to number 20,000. A policeman sought to make arrests but was stoned by the mob who "not content
with robbery, threw rocks at us too." The method remained unchanged:
"the advanced guard is led by young boys, who whistle and yell, and they
are followed by the actual robbers, among them very many youths in
gymnasium [secondary school] uniforms." Pogroms were, for many
youths, rites of passage, conceivably traceable, as one might speculate,
to anciently rooted displays of self-imagined victims' revenge for alleged
ritual murder threat. These looters were not from Messer's neighborhood, "for, having lived here four years, we would have recognized some
of them."

Many shops were run by women, in whose names they were often
legally registered. Their husbands were sometimes absent at the front.
Regine Lipmanowicz, candy shop owner, reported 2,641 Kr. lost, looters
leaving behind "half-eaten bake-wares." She could not identify attackers
"because all my neighbors are Christians and they refuse to give me any
information." When she saw the crowd approach, she closed shop and
retreated into her apartment building. She encountered in the entryway
fellow resident Marie Widerko, city employee's daughter, who called out
to the looters, "you'll have to plunder this Jewess's shop."

When I asked her if she would like that, and whether she would then be able to
take some thousand-Kr. notes for herself, she called in the looters from the street
and urged them to do their work.

Widerko, before female witnesses, struck Lipmanowicz in the face and
boxed her sister's ears. Salomea Haber, shop owner, lost 8,811 Kr.
Leading looters were "two men with iron bars." She ran from her dwelling
to summon police, "but the crowd fell upon me, beating me with clubs
and wooden sticks so that I began to lose consciousness." She added: "I
have a sick husband at home, who fell mentally ill at the front and was
mustered out, and four small children."

Ida and diabetic Zygmunt Gutfreund, delicatessen and spices shop
owners, lost 47,641 Kr. "The crowd sold robbed goods to ladies, who
gladly bought them." Such sidewalk trading was common, such as
when soldiers bought up Jacob Freier's plundered wristwatches. In
Gutfreund's case, a Jewish soldier jumped from a tram to offer help,
vainly seeking a policeman's aid. The crowd – estimated at 1,500 –
showered the officer with stones. He fired warning shots, then fled.
Robbers sought to force themselves into Ida's apartment, but she
managed to dissuade them. Reporting her plight at a police station,
Commissioner Tomasik remarked, "Jews themselves are guilty of
provoking such things."

Some shops and their owners' apartments were picked clean. Active-duty soldier Ignacy Rettig wife's shop was attacked by a crowd of 200, some bearing axes. The Rettigs not only lost movable goods, but also "furniture was destroyed, drawers and other things taken, even the telephone." The crowd seized Baruch Klappholz's family's entire wardrobe along with 9,900 Kr. in cash and jewelry.

The Jewish Club listed ninety-nine small losses, averaging some hundreds of Kronen, alongside thirty-one larger claims. The total was 876,420 Kr. Restitution, if made, will have been in small proportion. This pogrom, viewed through plundered Jews' eyes, was anti-Judaism actualized in ruthless and heartless plunder, with some physical blows and thrashings added, along with incalculable humiliation and embitterment. No one pointed to conspiratorial steering or to ideological motivation. Some looters were poor proletarians; others members of higher orders. Unlike hunger riots, many adult men were present, including soldiers and legionnaires. The antisemitic script such pogromists enacted, if unconsciously, declared Jewish social existence illegitimate, if not criminal, the material goods it rested on free for taking by righteous Christian sufferers. Jews' only recourse, the Christian state having abandoned or spurned them, was exodus to Zion, a journey many or most Poles would have thought, in moral self-congratulation, highly advantageous to all parties.

Scenes from the Final Dissolution

Press censorship and other official efforts to stifle discourses of national enmity among the monarchy's peoples muted ideological antisemitism in Galicia without silencing it. Straucher claimed the agrarian Populist Party's weekly *Piast* reported, "unhindered and unpunished," that a local district council had resolved that "Jews' immediate uprooting from Polish soil" was "the Polish people's urgent wish."[51] "Dejudaization" was certainly a familiar slogan.

In June, the Railroad Ministry investigated anti-Jewish violence on the Lemberg line. Jews were buying food in villages and "transporting it as baggage in train corridors." Passengers objected to this obloquy-laden "chain-trade," seemingly short-circuiting food requisitions for civilians. Fights erupted, Jews were manhandled, their goods hurled from windows. Railroaders doused them with cold water. Poor Jews testified they could no longer ride third class but sought safety in bourgeois second

---

[51] Ibid., No. 19867. Haus der Abgeordneten. 79. Sitzung der XXII. Session am July 22, 1918, p. 10. *Piast* (February 17, 1918).

class. Hunger-plagued and impoverished Christians harbored "strong aversion" to them, seeing them as unjustifiably "well-off."

Resentment's fires were stoked by such flyers as that which, in February 1918, railroad official Gilowski distributed in large numbers among colleagues and subordinates. Produced by the Lemberg publication, "Dejudaization of Galicia," and sold for pennies, it inveighed against the prospect of Galicia's joining Russian Poland in an enlarged German-satellite Kingdom of Poland. Displaying the double-headed Habsburg eagle "with a Jewish head," a moneybag and menorah in its two claws, with a "vulgar depiction of the male organ," its German-language caption read: "Austro-Polish state eagle, now being created by House of Austria with participation of Polish Jewish elements dependent on Austrian government and serving it body and soul."[52] Thus did antisemitism besmirch the "Austro-Polish idea," hated by Polish and Austro-German nationalists alike. Such images easily broke free of political anchors to roil other psychic waters.

The monarchy's devoted and trusting Jewish subjects were slow to conclude that antisemitism's tides were rising dangerously. But in mid-1918 Vienna's Israelite Religious Commune submitted to the War Ministry a resolution of 387 Jewish communes throughout the empire condemning political Judeophobes' "systematic work of undermining them." Foremost were Pan-German organizers of "German Folk-Days" taking place throughout "West Austria," at which "direct pogroms" were preached, while Jews' massive war contribution in soldiers, bond purchase, and charitable aid was denigrated. "Jew-hatred" was invading the army, "even at the front lines." Austria's Jews were a "state-sustaining element," and to threaten them imperiled the entire monarchy. In extremity, Jews would organize self-defense forces. Such were apprehensions not alone of Jewish nationalists and Zionists but also of liberal assimilationists and Orthodox conservatives.[53]

In mid-August the War Ministry, employing antisemitic code, found Galicia closer to social than nationalist revolution "because of extraordinarily difficult living conditions, uncontrolled spread of large-scale usury and capital concentration in few hands that it fosters, and corruption in all institutions." Polish socialists were coordinating with other Slavic parties, and with railroaders, in anticipation of an uprising. Home Defense Ministry tracked a mysterious Polish agitator – "supposedly a professor" – giving subversive speeches. When asked at a meeting in

---

[52] Ibid., No. 19867 (June 12, 1918).
[53] KMP, 1918 No. 52 – 27/1. July 29, 1918. Cf. Rozenblit, *Reconstructing a National Identity*.

Tarnów "who he was, what his name was, whom they were dealing with, he gave no answer."[54]

In September, Kraków General Staff saw no tunnel light. Pan-Germans were blocking the monarchy's last-ditch efforts at self-federalization. They presented themselves as "state-pillars, but their unmeasured criticism of Austrian conditions often strikes disloyal tones." People ignored dynastic holidays. Hopes for peace wilted before "the Entente's intransigent will to victory." Citizens observed the "administration's failure to provide police security," while "thefts and burglaries occur daily" amid "general insecurity and slide into primitivism." Soldiers openly denounced the war. The public was outraged at the "conscription, despite military law's clear provisions, of pupils of the Leipnik institute for deaf and dumb." Protest meetings against food shortages reached huge proportions – 12,000 in nearby Moravian Prossnitz.[55] Intelligence officer Njegovan reported on railroad workshop workers' desperate condition. Their exhausting nine-and-a-half-hour shifts earned them 11 to 12 Kr. daily (comparable to civilian typesetters' easier earnings), but a kilogram of flour or a large bread loaf cost 17 Kr. Potatoes alone, if available, were affordable. "Time is no longer distant when bayonets alone will maintain order."[56]

On October 7 the Polish-manned Regency Council in the German-steered Kingdom of Poland moved, amid collapse of the Central Powers' eastern armies, to proclaim Polish sovereign independence. On November 3 the new state, joining Galicia and Prussian-German Poland to the Warsaw-ruled center (Congress Kingdom), rhetorically bestrode the world stage, after 123 years of partition and foreign rule. It was born amid new armed strife – Poles now fighting Ukrainians over East Galicia and Germans over Poznania – and heightening social revolutionary waves. Galicia's last month of life – for the crownland as an earthly site was specifically Habsburgian and could not survive Austria-Hungary's fall – was chaotic and tragic, if also illuminated by heroic acts. Anarchy descended, during which pogroms exploded that darkened the skies over Poland's rebirth.

Events Austrian officialdom sought to understand but could not control swept it forward. Galician gendarmes reported rumors of a revolutionary underground cooperating with deserter-staffed forest bands that produced grenades, robbed trains, and planned assassinations to advance

[54] AVA. MdIP-G. Sign. 22. Fsz. 2119, No. 5222 (August 16, 1918); KMP. 1918. No. 5–5/ 37 (August 4, 1918).

[55] AVA. MdIP-G. Sign. 22. Fsz. 2119, No. 22061 (September 5, 1918).

[56] KMP. 1918. No. 52–5/59 (September 12, 1918); AVA. MdIP-G. Sign. 22. Fsz. 2119, Nr. 23485 (October 15, 1918).

Polish independence. Their "identification symbol," formerly a button-holed flower, was now "small cross with two letters over left breast." Soldiers sent against them deserted to their side. To this report was added, on November 9, an unwittingly comical expression of the fallen empire's bureaucratic otherworldliness: "in view of the political upheaval that has meanwhile occurred in Galicia, the Interior Ministry has been deprived of the possibility of pursuing this matter further."[57]

Intelligence officer Njegovan reported on reactions in the Polish-Ukrainian border city of Przemyśl to the Warsaw Regency Council's independence proclamation. "Everyone agrees this is the long yearned-for historic moment that generations of the Polish people have awaited." In the city council, while Ukrainian deputies abstained from voting approval, "they congratulated the Poles and remarked that Poles and Ukrainians must live together fraternally." Jewish deputies conferred with colleagues in the religious commune. "Great excitement prevailed," but finally agreement – probably agonized – emerged "to vote for sending [to Warsaw] the homage-address." Ukrainians warned their people's territory must not be incorporated into new Poland. Polish socialist Dr. Mantel, of Jewish heritage, spoke "in the national-Polish sense," demanding release from German prison of Józef Piłsudski (who on November 10 duly took power in Warsaw).

Professor Przyjemski pronounced the oath of homage and addressed a crowd of 2,000 outside Przemyśl's city hall. National hymns were sung along with "Red Standard," the socialists' anthem, with the socialists aiming for a "free republic." An embittered Habsburg official penciled "then they will surely go to ruin!" Among local Jews, "disquiet and a certain dejection were evident." Voices urged "Jews' emigration, some saying to Ukraine or Russia, some to America and England, some to Palestine." Rumors circulated, "especially among Jewish lower classes, of possible persecution and oppression" so that "the great mass of the Orthodox Jewish population receive all reports [of Polish independence] with great apprehension." Njegovan referred delicately to "a certain antisemitic tendency in Pan-Polish circles" and anti-Jewish boycotting their press preached.[58]

In Kraków, viceregal official Pluchard informed Vienna that Tarnów mayor and chair of the Galician city council delegation Tadeusz Tertil had expressed thanks for government sanctioning of October 9's independence parade (while also warning against military intervention). Bloodshed would only injure His Majesty "and drive Poland into a

[57] Ibid., No. 4371 (October 9, 1918).
[58] KMP Präsidium. 1918. No. 52–5/60 (October 12, 1918).

republic." The people were, Tertil said, in a state of "enthusiasm" (to which disenchanted Pluchard added, "of this there is little evidence"). Pluchard had loftily assured the mayor that if the imperial eagle were not besmirched, if no treasonous speeches were held, if no one tried to entice soldiers into disloyalty – "at these words Tertil sputtered" – and if there were no robbing and murdering, then security organs would hold back. "A few exultors will not upset our calm." But privately Pluchard was apprehensive; the prefect warned him people were restive, fearing the hated Hungarian army's arrival, while coal shortages threatened riots.[59]

Civilian Germans' bitterness over emergent Polish statehood radiated from Jochen Langewitz's letter to the War Ministry from Rzeszów. It was "indescribable" how Poles had "decorated and beflagged the city, celebrating the end of their Austrian captivity," singing and shouting that the two Kaisers would be hung by their feet and dragged about and forcing all others to join in. Polish officials were cleaning out the treasury. It was scandal.[60]

From Przemyśl, Njegovan filed his final, pessimism-laden report. People were "extremely nervous" because of "most unbelievable rumors." In the army, deserters' executions could not stem flight, while everywhere reconstitution of the armed forces along lines of ethnic-national exclusivity was occurring. "Hatred in Galicia of Germans (also German Austrians) knows no bounds." Among Poles, including now villagers, "the Austrian state-idea and feeling of belonging to the monarchy are already vanishing completely." No one interfered with transference of power and loyalty to new Poland. Among Ukrainians, Vienna's feeble acquiescence in Polish breakaway had led to "complete reversal in attitude toward the monarchy." They would pursue their own goals, whether separate East Galician crownland or secession to join "new Ukraine."

As for Jews:

The broad masses are buying up all possible supplies of food and consumption goods to reap the profit early next year which they expect the overall situation will yield. In politics they wait on events: the prospect the Entente holds out of creation of Jewish statehood [a reference to Britain's 1917 pro-Zionist Balfour Declaration] appears to strongly engage their feelings and awaken pro-Entente sympathy.[61]

In Vienna, Jewish Club president Straucher angrily protested to Prime Minister von Henlein press reports that the Polish Club had dispatched

---

[59] Ibid., No. 52–5/55 (October 16, 1918).
[60] KMP. 1918. No. 52–5/47 (October 12–13, 1918).
[61] AVA. MdIP-G. Sign. 22. Fsz. 2119, Nr. 24035 (October 17, 1918).

its member, Dr. Löwenstein, to speak, in Galician Jewry's name, what had evidently been Polonophile words to Emperor Karl. Löwenstein was no representative of the Jewish people but of a "foreign national organization."

Austrian Jewry is in enormous majority Jewish-national. The Jewish population's broad masses, including the great majority of Jewish workers, the greater part of the Jewish intelligentsia, academic youth, the great majority of almost all bourgeois, commercial, and economic occupations – with the exception of a very thin, tiny upper stratum – is Jewish-national. Even the overwhelming majority of conservative Jews are Jewish-folkish [*jüdischvölkisch*], but in Galicia they dare not – with few exceptions – openly display their convictions and views, since every Jew not devoted to the Polish Club is considered an "enemy" and object of various persecutions.

Straucher had earlier protested to the prime ministry against ongoing anti-Jewish Galician excesses. Presently, in October, they signal "the great danger to which Galician Jewry is exposed." Because the Viennese government had failed to quell it, Austrian Jewry "will be forced to inform the outside world of these events and so communicate the true state of affairs."

Altogether, Galician and Polish Jewry are frequently exposed to brutal, hateful and humiliating treatment, suppression, marginalization, and persecution in political, administrative, and social affairs. What dreadful misery, what terrible want and poverty, what unbelievable neglect prevail among the broad Jewish popular masses is well-known to the public.[62]

Such was the stage on which postindependence 1918 pogroms erupted. In Lwów/L'viv, clouds of Polish-Ukrainian war were gathering. The police commissar there informed the Interior Ministry that Polish social-political leaders had gathered at the Shooting Club, solemnly resolving that Lemberg was "a pronouncedly Polish city" that must be incorporated into the Polish state, to which end a delegation would depart for Warsaw.[63] The last, seemingly, to grasp the Habsburg monarchy's imminent dissolution were Lemberg's military and civil governors. The army reported on October 23 that nothing had changed in people's attitude toward itself, however much they wished Imperial Germans to vanish.

One may rest assured that the more troops here, the happier the population's majority, among whom fear of Bolshevism lodges in the bones. This is not openly

[62] Ibid., No. 23805 (October 14, 1918). Filed with No. 19687.
[63] Ibid., No. 24176 (October 24, 1918).

admitted, but it's a fact that even the most extreme Pan-Pole concedes in one-to-one conversation, and that the Ukrainian element also takes into account.[64]

Viceroy Huyn was frozen in irresolution, but soon he was gone, k.k. army but a memory. The Great Powers' war was over. Ethnically inflected social war in Poland and along its borders was bursting into flame.

[64] KMP. 1918. No. 52–5/51 (October 23, 1918).

3   Polish Dawn, Jewish Midnight
The November 1918 Pogroms in West Galicia and Lwów

Like a doomed tree falling to the axe, the Habsburg monarchy shivered, cracked, and crashed to the ground, its ethnic limbs scattering. Poles knew of the October 7 Warsaw proclamation, by the previously German-subservient Regency Council, of national independence within the boundaries of the prewar Russian-ruled Congress Kingdom heartland. But not until October 31 did a formal successor to Austrian rule in Galicia appear: the unsentimentally named Polish Liquidation Commission, a council of politicians headed by nationalist Peasant Party leader Wincenty Witos. They seized power dropping from Austrian hands, pledging to deliver it to the not-yet-existent government of soon to-be-unified Poland. On Sunday, November 3, Galicia's incorporation into the emerging Warsaw-ruled Polish state inspired celebrations both bright and dark. The k.k. army dissolved, and its Polish successor, which the Liquidation Commission began conscripting in Galicia after November 6, was slow to muster.

In Warsaw on November 14, charismatic war hero Józef Piłsudski accepted executive power from the Regency Council. Yet it was not until elections in January 1919 created a constitution-making parliament that national government encompassing the three partition zones gained pervasive recognition among Poles, even as Piłsudski's Endek rivals vehemently contested his authority as head of state. In Kraków, the Liquidation Commission only surrendered its Galician powers on January 10. Law and order lost anchorage in settled legitimacy. No civil authority of Habsburg genealogy commanded popular respect. Many demobilized soldiers stayed armed, often joining forest-based bands.

In this setting, West Galicia witnessed in November 1918 pogrom conflagration. The violence awaits definitive quantification. Leon Chasanowitsch, well-informed author of *The Polish Jewish Pogroms in November and December 1918*, published under Zionist sponsorship in Stockholm in 1919, listed 106 localities, all but four in Galicia. British Zionist Israel Cohen, having visited Poland in January 1919, identified

127 Galician pogrom sites in his valuable report, "Pogroms in Poland."[1] This chapter rests on these and other published sources but also and especially on unpublished archival documentation of anti-Jewish violence in forty-seven localities. The West Galician wave appears to have caused at least fifty-nine, and probably more, murderous Jewish deaths, not including those many who died in the colossal war-engendered November 1918 pogrom in East Galician Lwów/L'viv – subject of this chapter's final pages.

Doubtless many, perhaps most, settlements escaped anti-Jewish looting and assaults. Larger towns best mounted self-defense against pogromist mobs or rural-based marauders. The 1898 tumults engulfed more than 400 Galician localities. Possibly 1918's riots extended equally far. Sentencing villagers guilty of receiving Jewish property stolen in 1919, a Kraków judge observed in 1921 that they could hardly have been unaware of the source of their ill-gotten gains "in time of mass plundering and assaults throughout the entire region" and in face of "a movement of robbery that had engulfed a whole expanse of the [Galician] land."[2]

Galician pogrom documentation, as of 1914–20 anti-Jewish violence generally, falls into two main categories. Jewish social-political organizations and journalists, horrified at coreligionists' suffering, zealously assembled it as evidence for criminal charges, parliamentary protests, claims to governmental recompense, and, among Zionists, in support of building the Palestinian homeland. It undergirded demands for internationally enforced minority rights in newborn postwar East European states harboring large Jewish populations, preeminently Poland. It voiced pain and outrage directed against perpetrators, commonly seen as fanaticized dupes of behind-the-scenes manipulators. Resentment-laden animosity colored many such reports, which tended, in an atmosphere heavy with collective paranoia and hysteria, to exaggerate Jewish losses.

Official documentation – by police and judiciary, military and civil investigators – tilted toward minimization of violence's antisemitic intent while stressing perpetrators' criminal liability. Censorship – externally

---

[1] Leon Chasanowitsch, *Die polnischen Judenpogrome im November und Dezember 1918. Tatsachen und Dokumente* (Stockholm: Verlag Judaea, 1919), 27–31, and *passim*; CZA. L6/119: Israel Cohen, "The Pogroms in Poland," 15–25 and *passim*. Published version: *A Report on the Pogroms in Poland* (London: Central Office of the Zionist Organisation, 1919). See also Cohen's autobiography, *A Jewish Pilgrimage* (London: Vallentine Mitchell, 1956), 135–60. Izaak Grűnbaum, ed., *Materjały w sprawie żydowskiej w Polsce* (Warsaw: Biuro Prasowe Organizacji Sjonistycznej w Polsce, 1919), 19–25, sketches twelve West Galician pogroms. Konrad Zieliński compiled from JDC and other American sources a list of eighty-one sites of anti-Jewish violence, October 1918–January 1919. Zieliński, *Stosunki polsko-żydowskie na ziemiach Królestwa Polskiego w czasie pierwszej wojny światowej*, 429–32.

[2] SOKKr. S8/II. J 3541/20, fo. 42*ff.*

imposed by political authorities and internally born within partisan journalists' hearts and minds – greatly distorted ethnic violence's commercial press coverage. Yet foreign governments and journalists were also interested in anti-Jewish aggression in the Central Powers' empires and successor states, as were foreign social-political organizations. Israel Cohen acted as "Special Commissioner of the [British] Zionist Organization," while in 1919 the British government dispatched liberal notable Sir Stuart Samuel to report on Polish Jewry's plight. In the United States, President Wilson in 1919 similarly commissioned a pogrom inquest team headed by Ambassador Henry Morgenthau. Its report and related documents, valuable if sometimes ideologically distorted or credulous, will figure in the pages that follow.

This chapter analyzes West Galician small-town pogroms as illuminated by contemporary Jewish sources. This will, apart from its empirical contribution, convey widespread interpretations of the violence. It then considers November 1918's ethnic violence as it appeared in judicial proceedings in a Kraków court – from a non-Jewish governmental viewpoint. Finally, it turns to army-ignited pogroms in the fought-over major cities of Przemyśl and Lwów. Lwów's was these years' single deadliest and most damaging to Poland's reputation abroad.

The Jewish economic relationship to Christian Poles remained explosive. In independence's sunrise, the question of Jewish loyalty loomed ever larger – a loyalty that bloodshed could not engender, but intimidated instead. Christians' subliminal wariness toward Jews continued to wear its medieval masks, while beneath Lenin's and Trotsky's visages antisemites descried the familiar foul fiend in Jewish dress. In their minds' lucidity, as in the subconscious depths, Judeophobic nationalists saw themselves, as the Polish state emerged from history's tomb, in millenialist – even apocalyptic – war with Israel.

Independence Day and Its Aftermath in West Galicia

Eruptions were scattered and local, perpetrators the Jews' fellow townspeople or nearby villagers, usually also unruly soldiers or armed partisans. Here we look at a handful of pogroms, each different, but taken together displaying such assaults' ambit of aggression. In Chrzanów (Yiddish: Kshonev), a half-Jewish industrial town of 14,000 inhabitants, violence peaked on November 6, midway through independence's first week. Already on Sunday November 3 pogroms began exploding in medium-sized towns such as this and in smaller settlements, where notables and police could not – or would not – prevent rioting, unlike in most larger towns. Jewish eyewitnesses vividly recalled the violence as grotesque, hate-filled celebrations of Polish statehood's rebirth, ruining Jewish businesses and unseating Jewish urban officeholders from power. In our eyes, they figure as unself-conscious enactments of Christian self-liberation not only from Austrian but also from imagined Jewish domination.

The anonymously penned Chrzanów report, archived by Berlin's Zionist Central Office, was a joint product of local bourgeois Zionists, revolution-friendly labor Zionists (Poale Zion), and the moderate "Jewish Social-Democratic Workers Party."[3] As Austria fell, pogroms erupted in nearby villages, "and in the town voices multiplied among Poles that time for settling accounts with Jews would also soon come." The prefect (*starosta*) formed a new militia, supplanting dissolved Austrian soldiery. Yet mostly Jews volunteered, since many Poles, "influenced by systematic antisemitic agitation, viewed Poland's liberation as finally arrived opportunity to plunder Jews." *Kommissar* Bochański said that "Jews should hand over their wares, and then nothing would happen to them."

Count Mycielski, Habsburg-era Galician Sejm deputy and county commission chairman, declined rabbis' and other Jewish communal officials' pleas for more police. He self-deludedly declared that if anti-Jewish riots erupted, "the entire Polish intelligentsia, arms in hand, would stage most energetic resistance." But when small bands of outsiders/interlopers with sacks and wagons appeared and "loitered about with local Poles," officials and intelligentsia did nothing. Jewish militiamen alone held them in check.

On November 6, numerous peasant farmers and workers lined Chrzanów's streets "as if only waiting for the terrible witches' dance upon Jewish lives and property to start." Polish legionnaires, acting on Kraków army command to disband Jewish militias (which the civilian Liquidation Commission had previously sanctioned), disarmed Jewish defenders before three local clergymen's approving eyes. Judicial official Wierzbicki, who earlier alone among Poles supported the militia, now "curiously, incited legionnaires to this misdeed." Soldiers searched Jewish prayer houses for weapons.

Pogrom commenced, local Christians plunging in. In the familiar scene – sometimes imagined but often reflecting sad reality and certainly expressing Jews' sense of betrayal – the report charged that "some gentlemen among the so-called Polish intelligentsia strolled about with their wives among the plunderers, contemplating this strange spectacle with pleasure." These included the mayor, himself lawyer, and lawyer colleagues, also gymnasium professors, judges, and other officials. "More still: many of these gentlemen exhorted others to plunder and, as many witnesses aver,

---

[3] CZA. L6/110, fos. 1–11, (n.d. [November, 1918]); Chasanowitsch, *Judenpogrome*, 36–37.

enjoyed such stolen objects as bonbons, wine, and spirits." A city official and gendarme urged looters, "nothing to fear, people! Rob the Jews, rob the Jews!"

Somehow Jewish reporters learned of telephone calls between military commander Kaden in Chrzanów and his superior in Oświęcim, who offered Kaden forty additional soldiers. Kaden replied: "no need for help. I have a directive from a highly placed personage precisely not to intervene." Kaden instructed his subordinates: "don't send out patrols. This wave, it's strictly anti-Jewish, and will pass. It wouldn't be right to greet a free Poland with Polish corpses and Polish blood." Here was stark evidence, but probably only imagined – for who overheard the incriminating phone call? – that power holders covertly tolerated pogroms, if they did not orchestrate them.

While violence raged, Christians celebrated Polish rebirth. Jews trembled for their lives as stained-glass windows glowed and "the organ loudly sounded as if in triumph over 'victories' of the newly created Polish army and Polish people." Trains disregarded schedules to allow looters to bring booty aboard – another sign of social consensus over plundering. The reporters opined, perhaps implausibly, that "a single salvo, indeed just a determined show of Polish soldiers and intelligentsia would have sufficed to scatter robbing peasants' and townspeople's bands to the wind." A Christian looter – engaged in deadly pantomime? – was shot dead because he wore a "Jewish velvet hat, such as all Jews and only they wear hereabouts."

Next day a detachment of Kraków's Jewish self-defense force, dispatched by the Jewish Soldiers' Council, arrived to halt looting's resumption, but only until Christian legionnaires disarmed it. Chrzanów's Jews fled in panic, paying exorbitantly to board trains. There was "no Bolshevist character" to the pogrom: only Jewish houses and shops were plundered, including "totally poor Jewish candy stores and milk sellers." (Israel Cohen, visiting postpogrom Chrzanów, saw inscriptions: "Here lives a Pole," "Here lives a Catholic.")[4]

Officialdom blamed "foreign agitators" and "deserters and POWs," but all knew that plunderers were "practically the entire Christian population," also "nearby farmers, grown rich in war, and numerous workers in nearby mines, while the Polish intelligentsia looked on with pleasure, or even spurred plunderers on."

The wild bestiality of the horde's labors is indescribable. – Whatever furniture and equipment in shops and houses could not be hauled off was chaotically destroyed.

---

[4] Cohen, "The Pogroms in Poland" (CZA. L6/119). Further references to Cohen's report derive from this unpublished source alone, organized by locality.

In the Jewish cooperative store, petroleum was poured into honey. In other shops, spirits, wine and beer that could not be emptied were spilled in the gutter.

Ethnic cleansing's cruel spirit was abroad, seeking to make life unresumable for plundered Jews.

Next afternoon, as destruction subsided, an assembly chose a new city council, confined to Christians alone, though Jews purportedly outnumbered them two to one (in 1921, Jews comprised 55 percent). Under inegalitarian Austrian municipal electoral law, a majority since 1888 had been in Jewish hands, as was the mayorship (1899–1912). The new council then palavered with robber-band invaders, whose leaders and town officials confronted the chief rabbi, demanding Jewish surrender of "a hundred more sets of underwear, a great amount of linen, and 4,000 men's suits" in return for cessation of home plunder. When the rabbi declared this impossible, Jewish supplies having already been decimated, the mayor commanded him to buy the textiles ("at usurious prices") from the "Polish clothing warehouse," which was filled with goods earlier requisitioned mainly from Jews. "Cold jokes" such as these were pogroms' frequent embellishment.[5]

"So-called Polish militia," recruited from local "scum," were ordered to search Jewish houses and requisition valuables, a task they pursued "in indescribably merciless fashion." Meanwhile, Christian plunderers marketed their booty, farmwives sending off "whole hundred-weights of bacon" to Moravia under the militia's benign eye. It was particularly embittering that local farmers, war enriched with Jewish traders' help, should fatten themselves further with pogrom plunder. "In the town's Jewish back-streets cemetery-stillness prevails. Jews fear their own shadows, and hardly dare go outside."

The reporters claimed objectivity. "Let the public judge and decide what the Polish intelligentsia, Polish culture, Polish freedom really are!" Altogether, three Jews had been murdered, thirty wounded, mostly seriously. (Israel Cohen reported two deaths and twenty-eight injuries.) Eleven victims could name their attackers. Altogether 180 losses were registered, valued at 12,648,710 Kr., which Cohen translated into the huge sum of 520,000 British pounds. A further forty-eight losses totaling 1,462,900 Kr. occurred in seventeen nearby small localities.

Chrzanów's pogrom here appears as Polish Christian revolution against the Habsburg urban order granting Jews political and economic predominance. Their would-be protectors were aristocratic former Vienna loyalists, here embodied in Count Mycielski, whose promise

---

[5] On cold jokes as accompaniments of ethnic violence, see Jonathan Glover, *Humanity: A Moral History of the Twentieth Century* (London: Cape, 1999).

that the "whole Polish intelligentsia" would resist a pogrom proved lamentably and laughably empty. It was riot of plunder and destruction, beggaring many Jews and cutting others down so that Poles could rise above them. It was both ruthless collection of payback for what pogromists saw as Jewish war profiteering and invasion of Jewish space imagined to glitter with ill-gotten wealth. It was, as Jewish reporters believed, a carnavalesque event, a witches' sabbath of sorts, its participants showering themselves with luxurious food and drink while upgrading wardrobes. Some took pleasure in murder and battery and many others in witnessing physical violence, humiliation, and degradation. It was an assertion of Polish domination, at Polish freedom's dawn. It was revolution against "the Jews."

But, while it was all of these things, the Jewish nationalist interpretation very likely downplayed the role of rural-based bands whose invasion and coercive presence it could not deny. These mostly youthful former soldiers, uprooted armed peasants, and proletarians dotted the Galician and wider Central and Eastern European landscape, constituting in some places, at least in the eyes of alarmed newspapers and fearful bourgeois and upper-class public, "green" – or sometimes "red" – "armies" or "brigades." Suspected of "anarchism" or "Bolshevism" or "agrarian communism" but often nothing more than charismatically led brotherhoods living from violence and plunder, their suppression was a mighty challenge to postwar governments, including in Russia that of Lenin and Trotsky.[6] They will turn up repeatedly.

In Brzesko (Yiddish: Briegel) – 3,144 souls, two-thirds Jewish – a three-day pogrom claimed, by differing accounts, four to eight Jewish lives, eight seriously wounded, and four houses burned.[7] Here too Kraków-dispatched Jewish militiamen duly arrived, but in the night a forest band attacked the town's protective force of sixteen Polish and Jewish soldiers, overpowering them. During the battle,

starosta Dr. Cyga, who had warned against excesses, was surrounded by the band, which threatened to shoot him. The rifles were at the ready when out of the lawbreakers' ranks his brother sprang, placing himself between them and him. The mob forced Dr. Cyga to promise to hand over all weapons – and this saved him.

[6] Schnell, *Räume des Schreckens*, offers sophisticated analysis of such armed bands. Cf. Robert Gerwarth and John Horne, eds., *War in Peace: Paramilitary Violence after the Great War* (Oxford: Oxford University Press, 2012), 184–99 and *passim*; Robert Gerwarth, *The Vanquished: Why the First World War Failed to End* (New York, NY: Farrar, Straus and Giroux, 2016).
[7] The following account rests on www.sztetl.org.pl/en/article/brzesko/5,history/ (accessed April 20, 2014); CZA. L6/109: document C: *Nowy Dziennik* (November 14, 1918), "Pogrom w Brzesku"; CZA. Z3/178: Cohen, "The Pogroms in Poland."

Cyga, "whose behavior Jews had praised," then ordered militia disbanded, and looting began, townspeople joining in. Pogromists "hurled Meier Perlmann under a moving train." They plundered Goldmann's store and home and, because he had sheltered Jewish soldiers, fired five bullets into his head. "As he lay blood-drenched in agony, a soldier administered a bayonet stab in the heart, saying 'you, Jew, have suffered too little.'"

Finally, regular Polish soldiers arrived, but their commander said, "We won't shoot at our brothers. Nobody needs to murder, that wouldn't be nice for Poland. But robbery is permitted, for that not a hair will be rumpled." General Bolesław Roja informed the Liquidation Commission that dispatch of Jewish self-defense troops to Brzesko, Oświęcim, and Podgórze had only embittered local Christians. He commanded the Jewish units' dissolution, leaving their members only the option to join army or city militias (if these would have them).

As elsewhere, Christian soldiers and policemen easily succumbed to forest-band and local pressure not to defend Jews. Fear of exclusion from the Christian community for being, allegedly, in Jewish pay was deep rooted. Some determination was evident among Poles to stand together with Jewish fellow burghers against rural marauders, but it crumbled soon. That a Jew deserved to die – and was murdered – for not having previously suffered enough gave violent expression to the widespread pretext for antisemitic aggression among Catholics deeply convinced of their own profound misfortune.

Oświęcim (Yiddish: Oshpitzin), transportation hub and industrial city, counted some 52,000 inhabitants, including 6,000 Jews.[8] On November 9 it teetered on the brink of plunder by bandits and townspeople. A conference ensued among town authorities, local police, and Christian and Jewish civilians. According to the 1918-founded, intelligentsia-edited, Kraków-based, Zionist-oriented, Polish-language daily newspaper *Nowy Dziennik*, mayor Meisel proposed that Jewish merchants hand over wares to the county commission for sale at fixed prices "so as perhaps to still the unrest." Schoolteacher Baścik distinguished himself for aggressiveness, saying, "Jews deceive themselves if they see only the Polish population's scum behind this movement. It's a symptom instead of Poles' deep-rooted hate for Jews, who provoke the Polish people with their present behavior." Still, he offered, provided Jewish goods were delivered as the mayor proposed, to go "to the pogroms' instigators (*Veranstalter*) and explain" the

---

[8] www.sztetl.org.pl/pl/article/oswiecim/ (October 27, 2014); CZA. L6/119: Cohen, "The Pogroms in Poland"; CZA. L6/109: *Nowy Dziennik* (November 10 and December 9, 1918), Chasanowitsch, *Judenpogrome*, 19.

controlled sale "so that they should abstain from robbery and plunder," although their compliance was uncertain.

Jewish leader Dr. Pilzer said he would leave it to the military to decide if it accorded with their honor to negotiate with bandits. No one, he noted, was pressuring peasants to lower their prices. Security Police Chief Machniewicz protested "Jews' impudence to appeal to the Polish soldier's honor to protect them. They're only making concessions on prices under threat of pogrom. If we withdrew our military, they'd level you to the ground in a few hours." Pilzer, perhaps overconfidently, took this as proof that pogroms were launched "with intelligentsia's tacit or even express agreement." Yet Baścik and friends evidently knew armed band leaders and their urban friends (if any) or how to find them. Pilzer agreed that prices needed regulation, but this should apply to Christian merchants and farmers too. Jews would have to organize in self-defense.

It appears that the mayor's plan spared the town, although Israel Cohen reported subsequent attacks on synagogues and demolition of cemetery tombstones. Probably Oświęcim was too large and well defended for rural bands to storm, leading would-be pogromists to agree to buy at bargain prices Jewish goods Christian authorities forced on the market. If members of the Polish intelligentsia stemmed popular violence, it was evidently not always for lack of antisemitic sentiment. We see here how forested armed men could be frankly acknowledged as pogrom instigators, acting independently of political parties.

In Brzozów (Yiddish: Bresiv) – with 1,127 Jews among 4,160 souls – November 3's proclamation of Galicia's entry into the new Poland coincided with a massive invasion by some 5,000 plundering ruralites.[9] They pillaged 104 Jewish houses and shops and murdered Judge Richter. "Threatening his wife with a knife, they demanded money. To her appeal that she was a poor official's wife, they replied: 'you dogs have the most'" (or, in another version, "You accursed officials have the most money").

Next day an army officer arrived who attempted to actualize General Roja's early-granted permission to form Jewish self-defense forces, but militia and prefect resisted arming and admitting them to their ranks. Jews, with self-crafted weapons, protected themselves from raiders, irritating bedded-down Christian burghers by ringing night alarms when attackers' whistled communications were heard. Pogromists retreated, concentrating assault on Jews in outlying hamlets. Christian townspeople

---

[9] CZA. Z3/178, 8–9; CZA. L6/109: *Nowy Dziennik* (November 17, 1918); available at www.jewishgen.org/Yizkor/pinkas_poland/pol3_00071.html and www.sztetl.org.pl/pl /city/brzozow/.

were obliged to defend their *starosta,* whom bandits aimed to kill "because he had sent the Hungarians [the hated Honvéd] against them."

This attack left Jews in "deathly fright." *Nowy Dziennik* observed that "there are decent and law-abiding Poles here who would like to halt plunder, but they have lost all influence over the masses." When rumor arose that Jews had shot at peasants, "respected citizens" objected, saying Jews had no firearms. "But no one believed them, dismissing them as 'Jewish uncles.'" Jews had to pay for Christian protection, on the grounds – ignoring prefect's plight – that "for non-Jews there's no need for militia." Here, in Jewish eyes, the Christian "intelligentsia" – educated and propertied burghers – behaved honorably but were powerless against demotic masses.

In Radomyśl Wielki (Yiddish: Radimishil) – 2,500 inhabitants, 60 percent Jewish – a priest tried to halt pogrom.[10] At November 3's celebration, Father Łukasiński said of Jews during Poland's partition that "they too were slaves, but now are free." What did freedom mean? "Not robbery, murder, and the like. Poland's freedom demands unity and cooperation." The Liquidation Commission's local delegate directed Jews to bring forth their wares and sell them "at appropriate prices, for the Polish people won't stand for usury."

Reports circulated that plunderers would arrive on market day, Thursday. Local Jews sought to organize a religiously mixed militia, but town authorities trusted to the local eight-soldier army unit. Jewish merchants put out goods. The Provisioning Committee met, seating seven Catholics and three Jews. Father Łukasiński predicted that the coming pogrom would not stop with Jews but would endanger "the same gentlemen who now passively look on." He introduced a motion "that the entire local intelligentsia and citizenry assemble on central square next day, when pogrom was scheduled, and uphold order with their authority." But it fizzled.

Jews, denied inclusion in the town's now-widened defense force, organized themselves, armed "with ordinary clubs." A thousand villagers and armed men marched in, followed by women with baskets and wagons. "The clergyman Łukasiński, whose assistance Jews will never forget, went about zealously demanding that all be mindful of the moment's seriousness and remain peaceful. But his words failed completely, especially since no one among the Catholic intelligentsia came to help."

The militia tried to disperse the villagers. "Zabiarski, armed with [a] club, assisted, driving off peasants trying to plunder," striking one of

---

[10] CZA. Z3/178, 7–8; CZA. L6/109: *Nowy Dziennik* (November 12, 1918); available at www.sztetl.org.pl/pl/article/radomysl-wielki/6,demografia/.

them. Two militiamen fired shots in the air. But then the Liquidation Commission–appointed gendarmerie chief, "known antisemite," local judge Kuśnierz, ordered Zabiarski and militia to withdraw, unleashing comprehensive plunder. Twenty-one victims, some physically injured, suffered losses to 50,000 Kr. Here responsible burghers' ranks split, opening sluice gates to plunderers against Catholic priest's pleas.

In Bochnia – 11,000 souls, 80 percent Christian – Jews plundered and injured in the surrounding countryside flooded in. Major Dobrodzicki's "strong army units" held advancing marauder bands at bay. A local priest assisted him, "working continually to soothe spirits and inculcate in all the precepts of Christian neighborly love." Bandits also knew "that Bochnia Jews were strongly organized and would not allow themselves to be robbed." In nearby Proszówki, large bands lengthened their trail of destruction. Of one Jewish woman, Christian women cried, "Kill her, she's a Jew," while her children were stripped of clothing and shoes.[11]

In half-Jewish Kolbuszowa (3,000 souls), Judge Dr. Czarny ended Habsburg rule by disarming gendarmes. As peasants streamed in and stormed taverns for drink, "several important [Jewish] citizens" urged Czarny to organize a militia or allow them to do so, but he refused. On Saturday, November 2, carousing continued alongside Jews' physical abuse. On Sunday, full-scale plundering erupted. The Christian Gawron, criticizing pogromists, was knocked unconscious. A priest persuaded a group of armed youth to drive rioters from pubs, while Jewish wives' pleas moved gendarmes to resume their duties and drive back the mob with revolvers and clubs. "The peasantry" demanded punishment, on unstated grounds, of two young Jewish brothers, whom a policeman led to town hall for beating with knout by Christian youths. Here again the archaic script of public lashing was reenacted.[12]

Apologists and minimizers routinely blamed anti-Jewish violence on deserters and demobilized soldiers, especially non-Poles, and on social scum (*szumowina*), rabble (*tłuszcza*), dregs (*męty*), or plebeians (*pospólstwo*) who – together with sundry adolescents and women householders – often did indeed plunder and torment Jews. If peasants were involved, they were frequently labeled poor smallholders or landless – again, often true. In Żabno – 1,000 souls, half-Jewish – an "unusually large peasantry, mostly well-known respectable [*poważni*] farmers," invaded town, assaulting Jewish stalls and plundering shops and homes, rendering "prosperous citizens" into "homeless beggars." *Nowy Dziennik*'s informers said these were not "pranks of irrational youths or

---

[11] *Nowy Dziennik*, no. 126 (November 14, 1918), "Powiat bocheński."
[12] *Nowy Dziennik*, no. 129 (November 17, 1918), "Kolbuszowa."

riots of starving masses, but actions indubitably provoked by *underground agitation of persons without the courage to express their reactionary convictions openly.*"[13] Who might these persons have been?

In Rozwadów – 2,700 souls, two-thirds Jewish – an influential priest helped ignite pogrom. A Jewish militia sprang up, responding "to certain symptoms," perhaps menacing loiterers or shouters of inciting words, "pointing to impending pogrom danger." Next day, the provisional town council disbanded the militia on the frequently invoked grounds that "weapons in Jewish hands only provoke peasants." Lieutenant Greismann vainly urged his superiors, "on his knees," to send an army detachment. On market day, riot exploded.

"A thousand-headed crowd of bestial [*vertierter*] peasants broke into Kropf's hotel and plundered or destroyed everything." Local priest and agrarian social-radical leader Eugeniusz Okoń, conjuring with feudal imagery, addressed the pogromists, saying, "robbery is indeed not nice, but you are now the masters [*panami*] and soon we will divide among ourselves the wealth of these great lords [*wielkich panów*]!" He ended with "long live freedom!" The crowd poured into Silber's inn, militia's seat, seizing ten carbines, which figured as evidence of Jewish self-arming, justifying ensuing mayhem in which four Jews died: Hebrew teacher, rabbi's deputy, watchmaker, and war-widow, "both hands broken." The usual procession ensued of male looters followed by women loading booty on wagons.

Lack of police protection left Rozwadów's 500 Jewish families, gripped by "extreme pogrom-panic [*skrajnej panice pogromowej*]," lost in a "sea of hatred and hooligan-rage." A letter writer espied among plunderers "deserters and prisoners released from jails." Its author charged "nobility and clergy" with prepogrom exhortation to violence. Pogrom "arrangers" (*Arrangeure*) armed rioters. "Striking" was participation in the mayhem of "Polish officers, legionnaires and town militia." "From surrounding villages hard-pressed Jews stream in."[14] Here was a hotbed of anti-Judaism and Christian discord, where Polish notables sought to direct popular rage, in part toward themselves, against Jews, an exhortation the motley crowd was happy to follow.

Thus did West Galicia's November pogroms appear in (mostly nationalist and Zionist) Jewish eyes. Readiness to stand and fight in self-defense heightened anger and frustration over the Liquidation Commission's reversal of its initial policy sanctioning Jewish militias. Christian

---

[13] *Nowy Dziennik*, no. 120 (November 8, 1918), "Pogromy w Galicyi," (author's emphasis).
[14] CZA. Z3/178, 11–12; CZA. L6/119: Cohen, "The Pogroms in Poland," 68; Joint Distribution Committee, New York (hereafter: JDC). AR 14/18, file 136: Poland (localities 1918); www.sztetl.org.pl/pl/article/rozwadów.

pogromists appeared not only as "bestial peasant hordes" and urban "scum" and "hooligans" but also as cynical and heartless antisemites among upper classes. Yet there is recognition too of pogroms' divisive and harmful effect among Christian Poles, besmirching national independence's attainment and humiliating "serious" Poles – whether villagers, nobility, or urban intelligentsia – who strove to halt them.

These accounts display pogroms as colossal looting forays in which bodily injury or death resulted mainly from resistance. Why else were the murdered war widow's two hands broken? Plunderers' motives, these records say, were rooted in belief that Jews had avoided war suffering, profited from dealing in shortages, and amassed stocks of food and other necessities that they withheld from the market or sold usuriously. While doubts about Jewish devotion to Polish independence agitated Polish nationalists, they are silent here. Habsburg collapse undermined Jewish municipal office holding and political strength as Polish nationalist populism seized governmental control. But there is no sign that pogroms served, or were meant to serve, this end.

It was Galician – and Eastern European – Jewish fate to figure as merchants dealing in everyday necessities whose shortage had driven prices for widely impoverished common folk sky high. Had Jews not occupied this social niche, riots against them would have lacked economic impetus and would have required different justification. Efforts were made to block pogroms by politically controlled sale of Jewish-held goods, but in vain – whether because the suspected stocks did not exist or because pogromists reckoned they could be seized cost-free.

Christian belief was widespread that Polish independence and Habsburg breakdown left Jews defenseless – "excellencies" were no longer "protecting" them. Their possessions could be robbed or smashed to bits with impunity, their physical persons willfully humiliated or violated. Jews were not to be embraced in the new Poland but excluded and impoverished, if not obliterated. The roots of this cultural aggression were deep. In Jewish eyes, November 1918's pogroms were a sequel to the "Judas Fest" whose prewar celebration, as Marek Rapaport feared, anticipated them.

Pogromists in Independent Poland's Courtrooms

In February 1920, a county court found thirteen among forty defendants guilty of armed and forcible theft committed in November 1918 against Jewish tavern keepers in villages near Kraków. Prime suspects among these men – farmers, laborers, and blacksmiths aged eighteen to thirty – had been in custody for eight months. In February 1919, statewide

amnesty had reduced many categories of prison sentence by half, concession benefiting five defendants. Another five were now condemned to
sentences under one year. The worst offenders' punishment included one
day weekly "with a hard cot [*twardem łóżem*]."[15]

The court ventured little interpretation of motive. On November 2–4, a
band led by Józef Nowak, nicknamed "Klimczak," inflicted on five business owners and a Jewish-owned agricultural estate losses of 5,000 to
80,000 Kr. Much alcohol was stolen and drunk. Physical violence was
one minor head cut. References to antisemitism figured only obliquely.
Some defendants claimed, in time-worn formula, "it was permitted for
forty-eight hours to rob Jews." A defense lawyer described the crimes as
"Jewish pogroms." A 1919 police report observed that "much time has
passed since 1918's public excesses that broke out here and there, and
mental agitation [*podniecenie umysłów*] directed against Jews has calmed
considerably."[16] Obviously, Poles understood they had lived through a
period of widespread anti-Jewish hysteria.

The trial centered on a tavern and shop operated by Regina
Mondererowa, twenty-one-year-old daughter of Lejzer Monderer, in
Gruszów village. A gang appeared in military dress, armed with bayonets.
Ringleaders (*hersztowie*) were Nowak and Andrzej Dobrowolski, who,
"following plentiful drinking," demanded 15,000 Kr. from
Mondererowa. "Should she resist they would demolish the tavern." On
offer of but 2,000 Kr., they rampaged. Mondererowa fled on pretext of
fetching ransom.[17]

Defendant Kaleta claimed that "colleague Lenart ordered him to go
with the band to the tavern and threatened that, if he didn't, *the whole
village would push him away*." Yielding, he observed how Mondererowa
resisted paying full ransom. "Dobrowolski, dissatisfied, gave the signal for
robbery, shouting 'boys, blow your stacks' [*róbcie chłopcy luft*], and the
whole band began robbing." In the pub, villager Stram "tried to persuade
[Dobrowolski] to desist from robbery," but in vain. Dobrowolski,
"incensed, insulted him, shouting while shooting his revolver, 'get out,
son-of-a-bitch Jewish uncle.'"[18] In February 1919, a Kraków lawyer
appealed for codefendant Kwarciak brothers' jail release. Their parents
were "dignified and prosperous farmers." If they participated in "Jewish
pogroms" and "Jewish riots" (*rozruchy*), it was from youthful indiscre-
tion, not criminal instincts.

---

[15] SOKKr. S8/II. J 2581/20, fos. 529*ff*, 613–31, 927–42.
[16] Ibid., fos. 21*ff*, 104–5, 131–35.   [17] Ibid., fos. 21*ff*., 104–5, 159–62, 255–57, 523–27.
[18] Ibid., fos. 65–66, 71–72 (*idź skurwysynie żydowski wujek*).

The Gruszów gang paid a destructive visit to Moses Engländer, thirty-five, tavern keeper in another village. He knew they had been rampaging elsewhere and had stolen a gramophone from Salomea Federgrünowa, "and indeed they arrived in my tavern with the gramophone's trumpet [i.e., bell]," serving seemingly as jolly pogrom horn. To demands for drink, he replied that another band had emptied his stock. They tore off his wife's head cover – religious desecration – and threatened her with bayonets, "so I fled with the whole family from the house." Engländer's losses – 11,952 Kr. – were not trivial, pointing to the comparative well-being of some rural Jews.[19]

Krystyna Piechnik, sixteen, reported that she had been buying tea at Mondererowa's shop when the band of twenty to thirty men appeared. "The Jews immediately gave them wine." "Through the whole night we didn't sleep, since we constantly heard shouts and uproar at the Monderers." Bandits were going about with open flame in their house and barn, and "we feared they would start a fire that might endanger our house." Scheindla Monderer, fifty-eight, merchant in Kawec village, confirmed that her daughter had fled the plunderers in fear. Father Lejzer was sick and bedridden. He could not clarify events "since he left the house at dusk and has nothing to do with the shop, leaving that to his daughter."

His son Samuel, thirteen, reported that on the critical Sunday his parents, fearing for his safety, sent him and his brother to stay with a Christian neighbor, Wojciech Patela. Late at night, as they slept, four bandits came "and began asking us where our father stored his money and goods." Ringleader Nowak "threatened to chain us and both he and Lenart pressed bayonets against our chests." They claimed ignorance and were rescued when Jakób Banasik and housewife Patelowa "led them away from us." Another son, Moses, seventeen, fled with sister Regina and hid through the night in the fields, from where they could see plunderers emptying their house and store.[20]

Kawec headman, farmer Garczyński, forty-nine, said, "I heard uproar in the village and they told me that bandits were robbing Monderer, but I didn't mix in, because I knew I couldn't do anything about it." Around midnight someone told him that Nowak was threatening to torch Monderer's house, whereupon Garczyński went to the tavern "and reminded him of a conflagration's consequences for the commune. He

---

[19] Ibid., fos. 229–30, 235: two gold watches with chains, 3,000 Kr.; two fur coats, 2,000 Kr.; pearl jewelry, 1,200 Kr.; diamond earrings, 1,200 Kr.; men's and women's slippers, 300 Kr.

[20] Ibid., fos. 207–16.

told me he had no intention of arson because he was reasonable [*ma rozum*]. So I went home and saw nothing more."[21]

There were aftershocks, such as when, on November 10, bandits arrived at Markus Goldfinger's isolated rural grain mill, smashing his windows with their rifle butts at 2:00 AM. His servant opened the door. Goldfinger was dressed "because I expected robbery, a peasant having tipped me off." The miller fled to the fields, a bandit shooting at him. He was obliged to leave his wife and children behind. He lost all his furniture, the plunderers emptying his bedding of feathers. They took silver- and nickel-plated watches with chains and gold earrings. He reckoned his loss at 4,600 Kr. His wife Taube, thirty-six, testified that "when the bandits shot at my fleeing husband, I too wanted to escape, but the marauders restrained me, threatening to kill me if I didn't give them 'thousands,' shooting with rifles at my feet." She had but 740 Kr. They wanted more, plus Goldfinger's bicycle. "I replied [that it] was in the storehouse, where money was hidden" beneath the coal pile. "I said this so that I could escape while they were searching," in which this cool-headed woman succeeded.[22]

Plundered too was the Gruszów estate of Edmund Lewinger and Juliusz Goldberger, Jewish country gentlemen, who reported losses totaling 33,844 Kr., including three pigs highly valued at 8,000 Kr., along with hunting gear. Culprits were two of their estate laborers, who with other villagers made off with valuable livestock and equipment. Having confessed guilt, they justified themselves, saying that "they had nothing to wear, their employer gave them neither clothing nor footwear, so they took it for themselves."[23]

The county court's final sentences, pronounced in February 1921 – the 1920 Polish-Soviet War probably delayed them – fell most heavily on ringleaders Nowak and Dobrowolski, both given one year's imprisonment with one weekly "hard cot." Twenty-seven of forty defendants escaped punishment beyond whatever detention they may have endured. The court accepted testimony of four Jewish witnesses and one Christian. The court rejected defendants' self-defense on grounds of drunkenness, although it patronizingly and insultingly noted that their "inebriated state, low level of intelligence, and neglected education, as a result of

---

[21] Ibid., fos. 217–18.   [22] Ibid., fos. 315, 351.

[23] Ibid., fos. 309–10, 593–94. See also ibid., fos. 197–203, 221–25. Some additional loss inventories are suggestive of Jewish life: "a man's long robe" (800 Kr.); "two large pictures of Jerusalem," two prayer shawls (*tales*) "with silver collars" (1,500 Kr.); a Sabbath cap (500 Kr.); a silken Hungarian frogged coat (100 Kr.); and torn prayer books; a debt register – probably an oft-seized item (500 Kr.); 100 liters of rum (4,000 Kr.); 15 liters of plum brandy (600 Kr.); 150 liters of beer (480 Kr.), 145 liters of various wines (2,900 Kr.).

which the accused, during state revolution and security-force reorganization, succumbed to impulse and uncritically followed criminal exhortations." This judgment reduced anti-Jewish violence to the perpetrators' ignorance and lack of self-control, though allowing for leaders' possible recourse to anti-Jewish slogans for criminal gain.

This seems persuasive yet fails to accord villagers' will to plunder, humiliate, and abuse Jewish neighbors any cultural or psychological authenticity. Why they imagined it "was permitted" to rob Jews remained an enigma the court did not resolve but rather obfuscated. Such records show how weak-willed villagers let themselves be bullied into joining anti-Jewish assaults, fearing social exclusion. It happened that plunderers, whether conscience stricken or anticipating arrest, sometimes returned stolen goods. Among Christian elders, some chose more or less indifferent quietism. Others risked denunciation, in counseling against aggression against Jewish neighbors, as venal "Jewish uncles." Priests, intelligentsia, and other elites are off stage. Jewish women, often more active in economic life than their husbands, stood on front lines. Police and judiciary acted correctly, if slowly, rendering objective and even hard judgments but aiming mainly to throttle peasant anarchy and assaults on property, not anti-Judaism.[24]

Another trial record illustrates Christian-Jewish bonds that ethnic violence tested and often sundered.[25] In rural Krzyżanowice Małe, Haskel Silbermann, fifty-two, lived as "farmer and shopkeeper." On November 3, a youth band inflicted damage on him of 43,940 Kr. Kraków court ascribed their actions to "hatred" (*nienawiść*). As unlettered Christian laborer Adolf Winzelberg, eighteen, testified, "rumors spread that Jews would be robbed, so on request of victim's son [gymnasium student Izaak, sixteen], I overnighted at Silbermann's, since his father, for fear of attack, had traveled with his family to Bochnia." Later, two other Christian youths arrived, "who were there actually to help guard the house," but who later – gun in hand – joined a gang of plunderers arriving at 1:00 AM and returned again the next night for more looting.

Defendant Jan Trepa, twenty-four, living with his mother, testified that "a few days before the robbery *Jan Gawlik was inciting the boys to fall on Jews* and steal their things." Premeditation turned into action when "Gawlik talked us into going to Silbermann's to take away his revolver,

[24] Ibid., fo. 959. Of the pogromists' subsequent lives, nothing is known, except that in 1928 a priest wrote a "freedom testimony" for Stefan Kwarciak, possibly following release from prison on new charges. "He leads a life that is sober, moral, and industrious." He fulfilled his religious duties. "He understands his civil responsibilities, for he is busy building his own house." He deserved trust.

[25] SOKKr. S8/II. J3710/20, fos. 9–37, 65–66, 131, 139.

because he had threatened to shoot us" – again, the stereotypical pogrom excuse. Responding to standard interrogation, he admitted that he "felt" guilty but "acted under Gawlik's compulsion, who pressured me."

Jan Stachura, "called 'Tazbir,'" twenty-four, literate, previously unpunished, living with parents, said that "Gawlik threatened to thrash me if I didn't rob Jews." At Silbermann's, Gawlik stole money, sharing it around, and commanded on leaving that all windows be broken. Józek Gacek, war invalid living with parents, had been asked by young Silbermann to help protect the property, but Gawlik forced him into looting "since if we didn't go *he would beat us for keeping watch for Jews.*"

Ringleader Gawlik, twenty-four, literate, previously unpunished farmer, denied guilt, casting his actions as a justifiable search for Silbermann's (undiscoverable) gun. Prosecution was slow. In 1920, four of eight defendants were under arms against Bolsheviks. In March 1921, the above-named three were found guilty of "engaging in violence to vent hatred." The sentences of four weeks' imprisonment were halved by the February 1919 amnesty. They paid court costs. As in the Gruszów case, the judge took account of the miscreants' "neglected education, [Gawlik's] pressure," and drunkenness.

In this seemingly minor case, strangely little was made of Silbermann's 44,000-Kr. loss, which included 13,000 Kr. for clothing, 9,000 Kr. for linen, and 6,000 Kr. for furniture. Perhaps this booty was stuffed into outsider bandits' bags. Whatever hopes Silbermann invested in his young son's ability to recruit Christian acquaintances to protect the family's possessions proved vain, as – once again – threats of violence against (youthful) "Jewish uncles" trumped Christian obligations to Jewish neighbors.

Women were not immune from punishment for pogrom participation. In Księże Kopacze, thirty-six year-old ironically named day laborer Wojciech Szlachta, married with three children, with a postage-stamp farm and "two winters of elementary school," suffered imprisonment together with his wife Bronisława and three other adults for buying clothing, textiles, shoes, and furs knowingly stolen from Jakob Flaumenhaft. The women were underway in mid-November, "after the rioting had occurred," ostensibly to buy children's garments when they met deserters, who asked "why buy from Jews?" when they would sell cheaper. Bronisława bought goods for 400 Kr. Sentences ran stiffly from eight months' imprisonment with one "hard cot" monthly for two months, with time off for pretrial detention. Flaumenhaft identified his wares among gendarme-confiscated stolen goods. Here the above-mentioned judge recalled the "time of mass plundering and assaults throughout the whole region" and the "movement of robbery that had engulfed a whole expanse of the [Galician] land."[26] Defendants' stern punishment reflected less any (undetectable) judicial wish to suppress anti-Jewish violence than zeal to halt lawlessness and crimes against property among the laboring classes.

Finally, an exemplary tale of cold-blooded plunder and ethnic cleansing was heard from Ludwik Fischer, forty-nine, who lived with wife Rozalia and nine children in Brodłe village. Born there, he cultivated a few acres and housed a small store. Five neighbors demanded "food, tobacco, vodka and wine plus money on threat they would rob me of everything." He complied, but they returned at night with some "thirty people armed with axes and revolvers, forced me to raise my hands, and began robbing," taking his cow, linen, and children's shoes.[27]

Next night another band appeared. Discovering Fischer's wife at a neighbor's, "they forced her to give them the key, searched her and took a few hundred korony." Entering his house, they took "all furnishings, mirror, pendulum clock, tore straw from pillows and packed stolen items in them in a wagon standing ready." A servant of Fischer's relatives later saw his mirror and wall clock in a robber's house in another village – demonstrating that some plunderers aimed not to sell booty but to use it to elevate themselves socially.

That night Fischer's doughty wife kept guard in their garden against further robbery. She saw how, after the plunderers' departure, Brodłe's locals "threw themselves into robbing the entire house and harvested stocks." Among twenty, she recognized eight women, including Maria Gałdyn, "called Dukalanka"; Zofia Gałdyn, "called axe"; and Ulina Kałamacka, "who sold around the village kerchiefs robbed from me."

These Brodłe people even searched under the floor, which they tore up, and didn't spare themselves the trouble of tossing out from the basement four wagon-loads of beets to get to the basement's earth-floor, in which I had buried after the first attack a pot with 600 korony.

The Fischers took refuge elsewhere but later returned, "having nowhere to live" and planting time having arrived. Eight men, including three village councillors, came to his house, "where I had barely managed to put in doors and windows and set up the oven – for in the winter the Brodłe people had stripped practically the whole house of framing" and even roofs. The men proceeded to "besiege my house, throwing stones at it and the windows." One demanded he leave, saying "'you've got until noon tomorrow, and if you haven't moved out we'll tear you all

---

[26] Ibid., J 3541/20, fos. 3–5, (author's emphasis).
[27] SOKKr. S8/II J 2489/20: Brodłe. fos. 13–17, 133–35, 157–60, 169 (February 5, 1919 et seq.).

to pieces [*was rozniesiemy*],' while another shouted they'll 'drag us out feet first.'" Next day the Fischers went to the mayor, but "the people behaved so threateningly that, facing danger of beatings, we left Brodłe." On the road out they met Marcin Kołodziej, "threatening 'if you don't get out of Brodłe, I'll kill you all, it's nothing to me whether I kill or don't.'"

The court's list of eight defendants placed them in the thirty-six to fifty-seven age range, apart from one eighteen-year-old. All were farmers or farm laborers; three were women. They did not qualify as "adolescents" or "bandits" nor even as (conventionally understood) "scum." Six signed their names well, one shakily, one woman with X. In April 1921, Kraków's criminal court found, among the now only six defendants, five guilty of theft "during the mass plundering." Stolen goods were minutely specified, proof being required of discrete thefts. The sentences were of two months' imprisonment and payment of court costs, though following February 1919's amnesty, punishment was halved. The guilty parties were ordered to pay Fischer 600 marks (by then the new Polish currency, one mark equaling 1.66 Kr./korony). All defendants claimed innocence. Those found in possession of stolen goods did not know how they acquired them. No drunkenness defenses arose. In June 1921, the court released those still imprisoned under the second postwar amnesty law of May 1921.

Were Brodłe Christians better off materially without the Fischers? They failed to weigh this question when robbing and expelling them. They were, instead, exorcizing Jews' presence while inheriting rustic riches, some of which – like the wall clock – they flaunted in their parlors. Cavalier attitudes toward murder were war's legacy.

Insights from Lesser Pogroms

In antisemitic eyes, Jews' patriotic professions were worthless. In industrializing Trzebinia – 5,000 souls, one-quarter Jewish –

the Jews appeared en masse to express their loyalty and joy over Poland's rebirth. But hardly had their leader, Dr. Wald, begun to speak than, at a signal by [county physician] Dr. Dobrzyński, the cry arose [among the doctor's "hooligan" followers]: "out with the Jews!"

The doctor, "notorious for his Jew-devouring [*żydożerczej*] activities," held the militia passive before pogromists. Alone among the intelligentsia, elementary school director Geremuga protested, exclaiming, "By God, it's a disgrace to besmirch Poland's rebirth with pogrom blood."

Christians displayed images of the Divine Mother (*Matka Boska*), flanked by two burning candles, shielding homes and shops.[28]

In industrial Siersza, pogrom rumors led mine administrators to form a militia whose chief only agreed to nightly patrols after local Jews paid him 1,000 Kr. Next morning, peasants and "girls from Congress Poland," with "happy exclamations," leveled Jewish homes and shops. Militiamen fired "shots of joy into the air, crying 'long live Poland.'" The mob attacked a Jewish butcher, thinking he had wounded a pogromist. They pummeled him with clubs, truncheons, and rifle butts "until, amid indescribable torments, he fell dead." Jewish butchers – icons of religiosity, strength, and killing capacity but also villains in ritual murder imaginings – often figured at violence's forefront both as defenders and victims.[29] As in Trzebinia, here too industrialization did not inhibit anti-Jewish violence. In modernizing towns and cities, it was stronger and better disciplined security forces, not always present, that could block pogroms.

The fantasy of "de-Judaizing Poland" doubtless gripped many minds. Two Jews found "death decrees" in their mail. Sent by the self-designated "Bolshevik Government Supreme Council," they stated: "we command that after five days no Jewish person shall inhabit Przytkowskie land. Otherwise, all will be slaughtered [*wyrznięte*]." Looters of a Jewish-owned country estate warned its inhabitants to depart for Palestine within three days or face being driven out with blows. The imperious expellers' self-definition as "Bolsheviks" could have been camouflage or signal that they were revolutionary-minded agrarian radicals, for whom "Bolshevik" was ill-understood synonym.[30]

Occasionally, villagers held aloof from robbery bands. Hermann Gutter witnessed plundering in seven villages near Żywiec by some 200 armed men with booty wagons. They defied soldiery. "Officers were harassed, even disrobed." Yet "local farmers behaved decently toward Jews."[31] Such reports were rare. In Andrychów, textile town with a small "advanced" (non-Hasidic) Jewish population, peasant pogromists claimed eight (not two or three) days' official permission to plunder Jews. Priest Kotarby asked city councilmen: "where were you?

---

[28] *Nowy Dziennik*, no. 120 (November 8, 1918), "Pogromy w Galicyi"; ibid., no. 122 (November 10, 1918), "Wiadomości"; CZA. Z3/178; L6/119. Chasanowitsch, *Judenpogrome*, 37–38.

[29] CZA. L6/109: *Nowy Dziennik*, no. 124 (December 12, 1918).

[30] *Nowy Dziennik*, no. 121 (November 9, 1918), "Wiadomości o pogromach"; ibid., no. 124 (November 12, 1918), "Dalsze wiadomości."

[31] JDC. AR 14/18, file 136: Poland.

Five people could have saved the town."[32] In industrial Szczakowa, legionnaires loaded pogrom plunder worth millions onto trucks, ostensibly for military use.[33]

Virtually any Jewish political stirring could spark Polish antagonism. In Chmielnik, a largely Hasidic town of 5,908 souls, proletarian Poale Zion members held a synagogue meeting, after which they marched singing to the main square. Here Christian militia fired on them, killing three girls. "Following the shooting, a peasant crowd armed with axes and pitchforks arrived from suburbs and villages and began to revenge themselves for the [Jewish] 'attack.' The militia leader assured them that all was in order, and they retreated." Here Christian alarm over Jewish leftism triggered violence, which plunderers – self-righteously, deludedly, cynically – sought to exploit.[34]

In half-Jewish Nowy Wiśnicz (4,000 souls), Jews fell out among themselves over unseating the Habsburg-era official rabbi, who appealed to the local military commander for protection against this "revolution." Soldiers rounded up Jews on the market square. The lieutenant announced that every tenth man would be shot, marching them before machine guns. "Fortunately the priest's 'compassionate' heart awoke, as he recommended flogging instead. A whole group immediately responded to the lieutenant's call for volunteers to administer the punishment": beating victims on bare buttocks as they lay on benches in public view. One hundred and thirty Jews, aged from twelve to seventy-two, reportedly suffered this humiliating fate. "The victims' groans and their flowing blood seemed to hasten the 'work,' which offered the mob an enjoyable spectacle" – of three hours' duration. Here Polish nationalists and antisemites reacted sadistically – and anachronistically – to internal Jewish politics, generally thought mysterious and ominous.[35]

Ritual humiliation also accompanied plunder of eastward-lying Chyrów by eighty marauders. Cohen noted, "sick rabbi taken with bed into street in bitter cold; robbed of all. Over 100 girls and women, stripped of boots and stockings, forced to march to Felsztyn and compelled in turn to wade in ice-cold stream to bring out gun thrown by commanding officer" – seemingly a symbolic disarming of Jews.[36]

---

[32] *Nowy Dziennik*, no. 125 (November 13, 1918), "Andrychów"; CZA. Z3/178. Cf. CZA. Z3/178; available at www.sztetl.org.pl/en/article/baranow-sandomierski/5,history; *Nowy Dziennik* (November 17, 1918)

[33] *Nowy Dziennik*, no. 122 (November 10, 1918); CZA. Z3/178.

[34] CZA. Z3/178, available at www.jewishgen.org/Yizkor/Chmielnik/chm073.html.

[35] Chasanowitsch, *Judenpogrome*, 42 (November 28, 1918).

[36] JDC. AR 14/18, file 136 (Poland): testimony of Salomon Rotner in Vienna, November 8, 1918. Cf. CZA. Z3/178; L6/119.

The several brutal multiple murders that known documentation reports will not have been unique. A private letter reported that in Tuczempy, four women and an infant "were killed with knives." The writer's friend who sought to inform police was also murdered. Jarosław firemen exhumed the hastily buried bodies, while other authorities approved a Jewish self-defense force. In Jarosław itself, an eastern border town of some 20,000 (one-third Jewish), the gendarmerie and Polish-manned civilian guard halted incipient plundering. Later some sixty soldiers formed a Jewish militia. The larger the town, the more likely it was that such interventions would succeed.[37]

In Grochów village, unidentified attackers murdered Rabbi Grochower, his wife, and three sons. "Their Christian housemaid, because she served Jews, was hanged." In Łazy, villagers assembled "at the shopkeeper's house" – the locality's only Jewish family – "barricaded the windows and doors and set it ablaze." Father, mother, daughter, and three grandchildren perished. Reports such as these, stemming sometimes from anxious, even paranoid sources and appearing in mass-circulation Jewish publications, cannot always stand as empirically indisputable. But they may reflect brutal reality and certainly convey well-founded Jewish apprehensions.[38]

In Jasło, the National Council, supplanting Habsburg authority, had started out badly, searching Jewish houses and synagogues for weapons and expelling Jewish war veterans from the militia. In play were "usurpatory persons' machinations," former "toadies" for the Austrians, then for the Russians, now posing as "arch-patriots," using antisemitism "to advance their careers and gain new sinecures."[39]

Jewish appreciation of Polish support emerged from "unheard-of anti-Jewish rioting" in Pilzno, in which market plundering killed two men. "Bestiality" – oft-invoked word – "went so far that [murdered] Kranz's two-year-old child was abused in lowest manner." When gendarmes fired shots, the mob scattered.

Local clergy's behavior was praiseworthy, as was Captain Dr. Lewicki's ... At the critical moment they exhorted the masses to reason. Likewise may heartiest thanks go to other Polish fellow-citizens for energetic intervention on Pilzno Jews' behalf in capturing gang leaders.[40]

---

[37] *Nowy Dziennik*, no. 136 (November 24, 1918), "Dalsze wiadomości"; CZA. Z3/178; ibid., L6/119. JDC. AR 14/18, file 136.
[38] CZA. Z3/178: *Chwila*, no. 122; ibid., L6/119.
[39] *Handlanger*. CZA. L6/109: *Nowy Dziennik*, no. 124 (December 12, 1918).   [40] Ibid.

Here was precise juxtaposition – a strong tendency among conservative Jews, uninterested in democratic populism – of "bestial" antisemitism among common folk to educated Poles' enlightened protection.

Yet elite benevolence was unreliable and often ineffectual. Jewish religious authorities in Zator wrote the Liquidation Commission that pogromists streamed into town, crying "Get the Jews!" Band chieftains gave signals for plunder, drawing in many townspeople, "even respected and prosperous burghers." Bed-ridden women, some pregnant, were hurled to the floor, bandages torn away, bodies "in brutal fashion searched." Alcohol flowed. "In broad daylight people did not scruple, amid the delighted mob's wild shouting, to join in robbery." Mayor and priest sought, alone, "to calm the mob, but completely in vain." Pleading for food, denied by the Liquidation Commission, Jews wrote that "as winter approaches, a cry of desperation for immediate aid arises from our broken hearts and ravaged souls." Jewish communal president David Lipschütz told *Nowy Dziennik* that Zator's events "make hair stand on end and blood freeze." Not a single religious book was left intact. "Whoever among Poles defended Jews was beaten: parish priest Noks, mayor Bystrzanowski," and five militiamen "injured by fist-fighting [*bokserem*] in arms and head."[41]

In coal-mining Jaworzno, "local clergy incited peasant plunderers." A priest announced, "we cannot murder Jews, but we must rid ourselves of them." Referring to wounding of Christian workers by a certain armed Jew – seemingly because of job-site quarreling – the priest complained that "no Catholic has killed a Jew, but Catholic blood has been shed," whereupon his listeners began pogrom work. Cohen noted, "in January [1919] all 9 members of Town Council compelled to resign, and populace demanded exodus of entire Jewish community within a fortnight." This was another instance of anti-Habsburg revolt combined with an antisemitic wish for "de-Judaization."[42]

In sub-Carpathian Żmigród, with a venerable Hasidic community of some 1,000, villager pogromists streamed in for "cheap shopping." Christians pointed out Jewish homes so that "God forbid, no mistakes should occur." Soldiers, drawn by rumor that Ukrainians were attacking Poles, withdrew, seeing cynically that "only Jews were staging provocations. The intelligentsia (the teacher) 'calmed' the Jews by saying, 'you must believe it, this pogrom will be the last one, you must all leave.'"[43]

---

[41] CZA. L6/109, L6/119; Chasanowitsch, *Judenpogrome*, 38; *Nowy Dziennik*, nos. 122, 124 (November 10–12, 1918).
[42] CZA. Z3/178; L6/119; *Nowy Dziennik*, no. 122 (November 10, 1918), "Jaworzno."
[43] CZA. L6/109: *Nowy Dziennik*, no. 124 (December 12, 1918).

Elite perfidy surfaced also in Nisko. A letter from a local inhabitant who returned home in November bitterly lamented that

> fourteen-year-old lads carry guns. They plunder and carry off anything they find among Jews. They conduct pocket searches and take Jews' money ... Also the better "gentlemen" have agreed to demand 20,000 Kr. monthly from the Jews, or otherwise bad things will happen to us.

Here, too, wealthier Jews had fled for bigger towns' safety, leaving impoverished others who could not ransom themselves. People escaped with only their "naked life" because on trains everything Jews transported was seized, "even their clothes and underwear."[44] On the Kraków-Zator line, "enraged crowds of human cattle threaten" Jewish travelers. "Maddened" men threatened to hurl an elderly Jew from a high-speed train's window, onlookers shouting, "let's kill the Jew." Only the man's "terrible weeping" moved the conductor to hide him in a separate compartment. On another occasion, thugs beat a Jew in a car carrying priests, soldiers, and university students. "The students mumbled under their breath, 'how embarrassing [naprawdę wstyd],' but no one lifted a finger."[45]

In Błażowa, 200 Jewish families were plundered. The only Catholic damage was to apothecary Brzęcza's windows "because they took him for a Jew. For this they humbly apologized to him." *Nowy Dziennik* published Mielec Jewish Commune's disclaimer, "in [the] interest of truth" that the town's "citizens and militia had [not] taken any part whatsoever in robberies." Nor had they shown "where the Jews have wares or money." Was this Jewish retreat from fear of reprisals or conservative timorousness about pressing charges against pogromists?

The Galician press reported on anti-Jewish violence flaring elsewhere in Eastern Europe. In Prague, for example, an antisemitic mob threatened Jewish merchants, shouting, "Execute the Jews! Hang them! Lock them up! Let them eat war-bread and cabbage!" But Czech soldiers and Sokol gymnast youth protected them. In Lubomil, near Chełm in Volhynia, the disintegrating Austrian army's efforts to organize a civilian militia failed because of "the clergy's anti-Jewish agitation." Czech soldiers joined there in a pogrom with marauding peasants and deserters who had plundered the Austrian arms depot. Jakob Bialer reported that they shot him in both feet. "As he lay bleeding on the ground, the soldiers searched his pockets and took his assets, 10,000 Kr." His life hung in balance.[46]

---

[44] CZA. Z3/178. Letter of November 17, 1918.
[45] *Nowy Dziennik*, no. 122 (November 10, 1918), "Wiadomości."
[46] CZA Z3/178. Report by Zionist *Moment*, November 1918.

Bombarded with such reports, many Jewish voices expressed harsh condemnation of Polish rebirth and keen regret at Habsburg demise. Berlin ZO received a letter from Galician Meyer Leistyna, tobacco wholesaler's son. His father's workers, cooperating with pogromists, plundered the familial home and warehouse. Appeals to the prefect brought ten soldiers, but they refused to protect Jews and, "following abominations perpetrated by Polish culture-bearers [*Kulturträger*]," soon withdrew. Violence continued next day, when twelve Jews were severely injured. With most young Jews still under arms, no defense was possible against the "mob filled with blood-lust and lowest instincts." At night, terrorized Jews huddled in their basements, "citizens of once unfree Austria and now free and happily democratic Poland," fearful of "being killed by Polish neighborly love."

Such is the Poles' thanks for the lives that countless [Jewish] brothers laid down for their country's liberation. And such complete and half-wild Asiatics speak of freedom, equality and fraternity![47]

Military Pogroms in Przemyśl and Lwów/L'viv/Lemberik

Soldiers, whether demobilized warriors, legionnaires not yet subordinated to firm state command, or troops of the nascent new army, figured in much – perhaps most – anti-Jewish violence.[48] Armed bands of deserters and rural bandit plunderers were, with villager followers, also commonly chief instigators, engulfing towns in looting expeditions that Christian burghers and lower classes, alongside armed authorities of various kinds – soldiers, legionnaires, police – frequently joined. Among West Galicia's many explosions there erupted, three weeks after November 3, the most devastating single pogrom in the period 1914–20 and indeed in known Polish history before World War II. This was the assault on Lwów's Jewish quarter by soldiers, irregular fighters, and civilians following a desperate armed struggle between eventually triumphant Poles and vanquished Ukrainians for possession of the East Galician capital. The Lwów pogrom is the most fully documented of all that occurred in these years.

A certain prefiguration of this tragic and shocking event occurred in Przemyśl (Yiddish: Pshemishl), counting 48,000 souls, one-third Jewish.

---

[47] CZA. Z3/180. 9 (December 2, 1918).

[48] Jewish eyewitness reports often designated Polish fighters as "legionnaires," a term generally associated with Józef Piłsudski's and Józef Haller's armed followers, originally subordinated to the Austro-Hungarian army but whose wartime units were not present in Przemyśl and Lwów in November 1918. It seems to have often been a local synonym for irregular soldiers fighting Ukrainians.

Here on November 11–14 pogrom raged, ignited by Polish armed forces' expulsion of Ukrainian fighters. Following Habsburg collapse, Ukrainian armed forces tolerated Jewish militiamen confined to predominantly Jewish neighborhoods and pledged to neutrality between warring Christians. Poles grudgingly followed suit, although ferocious antisemitic posters appeared calling for "slaughtering the Jews and driving them out to Palestine." On November 10, Polish forces attacked Ukrainian troops across the San River, driving them from the city, initiating "orgies directed exclusively against Jews," charged with anti-Polish treachery. Jewish militiamen were rounded up and "bestially abused," forty-five of them together with 300 Jewish civilians marched under blows of rifle butts and knouts, stripped of clothes and shoes, for three days' imprisonment without food or drink. Meanwhile, Polish fighters and civilians unrestrainedly plundered Jewish property. "Furniture dealer Rotter was bestially dragged onto the street and killed by bayonet." While in one account this was the sole murder, Israel Cohen reported fifteen Jewish deaths, adding that pogromists "broke into the synagogue, dirtying it and covering the filth with prayer shawls and torn-up Torah covers."

The newspaper *Ziemia Przemyska*, later speaking for the Polish National Council governing the city, branded the plunder as civilian work the army had sought to restrain. It regretted "the crimes," saying it would give much "if such events had not besmirched recent days' history." But it could not refrain from victim blaming, both for smuggling and price gouging, "which generated great agitation and desire for revenge" for Jews being "good Austrians" who did their "military service behind the front"; for "proclaiming themselves, after the Austrian army's withdrawal, a distinct nation and decorating themselves with Zionist national colors"; and for breaking neutrality and siding with the Ukrainians. Yet "we cannot conceal that some Jews fought heroically on our side."

Polish authorities sought to whitewash the armed forces, saddling commoners with the pogrom, but soldiers' initiative and participation were unmistakable. Before withdrawing his troops to reinforce the fight for Lwów, Commanding General Michał Tokarzewski attempted to fine Przemyśl's Jews 3 million Kr. (£125,000 or $625,000) in admission of collaborationist guilt, even though the Polish National Council had conceded Jewish innocence. Israel Cohen reported that councilman Dr. Tarnowski defied Tokarzewski's emissary: "You will have to order firing at me and the Poles before you let soldiers loose against the Jews." The Galician Liquidation Commission halfheartedly repudiated the attempted blackmail, seemingly stiffened with the threat of renewed pogrom, saying that since Przemyśl's Jews had ostensibly promised future anti-Ukrainian loyalty, the fine was canceled, yet also denouncing Jewish charges that Polish soldiers had committed "outrages and plundering." It was hard for the new state to acknowledge its soldiers' indiscipline, taste for booty, and violent Judeophobia, let alone that military leaders might authorize or even command pogrom violence.[49]

Nowy Dziennik published revealing letters between Przemyśl's Jewish People's Council and the Polish National Council. The Jews angrily denounced the pogrom and Polish authorities' failure to throttle it. Instead, "in your silence you sanctioned it," for which Poles bore responsibility before God. The Poles chided the "Jewish gentlemen" for reckless charges. "You know yourselves that we only entered the city after the army stormed it, and then began forming the security guard. You will admit that we behaved toward you loyally and correctly." Before then, as hand grenades blew open apartment buildings' entrances, "robber bands began swarming."

Gentlemen: We did not create them, but rather four and a half years of pitiless war, poverty, general primitivization [*zdziczenie*], and demoralization, planned and deliberately launched from above, which we – our hands tied – could only weakly attempt to resist.

Evildoers, released or escaped from jail, flooded the city. "All shady individuals took advantage of conflict and fighting, in an atmosphere reeking of fresh blood and smoke, to rob and plunder."

Before then we tried to fight antisemitism's manifestations. Did you, Gentlemen, read our public denunciation not just of deeds but also of words of hostility directed against You? You know the broad masses' mood and the reasons for it. You know the proclamation was an act of civil courage on our part, against opinion's tide. After armed battle we made a superhuman effort to suppress anarchy. Nevertheless You claim that no one, in word or deed, stepped forward against it.

Guilt rested on both sides, especially their "benighted and irresponsible elements." The leadership committees should be not advocates but peacemakers. To this *Nowy Dziennik* replied that the decision for neutrality was "painful" but reflected responsibility for a 70,000-strong Jewish population, most living outside the city in Ruthenian-dominated land. General Tokarzewski's cynical effort to squeeze protection money from Przemyśl's Jews had greatly worsened Christian-Jewish relations.

[49] *Nowy Dziennik*, no. 131 (November 19, 1918); CZA. Z3/179; L6/110, fo. 5, L6/109, L6/119; Chasanowitsch, *Judenpogrome*, 23*ff*, 38*ff*. Cf. Wacław Wierzbieniec, "Zajścia antyżydowskie w Przemyślu pod koniec 1918 r.," in Krzysztof Jasiewicz, ed., *Świat niepożegnany: Żydzi na dawnych ziemiach wschodnich Rzeczypospolitej w XVIII–XX wieku* (Warsaw: Instytut Studiów Politycznych PAN, 2004), 573–80.

Now, after its withdrawal, "the possibility of positive work together arises."[50]

As these hopeful words were being read, and as the Lwów pogrom was ending, another Polish commander, Lieutenant-Colonel Swoboda, on November 24 confronted the Jews of Ustrzyki Dolne on the Polish-Ukrainian ethnic border with an ultimatum: either deliver 300,000 Kr. "within an hour" or suffer dynamiting of the Jewish district "with armored trains." Such was punishment for Jewish collaboration "with the Haidamaks" – bandits, referring to Ukrainian fighters – against Polish forces. The beleaguered Jews scraped together 59,337.82 Kr., including Frau Sophie Apfel's postal savings account of 2,000 Kr. Liquidation Commission director Count Lasocki pronounced this extortion by his military commander Roja's subordinate illegal, yet Swoboda squeezed 90,000 Kr. more from his victims (one murdered).[51]

The Polish armed forces' culpability in the Lwów pogrom was greater still. Yet it was far more than a rampage of antisemitic soldiers who were, as must be remembered, also members of society with complex cultural identities and not mere products of military socialization. War-saturated civilians may have been responsible for an incident reported to a delegation of "Warsaw assimilationists" who had come to survey their coreligionists' losses in the ravaged East Galician capital. "The attorney Levin," the appalled visitors heard, "was forced to load the objects plundered from him onto a wagon and then he was hitched to the wagon together with the horses. After pulling his way as a beast of burden through several streets he was gunned down together with his wife and old mother."[52] The pogromists had robbed Levin of his property and high social standing, stripped him of his humanity, and finally killed him and his kinswomen. It remains to confirm the authenticity of this cruel picture. Yet, because contestation of ethnic violence's memory and popularly received narrative is no less central to its historical force than the tangible losses it inflicts or than disinterested probing of its causes, the very circulation of stories such as attorney Levin's forms part both of the pogrom itself and of the problem requiring explanation.

---

[50] *Nowy Dziennik*, no. 136 (November 24, 1918), "Po ekscesach w Przemyślu."

[51] Chasanowitsch, *Judenpogrome*, 25; CZA. L6/119: Cohen, "The Pogroms in Poland," 28–29. An earlier account of the Lwów pogrom is William W. Hagen, "The Moral Economy of Popular Violence: The Pogrom in Lwów, November 1918," in Robert Blobaum, ed., *Antisemitism and Its Opponents in Modern Poland* (Ithaca, NY: Cornell University Press, 2005), 124–47; also in *Geschichte und Gesellschaft*, vol. 31, no. 2 (2005), 203–26. The pages below extend that interpretation with additional primary-source documentation.

[52] Cited from the "Warsaw Jewish press" by Chasanowitsch, *Judenpogrome*, 103.

This book highlights the element of social ritual, playing out – in "play's" sinister sense – public dramas designed to repair a society fallen out of the rightful order that perpetrators' communal convictions expected of it. Such social norms British historian Edward Thompson memorably termed the popular classes' "moral economy." Actions dramatizing and enforcing them often resembled the "carnivals of violence" familiar in the historical literature as early modern European communal rituals symbolically reversing social hierarchy and punishing offenders against cultural codes. These rites, usually jolly though sometimes rough, occasionally gyrated out of control into bloody violence, as symbolical contention turned real.[53] Analogous were the Lwów pogrom's ritualized forms or stagings, the social and cultural scripts it followed, and the messages it conveyed. These constituted the pogrom as spontaneous communal act, whose carnavalesque elements were central to its suprain-dividual character and purpose.

As attorney Levin's fate shows, the deliberate and intentional destruc-tiveness and brutality of pogroms unfit them for categorization as mere carnivals gone awry. Their violence crescendoed upward through random killings to maddened individuals' threats of comprehensive murder. The thought of massacre gained warrant from Polish nationalists' sense that their own community had fended off disaster in a moment of crisis during which, in their view, Jews deserted them. In victory's exaltation, the thought seized many Poles not merely to punish Jews humiliatingly and bruisingly but even – wishfully imagining them now irrelevant to Polish survival – to eliminate them altogether from their midst. This idea surfaced – as it did in earlier-explored lesser explosions – as threat of expulsion or of localized slaughter, sometimes with genocidal overtones.

Lwów's pogrom was certainly military sack by victorious armed forces – including many uniformed but irregular troops – of civilians marked as enemies. On November 1, Ukrainian fighters surprised the narrow Polish majority – in 1920, 51.3 percent of 219,000, the remainder three-quarters Jewish – by seizing power over much of the city, including predominantly Jewish quarters. Ukrainian nationalists' aim was to make their L'viv the capital of a post-Habsburg West Ukrainian republic, intended launch pad of a united Ukrainian state oriented toward Central Europe and away from Bolshevik Russia.

Polish nationalists counterattacked, first in waves of youthful armed volunteers, then in locally recruited units of the new national army, reinforced by soldiers of preexisting wartime legions. After three weeks

---

[53] On Thompson, moral economy, and social-political violence's ritualistic dimensions, see the Theoretical Footnote.

of street fighting amid dwindling food stocks, arrival from Kraków of regular army troops under General Roja secured Polish victory in the early hours of Saturday, November 22. Power now reposed ill definedly in the armed forces' hands, with Polish municipal authorities standing deferentially on the sidelines.[54]

On November 9–10, amid the fighting, Polish military and civilian leaders had joined Jews and Ukrainians – as earlier in Przemyśl – in sanctioning creation of a Jewish militia, here numbering some 200 riflemen. They would patrol the central Jewish district, warding off looters in the food-scarce, darkened, and lawless city and maintaining access to Jewish shops, where available essential goods were sold at fixed prices.[55] Already on October 28 a mass meeting of Lwów's Jews, many inspired by Zionist nationalism, had declared neutrality in the escalating Polish-Ukrainian conflict.[56]

---

[54] Christoph Mick, "Nationalisierung in einer multiethnischen Stadt. Interethnische Konflikte in Lemberg, 1890–1920," *Archiv für Sozialgeschichte*, vol. 40 (2000), 144. Mick's *Lemberg, Lwów, L'viv, 1914–1947: Violence and Ethnicity in a Contested City* (W. Lafayette, IN: Purdue University Press, 2016 [German original, 2010]), offers authoritative political and social history. On 1918's pogrom, see ibid., 158–74. On Lemberg's Jews, see Svyatoslav Pacholkiv, "Zwischen Einbeziehung und Ausgrenzung. Die Juden in Lemberg 1918–1919," in Alexandra Binnenkade et al., eds., *Vertraut und fremd zugleich: Jüdisch-christliche Nachbarschaften in Warschau–Lengnau–Lemberg* (Köln: Böhlau, 2009), 155–216.

Other valuable works include Golczewski, *Polnisch-jüdische Beziehungen 1881–1922*, 184–204 and chaps. 8–10, *passim*; Leszek Podhorodecki, *Dzieje Lwowa* (Warsaw: Oficyna Wydawnicza Volumen, 1993), 153–72; Włodzimierz Bonusiak et al., *Galicja i jej dziedzictwo*, 2 vols. (Rzeszów: Wydawnictwo Wyższej Szkoły Pedagogicznej w Rzeszowie, 1994–95), especially vol. I, 83–115; Peter Fäßler et al., *Lemberg-Lwów-Lviv: Eine Stadt im Schnittpunkt europäischer Kulturen*, 2nd edn (Köln: Böhlau, 1995), 46–112; Philipp Ther, "Chancen und Untergang einer multinationalen Stadt: Die Beziehungen zwischen den Nationalitäten in Lemberg in den ersten Hälften des 20. Jahrhunderts," in Philipp Ther and Holm Sundhausen, eds., *Nationalitätenkonflikte im 20. Jahrhundert: Ursachen von inter-ethnischen Gewalt im Vergleich* (Wiesbaden: Harrassowitz, 2001), 123–46; Harald Binder, "Making and Defending a Polish Town: 'Lwów' (Lemberg), 1848–1914," *Austrian History Yearbook*, vol. 34 (2003), 57–82; David Engel, "Lwów, 1918: The Transmutation of a Symbol and Its Legacy in the Holocaust," in Joshua D. Zimmerman, ed., *Contested Memories: Poles and Jews During the Holocaust and Its Aftermath* (New Brunswick, NJ: Rutgers University Press, 2003), 32–46; Nationalist tradition constrains some works from acknowledging the extent and significance of the 1918 pogrom, e.g., Rosa Bailly, *A City Fights for Freedom: The Rising of Lwów in 1918–1919* (London: Publishing Committee Leopolis, 1956), an otherwise encyclopedic work that takes no notice of the city's Jewish population or the pogrom. Maciej Kozłowski, *Zapomniana Wojna. Walka o Lwów i Galicję Wschodnią 1918–1919* (Bydgoszcz: Instytut Wydawniczy "Świadectwo," 1999), is defensive and apologetic on the pogrom.

[55] For text and signatories, both Polish and Jewish, of the neutrality agreement and the Lwów Zionists' interpretation of it, see CZA. A127/74, "Memorjał w sprawie pogromu we Lwowie, 1.XII.1918," fos. 1–6.

[56] CZA. L6/119: Cohen, "The Pogroms in Poland," 30.

Except to a narrow stratum of Jewish assimilationists, there was no decisive argument for taking Poles' side. Most of Galicia's 900,000 Jews lived among the largely Greek Catholic Ukrainian majority of 3.3 million inhabiting the eastern half of the land (along with its 1.4 million Roman Catholic Poles). Lwów itself was largely a Polish-Jewish island in a rural Ukrainian sea. Ukrainian reprisals were foreseeable outside the city for pro-Polish Jewish partisanship within it.

Many of Lwów's Poles, like Przemyśl's, burningly resented Jewish neutrality. They widely believed not only that Jewish militiamen had collaborated with Ukrainians in fire fights against Polish forces but that Jewish civilians also furtively fought them, shooting or pouring boiling water from windows.[57] A Viennese reporter wrote that "even my fellow lodgers, tolerant and educated Poles, pass on these fairy-tales," as many among the intelligentsia inclined to do concerning all pogroms. A Jewish lawyer who paid a Polish officer 1,000 Kr. to free his wife from a gun at her temple learned that it was the Jews' "treacherous two-facedness" that caused "Krakowers and Mazurians to thirst for Jewish blood."[58]

Rumors circulated that, in victory's aftermath, Jews would suffer for neutrality. On Saturday morning, November 22, Polish soldiery disarmed and interned Jewish militiamen, whereupon sacking of the Jewish quarter commenced that lasted through Sunday. On Monday, November 24, an army order, backdated the previous day, proclaimed martial law, halting increasingly bloody mayhem. Many victims and eyewitnesses later testified that rioting soldiers said their officers had given them, as reward for victory, forty-eight (or seventy-two) hours to sack Jews. A man told of meeting a soldier known to him and asking for help in arresting a plunderer. He replied, "too bad, but you won't be able to do anything about it, because it's been permitted to rob for forty-eight hours." An apothecary testified that "an intellectual" plundering his wares said: "it's not any fun, robbing, but there's nothing for it, orders are orders." A lieutenant whose protection a Jewish merchant had sought appealed to a fur-coated cavalry major, who replied: "you've done wrong. Gabriel Stark is a Jew, his shop may be plundered."[59]

Some, perhaps much robbery occurred on army command for military purposes (though, if so, it remains undocumented). Soldiers beat a Jewish

---

[57] Exemplary is Bujak's above-cited *Jewish Question*. Polish nationalist apologetics, replete with anti-Jewish accents, are on display in Leszek Tomaszewski, "Lwów–Listopad 1918. Niezwykłe losy pewnego dokumentu," *Dzieje Najnowsze*, vol. 25, no. 4 (1993), 164–73.

[58] Josef Bendow (pseudonym for Joseph Tenenbaum [hereafter cited as Bendow]), *Der Lemberger Judenpogrom November 1918–Jänner 1919* (Vienna: Hickl, 1919), 142 (eyewitness protocol 762).

[59] Ibid., 56–57, 114 (eyewitness protocol 263). CZA. Z3/179 (November 27, 1918); Z3/181 (November 29, 1918).

manufacturer, forcing him to open his cash box. Military vehicles were loaded over several days with his wares, taken then to army headquarters. Similar raids emptied grain mills, soap works, soda-water plants, and other factories. Legionnaires' trucks hauled away from Berger's and Katz's retail stores wares worth 400,000 and 215,000 Kr.[60] A family of large-scale clothing manufacturers was plundered, the father-owner murdered. Soldiers spitefully cursed him: "Mundek, you whore's son, hand over the 1,000 Kr. you charged for a uniform."[61]

The nearest thing to an official Polish government account of the pogrom was an unpublished report of December 17, 1918, prepared for the Foreign Ministry on the causes and consequences of the "anti-Jewish transgressions." Its authors were Dr. Leon Chrzanowski, Foreign Ministry legal specialist, and assimilationist Jewish journalist Józef Wasercug. "It was the conviction," they wrote, "of the entire Lwów population and army that the Jewish militia had not maintained neutrality," though such breaches (also undocumented) were at most rare. They emphasized the role played among locally recruited Polish armed forces of criminals the Ukrainians released from local prisons or who escaped in war's end chaos. These hard men, together with others drawn from Lwów's sizable underworld, seized weapons and uniforms Polish authorities were offering all volunteer fighters so as both to repel the Ukrainians and engage in plunder, especially of the large Jewish shop-owning and business class. A "tragic and vicious circle" arose, for such a soldier, though he might fight bravely for Poland, also "robbed at every opportunity and wherever he could." It was, Chrzanowski and Wasercug argued, these marauding jailbird fighters on whom Jewish militiamen fired.[62]

The analysts found that while army leadership formally ordered no "punitive expedition" against Jews, existence of such a command was generally accepted, so that soldiers and many officers joined uniformed criminals in attacking Jews. In January 1919, Jewish notables in Lwów told Israel Cohen that army Chief of Staff Jakubski said explicitly to a Jewish delegation protesting the pogrom: "It is a punitive expedition into

[60] Central Archive for the History of the Jewish People, Jerusalem (hereafter CAHJP), microfilm HM2/8299.14. fr. 1–2; ibid., HM2/8299.11, fr. 52. This and other CAHJP microfilm cited below derive from the Ukrainian state archive in L'viv, bearing the Soviet-era signature, GALO/g.Lvov/FOND 271/Opis.1/Od. 3B.446.

[61] Bendow, *Judenpogrom*, 25 (protocol 282), 156 (protocol 363).

[62] "Raport delegacji Ministerstwa Spraw Zagranicznych R.P. w sprawie wystąpień antyżydowskich we Lwowie," reproduced in full in Jerzy Tomaszewski, "Lwów, 22 listopada 1918," *Przegląd Historyczny*, vol. 35, no. 2 (1984), 281–85, quotations from 282. Typescript in CAHJP. PL578(4): Archiwum Akt Nowych, Warsaw (hereafter AAN), KNP sygn/ 2066/p. 144.1.

the Jewish quarter, which cannot be stopped."[63] Possibly this was the same Jewish group that announced to the Warsaw press that a "Polish delegation" had allegedly appeared at City Hall demanding that the town's vice-president, Jewish Dr. Schleicher, be handed over for execution. Schleicher evaded this fate by finding a "safe hiding place."[64]

Chrzanowski and Wasercug found that while "unheard-of agitation" gripped Polish opinion, "truly hellish orgies" and "terrible things" followed, which they proposed to detail in a subsequent confidential report, though, unfortunately, no trace of this has been found. "It was a true bestialization [*istne zezwierzęcenie*], altogether medieval." They concluded that "during the pogrom days" – words the government publicly avoided – "the authorities did not fulfill their responsibilities." In mid-December, Lwów's military and civilian courts had yet to pronounce a verdict against the forty soldiers and some one thousand "criminals" jailed for participation in robbery and murder. "Most lamentable, however, is lack of any clear evidence of real desire to immediately throttle the pogrom."[65]

Chrzanowski and Wasercug reckoned the Jewish community's losses as "at least 150 killed or burned to death," together with "over fifty two- and three-story apartment buildings lost through fire." In the Jewish quarter alone, more than 500 shops and businesses suffered total plunder. Homeless, and only partly lodged in temporary shelters, were 2,000 people. The Jewish Rescue Committee (*Komitet Ratunkowy Żydowski*), umbrella recovery organization, discovered seventy orphans who lost both parents. "A dozen and more rapes of women have been reported by parents," while "a certain number of others have been concealed out of shame." Altogether some 7,000 families had by December 13 registered themselves as victims of violence, theft, and destruction with the Rescue Committee, which, in a seemingly early reckoning, counted dead lower, at seventy-three, and wounded at 437. Material losses totaled 103 million Kr., equivalent of about £4 million or 20 million then-contemporary US dollars. Half this sum represented stolen commercial-industrial inventories.

Chrzanowski and Wasercug faulted Polish authorities for refusing to take seriously entreaties by Jewish and Christian-Jewish delegations to end the pogrom. They waited forty-eight hours before announcing the establishment of summary courts, guiltily backdating the order by one day. These courts' authorization of searches for arms, which commonly degenerated into renewed robbery, kept the Jewish population in

---

[63] CZA. L/119: Cohen, "The Pogroms in Poland," 38.
[64] Chasanowitsch, *Judenpogrome*, 103.   [65] Chrzanowski and Wasercug, Report, 283–85.

PREMIERS VICTIMES DU POGROME DE PROSKOUROFF, organisé par l'ataman de Petlioura, Semessenk le 15 février 1919.

Figure 3.1 Pogrom iconography. Here are displayed Jews murdered in the one of the Ukrainian land's costliest pogroms, that of February 1919 in Proskurov (today's defiantly named Khmelnytsky), which swelled to claim thousands of victims. Such scenes had been photographed since the Russian pogrom wave of 1881–84. Other iconic representations were those of caskets in which desecrated Torah scrolls were ceremoniously buried and photomontages of pogrom victims, especially those of students and other youths. If such pictures document the Lemberg pogrom, they have not come to light but will likely have perpetuated these visual traditions. Eastern European Jews widely and rightly viewed documentation of pogrom cruelty and injustice before the eyes of the Western gentile world as a potent means of self-defense and plea for protection.
Source: Bettmann. Getty Images, 515381242.

"constant fear" after pogrom's end. Nor did either summary civil courts or courts martial manage to pronounce verdicts before the Chrzanowski-Wasercug report was composed. An army proclamation to Lwów's Jews, though never published, was generally known to be a litany of anti-Jewish complaints justifying pogrom violence.[66]

---

[66] Ibid., 284. CZA. L6/119, "Der polnisch-ukrainische Konflikt und die Juden" (n.d.), reporting the Jewish Rescue Committee's statistics, which reckoned, among seventy-three dead,

Lwów's pogrom enacted several collective scripts or scenarios – keys to its meaning in perpetrators' conscious (if delusion-veiled) or unconscious minds. Military plunder and attendant aggression alone wrought great havoc. Yet, for many victims, noninstrumental and symbolical violence cut the deepest wounds.

Perpetrators' behavior and motives take shape, rarely unambiguously, from copious documentation. The Jewish Rescue Committee, administered by local Jewish notables and chaired by Lwów's assimilationist leader, Tobias Ashkenazy, scrupulously recorded some 500 or more depositions from victims and eyewitnesses. Some of these appear in full, while others were selectively presented in previously cited books by Chasanowitsch and Galician Zionist pogrom witness and social analyst Joseph Tenenbaum (pseudonym: Josef Bendow). In Jerusalem, the Central Zionist Archives house other – unpublished – testimony, while the Central Archive for the History of the Jewish People holds microfilm of Polish judicial records assembled by the Extraordinary Governmental Investigative Commission (*Nadzwyczajna Komisja Śledcza Rządowa*), which in 1918–19 gathered pogrom evidence.

Altogether this documentation captures pogromists' actions, constituting the scripts they staged and often too explanations their own words offer for anti-Jewish aggression. The question looms whether each reported word and deed mirrors empirical reality. While some may not, the mosaic pictures that come into view certainly display widely enacted patterns of violence and rhetoric. It is characteristic of crime that victims report it, while perpetrators deny it. Most of the evidence marshaled below is of Jewish provenance. But, while Polish and other scholars might question pogrom injuries' extent, few are disposed to wholly reject them. The vital questions revolve instead around interpreting the Lwów upheaval's meanings and significations.

Early modern Europe's carnavalesque rituals repudiated social hierarchy, turning "the world upside down." Among common people, Rabelaisian feasting and costumed finery temporarily banished hunger and want. As Polish expulsion of Ukrainian troops from Lwów drew nigh, Jewish bystanders observed a festive mood among Polish fighters, in

thirty-six merchants or traders, eleven artisans, four members of the intelligentsia, and twenty-two without occupation. Among 437 wounded were 121 merchants or traders, twenty-six artisans, five workers, fourteen commercial employees, and 271 "private persons" and children. Cohen, "The Pograms in Poland," 38, reported that the Jewish Rescue Committee had collected signed eyewitness testimony to 500 cases in which patrols led by officers wrongfully injured Jews and another 2,300 cases in which individual soldiers took part. Names were known of eighteen culpable officers and seventy-two soldiers. Cohen (16) reckoned the korona/Krone at twenty-five to the British pound. Tomaszewski ("Lwów," 280) overvalued it at four to the pound.

anticipation of the widely foreseen sacking of Jewish shops clustered around Kraków Square that was to be their soldierly reward. Tenenbaum caught their mood from the phrase, perhaps oft-repeated, "we're going into the land of Eden."[67] A thirty-six-year-old woman, member of a family owning a "big clothing warehouse" supplying – among other things – army uniforms, saved herself by convincing pogromists she was "poor housemaid and Pole." She testified that some thirty Polish soldiers, speaking in "West Galician dialect" and accompanied by a Polish Red Cross sister, burst into her familial apartment, crying "give us gold, silver, diamonds, millions." Thus did Jewish El Dorado appear to such plunderers (and murderers, for they killed the witness's sister). "The Red Cross woman," she added, "kept shouting 'shoot.'"[68]

Moses Weinreb observed legionnaire looters, led by a lieutenant. "Next to him stood a bugler, who gave signals." A merchant recalled that at 5:00 AM on pogrom's first morning, "I heard harmonica playing while [soldiers] pounded on the door."[69] A temple servant remembered an officer who searched a synagogue for evidence that Jews fired from it on Polish troops. "The officer struck a brutal pose. He had a cigar in his teeth and whistled a popular tune."[70] Still more sinister musical notes resounded next day, when soldiers, having plundered a Jewish family and killed the father, repaired to the landlady's apartment. There, as the victim's sister testified, "the murderer played piano very expertly for about an hour and a half, while his comrades danced. The murderer was thus a member of the intelligentsia from better circles, since I'm a pianist and must characterize his playing as very good."[71]

That the pogrom displayed, in Polish participants' and observers' minds, the character of public drama emerges from a Jewish lawyer's recollection that as he was walking on Saturday morning near Lwów's Jesuit Garden, he observed at its entrance "an elegantly dressed gentlemen wearing the town militia's armband and shouldering a gun. He spoke to the crowd that was standing about: 'why are you strolling here? You should go to Kraków Square, where a performance is being given free of charge.' Someone asked, 'has the spectacle already begun?' The guardian of order replied, 'it has begun and it will go on.'"[72]

Zionist Max Reiner, Galician-born Viennese journalist who found himself trapped in Lwów, having first looked in the mirror to assure himself that his "physiognomy" did not brand him as "suspicious," ventured "with beating heart" onto the street on Saturday morning. He

[67] Bendow, *Judenpogrom*, 30.   [68] Ibid., 155 (protocol 363).
[69] Ibid., 143 (protocol 114). CZA. Z3/181 (December 10, 1918).
[70] Ibid., 160 (protocol 265).   [71] Ibid., 158 (protocol 265).   [72] Ibid., 91 (protocol 56).

encountered "an elegant lady" handing out pastries to the Poles' libera-
tors, asking them "will there now be pogrom?" Into a barber shop, where
he was having his (seemingly telltale) moustache shaved off, a young
woman happily burst with two bottles of wine, given her by soldierly
liquor-shop plunderers. "And now I'm going to see what else there is to
be fetched."

Looting occurred as street comedy. Moustache-shorn Reiner
watched a furrier's shop's plunder. Soldiers threw precious goods
into the street

and in a flash ladies of working-class suburbs and the population of Łyczaków
district, which houses notorious street people [Plattenbrüder] and Rowdies, were
scrambling for them. Washerwomen and housekeepers threw off their shawls and
padded work coats and wrapped themselves in Persian lamb and seal jackets.

Nearby, "high-class gentlemen and society ladies watched these scenes
and laughed."[73] A female plaintiff, having accosted a woman dressed in
clothes looted from her shop, followed her into a barracks, where she
found "many legionnaires running about in furs robbed from her." In
response to her demand for return of the goods, legionnaires threatened
to shoot her, advising the female plunderer, if the plaintiff further harassed her, "to stone her."[74]

Another witness saw how "some civilians, foremost among them lame
'Edek,' a knacker's apprentice" – lowly outcast – identified Jewish-
owned businesses to civilian militiamen. Joined by some sixty soldiers,
they threw themselves into plundering. "Then the rabble arrived, and
among them many ladies with elegant hats, veils, and gloves. The
legionnaires fetched packages from the shops, each" – in a show of
Polish gallantry – "giving one to his lady."[75] A third plaintiff, a young
female bank clerk, told of her family's apartment house's soldierly sacking. Apart from her own painful loss of a rich bridal trousseau, "which
when acquired cost 5,000 Kr. but now is not to be had," the plunderers
tore away her mother's blouse, discovering 300 Kr. hidden there, whereupon they rifle butted her, demanding more money or they would
"shoot her like a dog." They pocketed the family's 8,000 Kr. "hidden
in the linen" and took three men's suits and four pairs of boots. "The
first three were very well-educated [intelligente] young legionnaires," but
the others were "less intelligent." Among her building's robbers her
uncle "recognized a [gymnasium] professor, who was very happy, and

[73] CZA. Z3/179: handwritten copy of article published November 26, 1918 in Neue Freie
Presse, Vienna.
[74] Bendow, Judenpogrom, 62 (protocol 479).   [75] Ibid., 144 (protocol 114).

who said: my boys too [his students] have already got enough, they've stuffed their pockets full."[76]

The carnival tradition warranted sexual license, which in pogrom's brutalized script often meant rape. Eyewitnesses were lacking, but Tenenbaum reported that as army reinforcements – the *Krakusy* – arrived on pogrom's eve, local irregular soldiers sang out: "Here comes General Roja with his boys, the Jews will be having a wedding" – they would be deflowered.[77] About the pogrom itself, he wrote that "women had to disrobe and stand naked, to the crude mob's delight. Lawyers' wives were treated like whores, university attendees grossly besmirched, their womanly dignity shamelessly trampled on."[78]

An eyewitness told how soldiers came across several girls in a house they were plundering. One said, "It's a shame to murder these girls. It's better to 'cuddle' them [*liebkosen*], whereupon soldiers threw themselves on the girls, to make them do their bidding." A young woman who refused was hit in the face. "They had, under threat of death, to kiss and cuddle with the soldiers."[79] Here was semimock violation of the taboo, normatively embraced by both ethnoreligious sides, against sexual intimacy. A Jewish lawyer asked a group of "elegant gentlemen" if the streets were clear. They told him, taking him for a Pole, "you may safely go ahead. The Ukrainians are gone and along with them 'the neutrals.' Now we're going to flirt with Jews," which Tenenbaum translated using a word (*anbandeln*) meaning both to flirt and start a real fight.[80]

Other scenes cruelly dramatized carnavalesque social reversals. A Jewish lawyer suffered maltreatment recalling attorney Levin's fate when five armed youths burst into his apartment at 1:00 AM, dragging him and his family from their beds and stealing, "apart from a fur, a large sum of money, which the lawyer was obliged to hand them on his knees."[81] Humiliations were staged, such as when the army, in pogrom's aftermath, seized Jewish gymnasium students on the streets for compulsory labor, including two "who were ordered to wash the floors" at a command post, "where pranks were played with them and they were forced to jump over tables." The Jewish Rescue Committee lodged another complaint about the army's "rounding up of Jewish intelligentsia and their assignment to the lowest kinds of work, such as stuffing straw sacks and cleaning latrines." Thus did nationalists ritually castigate Jews for their lack of Polish military exaltation. A Jewish merchant, brazenly robbed, protested to a higher

---

[76] CZA. Z3/181: deposition dated 28.XI.1918. Cf. Bendow, *Judenpogrom*, 91 (protocol 78).
[77] Bendow, *Judenpogrom*, 31.   [78] Ibid., 35.   [79] Ibid., 50 (protocol 425).
[80] Ibid., 91 (protocol 56).   [81] CZA. Z3/179 (November 26, 1918).

officer, who replied, "I have stopped being first lieutenant for you Jews. For you I am hangman."[82]

Many Poles entered the charred and plundered Jewish district on Monday, after martial law's imposition ended violence and tumults. Of them Reiner wrote bitterly that they "streamed in as to a festival scene, to survey their handiwork," even as corpses still lay in the streets.[83] Elias Nacht, another observer, told of seeing "a mob thirsting for lynching leading Jews through the streets in chains" and of "Poles' enthusiasm, streaming to the resting place of thousands [*sic*] of innocent victims like pilgrims to a holy shrine."[84] Doubtless such language reflected rhetorical choice, yet this was a time of numerous mass meetings, marches, and demonstrations on all sides. Reiner had witnessed, when Lwów's Jews resolved on neutrality in imminent Polish-Ukrainian fighting,

a great [Jewish] parade, thousands of persons, among them hundreds of Jewish officers and soldiers in uniform, moving from the theater through the city's main streets. Zionists celebrated this as a holiday. Tapestries and blue-white pennants hung from many windows, everywhere Herzl pictures were displayed. Men and women had pinned blue-white cocards on their hats, coats, and blouses.[85]

As they plundered and wounded, pogromists moved within a self-chosen framework of symbolic action that, in carnavalesque form, gave expression to a collective sense of celebration, triumph, cruel playfulness, and joy at Jews' dispossession, humiliation, and even murder. Such behavior we encountered earlier. How was it understood by perpetrators as justifiable or righteous? What moral economy sanctioned such ethical calculus?

The answer lies partly in pogromists' self-understanding as Christians and in the conviction that Jews *owed* them the goods (and even, at times, the lives) of which, by moral right, they were being dispossessed. Before the pogrom, Tenenbaum reported, "a Polish city functionary consoled those assembled before a shop: 'a few days' patience, people [*Kinder*]. As soon as we get to Kraków Square we'll take everything from the Jews and the poor children of Christ will have all in abundance.'"[86] Later, on Christmas eve 1918, Poles seized a Jewish candle dealer's stock "and distributed it among the Christian population."[87] A Jewish merchant reported that on pogrom Saturday, "financial official Zieliński" burst with son into his family quarters, exclaiming "now it's the Last Judgment for you, today you'll lose your heads."[88]

[82] Bendow, *Judenpogrom*, 147 (protocol 147).   [83] Reiner, 22.
[84] "Das Blutbad in Lemberg," *Allgemeine Zeitung des Judenthums*, no. 46, (December 14, 1919).
[85] Reiner, 4.   [86] Bendow, *Judenpogrom*, 31.   [87] Ibid., 119.
[88] Ibid., 91 (protocol 229); 114, 156 (protocol 363).

Jewish victims sometimes appealed to their tormentors' Christian sentiments. A girl successfully pleaded with her father's soldierly murderers not to kill her mother too, saying "the Mother of God would have taken mercy on us, but you don't." A soldier, "visibly moved, said to [the killer]: 'come, Jasiek, let's get out of here.'"[89] A less fortunate girl, fourteen years old, "with folded hands knelt before the sergeant," whom the above-mentioned Red Cross sister was urging to use his gun "and received a [fatal] shot through the mouth."[90]

Christian self-righteousness found expression in brutal street theater desacralizing and destroying Jews (whether symbolically or actually) in their specifically religious identity and holy sites. Common to pogroms were scenes such as that in Lwów on December 26, 1918, in which, led by a corporal, "legionnaires seized whiskered Jews, tugging them by their beards into Ziółkiewska Lane barracks where, to the rabble's delight, they were made to dance."[91] Probably most Poles knew that dancing figured in Hasidic and other Jewish ritual. A journalist reported that during the pogrom, soldiers drunkenly attempted to sever an elderly man's ear locks with their bayonets. When he resisted, a sergeant shot him dead and robbed the corpse. A synagogue keeper (*szames*) testified that two bodies lay bullet ridden before his building, both of young Jewish butchers' assistants, who seemingly had sought to defend it against fire. Hochberg, candy seller, died of a bayonet wound suffered as he tried, together with Stern (also murdered) and sons, to rescue the Torah roll from the main synagogue.[92]

Post-pogrom, soldiers halted Jewish funeral processions and opened caskets, ostensibly seeking weapons but treasure hunting too. At the Jewish cemetery, new graves remained undug because soldiers commandeered workers to open older graves and crypts in further arms hunts. Soldiers tore up the floor of the hall in which pogrom victims' corpses lay awaiting burial. They "meticulously" searched hearses returning empty from the cemetery. The not uncritical Israel Cohen accepted that numerous such incidents occurred in Lwów, including soldiers' opening graves of thirty pogrom victims, ending their work "by flinging mud upon the desecrated dead."[93]

Physical assaults on synagogues and their sacred paraphernalia packed murderous symbolic charge. The profanation they worked on Judaism stripped it in anti-Jewish minds of magical aura and spiritual legitimacy. In Lwów, pogromists torched two synagogues, one a historic

---

[89] Ibid., 168 (protocol 265).   [90] Ibid., 156 (protocol 363).   [91] Ibid., 116.
[92] Reiner; CAHJP. HM2/8299.11: fr. 86, 117.
[93] Bendow, *Judenpogrom*, 121–22; CZA. L6/119: Cohen, "The Pogroms in Poland," 42.

seventeenth-century structure and the other the "progressive temple." An eyewitness reported that "at the Great Synagogue I saw legionnaires hacking at the Torah roll with sabers" – sublimated human slaughter – "while Christian women wore the *Projches* [Torah cabinet veil] on their heads." At the progressive temple, "the officers led the action, playing clowns with *Procheth* on their heads."[94]

On pogroms' margins, even when staged within culturally defined boundaries, there stalked, in many minds and perhaps in wide social consciousness, phantasms of mass murder. Why this was so is a question that leads beyond Polish mentalities to the problem of Jewish presence and absence in Christendom's historically evolving self-understanding. The Lwów evidence reveals that many perpetrators and onlookers readily transformed discrete instances of violence into metaphors of comprehensive Jewish death. There are no signs that the genocidal shadows hovering around the Lwów pogrom arose from print-antisemitism's ideological intoxication.

The idea, whether dreaded or embraced, of death effacing whole cultures seems to flow, when it shows itself, from an apocalyptic or millenialist imagination (or potentiality) in Christian civilization and humanity in general.[95] In Lwów, as elsewhere in the Polish–Eastern European borderlands, Poles, fearing subordination to Ukrainian rule or a bloodier fate, could imagine themselves, however exaggeratedly, as having escaped a kind of collective mortal threat. On deliverance from such a menace, the wish to inflict crushing punishment on Jews quickened among some pogromists and sympathizers, whose aggressions toward Ukrainians faced the obstacle that bloody counterreprisals against the scattered East Galician Poles were certain.

Some pogromists succumbed to visceral murderous impulses. Stella Agid, twenty-four-year-old schoolteacher, reported to Bronisław Wisznicki, public prosecutor assigned to the Governmental Investigative Commission on the Lwów pogrom, how four army patrols stormed into her apartment. "The fourth was most ruthless: they robbed and destroyed everything, and one of the soldiers gave the impression of an enraged wild animal. Bloody, sweaty, with a broken rifle, he ran about shouting that he had to kill a Jew." Agid escaped with other women to a neighboring apartment house by climbing down a ladder. "But my husband Moses Agid, an older person, couldn't risk taking this route," and the enraged soldier murdered him with four bullets. Antonina Piątek,

[94] Bendow, *Judenpogrom*, 42, 146 (protocol 114).
[95] See, alongside previously cited broad-gauged studies, John R. Hall, *Apocalypse: From Antiquity to the Empire of Modernity* (Cambridge: Polity Press, 2009).

nineteen, witnessed the shooting and recalled that "before the murder, that person ran about the whole apartment, shouting that he had to kill one of the Jews, no matter who. After the murder, when one of the soldiers condemned him, saying he'd killed an innocent human being, he kicked the dead man and left the room."[96]

What possessed this murderer he may not himself have known, or known how to express. His action's message, like that of many other killings, is befogged. Conversely, other murders reflected one-dimensional banality, cynicism, and greed. An eyewitness saw a young legionnaire demand money from a female passer-by. She surrendered "a packet of money concealed in her bosom." Demanding more, he and another soldier threw her to the ground, discovering money in her stocking. As she struggled to keep it, "she was killed with a bayonet." Plunderers, having shot a man, remarked, "So, dad, you're still shouting. I'll give you another bullet, you whore's son."[97]

Jetta Donner, merchant Chaim Sender's twenty-nine-year-old widow, told Investigative Commission Director Rymowicz how she and her husband fled their apartment to take refuge with her sister. Returning, they met neighbor Ludwik Ciesiak, "a troublemaker [bosiak] who constantly quarreled with my husband." She added that Ciesiak "also speaks fluent Yiddish." Ciesiak again picked a fight, "threatening [Sender] by saying, 'you just wait, I'll show you where Poles stand.'" Later Ciesiak appeared in their apartment with soldiers, to whom he said, pointing to Sender, "that's the one." Sender's body turned up twelve days later, pierced by six bullets, among corpses at the execution grounds. Jetta lamented, "my husband had 1,000 Kr. on him, all our assets. This money disappeared, and so did the shoes he was wearing . . . From malice an innocent man was murdered." She added that "Ciesiak also used prostitute Halke Lang to threaten me. She said people told her that Ciesiak boasted that 'he treated Donner to some good plums.'" Though Ciesiak dressed his denunciation of Sender in nationalist colors, theft and malevolence were evidently his guiding stars. Command of Yiddish – and the emotional-psychological intimacy it conveyed – left him cold to Jewish victims.[98]

More typical was violence justified by lurid or fantastic charges of Jewish misdeeds and aggression. Among these Tenenbaum listed selling poisoned candy and cigarettes, giving millions to Ukrainians, and causing – together with "their Kaiser" – the war.[99] A Jewish robbery victim went to the army command post to file a complaint but was told, "it's right

[96] CAHJP, microfilm HM2/8299.11, frame 81.
[97] CZA. Z3/179 (November 27, 1918); Bendow, *Judenpogrom*, 158 (protocol 265).
[98] CAHJP, HM2/8299.11, frames 76/76od.   [99] Bendow, *Judenpogrom*, 101–2.

what's happening to you. People have to rob the Jews. You Jews robbed long enough, now it's time you were plundered."[100] Such comments were legion. But the "main legend," Tenenbaum wrote, "that never fell silent and like a thousand-headed hydra, though once slain, came back to life," condemned Jews for firing on Poles. This violated deep-seated insistence in Polish popular culture that Jews remain passive, powerless, and defenseless – reflecting a similar pattern in the segregationist US south, where black self-defense provoked lynchings. This was, seemingly, a condition Christian popular culture imposed on Jewish life to balance or neutralize the perceived power, both material and magical, Jews wielded in Poles' midst.

So serious were charges of furtive Jewish shooting and arms stockpiling that Dr. Waschitz took part as Jewish Rescue Committee representative in the civilian city militia's search of the Jewish quarter for arms caches. Present were some forty militiamen "from the best Polish social circles (lawyers, senior judges, etc.)" and many policemen under their commissioner. For three hours they combed a passage formed by three intersecting streets, but "nowhere was any trace of weapons or ammunition found."[101]

The provocation Jewish self-defense posed appears in testimony of a Jewish typist in an engineering firm. She told how a colleague excitedly exclaimed to "assembled villagers and [prisoner-of-war] Italians" – seemingly the firm's workers – that "we have to arm ourselves. I saw a Jewish boy with a gun." Later, when she questioned his vehemence, he said "the Jews are siding now with Ukrainians, and then they'll go with us, but we'll drive them away like dogs." During the pogrom, soldiers killed this same witness's brother in his apartment, even though he protested that he and his family should be spared, since he had just returned as Austrian POW from Russian captivity and was still wearing his military trousers. "We kissed the murderer's hands and fell at his feet, but he pushed us away, saying 'it's a shame to leave such a strong man alive, we have to kill him.'"[102]

A higher level of anxiety over imagined Jewish malevolence emerges from the Investigative Commission's interrogation of a market saleswoman, who was thought to have witnessed "a legionnaire's murder by Jews, who plucked out his eye." She admitted only hearing it from others but that both eyes were "dug out."[103] A female apartment house supervisor warned soldiers breaking through defenses behind which

---

[100] Ibid., 76 (protocol 253); cf. 77.
[101] CZA. Z3/181, Deposition 6 (December 6, 1918).
[102] Bendow, *Judenpogrom*, 159 (protocol 265).
[103] CAHJP. HM2/8299.11:53, frames 103/103od.

neighboring Jews had barricaded themselves that "here live nothing but brutes [*Hamans*], who rob, steal, and shoot at the legionnaires." In this bold psychoprojection, Jews became their own arch persecutor in the Book of Esther and Purim Theater, the Persian Haman, who sought their mass murder, a fate now imagined to threaten the Poles.[104] A family father told how soldiers stormed into his apartment at 3:00 AM. The commanding lieutenant ordered the victims shot, stipulating that "these disgusting Jews [*Rotzjuden*] are only worth one bullet." Rescinding death threats, soldiers drove the sons into the street, telling late-night passers-by and other legionnaires, "'these Jews wanted to kill us with axes,' whereupon everyone starting beating our children."[105]

An apartment house owner, hoping to save her burning building, begged a Polish firefighter "on my knees for rescue, offering him whatever payment he wanted. But he replied: 'We have orders not to save any Jewish houses. You Jews demanded 20 Kr. for a loaf of bread, and now you're getting pay-back.'"[106] Such willful destruction of Jewish property, apart from any theft motive, represented symbolic violence against Jews themselves. A female medical student said of soldiers' repeated plunder of her family's dwelling: "what they couldn't carry off in sacks they maliciously demolished like Vandals, with unbelievable fury, venting hatred of Jews."[107] As for avenging perceived Jewish misdeeds in violence's coin, this extended beyond property damage to physical injury. Before murdering the above-mentioned Jewish veteran returned home from Russian captivity, his killer told him (equating money lending with murder): "you people killed three legionnaires, and in return we're taking out a loan of 300 Jews."[108]

Pogrom fire, like premodern stake burning of heretics, consumed many lives. One witness recalled that army officials told a Jewish family alarmed by the spread of fighting-ignited fire, "we don't have any time for you," adding that "anyway, Jews can burn for the Polish cause" – burn to death if they wouldn't burn with zeal.[109] A fireman dismissed a woman's plea for help, saying "let Jews warm themselves up."[110]

Witnesses told of soldiers' and other pogromists' efforts to enclose Jews in burning buildings or prevent their escape.[111] Pogromists thrust a passer-by into a burning apartment house and forced a woman with two children into a burning prayer house.[112] An eyewitness recounted how some seventy Jews took refuge in a prayer house. Marauding soldiers

---

[104] Bendow, *Judenpogrom*, 112.   [105] Ibid., 150 (protocol 268).
[106] CZA. Z3/181, deposition 8 (December 3, 1918).
[107] Bendow, *Judenpogrom*, 151 (protocol 475).   [108] Ibid., 158 (protocol 265).
[109] Ibid., 139 (protocol 69).   [110] Ibid., 49 (protocol 725).
[111] CZA. Z3/18, deposition 2 (January 2, 1919).   [112] Bendow, *Judenpogrom*, 49, 81.

discovered them and demanded 2,000 Kr., but the poverty-stricken group possessed only a few hundred. The soldiers erected a gallows and announced that executions would begin.

As distraught victims began lamenting and pleading to be shot rather than hanged, Polish killer-thugs [*Mordbuben*] carried holy scriptures and Talmudic books to the middle of the room, piled them up and set them all aflame. They then left the synagogue, locking the door from the outside. Only thanks to the existence of a concealed passage through the wall, unsuspected by the legionnaires, could these people, condemned to death by fire, save their lives.

The heretic-burning scenario displayed carnavalesque elements in allusions to cooking of food.[113] Tenenbaum reported several "stereotyped answers" that pogromists gave Jews threatened by fire. "One heard the Polish crowd rejoicing: 'now they're getting roasted.'" Soldiers chanted, "let the Jews fry, there'll be Jewish bacon."[114] In this macabre vision, Jews would vanish, transformed by fire into prized, eminently Gentile food.

Such deathly theater was prologue to imagined aggression's last act against Jews, portending banishment or even systematic murder. Some pogrom scripts, even only of plunder, entailed murder or its threat, such as when thieving soldiers chased a woman from her apartment with the executioner's words, "lay down your head, Jew."[115] One victim reported that officers and soldiers stripping him of his possessions "shouted, 'There are too many of you Jews here. Go to Palestine or we'll wipe you all out.'"[116] A shop clerk told another that Jews "should go to Palestine, where they would get bread" and that "we have nothing for Jews."[117] A woman reported seeing troops escorting Jewish militiamen taken prisoner, including one who was wounded. A Christian monk cried out, "it's a shame to waste time with them. It'd be better to mow them down right away."[118] Tenenbaum heard of an incident in which "an officer, exclaiming 'what's the sense in keeping the Jewish brood alive,' proceeded to bash in [an] infant's skull."[119] An eyewitness told of a young officer who "seized a four-week-old infant lying in its cradle by the legs, twirled it around a few times with the intention of hurling it to the ground. He asked the mother, 'What are you doing with so many Jewish bastards?'" She rescued the child "only with greatest effort."[120]

These words, as was typical of such scripts, concealed Polish aggression behind rhetoric of Jewish guilt. Other such threats issued from hearts choked with wartime hatred. The above-mentioned father, whose sons a

---

[113] Ibid., 152 (protocol 475).   [114] Ibid., 39–40.

[115] CZA. Z3/181, Deposition 8 (December 3, 1918).   [116] Bendow, *Judenpogrom*, 120.

[117] Ibid., 46 (protocol 28).   [118] Ibid., 24 (protocol 674).   [119] Ibid., 35.

[120] Ibid., 46 (protocol 28).

street crowd pummeled, reported how soldiers then forcibly joined his boys to a column of Ukrainian, German, and Jewish captives. A military escort marched them through the streets, "where the Polish public dealt them continual blows. Elegant ladies, who themselves didn't strike out, exclaimed 'Away with the Jews! Hang them! Slaughter them! Shoot them down!'" When the father later sought his sons' release from military custody, an officer threatened to shoot him, while "other officers called out 'for Prussians a bullet, for Jews a noose.'"[121]

Thoughts of mass murder hung in the air even before pogrom erupted. A Jewish witness reported that a cavalry captain told him it was good he lived outside the Jewish quarter "because slaughter of Jews is approaching."[122] Another described how he and his family left the Jewish quarter to buy food in a government-controlled shop. "Standing in line," seemingly unrecognized, "we heard things that chilled us: 'the Jews, that pack of Jews, they're to blame for everything, these lepers [another ancient memory] ... just wait until we conquer the city, not one of them will escape alive,' and many other similar statements." Another Jewish family found itself caught in its apartment between Polish and Ukrainian fire. Poles captured the apartment building, and their captain "laughed grimly" at the family father, saying "'So, now we'll blow this house in the air with our cannons. Why did you give the Ukrainians signals, and shoot from your windows at us?' And the soldiers cried out, 'we don't want, we don't need any Jews. Let them all disappear. What good are these traitors. We'll show them, we'll murder them all.'"[123]

During the pogrom, legionnaires burst into a Jewish merchant's dwelling, led by city gasworks employee Banderowski and followed by "a crowd of men and women." They shouted: "we'll shoot you all, we'll burn the house down ... You stood with the Ukrainians, you shot at us." Other soldiers delivered Banderowski to an official for interrogation, at which the plundered merchant was present. He heard Banderowski say that authorities had permitted forty-eight hours of robbery and that Jews had suffered too little for opposing the Polish army and pouring boiling water on soldiers. For this "they will now all be slaughtered." Though the merchant thought Banderowski had been condemned to death, he later met him on the street. Banderowski "sought to excuse his robbery," saying he was under military orders at the time and that if the merchant needed anything, "he would gladly be of service."[124]

---

[121] Ibid., 150 (protocol 268).   [122] Ibid., 57 (protocol 705).
[123] Ibid., 139 (protocol 69).   [124] Ibid., 149 (protocol 147).

Teresa Stadler reported to the Investigative Commission that, among the three fighters who robbed her was trader Stanisław Boni, twenty-three, one of a poor tailor's six sons. The commission confronted Boni with Stadler. "The injured party bore witness, looking into Boni's eyes, that she recognized him as the robbery's third perpetrator, and repeated [her original charge] that even though she appealed to him, as someone she knew by sight, for rescue, he had replied: 'it's an order [to rob her] and after that they're going to shoot you all!'"[125]

All such assertions that Jews would suffer or die because of culpable actions during Polish-Ukrainian hostilities were political in inspiration and, given their basis in generalizations about Jews as undifferentiated community, obviously Judeophobic or ideologically antisemitic. A woman witnessed three soldiers storming a neighbor's apartment. The band included, as occurred in other cases, the apartment house manager's son (such people knew tenants well). "Replying to the plundered victims' plea for mercy, one of the robbers declared in a Kraków accent: We don't need any Jews. Why are they living in this world? We'll slaughter you all. We didn't come here from Kraków for nothing."[126]

Army command's martial law proclamation charged Jewish militiamen with "treacherously" resisting – with guns, stones, and boiling water – Poles' "victorious advance." Nevertheless, "Polish army command is suppressing the Polish population's and army's spontaneous [anti-Jewish] outburst." Everyone, including Jews, stands under "law's protection."

Responsibility rests on the Jewish population in general, however, to exert a moderating influence on that fraction among their co-religionists that has not yet ceased to act as if they were determined to bring an *incalculable catastrophe* upon the whole Jewish population. [The command counted on Jews, in their own interest,] to restrain co-religionists from outbursts of hatred against the Polish government and, by correct and loyal behavior, to enable authorities *and the rest of the Polish population* to introduce and uphold order based on right and law.[127]

Like many other pronouncements about pogroms, issued both by officials and political parties, this one cold-bloodedly and terrifyingly threatened Jews with "incalculable catastrophe" even as it denounced the violence, imagined   stereotypically   as   common   people's   righteous   and

[125] CAHJP: HM2/8299.11, frames 59–61 (November 22, 1918).
[126] CZA. Z3/181, Deposition 7 (December 3, 1918).
[127] CZA. L6/114. German text, released by the Polish Press Bureau in Bern. While Chasanowitsch, Jerzy Tomaszewski, and this version differ in dating the proclamation of martial law, it is clear that the pillage did not end before Monday, November 24. (Author's emphasis).

uncontrollable fury at Jews' alleged disloyalty and hate. The psychological projection such documents revealed was invisible to their authors.

Of martial law, Reiner wrote: "at once calm descended." Not one Pole expressed disgust at the pogrom, but rather all found punishment of Jewish neutrality "self-evident." The local Polish press was silent or wrote cursorily of bandit plunder. Crowds streamed into the Jewish quarter even as those corpses still lay in the streets that had not yet been gathered in the "big halls, where entry was forbidden." Authorities arrested leading Lwów Zionists, holding them in pogrom's aftermath as hostages. It was convenient that, in June 1919, the judiciary was able to charge a picture-perfect Ukrainian habitual criminal and prison escapee, his named Polonized as Wawrzyniec Zahorski, with robbing Jewish housewife Sala Poch. He was already serving his second long prison sentence for robbery and had also sat behind bars three times for habitual drunkenness, nine times for begging – he lacked a leg – and six times for vagrancy. He had been banished from Lwów but returned. He was ideal pogromist "scum."[128]

In December 1918 an obscure populist organization styling itself "Red Guard" composed two threatening letters and posted them to the Jewish Rescue Committee. Having intercepted them, military censorship delivered them to the addressees. They expressed wounded feelings about imagined Jewish power and well-being which, in many minds, it was pogrom violence's purpose to "turn upside down." One letter (in German translation) warned that

the Red Guard Committee demands you leave Lwów free of Jews by New Year's. And all your grand gentlemen can travel with you to Palestine. Leave! All your assets will be devoted to rebuilding Galicia, for without your millions, without your Kaiser with his Jewish mistresses, no such misfortune as now prevails would have come into the world.

The second letter decreed that

you may take nothing with you. You have caused the present universal misfortune [Weltunglück]. By New Year's Lwów must be free of Jews. Your baggage may consist of only a small package. In all of East and West Galicia blood boils for revenge for the long years of the Christian population's exploitation. A pogrom against the Jews must result, come what may. Let all the burghers, merchants, lawyers and doctors go buy land in Palestine.[129]

---

[128] CZA. Z3/180. "Die Pogrome in Lemberg," 22; CAHJP. HM2/8299.11.
[129] Bendow, *Judenpogrom*, 122–23.

Striking, apart from desire to reduce Jewish property to "small packages," is these letters' invocation of "misfortune" and "universal misfortune," of which the nation as a whole had, in these unsophisticated eyes, been victim until war's end and Lwów's reconquest. These statements conjure up the moral economy many November pogromists acted on: Polish suffering warranted pogroms and Jews' banishment from city and land. It was a worldview that was political in moral-absolutist rather than a party-program sense. Pogromists acting on such feelings had few or no words for state and officialdom, conceiving themselves instead as executors of a righteous people's will.[130]

[130] On traditions of populist subordination of pragmatic politics to sweeping moral-religious-ideological visions, see Thomas Simons, *Eastern Europe in the Postwar World* (New York, NY: St. Martin's Press, 1993), chaps. 1 and 2; George Schöpflin, *Politics in Eastern Europe, 1945–1992* (Oxford: Blackwell, 1993).

4   Reading the November Pogroms
Rage, Shame, Denial, Denunciation

This chapter is an echo chamber for voices raised on all sides – Jewish, Polish, Western European – lamenting, excusing, denouncing, explaining, and apologizing for the November pogroms in Lwów and West Galicia. It listens to politically variegated Jewish reflections on the pogroms' messages and implications. It pauses in this book's exploration of grassroots ethnoreligious violence to look more sustainedly into the ideas and emotions driving Poland's contentious political parties' approach to the Christian-Jewish relationship. It asks, how perceptively did the interpreters of this tragedy understand their own roles, and also, what shapes can we make out in the unexamined depths of their responses to the violence? For Poles, facing foreign – if not also their own – condemnation of the pogroms, national self-confidence was painfully at risk.

Aftermath in Lwów and in the Jewish Press

Weeks passed during which silence over the Lwów tragedy's extent, or its minimization, prevailed on the Polish side, while Jewish reports tended toward exaggeration. Berlin's Zionist Office telegrammed World Zionist Organization President Chaim Weizmann and journalist Nahum Sokolow in London. Citing Max Reiner's reportage – "absolutely reliable personality" – they reckoned the pogrom consumed 1,100 Jewish lives, including those burned alive in a besieged synagogue. "Polish population very satisfied at pogroms' ladies and gentlemen walking through streets like French gentry day after Saint Bartholomy night [1572] to enjoy gruesome spectacle." British leaders alone could "secure an intervention which would prevent entire extermination [of] Jews [in] Galicia [and] prevention of pogroms against Jews must no less than those against Armenians be international concern." Sokolow replied, chiding them for "journalistic exaggeration," which provoked "suspicion" in official circles. He wanted Warsaw Zionists to report on pogrom losses but added that the British government publicly commented on Polish pogroms "most satisfactorily."[1]

Sokolow's reservations were borne out by a Reuters News Agency–generated report published in the March 1919 British *Jewish Chronicle* summarizing "Allied Inquiry Reports." Not 500, but thirty-five deaths had been confirmed, with thirty more under investigation. Poorer Poles resented Jews "because during the war the Jews had been entrusted by the Austrians with large contracts, which enabled them to procure great quantities of provisions. The belief was that they sold these in an illicit manner at enormous profiteering rates." In Lwów, food became scarce, and "the rougher elements and criminals started desultory pillaging." Jewish militia opposing this were drawn into cooperation with Ukrainians, who thanked them publicly, leading Poles to believe Jews had broken neutrality. Though Jews claimed Polish officers led the plunderers, no actual case of this had, allegedly, been proven. "The disorders were undoubtedly serious, but they took place in a city demoralised by three weeks of fighting and having no police or properly constituted government. The accounts of the pogroms published in the Press are gross exaggerations and are condemned by the Jews themselves." Such deflating reports, unattributable to Polonophile subterfuges, clouded Western opinion.[2]

Lwów's Polish Socialist Workers Council promptly denounced on November 24 "the raging *soldateska*'s violence," albeit "Jewish nationalists did not comport themselves at the most difficult hour as we had right to expect." But that was not ordinary Jews' fault, and socialists would not be moved "to any acts of violence and terror, of which the civilized Polish people are unworthy."[3] In Warsaw on Hanukkah Sabbath, November 30, mourning ceremonies took place in synagogues, during which labor Zionists and other leftists branded pogroms the work of "black Polish reaction." They did not believe that "the politically conscious Polish proletariat's hands were spattered with our blood" and expected them to protest "this bloody carnage which with its horrors recalls medieval times."[4]

The nascent state's Minister-President Jędrzej Moraczewski (PPS) – who had publicly exhorted to anti-Jewish plunder in June 1918 – now officially condemned "most sharply" anti-Jewish violence, adding, formulaically, that Jews must remember duties as well as rights and "therefore avoid anything that might elicit embitterment in the Polish

---

[1] CZA. Z3/179 (November 29, 1918).
[2] CZA. L6/114: *The Jewish Chronicle*, March 14, 1919.
[3] Chasanowitsch, *Judenpogrome*, 75.
[4] CZA. Z3/180: *Nowy Dziennik*, no. 147 (December 5, 1918).

population."[5] A Socialist Foreign Ministry spokesman observed that "among Jews there are some irresponsible Bolshevik agitators who spark anti-Jewish attitudes. The passion-driven crowd does not know how to distinguish among the various categories of Jews." PPS leader Feliks Daszyński, in a December Kraków speech, faulted Jews for not having assimilated – "polonized themselves" – during their centuries in Poland, for staying enclosed in their ghetto, distinctive by dress, custom, and language. "A few hundred years ago Kraków was practically a German city, but we absorbed them long ago and their descendants today are excellent Poles." Jews were not only numerous – 13 percent of the whole population – but also heavily stamped urban life.

Imagine how in English or American cities such a compact foreign stratum would be viewed. Would people there like them? Would they entrust them with public office if they maintained their separateness and spoke a foreign language? Nor can we bear this. As long as they say that the Polish language doesn't concern them, as long as they occupy in such large numbers our towns, let no one be surprised that the nation and state cannot trust them and invest them with vital functions ... So long as things are not equal, there will always be Jew on one side, "goy" on the other. But this does not justify the pogroms for one moment. Everyone must condemn them as barbarism, as something that lowers us in the world's eyes.[6]

Daszyński's words well express secular-minded Poles' resentment at Jewish separateness, viewed less as religious self-segregation than as behavior of a foreign nationality living in their midst, just as the presence of non-Polish-speaking Germans or other ethnicities seemed unacceptable.

---

[5] Moraczewski was a former left-wing socialist Reichsrat deputy and veteran legionnaire. In June 1918 he delivered in Jarosław an ultraradical speech before a thousand-strong crowd. The Austrian police reported that "he branded as scandalous and disgraceful the government and its rationing system, Jews, estate owners, rich gentlemen and officials in the prefect's office, and exhorted the crowd to self-help. In particular, he pointed out that the prefect himself and all Jews had concealed great grain reserves. [The people should] throw themselves on these bloodsuckers and settle accounts." Moraczewski encouraged women especially to fend for themselves, saying that they would face no punishment. Police and high-ranking officials intervened, ordering Moraczewski to cease speaking and dissolving the meeting. But he persisted, denouncing the "enormous abuses of public functionaries, whereupon the assembled crowd assumed a threatening posture, heaping insults and warnings on the civil and military authorities," who retreated from the park. The reporter "noticed how even officials applauded the deputy. As the crowd hoisted and carried him off in triumph, they cried 'long live Bolshevism, away with district officials and Jews and their helpers! Let's throw ourselves on these gentlemen!'" Such a speech was unvarnished incitement by a revolutionary leftist agitator to plunder state food magazines and Jewish shops and warehouses, though without antisemitic ideological framing. Mercantile Jews, in Moraczewski's vision, were class enemies, not religious or supernatural menaces. AVA. MdIP-G. Sign. 22. Fsz. 2119, No. 16443 (June 21, 1918).

[6] *Nowy Dziennik*, no. 168 (December 28, 1918), "Daszyński." Chasanowitsch, *Judenpogrome*, 81, 87.

Lwów's "Civic Women's Committee" advocated law and order despite Jewish "provocations" that scorned the "generous protection they found in Polish lands." Archbishop Józef Bilczewski's pastoral letter urging pacification remarked, in old-established anti-Judaic rhetoric, that "if the Jewish people [not individual Jews] has made itself guilty of anything, the heavenly and earthly court will pronounce the just verdict."[7]

The Warsaw-dispatched Extraordinary Governmental Investigative Commission, active in Lwów January–August 1919, took a worldlier view. It functioned as prosecutorial office, supplying police and courts with evidence of actionable crimes its agents collected from pogrom victims. No record survives of convictions obtained, which disappearance of suspects and unreliability or evasiveness of witnesses will have diminished, probably greatly. In its internal discourse, and that of Lwów's police, the events of November 22–23 often figured straightforwardly as "pogroms" or "Jewish pogroms," though the Warsaw government preferred "so-called pogroms."[8]

The commission directed police to investigate alleged crimes, notably murders, but also lesser offenses. Unidentified plaintiffs charged that two men suspected of pogrom crimes "were living much more affluently than before," though "fear of revenge" kept accusers from supplying more details. Police reported back that one suspect had been drafted into the army. "As for showy lifestyle, the charge is untrue, for both live in poverty."[9] The commission found that military depredations were occurring well before pogrom's outbreak, such as when on November 5 soldiers robbed a Jewish sausage maker of stock worth 12,000 Kronen, destroying his machinery with bullet fire.[10]

Reversals of testimony suggest that some victims feared reprisals. Apartment house dwellers gave 2,000 Kronen to a Christian fellow tenant who promised to recruit Polish guards but then absconded. Yet they declined to press charges but rather "were grateful to Filipowski for his disinterested protection."[11] Some plaintiffs fled the scene of their losses. A middle-aged shop owner, reporting robbery to soldiers, testified that "my daughter told me of this. I was not present at the robbery, but had hidden myself." Because the day was Shabbat, he would not sign.[12] Police methods favored old-fashioned eye-to-eye confrontation of plaintiff and defendant and corroboration by third parties, but often neither alleged suspect nor witness came forth.[13] Yet some charges were proven and

---

[7] Bendow, *Judenpogrom*, 82–83.
[8] CAHJP. HM2/8299.11. fr. 110 (January 30, 1919); HM2/8299.10. fr. 1 (January 4, 1919).
[9] CAHJP. HM2/8299.11. fr. 26–28.   [10] Ibid., fr. 30.   [11] Ibid., fr. 47–50.
[12] Ibid., fr. 58.   [13] For example, ibid., fr. 64–65.

imprisonment, if not restitution, gained, such as when two Christian workers who pledged to defend their bakery-owning employer turned coat and plundered him alongside soldiers, both then landing in jail.[14]

The Jewish Rescue Committee supplied the Investigative Commission with charges to pursue. A list of twenty-two unresolved cases from August 1919 highlighted the prominent place among suspects occupied by apartment house manager-supervisors (*dozorcy*) or their sons: seven among eleven with named occupations (alongside waiter, servant, street hawker, and army captain's son). An allegation that an apartment house supervisor absconded with Jewish property entrusted to him during the pogrom was not unique. Another faced murder charges.[15]

The country did suffer in Western eyes, but Lwów's Jews, who experienced November's pogrom as "immeasurable misfortune," could only dream of revenge while struggling to stay alive in its aftermath. On November 29, various political organizations joined in launching the self-professedly nonpartisan, bluntly named Jewish Committee to Aid Victims of Riots and Robbery or, informally, Jewish Rescue Committee. A year later it published a lengthy report on its far-flung emergency aid and charitable undertakings. It amounts to an official appraisal of the pogrom's devastating economic and public health effects by Lwów's Jewish leaders, principally assimilationists and Zionists, chief among them the kaleidoscopically named Dr. Tobias/Tobiasz Ashkenazy/Askenase/Aszkenazy.[16]

Jewish bitterness was profound:
> The unforgettable November days were but the beginning of a long chain of torments, agonies, and persecutions which Jewry here had to endure. Hatred in no wise justifiable gripped a large part of Polish society, whipped up by a significant branch of the Polish press. Hurling slanders, it awakened the lowest instincts and widened ever more the gulf between Polish and Jewish populations opened by the November days. The [postpogrom] situation grew ever more intolerable. Attacks on dwellings, usually at night; theft of property; blackmail of various forms; capture on the streets on pretext of labor needs, sparing neither young nor old; continual inspections all brought about fearful panic and boundless despair.[17]

Alongside well-known anti-Jewish legends, fairy tales circulated about Jewish revenge, even of Jewish boys selling poisoned candy. Despite meticulous investigations – passing hint at Polish paranoia and efforts to expunge guilt feelings – no such charges had proved true.

---

[14] Ibid., fr. 99–100.   [15] Ibid., fr. 101–2; 120; 127.
[16] CAHJP. II.HM2/8300.1. fr. 85–120: *Sprawozdanie Żydowskiego Komitetu dla Niesienia Pomocy Ofiarom Rozruchów i Rabunków za czas od 25. listopada 1918 do 1. grudnia 1919* (Lwów, 1919), 1.
[17] Ibid., 6–7.

Jews suffered dismissal en masse from postal, railroad, and other public service, doctors and other medical personnel from public hospitals. Not only the pogrom's immediate victims required succor, particularly those ruined by fire, but also impoverished intelligentsia and refugee masses who streamed in from the 143 war-torn provincial Jewish settlements in East Galicia. Food prices had soared, necessitating "struggle against usury in foodstuffs." The Lwów rabbinate pronounced religious excommunication (*chejrem*) on Jews guilty of "rampant profiteering." Meanwhile, typhus raged.[18]

Aid from fellows Jews was arriving: 250,000 Kr. from Germany's Frankfurt/M. Orthodox Commune, a million Marks (1.66 million Kr.) from America's Joint Distribution Committee. The Rescue Committee looked beyond the present crisis to future tasks, especially – Zionist vision – "restratification through accustoming the [Jewish] population to labor on the land and improving handicrafts." Financial panic had caused "practically all wealthier people to depart the city," undercutting local fund-raising. "Our brothers in America" would have to give more.[19]

The Rescue Committee's huge effort at feeding the poor highlighted women's otherwise obscure role. This included maintenance of separate facilities for "discreetly" nourishing ruined intelligentsia and other formerly prosperous people, who could not be expected to queue up publicly alongside the ragged and unshod. In a year's time, *daily* free or low-cost meals averaged about 4,800. Clothing was distributed to 17,000 people, small loans were given to some 2,000 merchants and artisans, 476 cases of legal representation were accepted, 324 intelligentsia members received loans averaging 500 Kr., elaborate medical and educational aid was extended, especially to small children, at the cost through infection of some medical volunteers' lives. After "conscience-less elements" embezzled funds from the central office, it was rigorously disciplined. The Committee's Labor Department systematized government worker recruitment for military projects, including at front lines of the Polish army's eventually successful drive to conquer East Galicia. At its height, this involved 20,000 Jewish workers monthly, earning 20 to 40 Kr. daily (of which the army paid but 10 Kr.). "The numerous sacrifices in men killed and wounded in the course of these works demolished the legends about Jewish aversion to physical labor."[20]

Polish army commanders' defensiveness and aggressiveness toward Jewish civilians radiated from Colonel Władysław Sikorski, ascendant military hero, future prime minister, and leader of Poland's government-in-exile in Western Europe during World War II. On January 4,

---

[18] Ibid., 10–11.   [19] Ibid., 16–19.   [20] Ibid., 52–53, 19*ff*.

1919 he replied to Rescue Committee grievances, displaying his "sincere good will" by pointing to his introduction of "governmental security guard" and "field gendarmerie." His aim, to minimize anti-Jewish violence, was to shield civilians from "all annoyances, burdens, and pranks on the part of military personnel depraved by war and the numerous civilian criminals of all nationalities rampaging under cover of illegitimately worn uniforms." Yet it was an "indubitable fact" that Jews had, in war with Ruthenians ignited by "the Ukrainian coup," occupied from the start "a position hostile to us" and now appeal against Poland to President Wilson and the "whole civilized world" while forming "in larger centers Jewish '*revenge battalions*.'" That one of modern Poland's preeminent military leaders' imagination should be stalked by such menacing figments speaks starkly of the guilt-generated anxiety evoked among Christians by the pogrom-stricken and otherwise abused Jew.

Ominously, Sikorski complained that "the enemy is continually informed of our every military movement and order." He criticized the Rescue Committee for confining its charitable activities to victims of "so-called 'pogroms,'" deepening people's apprehensions of a Jewish "state within the state." He expressed his readiness to cooperate with the Committee in aiding the "POOR Jewish population" – implying that nonpoor were benefiting – but if his warnings were not heeded, he would, in interest "of the Polish army fighting on city terrain, dissolve the Committee and summon its guilty members to responsibility before a court-martial." This deadly threat provoked the Committee's immediate retort, abjuring hostile intent, to which Sikorski replied conciliatorily, probably content with having made intimidating points.[21]

The Haller army's arrival in early 1919 renewed Jews' torment. Austrian subject Haller, having bolted to the Entente in 1917, took command in 1918 of a blue-uniformed army of Polish volunteers from America, POWs in Entente captivity, and other Poles in Western Europe. Politically close to Dmowski's Polish National Committee, which Western powers accepted as the Polish cause's authoritative representatives, Haller's "blue army" moved in 1919 to the Eastern front, fighting both against Ukrainians and White and Red Russians. By then, many other Poles had joined its ranks, particularly from former Prussian Poland, where Endeks dominated political life. These uniformed "Poznanians" (*Poznańczycy*) were notorious for aggressive antisemitism, whose violent outbursts especially targeted Russian and Austrian Poland's religiously garbed and coiffed Orthodox and Hasidic Jews – patronizingly or contemptuously named "caftan Jews." Here

---

[21] CAHJP. HM2/8860.10. fr. 31–35 (author's emphasis).

Westernized and modernized Poles raged against the – to them – humiliating presence of such Jews (a rarity in Germany, where even conservative Jews had adopted Western dress) on the social landscape of the Polish state whose birth they had yearned for and of which they were now citizens but about whose formerly Russian and Austrian parts most knew little or nothing.

In Lwów, Poznanians' depredations found documentation in May 1919. Police Director Batorski encountered four drunken Poznanian soldiers who had stormed a Jewish store and were beating its occupants. The situation was dangerous, "given such a numerous crowd of Jews and also soldiers who gathered and incited the Poznanians to beat them." His efforts to lead the soldiers to barracks and obtain their leader's identity papers met drawn revolver. Since such incidents were the "order of the day," he requested incontestable authority to check such soldiers' papers and take command in tumults. The Rescue Committee's register of "Incidents of Physical Outrages by Hallerites" (*Hallerczycy*) for April 15–30 numbered thirty-seven: twenty-eight street thefts of money and nine cases of beating, crippling, wounding, and ear-lock cutting. A well-to-do woman, possibly Christian, viewing jeweler Zipper's wares, witnessed Haller soldiers' invasion. The salesgirl ran into the street, crying "*gevalt*" (*gwałt* [violence]) and "they're robbing," whereupon "a great many Jews came running to her" (more evidence of collective efforts to confront pogromists). Meanwhile, soldiers stole plaintiff's "brooch worth 20,000 Kr."[22]

Lwów City President Leonard Stahl protested to East Galician front commander General Iwaszkiewicz renewed anti-Jewish excesses, notably at the Jewish cemetery, "where horses are pastured, trampling graves of legionary officers who fell as Polish soldiers defending the Fatherland against hajdamaks." Vaults had been destroyed, and "the silver eagle was torn from the grave memorial of Goldman, honorable soldier of 1863." Poznanians had rampaged drunkenly in four Jewish streets, invading shops and seizing sweets and foodstuffs "which they distributed to the crowd of paupers accompanying them." Thus was insulted "a Jewish society that feels itself Polish." President Stahl pointed darkly to an unspecified "criminal hand" – whose he did not say – provoking soldiers to these crimes, to Poland's international disadvantage. Iwaszkiewicz replied that Poznanians had received appropriate orders, whose violation would "be punished most severely."[23]

---

[22] CAHJP. IV. HM2/8299.10, fr. 10, 12–13; HM2/8860.10. fr. 35–38.
[23] CAHJP. HM2/8860.10. fr. 39–41. On cemetery desecration, see also CAHJP. HM2/8299.13.

Many Jews fired from public-sector Austrian-era jobs petitioned to regain them. In October 1919, the Warsaw government created a Rehabilitation Commission to weigh claims of former officials who stayed at their posts during the "Ukrainian invasion" in Lwów and East Galicia generally. Having sworn a Ukrainian loyalty oath did not justify nonreappointment, provided petitioners had not "cooperated in the struggle against Poles." Among sixty documented cases, not many appear to have regained their jobs, though some did, occasionally with transfers to new localities. Ukrainian or Zionist loyalty (real or suspected) yielded such damning arguments as these: a subaltern tax official "willingly entered [Ukrainian] service [and] as [an] ardent Zionist, exploited his post to oppress Poles with property-seizures"; a Zionist "who was always challenging and rude to the Polish side"; "a prosperous [tax official] who, seeking personal gain and friendship with Ukrainians, performed his duties in Ukrainian language and reacted to Poles with prejudice, hatred, and ridicule"; others allegedly enriched themselves during the war, or were spies; one "joined a protest parade against the alleged pogroms in Lwów"; another "made fun of Polish speech."[24]

Gendarmes investigated twenty-five-year-old Lwów journalist Oskar Rohatyn, author of a Yiddish "Pogrom Song" that he reportedly performed at the Jewish Society for Self-Education and also sold to raise money for the injured. Rohatyn's poem differed from Hayyim Bialik's celebrated Hebrew-language poem on the 1903 Kishenev pogrom, "City of Slaughter" (1904), which castigated Jewish men and boys for – as Bialik thought – failing to resist bestial axe-wielding pogromists. Rohatyn shared with Bialik the emotional pathos infusing all Jewish protest against violence and discrimination but interpreted Lwów's pogrom in religious terms, as anti-Judaic assault by implacable Christian foes eliciting heroic Jewish self-sacrifice.

The murderers, the dark power, destroyed prayer-houses, burned holy books. In vain did we pray . . .
    Mercilessly Jews were killed . . . prayer-house in flames; a misery of fire. They murder, they rob Jews' goods.
    But in the prayer-house a loyal Jew risks himself to rescue our most holy treasures. In he goes and comes out with holy books in his hand.

A shot cracks and the Jew is stricken. He falls to earth, blood flows.

In the flames is he thrown to burn with the books.
    "May God have mercy," all say to themselves. The Jews weep bloody tears. It rends the heart to see the prayer-house burn.

[24] CAHJP.HM2/8856.7. fr. 42*ff*, 71*ff*.

Do we bear so much sin?

To destroy us completely is the son's thought [*Ynz genclich vernichten yz dem Sojnes Gedank*]! We are caught between the tiger's sharp teeth ... But to destroy the Jew – it cannot be done.[25]

Contemporary Jewish Interpretations of the Galician Pogroms

An early and poignant statement flowed from the pen of Lwów city vice-president, Galician Sejm deputy, and liberal-assimilationist leader, the aforementioned Tobiasz Askenase (1863–1920). Published in Lwów's progressive liberal *Wiek Nowy* on November 24, as pogrom fires still smoked, he described himself "as a Jew who from earliest youth stood unshakably under Polish flag." Advancing a proposal that "would halt the wave of destruction and fires of barbarism that engulfed Lwów," he directed his appeal to "conscience and reason of the thousands of those most noble Poles, known personally to me," to the "flower of the Polish intelligentsia" and "reasonable bourgeoisie of Lwów," and especially to the National Democratic and Socialist Parties, which had come to power in Poland and would be responsible for what happened there.

To quell evildoing, acts, not words, were needed. "Lwów's people are goodhearted and easily led and guided." But "refusal to grant Jews the right to their own nationality" had created a "constantly festering wound." It was "a great lie" that Jews must be either Poles or Ruthenians. "The huge mass of the Jewish people neither are nor want to be Polish or Ruthenian [*ruska*]; they are Jewish and want to remain so." Momentary battle lines cannot determine who should serve as Polish or Ukrainian soldiers. Otherwise brother is pitted against brother. Divine law and the right of self-determination demanded that Jews themselves choose their "national belonging." "This will remove a weighty source of the conventionalized falsehood, sometimes hypocritically embraced, sometimes unconsciously held, that poisons our public life," that is, that Jews were – or ought to be – Poles. Askenase, ardent advocate of Jewish self-Polonization, pleaded for acknowledgment that the majority of Jews were a separate nation living in cohabitation with Poles and Ukrainians, in whose wars Jews should be under no obligation to fight.[26]

In February 1919, under Lwów municipal auspices, a six-day "inquest" into the pogrom took place, attended by several dozen spokesmen from all sides. Conflicting positions found expression, rather than

---

[25] CAHJP.HM2/8299.16.

[26] *Nowy Dziennik*, no. 139 (November 27, 1918), "W sprawie żydowskiej."

violence's dispassionate analysis or a meeting of minds, much less hope of future cooperation. Disarray was evident in the Jewish assimilation camp. Some "Poles of Mosaic Faith," denying modern Jewry a culture of its own, insisted it should vanish except as a religion. Moderates followed Askenase's lead, advocating official benevolence toward self-administered Jewish "national autonomy" within existing communal-educational institutions. Zionism too was to be expected and accepted as a Jewish form of all-pervasive modern nationalism.

Zionist speakers clung to neutrality between Poles and Ukrainians, some suggesting that no progress in establishing a Polish-Jewish *modus vivendi* was possible with Polonophile coreligionists present. Orthodox Judaism's spokesmen rejected the assimilationist position, as did – more forcefully – Reform Rabbi Samuel Guttmann, who insisted on harmony in Jewish self-understanding of nation and religion and extolled modern Yiddish and Hebrew literature. No one spoke for Yiddishist nationalism anchored in existing East European settlements.

Non-Jewish Poles nearly unanimously agreed that embrace of Zionism disqualified Jews, if not for Polish citizenship – some proposed Zionists rank legally as "foreigners" or "Palestinian citizens" – then for public-sector employment. Some were self-professed "a-semites," striving for erasure of Jewish presence from secular civil society. Assimilationists deserved encouragement. Probably the Polish majority view was that Jews could rightly and understandably develop cultural individuality, but not to the detriment of linguistic and citizenly self-Polonization. Even Teofil Merunowicz, nationally well-known, long-established anti-semitic publicist, advocated Jews' full legal equality, condemning the pogrom as irresponsible rabble's deed.[27]

Before Lwów's explosion, Kraków's Zionist-leaning *Nowy Dziennik* had run an analysis of West Galician pogroms claiming the peasantry had no reason to assault Jews, having prospered from wartime commodity price explosion. "The Polish farmer – in contrast to the Polish townsman – is not, basically, an antisemite. This is proven by the fact that in numerous cases farmers protected the Jews of their own settlement against attacks from neighboring villagers" – which may have been true, but of which little evidence has surfaced. In this journalist's view, banditry caused the pogroms, especially by demobilized soldiers streaming in from Russian Poland.

[27] Pacholkiv, "Zwischen Einbeziehung und Ausgrenzung. Die Juden in Lemberg 1918–1919," 208–12. Speakers' full texts in Komisya dla Sprawy Żydowskiej, *W sprawie polsko-żydowskiej. Przebieg ankiety* ... (Lwów: Nakładem Komisyi rządzącej we Lwowie, 1919).

Bandits draw women and half-grown boys behind them and together stage pogroms. Farmers themselves mostly don't take part. It's not uncommon that fathers refuse to allow robbed booty in their houses and send it back to town for restitution to its owners. Farmers regret these incidents, and I'm convinced our relation to them in the future will be completely tolerable.

With townspeople, it was "much worse." They were "hostile to Jews purely on grounds of competition." It was worse still with officials and schoolteachers. Exaggeratedly, he claimed that except for judicial officials, superior in education and social form, educated professionals "were antisemites through and through." Although Jews welcomed independent Poland, "countryfolk have robbed us, townspeople have blocked our self-defense, and intelligentsia have excluded us from committees and commissions exercising executive power." Jewish prospects were therefore "very sad, indeed desperate."[28]

Nowy Dziennik reader Dr. Kornguth in Wadowice was more hopeful. He argued against segregating Jewish and Christian militias, since "sight of a Jewish militiaman now has the effect of a red flag on a bull." Yet the "time has come when it's not shape of nose but honor, character and good will that determine how people are treated." A week earlier *Nowy Dziennik* reported that Jewish merchants in Wadowice, faced with threat of peasant bands, "defended their possessions with gun in hand," while "brave action" by gendarmerie and militia ended excesses.[29]

A Yiddish-language letter translated in Berlin's ZO, from Galician *shtetl* dweller to German relatives, was truer to the times. All lived in fear of "bigger robber bands," who "just want to destroy Jews."

People have housewares packed. You only take out your bedsheets at night to repack them in the morning ... That's our reward for fighting four years for Poland and sacrificing our lives. The ignorant robber band think freedom means to plunder and murder Jews. Now, as I write, there's a mass of villagers gathered such as never before. Our numbers are unfortunately too small for us to defend ourselves alone.[30]

Assimilationist Herman Diamand, influential Lwów-based Galician PPS leader and one of independent Poland's coarchitects, surveyed the wreckage with cooler eye. Speaking to German-Jewish liberals, he said that excesses could have been avoided "if the Jews had not shown a certain aversion to the Poles," by which he principally meant the Zionist "National Jews," seen by Poles as an "internal enemy." The Jewish question in Poland could only be resolved "when Jews are more prepared

---

[28] CZA. L6/109: *Nowy Dziennik*, no. 129 (November 17, 1918).
[29] Ibid., no. 128 (November 16, 1918); ibid., no. 122 (November 10, 1918).
[30] CZA. L6/110 (n.d.).

to advance Polish interests." At present, "the Pole doesn't know where among Jews the Jew ends and the Pole begins."[31]

In Germany, Jewish liberals offered a 1920 appraisal, seemingly from prominent Galician journalist Benjamin Segal's pen, sounding a wistful note of disappointment over breakdown of the Polish-Jewish relationship.

Among Poles pogrom is something artificially introduced, something suggested from outside, grounded neither in their tradition nor their mentality. From the beginning of the Russian pogrom-era, which coincided with German antisemitism's rise and was causally related to it, Poles successfully fought against both [of these anti-Jewish tendencies] until Pan-Polish National Democracy grew strong. But just as foreign plants sometimes thrive better than native ones, so too has pogrom in Poland assumed more despicable, coarser, and meaner forms than elsewhere: beard-ripping, abuse and harassment are viler and more malicious than actual pogrom, and have a more embittering and long-lasting effect than plundering and bloodshed ... If Jews in Poland, and especially eastern Galicia, where in the towns they were the Polish cause's main pillars, can be massacred, and indeed by Poles, who always condemned pogroms, then there is obviously now nothing morally objectionable about pogroms, and they no longer besmirch the honor of a civilized nation awakening to freedom. The Lwów pogrom demonstrated to the world that under certain conditions a pogrom can be very welcome.[32]

The Violence in Poland's Governing Elites' and International Eyes

In these Jewish-penned analyses, prime danger was not so much sporadic physical assault, brutal though this was. It was, rather, ruthless antisemitic ideologists of Christian middle-class formation who, when state power stumbled, did not scruple to foment violence, finding ready enforcers among armed outlaws and compliant listeners among the "dark masses." How, though, did the bloody outbursts look in Poland's new governors' eyes? Benjamin Segal's dictum – "pogroms surprised not only Jews, but also Poles. They tried therefore to make excuses not only to the world, but to themselves" – found ample confirmation.[33]

Fusing Catholic religious sensibility, social conservatism, and ideological antisemitism, Lwów archbishop Józef Bilczewski challenged the

---

[31] *Allgemeine Zeitung des Judenthums* (hereafter: *AZdJ*), no. 42 (October 15, 1919), 475–76.
[32] *Im deutschen Reich*, no. 11 (November 1920), 340–46. Cf. William W. Hagen, "Murder in the East: German-Jewish Liberal Reactions to Anti-Jewish Violence in Poland and Other East European Lands, 1918–1920," *Central European History*, vol. 34, no. 1 (2001), 1–30.
[33] *AZdJ*, no. 25 (June 20, 1919), 265–67.

Zionist Jewish National Council for German-Austria's November 23, 1918, antipogrom protest.[34] He deplored war-induced disorder, misery, "general demoralization and, certainly not least, the four-year-long orgy of usury in all branches of commerce, three-fourths of which, with us, is in Jewish hands." He claimed the Kraków rabbinate concurred, publicly imploring "Jewish commercial circles to cease price-gouging and content themselves with more modest and just profit." Bilczewski charged that worse antisemitic violence occurred in Hungary than in Galicia and that antisemitic journalism was far more aggressive in Germany than in Poland. "Polish antisemitism lacks the heavy accentuation observable elsewhere, and does not derive from feelings of mutual racial antipathy. This confirms the Poles' many-centuries-long deep patriarchal relationship to the Jews, which unfortunately in our time has suffered disturbance" (but which Jewish nationalists remembered as domination).

Bilczewski bewailed life's dissoluteness "in the social depths" and the "masses' ever greater moral decline." The war's "senseless bloodshed frighteningly undermined morality's foundations." He ironized that "we are blessed with efforts, pursued with zeal worthy of better cause, to introduce Bolshevism among us, whose apostles and workers are almost without exception Jews." Equally disruptive of the church's efforts to "restore balance" was the worldwide campaign stigmatizing anti-Jewish violence in Poland as more furious and implacable than elsewhere. This was "with best will impossible to understand, or rather too easy to understand." Polish Jews must try harder to attain good relations with Poles, "for otherwise their existence would be called into question" – an ominous, if cloudy, formulation, possibly implying expulsion or renewed violence. The danger resided in "Jewish incitation against Poland in Europe," which it was not in the church's power to halt.

In New York, the American Jewish Committee had been meeting since spring 1918 with Polish leaders in hope of gaining the Paderewski-headed, Endek-slanted Polish National Committee's condemnation of anti-Jewish boycotting in occupied Poland and of antisemitic violence there, of which alarming reports were crossing the Atlantic. On the Polish side, the ensuing dialogue displayed a powerful impulse to absolve Polish society of Judeophobic rioting universally associated with execrated Russian pogroms of 1881–84, 1903–6, and 1914–18 and contemporary civil war–stricken regions. Allegations of pogroms would endanger future

---

[34] Here and below: CZA. L6/114, no. 2. This file misidentifies the archiepiscopal author as [Adam] Sapieha, then bishop of Kraków. The clerical letter is undated, and whether it was publicized is unknown. Unclear is its relationship to the pastoral letter cited by Bendow, "Zwischen Einbeziehung und Ausgrenzung. Die Juden in Lemberg 1918–1919," *Judenpogrom*, 82–3.

Polish state interests by outraging Western opinion before the peace settlement and by raising likelihood that the Western powers would heed Zionist calls for internationally enforceable Jewish minority rights in renascent Poland.

In the psychological depths, pogrom charges also menaced nationally minded Poles' self-image as noble, fair-minded, civilized Christian people who had sacrificed much in struggle for their own and other nations' freedom and whose forefathers had generously gathered into their own homes and for centuries protected the world's largest Jewish community. If violence occurred – American Poles reluctantly conceded it had – then it was at marauding soldiers' hands in a "sea of anarchy" (and Bolshevism). As for boycotting, Endek leadership had at war's outbreak repudiated it in its highly politicized 1912-proclaimed form, but that it persisted as an imperative in antisemitic minds was indubitable, even if Christian consumers often ignored it.[35]

In February 1919 the Polish National Committee, now the new state's official delegation at the Paris Peace Conference, issued an English-language press release, governmentally endorsed in Warsaw, entitled, "The Jewish Pogroms in Poland." Like the conversations in New York, it displayed denial, self-congratulation, and threat mixed with self-exculpation. Pogrom reports, "spread over the world through German press agencies," had proven, "luckily," groundless. Unspecified Jewish and mixed Christian-Jewish investigations had found "not a single pogrom of the well-known Russian type, that is, having as its object the destruction and murder of Jews only."

In Poland there occurred as in Hungary, Slovonia [sic], Moravia etc. during the months of November and December 1918 excesses caused by bands of soldiers, fleeing from shattered fronts and by hundreds of thousands of German, Russian and Austrian prisoners returning to their homes, and who were also joined by local bands of bandits, which were formed at war's end in Austria, composed of deserters. These bands, pressed by hunger and want, robbed stores containing food and clothing regardless of the nationalities of the proprietors . . . most of such stores belonged to Jews, thus giving such attacks a Jewish character, which they have not. It is a tragedy of the war, bringing to mind the return of the great army in 1812.

Civilian deaths, mostly occasioned by resistance to plunderers, were not numerous. Lwów was a special case, having been besieged and famished for weeks by "bands of Ukrainians." Some 400 "starved criminalists," released from jail, plunged into robbery, joined by Austrian deserter

---

[35] See the documentation in CAHJP. PL 578(4), from AAN. Komitet Narodowy Polski/ KNP 159, k. 91–95.

bands and "local blackguards." Fighting and excesses killed 340 Christians and seventy Jews, while over 1,000 Polish soldiers perished "fighting with Ukrainian-Bolshevik bands." In the aftermath, Polish authorities arrested some 1,000 rioters and brought another 150 before courts martial. "Peace and quiet" quickly descended, yet "Germans" had sought to rob Poland of "the civilized world's sympathy and lessen her chances at the peace conference."

Poland received Jews very hospitably in the 14th Century when they were persecuted everywhere and chiefly in Germany. Over the centuries the Jews have partaken in the fate of Poland and very many of them held positions of great respect and influence.

The pogroms instigated by Russia during the years 1905 and 1906 were stopped when they reached the frontiers of Poland [i.e., the Congress Kingdom], and in Russian territory the Poles hid the hunted Jews in their homes.

Pogroms are foreign and abominable to the Polish nature, and for that reason that charge made against them greatly angered the population, and Polish citizens and prominent Jews made public protest against such charges and such underhanded intrigues.[36]

Behind this statement loomed colossal self-deception and denial, particularly of widespread civilian pogrom participation but also of anti-Jewish propaganda's potency in Polish politics. Yet it was not conscious antisemitism but rather expression of political self-image, cultivated especially among the educated and propertied, highlighting historic liberality toward the country's Jewish population and Polish noble-mindedness in contrast to Russian brutality.

Anti-Jewish violence in Warsaw at Christmas 1881, in West Galicia in 1898, in Białystok and Siedlce in 1905–6 (though largely Russian soldierly, not Polish civilian aggression), and during the 1914–18 war darkened without utterly eclipsing this idyllic and self-congratulatory picture. What was absent, here and in nearly all other self-exculpations, was recognition of the towering wave of anti-Jewish propaganda set in motion since the prewar years by the Endeks, peasant-populist nationalists, and single-issue antisemites. It swept up masses of ordinary Poles, educated and privileged alongside "criminalists," "blackguards," and "scum." It authorized many to act on widespread, deep-seated, centuries-old Judeophobic anxieties and aggressions and plunge into 1918's anti-Jewish assaults alongside the ruthless armed men, whether soldiers/ legionnaires or bandits/deserters or peasant anarchists, who collectively wreaked greatest destruction on Jewish victims.

---

[36] CAHJP. PL 578(4), from AAN. KNP sygn/2066/144 (February 22, 1919).

In former Russian Poland, a brutal pogrom erupted – as will been seen – on November 11 in Kielce. It was the crucible in which Warsaw-centered Polish opinion on the postwar pogrom wave was forged, with anti-Bolshevism as most potent ingredient rather than the paranoia over Jewish loyalty and vengefulness toward supposed economic exploitation that pervaded discourse over Galician pogroms. As the renascent nation's capital, housing its mightiest political media, Warsaw would eclipse Kraków, Lwów, and other big provincial cities as the fountainhead of antisemitic propaganda and intermittent spring from which rebuttals flowed.

Shortly after Kielce's violence, the government's press agency (PAT) released a communiqué branding Bolshevism the "looming danger," imported from Russia (with German toleration) especially by "Polish Jews such as [Karl] Radek, Sobelson [actually Radek *was* Sobelson] and others who, exploiting their connections in Poland and with copious financial resources, send agitators to Poland." All democratic elements recognized that "far-reaching social reforms" were the best antidote to the revolutionary leftism of the prewar Social Democracy of the Kingdom of Poland and Lithuania (soon self-rebaptized as the Communist Party [KPP]), consisting "largely of Jews." Its campaign of denigration against the new Polish army – as in Kielce, where Jews allegedly shouted "down with the white goose [Polish eagle]" – provoked patriotic choler. If anti-Jewish violence had not erupted in Warsaw and elsewhere in the former Congress Kingdom, it was only because of Poles' "mildness and toler-ance." Wide circles of Jewish loyalists were struggling to suppress their coreligionists' Bolshevik onslaughts, and Polish authorities were promis-ing to help them.[37]

This pronouncement projected the Polish self-image as progressive and benevolent but also besieged by Jewish-Bolshevik enemies driven not only by revolutionary aggression but also hate-filled anti-Polonism allegedly drawing on Jewish financing in Poland and elsewhere. Zionist leaders Osias Thon, Itzhak Grünbaum, and Max Lesser, wrung from Minister-President Moraczewski's disavowal of PAT's press release. Responding to Zionists' demand for comprehensive official pogrom denunciation, Moraczewski replied that while Jewish fighting alongside Ukrainians in Lwów was a proven fact, the government condemned pogroms and would resist them "unconditionally." The Piłsudski-Moraczewski government had published its program on November 20, promising social democracy and protection of "those population fragments [*odłamów ludności*, i.e., ethnic minorities] that we inherited from the partition zones" and to

---

[37] CZA. Z3/179 (November 26, 1918).

"guard against all confessional and nationalist strife and struggle." The shaky new left-leaning government was weak and unwilling to single out Jews for protection.[38]

Zionist leaders met later with Piłsudski, protesting Galician pogroms and accusing the Liquidation Commission of having publicly condemned victims as black marketeers. Everyone knew, they countered, that it was agriculturalists who profited in the war and would not sell at reduced prices, "although they have already piled up cash-fortunes in fantastic sums." Why, too, had the government failed to track down the "bandits" and recover the plundered goods? The delegation demanded of Piłsudski restitution of material losses and cessation of all governmental anti-Jewish stigmatization, which only triggered "lynch justice."

Piłsudski said he had ordered the armed forces, seconded by individual commanders, "to protect Jews from pogroms." Of Lwów, he said that because Ukrainian troops had engulfed the Jewish quarter, it had been hard for Jews to behave loyally. The "rabble" staged the pogrom, which injured Christians too. Thon cited known instances of Ukrainian fighters shooting from Jewish dwellings, fueling anti-Jewish reprisals. Resisting their pressure, Piłsudski said he was "no autocrat ... The Jewish Question could not be solved until the Constituent had assembled." Grünbaum declared Lwów violence "the most terrible in the history of Jewish pogroms." Piłsudski invoked wartime brutality and many Jews' doubtful loyalty. The same day Moraczewski told them that "the Jews were sounding too many alarms. People abroad were thinking, 'God only knows what all is going on in Poland.'"[39]

A January 1919 circular from Interior Minister Stanisław Wojciechowski (PPS) to all prefects addressed "mistreatment" of Jews by state and military officials and civilians. Asserting that Jews possessed the same civil rights as the "native Polish population," he perpetuated, seemingly unconsciously, the myth that Jews, despite a half-millennium of Polish residency, were nonnative foreigners. "In free Poland there are no differing citizenly categories," as there had been among Russian subjects, but "everyone can live as he wishes, so long as he does no harm to Polish statehood."

The Polish people, oppressed for many years and unable to express their collective will, know how to value the freedom of those with whom their fate is linked. Poland has since olden times been synonym for freedom, its flag fluttered

[38] CZA. Z3/180: *Nowy Dziennik*, no. 150 (December 8, 1918); *Nowa Gazeta*, no. 483 (November 20, 1918), "Odezwa rządu."
[39] *Nowy Dziennik*, no. 143 (December 1, 1918), "Deputacja żydowska"; CZA. Z3/180: *Nowy Dziennik*, no. 147 (December 5, 1918).

everywhere where freedom and independence were at stake, it has remained true to its traditions and will therefore not besmirch its great and glorious past. It will gather unto itself all who seek protection and justice.

I warn, therefore, that all violence and arbitrary acts against the Jewish population, whether by administrative organs or civilians, will be investigated and punished with all the law's impartiality and rigor. In free Poland there is no place for injustice, violence, and arbitrary exercise of power.[40]

This not ineloquent profession, by a man of gentry roots who rose to the Polish presidency in 1922–26, well captures the self-image of the "noble, freedom-loving Poles." Their imagined relation to the Jews was paternalist, even intimate (as implied by use of the German term in a knowledgeable translation from the Polish of "*an sich schmiegen*," whose meaning extends to physical embrace).

The Zionist newspaper *dos Yiddishe Folk* coldly rejected Wojciechowski's preachments. He will know, it wrote, that for many Poles "barbaric assaults on Jews" had become "second nature." Assurance had "entered their blood" that anti-Jewish violence, even murder, was likely to go unpunished. Such was the fruit of the antisemitic press's long-running "bloodthirsty incitations." When government, church, and political elites once honestly resolve to take necessary steps – including confession of sins and succoring of injured – peaceful coexistence would prevail, but years were likely first to pass.[41]

In February 1919 Piłsudski and then Minister-President Ignacy Paderewski spoke with delegates of the Zionist-oriented Jewish National Council for East Galicia. Piłsudski said that when he returned from German imprisonment in 1918, "I was really surprised at the tremendous antisemitism that had spread among the Polish population during the war."

I myself was no antisemite but, having gotten to know the mood among the masses and the Jews' stance, I'm not surprised that partisans of Polish statehood view the Jewish element as a foreign body and try to exclude it. The pogroms in Lwów and Kielce don't even really express the true popular attitude to the Jews. That greater pogroms haven't occurred is only because the Polish peasant is not by nature inclined to violent deeds.[42]

Jews' posture toward the state, Piłsudski continued, could only be described as hostile. Proof was that pogroms were trumpeted about in the world. Asked to specify instances of Jews' "hostile stance," Piłsudski gave no details, saying only "such were the Polish people's feelings."

---

[40] CZA. Z3/181, trans. Berlin Zionist Office (n.d.), "Die polnische Regierung und die Judenpogrome."
[41] CZA. Z3/181 (n.d.).   [42] CZA. L6/112 (February 22, 1919).

Paderewski added that pogroms were deplorable and that discriminatory laws should not weigh on Jews. But they shouldn't expect the state to pay for Hebrew-language schools or to have their own organs of justice. To Zionist commentators, this unmasked Paderewski's ignorance because no Jewish groups demanded these things.

Whether or not these were Polish leaders' precise words, the attitudes they conveyed were not implausible, even if drastically expressed. That Piłsudski – or his simulacrum here constructed – could invoke, attempting to mollify Jewish critics, even fiercer pogroms seems to reveal the deep-rooted idea within Christian culture of Israelites' cataclysmic punishment. Of Piłsudski, Israel Cohen reported that "he candidly admitted to me that Poles were no philo-Semites, and the only hope he held out was that the present anti-Jewish hostility could not last." Paderewski told Cohen that "he was philo-Semitic" and that "stories about his being antisemitic were untrue and had done him much harm." He vowed to keep his promise to American Jewish leaders that he would do everything possible to improve Jews' condition. Yet it was an "unhappy omen" that Paderewski's speech at Warsaw Town Hall, "in which he appealed for a cessation of hostilities on the ground of race or religion, was omitted from the reports in nearly all papers." Nor was it propitious that "when I asked Count Szeptycki, Chief of the General Staff, whether any soldier had yet been shot by a Jew he replied that though they fired they missed." Stanisław Grabski, influential Endek, "said he was antisemitic before, but was so no longer, 'as no longer necessary.'" If Jews would only declare themselves in favor of a greater Poland including Danzig and Wilno, "he would arrange a Conference of representatives of all Polish parties and of the Jews to arrive at a peaceful understanding." Liberal-minded, anti-Endek Foreign Minister Leon Wasilewski said that the government, opposed to pogroms, "was trying to combat antisemitism, and that its task was made difficult by Jews in Western Europe calling [it] antisemitic."[43]

Cohen advocated a Zionist program of Jewish minority rights, including their own electoral college for the national parliament and a Secretariat for Jewish Affairs. He warned his British readers that if denied this, Jews would emigrate in hundreds of thousands "and crave asylum in the western lands that will be sufficiently preoccupied with problems of their own." Western Jews, though fighting for Eastern brethren, did not want them massing on their own doorstep. Cohen ended his report, if patronizingly, also not unwisely.

---

[43] CZA. L6/114 (February–March 1919), 3, 45, 47.

The Polish Jews have an oriental culture, a traditional mode of life, which cannot be broken up by forced methods; and the antagonism felt toward them by the Poles will not diminish until the latter become better educated and more accustomed to liberal institutions.[44]

Despite equivocations and anti-Jewish impulses, conscious and unconscious, renascent Poland's architects viewed pogroms as counterproductive and sought to suppress them. Yet their command of armed forces loose in the land was shaky, particularly over the anti-Piłsudski, pro-Endek Haller army. Moreover, public opinion, as crystallized in the politically influential press, was polarized: denying anti-Jewish violence, justifying it as righteous response to intolerable provocations, or condemning it but on grounds different from the Piłsudski government's.

Polish Ideological Camps and the November Pogroms

National Democrats' chief organ and most ambitious newspaper was *Gazeta Warszawska*, suspended in 1915 but revived at war's end. Tracing its origins to 1774 and the Polish Enlightenment, it grandiloquently posed as oracle of "interests of a hard-tested [*ciężko doświadczony*] nation," paladin of "Polish civilization," mouthpiece of "superb [*luksusowa*] political party," embodying "our forefathers' patriotism – most reliable arbiter and regulator in social and economic affairs," and enemy of all "anarchy and internal conflict."[45]

In it, Stanisław Głąbiński, Lwów-based Endek leader and gentry-born parliamentarian, cynically branded attempted Ukrainian power seizure as "Prusso-hajdamak invasion." Displaying Endek appetite for conspiracy theory, he darkly attributed its orchestration – presumably out of suspected antipolonism – to the faltering k.k. army. He charged Jewish militiamen with collusion with "so-called Ukrainians" (pejoratively distinguished from authentic and unpolitical Ruthenians) and expressed embitterment at assimilationists' acquiescence in Jewish neutrality. It revealed "their Polishness as duplicity and commercial speculation." Yet, though an "uncommonly painful disappointment for Poles," it could not provoke them to "deeds unworthy of the nation's dignity and culture." Perpetrators of "so-called pogroms" in Lwów and elsewhere "were people with no connection to Polish national opinion": alongside Ukrainians and the criminals they protected, "Polish and Jewish [!] dregs from suburban slums." Nor was the violence antisemitic but rather mirroring of German and Austrian armies' "war of plunder" passed on to

---

[44] Ibid., 49.
[45] *Gazeta Warszawska* (hereafter: *GW*), no. 1 (November 16, 1918), "Od Wydawnictwa."

deserters and bandits. Such deeds "will not end with Jews, but are an expression of anarchy, and must be unconditionally condemned everywhere." Nor, given their prevalence throughout Carpathian and Danubian lands, were they peculiarly Polish.[46]

Głąbiński's barbed views recalled the Liquidation Commission's November 27 dismissal of Jewish charges of overt or covert pogrom incitement by Polish antisemites, accompanied by threats that such anti-Polish calumnies might unleash the very violence Jews feared.[47] This pronouncement, as we saw, the Warsaw government quickly repudiated. But attribution of pogroms to bandits and social dregs remained nationalist interpretations' bedrock. With Poland's fate in Paris undecided, Endeks had good reason to abjure radical antisemitism.

The ND Party (*Stronnictwo Demokratyczno-Narodowe*) published its program on December 30, 1918, promising "true to historical tradition, full measure of freedoms and civil rights to all citizens, regardless of origin or confession." As for "other nations' branches" finding themselves in renascent Poland, Endeks invoked the "traditional principle, 'free with free, equal with equal.'" Regions they inhabited would possess "internal structure assuring complete freedom of national development." Evident again is the importance of Poles' self-conception as heirs to a deep-rooted culture of freedom and toleration.[48]

If these promises displayed Endeks' sunny side, evocative of faded debt to nineteenth-century bourgeois liberalism, their dark persona did not hide itself. It seems characteristic of all nationalist or racist paranoia that a self-understanding, such as Głąbiński's, as reasonable and benevolent coexists with more or less subliminal apprehensions of threat or endangerment expressed in belittlement or invective or even towering hostility. The Endeks' flagship newspaper lost no time running an article series, "Unmasked," expounding feverish Judeophobia. It conceded that assimilation could transform Jews into Poles, if correctly guided, and excepting Jewish Marxists, hostile to Polish Christianity and freedom. But socialism, steered by Jews, aimed at world domination and possession of earth's material goods.

World Jewry constituted a "pluto-theocratic national government, operating from hiding through the aid of organizations of Masonic type driving consciously toward realization of the Jewish nation's messianic ideals," above all, "rule of the world," a goal plainly announced in Old Testament passages, as *Gazeta Warszawska* earnestly recalled. Polish

---

[46] *GW*, no. 16 (December 1, 1918), "W Galicji Wschodniej."
[47] PKL text in ibid., no. 12 (November 27, 1918), "W sprawie agitacji żydowskiej."
[48] Ibid., no. 43 (December 30, 1918), "Deklaracja Programowa."

antisemitism had long obsessed over imperialist menace seemingly posed by Hebrew religion, while in secularizing Western Europe analogous Christian fears, such as they may have been, had paled. Biblical passages from the Book of Isaiah cited in "Unmasked" betrayed deep but unacknowledged anxieties over enslavement, forcible submission, and prostration – fears not surprising in a land emerging from political captivity, nor in a land in which successful Jews could seem a superior people, in relation to whom sadomasochistic impulses might well arise.

For the nation and kingdom that will not serve you will *perish*, and the nations will be *utterly destroyed*. (60.12)

You will *suck the milk of nations*, you will *suck the wealth of kings*. (60.16)

Strangers will come forward to *feed your flocks, foreigners be your ploughmen and vinedressers*. (61.5)

You will *feed on the wealth of nations*, you will *supplant them in their glory*. (61.6)

Kings will be your foster-fathers and their princesses, your foster-mothers. They *will fall prostrate before you, faces to the ground, and lick the dust at your feet*. (49.23)[49]

Anti-Judaic paranoia also pilloried Talmudic writings, mysterious and fearful in their Hebrew inaccessibility and foreignness, for sanctioning exploitation of non-Jews' "blood and sweat."

"The one antidote to Jewish messianism, wishing to yoke the whole world, could only be Polish messianism." This would alone succeed if (non-Jewish) "humanity" accepted the "categorical postulate of political and religious unification." For, as "Jewish Bolshevism" prevailed in Russia, Napoleon's dictum grew truer: "Europe will either be republican or Cossack" – that is, either "freedom, peace, justice, joy in the soul – in a word, the Kingdom of God on earth, or the Jewish yoke." Because it stood on the front line against Russia, "all humanity's fate hangs on Poland's decision," which – if correct – will lead to the "political Church of reborn, united humanity," "eternal salvation," and not "everlasting damnation."

"Do not fear, Polish people, the reproach of antisemitism." To combat Jewish imperialism was to be Jews' friend, enabling their moral rebirth and reentry into the "family of brotherly nations," whereas now they saw no other road "but their own obliteration [*zagłada*]" or rule over non-Jewish peoples. The true antisemite left Jews to their present devices, while the philo-Semite encouraged their transformation into "brother,

---

[49] Ibid., nos. 13–15 (November 28–30, 1918), authored by "Jednacz" (author's emphasis).

not lord," within the future "Pan-Human United State" (*Powszechnoludzkie Państwo Związkowe*).

In this apocalyptic vision, existential stakes for newspaper readers, jostling on bus or sitting at home hearth, could hardly be higher: salvation in a Christian-hued world order, to which Jews would subordinate themselves, or perdition under "Jewish Bolshevism," itself but a means to realize the age-old dream of Jewish world empire. Nineteenth-century Polish messianism, as influentially formulated by such poets and philosophers as Adam Mickiewicz and Andrzej Towiański and in which Poland figured grandiosely as "Christ among nations," joined hands in *Gazeta Warszawska*'s first postwar issues with fear of godless Bolshevism, whose appeal to common people and radical intellectuals was no less to be discounted than susceptibility of fallen humanity to sin itself.

Relief from feverish imaginings such apprehensions induced came in invective and scornful humor that antisemites regularly vented. The charge of hypocrisy frequently flew; Socialist Hermann Diamand was, allegedly, actually "estate owner and capitalist," "millionaire-proletarian," "son-in-law of one of the richest Galician Jews." Jews, having backed the Central Powers, lost the war along with them and sought revenge by provoking pogroms against themselves to discredit Poland in Western eyes and by stirring up internal revolution to cripple the new state. *Gazeta Warszawska* proclaimed mockingly, "Jews are Best," reacting to a Jewish newspaper's argument that were antisemites to expel Jews, other nearby peoples would stream in, but without Jews' virtues. Yet "comprehensive expulsion of all Jews is impracticable."

Polish politics must strive instead to halt the Jewish element's excessive growth and primacy by easing its outflow to Palestine, Russia, and Germany, which have few Jews, and by putting the Polish element in their place.

As for "reverse assimilation" of Poles through learning of Yiddish in commercial life, especially from Jewish women retailers (*żargonówki*), Jews must stop making jokes about it that spread "hatred of Poles."[50]

Such were the widely read and prestigious Endek press's self-exculpating, self-glorifying, self-defensive thoughts on the Christian-Jewish relationship. Social conservatives, especially among estate owners and bureaucratic intelligentsia, and particularly in Galicia, were more likely to read the venerable Kraków-based daily *Czas* (*Time*). In November 1918 prospect of Ukrainian conquest of East Galicia and violence the largely Polish landlord class faced from insurrectionary Ruthenian

---

[50] Ibid., nos. 7 and 12 (November 22 and 27, 1918), "Bałkanizacja Polski," "O czem żydzi piszą?"

villagers froze its readers' hearts far more than news of Jewish pogroms. East Galicia was land "whose every clump of soil has been for centuries soaked in Polish blood." As Lwów's Jewish district burned, not only did *Czas* express huge relief at the city's reconquest because its inhabitants were rescued from "Ruthenian armed banditry's atrocious behavior." It also rejoiced, more profoundly, because Polish society had mustered will to maintain its rule in historic "Red Rus" (East Galicia) against Endeks and others inclined to a Wilsonian, ethnographic concept of the renascent Polish state and against social revolutionaries fixated on radical social reform at the cost of abandoning the Eastern borderlands, where it was Polish nobility and intelligentsia whose fate was mainly at stake. Lwów's saviors had won a victory comparable in grandeur to their forefathers' seventeenth-century armed feats – "the first such victory, unfortunately, in many, many a day" but promising a new flowering of Polish – "alongside, as we wish, Ruthenian culture."[51]

Czas later reported blood-curdlingly on "massacres by armed bands in Ukraine," multiplying as the German-backed regime there of Hetman Skoropadsky was pushed aside by Symon Petliura's populist Directorate. Estate managers and Polish intelligentsia were falling victim to "the raging mob, while Petliura ordered Jews to be spared" (though he was to be assassinated in 1926 for complicity in the 1918–19 Ukrainian pogroms). Among fleeing refugees' reports was one of eleven estate officials immersed in water in a cellar and reduced overnight to icebound corpses. Insurrectionists told villagers, "if you murder all Poles, the whole land will be yours." The "wild rabble" (*zdziczała czerń*) had killed thousands, many of whose distinguished names *Czas* respectfully reported. Of other captives, marauders contemptuously said, "the Pole [*Lach*, a contemptuous Ukrainian term] will buy himself free."[52]

Czas showed typical nationalist sensibility in minimizing West Galician pogroms' antisemitism, claiming that many well-off peasants and rich estate owners also fell victim to bandits and their adolescent followers. Jews' alleged demand for "extraterritorial standing" such as they never possessed anywhere risked inciting "dangerous feelings."[53] Yet, when Lwów pogrom reports proved truthful, the conservative organ took refuge in the thought that Jewish trust in Ukrainians was misplaced, for "since days of Bogdan Chmielnicki [Khmelnytsky, 1648–49] and the massacre in Humań [Uman – by Cossacks of several thousand Poles and Jews in 1768] Ruthenians were most dangerous, because blindest, of the Jewish

---

[51] *Czas*, no. 512 (November 23, 1918), "Lwów w polskich rękach."
[52] Ibid., no. 545 (December 29, 1918), "Rzezie hajdamackie na Ukrainie."
[53] Ibid., no. 508 (November 19, 1918), "pogromy."

people's enemies." Overlooking earlier bloody urban pogroms in Odessa and Kishinev, *Czas* declared that virtually all pogroms in Russia were Ruthenian villagers' handiwork.

Czas reckoned 80 percent of Jews as conservative Orthodox, 5 percent assimilationists (*żydzi-Polacy*), and the rest "fighting Zionists." The latter, drawn from "intelligentsia and half-intelligentsia, students, shop clerks, and artisans," had allegedly fought alongside Lwów's Ukrainians. Nightmare-ridden Poles confronted the "monstrous circumstance" that armed Jews in league with Ruthenians "were hunting them down." This, along with such commonplace rumors as boiling water poured on Polish soldiers, goaded the "dark masses" to violence. "A few hundred slum bandits" had been arrested. No newspapers incited Galician pogroms. Once having erupted, authorities promptly suppressed them.[54]

By December, *Czas* was straightforwardly condemning anti-Jewish violence, calling for the Polish nation to join with Jews, "such a numerous and *powerful* element among us," to regulate their mutual relationship, whether in the direction of assimilation, exercise of limited cultural-religious rights, or "Jewish national autonomy (which in practice would be return to the ghetto)." Anti-Jewish violence had swept through much of the collapsing Austrian monarchy. "The miasma of brutal and plundering antisemitism is everywhere in the air." Still, "extreme Zionist and Jewish nationalist slogans" risked unleashing violence and required moderation, particularly by Jewish voices in Western Europe. Poles were, after all, "the only nation that never persecuted Jews, that alone in Europe received them in the fourteenth century."[55]

Polish conservatives booked no cynical gains in pogroms but found Jewish self-assertion unsettling, even "monstrous." Bolshevism, which they charged the proletarian Jewish Bund with actively championing on Polish soil, was no less a nightmare than bloody agrarian revolt in Ukraine. Upper-class *Czas* readers' fate was to bend their knee to the mass-based party promising them fullest protection. It could be Dmowski's or Piłsudski's.

Polish *peasants* found political voice in demotic parties hostile both to noble landlords and Jews. In 1918, the strongest was the moderate PSL (Polish People's/Populist Party), led by village-born Witos, Liquidation Commission chair and future prime minister. Behind its front ranks of middle- and small-holding peasants stood grassroots clergy and rural

---

[54] Ibid., no. 518 (November 29, 1918), "O 'pogromach' we Lwowie."
[55] Ibid., nos. 529 and 532 (December 10 and 13, 1918), "Pogromy Żydowskie," "'Pogromy' a Niemcy" (author's emphasis).

intelligentsia of cooperative-marketing organizers, schoolteachers, and local journalists. Its flagship publication was the Kraków-based daily *Piast* (reference to medieval Poland's putative peasant origins). Its rival was *PSL-Wyzwolenie* ("Liberation"), self-consciously leftist in agrarianist sense, keen on radical land reform, with strongest support in former Russian Poland.

Piast fused militant anti-Jewish sentiments with law-and-order nationalism not unlike the Endeks'. Its article, "Tolerating Riots Is Forbidden," sent a double message.

We all know that, especially during the war, hatred of Jews grew strong in Polish society. We don't need to justify this. The Jewish element is guilty of much and itself brought forth that hatred. In some parts of our land that hatred has begun to break out in a way that accords neither with the moment's solemnity nor our nation's culture. Against this we admonish most forcefully![56]

All efforts must concentrate on state building. "We must – we must – guard against all physical disturbances, all enactments of hatred, whether racial or economic." Anathema fell on "common banditry," which, as a threshold to worse things, required forceful suppression. Thus *Piast* tacitly acknowledged that West Galician pogroms had been peasant affairs, if often triggered and brutalized by bandits (mostly uprooted villagers).

On November 24, leaving Lwów unmentioned, *Piast* strove again to persuade its readers that "Jewish Riots Don't Make Sense."

Listen up, you peasants [wrote Antoni Budziak], to what I'll tell you about the Jewish "question" ... So far not a single Jew has lost a fingernail [*sic*], while some dozens of our people have died, whether murdered by Jews or poisoned by Jewish alcohol. Nevertheless, Jews around the world are telegraphing, especially to President Wilson, that in West Galicia people are murdering Jews. That in East Galicia Jews together with Ruthenians are murdering Poles – naturally this they're not telegraphing.

Christians were suffering more than Jews, who were losing "armfuls of rags and a few hundred Austrian coins," for which they would receive full restitution from "worldwide, millions-rich organization, 'Al[l]iance Israelite.'" They would also cite losses to justify raising prices "by 50 percent."

If you want to know the truth, Jews were ready themselves to provoke riots even when Austrians [*Austryaky*] were sitting in Galicia. Why? First, to massacre our nation [*naród*] with Austrian army and, second, under pretext of riots to occupy all

[56] *Piast*, no. 45 (November 10, 1918), "Nie wolno dopuszczać do rozruchów!"

Galicia with German [*szwabskiemi*] and Magyar troops, who would gobble up the peasant's last potato and steal his hidden valuables' last traces.[57]

Riots, Budziak continued, gave unfriendly Jews an excuse to brand Poles a "wild nation" and move the Paris Conference to create "a Jewish state inside the Polish state. Get it?" *Piast*'s readers should therefore organize citizens' militias in all villages and small towns. "Down with stupid riots and robberies!" Let the Liquidation Commission impose "maximum prices on Jewish wares."

Let's remember that we ourselves turned Jews into masters by giving them our last penny. Every class helped the Jews. The nobility protected them everywhere and gave them leasehold-concessions. The intelligentsia in government offices put Jews first in settling their affairs, because Jews knew how to talk. Peasants helped raise Jews to domination, buying and selling everything from and to them ... *Jews conquered us* – with their intelligence, their diabolical cleverness [*sprytem dyabelskim*], their endurance, organization and unity, their commerce and industry.

Here antisemites' often – if unconsciously – felt inferiority complex toward Jews appears in lapidary perfection.

When *Piast* belatedly addressed Lwów's pogrom, it branded it "disgrace for its [unspecified] perpetrators" but misfortune for which neither Polish state nor Lwów's inhabitants were responsible. Jewish losses had been distorted, *Piast* (inaccurately) claimed, by counting as pogrom victims corpses of those who died during preceding fighting but whose timely burial was blocked by Ukrainian actions and which then burned in pogrom fire.[58]

The massive peasant movement *Piast* represented took pains to avoid letting pogroms, peasant-inflicted to considerable degree, weaken its aggressively anti-Jewish posture and strategies. Villagers suffered under Jews, not the opposite. Pogroms were inopportune, not on principle – antagonism to Jews was justifiable – but because they hurt national cause and peasant pocketbook. *Piast* ridiculed "peasant yokels" (*chłopini*) who let Jewish middlemen cream off harvests and livestock-raising profits. "They split their sides laughing at your ignorance."[59] Jews divided common people from intelligentsia, for by (illicitly) gaining food they needed from Jews, "the official, the educated professional" could ignore villagers' plight – sore lack of essential manufactures – in effect, paying Jews' "protection money."[60]

---

[57] Ibid., no. 47 (November 24, 1918), "Rozruchy żydowskie nie mają sensu" (author's emphasis).
[58] Ibid., no. 52 (December 29, 1918), "Z oblężonego Lwowa."
[59] Ibid., no. 45 (November 10, 1918), "Chłopski zysk w żydowskiej kieszeni."
[60] Ibid., "Stosunek inteligencyi do ludu."

What of Christian morality? *Piast* bowed to it in schoolteacher Tatara's "Heart aches, despair descends." The "godly little folk" (*bożny ludek*) teachers sought to educate were proving "cold as ice, hard as glass" because "you permit robbery, you – unfortunately – yourselves rob others' belongings, and you have no heart for human misery." Tatara chided kin-ordered authorities: "you, Christian and Polish mothers," "you, elderly, honest farmer-proprietors," and "sisters of those who reach out their hands for others' property." It was from lack of courage "to properly condemn scoundrels." Wives did not exhort husbands to oppose plunder, nor did girls spurn boys who practiced violence. "Human wrong, whether Christian or Jewish, burdens their consciences." Nor do those who could do so offer a "piece of bread to poor landless people" whom even Austrian authorities had nurtured, if inadequately. They give no "flour to teachers, who are suffering hunger."[61]

How far such heartache pulsed is indeterminable, but stonier matters of self-interest overshadowed it, just as conservative *Czas* readers' preoccupation with survival of their privileges, and even their lives, weakened earlier elite advocacy of Jewish inclusion in Polish society. For the Polish Socialist Party (PPS), by contrast, anti-Jewish violence loomed very large, especially as reproach to the antisemitic right. PPS was the paladin of politically awakened Catholic workers, leftist intellectuals, and many assimilationist Jews and also the party from whose ranks Piłsudski had emerged and which now backed him against nationalist and conservative rivals. It also nervously watched its left flank, as revolutionary forces of still incalculable potency maneuvered for grassroots backing: PPS-Left, its own prewar offshoot, which would soon join Social Democracy of the Kingdom of Poland and Lithuania to form the Polish Communist Party; Jewish Bund, ambivalently attracted to Bolshevism; and similarly tempted Poale Zion. These revolution-minded forces would revile pogroms as bourgeois rottenness and mock the PPS for making compromises with the postwar Republic.

PPS's organ was Warsaw's daily *Robotnik* ("Worker"). Its first antipogrom salvo targeted a call in "the bourgeois press" for the "Polish-Catholic" (*Polak-katolik*) to wear an identifying sign "to ease orientation on the street." This was unvarnished preparation for pogrom action by "our home-grown Black Hundred." *Robotnik*'s rhetorical mode in addressing the November pogroms was, in Marxist tradition, scornfully ironical: the Warsaw press sought to cover them up, even though it cynically did not shrink from accepting paid advertisements from "dealers

---

[61] Ibid., no. 49 (December 8, 1918), "Ból serce ściska, rozpacz człowieka ogarnia."

in human flesh" or those seeking "paid thugs to dispose of certain inconvenient individuals."[62]

Robotnik ran an impassioned essay on Lwów's pogrom by Andrzej Strug, prominent left-socialist novelist-publicist and propaganda minister in Piłsudski's provisional government. Before the violence's "immensity and monstrousness the soul shudders." Strug refrained from expressing his own views on the "tragic Jewish question," aware that they would "displease many Jews and Poles alike." He wrote instead "in defense of Polish conscience's honor" and "to awaken our intelligentsia's vigilance, who have succumbed to *disturbing neurosis.*"

Strug assumed that Lwów's explosion claimed 960 victims, yet "Polish opinion knows nothing of it!" Did "terrible indifference" explain this or "shame before the world, before Europe?" Jewish journalists spread the news abroad, and while they might seem always to speak "with bias and falsely of persecution of Jews in Poland," now they spoke truly. Strug scorned blaming of bandits and prisoners, and if Jews had fought against Poles, they should have been opposed by soldiers, not pogromists. There remained "an infamous atrocity," a "terrible secret."

Engulfing Poland is not Bolshevism, which though corrupted and drenched in rivers of blood is stamped with a great idea. Instead Poland is descending into lawless and hellish strife and a war of all against all. Arbitrariness of the fist, insubordination of every armed band, rule of lies, slander, and thuggery in political life.[63]

The end will be foreign intervention, "as to a land of savages [*dzikich ludzi*]," crippling Polish independence. Here, again, we glimpse, in lurid metaphor, Polish self-doubt and defensiveness toward the West.

Strug detected no "great idea" informing Polish antisemitism. Yet he knew it demonized Bolshevism, whose family tie to socialism he was reluctant to sever. His semiofficial *cri de coeur* corroborated Segal's dictum – that the pogroms surprised Poles themselves – while pillorying the intelligentsia, so enamored of their own ideal vision of Poland, for refusing to face them.

Leon Berenson, lawyer distinguished for defense in tsarist courts of Polish socialists, explained the indifference Strug denounced as a consequence of National Democrats' "monopolization of the Jewish question," with the effect that dissenting Poles turned away from it. "The weak bourgeois left [Polish liberalism] in its bewilderment and lack of program" succumbed to Endek mood, while Polish socialism was struggling too hard

---

[62] *Robotnik*, no. 332 (December 4, 1918), "Agitacja pogromowa."
[63] Ibid., no. 47 (November 24, 1918), "Rozruchy żydowskie nie mają sensu" (author's emphasis).

for survival to fight antisemitism. In Lwów, Dmowskyites celebrated a "great victory," signaling successful cultivation of "instincts of the street, transformation of anti-Jewish aggression into national obligation."[64]

Robotnik followed Berenson's call for socialist counterattack with fellow lawyer and non-PPS Piłsudskiite politician Aleksander Babiański's revelation that mainstream Warsaw dailies, including bourgeois *Kuryer Polski* and pro-governmental *Nowa Gazeta*, had refused his antipogrom protest's publication. He, not Jewish, recounted his attendance, with "crowds of Jewish intelligentsia," at a memorial service at Warsaw's Tłomackie St. Great Synagogue. "When the speaker [eminent Rabbi Samuel Poznański] announced that [Lwów's] misfortune had provoked neither protest nor outraged society, but encountered only silence, shame reddened our faces." The press devoted itself instead to sedulously recording every excuse, viewing Jewish losses as nothing more than unavoidable, unintentional consequences of the anti-Ukrainian fight.[65]

A three-part report from Lwów crowned *Robotnik*'s coverage of November's pogroms. It was (it recklessly charged) Ukrainian legionnaires – allegedly though unexplainedly (as Endek Głąbiński had charged) with k.k. Austrian military backing – who ignited the fighting and, threatening to kill every tenth adult male Pole, created a terror-filled atmosphere. The prepogrom weeks recalled, to the socialist journalist, Paris's 1871 siege. Workers streamed "in crowds" to the Polish armed forces, where Piłsudskiite legionnaires led a counterattack, until joined by the government's expeditionary relief corps. It was, if a Polish triumph, also a tragic "slaughter of two fraternal peoples, accompanied by most atrocious wildness and bestialization," still persisting outside the East Galician capital with undiminished ruthlessness and ferocity. Guilty in first instance were Ukrainian nationalists.

Among Lwów Poles, *Robotnik* continued, Endeks now held power, fanning flames. They aimed to partition Ukraine, taking the historically Polish-dominated lands on the Dnieper's right bank and leaving the rest to Russia. To avert this outcome, Polish and Ukrainian socialists must cooperate, not quarrel. As for Lwów's Jews, on Polish victory day, "crowds threw themselves on the Jewish quarter and carried out the pogrom," displaying "complete inhumanity, complete bestialization," taking hundreds of lives in "unheard-of wildness, incomprehensible crowd madness," including holocausts of victims in burning buildings: "on victory day torches of Nero [sacrifices by fire] illuminated the city." Thus was the "Polish nation's good name sullied." Despite all Endek talk

---

[64] Ibid., no. 339 (December 8, 1918), "Z powodu Lwowa."
[65] Ibid., no. 344 (December 11, 1918), "Z powodu pogromów."

of bandits and prisoners, "it is fact that people belonging to Polish armed forces took part in shameful events, not hesitating to besmirch fresh Polish uniforms."

Moral responsibility fell "undoubtedly" on Jewish nationalists who allegedly fought alongside Ukrainians. But that in no way justified pogrom. The inaction of Polish commanders – Mączyński, Rozwadowski, Sikorski – suggested they sanctioned the pogrom. They and Endek politicians turned Lwów into anti-Piłsudski fortress, which the Warsaw government must promptly subdue. There must be political settlement with Ukrainians and replacement of the army with urban people's militia.

On December 20, *Robotnik* gave voice to the Union of Polish Socialist Youth, who expressed their outrage at the Endek-inspired "disgraceful [pogromist] gang[s] without honor or faith" who had "cast a shadow on the whole Polish nation." The young socialists (also defensive about self-feared Polish backwardness) harbored a patriotic love for the common folk (*lud*) that aimed "to equal that of the peoples of the West in its fostering of national spirit and humanity of feeling."[66]

Socialist interpretation of November pogroms began with moral strickenness and ended in confident, militant ideology. Respectable Warsaw bourgeois dailies equivocated. *Kuryer Polski*, founded in 1898, associated itself in December 1918 with liberal intelligentsia and their hopeful but short-lived political vehicles, Union of Polish Democracy (*Związek Demokracji Polskiej*) and National Independence Party (*Stronnictwo Niezawisłości Narodowej*). On December 9, *Kuryer* wrote of the "alleged pogrom" in Lwów, which had been "shouted about" across Europe. Jewish irregular fighters had, in opposing Polish reconquest, lost 100 men. Simultaneously, "the rabble came out of the woodwork and began robbing," though the army smartly put them down. The Jewish commune ungratefully refused the city government's – alleged (but miserly) – offer of a half-million Kr. compensation.[67]

In publicizing the Independence Party's program, *Kuryer Polski* struck new tones. "From one side Bolshevik invasion and ruin threaten us, from the other National Democracy's aggressiveness, wanting to oppose 'Bolshevism of the left' with its 'Bolshevism of the right' and responsible, through its past sowing of tribal hatred, for not a few of today's mob excesses." In short, pogroms were the work of Endeks and scum. The new party, conversely, advocated "harmonious co-existence with other nations, condemnation of all chauvinism and political exploitation of

[66] Ibid., no.362 (December 20, 1918), "Przeciwko pogromom."
[67] *Kuryer Polski*, no. 307 (December 9, 1918), "Zajścia we Lwowie."

tribal animosities, and so also condemns minimizing antisemitic outbreaks' abominations, which have supplied our enemies with weapons to slander us abroad."[68]

Kuryer Warszawski, widely read among Warsaw's centrist and liberal officialdom and intelligentsia, printed the government's none too conciliatory pronouncements on November's pogroms, to which on bloody November 23 it added a harsh attack on Jewish nationalists' anti-Polonism. This had allegedly soared along with German wartime victories, betraying Jewish backing for "our country's Germanization." Now such Jews sought international guarantees of separatist rights in Poland. How had they greeted Polish independence? "Jewish processions cried 'Down with Poland,' 'Down with the Polish Army.'" This had inspired assimilationists and the Orthodox to step forth with public dissents.

The Polish population treated all this, from war's beginning, with coolheadedness and patience worthy of a cultured nation. There were no anti-Jewish explosions, no use of arms against hostile Jewish street skirmishes[!]. Small-scale, bloodless clashes in some localities bore marks of commercial, not confessional or racial competition. Nowhere more clearly than here did the peaceful and self-controlled Polish temperament reveal itself.[69]

This illusion-rich, projection-laden, self-congratulatory self-portrait returned to earth with acknowledgment that "Jews will remain in Poland," even if they look for backing now, not to Russia's vanished Kadet Party, nor to German imperialism, but to Trotsky, or worldwide Jewish finance, or to "the naiveté of western democratic doctrines." One thing they neglect: "to offer tangible proofs of their attachment to this land and their desire for honest understanding with their real hosts in Poland." Here pulsed the resentment-laden antisemitism that had penetrated a bourgeois- and intelligentsia-based liberalism which had earlier been confident of patriotism among educated and propertied Jews. Now, after half-millennium's residence, Jews were disloyal, unfriendly lodgers in the house of foreigners.

The Assimilationist and Zionist Press

Warsaw's twice-daily *Nowa Gazeta*, founded 1906, was influential in Jewish assimilationist circles and among Polish liberal intelligentsia, many of whose prestigious authors wrote for it. It soft-pedaled Jewish affairs, describing its standpoint as a nonparty "organ of democratic, free-thinking opinion," though it viewed benevolently the new National

[68] Ibid., no. 310 (December 12, 1918), "Oświadczenie Związku Demokracji Polskiej."
[69] *Kuryer Warszawski*, no. 324 (November 23, 1918), "Ze zaślepieniem."

Independence Party, which advocated "strictly secular schools."[70] Its first comments on the Lwów pogrom repeated the Liquidation Commission's aforementioned denialist blaming of bandits and "Jewish cut-purses" while condemning more drastic accounts as German propaganda. Though *Nowa Gazeta* castigated Dmowski for his party's "fighting antisemitism," unfitting him as Poland's Paris representative, it redoubled its charges against Jews, both for firing on Poles in Lwów and, as Polish searches allegedly discovered, for hiding grenades, machine guns, rifles, and pistols in Jewish shops. "That was the reason for the so-called 'Jewish pogrom.'"[71]

But soon the paper's defenses crumbled: Lwów had indeed suffered a "massacre" by "the mob." It was true that "terrible things" had transpired. Despite Jewish pro-Ukrainianism, or "dishonest speculation" in daily necessities "which in the poorest and most benighted rabble inspired visceral hatred," violence was unjustifiable. There was antisemitism in Poland, as elsewhere in Europe. "We are fighting it." But it did not ignite Lwów's disaster, which was rather work of "social dregs" worsened by corrosive war fought by foreigners "over our living land." Strong government, such as Piłsudski promised, would clear streets of rabble and scum. Deprived of its myrmidons, Endek antisemitism would languish in its crannies, heartening Jews and other minorities to assimilate into a secularized, liberal-democratic polity.[72]

The leading Polish-language journal for the Zionist-minded was Kraków's *Nowy Dziennik*, founded July 1918 on initiative of Rabbi Osias/ Ozjasz Thon, who had journeyed from familial Hasidism through enlightened liberal-maskilic education to leadership of West Galician Zionism and political eminence in reborn Poland. His religious-political arc was paradigmatic for many Polish Jews, its middle phase leading to Polish language and preference for it even after embrace of Zionism, with its resignation from primary identification with the Polish nation. Together with *Nasz Przegląd* ("Our Review"), widely read popular daily launched in 1923, *Nowy Dziennik* spoke until 1939 for the rapidly expanding circle of linguistically Polonized, socially modernizing, largely city-dwelling Jews of varying religious piety who were coming to terms with Polish citizenship and identity while also rejecting assimilationism, partly in reaction to antisemitism, partly because of Jewish nationalism's appeal. Their path was that which, very probably, Polish Jewry as a whole – apart from emigrants to Palestine and elsewhere and the Hasidic core – would have

[70] *Nowa Gazeta*, no. 538 (December 20, 1918), "Nasze stanowisko"; ibid., no. 499 (November 29, 1918), "Program oświaty S.N.N."
[71] Ibid., nos. 503 and 509 (December 1 and 4, 1918), "Fałsz o pogromie," "Ostrzeżenie."
[72] Ibid., no. 511 (December 5, 1918), "Straszne rzeczy."

followed into the present, whatever interwar Zionist expectations might have been, had the Holocaust not catastrophically descended.

On November 3, *Nowy Dziennik* hailed Polish reunification and independence in rhetoric of romantic nationalism's "miraculous teaching": "when the state falls, but the nation lives, it will eventually rebuild it; but if the nation dies and the state remains, it too will disintegrate like the wooden coffin in which the corpse is laid." Mighty Zionist-led meetings had already expressed, "loudly and unmistakably," virtually the whole of Polish Jewry's loyalty to the new Polish state and willingness to bear their citizenly responsibilities.

Indeed, Poland's restoration is full confirmation of the national Jewish ideology which for two thousand years, despite sufferings such as no other human community has traversed, believes unshakably in rebuilding of its people's lost self-sufficiency, and day after day repeats with unbroken obstinacy: "I believe with complete faith in the coming of the Redeemer [*Zbawcy*], delayed though it may be."[73]

Such language evoked, deliberately or unconsciously, the parallelism of Polish and Zionist nationalist messianism.

Jewry's formerly "separate intellectual culture," *Nowy Dziennik* added, which had never been purely religious, had now become "completely secularized, completely worldly." This formulation avoided Zionism's reduction to a plea for religious freedom and entitled its followers to appeal to President Wilson, "to whose protection we submit ourselves, like all oppressed nations awaiting liberation," for "national autonomy" in new Poland. This would be no "state within the state" but rather personal autonomy of those signing their names on a national cataster so as to gain proportional political representation for the voluntaristically identified Jewish electorate, legal protection of Jewish languages, and pedagogical self-administration. Building on similar, promising efforts in the late Austrian monarchy – in Moravia and Bukovina – proportional representation for national minorities would end politicized nationality struggles, leaving each ethnicity to select within its own ranks political representatives to occupy a guaranteed block of parliamentary seats. Such "freedom of national confession," paired with Jews' "unconditional faithfulness to the Polish state," was Zionists' simple and honorable prescription for "both sides' salvation."

Galicia's Liquidation Commission had issued on November 5 an appeal – in the name of its Endek chairman Count Skarbek, Tarnów Mayor Tertil, and provisional Prime Minister Moraczewski – to Jews to

---

[73] *Nowy Dziennik*, no. 115 (November 3, 1918), "Polska a Żydzi."

join in building the state, in which they would enjoy fullest civil rights and freedoms such as were extended to Jewish populations "by all great and free civilized nations," adding that "we condemn all excesses and violence aimed specifically at Jews and will employ all means to prevent them or, should they occur, ruthlessly suppress them." *Nowy Dziennik* welcomed these words yet demanded recognition of Polish Jews as a separate nation (*naród*), expressing ill-informed confidence that in the United States, and new Germany and Austria too, formal recognition of Jewish nationality would soon be written into constitutional law.[74]

On November 6, as "news of anti-Jewish excesses reached us from all directions," Kraków Zionists organized mass demonstrations that unhorsed the hitherto dominant power holders in the Jewish religious community – stigmatized as "assimilationist-Jewish communalist clique" (*klika asymilatorsko-kahalna*) – whose relation to the Jewish masses *Nowy Dziennik* aggressively likened to that of "[Prussian] Junker landlords and army generals to the German nation." Jewish notables' unfortunate policies "had poisoned our relation to the Polish nation," which cannot now understand "that the Jew dares to claim for himself the same rights that every nation in the world demands."[75]

On November 8, the Zionist organ began a stream of reportage on "pogroms in Galicia," from which details on many above-mentioned instances derive. Disappointed in expectations that Polish authorities would squelch anti-Jewish excesses, the journal bitterly lamented:

The Black Hundred is at work in Galicia. Bands of hooligans, peasants, soldiers, deserters rob, beat, and plunder Jews ... At the dawn of Poland's reawakening to its own independent life, in this luminous historical moment, all society's scum, minds saturated with years-long antisemitic agitation, bestir themselves to a bloody feast.

Poles "always say with pride [that] there were no pogroms in Poland." But actually, there were no pogroms under the partitions (in fact, there were some). But now "all Galicia burns," while Liquidation Commission stands idle. The army must act in Polish honor and culture's name. Jewish militias must be armed. "The Jewish people, who in thousandfold demonstrations and deeds greeted Poland's resurrection, now suffer most horrendous cataclysm at organized and armed hyenas' hands." To this outburst the newspaper added last-minute news that the Liquidation Commission had recognized Kraków's Zionist-hued Jewish National

---

[74] Ibid., no. 117 (November 5, 1918), "Odezwa P.K.L. do Żydów"; no. 118 (November 6, 1918), "Za skąpo."
[75] Ibid., no. 119 (November 7, 1918), "Walka ludu żydowskiego o kahał."

Council (*Żydowska Rada Narodowa*) as Jews' political representative, proposing to cooperate with it against pogromists.[76]

Weighing blame, *Nowy Dziennik* charged that, while street-level pogromists were social scum, "guilt for pogroms having occurred rests on those at Polish society's pinnacle" who fattened themselves on "deepening racial differences." Pogromists acted on antisemitic calls to "dejudaize Poland." With few exceptions, the intelligentsia contemplate current violence "neutrally," while the press is mostly silent or blames foreign demobilized soldiers. Not common folk were guilty, but "so-called intelligentsia." To rescue Polish honor was not Jewish task. "We will defend ourselves and not let ourselves be physically beaten." Jews would avail themselves of the universal right to appeal to the Paris peace conference. This Zionists knew would deeply provoke Polish nationalists. "Pay heed! Pay heed!" they cried to them.[77]

Nowy Dziennik's interpretation of Lwów's "horror-inspiring" pogrom appeared on November 27.[78] When the army first swept into the city "the Polish population's joy was limitless." But with its command that all men aged 17–35 report for conscription "one could feel that something was cooking against Jews." Cries arose on the street: "the day of reckoning has come for the Jews." Robberies began. Jewish notables' pleas to town authorities were ignored. Jewish quarter having been cordoned off, officer-led patrols ordered apartment blocs to open their gates, locked during fighting by Ukrainian order. Behind them came patrols of six to twenty fighters in legionnaires' uniforms who went from dwelling to dwelling, among Jews only, carrying our "inspections," and "confiscating possessions – especially money – on threat of on-the-spot execution." Simultaneously, plundering began of shops, their shutters and doors hand grenaded. Carts and trucks hauled away goods and shop fixtures "under strong escort."

In crisis, Lwów's "Poles of Mosaic Faith" vainly sought authority's ear. Calls arose for Jewish communal leaders' resignation. On Saturday morning, army Commander General Roja heard a Jewish delegation's denunciation, aimed – diplomatically – at "uniformed bandits" rather than regular soldiers. Expressing his "deep regret," he issued sharp orders to the troops, promising introduction of courts martial with powers of immediate execution. Arrests began. Meanwhile, plundering seized the town center, where various luxury stores were looted, including that of the aforementioned Gabriel Stark, whom *Nowy Dziennik* paused to label a

---

[76] Ibid., no. 120 (November 8, 1918), "Pogromy w Galicyi."
[77] Ibid., no. 121 (November 9, 1918), "Kto jest winnym?"
[78] Ibid., no. 139 (November 27, 1918), "Masakra w dzielnicy żydowskiej Lwowa."

"baptized Jew." Habsburg-style coffee houses for upper classes, including the "New York," were not merely looted, but destroyed in demonstrative obliteration of Jewish presence at city's heart.

It must be said that many Poles, surveying this mindless and unprecedented plunder, indignantly called on pogromists not to besmirch Poland's honor with such barbarian deeds. The perpetrators [*ekscedenci*] replied that, as reward for Lwów's conquest, they had been given forty-eight hours to rob Jews.

In predominantly Catholic neighborhoods, pogromists forced apartment house supervisors on pain of death to identify Jewish tenants. By Saturday afternoon, plumes of smoke over the Jewish quarter were joined by streams of flames visible from afar. Polish Christian eyewitnesses told of how army units prevented residents of exclusively Jewish-occupied buildings from escaping the flames by shooting those who attempted it.

Nowy Dziennik later scathingly rejected the Liquidation Commission's self-exculpatory and antisemitic apology for the Galician pogroms (leaving Lwów unmentioned). Was it possible that it contained not a word of condemnation of the "'bandits' who besmirched Poland's name before the entire civilized world?" Nor one word of sympathy for victims of "bestial pogroms"? Galicia's "provincial caciques" lacked the intelligence and heart to comprehend the damage their "hatred of Jews" was inflicting on their own country. Did they suppose that pogromists were authorized to punish Jews for imagined pro-Prussianism? And if loyalism toward the Habsburg monarchy, while it ruled in Galicia, was a fault, did not Polish elites exhibit it to highest degree? *Nowy Dziennik* existed as a "mediating organ" between Jews and Poles, committed to search for agreement. "Two and a half million people cannot be murdered, or driven out, or even starved, without generating most fatal consequences for the perpetrator no less than for those who are crushed."[79]

We have heard Galician voices but not yet those from Warsaw, headquarters both of Polish Zionism and the Yiddish-language press. *Nowy Dziennik* reported on a thousand-voiced protest staged in Warsaw by Zeire Zion – Polish Zionism's leftist, antibourgeois wing. It denounced pogroms as work of "Polish black reaction" seeking to "drown in Jewish blood revolutionary flames that have engulfed all Europe." It expressed confidence that the "conscious Polish proletariat" had not stained its hands. Principal speakers were nonrevolutionary Rabbi Thon, speaking in Hebrew and "the Jewish language," and Warsaw-born journalist-politician Itzhak Grünbaum. The mood in Jewish Warsaw generally

[79] Ibid., no. 140 (November 28, 1918), "P.K.L. o pogromach."

was "exceptionally stricken," but huge efforts were aiding Lwów victims.[80]

The Zionist Organization addressed the assimilation question in a press release of the preliminary conference that was preparing a nationwide Jewish assembly in January 1919. Its English-language version said that "the opinion of Polish politicians and diplomatists sentenced Jews to amalgamation with the Polish surrounding."

Also from the Jews' side this policy has been defended by the assimilators, who have seen their highest ideal in the decay of the Jews as a separate community, as a nation with its own forms of life, ideal hopes and wishes. Like a wall they stood between the Polish and Jewish nations [and] falsified Jewish public opinion, concealed the actual shape of Polish Jews, their real wishes and demands.

Already before the war, "a terrible antisemitic hunt was cultivated, a boycott of the economic and social branches of life organized." Poles were complicit in tsarist antisemitism and in "espionage affairs in the first year of this war, which cost the Jews much blood and many victims." Poles had lost belief in "the possibility and [desire] of the Jews to assimilate ... and the call to assimilate only remained as an excuse."[81]

Warsaw Zionists' memorial to the governmental commission investigating the Lwów pogrom saw Galicia's separation from Austria as a "cardinal change" in Poles' relation to the former crownland's Jews. "What had previously run deep in the soul of an important part of Polish society and had been covered with a varnish of European culture suddenly broke to the surface. The Jews, deprived of the protection of a well-organized and strong state, were thrown as prey to mob instincts." Decades of anti-Jewish agitation by "the most powerful and numerous group in Polish society, the National Democrats, attained a splendid result," for simultaneously with Poland's liberation pogroms erupted practically everywhere.

The Zionist memorial documented acceptance already on November 10 by the Polish military's chief of staff Stanislaw Łapiński of Jewish neutrality in Lwów, as well as the predominantly military character of the subsequent pogrom. "It was mainly officers and the army that plundered," using military vehicles and Red Cross wagons. "The wild horde of uniformed bandits was so far bestialized as to throw living people into the flames." Torah rolls and other sacred objects were hand-grenaded and bayoneted. Czesław Mączyński, Lwów Poles' military commander, now continued his "repulsive agitation" from university lecterns. Everything

[80] Ibid., no. 147 (December 5, 1918), "Echo pogromu lwowskiego w Warszawie."
[81] CZA. L6/114 (n.d.), "Political Declaration of the Preliminary Conference."

pointed "to the pogrom's organization by certain [unspecified] circles, to criminal passivity of the military authorities."[82]

On December 9, the Central Committee of the Zionist Organization in Poland unfurled a livid proclamation, "To the Polish Nation." It was meant to accompany a one-day countrywide Jewish work stoppage and to be read in synagogues and meeting halls. It branded the "anti-Jewish terror raging throughout the land" as "bloody bestialization." It denounced various efforts to justify "such slaughter, slaughter of elders and children, burning of people alive, rape and murder of women" without "a single Pole coming forward publicly to condemn this monstrous crime without reservation," with no one to oppose those "who ceaselessly set dogs on Jews and continue to do so." With four dead in Kielce and "960 corpses of atrociously murdered Jews in Lwów," Poland's "populist government" had still not issued the powerful condemnation that might "somewhat wash away bloody stains of disgrace from resurrected independent Poland."

At the grave of those burned alive, murdered, butchered and shot we express our pain and rage against those who, with their incessant baiting of Jews, prepared the [Lwów] pogrom, against those who with aid of false distortions and silence of indifference want to veil and justify the crime.[83]

The proclamation ended with an oath, swearing no rest until "our captivity's chains are broken and Jews' bloody road in exile" ends, until Jewish rights were secured, the Jewish people liberated, and "our fatherland [*ojczyzna*], our Israelite land" rebuilt. More militant words are scarcely imaginable, nor greater contrast with the concept of "Pole of Mosaic faith," ideal of Jewish assimilators and Polish Christians friendly to their Jewish fellow citizens.

---

[82] CZA. A127/74, "Do Zwierzchniej Komisji Śledczej."
[83] CZA. A127/73 (December 9, 1918).

Part II

National Independence's After-Tremors

5   Jews in Russian Poland, 1914–1919
German Friends, Russian Enemies, Polish Rivals, Zionist Prophets

This chapter bridges the Galician turmoil and tragedies we have so far contemplated and troubles to come in independent Poland and its eastern borderlands. It introduces Zionists in former Russian Poland, whose Warsaw-centered organization and politicians would figure crucially in stamping Polish-Jewish relations. It marshals new evidence on Jewish immiseration in German-occupied Poland and on early wartime Russian-provoked anti-Jewish violence that compounded it. It ends with November 1918's Kielce pogrom, a baleful prologue to subsequent assaults carried out under the anti-Bolshevik banner, suffused with wild paranoia over Jews' presence in resurrected independent Poland. Polish nationalists, despite their bravado, were beset by anxiety that their newly regained state might fail, or fall to Bolshevism, whether imposed by the Red Army or by clandestine Jewish-driven machinations within the country. November 1918 – and the next two years – were, for Poles, an apocalyptic moment between self-achieved triumph and fear of defeat by newly arisen specters beyond their ken.

The War's Uncertain Futures

The Habsburg monarchy's fall spared its subjects' blood, even if they fought over its severed limbs. The Romanov Empire expired in anarchic and murderous civil war, darkened by internecine terrorisms unknown in Europe since Robespierre's day. The lands of historic Poland that had been absorbed entirely into the Russian state – Lithuanian Grand Duchy and right-bank Ukraine – were swept into revolution's vortex. The Warsaw-centered Congress Kingdom – ethnographic Russian Poland – escaped this fate while witnessing at close range the Russian Revolution's savage workings. After the Polish state's rebirth, struggle over the eastern borderlands ignited clashes with Russian armies, from which Piłsudski's soldiers emerged more than half-victorious: they repulsed the Red Army from Warsaw's outskirts and successfully planted their flag on a line far

east of Polonophone heartland, from Wilno/Vilne/Vilnius south to Lwów/
Lemberik/L'viv.

By these various strokes of fate, some 2 million Jews – apart from
Galicia's near-million – found themselves tenants in a many-winged
Polish-ruled mansion. Some, understanding themselves as historic
Polish Jewry's heirs, thought this exilic abode appropriate and inevitable. Others, whose ties to the Polish-ruled past had frayed and
broken during partition or whose soaring Jewish self-identity demoted
other loyalties, found the prospect of Polish citizenship, in a
political culture roiled by antisemitism, daunting, discouraging, and
alarming.

After 1914 and before Piłsudski took residence in 1918 in Warsaw's
Belvedere Palace, other futures were imaginable. One was continued
Russian rule, amplified by conquest of Austria's Ukrainian-inhabited
East Galicia and Bukovina – a possibility not ruled out before the
tsardom's 1917 fall or before 1920's Polish-Soviet showdown.
Another was recasting of Russian Poland and its eastern periphery
into a German satellite state. This vision Berlin pursued after con-
quest of Warsaw in summer 1915, as unveiling of its protectorate
"Kingdom of Poland" in November 1916 showed. This new state's
eastward expansion was stymied by German hopes of creating a
second, multinational dependency in the Lithuanian-Belarusian-
Eastern Baltic occupation space of army-ruled "Ober-Ost" and by
German godfathering in 1917–18 of yet a third client state, in Ukraine
under conservative Hetman Skoropadsky. Not before the Central
Powers' November 1918 defeat and retreat from occupied Poland
was it certain that a chain of German satellites would not span
Eastern Europe.

Unlike wartime Galicia, where Austria's Jewish subjects were duty
bound to abide under Habsburg rule, Jews in Russian Poland balanced
on multiple knife edges of loyalty. Temptation to render nothing more
than what momentarily enthroned Caesars demanded was great. Discreet
entertainment of better prospects beckoned. Among Russian-ruled Jews'
most ardent suitors were German coreligionists, mostly Zionists but also
German patriots "of Mosaic faith," who mobilized at war's outset as the
"German Committee for Liberation of Russian Jews" but who soon
adopted the stealthier title of "Committee for the East."

These German-Jewish missionaries to Polish Jewry discovered that
their eastern coreligionists were cold to colonialization from Berlin.
Kaiser Wilhelm's officials in Russian Poland benevolently extended lib-
erties to their new-won Jewish subjects unattainable under tsarism: education and newspaper journalism in Hebrew and/or Yiddish and freedom

to form civil-society associations and political parties. But in Berlin and Vienna, recruitment of Christian Polish collaborators in the "Kingdom of Poland" project outweighed patronage of Jewish interests. Conservative-monarchist Poles, tempted by the Central Powers' overtures, were loath to be branded conciliators of Jews, for populist antisemites already scorned them as advocates (and secret agents) of German-Austrian victory and enemies of Polish independence. The greater the self-governing powers the occupiers devolved on Poles, the shakier was Jews' sense of protectedness.

By 1917–18, Congress Kingdom Jews were Berlin's and Vienna's unloved step-children at best. German authorities began scapegoating the eastern Jewish masses. They stigmatized them as disease ridden, roughly disinfecting them and their dwellings. They blamed Jewish merchants ("smugglers") for faltering civilian provisioning, closing the border with Germany to them. They recruited them into strenuous, even brutal war-economy labor. The Austrians, desperate to control dwindling food supplies and raw materials, marginalized Jewish merchants and wholesalers, who yet bore the brunt of shoppers' rage. The entire Congress Kingdom population, except upper classes, succumbed to gnawing hunger. Even though the occupiers maintained sufficient discipline to forestall anti-Jewish collective violence, few Jews here, unlike in Galicia, regretted the Central Powers' 1918 defeat and ignominious flight.[1]

Polish Zionist Hopes and Fears

Zionism bestrode Russian Poland's political stage only under German occupation, after enduring tsarist outlawing of Jewish political movements. It leaned under Warsaw-housed Heschel Farbstein's leadership toward Hebraist purism and Palestinianism. But Jewish coexistence with Poles was daily reality, and as prospects of postwar Polish statehood brightened, crystallization of a Zionist domestic program grew pressing, especially as widely popular Yiddish-favoring Folkists and Bundists both

---

[1] On the war in Russian Poland, see Robert Blobaum, *A Minor Apocalypse: Warsaw During the First World War* (Ithaca, NY: Cornell University Press, 2017). On these pages' German dimension, see Steven Aschheim, *Brothers and Strangers: The East European Jew in German and German Jewish Consciousness, 1800–1923* (Madison, WI: University of Wisconsin Press, 1982); Liulevicius, *War Land*; Frank Schuster, *Zwischen allen Fronten: Osteuropäische Juden während des Ersten Weltkrieges (1914–1919)* (Köln: Böhlau, 2004); Conze, *Polnische Nation und deutsche Politik*; Egmont Zechlin, *Die deutsche Politik und die Juden im Ersten Weltkrieg* (Göttingen: Vandenhoeck & Ruprecht, 1969); Prusin, *Nationalizing a Borderland*; and Zieliński, *Stosunki polsko-żydowskie na ziemiach Królestwa Polskiego w czasie pierwszej wojny światowej*.

prized Jewish life in East European diaspora – *Doykheit* ("being here") – above emigration to Palestine.[2]

So too, for religious reasons, did the emergent Orthodox Jewish political party, Agudat Israel. Growing from several historic roots, reaching back from the party's 1912 founding on German Orthodox initiative in Katowice/Kattowitz to Orthodoxy's nineteenth-century confrontation with *Haskalah* and forward to launching of its Polish branch in Warsaw in 1916, it sought to give religious Jews political voice through rabbinical leadership, including that of charismatic Hasidic rebbes. Religious authority would supply answers Jews – community of faith and culture, not political nation – needed to confront modernity. Friction with Christian Poles could be minimized by limiting Jewish political objectives to religious needs.

Agudat Israel accepted Yiddish as quotidian reality but, in opposition to prominent journalist Noach Prylucki's *Folkspartey*, rejected Yiddishism as definitive of an emergent ethnocultural Jewish nation in Eastern Europe. In Warsaw's 1916 city council election, whose districting and taxpayer curias underrepresented Jewish voters while advantaging prosperous over poor, among twenty Jewish deputies (of ninety altogether) twelve were "assimilators," alongside three representatives of Orthodoxy, including two from Agudat Israel. In the demotic sixth curia, the *Folkspartey* (8,680 votes) won four seats, Zionists (1,920 votes) but one. Agudat Israel's relation to German authority was good because its goals were far easier than secular Jewish parties' to fulfill.[3]

German Zionists, deep-dyed in Germanophone culture, were active in conquered Russian Poland, struggling mainly against undesired futures for Polish Jews (especially their linguistic and cultural Polonization) and against Polish antisemitism. Their Berlin Organization (ZO) recorded a

---

[2] Ezra Mendelsohn, *Zionism in Poland: The Formative Years, 1915–1926* (New Haven, CT: Yale University Press, 1981); Ezra Mendelsohn, *The Jews of East Central Europe Between the World Wars* (Bloomington, IN: University of Indiana Press, 1983); Marian Fuks, *Żydzi w Warszawie* (Poznań: Sorus, 1992); Israel Gutman et al., *The Jews of Poland Between Two World Wars* (Hanover, NH: University Press of New England, 1989); Polonsky, *Jews in Poland and Russia*, vols. 2 and 3; Robert Blobaum, *Rewolucja: Russian Poland, 1904–1907* (Ithaca, NY: Cornell University Press, 1995); Blobaum, *Minor Apocalypse*; Scott Ury, *Barricades and Banners: The Revolution of 1905 and the Transformation of Warsaw Jewry* (Stanford, CA: University of California Press, 2012); Keith Weiser, *Jewish People, Yiddish Nation: Noah Prylucki and the Folkists in Poland* (Toronto: Toronto University Press, 2011); Bernard Johnpoll, *The Politics of Futility: The General Jewish Workers Bund of Poland, 1917–1943* (Ithaca, NY: Cornell University Press, 1967); Zvi Gitelman et al., *The Emergence of Modern Jewish Politics: Bundism and Zionism in Eastern Europe* (Pittsburgh, PA: University of Pennsylvania Press, 2003).

[3] Gershon Bacon, *The Politics of Tradition: Agudat Yisrael in Poland, 1916–1939* (Jerusalem: Magnes, 1996). On elections, see Zieliński, *Stosunki polsko-żydowskie*, 267–68; Blobaum, *Apocalypse*, 159*ff*.

1915 meeting in Stockholm of Zionist representatives Dr. Ehrenpreis and Warsaw attorney Patek with PPS leader Ignacy Daszyński and other Western-oriented Polish independence seekers. They gathered at the home of Countess Julia Ledóchowska, Ursuline nun (later sainted) and sister of Jesuit General Włodzimierz Ledóchowski. In this high realm of Catholic Poland, Patek reported on a visit with British Zionists Baron Edmond Rothschild, Claude Montefiore, and Lucien Wolff. To Patek's modest proposal that Polish Jews should attain civil equality, "the gentlemen replied" – benevolently but conservatively – "that they wished the Polish Jews to be such good patriots for Poland as they were for England." Ehrenpreis condemned "Poles' criminal treatment and sinful behavior toward Jews," but Daszyński denied it, blaming incidents Ehrenpreis cited on Russians and producing a corroborative published statement by "patriotic Polish Jews."

As for Jewish national autonomy in future Poland, the Poles present said "they will neither fight it nor satisfy it, whereupon Daszyński sought to heap ridicule upon it by reference to Yiddishist aspirations for linguistic autonomy." Poland would guarantee full civil equality. "If the Jews want to use this to develop their national individuality, they may do it. That's your affair, we won't hinder it, but we won't advance it. We're looking out for Polish identity." Yet their present mission was to seek "closer relations and understanding with Jews," which Ehrenpreis applauded.[4]

Countess Ledóchowska was Poland's formidable advocate and red flag to Zionist bull. She undertook Scandinavian tours, presenting herself as "grieving Poland." She spoke with "gushing eloquence and fanatical forcefulness," now in Swedish, now German, now French. An account of wartime antisemitism submitted to Warsaw's notables-studded Citizens' Committee Chair Prince Lubomirski by Yiddish and Zionist Hebrew newspapers complained that her presentations were silent on "enormous sins Poles have committed against the Jewish popular masses." Germans having opened Warsaw's public parks (against tsarist practice) to traditionally garbed Jews, Poles had stoned and beaten them, exhorted by the Endek press, which accused such Jewish strollers of spoiling "good Polish weather." After German conquest of the Congress Kingdom, Jewish expellees and refugees returning home found their houses and shops in the hands of Poles who would not relinquish them. Nor were Jews allowed to resume their seats on Warsaw's suburban town councils. Endeks wanted emigrant Poles to come from America to take uprooted Jews' place. Jews could serve only in Warsaw militia's lower echelons, while Christian militiamen beat civilian Jews unconscious with rubber truncheons, stole their

---

[4] CZA. L6/102 (meeting of July 16, 1915).

wares, and "drove them through the streets like a school of herring." Jews were expelled from food-ration centers by harassment, even pogrom threats by men brandishing knives. The shop women said, "there's nothing here for Bailisses [*sic*], only straw." Preachers of hate "would hang whole masses of Jews if they could." Such was the outrage with which the big-circulation popular Jewish press denounced antisemitism high and low.[5]

In October 1917, shortly before November 7's Bolshevik power seizure in Petrograd and the Balfour Declaration's November 9 publication, the Polish Zionists' third national conference met in Warsaw, assembling some 360 delegates (including forty religious Zionists from the Mizrachi affiliate). A triumphalist mood concerning the "Jewish Question's internationalization" prevailed. Herzl was apostrophized: "Great Leader! Victory has finally arrived! Thy will and Thy sacred truth hath vanquished all opponents. Now the emissaries of his people stand before the memory of his name with bowed heads. (Stormy applause.)" That Poland was recently liberated (from Russian rule), "that an enslaved people regains its power and independence, is also our victory, a victory of our principles."

"Dark clouds" still overhung the Polish-Jewish relationship, as Yehoshua Gottlieb lamented, offering psychological explanation stressing Russian influences.

The chains of Poland's external oppression are sundered, but not fully broken is the power of dark prejudice's inner compulsion, expressing lingering pains of hard times endured. This befogs and blinds a large part of the Polish people, releasing in them feelings of enmity and embitterment toward Jewish fellow-citizens. We are seized by deep pain when we see what little recognition our citizenly loyalty and devotion find in influential Polish circles, how little understanding for our Jewish needs and demands, not only for civil equality but also full right of self-determination of our national individuality and self-administration of our cultural affairs. (Stormy, prolonged applause)[6]

Yet the February 1917 revolution's ending of tsarist discrimination had wrought "a happy turn in Russian Jews' fate." As for Palestine, while most diasporic Jews could not live there, Zionism aimed to create "a strong, normal, and healthy Jewish core, whose political and spiritual significance will exert influence on Jewish life in exile." Zionist work in Eretz Israel would strengthen the Ottoman Empire, transforming "half-desert land into fruitful soil sustaining rich industries." Imperialism was foreign to this enterprise. Arab interests would not suffer. "Arab claims were never

---

[5] CZA. L6/103 (December 6, 1915); L6/106, Report (n.d.), from *Hajnt, Moment*, and *Hazifirah*.
[6] Here and below: CZA. Z3/146 (October 28, 1917).

focused on Palestine." The few hundred thousand living there had never sought to develop the land. Jews and Arabs shared, like their languages, a "common Semitic descent."

In Poland, Jews had two languages – Hebrew and Yiddish (Polish absent). Zionism would defend the "rights of Yiddish, our people's tongue, the Yiddish popular masses' everyday language." There must be democratization of public life, including Jewish religious commune, but women's rights – contentious point not only among religious traditionalists – went unmentioned (as did Russian Poland's German occupiers). Zionist anthem *Hatikva* resounded.

A 1918 Berlin ZO report following announcement of German cession to Ukraine of Chełm district argued, wishfully, that the Bolshevik Revolution had undermined Endeks' pro-Russianism, forcing them to seek paths of cooperation with the Central Powers. This portended muffling of antisemitism, as the Kingdom of Poland's nonpartisan prime minister, respected historian Jan Kucharzewski, had recently attempted. But when "Trotsky's agitational speeches began stirring up sympathetic ferment among Polish workers, the Polish press opened a campaign against the Bolsheviki, employing the proven method." Old epithets – "Beilis" and "Jagiełło" (Polish Socialist elected to 1912 Duma with Jewish voters' backing) – yielded to "Trotsky" and "Joffe" (Jewish-born Bolshevik negotiators at Brest-Litovsk).

Here was early evidence that antisemitic propaganda was shifting emphasis from Jewish economic behavior and loyalty to Poland to obsession with the "Judeo-Communist" threat from abroad. "Well-known Jew-devourer [*Judenfresserin*] Izabela Moszczeńska," prominent Polish feminist who had joined the Endeks, was again fomenting Judeophobia. But this report supposed that Polish nationalists, to escape dependency on Germany, would have to work toward negotiated peace between Central Powers and Entente and so would need to repress antisemitism. Here anti-Jewish agitation figured as tactical, switchable on and off rather than an irresistible force in Polish politics.[7]

A February 1918 letter from Warsaw to Berlin ZO reported how Polish newspapers explained Chełm's loss by war-profiting Jewish interests pressuring Austrian Foreign Minister Czernin behind the scenes. Polish Zionists felt obliged not to hail the Balfour Declaration for fear of drawing German reprisals. The unsigned author eccentrically supposed that the English saw themselves as descendants of Israel's ten lost tribes, obliged to missionize Jews, as they were deviously doing with their Palestine offer. Polish students at a respected private technical school refused to join

---

[7] CZA. Z3/148 (n.d.).

mourning ceremonies for a Jewish fellow student: more evidence of "extraordinary heartlessness" crushing assimilationist circles.[8]

In June 1918, Warsaw Zionists informed Berlin that there was "hardly a trace of Zionist activity" in the Congress Kingdom's Austrian occupation zone, including such important cities as Lublin, Radom, and Kielce. This was curious because Jews there were "much better situated and financially stronger than in the German area" (though arguably this was contributory explanation).[9] By September, Warsaw ZO was lamenting that the Imperial German General Government (GG) "does nothing to secure Jews' rights." The Germans deal only "with a few assimilationists." In twenty Jewish-funded Warsaw middle schools, language of instruction was Polish, but with two hours of daily Hebrew instruction. "All authoritative political personalities in Poland, whether [pro-German] activists or [anti-German] passivists, are united in aversion to Jews."[10]

Near war's end, Warsaw ZO informed Berlin that Congress Kingdom Poland now counted 200 Zionist local organizations. In 1917 there had been 40,000 members, but now Zionist sympathizers were robustly estimated at quarter million. The Zionist, though "he carries inside him the ideal of [Jewish] nationality standing isolated and alone," was able and wished to carry out his duties in his diasporic homeland. Assimilation was guilty – in a psychologically revealing metaphor – of having created "hermaphroditic [zwitterhafte] and morally homeless people," inspiring in Poles "unfulfillable expectations" of mass Jewish integration into Polish culture. In Warsaw, "the most extreme reactionary form of Jewish Orthodoxy" banded with assimilationism against Zionism. In Russia, "where there are [as was wishfully but wrongly claimed] no tsadiks or assimilationists," Orthodoxy was firmly national minded.[11]

In Łódź, Ch. Lifschein, signing herself "longtime enthusiastic Zionist," penned on November 1, 1918 a passionate German-language letter to Berlin headquarters. Having heard prominent speakers at a meeting, "it became clear to me, in these unforgettable moments, that the Zionist idea is no longer a utopia, a legend, overheated imagination's child, folk-tale or fairy-tale for lulling a child to sleep."

This hour of all nations' destiny strikes also finally for *our* poor people, who have languished in thousand-year servitude ... A great, thousand-year-old longing advances toward fulfillment of a people's most beautiful dream.

Fully analogous to the long history of the Jewish people's suffering is the Jewish woman's history. As Jews were everywhere pariahs among peoples, so were women pariahs and slaves of their people ...

[8] CZA. L6/122 (February 25, 1918).   [9] CZA. L6/108 (June 27, 1918).
[10] CZA. Z3/150 (September 14, 1918).   [11] CZA. Z3/150 (October 21, 1918).

It suffices according to Jewish ritual for the wife to burn the porridge 2–3 times to be suddenly wholly abandoned by her marital master (*Eheherrn*). It suffices no longer to be the most beautiful in the eyes of her commander (*Gebieter*) for him to be entitled to divorce her on the spot, etc. etc.[12]

In the name of "the whole legion of our unjustly oppressed sisters," she appealed to the "great men, who are entrusted with leading their people into the promised land" to show the way to a more just conception of life among future Jewry. She pleaded that the Jewish women's question receive attention at the peace conference. "We Jewish women have also learned to think and feel as human beings. We too ask for equal rights, of which we are all completely worthy today, and of which we shall show ourselves even more worthy in the future." Unfortunately, Polish Zionism in independent Poland, yielding to pressure from religious traditionalists (and its own impulses), could not fulfill her fervent hopes and suffered a serious deficit of female support.

Poverty and Disease among the Jewish Poor

We turn now, briefly, to the drastically deteriorating living standards of Jewish workers and the unemployed in the German-Austrian occupation zone. A death-stalked wartime environment had emerged, unprecedented in recent memory, devaluing life, normalizing suffering, and subliminally warranting lawless brutality toward ethnic outsiders.[13]

A speech, seemingly of mid-1916, delivered to Scandinavian audiences by Warsaw City Councillor and chief Polish Zionist leader Heschel Farbstein painted his coreligionists' worldly plight in darkest light. Amid industrial standstill, rampant shortages, and inflation, "the broad middle class is impoverished. People who possessed 50–100,000 rubles must – after selling furniture, clothes, even underwear, and driven by hunger, after hard struggle within their soul – ask for public assistance." Among the broad masses, "parents often conceal a child's death for many days, to use up its bread-ration card." Disease spread. Children of five or six years were too weak to walk. "The body collapses and grows soft – jelly-like." Body fat consumed by hunger, the skeletal framework hollowed out. Ninety thousand Warsaw children needed care, but charitable institutions provided it for only 21,000. The rest were on the streets, where – as when girls begged from soldiers – they soon "go to physical and psychic ruination."

---

[12] CZA. Z3/150 (November 1, 1918).
[13] Blobaum, *Apocalypse*, is authoritative on the socioeconomic crisis in Warsaw. The quantitative data cited below reflect wartime understandings.

Widows and absent soldiers' wives suffered mental breakdowns because they could no longer support their children. Corpses were buried in paper for lack of linen shrouds. Of Warsaw's 340,000 Jews, 220,000 were dependent on charity, apart from unregistered "shame-stricken needy, who commit suicide or literally die of hunger to avoid public assistance's disgrace." The poor were "naked and barefoot." American aid had been lacking for months. "The Jewish population in the occupied areas stands before a catastrophe such as world history has never witnessed."[14]

American observer, Dr. Bernard Kahn, high-ranking Joint Distribution Committee emissary, on completing his trip to Warsaw in December 1916, expressed himself hardly less drastically: "the Jewish population's impoverishment goes on at terrifying pace." He said, of lack of shoes and clothing, "adults are often prevented, in Warsaw as well as in the rural districts, from going out to the kitchens to get warm soup for themselves; and the children cannot go to school." With schools half empty, charitably provided midday meals could not be consumed. Two million German Marks ($500,000) would be needed, in the General Government, Ober-Ost, and Front District, for clothing and footwear alone.[15]

A 1917 Zionist report on Jewish artisans in Łódź evoked crisis, some war induced, some technological. Endek-preached boycott was shrinking demand, and Jewish customers did not always offer "requisite support." Jewish employers "not seldom preferred to employ non-Jews." Textile trades had lost markets, pinching the 5,000 handloom weavers and 10,000 apprentices and the 1,000 ladies' underwear sewers. Furniture makers were profiting from an "increase in marriages," reference possibly to efforts to evade military or forced-labor conscription. Many trades with high Jewish participation would only survive through reorganization into cooperatives with savings-bank funding.[16]

Warsaw's ZO reported in mid-1917 on Jewish health. Among 3,000 children, average weights in the first five years were around 60 percent of prewar figures. Most four-year-olds could not run. Many suffered from severe rickets, induced by vitamin deficiencies, "with all possible deformations." Scrofula and tuberculosis were "extremely common." Birth rates were falling, mortality rising, especially from tuberculosis, exhaustion, and "hunger tumors." There was evident "tendency toward the

---

[14] CZA. L6/106: "Die Lage der jüdischen Bevölkerung in den okkupierten Gebieten."
[15] JDC. AR 14/18, file 129(1) Poland, "Report on Trip of Dr. Kahn to Warsaw in December 1916."
[16] CZA. Z3/149, "Bericht über die Lage der jüdischen Handwerkschaft in Lodz" (n.d. [1917]).

Jewish population's dying out," stricken by "physical exhaustion and degeneration."[17]

From Pinsk, in Ober-Ost, an unidentified German soldier wrote in mid-1917 that Jews "rejoiced two years ago in happy expectation at German entry." But as people now said, "we awaited Messiah and the knout came instead." Under the Russians, food and supplies were available, "only the notorious Cossack days were unpleasant." But under Germans, plunder was organized as requisitions, paid for in promissory notes no one accepted or lent against. Immiseration played no favorites: "whether rich or poor, ignorant or educated, they've all become beggars." German authorities provided work, but at such pay that daily wages bought only half-pound breads, and in winter prices would double. "People have to wrap their feet in scrounged-up rags. In summer, people whose nakedness was covered with but a frazzled cloak were nothing unusual."[18]

An October 1917 report on GG and Ober-Ost by the anti-Zionist German-Jewish Relief Organization warned that while previous "abnormally high mortality" had abated following good harvests, fuel was disastrously short as winter loomed. The well-to-do will be hard pressed; "for the poorer, heating will be almost impossible." There were no shoes. American Jews "are shouldering a huge responsibility by their peculiarly dilatory handling of money transfers." In provincial towns, Jews' situation was still "relatively good." Polish peasant farmers "have earned much money and attained great prosperity," benefiting Jewish business. But in big towns, one-quarter of Jews would likely not survive the coming winter if American and Russian relief didn't arrive. Of masses of war-uprooted refugees, 15,000 remained in the GG in miserable condition. Relief agencies left provision of work to the German army, conditions of which rightly frightened people off. Nor should they be expected (seemingly for dietary reasons) to accept the work. Yet "the system of unconditional charitable support turns them into moochers [*Schnorrer*]."[19]

German exploitation of occupied Poland's resources extended to recruitment of workers for homeland German industries. Though it was voluntary, war-induced unemployment in Poland left many men little choice if they wished to escape soup kitchens. By 1918, hundreds of thousands of Polish Christians and Jews found themselves in laborers' barracks in Germany, while large numbers were similarly housed in the

---

[17] CZA. Z3/147, "Gesundheitszustand der jüdischen Bevölkerung in Warschau" (n.d. [1917]).

[18] CZA. L6/106 (n.d. [fall 1917]), "Bericht über Pinsk."

[19] CZA. Z3/172 (October 16, 1917), *Hilfsverein der deutschen Juden*: "Jüdisches Hilfswerk in Polen."

German-occupied east. On expiration of their contracts, they were free to quit and return home, but until then, they lived as semicaptive laborers in foreign environments. Reports on labor-conscripted Jews show the skilled among them earning, by Polish standards, good wages in Germany and easily switching from Yiddish to German.

In July 1918, German Zionist Julius Berger reported on Jewish workers conscripted by the Warsaw GG Labor Office, which had, as a welcome concession, recently shortened its contracts to four-month stints. He found good circumstances – pay, food, treatment – among 300 workers at an Upper Silesian industrial firm, while conditions for 190 forest workers in eastern Poland were "absolutely outstanding." Here workers lived in empty[!] farm houses, "earn[ed] a lot of money," and received uncooked food "but in very generous quantities."

Conversely, Jewish railroad workers' circumstances at Neustadt near Memel, on the Baltic, were the "most unfavorable imaginable." Previously compulsorily but now voluntarily recruited, workers still lived "in camps behind barbed wire under military watch." One supervisor, a sergeant-lieutenant, admitted to beating recalcitrant workers. Absconding had reduced the original force of 2,000 workers to 400. Escapees found shelter among coreligionists. The camp suffered repeated epidemics.

People look terribly run-down and ragged. Most of them work without shoes, in most miserable rags. Most have only one completely worn-out suit of clothes. The whole company makes a terribly sad and depressing impression.

Food was inadequate, something between that of prisoners and soldiers. For people throughout Ober-Ost and the GG, "Neustadt has a terrible ring." Yet most private employers sought good relations with conscripts. Even at Neustadt, workers could get an extra pound of bread daily, beyond rations, for 1.10 Marks. German officials tolerated black marketeering to supply workers' food, also in public-sector firms.[20] It was a sign of burgeoning antisemitism on the German home front that recruitment there of Polish Jewish workers was halted in spring 1918 on the pretext of fighting the spread of typhus and other diseases.[21]

Developments in the Austro-Hungarian GG, encompassing the southern, less industrialized and urbanized part of the Congress Kingdom from Kielce across to Lublin, followed a separate path. Vienna's Zionists archived an embittered account of its 800,000 Jews. At war's outbreak, 95 percent of trade and commerce was in Jewish hands, and 70 percent of artisans were Jews. Endeks had agreed to end boycott calls. Polish estate

[20] CZA. Z3/173 (July 6, 1918).   [21] CZA. L6/106 (January–February 1917), *passim.*

owners, turning their backs on their lassitudinous "national romanticism" and bankrolled by Jewish financiers, had in the late nineteenth century developed sugar beet and liquor production. Jewish capital was strong "insofar as it was not nationalized in Polish sense through baptism of its carriers – a few families of high finance pursuing *szlachta* allures, living at farthest imaginable remove from the Jewish people." Among Poles, a bourgeois element arose amid small-town farmers and petty gentry uprooted by peasant emancipation. These would-be capitalists were unscrupulously hateful toward Jewish rivals, adopting "a discourse of brutal shamelessness" in the nationalist press and boycott literature. Consumer cooperatives organized by parish clergy mushroomed. By war's eve, "every root of Jewish business life was chewed up by the boycott." Jews were "economically weakened and shaken in their trust in the law."

Now, under Austrian occupation Chief General Stanisław Szeptycki, control of the "Polish Central Trading Office," with its monopolistic powers of requisitioning, distributing, and rationing agricultural products, had been handed over to influential aristocrats. Their great estates profited from fixed prices, while they blamed Jews for smuggling and black marketeering. "Poor Jewish traders" were asking:

Where's the *Schmiggel* and who's responsible? All I know is that the peasant and the landlord won't give their crops to the *Zentrale*. They either sell [illicitly] at highest price or let harvests rot. I have to buy or die of hunger. If I don't buy, just let them shoot me, it's all the same.

As for rationed retail food and manufactures, Jews were squeezed out, not receiving necessary raw materials, as among Lublin's bakers and shoemakers.[22]

A late 1917 report enthused about Warsaw Zionists' relief work, "great trust" in which opened purses of both Jewish and non-Jewish donors. The city still housed 62,000 Jewish refugees, mainly from Pinsk and Brest-Litovsk. Throughout the GG, Zionists had "trustworthy comrades and activists, even in the smallest villages." Their competence had compelled the assimilationist-controlled Jewish religious community to admit them as relief partners. Zionists had organized an American Section, funneling money sent to war-stricken relatives. War's "worst impact" was on the larger cities' middle class. "Countless families formerly living in very good circumstances were at one blow ruined [and] reduced to beggars." Jewish manual workers could adjust to jobs available under German occupation

---

[22] CZA. Z3/149, "Über die Lage der jüdischen Bevölkerung im öesterreichisch-ungarischen Okkupationsgebiet Polens."

– forestry, military construction, factory work in Germany – but not the merchant, small shopkeeper, salesman, unaccustomed to heavy physical labor. "The Zionists have always been in contact with the middle class," and must help them now, though the aid "must, naturally, be provided confidentially."

While the ZO maintained seventeen schools and children's homes caring for 3,000 children, the great problems were "full orphans" and those sent out to beg. Orphans "lie begging day and night on the streets, sick and in rags." All such children "succumb to early moral and physical ruin." Such children, often lice-ridden, infected caregivers and were now being "disinfected and cleaned in halfway-stations."[23]

In May 1918, Warsaw Zionist Dr. Rosenblatt wrote pessimistically to Berlin ZO on Jewish pauperization in the face of robust and aggressive Polish antagonists. He tried to explain the "fact that, unfortunately, spotted typhus claims its victims especially among Jews," a circumstance antisemites in Germany and Poland were ruthlessly exploiting. While "the louse" was commonly seen as cause and carrier of typhus (present-day medicine targets fecal contamination), Dr. Rosenblatt was skeptical, pointing instead to disastrous worsening of Jewish diet. Before the war, poor Jews were no cleaner, no campaigns were waged against the louse, yet typhus was rare.

Hunger was unknown! Bread, vegetables, even meat, bacon[!], milk, butter were so cheap and plentiful that the poorest could eat their fill. Pure rye-bread cost 5–6 pf., meat 25 pf. There was nobody among us who did not eat meat at least once weekly. One did see people in rags, but never pale faces gnawed by hunger! It was not necessary to work hard to earn one's daily bread. The greatest idler could nourish himself and his family on one Mark daily. And these poor Jews, beset by lice but with full stomachs, were immune, resistant against louse-bites, against spotted typhus. A pound of soap cost 20–28 pf., one could wash frequently, keep one's clothes clean. Incidentally: what poor man did not own 2–3 shirts? [Now, in war,] people in Germany haven't the faintest idea of the literal hunger and misery prevailing here among the Jewish population. It's no exaggeration when I say that poor Jews are literally dying out from hunger ... You see on the street tottering people, without the strength to remain on their feet ... The poor wear no under-clothing, dress in dirty rags.[24]

From the Jewish religious commune the poor received but 120 grams (4.2 ounces) of bread daily. Christians were paid their wages, at least in the war's first two years. They could return to relatives in villages. "The rural people, the Christian population's predominant part, have grown

---

[23] CZA. Z3/172 (n.d. [mid-1917?]), "Hilfstätigkeit der Warschauer Zionistischen Organisation."
[24] Here and below: CZA. Z3/172 (May 30, 1918).

fabulously rich during the war ... For the peasant-farmer nothing is too expensive."

Rosenblatt addressed German anxieties, conceding that "the masses among eastern Jewry have deteriorated physically during the war ... The louse bites with sure effect these dirty, unwashed, naked bodies, dried out by hunger and misery." Typhus follows. He added that in 1915 he was attached to a Warsaw military hospital where soldiers, though lice ridden, suffered no typhus. Among Jewish refugees from the Eastern front who remained well clothed and adequately fed, typhus also was unknown. Rosenblatt argued too that typhus and malnutrition were found together in war-torn Russia.

An anonymous mid-1918 report found that 73 percent of 15,871 spotted typhus cases in 1917 Warsaw occurred among Jews, though mortality from it was, at 5 to 7 percent, half that among non-Jews. The disease entered the Congress Kingdom with the Russian army in 1914. It had nothing to do with "racial characteristics." In Russia it raged worst where no Jews lived. Principal victims in Poland were refugees. Its carrier was the "clothes louse," so fears of infection from men's beards and women's hair were unfounded. German-ordained "compulsory shaving of beards" only led to "concealment of the sick."

Some classes of the Jewish population try to evade the sanitary regulations (disinfection and isolation) because of abusive treatment by low-level sanitation personnel and some requirements' counterproductive severity.

This report ended defensively, fending off antisemitic charges, by holding that Jews' lower mortality rates were due to "inherited resistance" and "absence of alcoholism."[25]

Impressions of Jewish life in the Austrian zone near war's end emerge from a Zionist report focused on Lublin, which was profitably mediating trade farther east. The economy was "notably better" than under the Germans. Millionaires multiplied, middling businessmen too, food cost half what people in the Warsaw-centered GG paid. There was in larger towns an "'American' get-rich fever."

The not numerous assimilationist intelligentsia in the provinces emulate the Warsaw assimilationists, and if they exercise a strong influence, it's attributable to the indifferentism and the weak social experience of the "new" [Jewish] bourgeoisie, which has only now grown strong during the war and possesses neither the traditions nor the sturdy ambition of the older generation of Jewish 'g'wirim' [notables].

---

[25] CZA. Z3/173 (n.d. [July 1918?]), "Protokoll über Flecktyphus."

This was evident in Jewish underrepresentation on the new city councils, though it was an impediment that Polish literacy was prerequisite for serving (even if not all Christian officeholders could satisfy it). Jewish artisans, starved for raw materials, turned to risky and price-raising illicit commerce. Relations were tolerable with Austrian military authorities, among whose officers "there's a great many Jews." But in local civil administration there were numerous antisemitic officeholders "of Slavic origins/Czechs, Slovaks, etc. In their relation to Jews the Slavic branches are all one."[26]

The frustration of fighting a losing war burst into a warning Austrian army command at Ukrainian Kherson sent to local rabbis in August 1918. Entitled, "Influence of Jewry on the Troops," it took as "proven that members of the Jewish nation" sought to lead soldiers into political crimes (Bolshevism) and illegal trading, especially in weapons. Individual offenders being hard to apprehend, it was necessary to hold all Jewry responsible, particularly considering "how tightly [they] stick together." "Benevolently minded and decent Jews" must restrain bad elements from "destructive activities." Otherwise, all will face "special measures and levies." The note euphemistically cautioned that Jewish criminality might well "release against them the old attitude [*alte Stimmung* = 'pogrom mood']". Rabbis were responsible for Jewish reputation and tranquility. "This has nothing to do with religion."[27]

At war's end, Kraków's Jewish National Council informed a Dutch committee distributing American relief funds that among the 45,000 local Jews, businesspeople, artisans, and laborers found ample work and rising earnings during the war.

But after demobilization, stark immiseration struck those groups that performed war services, or who themselves and their families received state support. After their return, demobilized small shopkeepers and merchants, artisans, commercial employees and officials, also educated professionals, find no appropriate work, no workshops with machines and tools, no shop-space or wares for sale, no jobs as bookkeepers, clerks, scribes, jurists, etc.[28]

Kraków counted some 3,000 such Jews needing aid, mostly "family fathers of 3–8 children." The same proportion of Jews elsewhere in West Galicia required support, the more urgently because so many other Jews had been ruined in November's pogroms.

The disastrous, discrimination-worsened, even lethal condition into which war plunged Poland's multitudinous Jewish poor and impoverished, uprooted refugees had dire political consequences. In antisemitic

[26] CZA. Z3/150 (n.d. [late 1918]).   [27] CZA. Z3/188 (August 25, 1918).
[28] JDC. AR14/18, File 136 Poland (December 1918).

eyes, the Jewish presence appeared even more of a curse on the land than it had in peacetime. The militant, revolutionary politics that found echo among Jewish proletarians were unnerving to Polish nationalist ears. Yet Jews, conventionally seen in hostile eyes as physically weak, appeared ever more defenseless and open to attack. For their enemies of (conscious or unconscious) sadistic bent, widespread misery made defenseless Jews an easier target for violence and other reprisals. Already in the war's early years Russian armed forces hammered Jews in their path with pogroms, setting an ominous example.

Russian-Perpetrated Wartime Pogroms

In its 1914 invasion of Galicia, the Russian army, as we saw earlier, staged widespread assaults on Habsburg Jews, even as tsarist authorities, fearful of treachery, uprooted masses of their own Jewish and German-speaking subjects within the Pale of Settlement near the western front, brutally expelling them into the Russian interior. A 1915 inner-bureaucratic circular of the Finance Ministry called for investigation of rumors, still unconfirmed, that the German enemy "intends to destroy the Russian peasantry's well-being," devising "specially produced machines to destroy the whole harvest ['the bread'], and they have even sent out arsonists." Russian-ruled German and Jewish collaborators were said "to have been won over by bribery."[29]

Berlin Zionists learned in 1915 that, near Kiev, "persistent rumors circulate among the common people that Jews buy up all small-denomination money and hide it." Kiev's police chief telephoned a rabbi, demanding he halt the abuse. An army general threatened another rabbi with hanging. The regional governor told Jewish sugar beet processors: "People are excited. Excesses are possible. I won't permit pogroms," but steps must be taken.[30]

Wartime anxiety over intimidating new technology's destructive power, from airplanes to telegraph, was rampant, extending to nonexistent "infernal devices." In Congress Kingdom's Łomża, Russian counter-espionage agent Tschupanjuk accused Eisenbügel, a Jewish film-maker, of telephoning Germans. The defendant's Jewish friends learned of Tschepanjuk's liaison with a Jewish woman and through her gave him a ring and bribe offer, simultaneously informing his superiors of his venality. Trapped, Tschepanjuk was sentenced to six years' labor in an *Arrestanten-Compagnie*, while Eisenbügel walked free.[31]

---

[29] CZA. L6/763 (July 23, 1915).   [30] CZA. L6/763.
[31] CZA. A120/409 (n.d.), "Der Prozess der antisemitischen Provokateure."

Few cases of anti-Jewish persecution ended so happily. Pogroms flared when Russians – of Great Russian ethnicity alongside soldiers of many other nationalities, Poles included – retreated from occupied Galicia in mid-1915, again when 1916's Brusilov offensive returned them to Lwów, and when finally they abandoned Galicia in mid-1917. Witness of these bloody waves was famed Russian Jewish playwright (author of *Dybbuk*, a Yiddish-language masterpiece) and journalist S. Ansky/An-ski (Shloyme Rappaport [1863–1920]). As militarily credentialed Jewish relief officer, Ansky crisscrossed war-torn Galicia dispensing funds, interceding with Russian authorities, and chronicling *The Destruction of Galicia*, as his posthumously (1920) Warsaw-published, Yiddish-language book was entitled. No other work so vividly and passionately depicts the Galician tragedy from the battle lines' Russian side.[32]

Before contemplating Ansky's picture gallery, another perspective on anti-Jewish violence under Russian baton will prove illuminating. This was penned by M. F. Seidman, reporter for New York's "Forward." He toured German-occupied Congress Poland sometime after October 1916, producing a German-language account of earlier Jewish suffering that found its way, unpublished, to the Zionist archives.[33] Seidman depicted victimized Jews as generally passive and powerless, except insofar as bribery was effective or divine forces intervened. Hopes fastened on Russian authorities' possible goodness, reining in terrifying and beastly Cossacks (although rape by Russian soldiers alongside Cossacks appears commonplace). Germans, though off stage, figure as Jews' protectors. Poles were mostly bad, except for socialist workers. In Anna Kahan's Siedlce, Seidman learned that a Pole had disguised himself in "old-fashioned Jewish clothes, pasted on side-locks and beard," and shot at Russian guards, hoping (in vain) to trigger pogrom.

Russian officers could not control their fighters but forced Jews each to pay 30 rubles to buy off Cossack plunderers. Polish Christians cursed Jews as "Beilis" and "Willusch" (Wilhelm). Seidman attributed pogrom absence to the presence among Russian officers of "more or less decent people, who exerted themselves honorably to avoid big riots." Nonetheless, when Germans arrived, Jews celebrated "as on Beilis's acquittal day." Jews were "completely secure against pogroms, rapes, and riots under German barbarians' rule," although the Polish-dominated municipal Citizens' Committees discriminated against them.[34]

---

[32] S. Ansky, *The Enemy at His Pleasure: A Journey Through the Jewish Pale of Settlement During World War I*, trans. Joachim Neugroschel (New York, NY: Metropolitan, 2002). Wiese, *Pogrome*, insightfully builds on Ansky's reportage.
[33] CZA. Z3/173 (n.d. [1917]).   [34] Ibid., 1–4.

In Sterdin *shtetl*, Cossacks broke into the rabbi's house, shouting "give money, you dog." The local nobleman and town lord bought himself and other Christians free. Russians, having forced Jews there to fire their own houses, prepared to execute them when an officer shouted *"Germantschiki,"* whereupon the Russians fled. Jews said that the crier "looked completely different than before. It was certainly no Russian officer, but rather Prophet Elias's spirit." Such miraculous religious interpretations were common among pious Jews, as when in Lasowo mill-owner Mühlstein emerged from hiding to ransom women threatened with rape. People said the "Jewish God" showed his thankfulness when, Cossacks having set his mill alight, "it refused to burn. The Jewish women's tears extinguished the fire."[35]

Seidman found that in Żarnów, the Russian commandant successively dishonored twelve young women, having their fathers beaten and sending their disrobed daughters home through the streets. The town's men were sworn to silence on pain of mass execution. Near the front, Russians expelled Jews while their houses and shops were plundered, local Poles taking them over. Rabbis were whipped through their towns' streets, elderly women drowned in streams, a man who suffered twenty-five lashes in his rabbi's place later died, a rabbi accused of sending "fire signals" to Germans was tortured to death, three Jewish families were murdered for sending lamp signals from their verandas, thirty Jewish hostages were taken to discourage cutting of telegraph/telephone wires, though some freed themselves for 1,000 rubles. Russian soldier-pogromists destroyed a Jewish cemetery, even unearthing a recently buried corpse and hanging it on a tree.[36]

In industrial Żyrardów, Jews had prospered but then were suddenly expelled to nearby Warsaw in jam-packed freight cars. "A crowd of 7,000 souls occupied the railway-station environs. Among them were many respected citizens, a few days earlier rich and prosperous, now poor and without house or home, tired and desperate, and everywhere shrieking children, disgraced women. Older men and women could stand it no longer and lay in the streets." The town's factories were burned. Yet now, in Żyrardów, among Poles and Jews, "friendliest and most agreeable relations prevail" because Christians are workers and socialists who, cooperating with the German commandant, tried to restore plundered Jewish property.

In Mszczonów, after Grand Prince Nikolai Nikolaevich's August 1914 proclamation promising rebirth of unified Poland under Russian over-lordship, "free in its faith, language, and self-government," Polish-Jewish

---

[35] Ibid., 6–7.   [36] Ibid., 8–25.

relations greatly worsened. "People said openly and loudly that, as soon as 'future Poland' was established, Jews' destruction would occur." In once-prosperous Grodzisk Mazowiecki, Poles took over Jewish businesses, but "of course" Germans would restore them to their owners. In Skierniewice, assimilated Jews could stay while others were expelled, though one baptized medic chose to leave with his former coreligionists. In Grójec, Frau Willner, resisting rape, had her throat cut. In Tarczyn, Jews were beaten bloody and expelled, among them military supplier Besserglick ("Better Luck"), who went mad in Warsaw, falling under auto wheels. The rabbi's wife wrote statements for raped women, saying they were guiltless martyrs and saints. These would enable future marriages. Now "German soldiers maintain order."[37]

Seidman's was the view from the pious Yiddish-speaking proletarian street. Jews were helpless but virtuous, trapped in a morality play casting them as victims occasionally shielded from barbarism by unpredictably benevolent gentiles (or God Himself) and eager to huddle behind mighty Russian autocrats' or German occupiers' disciplined soldiers. Ansky, the dramatist, saw tragedy with little catharsis. On his 1914–15 Galician tours,

fear of death lurked in every corner ... [Victims] had survived recent mortal terror and were shocked and nearly crazy with despair. I found people who were virtually "shattered tablets," with blood pouring from every "break" ... Hundreds and thousands of lives had been cut short, fortunes destroyed, great cultural treasures wiped out. But the storm had not yet reached the depths of the soul, not yet annihilated human dignity ... In its vast scope, in its acuteness, there was a severe beauty that transformed these human sorrows and sufferings into an epic tragedy.

But, in 1916–17, even in undestroyed towns,

the heroes of the national tragedy had become professional beggars ... anxious about a piece of bread, a heap of barley. People had grown accustomed to constant hunger, to rags, to lining up for hours at the food centers. They roamed about, neglected, silent, despondent, indifferent to their dreadful situation. The few remaining members of the intelligentsia had likewise gotten used to their isolation from any sort of culture, social life, spiritual and intellectual pleasure. And all these living corpses trudged past me not as shattered tablets but as tablets from which the letters had been erased. These people had lost the supreme sanctity of human dignity.[38]

Ansky offered no pogrom statistics but wrote that plunder, rapine, and murder everywhere shadowed Russia's polyglot army. Among soldiers, "bestial antisemitism" prevailed. Drink-crazed new recruits ritually beat Jews, even killed them. Whole divisions – especially Bessarabian –

---

[37] Ibid., 26–45, *passim*.   [38] Ansky, *The Enemy at His Pleasure*, 250–51.

belonged to Black Hundreds, which swept into occupied Galicia, often led by fanatic priests. "Lunatic" Grand Prince Nikolai Nikolaevich instigated cruelties – mass expulsion of Jews from Kovno and Grodno – from which even the tsar recoiled. The tsar's brother, Mikhail Alexandrovich, commanded the "Wild Division" of Georgians, Chechens, and other Caucasians – their music "melancholy and monotonous" – who "excelled in barbaric cruelty," as Ansky wrote with Orientalist flourish. Everywhere Cossacks committed "bloodcurdling atrocities."[39]

As culturally and politically Russified Jew, Ansky's revulsion at such anti-Jewish violence collided with the Russophile inclination he ascribed to many Jews and which stirred within him too. It was not merely that "decent" Russians stood out against barbarous deeds. Ansky encountered many who believed, as a young Russian intellectual said, that "for all his crudeness, the Russian is filled with idealism and humanity. The Ruthenian and the German can't hold a candle to him." Russians were "simple" and "savage" but also "generous" and "humane." Even cultured Lemberg Jews preferred their rule to Austrian "clericalism." Russian brutality in Galicia was calculated from top down: the tsar, intending its annexation, aimed to cripple its Jewish inhabitants' influence there beforehand. Yet, in the end, it was Russians' illogic, impracticality, and unpredictability, their "wild nonsense and bestial games," their savagery and capriciousness, that doomed them to defeat and imperial collapse. Ansky offered no explanation for such essentialized traits. Ethnoracial character was fate.[40]

In Poland, "with its dense and lethal antisemitic air," it was Christian nationalists who stigmatized Jews as antitsarist traitors. They claimed that Jewish spies spoke to Berlin by telephone, yet it was Countess Zamoyska whom Russian soldiers discovered doing so in her palatial basement, whereupon she was "strung up immediately." At war's outbreak, Catholic priests urged from the pulpit "to kill the Jews." Ansky attributed the Black Hundreds' antisemitism to a Polish theoretician – he will have been thinking of aforementioned Polish-born but Orthodox Russophone Vladimir Purishkevich – who had enflamed the Romanovs with Judeophobia. The Polish gymnastic Sokół chapters instigated pogroms, though occasionally "decent Poles" blocked them – from personal integrity, not political principle. Yet Ansky thought that Galician Poles and Jews solidarized under Russian occupation, unlike in the tsar's provinces.[41]

---

[39] Ibid., 32, 73, 90–91, 108, 116, 130, 150, 206, 308. Cf. Babel, "1920 Diary."
[40] Ansky, *The Enemy at His Pleasure*, 106, 122, 149, 258, 272–73.
[41] Ibid., 3–5, 16, 21–22, 46–47, 78.

As for Germans, Ansky mutedly noted their losses in the 1914 pogrom against them in Moscow and in their evacuation – in huge possession-laden oxcarts – from the war front in Galicia and Volhynia. The German army was capable of cold-blooded murder, as when an epidemic-ridden field hospital with its patients was torched. But under German occupation, Jews were safe from massacres or pogroms. Still, "their harshness and scorn" were "hard to bear."[42]

Like Seidman, Ansky encountered magical thinking both among Jews and directed at them. "In most dreadful despair, when Jews lost hope of salvation, they were drawn with passionate faith to the ancient channel of national deliverance and revival – the Messiah." One rabbi predicted his arrival in the year 5684 (1924). Stories circulated such as that about Russian soldier Srulik Vaisbrod ("White Bread"), who supplied a *shtetl* with food and money for six months because his father ordered him in a dream to do so or because, far better, he was really the prophet Elijah. More potent were Judeophobes' imaginings: that Jews possessed ointment shielding them from bombs; that Jewish shoe-makers accompanied German pilots, pointing out Russian targets; that pogroms were justifiable revenge for Jewish girls' – frequent or habitual – shooting at soldiers from their dwelling windows; that Jewish coffins were filled with gold. The sight chilled Ansky of a crucifix erected inside a plundered synagogue.

He criticized Hasidic tsadiks' aristocratic distance from Jewish suffering, as when the potent Gerer Rebbe allegedly declared that "it was better for the Jews to starve to death than eat with Christians." He searingly condemned well-to-do Jewish black market-eers for selling alcohol ("mead") to pogrom-hungry soldiers. He scorned stories that Jewish estate owners complained to Governor Bobrinskyi that their peasants wouldn't kiss their hands and reported that Cossacks had forced such Jews to kiss their peasants' backsides instead. Ansky's sympathies lay with the common folk and ruined middle classes. He encountered village Jews who solidarized with Christian neighbors.

Above all, he empathized with Jews' suffering, their "bitter wailing" and "torrents of tears." He was stricken by plunder of beautiful "big, cultured European cities" such as Brest-Litovsk or Tarnopol, whose destruction amid Jewish evacuation suggested to Ansky a "huge, healthy animal whose veins have been opened, releasing a hot torrent of blood." In pogrom-ruined *shtetl* Janów,

---

[42] Ibid., 25, 272–73.

not a single shop had survived; but at the entrance to the town there was a row of small tables where wraithlike figures, mainly women, were vending bread and cigarettes, while naked, barefoot youngsters were milling about. The faces of both adults and children were marked by the savagery of hunger; I gave each women a few rubles.

Nearby were uprooted peasants: "They sat there grim, motionless, coated with dust, their eyes lifeless, their faces stony."[43]

Against this background, and amid society-wide immiseration, the probability of anti-Jewish violence sweeping in toward Warsaw from Galicia and the eastern front must have seemed, as indeed it was, high.

War's-End Violence in Warsaw and Kielce

Yet, when in November 1918 the German-Austrian occupation collapsed and as Piłsudski's provisional government struggled for mastery, no pogrom wave engulfed the former Congress Kingdom as it did Galicia. Further research remains to explain this outcome, which presently existing literature factually confirms.[44] Conceivably, local Polish authorities established under the Central Powers, sometimes as Polish-Jewish condominiums, commanded sufficient power and respect to maintain order. A serious pogrom nevertheless erupted in Kielce, while Warsaw witnessed endemic street violence, probably replicated in many other Congress Kingdom localities. Poland's resurrection will have been a perilous moment everywhere in the former Russian partition zone.

In mid-1918, a shadowy "Liberation Army" showered German-occupied Warsaw streets with what its socialist enemies derided as "paper rags" inciting anti-Jewish violence. One conflated the confiscatory German occupation with Jewish bandits, dismissing leftist revolutionaries as paid Jewish stooges. "God is our witness that we don't wish to shed blood, but let us imagine the defeats that await our fatherland if we don't put an end to this Jewish insolence." Another asked what were current public-sector strikes "if not low-down provocation by Jewish speculators," pushing prices up by halting delivery of food to Warsaw. "These Jewish monsters are smoothing the path for the financial and political career of the Trotsky gentlemen." There had (allegedly) been many Jewish *agents provocateurs* among 1905's socialist revolutionaries. "The

---

[43] Ibid., 15, 20, 39, 58, 80, 124, 136–37, 182, 208, 234, 259–60, 279*ff.*

[44] Zieliński, *Stosunki polsko-żydowskie*; Blobaum, while discovering pogrom-like violence during the 1915 Russian retreat in Warsaw's hinterland, finds its absence in Warsaw following German defeat attributable to lack of armed conflict in the city, Piłsudski's adroit assumption of power, and the disengagement of many Poles and Jews from ethnicized politics. Blobaum, *Apocalypse*, 169–70.

Polish people know the Jew sucks out their life fluids." But they could no longer hide their "earlocked faces." The public understood what "Jewish Social Democracy's devastating banditry" had done to Russia: "because of Jewish Bolsheviks' robbery and destruction of employment, Russian workers and peasants are dying of hunger" while foreign power rules. "The ruthless enemy in Jews' form aims to deal us the same fatal blow. Manly and determined, we must repulse our enemy!"[45]

Social Democracy of the Kingdom of Poland and Lithuania replied, branding these incitations, implausibly, as work of the *German* political police (*Ochrana*). Fearing explosions of hungry masses, German occupiers aped tsarist strategy, steering "the masses' rage into Jewish pogroms." Polish "Black Hundreds" collaborated, seeking "to enflame antisemitic instincts." But "we will not permit revolution to drown in pogrom-swamp." The proletariat would remain united. Despite such militancy, this riposte avoided any defense of Russian Bolshevism, widely unpopular and feared among Poles.[46]

Obsession with "Judeo-Bolshevism" (*żydokomuna*) was soaring. Yet older religiously rooted antisemitism still thrived, as exemplified in a vile (and self-pitying) travesty published at Easter 1918 in *Muchy* ("The Flies"), a gutter imitation of the reputable satirical weekly *Mucha*: "Christ, murdered by Jews," ascended to heaven and sadly surveyed the world: "Jews, who must expiate the grave sin of crucifixion, muck about in wounded humanity." Yet – reference to the Balfour Declaration – God miraculously bestowed on them the Promised Land. "None of the nations have gained anything from the war, while the Jews have gathered the whole world's gold in their hands and conquered Jerusalem." But God's will has so worked that "these vermin, swollen with Christian blood, will leave our unhappy fatherland." Let "Judas's sons depart for Palestine," inspiring "hosannas from all Poland."[47]

As Warsaw witnessed mid-October celebration of impending independence, anti-Jewish rioting erupted, if on a small scale. A proclamation by Grünbaum and Zionist colleagues charged that "unknown hidden forces" had put up posters "signed by a certain Orski, calling for pogrom against Jews and Bolsheviks." It was even claimed that this was Piłsudski's pseudonym (which the Marshal, meeting later with Zionist leaders, indignantly denied). The proclamation warned against failure by police and army to quell disturbances accompanying Poland's liberation – in addressing Piłsudski, Grünbaum spoke of its "resurrection" (*zmartwychwstanie*). It exhorted Poland's Jews to defend themselves "as free and proud Jews,"

---

[45] CZA. Z3/172, "Übersetzung eines Pogromaufrufes in Warschau."
[46] Ibid. (June 2, 1918).   [47] CZA. Z3/172 (n.d. [1918]).

adding, "let all know who should know that we will defend ourselves with all our powers if they try to attack us."[48]

In Warsaw, a Viennese university student reported witnessing on November 11 "national revolution." Poles disarmed German troops and staged anti-Jewish excesses. In two days, furtive rifle shots killed three Jews. Others were beaten or robbed on the street by youths or legionnaires, cursed in streetcars, or denied entry. "Everywhere inflammatory speeches against Jews were proclaimed to the masses. No one dared to take Jews under protection, for otherwise people thought Jews had bought them." Not even socialist PPS admitted Jews into its revolutionary Workers Council. Legionnaires broke up Jewish meetings.[49]

A well-informed Warsaw source informed Berlin ZO that "the Polish Freedom Movement was accompanied by terrible agitation against Jews." Nine Jews were dead, many wounded, theft and plunder were common. Principal offenders were armed youth, including legionnaires of the German-organized armed forces of the now-defunct Kingdom of Poland. Piłsudski's soldiery abstained from antisemitic violence, discharging their fury instead on the departing Germans. Their behavior toward Jews, like Piłsudski's own, was "correct."

A second category of offenders was "nationally minded young people from middle-class circles," especially students of higher and lower grades and boy scouts. Easily stirred by Endek journalism, they were "naive and reckless" but were calming themselves in response to Piłsudski's commands. Most dangerous were soldiers in Dowbór-Muśnicki's army, which had formed in Russia under Kerensky to fight Germans and, later, Bolsheviks and which was now, despite an anti-Piłsudski attitude, contributing seasoned fighters to Poland's new army. "This category is inspired by most terrible Jew-hatred and does not shrink from most horrible bloody deeds."[50]

On November 9, soldiers beat Leonard Himelfarb, law student, with buckled belts but fled on seeing his bloody injuries, which a Jewish field medic treated. Himelfarb testified that soldiers were assaulting Jewish students "because of their attitude toward the present army," presumably thought unenthusiastic.[51] It did no good that the Security Committee of the Jewish Population issued a strong affirmation of Polish independence, paired with protest over "the terrible sight" of Warsaw's streets.[52] Other sources reported anti-Jewish assaults, raids on Jewish property and synagogues, reckless shooting in the Jewish quarter, and military conscription

[48] Grünbaum, ed., *Materjały w sprawie żydowskiej*, 4–5, 13 (October 28, 1918).
[49] CZA Z3/178, "Warschau."   [50] CZA. Z3/179 (n.d.), "Bericht aus Warschau."
[51] CZA. L6/110 (November 9, 1918).
[52] Cited in Chasanowitsch, *Judenpogrome*, 31–32.

of forced Jewish labor extending from November 1918 through January 1919.[53] Israel Cohen wrote of his January visit: "I was astonished at the state of lawlessness that seemed to prevail in Warsaw. Soldiers repeatedly raided houses and shops in the Jewish quarter on the pretext of searching for weapons, and 'requisitioned' money, valuables, and anything useful."[54]

Cohen's informants told him that Kielce's pogrom of November 11–12 claimed among Jewish victims four deaths and eighty wounded, but casualties by other accounts were still higher. It was eminently political, though not without murder and maiming and accompanying plunder. It enacted the increasingly predominant pattern of anti-Jewish violence in formerly Russian Poland, whose pretexts were Jewish disloyalty and threat of "Jewish Bolshevism." It was bad enough that the land was home to revolutionary Jewish leftists of non-Bolshevik tendency. On November 10, Bundists in eastern Siedlce, distributing leaflets in Yiddish and Polish, drew attack from army recruits and legionnaires who, shouting, "Hurra! Let's get the Jews!," sparked a fight in which a fourteen-year-old pro-Bund boy was killed and ten of his comrades injured. Folkist Yiddish *Moment* reported that "gymnasium students played an especially enthusiastic part, fatally wounding their own Jewish fellow-students."[55]

Kielce (Yiddish: Keltz) had lain in Austria's GG. Burgeoning textile town, Jewish settlement had long been prohibited or legally contested. From the late nineteenth century its Jewish population ballooned from 1,000 to 15,000 in 1921, comprising nearly 40 percent.[56] As in Galician Żywiec, such history of Jewish exclusion made later antisemitism more virulent. It also seems probable that, in the war's last days, Austrian authority collapsed more swiftly than did the Germans', at least until revolutionary insubordination penetrated their ranks after the Kaiser's November 9 abdication.

Earlier, the local k.k. army commander had threatened Kielce's Jews. A man fleeing through town with a sack was arrested. As he was led away, "the Jewish crowd, amid great noise, pelted gendarmes with stones and bricks." This "unheard-of provocation" earned them collectively a 5,000-Kr. fine. The bag was found to contain illicit white bread. The commander wrote "that the Jewish population here have for a long time been stiff-necked and rough toward gendarmerie." If the fine were not promptly paid, "I will take hostages."[57]

---

[53] CZA L6/119.   [54] CZA. L6/114, 45.

[55] CZA. Z3/178, "Siedlec"; CZA. L6/119 (November 10, 1918).

[56] www.sztetl.org.pl/pl/article/kielce/6,demografia/ (accessed February 8, 2015).

[57] CZA. Z3/149 (n.d. [after July 15, 1918]), "Kreiskommando Kielce."

Prominent Lemberg attorney and Zionist Adolf Rothfeld, employed at Kielce's k.k. Military Court, penned an eyewitness pogrom account. Speakers, including Rothfeld, at a November 11 mass meeting of "all Jewish parties" welcomed Polish rebirth in a friendly spirit. They also demanded "the Jewish nation's recognition in Poland and granting of national, economic, and political autonomy." They promised to work "happily" in building the new state. Jewish soldiers were present, but only in their role as "Polish citizens of Jewish nationality." At meeting's end, a street crowd of "young Poles armed with clubs" attacked departing participants. In the theater hall the town militia commander escorted women to safety. Claiming to waiting men that the riot had been triggered by Jewish shots at a legionnaire, he ordered a weapons search, discovering none. Meanwhile, the mob surged into the theater, assaulting some 200 defenseless victims. It moved then into the Jewish quarter, smashing and plundering shops. Soldiers summoned to suppress rioters joined them instead and were withdrawn.

Signal expression of Polish hatred, Rothfeld wrote, was Dr. Jankowski's reaction to a wounded Jew he was called to treat. "He's already croaked," he said, "and departed without helping the wounded man, though he was still alive." Rumors circulated among rioters that anti-Polish speeches had been declaimed with such calls as "long live revolution, long live Lenin and Trotsky," which Rothfeld denied.

Next day pogrom raged from noon to nightfall. Over 500 Jews were wounded, of whom fifteen eventually died. Rothfeld submitted names of 103 wounded and three dead. When the meeting's organizers, released from overnight arrest, requested armed protection, the mayor replied that 100 militia men would cost them 300,000 Kr., while another official demanded 2,000 ells of linen for the army. In the end, nothing more was done than to impose a 9:00 PM curfew. Rothfeld proposed that Jewish soldiers form a self-defense force, but after Polish soldiers demanded that Jewish colleagues be "removed," their commander refused to vouch for their safety. Jewish soldiers were roughed up, the Polish eagle torn from their caps.[58]

At the November 11 meeting, the Provisional National-Jewish Representation of the City of Kielce declared that "we must raise our voice before the whole world and demand recognition of Jews, strewn about the whole world, as unitary nation, of which we Jews in Poland are part." They proclaimed their right to "our old homeland in Palestine," to cultural and economic autonomy in Poland, "which should be built on

---

[58] JDC. AR 14/18, file 136 (Poland), Kielce: Adolf Rothfeld, report of November 19, 1918. Reprinted in Chasanowitsch, *Judenpogrome*, 33–36.

the personality principle" – allowing Jews to opt individually for inclusion in the Jewish nation in Poland. Jews should have an electoral curia and their own Constituent Assembly.

We greet with joy the rise of united and independent Poland and declare our readiness to join in state construction ... We confidently hope that the Polish nation understands our intentions and, in its own well-understood state interest, will not turn away the three million Polish citizens of Jewish nationality from the state-building workshop. Long live the Jewish people![59]

How far the meeting's participants shared these maximalist Zionist sentiments is unclear, but possibly they predominated.

Nowy Dziennik later reported that although the army withdrew soldiers sent to contain the mob, Lieutenant Dr. Temką "arrived with a military unit on the scene, and thanks to his energetic action, animated by burning wish to suppress the pogrom, hooligans' bestiality did not claim more lives. His unit also suppressed plundering of Jewish shops." Deaths were seven, with eighty wounded.[60]

A compilation of various press reports sent to Berlin ZO described pogromists' weaponry as "truncheons and knives," with which "one of the most respected citizens" was killed in the meeting hall. With "knives dripping blood," they poured into the street, breaking into dwellings, slashing open pillows in mad search for valuables, and beating defenseless inhabitants. November 12 was market day, and incoming villagers, "incited by agitators," joined in the "terrible work." By evening, "cemetery quiet" prevailed. "Only hooligans with drawn knives strolled the streets, gazing with a lantern into every passer-by's face, to see whether he was a Jew. Every Jew, they said, must be killed and thrown out the window."[61]

On November 26, the official Polish Telegraph Agency distributed the aforementioned unsigned government communiqué on Kielce's pogrom, highlighting dangerous, allegedly Jewish importation of Russian Bolshevism, castigating Jewish cries of "down with the white goose," extolling Polish "gentleness and tolerance" in the face of such provocations, and promising aid to "Jews who stand loyally with the Polish state" in foiling "Bolshevik onslaughts" by their coreligionists.[62] Such reckless words doubtless reflected widespread paranoia and antisemitism. The army quailed before pogrom's challenge. That things could be otherwise emerges from *Nowy Dziennik*'s report that military commanders in

---

[59] JDC. AR 14/18, file 136 (Poland), Kielce: n.d., "An die jüdische Bevölkerung."
[60] CZA. L6/109: *Nowy Dziennik* (November 16, 1918).
[61] CZA. Z3/178 (n.d.), six-page summary of press reports on pogroms.
[62] CZA. Z3/179: no. 10 (November 26, 1918).

Radom, also an important industrial city, had issued an effective public warning against anti-Jewish violence, for which the Zionist newspaper expressed its gratitude.[63]

Jewish memory, particularly in the aftermath of the traumatic post-Holocaust 1946 Kielce pogrom, was deeply embittered, as the Kielce *Yizkor* ["Memory"] *Book* (Tel Aviv, 1957) shows.[64] The following extended quotations demonstrate how such a pogrom figured in later Jewish imagination, with accompanying normative judgments and metaphors. To begin with, the theater meeting appeared not as effort to harmonize Jewish with Polish interests at independence's dawn but as defensive action.

The Jews of the city had gathered in the local theatre to discuss the founding of a national local council. Participating in this meeting were representatives of all of the parties and factions, from the "Bund" to the "Aguda." The meeting was being conducted in quiet and order without any disruption. Everyone felt the seriousness of the hour, that Polish Jewry was standing before many dangers, and it was essential to organize and create a representation of Polish Jews, to stand on guard and protect them from having their rights injured.

The pogromists figure as brutal, seemingly unpolitical aggressors.

Meanwhile, a large gang of Polish thugs organized, all of them equipped with thick sticks and iron gloves, and among them also Polish soldiers ... it never occurred to [the Jews] that a pogrom was being plotted against them outside.

Suddenly ... horrifying rumors reached the ears of the audience. A voice passed through the boxes of the theatre: "They are beating the Jews! Pogrom!" ... A mass of men and women burst out in the direction of the doors; but in the corridor and on the steps stood "Szkejcim" [untraceable word, evidently for Gentiles] and showered those bursting out with heavy blows ...

[Pogromists] exploded glass panes in windows of Jewish homes. The Jews closed the gates of the houses to keep the destroyer from entering their courtyards ... The Jewish passengers who arrived on the night train had no idea of what was going on in the city and when they entered the station, fell victim to the blows of the rioters. Once the destruction was given license, it did not discriminate between the Jews of Kielce and the merchants who came from other cities for purposes of business. Every Jew, who fell into their hands, came out broken, shattered, injured and bleeding.

A need for self-explanation emerges.

Self-defense on the part of the Jews was not possible: first of all, the assault was sudden and there was also no time for orientation and to understand what was going on. Secondly, the crowd gathered there was made up of men, women and

---

[63] *Nowy Dziennik*, no. 132 (November 20, 1918).

[64] Here and below: *Book of Kielce*, translation of *Sefer Kielce*, ed. Pinchas Cytron (Tel Aviv, 1957), available at www.jewishgen.org/Yizkor/kielce/Kie047.html (accessed February 7, 2015), pp. 49*ff*. On the 1946 Kielce pogrom, see Gross, ed., *Fear*; and Zaremba, *Wielka Trwoga*.

the elderly as well, who were not in a state for defense without any tools, objects with which to defend themselves. The confusion that arose at the start of the assault had its effect. Everyone searched for an escape from the trap, and fell into the pit.

The Yizkor book bypasses the plundering other sources mention to high-light the pogrom's political-psychological function.

It was a fearful night for the Jews of Kielce. The Jews did not suffer from theft and looting on that night. In this sense, this pogrom was different from the rest of the pogroms in the cities of Ukraine and Russia. The Poles meant only to teach the Jews a lesson, that they should understand and recognize that from now on they were the masters, and the Jews would not be allowed to stand tall and demand rights. From now on the Jews were slaves who lived in hopes of charity from the masters of the land.

The workings of Polish authority appear mysterious.

The next day, when the news reached the farmers of the area of the license given to Poles to assault the Jews and beat them, they arrived in masses equipped with sticks and clubs to beat and take their part of the loot and property of the Jews. However, apparently, the local authorities received certain instructions from the central government regarding the scope of activities that they were permitted, and to exceed its boundaries was forbidden. In the morning, shifts of guards and soldiers were stationed in the market and on the streets who dispersed the gathering crowds and order was restored.

The pogrom narrative ends with bitter denunciation of Polish malevo-lence, which infused the pogrom with far-reaching antisemitic political design.

Democratic Poland – the Polish press [proclaimed] hypocritically – which had been reborn after hundreds of years of bondage, needed peace and quiet, and such events brought shame upon the Polish republic. In this announcement and in the distortion of the facts, this press wanted to absolve the Poles of blame, and attempted to show the world its pig's foot and say: "See, we are entirely kosher, we are civilized people and such actions are foreign and mysterious to us" ... The Poles were already known as hypocrites, doing any abomination and showing their hooves to show how kosher and unblemished they are ...

The intent of the Poles was [to] stifle, by terror and fear ... any aspiration in the hearts of the Jews to full civil life, to equality and the rights of a citizen in the country.

The Zionists had aimed for more than that. Finally, the Yizkor book leaped forward to the mid-1919 peace settlement.

Although, according to the Versailles Treaty, they were bound to recognize the rights of the minorities, including the Jews, the Poles wanted this recognition to be "Halacha [Rule of Law] – upon which we do not act"; that the rights would remain on paper, and in reality, the minorities would be oppressed in the state. They wanted to demonstrate that they were the masters and the government was in their hands.

Distortions notwithstanding, there is insight in this account, for Poles indeed widely feared and resented Jewish aspirations to their own nationhood within the Polish national state. Paranoically and guiltily assuming Jewish ill will, they anticipated that Jewish national autonomy – and "Jewish Bolshevism" even more – would disadvantage new Poland. The November 1918 pogroms doubtless did aim, alongside other objectives – some conscious and instrumentally rational, some just the opposite – to show Jews that Poles were masters in their new house.

6   In National Freedom's Morning Light
Disarray in Warsaw, Social War in Galicia

The newborn Second Republic – *II. Rzeczpospolita* – reembodied a freedom assassinated in 1795. Poland rejoined the sovereign powers' ranks clad in bemedaled uniforms and silk top hats but also bloody bandages and poverty's tatters. Menaced within and from beyond its eastern borders by peasant uprisings, wedged between plebeian revolutions east and west, and representing in its independence stinging defeat of German and Russian great-power ambitions, its foundations were shaky, its skies stormy to apocalyptic. In 1918–20 it was less a state than the promise of one, if army and police could be disciplined to secure its sway and if its 24 million people could be brought to acknowledge its birthright.

Among them, 3 million war-battered inhabitants of Jewish heritage found themselves subject to rule by a Christian people whose political sovereignty had long appeared extinguished and whose benevolence toward them was hard to detect and often imperceptible. Worse still, the new Poland soon marched into war to extend its boundaries eastward into Ukraine, Lithuania, and Belarus and – with Western blessings – to help slay Bolshevism's dragon in Russia. Here, in the former Pale of Settlement, millions more Jews lived with little prospect of escaping circumambient menace and destruction. Already since 1917 tens of thousands had perished in assaults by Cossacks, peasant rebels, turbulent soldiers, and other murderous interlopers. The civilization of manor house and bourgeois villa, of Christianity and Judaism, even of the comfortable peasant was going up in flames.

Ill-armored Jews' only hope was for fighting to end and orderly state power's sword to acquire a deterrent edge in all subjects' defense. This occurred, in Poland, only in 1920. This chapter and those following traverse the months from January 1919 to October 1920, when truce ended the Polish-Soviet war. They concentrate on recurrent pogrom waves, especially in spring 1919 and summer–fall 1920. A glance at Jewish politics and social welfare in early 1919, extending a landscape surveyed in Chapter 5, reveals more Jewish vulnerabilities on the eve of this chapter's central drama: a formidable new wave of West Galician pogroms, widening into virtual social war against the new Polish state.

Interpretation of these two years' tumultuous and tragic events has been throttled by patriotism-stricken denial or minimization on one side and by reduction of perpetrators' motivation to implacable antisemitism, even "bestialization," on the other.[1] This book unveils a dark theater of violence but show too that its shadows intermixed with light, often only wan, of Christian Poles' efforts to contain and suppress it. Pogroms were enemies of waging war and state building. In the social and cultural scripts that anti-Jewish violence enacted, the indifference of many ordinary Poles to these great political projects, or their investment of them with meanings congenial to their own demotic culture, stands revealed. We will see, too, that for Poland's power holders, in civil or military dress, the nation's rebirth was as much a matter of conjuring with dreams and phantasms as exercise of raison d'état.

Jewish Politics in Independence's Dawn, January 1919

Catholic Poles must cease treating Jews as second-class citizens "who can be mishandled and robbed without penalty, whose blood is freely available to quench flames of sundry political and social conflagrations." So in January 1919 did Warsaw Zionists' self-proclaimed Provisional Jewish National Council denounce, in *dos Yidishe Folk*, anti-Jewish violence as Machiavellian weapon in internal Polish politics. Jews must rally around Zionist leadership in the January 26 election to the National Constituent Assembly. Otherwise, "the politics of forced assimilation will continue, which – faced with our unavoidable resistance – must lead to a politics of exclusion and extermination." Targeted here were assimilationists, scorned as "Jew-Poles," accused of obliterating Jews as a "people with its own life-forms, hopes, and strivings." In Zionist-favored imagery,

---

[1] For omission of anti-Jewish violence, see Agnieszka Knyt et al., *Rok 1920. Wojna Polski z Rosją Bolszewicką* (Warsaw: Karta, 2005). Fot its minimization, see Norman Davies, *White Eagle, Red Star: The Polish-Soviet War, 1919–20* (London: Madonald, 1972); Norman Davies, *God's Playground: A History of Poland* (New York, NY: Columbia University Press, 1984), vol. II, chaps. 18 and 19; M. Kozłowski, *Zapomniana Wojna*. For important works acknowledging widespread violence but offering only cursory treatment of it, see Witold Stankiewicz, *Konflikty społeczne na wsi polskiej 1918–1920* (Warsaw: Państwowe Wydawn. Naukowe, 1963); Tomaszewski et al., *Najnowsze dzieje Żydów w Polsce*, 132 et seq.; Szczepański, *Społeczeństwo Polski w walce z najazdem bolszewickim 1920 roku* (Warsaw: Naczelna Dyreckja Archiwów Państwowych, 2000). Cała, *Żyd*; Cała, *Image*; Michlic, *Poland's Threatening Other*; Michlic, *The Neighbors Respond*; and Polonsky, *The Jews in Poland and Russia*, concentrate on ideology and politics, as does Brian Porter, *Poland in the Modern World: Beyond Martyrdom* (Chichester: Wiley-Blackwell, 2014), chap. 3.

assimilationists "stand like a partition-wall between Polish and Jewish ethnicity, falsify Jewish public opinion, conceal Polish Jewry's true shape, its real wishes and ideals."[2] Turning to their other battlefront, these same Zionists protested angrily to the government the "wildest of pranks [*wybryki*]" being played in Warsaw on Polish Jews – soldierly barracks rapes of women, protection money extortion, theft, beatings and whippings, and discharge of weapons in the Jewish Nalewki district.[3]

Such was the clinched-teeth mood of Jewish nationalists stepping into resurgent Poland's first new year. They had sought to concentrate their influence in a Zionist "Pre-Conference" of December 26–31, aiming both for Jewish unity in the January 26 elections and a Jewish National Congress to be convened in March. While the preconference assembled 498 notables from 144 communities, the workers' parties stood aloof – fearing Zionists' popularity, it was said, and in opposition to a bourgeois-dominated Jewish National Council. Orthodoxy also resisted. "There were towns whose rabbis had to be forced to attend the conference." Combative Zionist paladin Itzhak Grünbaum thought Orthodoxy's stand put it on an assimilationist path "that will inescapably provoke the Jewish popular masses' rage."[4]

Nor at the preconference was Zionist unity forged. In the January 26 national Constituent Assembly election, no fewer than nine Jewish parties offered voters seventy-seven candidates. The Bund abstained, leaving its followers to vote if and as they wished. Eventually, and partly because of such splintering, the newborn Parliament (Sejm) seated but sixteen deputies for Jewish parties, leaving Jewish Poland disappointingly underrepresented. Among 455,000 specifically Jewish votes cast in former Congress Kingdom Poland, 180,000 fell to Zionists of all stripes, 97,000 to the conservative religious party Agudat Israel (also designated Agudas Shlome Emune Israel/*Agudas Haortodoksim*), 59,000 to Folkists, and 52,000 to leftist parties (Poale Zion, Jewish Independent Social Democrats). No assimilationists – notables with few foot soldiers – gained seats. From Galicia, where Zionists and Orthodoxy roughly split the electorate, Habsburg-era deputies were seated where polling was impracticable.

It was Zionists' talented leaders' and high-quality press organs' stalwart opposition to antisemitic discrimination and violence, more than their controversial positive program, that won them political primacy among Poland's Jews. But the Jewish press widely read the election as defeat. The

---

[2] CZA. Z3/151 (January 9, 1919); Z3/184 (January 4, 1919); Z3/151, *Haint* (January 2, 1919).
[3] CZA. A127/73, (n.d. [January 1919]).   [4] CZA. L6/114 (January 3, 1919).

Zionist Provisional National Council denounced gerrymandering of districts to foil Jewish success: "the Jewish masses, who for the first time in Polish history would have been attracted to State-building work, were simply horrified by the election's results and have begun to understand that so-called people's government has in fact deprived them of their civil rights."[5]

In February 1919's democratically structured municipal elections, Jews in Warsaw ran on thirteen different slates, non-Jews on only eight. With twenty-seven seats among 120, Jews – comprising some 40 percent of the capital's population – were again underrepresented. Agudat Israel won eight seats; Bund, Folkists, and Zionists each won five; Poale Zion won two; the party of Jewish landlords and the assimilationist Party of Equal Rights each won one seat. In Łódź, Zionists outpolled rivals; in Lublin, leftist parties prevailed. In Lwów and other Galician cities, a not yet abolished Habsburg-era *numerus clausus* rule capped Jewish representation at 20 percent.[6]

The mainstream General Zionist program sought, as we know, introduction of a Jewish-administered personal cataster, registering individuals wishing to partake of Jewish collective autonomy and pay corresponding financial levies. Religious commune affairs were to be secularized and democratized. Yiddish was to be admissible as instructional language in state-funded schools. Polish was to be learned, but the supreme goal was Hebrew's inculcation as "national language." A governmental Secretariat for Jewish Affairs was to be established, its chief appointed by the head of state from a list of candidates presented by the yet-to-be-created Jewish National Assembly, seating delegates elected among catastered Jews.[7]

Noach Prylucki's Folkists, popular especially in Warsaw, shared the program of "national-personal autonomy" and Hebrew-language propagation but otherwise viewed Yiddish-speaking East European Jewry as a territorially enduring, culturally evolved *nation*, not only a religious confession. Prylucki, born in the Pale and scorned as Litvak by Christian Polish nationalists (and Jewish assimilationists), wielded sharp rhetorical tools. Yet he could declare in the 1919 Sejm that "all Jews were Polish patriots, while simultaneously belonging to the Jewish nation and religion." As a member of the February 1918–elected faux-parliamentary State Council, he had pressed for institutional democratization as an antidote to violence emanating from antisemites' "medieval darkness."

---

[5] Quoted in Isaac Lewin and Nahum Gelber, *A History of Polish Jewry during the Revival of Poland* (New York, NY: Shengold, 1990), 94.

[6] Ibid., 111.

[7] "Das programm einer personellen, nationalen Autonomie der Juden im poln. Staate." CZA. Z3/151 (January 6, 1919).

Only secularized democracy could "get rid of the superstitions, prejudices and reactionary customs which now poison public life in Poland."[8]

Agudat Israel emerged, as we saw, from Polish Orthodoxy's exposure to its 1912-created German counterpart. It embraced Polish independence, speaking through its Yiddish-language organ, *Der Yud*. Its leaders emphasized Jewish nationhood as embodied in the religious community. Crucially, it won backing of the Congress Kingdom's fourteen chief Hasidic rabbis, led by those of Warsaw's Gur/Gerer and Łódź's Aleksandrów courts, who formally admonished the faithful to vote for Agudat. A figure popular both with Jews and Poles was the party's 1843-born Warsaw Rabbi Zvi Perlmutter, white-bearded patriarch. In July 1918 he had declaimed in the State Council:

You may ask: "Does everyone come in the name of the Lord?" The answer is yes – because we believe firmly that Providence, and not blind power, directs the fate of the world, both of societies and of individuals.

Who would have prophesied to the Polish nation that our old Mother-country, awakening from a long sleep, would speak and say: "Children, you are entitled to hope that soon you will be fed by the milk of your resurrected Mother?" [He cited] Ecclesiastes 7:8: "the end of everything is better than the beginning" [and closed, saying] May the sun of our fortune never set again. May Poland live! (Long and stormy applause)

With such words, leading Orthodox Jews greeted the new dawn, already brightened by the Temporary Council of State's early 1917 proclamation that "the new Polish State will continue the interrupted historic tradition which has been characterized by religious tolerance, and will guarantee the Jews who inhabit Poland, as in the past, the right to live ... in accordance with their old faith ... as its citizens with equal rights."[9]

In debate with Prylucki, Agudat Israel representative Moses Pfeffer (Łódź) needled his antagonist with veiled charges of Litvakism and even pro-Bolshevism, while saying

we will get along with the Poles. We have lived with them for hundreds of years in peace. We sympathize with them, and we will be citizens of this country ... Our task, the task of religious Jews, is to love God and the State ... If there have been misunderstandings between us and the Poles, it is due to people like Messrs. Prylucki and Yatzkan [Folkist journalists], who have incited the Jews to create conflicts and have caused calamity. [This elicited applause.] We do not want to build a state within a state.[10]

---

[8] Quoted in Levin and Gelber, *Polish Jewry during the Revival of Poland*, 25, 111. See also Weiser, *Jewish People, Yiddish Nation*.

[9] Quoted in Levin and Gelber, *Polish Jewry during the Revival of Poland*, 41–45, 14–15. See also Bacon, *The Politics of Tradition*.

[10] Levin and Gelber, *Polish Jewry during the Revival of Poland*, 37ff.

The Orthodox party's remonstrances to Piłsudski over anti-Jewish violence wrung from him, as they reported, the confession that "he would be ashamed to be called a Pole if pogroms against Jews would take place in Poland" (though he earlier acknowledged their occurrence, or at any rate anti-Jewish violence, without apology). Following old practice, the Orthodox fervently sought strong state protection. In Hobbesian spirit, Samuel Blumenkranz quoted Mishna in the State Council: "Pray for the welfare of the government, for were it not for the fear of government, men would swallow each other alive."[11]

Assimilationists lost through electoral democratization the strength in parliamentary bodies and Jewish communal life that prewar voting weighted by tax payment had lent them. Zionist and Folkist challenges and, equally, anti-Jewish violence had thrown them on the defensive. The Party for the Equality of Rights for Polish Jews, founded in 1918 by leading Warsaw integrationist Bolesław Eiger, gained but one seat in the 1919 municipal election. In Constituent Assembly polling in Warsaw, among 75,000 Jewish voters, 4,400 chose assimilationists. They championed replacement of Yiddish by Polish in school and daily life but had learned to tread lightly, aware of popular attachment to the Jewish language, ever more finely honed as a literary tool. Still, they pushed for Polish-language instruction in religious schools (*chederim*) and stigmatized the idea of state-funded Jewish public schools as ghetto perpetuation. In *Kuryer Warszawski*, they sometimes appeared as the "Group of Polish Patriots of Mosaic Confession." They recalled Jewish support for nineteenth-century Polish revolts and criticized immigrant "Litvaks" for weakening Polish Jewry's devotion to Poland in favor of Yiddishism and Hebraist Zionism. In this, they failed, willfully or blindly, to recognize these attractions' native Polish roots.

In May 1919, 438 assimilationists convened in Warsaw, under prominent Lwów deputy Dr. Nathan Loewenstein, forming the Union of Poles of Mosaic Confession of All Polish Territories. When on June 6, 1919, the Sejm voted symbolically against the Minority Rights Treaty on which the Paris Peace Conference made Polish sovereignty depend, Jewish integrationists stood with the near-unanimous majority (against which only militant Zionist deputy Apolinary Hartglas voted, while other Zionists absented themselves).[12]

Jewish leftists agonized over their relation to the larger Jewish community but tended strongly, particularly in these revolutionary years, to class consciously stand apart from conservative Orthodoxy and bourgeois Zionism and indeed from the whole enterprise of Polish state building.

---

[11] Ibid., 125.   [12] Ibid., 34–35, 57, 91, 95, 125, 174.

They trusted instead – though with time this faded – to a vision of transcendence of nationalism and ethnic strife through proletarian revolution. Yet they militantly denounced antisemitism and accompanying violence and often sought to organize Jewish self-defense forces against it.

Before June 1919, Jewish nationalists of all stripes fixed hope on the Paris Peace Conference's imposition of minority protection treaties on Poland and the other new Central European states. Meanwhile, they fought in national Parliament against grassroots anti-Jewish violence and Endeks' and agrarian populists' hostile propaganda. Religious conservatives and assimilationists, fearing that Jewish pursuit of "national autonomy" would backfire, could only hope to persuade Piłsudski's government to vigorously extinguish antisemitic brushfires and lock up such arsonists as could be found behind them.

American Relief Workers' Views of Polish Jewry's Plight

In June 1919, the Joint Distribution Committee's director of Jewish relief in Poland, Dr. Boris Bogen, penned an anguished report on conditions in Warsaw. From 1915 to March 1919 the JDC had spent in Poland $7.6 million and in the following four months $3.5 million. It had shared one ethnically neutral relief shipment, oddly called "Westward-Ho," with the American Polish Catholic agency. There were now eight charitable soup kitchens cofunded by Jewish notables, led by integrationist Stanisław Natanson, together with the Warsaw city government and JDC. In 1918 the city had contributed 850,000 Polish marks, the JDC 250,000 marks. A standard meal comprised 0.66 liter of soup, containing 0.65 pound of potatoes, 1.6 ounces of cereal, and 0.03 ounce of fat. Of a visit in February 1918, he wrote:

The things I see here are driving me crazy. The people in a line in a dirty half-lighted hell, shivering with cold, covered with rags, covered with mud and filth, with anxious faces – something horrible. The kitchen proper filled with steam through which I could discern faces of dilapidated humanity, the cooks and workers – then again a miserable dirty hall, and then a dining room, filthy plain wooden tables not remotely scrubbed, and wooden benches. Rare cabbage soup and bread was the menu ... The people here say that they are used to the sights and that they do not affect them. The streets are full with beggars, barefooted, with sores of every description, moaning, running after people, asking in a sing-song, "bread, just bread."

While people told Col. William Grove, Bogen's friend and head of the official US Relief Mission, that streets were unsafe for Jews, "he himself went on Nova-Swilt Ultiza [fractured rendering of fashionable ulica

Nowy Świat] at night and saw a good number of Jews on the streets and in restaurants." But danger lurked near army barracks.[13]

Municipal workers were striking, including cemetery personnel, "so that the dead could not be buried – a horrible situation." Yet "the public and even the poor seem to take it quite lightly." Bogen spoke to Dr. Posnanski (Poznański), Great Synagogue rabbi: "He shrugged his shoulders but could not suggest any remedy." Bogen, visiting the poorest Jewish district, struggled to sustain American optimism.

It is a nightmare – a sight that hurts me. Children sitting in the gutters, begging in a pitiful sing song in Yiddish – dirty, with exposed bodies, looking through the rags in which they are attired. [This was becoming a profession, and children skipped school for it.] And you ought to see their faces – only the eyes reflect a deep hopeful soul, the rest is misery personified. And then the women with their careworn faces, dressed in God knows how many garments, all rags, and still not protected from the cold. The men standing or walking aimlessly – every type, Galician, Russian, etc. – it is only incidentally that you meet the properly clad individual . . . the houses are a horrible sight – the windows without panes, covered with rags and paper – impossible streets and still more impossible courts, dirty dilapidated entrances, broken steps – Poverty is king here.

I know my description may strike you as a poor attempt of being dramatic, but when I recall what I saw today, I am all shaking and feel like crying. These conditions cannot remain as such, and our people in America will have to apply themselves in healing these unfortunates, not only with money but with men and women who must come here with our own methods and start the work of real reconstruction.[14]

Jewish communal officials informed Bogen that their funds were exhausted. At a school, taught by "a fine type of woman," he (perceptively) found it "pathetic to be present at a lesson where the hungry, miserably clad students embibed the knowledge of anatomy, illustrated through the medium of an actual skull." Elementary teachers earned 350 marks monthly – making it "absolutely impossible" to meet minimal expenses.

Bogen visited Poale Zion's workers' kitchen and club. They were "not much different than the gathering places of our own working-men in the East Side." A good crowd was present, "and all of them seemed in a much better shape than the other groups," talking keenly of impending municipal elections. Their organization, which maintained a school and other institutions, was in deficit and now losing its previous 16,000-mark monthly municipal subsidy. Bogen noticed nothing radical about them.

---

[13] JDC. AR 19/21, 188 (Poland), "First Draft of a Memorandum on the Present Situation of the Jews in Poland," June 30, 1919; Bogen's report of February 1919, 80–94; here: 88–89.
[14] Bogen's report of February 1919, 86–87.

He learned that the Union of Leather and Fancy Goods Laborers was, exceptionally, in a relatively strong position, their wares in strong demand from the army. They worked eight-hour days, four days weekly, earning up to 60 marks a shift. They suffered from a "secret boycott practiced by the Government against the Jewish Manufacturers." The Union of Clothing-Trade Workers, with 1,300 members, reported 47 percent unemployment. The Labor Ministry paid relief money in March 1919 of nearly 30 million marks, mostly to the unemployed.[15]

In February 1919 Bogen's colleague, Professor Simonsen of Copenhagen, concluded that, throughout Congress Kingdom Poland, half or even three-quarters of Jews required charitable relief. Virtually all were underfed, public health was everywhere very bad, prices sky-high. Sugar, kerosene, soap, and candles were sometimes altogether missing. "Garments are ... not to be had in Poland; and so with footwear," or if available, only at exorbitant prices. Bad shoes might cost 300 to 400 Kr.[16] Traveling in late March with Col. Grove through Dąbrowa industrial basin and Łódź, Bogen found people "suffering from the present uncontrollable epidemic of Typhus." Tuberculosis stalked the poor, claiming in Łódź 70 percent of the dying.

Summing up in mid-1919, Bogen made finer distinctions, having learned that "the hundreds of thousands of Jews uprooted on the Russian side and unable to settle down elsewhere in Poland stand at the heart of present crisis." Many of these were inhabitants of towns surrounding Warsaw. In January 1915 Jews had been expelled from some forty suburban towns, leaving goods behind "abandoned to the mercy of the unbridled soldiery and rabble." Already by 1914's end, 80,000 refugees swelled Warsaw alone. In spring 1915, 200,000 more Jews were expelled from Suwałki, Grodno, and Courland. Again, the expellees' possessions "were plundered by the excited rabble even before the Jews had left their home-steads." Russian-ordered expulsions had continued through 1916's end, the Jewish Central Auxiliary Committee in Petrograd aiding 250,000 refugees within Russia's then borders, a number that excluded those Jews – *ca.* 20 percent of all expellees – who had cash and could support themselves.[17]

If those now homeless and unemployed could not find work, there will "arise a great army of human beings who will look for their rescue in an over-sea emigration" – to America, an outcome Bogen evidently wished to forestall. Hardest hit were the lower middle class plus "the great classes without any means, merely existing in a miserable way," and the workmen. Polish antisemitic parties targeted the economically stricken Jewish

---

[15] Ibid., 81–93.   [16] Ibid., "Appendix," 3–6.   [17] Ibid., 2–3.

middle classes, "and this Jew-baiting has taken away all their powers of resistance." Jewish cooperative associations required rebuilding, having proved vital, as Bogen wrote in a familiar vein of Western apprehension and condescension, "all over the East, as well as in Poland, to maintain the existence of the penniless classes, to keep them steadily working, and to bring them peace of mind, so that they shall/may give up their aimless travelling/wandering." In Łódź, raw materials were again reaching the thousands of Jewish hand weavers' hands. Before the war, the ready-made clothing industry had thrived there, despite low wages and tough competition. There had been masses of tailors, "as there was always plenty of work." But many Jewish "mechanics" (artisans) had been "badly affected by the boycotting," forcing them to work within the Jewish community alone and driving many into emigration.[18]

Such was the Jewish landscape in American eyes, foregrounded by uprooted and impoverished multitudes. From other angles, the desperate straits were less visible, but economic history imposes gloomy judgment on war-ravaged Poland, about to enter an inflation hardly less destructive of unprotected assets than Weimar Germany's. The interwar years, despite wan mid-1920s sunshine, would witness steady erosion of the weakest Jewish existences, whether middle class or proletarian. Around them, predators gathered, unnerved themselves at some psychological level – or provoked to attack – by the social defeat and abandonment immiserated Jews embodied.[19]

Casualties of Social War: Spring 1919 Galician Pogroms

Forest-based armed bands had frequently launched November 1918's West Galician pogroms, mostly within small-town and village precincts, assisted by peasant looters; hunger-beset, riot-prone poor folk; and plunder-driven, often drunken, aggressive, and sadistic youth. Craven bystanders cheered pogromists, while Christian authorities, when they did not join them, commonly put up but grudging and bumbling resistance. Outgunned Jews sometimes stood and fought but more often tried to hide or flee.

In spring 1919, central Galicia exploded again in pogrom violence engulfing even Rzeszów, the region's principal city. Nor were Jews alone targeted. Villagers, with hopes frustrated of widening meager acreage through parliamentary-sanctioned land reform parceling out large

---

[18] Ibid., 6–11, 44–45.
[19] See, *inter alia*, Hagen, "Before the 'Final Solution:' Toward a Comparative Analysis of Political Antisemitism in Interwar Germany and Poland," *passim*.

estates, plundered and terrorized big landowners and their agents. Agitators among radical agrarian populists incited to violence in rhetoric often indistinguishable from Bolshevism. Paltry 1918 harvests left many villagers and townspeople by ensuing springtime on starvation's brink. Countless uprooted men continued their furtive, well-armed sylvan ways. Nor could the Habsburgs' execrated German ruthlessness be blamed for new Poland's birth pangs. The pogromists now shook their fists at sovereign Polish officials, threatening them along with Jews and "lords."

This section draws on extensive, often scrupulous and insightful official inquiries to deepen this book's picture of demotic anti-Jewish riots and to plumb their now more visible political and social-psychological depths in the aftermath of the partitioning powers' – here, specifically, Austria's – retreat. This rich documentation has so far been left unanalyzed, if not unnoticed. Jerzy Tomaszewski observed in 1999 that while peasant radicalism in these years attracted communist-era historians' interest, "its antisemitic aspect, which collided with their simplified view of Polish revolutionary traditions, was avoided or mentioned only in passing."[20]

Pogroms were taking on more homegrown features, even as war-learned lessons in ruthlessness and revolutionism were being applied. It will be seen later that, especially in former Russian Poland, military-driven pogroms were raging, both before and, more fiercely, after the new Galician wave. It was only in western, once-Prussian Poland, where German-Polish rivalry had hastened Jewish emigration westward until but a few thousand self-identifying Jews remained, that anti-Jewish violence – despite widespread, deep-dyed Endek antisemitism – did not inflame liberated Poland's 1919 skies.

In four principal sections, the pages that follow contemplate, first, a *shtetl* pogrom swirling about the hoary ritual murder charge and, second, the elusive relationship between radical agrarian political agitation and anti-Jewish violence. They move next to the worst of this pogrom wave's explosions, in Kolbuszowa, which foreshadowed comprehensive urban-rural war. Finally, they address a rare urban pogrom in Rzeszów. These upheavals, alarming to Poland's governors, generated official inquests yielding interesting insights into popular motivation and ruling-class perceptions. The inseparability is striking of Judeophobic imaginings

---

[20] Jerzy Tomaszewski, "Zaburzenia antyżydowskie na Rzeszowszczyźnie wiosną 1919 roku," *Kieleckie Studia Historyczne*, T.15 (1999), 108. For an English version, see "Spring 1919 in Rzeszóv: Pogrom or Revolution?" in Tamás Csató et al., *Challenges of Economic History: Essays in Honor of Iván T. Berend* (Budapest: Budapest University of Economic Sciences, 1996), 183–91. Above-cited Stankiewicz, *Konflikty społeczne na wsi polskiej 1918–1920* (1963), is valuable, but its brief account of the May pogroms (159–68) confines itself to description.

from the social traumas and political disorientation gripping the pogromists and their human environment. We see that, caught in historical
crisis, the pathway out of its labyrinth appeared to many people, quite
naturally, to follow the red thread of anti-Jewish violence.

Easter Pogrom in Strzyżów

Cries of ritual murder ignited violence on April 21, Easter Monday and
Passover's final day, in the *shtetl* of Strzyżów (Yiddish: Strizev). This
small, half-Jewish county seat (2,200 souls in 1912) had witnessed
violence in November 1918 when, as Israel Cohen recorded, thirty-four
Jewish properties were plundered. Ritual murder panics – whether contrived and insincere or not – accompanied anti-Jewish Galician violence
in 1897–98, but Habsburg authorities refused to entertain them seriously.
Would Polish officials do so now?

The Kraków-based United Jewish Committee for the Protection of the
Jewish Population presented the Warsaw cabinet with its reading of
Strzyżów's pogrom. Penned by attorney Adolf Gross, it mentioned the
committee's protests over previous postindependence anti-Jewish incidents, fruitless "because courts release suspects arrested by gendarmes,
so that peasants see that nothing happens to them." Now there were
"formal pogroms," as in Strzyżów, where rumors circulated that "in
Ozyasz Seligmann's basement his daughter Golda Horowitz, who had
come to visit him, tried to carry out ritual murder of a certain thirteen-
year-old girl named Dziadoszówna (or Szafrańska)." Horowitz was
arrested along with "one of the Jews, red-bearded," as the girl had
described her intended killer. (In European folk tradition, supernatural
evil often displayed red hair.)

Nearby Rzeszów's district court investigated the ritual-murder charge,
"in which Strzyżów's intelligentsia also believe, in all seriousness," as
Gross irritably wrote, adding that, in this way, those with interest in
developing the murder story remained in control. But "it would have
sufficed to interrogate the girl in another locality without the presence of
agitators, and it would have emerged on whose initiative she had launched
the whole business." Here, again, Jewish charges of manipulation for
political purposes could not be supplied with substantive proof or even
plausible hypotheses about probable instigators.

Now eight pogromists arrested for robbery had been, as Gross heard,
released. Violence was spreading. In nearby Niebylec, thugs assaulted
Jews with metal rods, injuring some sixteen, three later dying. The central
government must act, "for we are threatened with a second Beilis case,"
and local officials failed to appreciate "how this could compromise

Poland's name abroad." Army reinforcements were needed, "for anti-Jewish riots threaten the whole of Galician Jewry." Meanwhile, the Zionist Yiddish press publicized riots "with ritual basis," in which Jews were charged with "the wish to kill a girl to use her blood for matzoth. Excitement has gripped the whole county."[21]

County prefect Biernowski traced the "antisemitic movement" to November's "uprising," when security organs collapsed. Since then, "agitators" at public and secret meetings had instigated in a dozen or more communes boycotts prohibiting work on Jewish-owned land, "the goal being to eliminate Jews in the villages and take possession of their lands." Villagers were also brazenly grazing livestock on large estates' meadows and pastures, even when Christians owned or leased such properties. Arsonists were at work, despite gendarmes' presence. Although Parliament aimed for land reform, "conscienceless agitators" misrepresented its work, inflaming village anger. Handwritten proclamations – telling evidence of grassroots inspiration – surfaced calling for pogroms.

Strzyżów's ritual-murder charge was, the prefect averred, "exclusively local teenagers' doing." The pogrom injured thirteen Jews, with one resulting death. In Niebylec, a crowd of 3,000 "peasants of both sexes" was repulsed by police, but rioters tracked down Jews who had fled the town to hide in the countryside, severely beating fourteen, with two subsequent deaths, while plundering some dozen houses.

Such, the *starosta* wrote, was the fruit of agitation aimed "in lesser degree also against Christian propertied classes and gendarmerie and army," who were held responsible for food shortages and allegedly "stood at the Jews' service." Great dissatisfaction raged among "poorer people, who are a sizable percentage." Their complaints were just, for since November the county had received but seventy-four hundredweights of American flour and little or no sugar. "Because of 1918's long drought and subsequent harvest storms, there was a catastrophic crop failure, so that food is lacking not only in the towns but in the rural communes." Absent relief, "hunger riots" were likely, "especially when Christians completely lacked flour and sugar while Jews received these items for their holy days." Christians finally gained one wagon-load of flour for the whole county, while Jews, though a minority, got the same amount free of charge from the Jewish relief committee for themselves alone, "which became the source of great embitterment among the

---

[21] AAN. Prezydium Rady Ministrów (hereafter: AAN. PRM), 5990/21 (May 12, 1919); CZA L6/119: Cohen, "The Pogroms in Poland"; CZA. Z3/181, "Dos judisze Folk" (April 27, 1919).

Catholic population." So too did lack of American subsidies for Polish artisans, and army requisitioning without proper payment of peasant draught animals.

Notable preachers of "hatred toward Jews" were two schoolteachers, one paid by Stapiński's Populist Party, the other "a student, private tutor and previous county administrator's brother-in-law," the latter not scrupling to criticize the government at rallies. Lutcza priest, Father Bolek, also exerted "harmful influence" and bears "great guilt." Worse still were "inflammatory sermons" of Father Franciszek Strzępek in Niebylec, responsible for pogrom there. Local courts were guilty of "passive conduct," having in March released twenty-eight plunderers of two Jewish manor farms after Stapiński and local allies succeeded in blocking their prosecution. Armed robbery and murder occurred repeatedly. Release of arrested suspects "mocks the gendarmerie, who are discouraged from service. Many have quit for lack of backing." The *starosta* called for immediate transfers of the populist teacher and priests. His surveillance had already driven the antisemitic tutor away. For the poor there should be three monthly wagon-loads of flour and one of fats. Roads in this railway-poor land needed improvements and police forces beefing up.[22]

Prefect Biernowski, dismissing ritual murder charges as child's play, acknowledged the force of popular hatred of Jews, which, if often dormant, was readily whipped to a frenzy by priests (although attorney Gross, perhaps concerned not to challenge Catholic power head-on, disregarded their agency) and other agitators. It was extreme postwar circumstances – hunger for bread and land, banditry, disarming of state power – that unleashed the pogromists. Yet, with food provisions and soldiers, order was restorable, and popular violence's well-springs capable, if not drainable.

Other interpreters accorded pogromists' arguments more weight. A report to the High Ministerial Commission in Strzyżów – evidently a Warsaw-dispatched investigative body – flowed from gendarmerie Chief Lieutenant Stepak's pen. As Habsburg authority crumbled, people disarmed the police – hated for enforcing food requisitioning and pursuit of deserters – and plundered shops. It was "generally known" that Jews had shirked war duty. "At the front people often said, 'here we have to shed blood while Jews sit in the hinterland and do good business, but just let's return and we'll get revenge.'" Recent flyers inciting violence spoke this language. It was ex-soldiers' and present new recruits' "hatred of Israelites" that explained the pogroms, as well as (falsely) that Jews did not purchase war bonds – hence numerous village resolutions to boycott

22 AAN. PRM, 5990/21, fos. 95–98 (May 20, 1919).

Jews in sales and purchases. While it wasn't "out of the question," as this seasoned policeman wrote, that individuals organized riots, more likely they were "spontaneous and instinctive actions" expressive of accumulated resentments and psychologically overwrought reactions to ritual-murder charges. The author thought this explanation found support in ex-soldiers' and adolescent boys' prominence in the violence.[23]

Self-exculpatory notes sounded here, as well as disinterest in making arrests, even though this report's tally of losses counted three dead across the county and thirty wounded. Jewish religious commune spokesman, attorney Dr. Gabryel Wasserman, felt obliged – absurdly – to deny that "the incident with Szafrańska" could have been a "provocation from the Jewish side, because the Jewish population suffers consequences too great from pogroms." They were a small exposed group "who count themselves the Polish state's most loyal citizens." He requested that, on market days and religious holidays, warnings be posted of "summary courts" (pro-claimed in November 1918 but largely inactive) and that police patrols be reinforced. The Strzyżów pogrom only ended after two days, "thanks mainly to lieutenant Detloff," who sent with troops from Kraków.[24]

Jewish merchant Michael Schütz was an immediate eyewitness.

About a week before the holidays and the Jewish Easter [*Wielkiejnocy /żydowskiej/*] rumors circulated of possible unrest during Jewish holy days and warnings to certain Jews to leave Strzyżów. But no one believed these rumors and no one left town.

Jews were reluctant to accept pogrom predictions partly because fleeing was perilous and untended shops invited plunder. Schütz's formulation signals confusion about Passover holidays' relationship to Easter. To some Christians, certainly, Judaism appeared less a free-standing religion than a heresy, both Christian and anti-Christian in nature. The proximity of the two celebrations encouraged this thought and heightened aggression's danger.

Schütz recalled that "the second Jewish holiday" – April 21 – proceeded tranquilly until two Christian women appeared at a Jewish prayer house, shouting "hand over the girl." Schütz saw policemen lead the girl, followed by a small crowd, to Seligmann's house. As they inspected it, the crowd began pelting its occupants and Jewish passers-by with stones. Schütz took refuge in the synagogue, but it too was stoned, and he escaped through a window. On that day Seligmann's house was robbed.

Next day, Schütz sought intervention by the prefect's office, where assistant *starosta* Bigniewicz and gendarmerie chief Stepak had ordered

---

[23] Ibid., fos. 99–100 (May 20, 1919).   [24] Ibid., fo. 101 (April 20, 1919).

Jews to stay home. Those on the streets were being injured by locals with stones or clubs. Assaults on dwellings began, including Schütz's, where he was thrashed. On April 23, villagers streamed in (including, as another witness averred, "farmer elders"). They joined local students and adolescents in attacking and beating Jews in their homes and robbing them. Schütz lost three men's suits and part of his linen, plus sixty liters of wine, sugar, and matches. He reckoned fifteen Jews seriously wounded, twenty lightly, and one dead. During the three days, half the Jewish population fled on trains in all directions. Although the town was patrolled, beatings continued, and even now boys stoned Jews.[25]

Christian farmer Wladyslaw Stachura testified that he regularly attended church and many times witnessed how priest Strzępek had, since fall 1918, "delivered sermons not on religious themes but always incited the people, criticizing the government – that it protects Jews, that since Moraczewski's appointment only dregs and scum join the army. He says gendarmes are Jewish uncles" and that soldiers sent in March 1919 to quell plundering in Niebylec were wrongly stationed there, and "those Jewish uncles" who summoned them should alone have to support them, not the commune. "Often after mass, neighbors discussed these sermons and considered whether they should continue attending church in view of what the priest was preaching."

Wladyslaw Mazur, Niebylec shoemaker, confirmed this testimony, adding that the priest from the pulpit "called all men returning from the front Bolsheviks, criminals, etc. and generally used the word Bolshevik on every occasion, which produced great indignation and displeasure among those assembled." The shoemaker quoted the priest as saying, in election season, "if you kill your father or brother you haven't sinned so greatly as if you had voted for the opposing party." Senior farmer Jan Majcher further quoted the priest: "let commune and farmers give the army nothing." His colleague, Wojciech Stachura, remembered hearing the priest say, at a farmyard electoral rally, "if someone took something from Jews, it was no sin." On another occasion he said, "Poland fell because of the Jews."[26]

A six-person delegation of Strzyżów officeholders, half women, averred that the pogrom's immediate cause was agrarian populists' meetings. Chief agitators were two teachers and Stapiński's operative. Difficulties in food provisioning, though weighty, were not the trigger. Yet "the delegation," betraying anti-Jewish paranoia's pervasiveness, "regards the secret occurrence with Szafrańska as Jewish-Bolshevik provocation, to trigger anarchy and then move against the existing social order."

[25] Ibid., fos. 102–4 (May 20, 1919).   [26] Ibid., fos. 105–6, 7 (May 13–14, 1919).

Townspeople did not participate, apart from "irresponsible adolescents. Balbina Kruczek was even beaten, as she tried to calm excesses' perpetrators." It seemed to the delegation necessary "to stipulate that the riots broke out exclusively for antisemitic reasons," proof (allegedly) being that on earlier Christian holidays Jewish devotionalia sellers were plundered.[27]

The *shtetl*'s Christian politicians saw no disgrace in emphasizing prevalence of antisemitism and pogrom violence – facts of life – though they blamed country folk and Jews, not themselves. In abjuring antigovernment resentments, specifically over poor food provisioning, they distanced themselves from charges of disloyalty or Bolshevism and shielded themselves from official reprisals. Viewed from this politically safe angle, ritual-murder charges might just be Jews' anarchorevolutionary tactics.

Strzyżów pogrom's last documentary appearance was in October 1919, when the *starosta* proposed to the Galician governor (*Namiestnik*) in Lwów that payments be made to families of the three men murdered in the pogrom. Droshky driver Sender Kimmel left a wife and five children "in bad circumstances." They deserved a 3,000-Kr. award. Jakob Rath left a widow and three children similarly, qualifying for 1,500 Kr. Mailech Schaffer left a family "in good financial condition," nullifying payment. These awards, if granted, fell in the range of workingmen's yearly wages.[28]

Pogrom Incitation by Agrarian Populist Politicians?

The Galician pogroms of 1918 drew some unquantifiable degree of ideological inspiration from antisemitic incitation in Endek and agrarian populist press, though conceivably many pogromists knew little of this, relying instead on homegrown "common-sensical" justifications. Spring 1919's pogroms, of which Strzyżów's is emblematic, exploded on a landscape carved out by radical agrarian populist agitation, which peaked in the short-lived "Tarnobrzeg Republic," centered on that town, proclaimed on November 6, 1918 and suppressed by the Polish army in January 1919. Its founders were post-Habsburg gendarme commander Tomasz Dąbal and priest Eugeniusz Okoń. Both were self-professed leftist radicals, promising peasant democracy and land reform. One of their critics, accusing them of treasonable radicalism, said that, at meetings, the priest demanded "expropriation of [estate] land at 100–200 korony compensation per acre [*morga*], while Dąbal wanted total

---

[27] Ibid., fo. 107 (May 20, 1919).   [28] Ibid., fos. 201–2 (October 27, 1919).

expropriation of noble estates, communal lands, priests' and bishops' lands without compensation."[29]

Their assemblies attracted giant audiences of 30,000, in whose midst the Tarnobrzeg "republic" was proclaimed to block flow into the emptied Habsburg space of new Polish state power that would oppress peasants anew. Both men were colorful, oft-incarcerated figures who gained parliamentary seats in January 1919's elections. Dąbal (b. 1890) drifted from Stapiński's populism to PSL-Left into communism, landing in the Soviet Union where, after a success-crowned career as Polish and Belarusian Bolshevik, he perished (as "Polish counterrevolutionary") in 1937's purges. Okoń (1881–1949) emerged into pre-1914 social Catholicism under aristocratic patronage with Endek connections to follow Dąbal's path, though stopping short of Sovietism, moving then into anti-Nazi resistance and final years in Communist Poland, hounded but posthumously lauded for his maverick radicalism.

During the January elections, Father Okoń was temporarily jailed "for inciting rural dwellers against manor-houses, officials and police," resulting in robberies, even murders, unlawful cutting of estate forests, and grazing of estate meadows. It took a "punitive military expedition" to halt these transgressions.[30] Dąbal's and Okoń's speeches at spring 1919 mass meetings were often cited as pogrom triggers or accelerators. A good account, filtered through policeman's and peasant's eyes, survives of a market-day assembly of 2,000 villagers in Mielec on April 3, 1919. The gendarme observer described Dąbal's three-hour speech as "jarring" and "provocative." The orator demanded sacking of ethnic Ukrainian gendarmes and others who were "hostile to the people." When he himself was Tarnobrzeg police chief, Dąbal acted "without permission of higher authorities and all was good." Civil officials should likewise know that "when the yardstick is passed to the people, they will measure justice for themselves. Revolution hangs in the air, and while villagers don't want to gain their rights with clubs in hand, they won't suffer much longer."

With an antisemitic flourish, Dąbal observed that "when Jews arrive in pan starosta Różecki's office, he gives them a chair and asks them to sit, but if a peasant appears he doesn't see him." (If Dąbal and friends on this occasion fired off other anti-Jewish blasts, police did not report them.) When cooking fat and bacon, flour and sugar arrived from America, it went to officials and well-off townspeople, "while only so much was given to the poor as to get rid of them, and villagers were left to starve." Attacking the moderate Piast Peasant Party, Dąbal charged their local parliamentary deputy with diverting 600,000 korony to his election

[29] Ibid., fo. 143 (May 22, 1919).   [30] Ibid., 2.

campaign, at cost of securing local food subsidies. Piast leader Wincenty Witos "is a millionaire and goes hand-in-hand with gentlemen lords." He charged Okoń with deserting Dąbal's Stapiński party for fat pay.

Police archived farmer Piotr Kalisz's rustic reportage. Of gendarmes, Dąbal had said that they lay in wait and horribly beat a seventy-year-old villager. Manorial land and forests belonged cost free to peasants, "who should take them by force." He threatened the noose against hostile Habsburg-era officials. His words "incited the uneducated nation [*podjudrały ciemny narud*] and gave voice to pillage and robbery."

I am a born farmer, I count sixty-five years, and have interested myself in politics for almost forty years, and was at elections, every election, in Europe and even America. But I never heard any such speech or rabble-rousing. That's incitation against authorities and public. That man was stirring up banditism with his speeches.

Any peaceful farmer or townsman [*bużarzie*], and the whole nation, will suffer great distress because of this person's disreputable words, and won't be able to peacefully work. As for gendarmes' chaining of that Kolbuszowa elder, I haven't been able to confirm it and regard Mr. Dąbal's words as incitation against Polish Gendarmerie. This person isn't worthy and shouldn't hold a deputy's mandate. The same applies to the other deputy from Mielec, *pan* Krempa, who also greatly harangues the people. And particularly all priests, which all honorable farmers find a great demoralization against Religion.[31]

Police also cited a civil engineer's report that Dąbal had told judge Otowski that "not a single educated person [*intelligent*] will survive in Mielec if peasants don't get free farm plots." It required only invocation of Jakub Szela's name to tie this remark to 1846's infamous *rabacja*. A witness informed an information-gathering team from Warsaw's Sejm that Dąbal's April 1 Kolbuszowa speech exhorted unequivocally to violence: "you know what you have to do with the Jews. You'll only get justice when you grab your scythes."[32] Mielec's pharmacist said he overheard Dąbal threatening class war in a restaurant conversation, while another informer claimed that Dąbal declared "the Bolshevik movement is spreading among peasants." Yet an article Dąbal penned in January 1919 for *Peasant Unity* (*Jedność Chłopska*) confined itself, amid heavy Catholic Christian imagery, to electoral propaganda against the Piast Party.[33]

A Tarnobrzeg gendarme recorded deputy Dąbal's April 10 speech. Land reform and other promises remained unfulfilled, he conceded, but there was hope. Unfortunately, his ally Father Okoń had, he claimed, gone over to PSL-Piast. He urged listeners to reject state gendarmerie, "who permit themselves murder and beatings," in favor of people's

---

[31] Ibid., fo. 127 (n.d.).   [32] Tomaszewski, "Zaburzenia," 97.
[33] AAN. PRM. 5990/21, fos. 131–32 (May 15, 1919).

militia. Should a gendarme attempt farm inventorying, villagers should "put up active resistance, fight back, refuse to be harnessed [*roztrząskać łeb*], use their axes" – flourishes earning cries of "long live Dąbal, bravo!"

He pilloried *starosta* Dr. Łącki for allowing food exports from the county "to reward profiteers" and for failing to properly distribute a transport of fats and bacon, leading Dąbal to intervene. He condemned a former Habsburg gendarme, now absconded, "who built latrines for Jews and fenced in their homes and gardens," while "for you, brothers, he built nothing, so that you must live in broken-down houses." In Warsaw, "lord deputies" resided in Hotel Bristol, at 60 marks nightly, while daily living expenses only paid 50 marks. Dąbal, "wearing borrowed cap and fur-coat, was sent by the lords with other colleagues to house in a venereal hospital, so that we would breathe our last. But instead, two grand gentlemen died and none of us!" Lesser voices denounced news sources other than left-agrarian *Przyjaciel Ludu* ("*People's Friend*"). Father Okoń had "gypped [*ocyganił*] the people" and should be beaten if he returns. As for land reform, peasants should reject leaseholds and settle only for full ownership.[34]

Father Okoń braved threats and spoke in Tarnobrzeg two weeks later, with Dąbal on the platform. He addressed his audience as "brother peasants!" (*Bracia Chłopi*). He knew that because of Dąbal's criticism, "you wanted to throw me in the Vistula," but he hadn't betrayed them for a parish living. He condemned the government "for sending soldiers to suppress us while Lwów drowned in blood. They beat us, herded us to jail, where dirt and vermin gnawed us." They don't fear the peasant, "but his patience is running out." In Parliament, Okoń backed abolition of physical judicial punishment, intolerable insult to "the honor of a free republican and citizens of Poland. It's forbidden to beat and cane free citizens." He had called for new railroad lines and roads, rural schools, basket-weaving schools, textile factories. "This will spare us the Bolshevik conflagration, that terrible plague," which shakes the mighty Russian state and is spreading in Hungary and German lands. Meanwhile, Poland's government was paralyzed. The *szlachta* and their mouthpieces fought land reform doggedly, asking for sky-high compensation. Forests should be nationalized. American flour and fats never reached peasants, "only lords, Jews, officials and *starosta* agents."

Dąbal then spoke, urging formation of a single peasant party. Congress Kingdom brothers held back, thinking they were better off than Galicians. Villages should have clean, nonpolitical administrators, free of bribe taking (*kubaniorstwo*). "The *szlachta* of old governed dishonestly and

[34] Ibid., fo. 146 (April 10, 1919).

perished. Bad headman, bad administrator – throw him out, even if he's my brother." The lords' press defamed the Tarnobrzeg Republic. "They see every peasant here as bandit and every parliamentary deputy as robber chieftain."

But you gathered here in good number, and we're not causing any trouble, we're not murdering or robbing anyone, we're just demanding honesty and justice from officials. We're protesting villainy [łajdactwo].

Why was the army here, enforcing a state of emergency? Rumors of Bolshevism were false. "The days of government by *szlachta* and lords are gone – big landed property is dying ... I, as far leftist, demand total expropriation in peasants' favor." Does the audience approve his membership in Stapiński's party? "A few voices: yes." Dąbal ended nationalistically: "The Czech wants our Silesia; the Ruthenian – the oil of Borysław, and Lwów, our ancient possession; the German – Gdańsk; but no one will dare or be able to tear these away, because we will succeed in securing our borders." Okoń seconded this patriotic salvo. The meeting endorsed land reform favoring peasants and Polish possession of aforementioned regions, plus snippets of Slovakia. Alluding to just-passed Easter, Okoń blessed the audience: "May the Lord's Resurrection day bring you consolation and solace."

A master of ceremony asked for a vote of confidence in the deputies, "to which some voices cried out: 'we confer it.'" The police recorder wrote: "here followed the meeting's humorous side." It was a parody of the old *szlachta* republic. "Jajko [moderator] turned to Father Okoń and, placing his hand on his head, said 'we give you our vote' [*udzielamy Ci votum*]. Those present snorted with laughter." Responding to Okoń's joking response and referring perhaps to his hearty appetite, someone cried out, "can't he stop talking rubbish? He wants *traife* [*treyf*: Yiddish for nonkosher food] in Tarnobrzeg, that's why he babbles – and he'll get it."[35]

Antisemitism was absent from these meetings' police transcripts, where Jews figured as recipients of governmental favor at peasant expense. The real bogeymen were large landowners, "lords" (*panowie*), the peasant-devouring conscription-based standing army, gendarmes, and unjust and corrupt officials, high and low. Yet such meetings undoubtedly inflamed anti-Jewish impulses. Israel Cohen noted of a November 1918 Tarnobrzeg riot: "several Jewish families beaten and robbed by mob incited by National Democratic priest."[36] And in May 1919, a Jewish religious commune's delegation in Tarnobrzeg (3,000 souls, two-thirds Jewish) "ascribed present occurrences," seemingly looting without physical injuries, "almost

---

[35] Ibid., fos.147–50 (April 23, 1919).   [36] CZA. L6/119.

exclusively to agitation by deputies Dąbal and priest Okoń." At a meeting in nearby Majdan Kolbuszowa, "there were outright calls for violence against Jews ['up and at them!']." The delegation added that

by strange coincidence, riots usually broke out following Dąbal's meetings, e.g., in December 1918 and January 1919, when, however, army units assigned to us blocked the crowd's entry into town. Disappointed in hopes of robbery, the bands then (January 10) plundered Count Tarnowski's Mokrzyszów manor-farm. The authorities fulfilled their responsibility to protect the town and its inhabitants beyond reproach.[37]

Here too Jewish witnesses did not – or could not – precisely link violence to its supposed instigators. It was perhaps repugnant in Jewish political circles, but probably a realistic thought to ordinary Jews, that socially explosive agitation, even in the absence of exhortations to violence, easily moved Christian common folk – culturally and, in their individual personalities, psychologically often predisposed to it – to anti-Jewish aggression. But that appears to be how many pogroms occurred: political agitation (or ritual-murder charge or other ostensible provocation) sparked collective will to plunder and assault not because demagogic speakers explicitly incited crowds to it but because such gatherings were launch pads for pogrom-hungry hotheads among the homespun audience. Strzyżów gendarme Stepak, as we saw, thought action in such cases "spontaneous and instinctive."

Social War in Kolbuszowa: "First the Jews"

This also was true of Kolbuszowa, where for five days (May 3–7) one of modern Poland's costlier pogroms raged, claiming eight or nine Jewish lives, with seven "hooligans" also dying. Some 100 Jews were injured seriously, and 350 of 416 Jewish existences plundered. Counting outlying Jewish households, 465 persons suffered robbery, at a cost of 7,571,974 korony. "Such a large sum," explained attorney Rabinowicz, "results from Jews' not trusting *korona*-currency, so that they invested their whole capital in merchandise and had big stores of accumulated goods."[38]

---

[37] *Bierzcie się do nich.* AAN. PRN, 5990/21, fo. 138 (May 22, 1919). Kraków's *Judisze Folksceitung* reported that on May 5 Majdan Kolbuszowski experienced a "horrible pogrom," in which peasants, having disarmed gendarmerie, invaded a prayer house and destroyed Torah rolls, "trampling them with their feet." Fourteen were seriously wounded; losses were estimated at 3 million korony. CZA. Z3/181 (May 16, 1919). Israel Cohen noted November 1918 violence there: CZA. L6/119.

[38] AAN. PRM, 5990/21, fos. 173–75. For a superb portrait of Jewish Kolbuszowa, see Norman Salsitz (Saleschütz), *A Jewish Boyhood in Poland: Remembering Kolbuszowa* (Syracuse, NY: Syracuse University Press, 1992).

Kolbuszowa (Yiddish: Kolbishov), northwest of Rzeszów, counted some 3,600 souls in 1914, half Jewish. The town's emblem displayed two hands shaking, symbolizing Christian-Jewish cooperation. An official (seemingly *starosta* Stanisław Tyszkowski) sketched 1918's nationalist power seizure in hostile strokes. On November 2, unnamed activists held a meeting

to which they dragged by force and terror some nearby farmers and rabble comprised of adolescents. This crowd, whipped up by agitators who even[!] incited to murdering officials, cheered *pan* Dr. [Judge] Kazimierz Czarny and, on agitators' motion, appointed him chairman of the county National Council.[39]

His authority was later reconfirmed by "a crowd of urban scum," youngsters, farmers in town by chance, and Dr. Czarny's partisans. Israel Cohen recorded four-day plundering here: "not until Nov. 4th, after the third call of a Jewish deputation, did [Czarny], the virtual mayor, agree to form militia. The Polish educated classes, when threatened themselves, organized 100 armed men."[40]

In March 1919, notorious radical Dąbal spoke in nearby Majdan Królewski, but official notes betray no antisemitic accents. His antagonism to estate owners, priests, and PSL reflected their resistance to his land-reform bill, including distribution of land and building materials to the wholly landless. He backed railroad extension to connect Kolbuszowa to the wider world and raising soldiers' pay "so they might bring some savings home with them." He inveighed against "Ruthenian gendarmes," targeting officer Piątek ("known," as the police reporter noted, "as an energetic gendarme, especially in nabbing thieves and deserters"). Gendarmes generally, Dąbal thundered, "stand in lords' service with bayonets aimed at peasants' chests, but peasants will hammer their scythes into lances and drive them out." Policemen should be peasant sons. Next day in Kolbuszowa he assailed requisitioning of peasants' horse-drawn carts. "Let lords and officers walk, and not smash up farmers' wagons," whereupon two villages abjured such service.[41]

On Kolbuszowa pogrom's eve, newly moderate Father Okoń "repudiated his previous system, his agitational speeches, and now calmed the people, warning against deputy Dąbal and his meetings, which only stirred people up." The priest confined himself to criticizing authorities for poor provisioning and low requisition payments. He discussed the agrarian question, "but very peacefully."[42] Here, too, antisemitic demagoguery was apparently absent, yet the meetings obviously gathered

[39] Jerzy Tomaszewski, "Zaburzenia," 95. Cf. 95–109, *passim*.   [40] CZA. L6/119.
[41] AAN. PRM, 5990/21, fo. 165 (March 31, 1919).
[42] Ibid., fos. 165–66 (April 25, 1919).

excited crowds from whose midst, without speakers having directly called for it, pogrom violence soon erupted.

Prefect Tyszkowski reported again, evidently to a governmental investigative commission like Strzyżów's, in terms corroborative of Thomas and Znaniecki's account of peasant psychology. From November 1, 1918, country folk's minds had been "unnaturally excited" by completely unanticipated governmental collapse. "Inborn troublemaking" or power lust drove certain upstart leaders, notably Judge Czarny and a building contractor, *Trafik*-kiosk operator, and schoolteacher, to fiercely denounce old-regime officials while disarming gendarmerie. "Local farmers and town's petty burghers, hearing such speeches from intelligentsia mouths," decided that "henceforth no authorities need be obeyed except communal organs, and documented their imaginings by starting to rob Jews in the small towns." This venture met blockage by reorganized gendarmerie with soldiers' backing.[43]

With the people's "ostensible approval," nationalist hotheads dethroned Austrian-era *starosta*, while villagers repudiated their leaders and "headed for anarchy." After Tyszkowski's appointment, calm returned, even during January elections. But discontent boiled up as Kolbuszowa's parliamentary deputies Okoń, Dąbal, and others held meetings attempting to explain why their earlier promises of "immediate parcellation of seigneurial lands and forests" hadn't been fulfilled. After such assemblies, "communal livestock-pasturing on seigneurial meadows and wild cutting of timber" regularly occurred. Villagers' refusal to transport officials meant that food supplies could not be brought from the railroad station twenty-two kilometers distant. Armed villagers overpowered gendarmes searching for weapons.

"Around Easter holidays rumors began circulating of intended slaughter [*rzeź*] of Jews," especially after Dąbal's assembly, "so I had to calm a Jewish deputation and promise them every sort of defense." On May 1, news arrived that plundering of Jews had begun in other counties, allegedly "with permission and on recommendation of Sejm and Warsaw government." On May 2, in the *starosta*'s office building, Kolbuszowa communal headman (*wójt*) Fryc "warned the Jewish ritual slaughterers that, starting next day, they should hide themselves well if they wanted to avoid danger." Saturday, May 3, was Poland's prime national holiday.

Although Tyszkowski held police on barracks alert that day, "bands of youths from outlying communes, clubs in hand, began breaking into Jews' dwellings. I advised them to close shops and taverns through Sunday and Monday." He canceled Tuesday's market day as well. On

---

[43] *Urodzone warcholstwo*. Here and below: ibid., fos. 153–60 (n.d. [after May 7, 1919]).

Sunday he learned of robberies in nearby Raniżów. "Then I had to recognize that the projected assault on Kolbuszowa on Tuesday would surely happen." He called to Rzeszów and Tarnów for military assistance. Meeting with refusal, he resolved to muster all policemen, thinking that if armed entry could not be prevented, they could block plunderers in the town.

Next day he learned that bands had disarmed police in Majdan Kolbuszowa and staged "wild robbery of Jewish shops."[44] Warsaw's General Delegate in Rzeszów now dispatched twenty soldiers, seemingly those who had been posted on a nearby large estate to protect its owner and officials and to guard against depredations on meadow and woods. Certain of impending pogrom, as he plainly wrote, Tyszkowski stationed his forces at town entrances, cautioning against unnecessary shooting. At 9:00 AM on Tuesday, "all the roads leading into town filled with incoming bands of young peasants armed with clubs and canes and some with rifles." In their van were the usual "masses of peasant women with carts and baskets." Policeman Stobierski commanded the crowd to halt, but it swept past, driving him and his men into "disorderly flight." Stobierski was chased to his house, where he hid. Municipal clerk Brkarta, leading armed men on another road, found himself surrounded. Shots rang, and "an attacker lay dead." Brkarta hid two hours in the jail attic as pogromists searched, threatening his death. "This official consequently developed heart illness and heavy neurasthenia."

At another crossroad, subofficial Dr. Schnitzel and his men fired salvos, then fled. "He barely saved his life, as the band chased him with clubs, amid incessant fire." Elsewhere, "soldiers voluntarily let themselves be disarmed, while the crowd thrashed official Augustyn painfully, crippling him." By noon, Kolbuszowa's armed forces had dissolved. One soldier and one policeman were dead, twenty-seven rifles lost. The remaining soldiers barricaded themselves in barracks.

By evening, all Jewish shops and homes were thoroughly plundered, "nine Jews murdered, their corpses pitilessly mistreated" – dehumanized, desecrated, demystified. Some 100 others were injured. Two Catholics were robbed: forester and judge.

To rob Catholic shops of Zach and Karakiewicz without punishment they fired Jewish homes flanking them and not only did not extinguish the flames, but stopped others, threatening *starostwo* official Lasota, who was organizing a rescue action, with being thrown in the flames. Only when priest Father Bardt, kneeling on the town square, called for help, did the crowd allow the fire to be localized, so that only one house burned. Because of powerful wind it might have consumed the nearby

---

[44] CZA, Z3/181, "Fala Pogromowa w Polsce: Majdan Kolbuszowski."

church and whole town square. The crowd burst into jail, freeing all prisoners, then robbed and drank all plundered alcohol late into the night, threatening that next day they would slaughter [*wyrznąć*] officials and especially prefect [Tyszkowski], who – as they shouted – had been bought by the Jews and had called in troops and ordered them to shoot, even though government ministers had [they claimed] permitted robbery of Jews and had issued a prohibition on gunfire.[45]

Soldiers from Rzeszów, armed with machine guns, arrived at night and drove pogromists from Kolbuszowa. Next morning the attackers returned, "in strict war formation, with lines of shooters" to break into town "and exact vengeance on officials" but were repulsed. One soldier and three villagers died. Local doctor Cierpielowski, "an old man of seventy-six, self-sacrificingly attended the wounded, risking a bullet."

Tyszkowski reckoned the town could not withstand another attack, expected on May 11. Rzeszów sent more soldiers, while in Sokołów, thirty kilometers distant, police repelled attackers "with constant fire." After May 12, order prevailed. A court martial found a villager guilty of assault on the forester's house and had him immediately executed by firing squad. Eight further jail sentences of five to twenty years were pronounced; other arrestees awaited trial in Rzeszów. Villagers were resisting weapons searches, as proven by a lieutenant struck in the head by a bullet and a boy's firing on a gendarme.

A "Red Guard Organization" (*Organizacja czerwonogwardista*) had been discovered in the forest, with some fifty young peasants well armed and provisioned. It would take strong soldiery to subdue them. They kept military order, with patrols and uniforms, including shirts "with sewn-on Red Guard patches (red plush)." The region's village-dwelling Jews were thoroughly plundered. Chaim Blitzer was killed "with wheels," his murderer sentenced (only) to prison. Jewish estate lessees lost everything, greatly weakening local food provisioning.

Tyszkowski heatedly concluded that "the whole movement was doubtless initiated by foreign Bolshevik elements, whose program [prescribes] chaos and bloody riots." More proof lay in their "outstanding organization," especially of the 8,000 men (or so he thought) attacking Kolbuszowa, led by "completely foreign individuals" and including "peasants from very distant parts" of three local counties. The bands evidently had their agents in Kolbuszowa county and took advantage of "the benightedness and indigence of the people here," including ex-soldiers and POWs. Fired by hope of booty, "these elements easily let themselves be persuaded to join pogroms, and they draw along with them the generality of peasants very eager for plunder and theft."

[45] AAN. PRM, 5990/21, fos. 155–56.

Tyszkowski addressed the ideological question, saying "there could be no talk of typical antisemitism, but rather the riots' essence is banditism, which first exploded against Jews." Nor could he say "that the riots were especially provoked by Jews."

The exploitation and profiteering they practice evokes here, as in all Poland, indignation. The behavior of Jews here, as throughout the State, is stamped by aversion to our idea of rebuilding the State. The young generation of Jews is imbued with a spirit of outright Bolshevism and fanatical hate of everything Polish. Yet all these phenomena don't exert any great influence on the thoughts of peasants, who are unenlightened and completely indifferent to the national cause [*włościan nie uświadomionych a zupełnie obojętnych na sprawę narodową*].

The clergy, "constantly prey to rumors and threats of loss of land," largely remained passive. Teachers held "extreme radical convictions" and did not rise to their obligations, for not only did they do nothing to stop the pogrom, but none told Tyszkowski of impending danger, though some, working constantly among the people, must have known of "secret machinations" (*knowania*). Townspeople, also passive, sympathized with pogroms. Some joined looting, and the court martial sentenced one to twenty years' imprisonment. Another urged the attackers to shoot Tyszkowski.

These pogroms were, in his view, the first of a series of criminal actions. "The peasants' pogroms against lordships and urban intelligentsia weren't abandoned but only postponed" owing to army arrival. Rumors of vengeance against "lords and officials" were multiplying as peasant aversion to Polish army service turned, through recent repression, "into irreconcilable fanatical hatred," which, if not blocked, "will break out with full force in a manner far more dangerous than the Jewish pogroms."

Hunger was rampant. Schoolteacher-preached boycott by Christian laborers of Jewish landlords or estate lessees undermined food supplies. Farmland was bad. The 1918 potato harvest failed. Many were starving and, were it not for the army, would commit desperate acts. The prefect could distribute but a half kilo of flour per person weekly and had no potatoes. Tyszkowski recommended military campaigns to capture bandit leaders and use of "competent detectives to investigate links between this county and Bolshevik agents around Lublin." Cash should be paid for requisitions; public employment provided for the landless. He sought his own transfer and that of other riot-compromised officials.

Tyszkowski's disillusioned view of his county's subjects, including Jews, made a locally grown agrarian revolution seem plausible, yet he targeted Bolshevik outside agitators. Like many others, he thought of Bolshevism not as revolutionary proletarianism but as war cry of land-hungry, landlord- and official-hating insurrectionary peasants. His gendarmerie chief, doughty Lieutenant Konopki, concurred. To the loss statistics he added, "it was learned through confidential channels that five young Jewish girls were raped." He confirmed Tyszkowski's warning that insurgents aimed to return to attack "the gentlemen," though the army blocked them. The pogroms' Bolshevik character was evident in the multitude of agitators streaming in from outside. "Because antisemitic frameworking [tło antysemickie] is most effective among unenlightened farmers here, it was used to more easily call forth riots that undoubtedly would have later turned against intelligentsia and bourgeoisie." Bands were waiting in the forest for further assaults.[46]

County official Augustyn, who had led eight soldiers against pogromists, reported that they shouted: "the lords [panowie] take potatoes and don't pay us" and "you took money from Jews to protect them."[47] He was struck on the head and lost consciousness. Czapliński, twenty-year local treasury official well-acquainted with "this people, their character and disposition," testified to peasant women's incitation to violence. Talking with people at pogrom outset, he learned that "today only Jews would fall victim." The starostwo office building was locked and – as was later revealed – "full of concealed Jews." At the police station he found fifty-four soldiers and their officer, who asked him to telephone Rzeszów for permission to withdraw, since "the crowd was threatening him for killing six people." Christian townspeople attempting to protect their property from fire, when blocked by pogromists, declared "they would come themselves to burn the villages if the town burned down," whereupon the crowd relented. Drunken plunderers announced that "they would come the next day to slaughter the lords, officials, and bourgeois. This threat I heard a few times."

I also saw bestial tormenting of Jews. There were a few of us witnesses, but because of the danger the crowd posed – had we tried to help them – we had to abandon all aid. I also talked with people who in fact did not rob and condemned murder and plunder . . . A few times I encountered the claim that parliament and our deputies had permitted murder and robbery.[48]

Lipnica, deputy Sudoł's home village, joined the pogrom en masse, until it confronted soldiers' machine guns.

The people here are benighted, superstitious and mistrustful of the gentlemen, i.e., intelligentsia and officials, especially the latter, since in pre-war Austrian times they were treated loftily by them as vulgar boors (cham[y]), during the war

[46] Ibid., fos. 161–62.   [47] Ibid., fo. 164 (May 22, 1919).
[48] Czapliński's testimony, here and below: ibid., fos. 167–69 (May 11, 1919).

exploited with requisitions, and if they needed something – swindled. Demoralized by war and invasions on several fronts, where they witnessed only murder and plunder and took part themselves in it; with priest Okoń and his followers Dąbal, Sudoł and others sowing mistrust and preaching resistance to police and soldiers with scythes and flails; the people stood there with firearms from the war, knowing how to use them: a big percent of them served militarily, they know the muster, commands, and with foreign elements' taking advantage of the parliamentary deputies' incitations, they betook themselves to plunder, firstly of the Jews. [The towns were attacked with military precision,] with reconnaissance patrols, a command hierarchy, and with whistled signals.

When the soldiery, some of them local residents, initially tried to halt the town's invasion, "people began calling on soldiers, even by name, having recognized them, and approaching them tore away their guns and ammunition." There was hope, seasoned tax man Czapliński thought, that as popular excitement abated,

more reasonable countryfolk, those thinking healthier thoughts, those who are richer, in fear that this violence-wave might destroy them too, will, little by little, provide authorities with clues. Offering a large monetary reward for identifying the actual pogroms' organizers could yield additional results, for the peasant, avid for a penny, will for a few thousand korony turn someone in, especially an outsider.

He saw how deputy Sudoł visited Kolbuszowa from Warsaw, "observing his political handiwork's consequences, his head drooping, his hat pulled over his eyes." He escaped "unrecognized and uncursed as one of the chief perpetrators." Captain Jakubiczek, punitive expedition commander, gathered "a dozen or so village mayors, and these people themselves, some of them serious and honorable, called for armed suppression of this Bolshevik uprising." Otherwise, seeing it unpunished, people would repeat it.

The government's investigative commission collected testimony from various citizens.[49] Shoemaker Cibicki opined that "the riots were because of lack of work and young village boys' idleness." The pogrom was a village affair, without urban participation. It was aimed not at Jews alone, "since it was generally known that the plan was to attack the townspeople and manors after the Jew." In the villages were numerous bandits, "who terrorize peaceful people and who are" – here a rare concrete identification of pogrom instigators – "*organizers of all the upheavals.*"

Vice-Mayor Draus couldn't specify riot causes, "but I often heard complaints about price rise because of Jewish speculation." His colleague, Przywara, also didn't know the causes, "but it would not have come to

[49] Here and below: ibid., fos. 173–75 (May 21, 1919).

such explosions if it weren't for the foreign people from other counties who came to the Kolbuszowa's yearly market festival in large numbers." The Jews knew beforehand, he claimed, of coming riots "since in the night they hid their wares, taking them to attics and basements and also to village farmers." A Jewish estate lessee spread his horses and cattle among several villages before the pogrom. Another witness heard that "a certain Jewess was said to have sewn red badges with inscriptions for the village boys to use as soldiers." Estate manager Skrowaczewski said that the "movement against Jews was planned well in advance, as I know, because we hear what's going on at the manor farms, and on pogrom eve I saw a dozen or so young men in Rudy Głogowskie village armed with clubs."

Lawyer Rabinowicz saw the "May riots' cause almost exclusively as deliberately planned anti-Jewish agitation." Before November 1918, Christians' relations with Jews were "entirely good." Before Austria's fall, some provisioning – as of fuel oil, sugar, and candles – was in Jewish hands, but thereafter Polish authorities took control of wholesaling such items and put their sale in Christian hands.

The riots were therefore not caused by conditions in provisioning and were not revenge for price-gouging, the more so as rich Jews paid ransom and were not robbed at all ... Taking part were mainly young village boys, and also older farmers and farm-women, mainly from the landless sphere, although there were also rich ones.[50]

(That "rich Jews paid ransom" may have described estate owners, but in light of some merchants' heavy losses, probably exceptional among townspeople.) In relation to pogrom-stricken Jews, "clergymen acted very correctly, townspeople in general sympathetically, teachers with indifference – one (a correspondent of *Piast*) published inciting articles."

Salomon Sonntag, religious commune leader, likewise identified "conscious and planned agitation" as riot cause. Participants were country folk, not townspeople. His testimony's brevity seemingly evidenced embitterment and aversion to dealing with Polish authorities. Communal assessor Ostniak sounded antisemitic tones. "Previously the county was very peaceful." Then came price rises, black marketeering, propagandizing of the "benighted people." Jews themselves "behaved provocatively after the November revolution, saying 'you wanted Poland, now you have it, so pay up'" (*"chcieliście Polskę, macie, płaćcie"*). Merchant Ekstein, like fellow Jews, stressed systematic antisemitic agitation, "which had very fertile ground, for common folk are benighted." Even before the riots people spoke openly of the pogrom

[50] Ibid., fo. 173.

plan: Monday – Majdan; Tuesday – Kolbuszowa; Wednesday – Sokołów; Thursday – "rest-taking"; Friday – against lords; Saturday – against officials and burghers. "I suppose the riots had a definite Bolshevik basis, but still they were directed in first instance against Jews." Town council official Serednicki recalled the November upheaval's radicalism: new electoral committees "reminded one of Soviets." In April, deputy Sudoł incited to manor house plunder: "take up your scythes and flails."

Starosta Tyszkowski faced in violence's aftermath the town council's complaint that city hall had been plundered, its official rubber stamps stolen, along with firemen's uniforms. In fall 1919, he recommended awards of 5,000 Kr. to the seven murdered Jews' widows, mostly shopkeepers, and to one gendarme's widow. Two masonry houses in Jewish women's possession burned, one valued at 100,000 Kr. with wares, the other at 115,000 Kr. Both deserved compensation of 20,000 Kr. The Saleschütz family, whose son Naftali survived World War II to author a masterful evocation of interwar Kolbuszowa's Jewish life, suffered losses of 52,000 Kr.[51]

A Yiddish-language press report stressed the "unusual size" (some 7,000) of the "wild horde" engulfing Kolbuszowa. "It must be said that both Polish intelligentsia and [the] army did what they could to calm the mob." Afterwards, "the local intelligentsia gathered to themselves injured and homeless Jews." Three medical doctors arrived, solicitously, from Rzeszów.[52] Such a perspective, paired with previously cited Jewish notables' acknowledgments of Polish authorities' antipogrom exertions, suggests that Jewish observers recognized that the Galician troubles, though lethally anti-Jewish, could not be summarily attributed to antisemitism alone. Instead, they expressed country people's social-revolutionary aggression against Jews and Christian power holders, in which folk-cultural Judeophobia and ideological antisemitism, as mediated by agrarian populism, justified violent, even murderous actions, particularly when commanded by hard-bitten forest-band chiefs.

The Rzeszów Pogrom: Urban Paupers, Village Revolutionaries

Rzeszów alone, among Galicia's more populous towns, suffered a May 1919 pogrom. Raysha (in Yiddish), lying on the road east from Kraków to Lwów, in 1918 counted 24,000 souls, 42 percent Jewish. On May 3, the

---

[51] Ibid., fos. 203–13 (January 6, 1920). Saleschütz, born in 1920, mentioned the 1919 pogrom only in passing, (Saleschütz, *A Jewish Boyhood in Poland*, 35), noting deaths and destruction and saying it inspired one brother to emigrate.

[52] CZA. Z3/181, *Judisze Folksceitung* (May 1919).

town's Christian poor staged an antisemitic hunger riot, soon joined by irruption into town of peasant masses. It was, though no Jewish lives were lost, Kolbuszowa writ large, infusing fear into authorities' veins that a stronghold of government and economy might capitulate before proletarian-hurled bricks and peasant pitchforks.

In Rzeszów pogrom's aftermath, both government and Parliament dispatched investigative commissions. Among evidence collected were two wall-posted "declarations," signed pseudonymously by "Jan Krzyszkowski" (John of the Cross). They read in entirety:

Revolution in Rzeszów. I call on peasants on May 1. Let's join up and give it to the Jews on their hides. Because the Yids want to kill off the peasants like scabby cats. Take your pop-guns [*pukawki*], whoever has one, and let the Yids know that they're finished with you. Whoever escapes to Palestine will live. I call you on May 1 in Rzeszów-Strzyżów. Jan Krzyszkowski.

Revolution in Rzeszów county and the same in Czudec village. It's all up now with these scabby Jews and their whore-matzo. They're strangling the Catholics. We peasants will get together and go to them. The army won't say a word, because the army sees it the same, that things have to be settled between these whoresons and us. I call on peasants on May 1 from Rzeszów county: come all and we'll make order with the Jews. Revolutionary commander Jan Krzyszkowki.[53]

We encountered similar sentiments among Lwów pogromists, but here defensiveness and paranoia were higher still. The antisemitic epithet "scab" (*parch*) was projected back on the peasants themselves, as they imagined their victimization at Jewish hands. Likewise the pogromists' genocidal fantasies were reversed in that they pictured themselves as slaughtered cats. Resentment glared over Jews' enjoyment of Passover matzo. The language of illegitimacy sounds: *kurwa* is drastic and far-reaching obscenity. The villagers' firearms were, guilt-diminishingly, transmuted into harmless playthings. Jews faced a stark choice: their own disappearance, that is, ethnic cleansing, or death. Christian John of the Cross figured as revolutionary – "Bolshevik"? – leader.

---

[53] ANN. PRM, 5990/21. fo. 81:

1. Obwieszczenie
Rewolucyi w Rzeszowie 1. maja chłopi upraszam trzymajmy się kupy a dać żydom po skórze bo żydy chłopow kco wybic do jednego parcha kota bierzcie pukawki, kto macie macie żydy wiedzieć że z wami już koniec, który uciekł do Palestyny ten będzie żywy chłopi prosz o na 1. maja RZESZOWA-STRZYŻÓW. Jan Krzyszkowski.

2. Obwieszczenie
Rewolucya w rzeszowskiem powiecie w Czudcu to samo będzie przecie raz tym parchom sie skończy kurwa ich mac//one katolików duszą a my chłopi jazdz na żydow trzymajmy się kupy. Wojsko nic nie będzie mówić bo wojsko samo tego patrzy żeby juz było z tymi żydami kurwymisynami. Upraszam chłopi na 1. maja z rzeszowskiego powiatu przyjdzcie i z żydami zrobimy porządek. // Dowódca rewolucyjny // Jan Krzyszkowski.

Such fevered sentiments bubbled in Rzeszów's hinterland. But now it was urban dynamite that exploded first. Polish nationalists set a bad example in November 1918. As Israel Cohen noted, "all Jews who applied for travelling permits were stripped, robbed, and stretched on benches, to which they were tied, and then flogged ... 2 Jews shot. Local authorities ignored decree of martial law for Rzeszów issued by Cracow government." The victims were probably traders, accused of profiteering. *Nowy Dziennik* reported that Rzeszów's post-Habsburg National Guard confined its red-white badge-bearing ranks to "Christian Poles."[54]

Authorities sensed coming onslaught. The prefecture posted large-format warnings dated May 3, 1918 – pogrom's first day – proclaiming curfew and recalling the Liquidation Commission's November 27 authorization of courts martial, to whose firing squads the warning's violators exposed themselves. "Guilty of crime is not only he who commits it, but he who encourages and incites it." "Sharp" firearms regulations promised live ammunition. References were absent to ethnoreligious conflict. Signatories were Mayor Dr. Krogulski, local army commander Lieutenant Zawada, and *starosta* Koncowicz.[55]

The *starosta*'s pogrom account began with a morning crowd's plundering of Jewish shops after hearing from the mayor's office that sugar and bread rations, the latter having fallen to but one pound weekly, could not be increased for lack of supplies. Koncowicz sent a "small armed force" to quell riots, but many were unwilling. "Voices of indignation were even heard among soldiers that they should defend Jews, and many observers later reported their participation in robbery." Army reinforcements marched in. Toward evening, rural bands arrived, intent on attacking officialdom's strongholds. Government defeat was looming when Haller army troops, waiting for rail connection, were sent to assist. "Thanks to these soldiers' decisive stand, further plunder was halted and some dozen bandits arrested." By the troops' late-night departure, policemen had arrived from Jarosław, blocking all roads into Rzeszów.

Plunder resumed the next morning, met by armed forces strengthened by eighty-eight more soldiers from Kraków. At one point marauders seized thirty-one rifles at the militia arsenal, but Koncowicz's men recovered them. "Loss of life confined itself to killing of well-known bandit Nędza ['poverty/misery'], who burst into Lt. Rydz's quarters, threatening him with revolver, and death of two youths who entered a basement for robbery, opening a poison gas-valve." Several dozen stores and nearly 200 Jewish dwellings were plundered at million-korony cost.

---

[54] CZA L6/119, including "Summary," 3; ibid., Z3/174 (November 16, 1918).
[55] AAN. PRM 5990/21, fo. 1.

These riots occurred on pretext of provisioning deficiencies and were aimed at Jews. But their staging on May 3 holiday, and one bandit's possession of two bags of gunpowder and many rioters' iron bars wrapped in leather testify that extremist elements planned this action in advance – to avenge May 1's not being recognized as a national holiday.[56]

More supposed proof lay in pogroms' near-simultaneous outbreak in nearby towns.

Koncowicz's theory seems far-fetched, for no evidence of socialist instigation surfaced. Possibly he believed forest bandits were leftists or lazily took refuge in bureaucratic red baiting. Urban plunderers could easily have armed themselves. The irony was salvation of Piłsudskiite order by Haller troops, who soon would be wreaking antisemitic havoc in Warsaw and vicinity. The rural incursion's strength is evident in hurling of five separate soldierly forces – some big – into the breach against it.

Lieutenant Kazimierz Łukasiewicz, military police commander, remembered arriving on November 4, 1918, losing seventy of 120 men to desertion in the first clashes with forested fighters. His task grew harder as political radicals – town councillor, former gendarme, former Reichsrat deputy – mounted the local stage, urging violence against gendarmerie and police. January elections spurned them, but tensions persisted, heightened by "the Jews' situation, employing themselves almost exclusively with black-marketeering, secret warehousing of goods, etc." Then at April's end, "influx began of whole communities of Jews from small towns, triggered by events in Strzyżów, also the eastern military situation. The excessive number of incoming Jews bought up already meager food reserves."

PPS socialists paraded on May 1, urging peacefulness but hinting at trouble. Railroad functionary Krwanicz spoke, saying, "we'll wait for now, but if they don't give us our rights, we'll take them." Lieutenant Łukasiewicz believed May 3 tumults "were incontestably linked to the Sejm's decision not to recognize May 1 as a workers' holiday." This he knew from "my agents and talk circulating among workers." How the pogrom related to Bolshevism he wasn't sure. But in mid-April "Izrael Reinbeck-Litwack, friend of [Bolshevik/Communist] Radek-Sobelsohn, consorted here" until, "noticing police were observing him, he vanished." Also, before "the events," men circulated in Rzeszów who, "judging by their caps [they wore blue visored caps] were from Congress Kingdom." As for ex-gendarme Lew, suspect in pogrom incitement, "he has no means of support, but he lives prosperously, often gambles, raising suspicion that he draws his income from murky sources."

[56] Ibid., fos. 109–10.

Here pogrom causation was also murky, for hunger rioters can hardly have been PPS operatives, nor was shadowy Lew unmasked as their demagogue. That the PPS, even at local level, would have seized on pogroms as a political tool strains credulity. But Łukasiewicz's insistence on leftist agitators' stirring resentments to a boil in post-November months is plausible.[57]

Leon Wiesenfeld, editor of the *Jewish People's Gazette*, informed investigative commissioners that after October 1918's "resurrection of the Polish State, total peace prevailed in our city." But when nationalists "unnecessarily" forced debate on "the Jewish question" in city council, they launched slogans aiding "destructive work of *second-rate antisemitic agitators, still not identified*." The antisemitic Kraków press, not excepting *Piast*, chimed in. Then "suddenly, before May 1, rumors circulated through town that it would be permitted to beat and rob Jews." Especially after Strzyżów's pogrom, isolated beatings of Jews occurred at Rzeszów rail station and elsewhere. A pogrom mood was rumbling. On May 3, the crowd, after haranguing the mayor's office, moved to "where prayer houses and synagogues stand." They attacked one holding Sabbath service, bombarding it with "stones weighing 2–3 kilos, severely wounding [many] worshippers." The building emptied, pogromists entered, ripped Torah rolls to bits, and otherwise demolished everything. "Thereafter began a regular, systematic pogrom." Troops that *starosta* Koncowicz mustered arrived ninety minutes later, after many shops were plundered. Only the next day did newly arrived troops halt destruction.

Wiesenfeld evoked a dynamic picture of unfolding violence, in which rumors of pogrom permission, isolated violence, symbolic destruction, and religious desecration (breaking Jewish magical strength) preceded plunder. The antisemitic agitators he scornfully mentioned may have been brothers-in-arms of "John of the Cross." Such indistinct and humble demotic orators, placard makers, and riot captains played a more consequential role in detonating pogroms than print-antisemitism's exhortations. It was, seemingly, their very obscurity that enabled them to evade police dragnets or other capture, while police agents, such as Lieutenant Łukasiewicz's, might well have penetrated violence-bent organizations and discovered their foot soldiers.[58]

Still, when educated classes embraced antisemitism, like-minded commoners took heart. Though activist himself in anti-Jewish cooperative marketing, Franciszek Mackiewicz told the Sejm's investigators:

---

[57] Ibid., fos. 111–13 (May 20, 1919) (author's emphasis).   [58] Ibid., fos. 114–17.

I see the antisemitic current originating, not from below, but among the middle classes who disseminated these slogans and still do. On the city council, instead of dealing with provisioning, eight sittings were devoted to the Jewish question. They debated whether to expel Jews or keep them. Jews were characterized as bacteria devouring the Polish organism. Obviously, after hearing such arguments, the gallery listener will leave the city hall as an antisemite, and will praise him who talked of bacteria in such words as: "that speaker deserves a glass of rum" (I quote what I heard myself).[59]

In Wiesenfeld's memoir, published in 1967 in the Raysha/Rzeszów *Zakhor* book, he recalled how, amid May 3 plundering, he observed Colonel Jędrzej Zawada, local army commander (who had cosigned the stern antiriot announcement), "standing calmly between two good-looking Polish women, chatting happily," oblivious of his troops' passivity toward the rampaging crowd. As Zawada's acquaintance, Wiesenfeld asked him why he did not suppress the robbery. The colonel, usually friendly, "reddened like a beet. His eyes flashed. He looked at me with wild hatred. The ladies exploded in laughter. Zawada turned his back, exclaiming 'such Jewish impertinence.'"[60]

Attorney Adolf Schune, Rzeszów's Jewish religious commune president, testified that rumors of impending "anti-Jewish riots" circulated a week before May 3. "Even my eight-year-old child returning from school told of having heard them." He could not determine their source, but consulting authorities, he learned they knew of the rumors and were taking precautionary measures. May 1 passed without incident. On May 3 he observed a crowd of several dozen "mainly women and paupers" before mayor Krogulski's dwelling – "deputation demanding higher bread-rations." Schune found them unmenacing and unworrisome. He learned thereafter of synagogue attacks. Word that three doctor-titled colleagues had been "severely beaten on central square" restrained him from investigating. But he later observed soldiers' and policemen's passivity, "giving [plunderers] the impression their actions were permitted." Before his eyes, "paupers, women, and peasants carried bundles about the streets with stolen items." He urged the prefect to put civilian officials in charge of soldiers, expecting them to intervene more decisively. Robbery continued late into Saturday night. On Sunday morning, shots finally dispersed a big crowd.

Protocols of victims showed that 300 Jewish families lost goods worth some 4 million korony, with 100 remaining to interview. Some dozen were severely beaten, many others less drastically.

---

[59] CZA. A127/82, quoted in Tomaszewski, "Zaburzenia," 101.
[60] Tomaszewski, "Zaburzenia," 103.

As these incidents' deeper cause I consider agitation at assemblies, also incitation by much of the press, which for example told fairy-tales about events in Rzeszów that unenlightened people believe. As immediate cause I consider some sort of covert action which sought, through spreading ritual-murder rumors simultaneously in several localities, to stir up large-scale disturbances, as suggested by the riots' announcement in advance. On Sunday, rumors were exploited that Jews had poisoned some boys with gas.[61]

Schune took a tough view of the "paupers" and "unenlightened" commoners who plunged into looting, as if by nature. Armed authorities existed, among other purposes, to protect him and coreligionists from them. Speaking to Sejm investigators, Schune faulted the press for spreading falsehoods, such as that in Rzeszów "Bolshevik manifestos had been distributed. I'm not aware that any Bolshevik proclamations were found on any Jewess's person." He added that while he believed Rzeszów's riots were "organized and pre-planned, I can't testify by which elements."[62]

Military policeman Franciszek Pryga reconstructed the "paupers'" worldview.

The war years demoralized our youth, deprived of school and especially of fatherly care. A twelve-year-old boy walks the street calmly smoking a cigarette. It happens that young children steal by pickpocketing. Already they even know criminal slang.[63]

Townspeople shivered in underheated quarters. "There's coal at the dealer's, but only in exchange for grain, flour, or bacon, etc." Coal theft from rail cars was rampant. Though a crime, "when the intelligentsia too start to freeze, they must buy coal from the thief." Wartime train-robbing spread, with sales of stolen goods to the public at "fairy-tale low prices" by "local Jews (known in criminal slang as 'coverers' [blatników])." Gun battles crackled between railroad police and robbers. War's-end soldier deserters, though popularly welcomed, drifted toward criminal scum for lack of work, swelling Rzeszów banditry.

Following Polish independence, radical populism (Stapińszczyzna) was reinforced by returning POWs mouthing Bolshevik slogans. In and around Rzeszów were 15,000 to 20,000 embittered and dissatisfied invalid soldiers. One, living with his impoverished family, told Pryga, "Austria gave at least a few Kronen, now I have nothing." Better-off landowning farmers, artisans, and officials – dissatisfied too – "didn't try as they should have to restrain the growing ferment."

---

[61] Here and below: AAN. PRM 5990/21. fos. 118–20.
[62] Quoted in Tomaszewski, "Zaburzenia," 101.
[63] Pryga's analysis, here and below: AAN. PRM 5990/21, fos. 121–24.

Bolshevik agitators seemed to have been at work. Villagers arrived in town on May 1, asking if there would be "a movement today." The answer was: no, because it's workers' holiday. "Stubborn rumors circulate, which I haven't succeeded in verifying, of Bolshevik agitation by a Czech Jew." A village Jew allegedly urged looting with promises of buying stolen goods. On May 3, Pryga heard street cries of "let's start with the Jews" and "beat and rob the dogs'-brothers [*psubratów*]." On May 5 one still heard agitators saying, "we ourselves, comrades, will make order" and "true, government and Sejm are no longer the lords, but the lords' lackeys, and lackey is worse than lord."

Here Galicia's social structure must be remembered: the merchant, the middleman, is a Jew, everybody knew that everything[!] could be bought from him. The wealthier farmer, not wishing to be known to possess money, gladly plies exchange trade for tobacco, sugar, spirits, leather, etc. The town-dweller, having nothing to exchange, must pay black-marketeers' price ... It was known that in their storerooms there was food, clothing, linen, shoes.

Everyone expected a pogrom on May 1. "Street rabble" talked of it. A May 1 PPS speaker promised a delegation would confront the mayor next day, but it only happened on May 3.

Pogrom participants were "*Lumpenproletaryat*" and adolescents from town and village – "and Jews" (though these latter, if real, will have been an execrated few). Members of other classes were sparse. "These bandits divided into groups, which under a few well-known bandit-leaders proceeded to robbery." Pryga, halting one such band, found himself facing Kaczmar Wawrzyniec, Ukrainian, now under arrest, who incited to excesses, crying out, "don't listen, tear off his uniform, rip off his insignia (I was in military dress)" and harangued the crowd to disarm the police.

Curiously, poorest shops were looted, richest passed over. The rich were only robbed by professional breakers-in and bandits, and then at evening or night. Or the bandit leaders didn't want to take on too much or they spared them for pay-offs. It was typical that the bigger stores' owners strolled calmly about the streets.

(Yet in November 1919 the *starosta* proposed governmental compensation to three merchants whose losses reached 20,000 to 100,000 korony.)[64]

It was difficult, Pryga wrote, in such upheavals to point to "Russian Bolshevik agitators" as perhaps governmental investigative commissions wanted local authorities to do. Suspicious people disappeared, leaving traces at most. But he thought it relevant to say that Rzeszów's "Zionists have long been organized in secret fighting units" – the word "fighting"

[64] Ibid., fos. 201–2 (November 21, 1919).

added as afterthought. Among non-Jewish socialists, extremism was propagated, and "L., one of their most zealous agitators, maintains financial relations with the Jewish plutocracy." As for pogrom losses, "one of the Jews says himself the Jews make too much uproar [*gwaltu*], since they buried their best things because they knew of the pogrom beforehand." Still, Pryga reckoned, damage ran to 5 million korony.

Here was an unself-consciously antisemitic effort to blame the pogrom's victims and minimize their losses, though it's hard to know what Pryga thought his superiors wished to hear and what he himself believed. Why "Jewish plutocrats" should bribe Polish socialists to foment pogroms loomed unanswered but figured in world-conspiracy theories hawked in the Judeophobic press. Nor could Pryga, despite his ear to the ground, point to specific pogrom instigators but conjured with rumors of Czech Bolshevik Jews – red-bearded, perhaps.

Official commentators on Rzeszów's pogrom and Jewish witnesses, too, discerned clearly the landscape of penury and uprootedness urban and rural pogromists inhabited. They saw also that antisemitic politics trickled down to legitimize thoughts of plunder and ethnic cleansing. Yet, although one might suppose they understood the popular psyche, they searched in improbable places for violence's triggerers – shadowy and elusive outsiders, some leftists, some Jewish, some both – rather than tracing the impetus to demotic convictions of righteousness in assaulting Jews, shamefully protected in possession of their riches in food and clothing by corrupt authorities. But certainly officials like Pryga, or Judge Sypowski in Wieliczka, did – so to speak, "instinctively" – understand the turbulent people, for their minds too knew thoughts of Jewish magic and power which they – in the name of law and order, national honor, and, possibly, enlightenment – were formally obliged to abjure. Yet, as soldiers' and officers' halfhearted resistance to rioters and civil officials' unthinking recourse to antisemitic motifs showed, repressed thoughts and impulses find ways to return.

Insights from Galicia's Other May Pogroms

In Baranów Sandomierski (1,800 souls, 42 percent Jewish), plundering broke out on May 5. As three Jewish notables reported, "shoemaker Piejko's daughter, thought to be Jewish, was beaten." The town's Christians rushed to her aid, causing pogromists, after four hours of pillage, to withdraw. Next day they returned, until soldiers drove them out. In the tumult a Christian girl was killed. "Here we must observe that a certain man rode horseback from village to village, urging people to attend the Baranów market because Jews would be robbed." Looters numbered several thousand. Queried about pogrom's cause, witnesses cited Okoń's and Dąbal's meetings and antisemitic Kraków-published *Illustrowany Kuryer*. Losses among some twenty-nine victims, mostly business owners, totaled 274,830 korony. Eight had been beaten, including one severely wounded. Of sixty-nine soldiers occupying Baranów, Jewish notables said they "can't support themselves on their pay in the present price-inflation, so the Israelite commune must cover their daily costs of 400 korony. But because commune members are poor, having been comprehensively robbed," they asked that the whole town share the burden.

A local gendarme saw the riot's cause as after-shock of Rzeszów and Tarnobrzeg pogroms. Populist agitation was not the cause, but people's embitterment over Jews' buying up food supplies and selling them usuriously. Deserter bands aimed through plunder to arrive at "more favorable material circumstances." He advocated immediate severe punishments. In December 1919 the *starosta* recommended compensation of 500 to 800 korony each to three poor Jews – one a man and two "workers' ritual wives."[65]

Christians' rescue of their mistakenly beaten coreligionist shows, glaringly, that concerted action by unarmed citizenry could stop a pogrom, but nowhere else in these pages did this happen. Nor did Jews' Christian neighbors wish to share costs of quartering soldiers protecting their town. While Jews inclined to blame political agitation for pogroms, policemen could dismiss such influences, stressing instead ideologically unvarnished popular rage toward Jewish merchants. We observe, tellingly, homespun pogrom riders galloping across the countryside, rallying villagers to stream into town. Once again, no trigger pullers showed their faces.

In Mielec (Yiddish: Melitz), a half-Jewish town of 6,000, pogrom raged on May 1, when some 4,000 people, "mostly unemployed" and armed with clubs, plundered Jewish shops. Israel Cohen recorded that in November 1918 a hundred-strong peasant band robbed twenty-seven Jewish shops. Cracovian Jewish militia men suffered disarming by Mielec's Christian militia, who then joined the looting.[66]

In May 1919, violence spread outward from Mielec for a week, "not limiting itself only to Jews, but also falling on rural settlements and manorial farms." Policeman Wertz wrote that "a Bolshevik movement from outside could not be ascertained." He had for months followed local agitation "aiming to cause tumults." Mostly propagated at electoral

[65] Ibid., fos. 139–40, 142, 151, 201–2 (May 22, 1919; December 16, 1919), *"ritualna żona zarobnika."*

[66] CZA. L6/119, 1 (November 7–8, 1918).

assemblies, it "greatly excited rural people's minds, and especially those individuals who, from lack of work or – especially – distaste for work, listened to agitators' improbable promises. *Stirred-up people thought mainly about changing the social order.*" The culminatory point was late April. "Because of agitation the generality of country-folk expected a revolution in nearest time, and the Jewish population reported that, according to circulating rumors, its outbreak would be directed first against them."[67]

Here a seasoned observer unequivocally ascribed pogroms to agrarian populist propaganda working on idle and trouble-seeking minds. Mielec's Mayor Józef Kołasiński thought differently: "May riots had exclusively Bolshevik character." Anti-Jewish violence aimed to unleash anarchy. The whole action was "undoubtedly pre-planned." He thought one detail proved his point: in Pławo, "the farmer Józef Flis walked about the village beating on a wooden box he had slung about him as on a drum, calling out 'peasants to Mielec' and 'before noon we'll beat the Jews and after noon the lords.'"[68]

This plausible image, paired with the pogrom rider's, argues instead that it was among villagers themselves that electoral agitation's violent implications underwent transmutation into pogrom campaigns and – if time permitted, as cynics might say – attacks on manorial lords' properties. But lest the May pogroms' archaic, peasant-cultural side be exaggerated, we note that in Raniżów, near Kolbuszowa, modern technology ignited plunder. Jews there reported to Kraków's *Judisze Folksceitung* that "the pogrom plague" had not spared their diminutive *shtetl*, harboring some 800 Jews alongside Catholics and some Lutherans. "On Sunday the beasts ran amok." Signal was a telegram from Rzeszów announcing pogrom there. "Postmaster Czubek communicated this news around town, adding that in Rzeszów it was permitted to smash [*gromić*] and beat Jews." Jewish youths tried to resist the mob but were overwhelmed. Gendarmes stood idle. When asked for help, commanding Sergeant Cybulski replied that he couldn't oblige because "it's customary today [Whitsuntide] to beat Jews. His own wish did not allow him to direct his underlings to intervene." Not until two days later "did the police bestir themselves somewhat."[69]

---

[67] AAN. PRM, 5990/21, fo. 133 (author's emphasis).   [68] Ibid., fo. 126.

[69] *Bestje rozhulały się*. CZA, Z3/181 (May 16, 1919). Cf. Cohen, "The Pogroms in Poland" (CZA Z6/119): Raniżów, November 7, 1918: assaults and looting "by mob led by village-chief, Wojciech Stec"; www.sztetl.org.pl/pl/article/ranizow/5,historia/.

Governmental Interpretation of Rzeszów Area Pogroms

The Warsaw-decreed Extraordinary Commission, dispatched in mid-May, generated most of this chapter's evidence. Its concluding May 31 report offered a synthetic view of the whole pogrom movement, in part enduringly insightful, in part illustrative of how well-educated and serious officials – Ministerial Councillor Dr. Juljusz Dunikowski and civilian colleague, also Captain Kazimierz Rettinger – sought to comprehend the violence raging at Poland's rebirth.

The commissioners identified the rural bands as, collectively, the "Green Guard" (*zielona gwardia*), after their forest lairs. Whether they or other Poles knew that such postwar guerilla forces, with similar names, had multiplied in woodlands from Austria eastward into Russia is uncertain. Polish and Jewish journalists seemingly neglected the subject. Near Rzeszów, forests were suitably vast. Here too plundering of estates owned or leased by Jews had reached its peak and with it populist land-reform agitation "at public assemblies and secret meetings."[70]

After Strzyżów's explosion, pogrom agitation spread powerfully, including "with help of the so-called 'butterfly' (pogrom proclamation attached to rod carried from hut to hut)." A certain Sikucki, later arrested, had composed announcements exhorting to anti-Jewish violence, signed in Piłsudski's name, and bureaucratically rubber stamped "Committee of the Pogrom of Jews" (*Komitet Pogromu żydów*). Here is further vivid evidence of grassroots pogromists' self-motivation and of the legitimization of their intended violence by officially framed appeal, however artless and implausible, to Piłsudski himself. Following armed forces' suppression of Rzeszów's pogrom, rumors spread that "the *starosta* had been killed and a successor elected by the crowd, who permitted robbery until May 15."

The Commission reckoned larger plunderer throngs at 3,000 to 4,000 persons. In Mielec, such a vast crowd was joined by a 200-strong party armed with clubs and cudgels, who arrived by rail but who were arrested and confined in a school until a train could remove them. Elsewhere the army foiled pogroms by fixing bayonets and firing machine guns. In the Baranów shooting, a girl died, "daughter of a known bandit." Christian losses in Kolbuszowa were unknown because retreating bandits took the wounded and dead with them. Here, as elsewhere, bandits displayed

---

[70] "Sprawozdanie komisji nadzwyczajnej wysłanej z ramienia rządu w sprawie rozruchów w okręgu rzeszowskim w maju 1919 r. na podstawie uchwały Rady Ministrów z dn. 13 maja 1919 r." Signed on May 31, 1919 in Warsaw by Dr. Juljusz Dunikowski, Zygmunt Biernacki, and Kazimierz Rettinger-Kapitan. AAN. PRM 5990/21. fos. 1–2. The contemporary term "green garrisons" also described such bands. Tomaszewki, "Zaburzenia," 96. The report noted pogroms also in *shtetls* Tyczno and Głogów.

seasoned military discipline. Around Raniżów, disarmed fighters were found to be wearing "amaranth-colored badges – traces of Bolshevik organization."[71]

The Commission judged prepogrom Rzeszów-area army and police forces weak. On May 7, the government dispatched a general-led army "pacification action," but with only three infantry and two light cavalry battalions – too little to tackle forest bands. They surrounded villages, confiscating 127 carbines and revolvers, sixty-three bayonets and swords, 814 cartridges, and three hand grenades and arresting thirty-three deserters, forty-five army recruits evading induction, eighty-nine criminal suspects, and thirty-two pogromists.[72]

The investigators wrote lengthily on riots' causes. First came war's destructive effects: reduction of "moral resistance and brutalization of manners," "loss of feeling" resulting from constant exposure to danger, and "contempt for death." "Idle and careless life spent in trenches, with certainty that others must care for food provision, quarters, clothing, etc., causes people to succumb very noticeably to laziness and aversion to systematic work." They learn, too, of the easy and disproportionately high earnings of wartime speculation, disinclining them to everyday wages. Tender souls of unschooled and fatherless youth are exposed to "everything evil, which in wartime appears in such drastic form."

Austria's "wild demobilization," following its army's collapse in Italy, brought "a whole swarm" of well-armed deserters to Rzeszów's forests, while POWs returning from Russia brought with them "Bolshevik plague's miasma." If communist doctrine was rarely absorbed, what Russophobic Poles – and these commissioners – called "Russian maximalism" (extremism) left its impression.[73] As for "unenlightened peasant masses, long and passionately awaited freedom was completely falsely understood." In a formulation echoing earlier examples of demotic conflation of freedom with conflagration of law books, the investigators wrote that

in their imagination the concept of authority was so closely associated with Austrian statehood that they translated the Austrian State's fall into end of rule by *starosty* and gendarmes, so that freedom for them was equivalent to these powers' complete removal. This was to be the first stage in further enjoyment of freedom, which would express itself . . . in division of lords' lands and forests.[74]

Prisons were so crowded that Poland's new courts released numerous laboriously captured criminals, many "escaping into forests and resuming banditry." The commissioners were drawn to the seemingly bloody idea

---

[71] AAN. PRM. 5990/21, fos. 3–11.   [72] Ibid., fo. 37.   [73] Ibid., fos. 38–40.
[74] Ibid., fos. 40–41.

that "very swift and determined administration of justice might have brought about cleansing of the overheated atmosphere." Jury trials frequently failed in their purpose as farmer-jurors were swayed by kinship or fear. Courts martial, though proclaimed in November, only began functioning after May's pogroms. Populist politicians, led by deputy Stapiński, pressured courts to reduce charges, "undoubtedly strengthening criminality" and leading to the present catastrophe. The sight of public officials, such as Judge Czarny in Kolbuszowa, participating in incendiary meetings weakened common people's respect for new authorities.

Apart from banditry, the landless population's lack of employment, as industry faltered in wartime, and inability further to migrate seasonally to Germany or emigrate to America, plunged them into hunger and misery. During Rzeszów's pogrom, "poverty-stricken children were observed eating plundered provisions with inordinate greediness." Nor did the commissioners spare "unconscionable speculation of various merchants." Masses of refugee Jews had migrated into Polish Galicia from the east.

The Rzeszów region's people, far from railroads, were "benighted and unenlightened."

Among Kolbuszowa county's population – living in remote forest corners, which the wide world's echoes hardly reach – old prejudices and superstitions live on. Understandably, only among this uncultured people could such agitational means be employed as invoking permission by Head of State [*Naczelnik* Piłsudski] to beat Jews for 3 days, or *starosta*'s permission to rob, etc.[75]

The effect of the populist politicians' agitation was of "fire on gunpowder."

A few meetings, a few appeals to the peasantry to disobey the gendarmes, to hasten land reform with flail and scythe in hand, sufficed to fan the flame of revolt red-hot and cause the ship of state to crash on social antagonisms' reefs.

Here the commissioners' appreciation of the harm Galician social wars inflicted on Polish state building found agitated expression. They did not hesitate to assign "moral responsibility" to Deputies Dąbal, Okoń, and Sudoł. Such politicians possessed huge authority. In another formulation confirming Thomas's and Znaniecki's peasant anthropology, they wrote:

The peasant's simplified logic burdens his representatives' shoulders with responsibilities beyond human power, but endows him too with suprahuman rights, for each of his utterances, every rhetorical flourish, is treated as infallible dogma and embraced uncritically.

---

[75] Here and below: ibid., fo. 45.

Priests Bolek and Strzępek preached sermons "inciting people to pogroms, and to resistance to army and prefect." So did certain school-teachers. It is no surprise that "all educated elements in contact with rural people worked on peasants' minds in terrorizing fashion, awakening in them evil instincts, and that peasants harkening to such voices let themselves become tools in conscienceless agitators' hands."

About Dąbal the commissioners heard damning testimony from Franciszek Sładnik, former government municipal agent in Grębów. Here on May 4 Dąbal spoke for two hours. Castigating the Sejm's indifference to populist concerns, "he announced that he and his comrades would withdraw from such a parliament and make a revolution in the whole state." Present at the assembly was "celebrated bandit-deserter Józef Gądek with his band, and notably brothers Janoczki (nicknamed 'Żwawy' [the jaunty ones])."

After the meeting, Dąbal repaired with bandits and a dozen farmers to Ludwig Josse's tavern, where they "treated themselves to drinks for an hour." One imagines this a likely setting for agreements to foment trouble. Witness Sładnik informed a gendarme of bandit Gądek's presence. Asked to identify him, he said "in consideration of my personal safety I can't point to him in the crowd." During the assembly, Sładnik had accused Dąbal of "roaming about villages, inciting people, making unfulfillable promises instead of sitting in parliament." He was thereupon seized by "bandits Janoczki, Tyburski and Czerepak (nickname *Gwardzista* ['Guardist']), who wanted to take me with them, but then, probably fearing gendarmerie intervention, set me free."[76]

Yet the commissioners concluded, "above all other causes there towers that which most strikes the eye, namely, antisemitism." Even if the Jewish press and associated interested parties represented violence as exclusively antisemitic, which was not entirely true, it was, they averred, undoubtedly central. Yet witnesses had all converged "unanimously" on the proposition that "the relationship of the Christian to the Jewish population up to the moment of the November upheaval left nothing to be desired and was completely correct." Evincing repressive self-censorship's power, the commissioners betrayed no memory not only of the widespread 1898 pogroms (many in the Rzeszów-Tarnów region) but also of the anti–Brest-Litovsk pogrom wave in spring 1918, a year previously. More fundamentally, the investigators were somehow oblivious to the profound ambivalence in Christian popular culture – and in themselves – toward Jewish presence, sometimes conceiving it positively, if from a position of domination, sometimes in most ominous negative colors.

[76] Ibid., fo. 92.

Only recently, they wrote, had "aversion to Jews" assumed large proportions, first, because from war's start "Jews evaded in very large numbers service at the front" and, second, because "blame for unprecedented
price-inflation, resulting mainly from speculative orgies of wartime 'heroes of industry,' was chalked up to Jews," who "have in their hands
practically all trade." As Kolbuszowa's attorney Rabinowicz said, Jewish
merchants, distrusting the currency, held much of their assets in various
consumer goods and food provisions, even though ordinary people had
gone months or years without them.[77]

Especially among Christian townspeople, anti-Jewish sentiment
swelled because of the allegedly "unfriendly attitude" Jews had mostly
assumed toward the new Poland. The commissioners recalled the sarcas-
tic sentiment ascribed to Jews that Poles would now have to pay dearly for
the free Poland they had yearned for. This and other "small but characteristic details" coalesced in the "general opinion about Jews' hostility
to Poland." The May pogroms should have surprised no one. Strzyżów's
ritual-murder charge was wholly separate. "It has been proven the Marja
Szafrańska actually was imprisoned in the basement." This (tendentious)
finding was not evidence of impending ritual murder but, as the commissioners opaquely said, of "willful provocation by elements" – were Jewish
nationalists or revolutionists meant? – "seeking to disturb public tranquility." The matter was so doubtful and unclear as to disqualify it as pogrom
cause. The commissioners further softened emphasis on antisemitism,
citing several "unprejudiced Jews" who accepted that violence targeted
Christians too.[78]

They concluded that the pogroms' immediate cause was "planned
action, excellently conceived, worked out in smallest detail and led by
as yet undetermined and unrevealed individuals." Their grounds for
believing this were that, apart from Strzyżów, the pogroms began at
roughly the same time; the same pogrom call (*odezwa*) was repeatedly
used, which claimed violence was authorized from above (though this was
hoary pogrom custom); when pogroms occurred, great throngs materi-
alized, often from considerable distances; the assaults were organized
militarily, with leaders on horseback and whistled commands; army
units, as they approached pogrom sites, were systematically observed by
forest bandits.

The question was crucial whether the pogrom wave was Bolshevik work
or that of local actors "without farther-reaching plans." Though still
unresolved, "everything points to its being conscious effort to call forth
anarchy" and thereafter introduce Bolshevism – hence pogromists'

---

[77] Ibid., fos. 48–50, "*rycerzy przemysłu.*"   [78] Ibid., fos. 45*ff*, 50–51.

discrediting of officials and police and forested fighters' self-designation as "red patrols," modeling themselves on the Russian Red Guard.[79] Viewed through commissioners' eyes, it could not have been "dark and superstitious" villagers who masterminded the pogrom wave's "planned action, excellently conceived, worked out in smallest detail." It was, instead, sophisticated, saddled Bolsheviks, undermining new Poland by stoking peasant hatreds.

Among riots' effects was "terrorization of authorities." Officials feared that should the army withdraw, peasants would attack them. Villagers thought their belief confirmed "that administrative authorities and gendarmes have been bought by the Jews (Jewish uncles), which has induced deep hatred of the authorities." The *starosty* were especially despised for calling in soldiery. A "colossal worsening of village-manor relations" had also occurred, leading to wild devastation of estate forests and meadows throughout central Galicia. The atmosphere was now so flammable that any new "destructive work" could count on success.

The Commission recommended protective transfers of officials at personal risk and punitive transfers for disorder-fomenters such as Judge Czarny and various priests and teachers. Armed forest patrols were necessary, while secret agents should ferret out bandit ringleaders. Jury courts should yield to official tribunals and courts martial. Requisitions from peasant farms should be remunerated in cash. Victims of material loss should be compensated. Public works programs should build roads. The appearance in the Rzeszów district of their own prestigious investigative commission made a "very positive impression" that should be deepened. In the pogrom crisis, all officials, except for those the report singled out, had acted correctly.[80]

General Józef Szamota, distinguished tsarist army veteran and Tarnów military district commander, who had arrived on May 7 in Rzeszów to supervise antipogrom operations, later submitted his own report to the investigative commission. The urban "masses" had expected war's end to improve their lot, and January's election campaign led them, in their "superficial way of looking for easy explanations," to blame Jews for their disappointment. But in the small towns and villages, the pogromist was the peasant "who suffered economically relatively little during the war." His motive was "the agrarian question." Led by "dishonest agitators" to anticipate seizure of estate land, he turned against Jews – "as the class in society that is least resistant to such violence." Still, the general – mindful perhaps of his own landlordly interests – saw the peasant threat aimed principally at large estate owners, who were safe only behind army

---

[79] Ibid., fos. 52–53.   [80] Ibid., fos. 54–57.

shield. Common folk attacked Jews because of "inborn antipathy." Spurning theories of top-down instigation, he saw pogrom leaders as "various obscure individuals." In Rzeszów, Szamota (groundlessly) blamed socialists for triggering the May 3 riots (a view the local Endek leader, a secondary school principal, shared).[81]

In Rzeszów military district, encompassing five counties, there were but forty-six officers and 654 soldiers, with eight "machine carbines." Fewer than half were free to move away from fixed positions. Such soldiers, many young and inexperienced, could not confront "enormous throngs." Thirty-two soldiers from Kolbuszowa drifted away – "probably they ran home." It would take more troops and long weeks to subdue the forests. Soldiers complained that this duty paid less and was harder than at the front. Deputy Okoń had protested soldiers' beatings of peasants and erection of a scaffold in Kolbuszowa. Szamota replied that he had stopped the beatings. The scaffold was only "to frighten." "I heard repeatedly that out of fear people returned stolen objects."[82]

Of Szamota's and the commissioners' pogrom understanding, we observe, once more, belief in pogrom planning, even with Bolshevik intent, together with inability (or unwillingness) to specify planners, excepting "obscure individuals" – presumably those who composed pogrom manifestos and otherwise drew attention to themselves as grass-roots activists inspired by fanaticism and obsessiveness. No evidence has surfaced showing that state authorities ever succeeded, either here or elsewhere, in prosecuting anyone for large-scale pogrom leadership, though many were charged with participation.

The commissioners purveyed intelligentsia versions of common anti-semitic recriminations while deploring ordinary people's benightedness and susceptibility to anti-Jewish scapegoating and demonization. They and General Szamota had no doubt of popular anti-Jewish animosity's depth, yet it alone did not, in their view, generate pogroms. This was, rather, the effect of revolutionary agrarian populist demagoguery, widely preached by rural and small-town intelligentsia of politicians, teachers, priests, officials, and journalists – but also by Bolshevism's seasoned apostles among forested Red Guard leaders. It was government's job to suppress sylvan banditry, discipline its public-sector servants, and muzzle revolutionaries. Order would return and with it the perennial problem of limiting provocations that Jews, commerce's seeming masters, flung in poor folks' faces. That lower-class Christians would abandon such anti-

[81] On Endeks, see Tomaszewski, "Zaburzenia," 104.
[82] AAN. PRM. 5990/21, fos. 13–15 (May 23, 1919).

Jewish resentments as future hard times might inflame was beyond imagining. But, with a strong state, social order was possible.

Central Government Actions

The Council of Ministers swiftly responded to the Investigative Commission's report. On June 6, 1919, it resolved that Rzeszów area riots exhibited "very serious character." Officials "who during riots' suppression antagonized the population" should be transferred "to restore a normal relationship between authorities and people." This applied foremost to Kolbuszowa *starosta* Tyszkowski and his staff but also to offending priests. Incendiary Dr. Czarny landed softly in a new judgeship in Tarnów. Among commissioners' recommendations, the Council did not agree it should compensate pogrom victims, charging Galicia's governors in Kraków and Lwów instead with this task. The Council ordered investigation of firebrand populist parliamentary deputies.[83]

The Ministry of Religious Confessions and Public Instruction concluded about Lutcze's father Bolek that "he exerted very harmful influence on local people," by whom "two manor-farms belonging to Jews were robbed and burned." Father Strzępek incited to the Niebylec pogrom, yet in August 1920 it was decided to leave him at his post, the country having been pacified. Agitators, never lacking, might claim that he fell victim to Jewish influence, "although *ks.* Strzępek enjoys no sympathy in the parish."[84]

Galician Governor Gałecki in Lwów recommended granting 1 million korony as "partial compensation to riot victims or to family members surviving them." Seemingly, the Council of Ministers sought to raise this sum to 2 million, but the Treasury Ministry objected. In January 1920, Galician authorities wrote the Council that if it were now thought undesirable to pay cash compensation and thereby set a precedent for governmental responsibility for all such losses, and in view of the government's bad financial situation, then the proposal of the Relief Committee for Polish Jews in Kraków should be honored. This would have granted victims access to loans from a 20 million korony account at the Wartime Credit Agency.

Governor Gałecki soon thereafter informed the Council that since more generous terms had been vetoed, he proposed ceilings on material losses of 3,000 korony, with 5,000 for survivors of murder victims.

---

[83] Ibid., fos. 71–71a (June 6, 1919); fo. 177 (June 16, 1919).
[84] Ibid., fo. 80 (n.d.); fo. 217 (August 26, 1920).

Considering that full losses were running at 10 million, his earlier recommendation of 1 million now looked "moderate." Finally, in March 1921, the Treasury Ministry approved extending "non-repayable assistance" of 1 million marks to those injured in the "May events," "without regard to religious confession" and observing individual limits of 3,000/5,000 marks. At mid-1918 exchange rates, these sums equaled 5,000/8,300 korony, but by 1921, Poland's rampant inflation, comparable to Weimar Germany's, was beginning. Conceivably, by the time compensation recipients banked their payments, they were virtually worthless.[85]

Evidently some high officials sought honorably, if unheroically, to aid pogrom victims, while others worried about emptying the treasury, eliciting a landslide of other claims, and appearing to favor Jews. But what of punishing murderers, cripplers, and plunderers? An inmate register of May 19, 1919, seemingly from Rzeszów prison, shows that, among 356 prisoners (in a jail meant for 180), 136 had been arrested as May pogromists, mainly from Rzeszów itself (eighty-four) but also from Kolbuszowa (twenty-five), and Tarnobrzeg and Strzyżów (twenty-seven). Among all prisoners, only twenty-two had received sentences.

In October 1920, the Justice Ministry tallied lawsuits over rioting/pogrom involvement in Galician appellate courts. In Kraków, of 1,026 appeals, 397 had been decided, 295 rejected, 165 were in process, and 169 under investigation. In Lwów, outside the May riots' range, of 129 cases, eighty-five had been adjudged, seven dismissed, and the rest in process. While these figures omit convictions, it's clear that the number of persons arrested and tried in court was not inconsiderable. They were not charged as perpetrators of Judeophobic violence but for murder, assault, robbery, and insurrectionism. In dealing with the "May events," high bureaucrats absurdly and allergically – probably also ashamedly – shunned the words "pogrom" and "Jewish."[86]

An Urban Variation on Ritual Murder

Antisemitism's uncanny nature, and its propensity to mutate and spill over into new territory, came to light in a May 1 pogrom in the small town of Miechów. It was a semimanufacturing center of some 6,500 (40 percent Jewish) lying near grimy Dąbrowa industrial basin and Russian Poland's Kielce. Its social profile differed from agrarian Rzeszów region's,

---

[85] Ibid., fos. 178, 200, 211, 214.
[86] Ibid., fo. 93 (May 19, 1919); fo. 213 (October 2, 1920). Tomaszewski reported in 1996 that trial records from 1919–21 were inaccessible. Tomaszewski, "Spring 1919," 191.

yet the anti-Jewish explosion there coincided with holiday riots farther east, even if pogrom erupted out of Miechów's local depths.

The Directorate of the Israelite Commune communicated Miechów Jews' experience to Kraków's Provisional Zionist National Council. The earth began shaking on April 28, when numerous army recruits arrived. "We Jews have been accustomed for years to recruits' assaults." They kept out of sight, for "every Jew seized by the soldiers was beaten by clubs or fists."

Every blow suffered by a Jew was accompanied by local inhabitants' Homeric laughter, which struck us right away. For previously they had come forward in our defense.[87]

Once again, we observe mercurial shifts in Christian-Jewish perceptions of their interrelationship.

Jewish torment continued three more days, with youths joining recruits in administering beatings. By the fourth day, Polish burghers were identifying Jews on the streets "as if it were the most pressing matter." Such danger from townspeople pointed to impending pogrom. "A certain official, *pan* Gliński, told his Jewish landlord, *pan* Lis: 'expect riots on Thursday.'" On that same evening, county assembly elections took place, with a Jewish candidate in the running.

This provoked such indignation among Christian city councillors (stemming mainly from the intelligentsia) that Abram Sercz, informed of the uproar, escaped unnoticed from election hall by a back door, leaving the councillors hotly debating the matter, excitedly gesticulating.

Jews slept that night uncertainly, for news began circulating of furtive murder committed on the Christian Targowski. The rabble suspected a Jew. Next morning, May 1, robbery commenced. Hooligans smashed the synagogue, injuring worshippers. The mayor had posters affixed to town walls, ostensibly to quiet the agitated mob, but Jewish officials doubted whether this was their true purpose, for they said:

"the bestial manner of the murder of our town's citizen, *pan* Targowski of blessed memory, plunges us all in mourning. We feel together with you the just outrage of the public," etc. Those few officials deserve praise who tried to suppress the riots, above all local *starosta*, *pan* Stanisław Kulesza. Unfortunately, there were too few noble people, and the pogrom, which could have easily been stopped, assumed ever larger proportions.

Though troops arrived from Kielce, riot raged two more days before their shooting ended it. More than forty Jews were injured; one had died.

---

[87] Here and below: CZA. Z3/181 (n.d.).

Two Miechówers told Kraków Zionists that the pogrom flared as striking workers joined visiting peasants in breaking Jewish windows. Jews barricaded themselves, "but the crowd, armed with axes and crowbars, broke into homes and shops." Having stolen stocks of leather, manufactures, and apparel, "the mob destroyed household furnishings with unbelievable fury. Chairs, mirrors, wardrobes were smashed, bedding torn, and everyone beaten, not excepting women and children." Losses were 1 million korony. Organizers' names were known, and if investigated, "the guilty could all be exposed."[88]

Kraków's antisemitic *Ilustrowany Kuryer* headlined the story, "Bestial Murder and Lynch Law [*Samosąd*] in Miechów. Agitators from Dąbrowa Góra Incite Mob to Excesses." At 3:00 AM on May 1, "Israel and Fajwel Płoński, local draymen and smugglers," attacked militia man Targowski, guarding an automobile garage. "The butchered him in bestial fashion with axe and knives." They aimed "to set the garage afire to destroy the automobiles that were intended to carry passengers from Miechów to Kraków," in competition with their own horse-drawn carriages. "At 10:00 AM, Targowski died in terrible agony (among other things he lost his eyes)."

News flew about town. Facing town militia, "the crowd threatened lynchings." The sight of some Jewish gendarmes "irritated the mob further, which had been joined by the scum, always eager to be fed." When soldiers reinforcing gendarmes fired in the air, an "innocent farmer" fell dead. Driven out of town, peasants vowed to return in greater numbers. Search for the Płoński brothers was underway. "The excesses were characterized exclusively as revenge for their atrocious crimes and for disfigurement of the dying militia-man. Contributing to the excitation were a few individuals from Dąbrowa Góra, who incited the crowd."[89]

Zionists collected known pogromists' names. First on the list was "country gentleman" Krapiński, released from arrest on bail, whom a Jewish couple identified as leader of a robber band inflicting 50,000-korony loss on them. Another witness saw him severely beat two Jews "with iron rod." Aron Gersztenfeld reported that Krapiński led forty soldiers to his restaurant, "ordering him to serve them drinks in the value of 10,000 korony, which money he naturally did not supply." It was this band that attacked the synagogue and Jews within. There must have been many other such gentlemen pogromists in these years.

Also free on bail was Okulsznikowa, "who led a throng of women and agitated heatedly." Helena Ples was seen by Szmul Miebelski and others as she "held a knife in hand and criminally summoned the mob, crying

---

[88] Ibid. (May 5, 1919).   [89] Ibid., *Ilustrowany Kurjer Codzienny* (May 5, 1919).

'let's slaughter Jews'" ("*chodźmy Żydów zarzynać*"). Attorney Korczak was seen "calling for plunder from his balcony. He cried: 'slaughter the Jews while there's time!'" ("*Rżnąć Żydów póki czas*"). To him, "plunder" and "slaughter" were, seemingly, equivalent or interchangeable terms. Cabinetmaker Buneberg was "generally blamed as main pogrom leader." Parents watched passively as children broke synagogue windows. A certain Małecka had earlier told her Jewish acquaintance Szajntal "that in May there would be something new." On May 1 she reminded him "that her prediction had come true. She added that some people had come from [nearby] Ołkusz who had incited pogromists." Pogroms were magnets, drawing fanatics from all directions.

Altogether, the twenty-three alleged rioters included one country gentleman, two village shoemakers, two locksmiths (useful in pogroms), a lawyer, a food-provisioning official, a house concierge, a pork-butcher, a "villager," a woman official, a gymnasium teacher, a cabinetmaker, a bookbinder, a prison guard, a water carrier, and a town councillor – nineteen townspeople, mainly of middle and lower middle class, three nonfarming country dwellers, and one villager. Confirming social-historical expectation, an artisan master was leader.

An anonymous pogrom announcer sounded the final note, sending a letter dated May 11, heavy with repressed aggression, to Koplowicz, market-square resident:

I warn the Jews, because it won't be long in this month, indeed, until they're going to beat you again. They're going to rob you a little, so tell everybody. Don't reveal this. Give the signal to all Jews and watch out, because they're going to slaughter [*rżnąć*] you and the women and children.

If no further pillage transpired, this threat – also reflective of the rhetorical continuum of plunder and mass murder – will have unsettled Koplowicz's and friends' minds, unless they were hardened to such curses and contemptuous of them.[90]

As we know, Jews could not count on the educated class's protection. In April, in Kuszmirów near Kraków, a crowd had attacked Jews buying railway tickets, throwing stones and snowballs at them. A victim, protesting to a "member of the intelligentsia standing nearby" that the mob should be restrained, heard in reply,

What's happening to you is right ... The time has come for revenge. You're in our hands, we can do to you whatever we like.[91]

---

[90] Ibid. (May 11, 1919). Zionists reported that "on May 8 flyers against Jews were distributed to farmers" near Kraków. CZA. L6/116 (May 17, 1919).

[91] CZA, Z3/181, *Dos Judisze Folk* (April 18, 1919).

Conclusion

The "May events" were not the finale in the Galician tragedy of anti-Jewish violence. According to Kraków Zionists' reckoning, they brought the number of pogroms since Polish independence to 227 – a not implausible figure if every flare-up of group-perpetrated violence counts as pogrom.[92] There would be a scattered few more before the Polish-Soviet War's 1920 end. In 1939 and 1941, Lwów witnessed devastating pogroms, mainly at Ukrainian hands, as, first, the Polish state collapsed and, second, Hitlerite forces expelled Soviet occupiers of 1939 from the city. In Kraków and Rzeszów in 1946, Holocaust survivors suffered violence. During the German occupation, horrendous massacres and murderous hunts occurred, often with complicity of Polish villagers and townspeople, even while others – fewer – aided doom-hounded Jews. Armed bands reappeared in the forests, anti-Nazi and anti-Soviet, commonly also anti-Jewish.[93] But the widespread 1918–19 pogroms found no repetition in the Galicia – now officially "Little Poland" (*Małopolska*) – of the interwar Second Republic.

The "May events" showed an archaic face in villagers' collectivized and ritualized assaults on Jews, individually resistible on the Christian side only at risk of self-branding as a venal "Jewish uncle." Forest-based banditry, associated with defiant mountaineers, "hajdamaks," and Cossacks, was an ancient pendant to settled peasant life. While ritual-murder panics, however induced, were rare, they seem to have lain ready to erupt below life's surface, just as the alleged diabolic slaughter of the Miechów militia man, guarding an auto garage, showed how ancient horror tales could be fitted to modern urban-industrial settings.[94]

One of antisemitism's most dangerous features shows its enigmatic face repeatedly in these pages. It was, so to speak, both there and not there. The *Illustrated Daily Courier*'s reportage on the Miechów pogrom simultaneously incited "bestial murder" and disavowed "lynch law," "scum," and "outside agitators." The Investigative Commission's and General Szamota's report condemned anti-Jewish actions yet invoked antisemitic arguments. Even when the reported speeches of agrarian populist

[92] CZA. L6/116, (n.d. [May 1919]).

[93] Jan Grabowski, *Hunt for the Jews: Betrayal and Murder in German-Occupied Poland* (Bloomington, IN: University of Indiana Press, 2013 [Polish orig. 2011]). Anna Cichopek, *Pogrom Żydów w Krakowie 11. Sierpnia 1945 r.* (Warsaw: Żydowski Instytut Historyczny, 2000). Cf. Zaremba, *Wielka Trwoga*.

[94] Jerzy Tomaszewski ascribed the ritual-murder charge in Strzyżów to "the fantasy of a psychically unstable girl." Tomaszewski, "Zaburzenia," 99. Whatever her condition, ritual-murder accusations were components of deep-rooted and highly structured cultural practices that commanded serious attention from public and authorities when raised.

demagogues made few or no references to Jews, they served to authorize anti-Jewish violence. Such ambivalence is observable in virtually all educated Poles who expressed themselves on the Jewish presence. It undoubtedly hampered intervention against pogrom violence, which might otherwise have been frequently blocked. As Kraków Zionists telegrammed to Copenhagen in May 1919, concerning the town Książę Wielki, "military stepped in against rioters on local priest's intervention."[95]

May's pogroms were social war waged by poor villagers and deracinated soldiers against state power, even when reorganized in common folk's collective name. They were inseparable from the impulse to attack the landlord class, yet knowing that the state would deploy its soldiers to defend estate owners (even those who were Jewish), villagers unloaded their aggression mainly on *shtetl* Jews. They knew, as General Szamota said, that Jews were "the class in society that is least resistant to [mob] violence." Pogroms were, to refashion influential scholar of peasantry James Scott's phrase, "weapons of the weak – against the weak."[96]

This book weighs pogromists' social-cultural motives, conscious or not, against their amoral "rational interest" in material self-aggrandizement through violence. It is doubtful that many participants in May pogroms reaped much financial or other material gain from robberies. Even when Jewish businesses' losses climbed into the tens of thousands, it's probable that when all shares were divided and all attendant costs covered – for example, bribes to officials, or discounts to receivers of stolen property, or redistribution among village peers (acts we surmise but cannot document) – not much will have remained in individual village plunderers' hands. Jewelry or fine clothes will have been prized, though often marking their wearers as plunderers. But sometimes their booty was worth no more than cheap circus prizes, which they may have been ashamed to hang on the wall. We have repeatedly encountered the belief that wealthier Jews were best able to defend themselves, if only by paying protection money, while poor Jews, easily plunderable, possessed far fewer assets. All, however, were vulnerable to physical abuse and destruction of homes and furnishings. Pogromists' rabid destructiveness reflected not only hope that riches lay hidden in Jews' feather bedding but also simulated – and stimulated – ethnic cleansing and often symbolized murder.

---

[95] CZA. L6/116 (May 7, 1919).

[96] James Scott, *Weapons of the Weak: Everyday Forms of Peasant Resistance* (New Haven, CT: Yale University Press, 1985). Tomasewski judged the May events "a certain type of peasant revolution," inflected by "antisemitic prejudices." Tomaszewski, "Zaburzenia," 105. Similarly, Stankiewicz, *Konflikty*.

What mattered was less plunder – though to starvelings a sack of potatoes is precious – than pogrom participation. This was not so much a realization in action of antisemitic or anti-Jewish *ideas* or *beliefs* (though it *was* this too) than reaffirmation, in pogromists' psyches, through *performance* of strength of peasant *identity* and *solidarity*, both in the village and across the land. Peasants – oppressed by rents, taxes, tithes, bad trading terms with towns, army requisitioner and recruiter – desperately needed self-validation. They sometimes bitterly reflected that the era of unpaid feudal labor services – *pańszczyzna* – had yielded, to their disadvantage, to subjugation to Jewish interests – *żydowszczyzna*.[97] Temptation to show they could dominate towns – the sphere of commercial capital, stereotypically Jewish – through their vast numbers, boldness, and physical strength was enormous. Their gratification would have been greater still had they been able to overthrow landlords and drive out officials and army, but such Herculean deeds were beyond them, as all but the most fiery Red Guardists knew.

[97] Tomaszewski, "Zaburzenia," 96.

Part III

Pogroms' Path Eastward, 1919–1920

7   Soldierly Antisemitism, Pinsk Massacre, and Morgenthau's Mission

"Pranks," Exorcisms, Explanations, Exculpations

Pogroms lethally mixed armed men and civilians. In some, as in Kraków in April 1918, Christian townspeople plundered Jews in defiance of police and army, whose guns eventually turned on pogromists. In others, as in Lwów in November 1918, soldiers blazed their way into Jewish neighborhoods, robbery-bent civilians in tow. Or, as in Galicia's 1919 "May events," armed bandits, defying government forces, fought their way into *shtetls* amid peasant throngs, to be joined inside town walls by "rabble" and "scum."

When in 1919–20 renascent Poland plunged into war to expand its borders eastward and challenge Bolshevik expansion westward, salience spiked of government-commanded soldiers among Jews' tormentors. We have contemplated soldierly antisemitism before but now descend, in this book's remaining pages, deeper into its dark passages. Two dimensions predominate: old-established culture of soldierly antisemitism, expressed especially in "pranks" at Jewish expense, and antisemitic violence understood by its perpetrators as just (and obliterative) war against Bolshevism. "Pranks" often turned lethal, while anticommunism's inner anxieties clouded judgment and stoked aggression.

Did military authorities tolerate the rank-and-file's accustomed Judeophobia or seek to suppress it? Were Poland's newborn, politically multicolored military forces amplifiers within the larger culture of anti-Jewish violence? In this chapter, whose culminatory theme is an internationally scandalous massacre by Polish soldiery of alleged Jewish Bolsheviks in Belarusian Pinsk and its investigation by American emissary Henry Morgenthau, it will be seen that Christian Polish authorities both strained against anti-Jewish violence and – as if unwittingly and against their will – unleashed it. Such ambivalence – already familiar to us – beset even those Polish nationalists who sought, in their well-educated and rational minds, a sustainable and defensible relationship with the Jews in their midst. What clouded their minds and lamed their judgment were both anxiety of vulnerability and hubris of command, embedded in subliminal conceptions of Jewish malevolence. What were the limits to permissible Christian Polish self-defense against Israelites' uncanny powers? This unspoken question looms ever larger in the chapters that follow.[1]

Rehearsal for War: Recruits' First Encounter with the Enemy

A crystalline example of army recruits' abuse of Jews involved thirteen young Galician villagers making their way, in March 1919, from their villages to induction in Tarnów. As gendarmes reported to military judges, the men's transport wagons encountered seventy-year-old Hirsch Geller on the road. Józef Chronowski "assaulted him, striking him with a blunt instrument on the forehead between the eyes," from which blow and "by being thrown down a two-meter bank he was killed." Proceeding to Wiśnicz Nowy, "the perpetrators stormed sweets seller Raca Braff's stall, and when she asked them not to harm her, they threw her to the muddy ground." Seizing her wares, they traveled on, beating various Jews so that doctoring was required. At a village tavern they drank without paying, slapping the owner's face. Proceeding farther, bullying Jews as they went, they were arrested in Bochnia.

Murdered Geller's wife testified that returning from shopping, "she heard the traveling recruits' singing [carnavalesque touch] and in fear of them hid at a [Christian acquaintance's] house." When they passed, she discovered her murdered husband, killed "by wooden canes [*kijami*]." A Jewish couple reported that as they carted coal, the accused "severely beat them with canes." Four others suffered the same fate.[2]

Chronowski – twenty-one, bachelor, farmer's son, literate, property-less, parents dead, previously unpunished – later reported that "I feel [plead] guilty," adding that he had been drunk. When he saw the "old Jew,"

I jumped from the wagon, ran through the ditches, seized the Jew by the beard, the Jew fell in the ditch . . . What happened to him I don't know . . . I had no intention of killing him but only, being drunk, wanted to scare him a little . . . I had a stick

---

[1] The historical literature counts no widely recognized scholarly work devoted to the Polish armed forces' relationship to antisemitism and anti-Jewish violence in the 1918–20 years, although, as will be seen below, some issues have been preliminarily investigated. Many above-cited works – notably those of Budnitskii, Golczewski, Kenez, and Klier et al. – address soldierly staging of anti-Jewish violence but largely in the Russian context and mainly as instrument or expression of trickle-down print-antisemitism rather than analyzing it as free-standing phenomenon expressive of soldiers' own aims and mentality. Wiese's *Pogrome* differs in offering analysis of Russian recruitment pogroms, including in their ritualistic aspect (chap. 4).

[2] SOKKr. S8/II. J 2210/20, fos. 7–14 (March 11, 1919).

[*patyk*] but I didn't hit him with it ... I remember that between Wiśnicz and Bochnia I struck maybe one or two Jews with the stick.[3]

His unapologetic references to scaring and hitting show that he thought such acts trivial and permissible.

Further interrogations showed that Chronowski's fellow recruits were all literate (and "of strong build"). They were neither ignorant peasants nor "scum." Farmer's son Tąfara saw Chronowski pull Geller's beard but not push him. "I did have a thin stick [seemingly army recruits' obligatory, more or less lethal surrogate saber] but hit no one."

Tavern keeper Schiffeldrün said the "lads," when refused rum, tried to seize it, but he recovered the bottle "and my wife voluntarily gave each one a glass, then they left peacefully." A merchant said that "when the lads saw us they left their wagon and began to beat me and my son with their canes so that I'm sick to this day from it." Widow Braff, eighty, reported that they took her stall-cover posts along with them as weapons. Recruit Dziedzic denied Chronowski beat old Geller, yet he damningly added that farther down the road "he twice more jumped from the wagon and beat Jews."

The police file ended with an October 1920 notice that the men were inducted, Chronowski dying in uniform.[4] It's clear that army recruits thought such tormenting of Jews acceptable fulfillment of "desire" (*ochota*) that seized them in their song-accompanied drunken revelry. Why were Jews the target? The script the recruits enacted – not their unknown private thoughts – shows that becoming a soldier led directly to aggression against Jews. The soldier's business was to beat Jews. The Jew was, in effect, first enemy, or surrogate enemy, or both. Soldiery was, among other things, war against Jews – deadly war, for the Christian himself might die.

The Recruitment Riot

Custom was ancient for new army recruits to drink heavily and engage in unpunished mischief. It was anarchical last fling before submitting to sergeant's lash or gunfire's hail. Where Jewish settlement was thick, as in Poland, anti-Jewish "pranks" (*wybryki*) were common, though their historical genealogy remains to be traced, as does their geographic compass. By World War I's time, collective soldierly assaults on Jews had become cruel and damaging. Whether they were infused with ideological antisemitism is a question, but none was detectable in Chronowski's case,

---

[3] Ibid., fo. 43 (March 29, 1919).
[4] Here and preceding: ibid., fos. 47, 51, 73, 87, 89, 91, 95, 97, 129.

where Jewish victims figured as scapegoats for soldiers' misfortune in having been forcibly summoned to face death and as surrogate battlefield foes.

An exemplary recruitment riot occurred in salt-mining Wieliczka, whose spring 1918 pogrom we earlier witnessed. In February 1919, soldiers and urban crowd ran amok. The prefect wrote that

in the morning, groups of drunken draftees undergoing conscription gathered on town square where, strolling and staggering about, they attacked passers-by, battered shuttered shops, broke into wall-showcases, and bullied Jewish pedestrians. They were joined by crowded onlookers – adolescents, women and especially social dregs from here and nearby.

From the general mood among the numerous throng watching the recruits' pranks, and from shouts from the crowd, the impression arose that the disturbances were mostly staged to encourage and incite the crowd, that among the onlookers there circulated elements trying to provoke evil human instincts and elicit hatred toward local Jews, who had not the previous day reported for military induction.[5]

The *starosta* found it suspicious that "among the troublemakers were individuals simulating drunkenness and riotousness" but who "moved among the excited crowd, and whenever military patrols came to arrest troublemakers they protected them," driving the soldiers away. "Yet, until noon, it seemed these were customary draftees' excesses." Later, recruits joined by newcomer villagers descended on Einhorn's tavern, demanding drinks. "When these, pursuant to alcohol sales ban, were refused, they invaded and robbed the cellar, beating Chaim Süssholz who lives there," stealing 2,000 korony in cash, destroying electrical fixtures and taking liquor worth 3,000 korony. As these pranks grew uncontrollable, the *starosta* telephoned the local army commander to quell the uproar.

Policeman Filar found himself facing troublemakers who, with clenched fists, knives, and whips (*bychowcy*), said that "if he was going to defend Jews, they would settle accounts with him." More patrols arrived, one led by "Pinkas Salomon (Jew)," who was attacked, disarmed, and severely beaten. As troops formed a firing line, "miners present, shouting to the crowd 'we'll get our rifles,' ran off toward the mining office." Because of "soldiers' uncertain standpoint" and "to avoid an armed clash with miners," they were marched to barracks, while Filar telephoned for reinforcements. Full-blown pogrom erupted, as the crowd disarmed an army patrol, firing their confiscated guns in the air "to spread fear."

---

[5] SOKKr. S8/II. J 708/20, fos. 1, 29–35 (February 7 and 14, 1919).

Plunderers followed signals from leaders (*prowodyrze, herszty*), moving from neighborhood to neighborhood, women and children collecting and stashing booty. Bursting into butcher Grossmann's apartment, a pogromist "seized the pot of boiling liquid [noodle soup] in the kitchen and flung it in Grossmann's face, scalding his eyes so that he is now blind in one and lingers in recovery" (boiling water, as we know, often figured in pogrom justifications). His material loss tallied 20,950 korony. The mob stormed the Bank for Commerce and Industry, Józef Palmowski jumping through the window and pointing a revolver at Director Schinagel, "crying, 'hand over the dough [*dawaj diengi*].'"

Seven suspects sat in jail; six others were wanted. Twenty-seven witnesses were on hand. Total losses amounted to 300,000 korony. The *starosta* vainly pleaded for summary trial. Policeman Filar testified that pogromists, whose leaders he thought were only simulating drunkenness, cursed him and his men as "sons-of-bitches, Jewish uncles." He warned against releasing suspects, creating the impression that pogroms went unpenalized. "Similar disturbances occurred in May 1918, and have repeated themselves mainly because they passed unpunished."[6]

A good illustration of extortion accompanying pogroms emerges from testimony of Mateusz Klinghofer, Lwów merchant visiting his brother Mojżesz. Into their apartment burst a "tall thin man, in jacket and round hat." He asked if Mateusz "was a Jew." Learning that he was, he said "I had to give him money." Facing his knife, Klinghofer let him empty his wallet of 350 korony. A second man burst in, in legionnaire's uniform, recognizable as Krysiak, also demanding money, saying "that he would not serve on my behalf in the army, threatening to kill me." Krysiak, believing Jews evaded conscription, spurned risking his life for them. Klinghofer's sister-in-law proposed to borrow money. A third intruder arrived, rummaging through their drawers. Mateusz managed to flee "to the fields." When he returned, he saw that the "kitchenware and cabinet had been destroyed." Was this kosher cooking's apparatus?

The sister-in-law repaired to the apartment of Matusiński, liaison official to the Lwów governor in the local *starosta*'s office. He too had seen the "tall man," who had warned him off with cudgel shake. Matusiński asked him his business. "The Jewess has to give me 1,000 korony." Asked why, he replied, in *double entendre*, that "he wanted 'to celebrate [*urżnąć* – "cut up"].'" Ominous word play, for *urżnąć* is

[6] Ibid., fos. 89, 103, 113–4 (February 26–27, 1919); fos. 221–22 (March 31, 1919); fos. 241–43 (April 1, 1919).

cognate with *rżnąć*, meaning, preeminently, "slaughter," a popular word in pogrom discourse. Matusiński refused Klinghoferowa's loan request. The tall man threatened to injure the Klinghofers. Matusiński's housekeeper testified that the men were not drunk, but Krysiak later insisted he was.[7]

Real estate owner and kiosk operator Sass, robbed twice in 1918, now lost goods worth 30,000 korony plus his violin. A spice dealer watched from her darkened window as robbers plundered her goods. Bookbinder Feig saw Kułakowski in legionnaire's uniform leading other men in tearing off a shop's door. "Seeing I was observing, he ran over and shouted, 'what are you looking at,' hit me in the face and chased after me. In my flight I lost my cap."[8]

In September 1920, Kraków criminal court found three women guilty of witness-corroborated theft or receiving stolen property. Sentences were one month's imprisonment, in two cases aggravated by "hard cot." The 1919 state amnesty halved sentences, but court costs remained. Various male defendants, serving in the army, were "excluded." The two who were tried, having been temporarily held in jail and later served in the army, were acquitted, no witnesses having testified against them. The women's appeals were rejected in February 1921. A January 1920 letter from defendant Kułakowski to his "beloved parents" in Wieliczka announced that he was in Kraków army hospital. "Let dad come to me because I'm going crazy with hunger. Dad's got a few korony from me, let him buy cigarettes and bread." He wanted acquaintances to be reminded that on pogrom day "I was with them and not in any robbery."[9]

The case's file encompassed nearly 600 pages yet yielded little justice. Seemingly, the chief offenders' army service, temporary jailing, and witnesses' reluctance to risk incrimination as "Jewish uncles" explain the outcome. The *starosta*'s suspicions of pogrom incitation found no judicial echo. Doubtless there were voices in the crowd calling for aggression not as coldly calculating entrepreneurs or paid agents of ethnic violence but because the pogrom script, known demotically to all, required that groundlings raise the drama's curtain.[10]

---

[7] Ibid., fos. 93–97, 457 (February 21 and 26, 1919).

[8] Ibid., 121, 123, 125, 127–28, 141–42 (February 27–28, 1919).

[9] Ibid., fos. 483–84 (January 19, 1920); fos. 517–21 (September 4, 1920); fo. 537 (February 7, 1921).

[10] For similar inductees' riots, see Będzin (CZA, Z3/181: *Dos Judisze Folk* [April 28, 1919]), which Jewish porters attempted to stop. Police restored order. Also for Sosnowiec, see CZA. Z3/181: *Dos Judisze Folk* (March 3, 1919). Jewish butchers resisted would-be pogromists. Police restored order. For Sochaczew, see CZA, Z3/181: *Dos judisze Folk* (April 27, 1919). Jewish town councillors halted tumult.

Military Authorities and Soldierly Antisemitism

Did uniformed pogromists ever act with superiors' sanction? There is no unambiguous answer partly because resurrected Poland's armed forces were multifarious. There were the Piłsudski-Paderewski government's divisions, the Endek-inspired Haller army, and – on eastern fronts – allied but uncontrolled partisan or irregular forces, each distinctive in anti-Jewish potential.

Piłsudski, Paderewski, and their ministerial colleagues disavowed and condemned pogroms and other anti-Jewish violence, even while sometimes excusing or justifying it by alleged Jewish anti-Polonism. They insisted, too, that the state was not yet strong enough prevent all such excesses. We know that soldiers often disobeyed superiors, refusing to suppress civilian pogroms and instead allowing themselves to be disarmed or joining the rioting.

The Piłsudski-Paderewski government's arguments against pogroms were voiced by army officers in civilian rioting's aftermath in half-Jewish Wieluń, industrializing town of 11,000. In March 1919, local army commander Lieutenant Colonel Łapiński publicly condemned the violence in high-flown words (self-critical and psychologically notable passages italicized):

Yesterday showed *how little we understand* citizenly responsibilities. [When Poland is rising again] and our brothers are shedding their blood for the eastern and western borderlands, are you, Citizens, to occupy yourself with murder and robbery? Are we to show, at this moment when *all Europe's eyes are on us*, that *we are so benighted* that we cannot manage to devote ourselves to building the Polish State, but that *the foreign invader's cudgel must constantly keep us in bounds*? No, Citizens! Our responsibility lies elsewhere . . . Just look where Russia was led by settling its internal accounts by crime and violence. If we don't break free of this immediately it could soon be too late.

You don't realize, Citizens, that *you're puppets* on strings of agitation in foreign pay. [Germans and Muscovites want to recover the lands they've lost to Poland.] There will be *time later on to settle personal accounts* . . . Do not push the State into collapse, so that *we fall again into foreign captivity*. Resist vile agitators! Work through the political process! Turn them over to the authorities! Thus will you serve the mother- and fatherland [*Matce ojczyźnie*], which expects help from you, Citizens, for otherwise *it will perish*.

Remember that Poland now being reborn extends to you hands *swollen by shackles of many-yeared captivity*, that the whole world's eyes are on us as forefront, *defensive wall*, against an *anarchy* out of Russia that aims to engulf Europe.[11]

The army's plea sought to ascribe Wieluń's violence to Bolshevik and German nationalist intrigue (puppet imagery was also endemic to

---

[11] Here and below: CZA. Z3/181 (n.d.).

antisemitic discourse). Victims' Jewishness went unremarked, reflecting (apart perhaps from shame) official avoidance of specifying identities other than citizenly. That acting on anti-Jewish resentments could be described as "settling personal accounts" unconsciously perpetuated violence's rhetoric, if it was not cynical promise that Jews would later pay for alleged misdeeds. The proclamation recognized anti-Jewish accusations and the legitimacy of raising them. But state building came first, demanding citizenly understanding of new authorities' limitations. Poles were reminded too of their land's historic self-image as (Western) "Christendom's rampart" against Eastern aggression and civilizational chaos.

On May 6, 1919, a military order, in Piłsudski's name and cosigned by Haller, summarized under thirteen headings soldierly delicts and prescribed punishments. Entailing death by hanging or firing squad, following adjudication by field court martial, were murder, manslaughter, arson, and armed robbery; also the "crime of theft, if damage inflicted exceeds 1,000 korony"; and plundering in excess of 100 korony. This draconian order (whose implications concerning rape were unclear) was to be read three times to all units at three-day intervals. It conveyed, in effect, zero tolerance for these common pogrom crimes.[12]

Doubtless such orders were issued with one eye on Poland's Western allies, who sometimes wrung hands contemplating Polish pogroms. Probably soldierly plunder of Jews seemed unavoidable and partly justifiable to military authorities, but bloodshed was another matter, and rampant criminality crossed their purposes. Yet, granting seriousness to Piłsudski's and Haller's pogrom-fighting motives, soldierly compliance and grassroots enforcement were questionable.

Soon thereafter, Haller army Lublin headquarters issued a *note de service*, seemingly for general proclamation. It read in full:

On May 10 on one of Lublin's main streets, around 8:00 PM, soldiers belonging to Headquarters attacked Jews, without having been provoked by them[!].

Soldiers belonging to the army of General Haller ought to distinguish themselves by good behavior and respect for others.

They should create the impression and leave behind memory of soldiers devoted to a great cause, inspired by but one thought – creation of a fatherland ever larger and more beautiful.

Stern measures will be applied against soldiers who do not comply with these regulations.[13]

---

[12] Centralne Archiwum Wojskowe, Warsaw-Rembertów (hereafter: CAW). File no. I.123.1.324: J (May 6, 1919).

[13] Ibid., G (May 12, 1919).

Lublin had recently suffered when recruits, secondary students, and "bestialized rabble" plundered and bludgeoned Jewish merchants and pedestrians. *Dos Judisze Folk* reported that "worker N. urged the crowd to peace, but was whistled down and accused of selling out to Jews for money," while "gymnasium teacher N. summoned the crowd to settle accounts with Jews." Army patrols moved in, but the retreating mob continued its plunder. One Jew died; fifty-four were robbed and/or injured. Droshky-transported student Rozenryb "was fallen on by peasants who beat him with wooden clubs, knocking out two teeth." Here soldiers suppressed pogromists yet two weeks later, by army admission, ran amok themselves.[14]

Haller's army arrived in former Russian Poland in spring 1919 with French army liaison officers. Many soldiers were French citizens of Polish immigrant background, while others were American Poles. Some will not have spoken Polish. For their edification, and to maintain French government favor, proclamations also appeared in French. On May 15, Haller's First Army headquarters issued bilingual Order 35, for reading to all troops. Praising their bravery under fire, it asked them now "to defend the peaceable[!] civilian population," remembering that "you are soldiers of POLAND, which never oppressed any nation or religion." Soldierly "excesses" and "requisitions" were forbidden. Marching eastward, they would see how the enemy had ravaged Lithuania, East Galicia, and Belarus. "You will see the Polish peasant plundered of his possessions. You will see misery and disorganization everywhere!" The population there must be protected "without regard for rank or nationality." All violations would be punished by *Conseil de Guerre*.[15]

Haller sent his officers a confidential message. He commanded them, addressing them in the plural familiar voice, "to live close to the soldier and care for him as brother." All infringements and excesses were to be punished "unconditionally, but justly."

Explain to the soldier that the greatest enemy of his family and himself is every kind of anarchy, lack of authority and government, which lead to disorganization of family life, undermining of all labor, to hunger and total misery.[16]

These were prime peasant values and fears. Officers should also raise soldiers' national consciousness, speak for all classes, and represent the Sejm as "highest authority and Head of State as highest executive." In

[14] CZA, Z3/181: *Dos judisze Folk* (April 27, 1919).
[15] CAW. File no. I.123.1.324: I (May 15, 1919). In July 1919, Haller authorities promised punishment by *Conseil de Guerre* of major alcohol theft. Ibid. File no. I.123.1.321: D (July 16, 1919).
[16] Ibid., K (May 19, 1919).

these instructions, Haller advocated liberal-democratic values, breaking with the partitioning powers' authoritarian military traditions, still alive in many minds.

Haller army's Department of Justice filed another of the commander's orders for reading to soldiers. "Complaints have reached my ear from the Jewish side that Polish soldiers are behaving toward them in a way incompatible with the Polish soldier's valor and honor, for example: *beating, tormenting and wounding the defenseless* and also *destroying their possessions.*" The commander promised that "I will sternly punish and hand over to court-martial all those guilty of the persecution of any population group."[17]

If high command's orders were followed, Haller's soldiers could hardly claim ignorance of Western liberal military norms. Yet Captain Giedrojć, chief of Haller's Justice Division, later wrote to the North-West Front Quartermaster saying that soldierly violence against Jews in the Warsaw region could not be prosecuted because victims could not identify attackers. He added: "to work against *constantly recurring excesses* against the Jewish population, regulations and instructions are being distributed to the separate unit commands to prevent future soldierly license." This was a confession of failure of Haller army efforts – which, despite appearances on paper, may have been half-hearted – to rein in troops' aggressive anti-Judaism.[18]

Hallerite Pranks in Zakroczym

Army leaders invoked liberalism, but at heart many shared the soldiers' Judeophobic spirit. This is evident in the French-language report compiled by Lieutenant de Worvan-Nawrowski, assigned to investigate "our soldiers' alleged [*pretendus*] pogroms of Jews in Zakroczym." This and adjacent Nowy Dwór were predominantly Jewish towns hugging the Napoleonic Modlin fortress near Warsaw. Here two French-commanded Hallerite companies were housed. Nawrowski found it relevant that many Jews were prewar immigrants from the Russia Pale ("*Latwaki*"). Local Poles greeted Hallerites enthusiastically, informing them of Jews' misdeeds: collaboration – first with Russians, then with Germans; "incitation against Haller soldiers as representatives of reaction; black-marketeering and export of food."

The soldiers, "of simple nature," mostly Poznanian and American, unfamiliar with everything in their *patrie* (as Nawrowski imagined

---

[17] Ibid., H (May 20, 1919), (author's emphasis).
[18] CAW. File no. I.123.1.321: E (July 23, 1919), (author's emphasis).

Russian Poland to be), "let themselves be led naively by sentiment and reflex to express their indignation, and slapped the faces of 3–4 Jews in Zakroczym and 3–4 in Nowy Dwór." Nawrowski interrogated the fortress commander, Polish officers, Christian mayors, priests, and rabbis. All assured him no "excess *en masse*" occurred. The soldiers' behavior was typical worldwide. Jewish parliamentary complaints and press reports were "very blundering and unfortunate." None of the supposed victims wished to file a complaint. "Our soldiers in general appear very disciplined and under control, well trained and polished; they never plundered, invaded or burned any Jewish house in Zakroczym." No further steps were necessary. "Everyone says Jews deliberately exaggerated insignificant facts, aiming on pretext of alleged danger menacing them from our troops to elicit intervention against them of local troops!" – Piłsudskiites versus Hallerites.

Nawrowski found that soldiers had underpaid for Jewish-owned merchandise, including alcohol. They found two Jewish-driven vehicles loaded with food, whose export was prohibited, and conducted them to city hall. The soldier who administered blows, "with best intentions," had already been punished. Other soldiers tore down, amid blows, a Jewish shop's German-language signage. Jewish town councillor Motyl opposed drawing the Sejm's Jewish Club into these insignificant incidents, while those who publicized the affair "are owners of a mechanical sawmill under sequestration!" – moved by vulgar self-interest.[19]

Such was the condescending and dismissive attitude of an evidently upper-class Franco-Polish officer. Seen through Jewish eyes, soldiers' assaults were agonizing. The (Zionist) National Club of Jewish Sejm Deputies recorded victims' experiences, contradicting Nawrowski's account and crediting a French cavalry commander with halting week-long excesses. "Many beards were cut off or ripped out. Hardly fifteen remain [in Zakroczym]." Some ten were beaten, including old men now lying in bed with bruised feet. Synagogue and rabbi's house were damaged but not successfully conquered. "Civilians pillaged under Haller army protection. Town militia remained passive." French General Petitdemange said that "soldiers' excesses against Jews were an absolutely incomprehensible surprise" and therefore could not initially be prevented.[20]

Twenty-eight injured Jews testified, all older men. Eighteen reported beard cutting, though all may have suffered it. The procedure had a markedly theatrical or carnavalesque, comic, or burlesque quality. Soldiers dragged Goldman, seventy, into the street "and began amid

[19] Ibid., F (May 5, 1919).   [20] Here and below: ibid., E (May 21, 1919).

crowd's hoots and whistling to cut his beard. Thanks to intervention by priest and army command, towards whom the crowd was mightily rude, the priest was able to get the old man to the convent." Soldiers cut Wolfowitz's beard with their bayonets, forcing him to shout "long live the Haller army" and "death to the rabbi."

Soldiers pierced elder Feigenbaum's bedding with bayonets and then pulled him into the street and cut his beard "to people's laughter." Sztalman suffered beard cutting before being chased and beaten. "This did not satisfy our good Catholics of Zakroczym." They returned with fifty soldiers, saying Sztalman's father had evaded beard cutting and beating, an oversight they corrected. Seeing that Sztalman had "a soda-water factory," they took 350 bottles of lemonade and other drinks, "giving them to the crowd of civilians following them." "Pitiless toward my age and pleas," eighty-year-old Glohn testified, "they cut half my beard with their bayonets." Next day a boy brought them back, saying he still had half a beard. "Hearing my 9-year-old grand-daughter's cries, a gendarme wanted to defend me, but assailants threatened him with bayonet," also beating the girl's mother.

Soldiers found the rabbi hiding in the synagogue and, "to cheers of Hallerite soldiers and other individuals from society's dregs," cut his beard while robbing him of 8,000 marks cash and 10,000 marks in jewels. They forced their way into eighty-year-old Gretler's house, stealing his spoons and forks and "offering them to civilians." Guiding soldiers was his faithless house guardian. Kleinman reported that a soldier invaded his house, wishing to violate his daughter, whose cries were joined by her mother's. "Another soldier came and made the first one leave. This saved my daughter."

Rampaging Hallerites encountered policeman Kamiński dispersing soldiers' youthful followers, who were removing signs from Jewish shops. "They surrounded him, seized the signs and hurled them to the ground, and severely beat him." The rabbi issued a damning but circumspect public statement:

Excesses in our town were the work of "Hallerites" and occurred under influence of instigations and incitations by Polish society's outcasts [*wyrzutków*]. Jews were beaten, beards cut, goods seized without payment. There was no pogrom: what actually happened bore the character of individualized attacks.[21]

Like non-antisemitic Poles, the rabbi wanted to distance respectable, law-abiding Polish society from violent and anarchical "scum," here called "outcasts." In his mind, "pogrom" evidently meant collective communal

---

[21] CZA. Z3/181 (April 22, 1919).

action. A Nowy Dwór newspaper corroborated the rabbi's claims, saying, "the [Haller] army is constantly incited against Jews by local antisemitic elements . . . Thanks to energetic actions of fortress commander Malewicz and town commandant Robaczewski disturbances were localized."[22]

Hallerites were enacting, through beard cutting with bayonets, a symbolic slaughter of religious Jews, akin to the "Judas Fest." They were redistributing Jews' ill-gotten gains among joyous Christian poor (keeping better booty for themselves). Their civilian followers, and they themselves, laughed uproariously at elderly Jews' misery. They tried, though failed, to demolish the synagogue and the rabbi's house. They proclaimed, through their victims' mouths, the rabbi's death. On their pranks' fringes hovered specters of rape and murder.

Why was this brutal spectacle necessary? Jews' symbolic removal from Christian life fulfilled deeply satisfying fantasies: bloody eradication of Jewish theological dissent, whose existence relativized and cast doubt on Christianity itself, and exproprietors' expropriation, overturning of commerce's masters, price gougers and black marketeers. Their demise opened to the Christian poor the realm of plenty without prices, medieval peasants' "Land of Cockaigne" or *Schlaraffenland*, free spoons and forks and sparkling drinks.

These scenarios were the work of Poles from the West – France, America – and from Poznania, Germany's piece of old Poland, where Polish society had modernized itself while ruthlessly rejecting brotherhood with the long-settled local Jews, who mostly took sides with Germans or emigrated westward. Hallerites may have known nothing of their Russian Polish *patrie* or of Galicia, but evidently it shocked them in their psychological depths far more to encounter there the "eastern caftan Jew" than the Westernized, Polonized Zionist or assimilationist. The traditionalist Jews' presence was humiliation to them, proof of Polish backwardness and inferiority. Removal of "medieval Jewry" would fit Poland to stride into bright modernity, cleansed of historic blemishes.[23]

Hallerites' Railway Pranks

Hallerites enacted similar scripts in rabid assaults on train-riding Jews. In mid-May, the office of Zionist Sejm Deputies (or Zionist Club) forwarded to Haller army command victims' testimony to Warsaw violence.

[22] CZA.Z3/181: *Kurjer Nowy* (April 29, 1919).
[23] For a complementary perspective, cf. Steinlauf, *Bondage to the Dead*.

It warned that Haller soldiers were threatening that new rampages "will be staged [*potworzony*], and on wider scale."[24]

Tormenting of Jews on trains, like other anti-Jewish violence, was multicausal and polysemic. But Jewish presence in this setting of techno-logical modernity – and of public community and individual equality within passenger classes – clearly unleashed aggression. Icek Auerbach observed "a few peasants" entering his train car, where he was the only Jew, telling passengers "with a laugh that they were beating Jews at the station."

The peasant sitting next to me shouted from the train window to a passing Haller soldier: "a Jew's sitting here!" The soldier jumped into the train, demanding that I get out immediately. A lady asked the soldier not to beat anyone in the train, whereupon the soldier pulled me from it. Fleeing, I ran through the fence, trying to get to town. The train-station guard chasing me demanded I return; otherwise he threatened to shoot. Running, I got caught on the barbed-wire, ripping all my clothes: pants, linen, overcoat.

This story reminds us that "peasants" frequented big cities and that "ladies" preferred not to witness beatings, though unseen thrashings might be tolerable.

Frajman Hersz, arriving in Warsaw, found Hallerites "beating pitilessly every train-exiting Jew, shouting and bullying most brutally. This occurred under higher-ranked officers' eyes." Staggering from a head blow, he fell into other soldiers' hands. "One tried to pull off my shoes, saying 'he's got good shoes, they've got to be taken.' By some miracle I escaped."

Goldberg reported, "dripping blood, I collapsed." He felt his pockets being rifled. "I saw people in mortal fear running to hide in the train, but a policeman barred their way. Merciful people [*litościwi ludzie*] led me to a First Aid station, where my head and face wounds were treated. Now, three hours later, I report money loss of 1,000 korony and 500 marks."

Markusfeld heard railroad officials feeding Hallerites anti-Jewish rumors, spurring them to threaten Jews present, who "instinctively" moved to the waiting hall. Officials closed doors from platform to hall, trapping Jews outside, where Hallerites beat them. Trainmen answered Jews' pleas with "so what? They're only beating with fists." Soldiers stole Jewish goods while railroad police passively watched, until other police arrived with rifles and halted the mayhem. Hallerites pulled Edelsztejn from his train, shouting, "Jews to Palestine." As he ran, a knife slit his overcoat's back. He lost two valuable silk robes (*kapoty*) worth 1,500

---

[24] Here and all further references in this subsection: CAW. File I.123.1.321: A (May 12–13, 1919).

marks, two prayer shawls, a fur-trimmed hat (*sztrajmel*), and groceries, altogether worth 3,018 marks. Travelers bribed trainmen exorbitantly to prolong their trips to safer stations.

Landau, robbed of 3,500 marks in goods, bravely complained at the nearest police station. Frenkel reported that in the moving train, Hallerites cut all Jewish beards. "They threw me down, beat me, tore out my hair and beard, and ripped my suit and shirt." They made another shout out, "may the Haller army perish!" "I replied that I would rather they beat me than say that. One kicked me, then they left me in peace." Later, when he was walking on respectable Senatorska Street, a soldier "hit me with full force in the face." Soldiers demanded, after cutting his beard, that Uszer Gewis say "thank you." Responding to their theatrics with his own, "I said: merci." But it was also an old custom for victim to thank executioner. Hallerites stopped every Jew at the "army ramp" in the Aleje Jerozolimskie. "The burned their beards with matches, cut and tore them out simultaneously, along with the skin, beat them, etc. Clustered around them were adolescent youths, who helped beat and rob." Then they dispersed, pilfering shops with "street-mob's" help.

A Kraków court trial involved army sergeant Morawski, who wrote that in a crowded train soldiers "were jeering, singing in Yiddish[!] and shoving an Israelite, who in complete calm endured mockery of a few soldiers amused by him. He sat on a bag, making jokes according to their commands. They made him call out 'long live General Haller's army,' 'long live the Polish army.' They made him curse like a soldier." On hearing the victim's cry, "help me [*gevalt*]," Morawski "ran down the wagon, opened his compartment door, and saw the Jew with half cut beard and bloodied face."

I went to his compartment not in defense of a Jew, but of a peaceful human being, who absolutely did not deserve anything like this. I went to instruct soldiers in a dignified way that they should desist, because it doesn't befit a Polish soldier to beat an unarmed and totally peaceful person.[25]

For this they took him for a Jew. "I replied that I was in no way Jewish but a human being like him, pointing to the beaten Jew." One of the soldiers responded:

Don't bark [*psykować*] so much, because you too, son-of-a-bitch, can get knocked around. Our lieutenant ordered us to beat Jews and here a sergeant sticks his head in.

Morawski withdrew, warning them that if more beatings occurred, he would order their arrest. Hearing the victim's cries anew, he led him to

---

[25] Here and below: SOKKr. S8/II. Vr 986/23, fos. 9–10, 13, 27–28 (October 1–9, 1920).

his compartment. In Bochnia, he succeeded in having them arrested. Plaintiff Wiesenfeld, Kolbuszowan, dealt in leather goods, two packages of which, worth 3,000 marks, his tormentors seized. He credited Sergeant Morawski with speaking "sharp words" before finding a patrol to arrest them. The defendants were a farmer and a miner with minimal education.

Lessons of Further Hallerite Excesses

Skierniewice resident Ickowicz reported that Hallerites appeared, cutting Jewish beards "in company of local hoodlums [opryszków]."[26] He and other Jewish leaders went to the town's military commander, along with Dayczer's "daughter Zofja Dayczerówna as translator." The general received them "exceptionally politely," later showing himself in the Jewish quarter where Hallerites were assaulting Jews. A soldier, unaware of the general's presence, pulled a Jew's boots off. "The general immediately ordered his soldiers to disperse them and return them to barracks."

Peace then reigned until a Hallerite cut an elder's beard. Gincburg protested, and a gendarme attempted to take the soldier into custody. A mass of Hallerites, reportedly 1,000, freed their comrade after the gendarme fired his gun, wounding three before taking refuge. "The rumor spread immediately that a Jew had disguised himself as a gendarme and killed three Hallerites." Soldiers began hunting, while Jews locked doors. Breaking into a house shouting, "hura," soldiers seized Kuperman, eighteen, visiting on business. Accused of being the disguised gendarme, he was "pitilessly beaten." "He received so many wounds on his whole body that even the malefactors were convinced they had killed him, and shouting 'vivat, we killed a Jew' they departed." Many others were beaten before French officers dispersed the crowd. Jewish notables complained of antisemitic propaganda roiling Skierniewice. The police chief agreed that Kuperman was innocent and that no one disguised himself as a gendarme but refused Jewish pleas to announce this publicly. "The mood in town is nervous, Jews live in fear."

Haller's Justice Division investigated the incident, finding it began when troops, bent on "soldierly jokes" (żołnierskich figlów), accosted an "Israelite," who responded by "scuffling." To his aid came a "would-be gendarme (disguised Jew)," who fired his revolver. A group of "unsober" Hallerites piled on the imposter, now deviously in civilian dress, and "severely injured him." He had arrived from Łódź with much money, earmarked "for unknown purposes." The judicial officer concluded: "I

---

[26] Here and below: CAW. File no. I.123.1.321: C (June 29, 1919).

consider the whole affair the result of machinations of certain leftist insurrectionary groups. It undoubtedly must be judged a provocation."[27] On display here is the paranoid – and conveniently self-justifying – idea that any opposition by government agents to street-level antisemitism was ipso facto evidence of state subversion or infiltration, whether by "Jewish leftists" or through bribery of "Jewish uncles."

Hallerites' "pranks" and "jokes," well documented around Warsaw in May and June, targeted Jews everywhere. In eastern Chełm, they "burst into the prayer-house and beat Jews there." They "stabbed and ripped the prayer-books with their bayonets." On the streets, they tormented two Christians "by mistake because of their Jewish appearance." A "people's commissar calmed the situation, but Jews' mood was "anxious."[28] A Berlin silk merchant witnessed Hallerites rampaging near Częstochowa. "They stabbed men in their beards, cut them with knives and shears and tore them off with main force. I saw repeatedly beards with strips of flesh and blood in the soldiers' hands." French and British officers standing on train platforms (allegedly) watched passively.

In Częstochowa, pogrom raged earlier the same day, claiming six Jewish lives and wounding 1,000 (as some thought). A Polish doctor ordered a Jewish medic to tend the injured. Fearing to enter the doctor's house alone, he went with a policeman. When the crowd saw them, it assumed the medic was under arrest and attacked "and tore him in pieces." The Committee for the East reported that "five terribly disfigured" bodies lay in the Jewish hospital, "face and body are mutilated beyond recognition." "Terrible scenes were enacted" at a kosher slaughterhouse and synagogue. (German) Jewish fears seemingly inflated these accounts, but they confirm what pogromists' words and deeds frequently revealed, that over anti-Jewish tumults hung shadows of chilling ominousness.[29]

Haller soldiers arrived in Kraków in June and, according to Zionist reports, launched together with a civilian mob a three-day rampage of plunder, injuring some seventy people, including policeman. Zionists believed their leader rabbi Thon's intervention with General Haller stopped the pogrom.[30] In its midst, a "huge crowd" gathered before the Chamber of Commerce, protesting high prices. A woman insulted authorities "because they care nothing for poor people, while Jews have

---

[27] Ibid., L (June 27, 1919). In July 1919, Hallerites plied their anti-Jewish ways in Łódź, prompting the city council to denounce "soldierly license." But a policeman noted that for three weeks city officials took no steps to curb the troops' "pranks." CAW. File I.123.1.321: B (July 6 and 22, 1919).

[28] CZA. Z3/181 (n.d.), Chelm.   [29] Ibid., L6/119 (n.d.); L6/116 (June 3 and 11, 1919).

[30] Ibid., L6/116 (June 10–12, 1919).

everything." Tumult ensued, and a policeman arrested her, only to be assaulted and disarmed by two Hallerites. This happened before ex-legionnaire Słomiany's stationary shop. Protecting his glass windows, he cried out, "the best thing would be to put a mine under these Jewish-uncle policemen and blow them sky-high." These words, recorded by police, led to charges against Słomiany of endangering public order. Interrogated, he backtracked, saying he meant that the tumult makers should be blown up. In trial, he was – improbably – found innocent. Yet, in Kraków at least, condemning officials as "Jewish uncles" was an actionable offense.[31]

Hallerites were not the only uniformed pogromists. An eyewitness wrote to Berlin's Zionists from industrial Dąbrowa Góra, where Polish workers attempted a general strike "demanding bread from the present reactionary government." Mounted army troops charged them. In the ensuing fight, Jewish-born officer Dr. Turin was killed. Rumor spread that Jews had murdered him "because he joined the Polish army." Thanks to previous antisemitic agitation, "it was understood that the long yearned-for moment had arrived to break loose against Jews." It would have been hypocrisy's summit for Polish soldiers to plunder Jews with a fallen Jewish comrade's name on their lips. "The district commander declared himself helpless in face of the degenerate soldiery and, since they refused to obey, wanted to resign." Some 100 Jews suffered broken bones and head cuts. "Thanks to the local militia's admittedly late inter-vention under Police Chief Lipiński, the plundering masses could be dispersed," but they returned next day, when a butcher trying with police escort to recover his wares was murdered by the "pogroming soldiers."[32] Here local police moved against the army just as, occasionally, the regular army confronted Haller troops. As these pages show, there was more than one Chief Lipiński, but still too few.[33]

Military Pogroms' Eastward Trail

Germany's withdrawal from the lands between ethnographic Poland and historic Muscovy opened them to many-sided claims by local nationalists of various ideological stripes – Lithuanian, Belarusian, Ukrainian – along-side eastward-marching Polish expansionists and westward-marching Bolsheviks. Memories of Poland's 1772 borders fired Piłsudskiites' minds. They aimed to annex East Galicia, the Wilno region, western Belarus, and, beyond that, to construct a wall of friendly satellites, from

---

[31] SOKKr. S8/II. J 2491/20, fos. 1–11 (June 22, 1919 et seq.).
[32] CZA, Z3/181 (March 1919).   [33] Ibid., L6/116: *Zeitschrift K. f.d. O.* (June 11, 1919).

right-bank Ukraine through eastern Belarus to Lithuania and its northern Baltic neighbors, blocking Russian expansion and making of Poland (once again) an East European imperium.

Polish-Bolshevik clashes flared over Wilno and Belarus from December 1918. By mid-April 1919, Piłsudski's troops commanded Belarusian Pinsk and Lithuanian-claimed Wilno. An offensive launched in May to seize East Galicia from its wobbly West Ukrainian Republican rulers ended victoriously in July. Farther east, Piłsudski palavered with Russian Whites and anti-Bolshevik Ukrainians before full-scale Polish-Soviet War erupted in April 1920. The Poles won and lost Kiev, were driven back to Warsaw's suburbs, and then counterattacked to repel the Russians and reach an October 1920 ceasefire. At Riga in March 1921, internationally brokered peace divided Ukraine and Belarus between Poland and Russia. In October 1921, Poland unilaterally tore Wilno from Lithuanians' ill-armed hands.

These violence-soaked power plays rained intermittent misery on Jews in every army's and every armed band's path. The farther east Polish armies moved, the less Polish and more Litwak-like or Russian or Ukrainian were the Jews they encountered. The fewer they saw of eastern-settled Poles – themselves a vulnerable minority widely hated in their upper echelons for their ancient landed property, higher education, haughty pretensions, and Catholic religion – the fewer were the partisans of Polish expansion who might be inclined on political grounds to defend Jews as neighbors and fellow citizens. Some borderland Poles joined with Bolsheviks, striving to establish multiethnic communist regimes to Poland's east and prepared to clasp comrades' hands in erecting a revolutionary communist state in Warsaw itself, once Piłsudskiites, Dmowskiites, clericalists, and so-called rich-peasant kulaks had been marched into history's lumber room.

Beyond the zone of contiguous Polish settlement – which ended on a north-south line roughly from Białystok through Brest-Litovsk to Przemyśl – the greatest Polish threat to Jews were soldiers. These acted more brutally for being invaders who would eventually withdraw westward and for seeing eastern borderland Jews as Bolsheviks or, at best, Polonophobic enemies. Scruples restraining violence were narrower, room for murderous fantasy ampler.

The Berlin ZO reported, in stilted English, that after Polish soldiery occupied East Galician Stryj in May 1919,

especially on Sabbat days, the Jews are the object of regular chases, their temples are surrounded, and the Jews in their praying costumes are dragged to work ... The Poles consider every Jew as a Bolshevist, which must be destroyed.

Symbolically, such abuses – undoubtedly widespread – both stopped Judaism's practice and "productivized" Jews, forcing them into hard physical labor and so satisfying many Christian Poles' deep village-derived wish that Jews ought to work as work should be done and that the commercial sphere of capitalist circulation – Jews' sphere – should cease to exist.[34]

In Wilno, where in early 1919 a fragile but violent pro-Bolshevik regime had prevailed against both Polish-leaning and Lithuanian-friendly Christians and Jews, Polish troops victoriously irrupted in mid-April. Lieutenant Wollstein had previously written to Berlin:

Terrible, total chaos rules Jewish life. The [leftist parties] Bund, Poalei Zion, and United Socialists [having withdrawn from the city council] fall ever more into Bolshevism's tow. The Bund has declared for dictatorship of laboring masses. Common people grow daily more Bolshevist. Zionism, seen as reactionary, loses ever more ground. [Freedom of speech and assembly persist, but were] under intellectual pressure generated by fear of *Bolschewiki*.

Zionist leaders sided with Lithuanians rather than Poles, seeing a chance to achieve "Jewish-national autonomy" (as independent Lithuania promised its Jews, without fully delivering).[35]

Before Piłsudski's personal arrival in Wilno, a military pogrom, spearheaded by Haller's "Poznanians," plundered the large Jewish population for several days. Another pogrom ravaged Jews in Lida, where numerous able-bodied men from Wilno were interned. Zionists reported fifty-four Jews murdered in Wilno, thirty-five in Lida. Some Catholic Poles were lynched as Bolsheviks. A German Jewish eyewitness wrote that Hallerites whipped Jews to force 1,500-ruble ransoms from them. Wilno's Jewish religious commune declared itself "shattered by insults (dishonorings), robberies and murders." Jews' "personal inviolability, Jewish honor, Jewish property" must be secured.[36]

London's ZO exaggeratedly wired New York that 2,200 Jews died in the Wilno-Lida pogroms. After Piłsudski's Wilno entry, four Jewish businessmen gained city council seats, "to make [the] public believe Polish sympathy. Nevertheless, Poles boycott Jews, sell no foodstuffs, so that

[34] Ibid., A126/560 (n.d.).   [35] Ibid., L6/113 (January 17, 1919).
[36] Ibid., L6/118 (May 6, 1919). Valuable evidence of Russian archival provenance on the Wilno and Lida pogroms is offered in Sarunas Liekis et al., "Three Documents on Anti-Jewish Violence in the Eastern Kresy during the Polish-Soviet Conflict," *Polin*, vol. 14 (2001), 116–49. Deaths are reported at sixty and thirty-eight, respectively. Polish military authorities rejected charges of pogrom atrocities. On Wilno, see Joanna Gierowska-Kałłaur, "Żydzi i Polacy na Wileńszczyźnie i Grodzieńszczyźnie w latach 1919–1920," in Jasiewicz, ed., *Świat niepożegnany*, 354–63; Andriej Czerniakiewicz, "Ekcesy antyżydowskie wojsk polskich na Kresach Północno-Wschodnich RP (IV-VIII 1919 roku)," in Jasiewicz, ed., *Świat niepożegnany*, 573–80.

terrible famine [prevails]. Afterwards town bombarded by Bolsheviks who threatened [to] kill whole bourgeoisie." Copenhagen's ZO informed New York's Joint Distribution Committee that "the Polish pogrom-press reported that the Jews had murdered a certain Polish officer, and had cut out his heart."

The JDC's Paris office's Harriet Loewenstein cabled New York, saying Wilno Jews had received no bread for eight weeks. Only American aid offered hope: "250,000 Mks left in city with reliable person for emergency relief." People "are actually starving. They are reduced to making soup from poison ivy ... Children in public institutions look like skeletons." Ten trucks were dispatched from Paris carrying large shipments of US government hardtack. "Situation in Lithuania and White Russia already visited, so much more terrible than had been deemed possible."[37] Amid such lengthening Eastern shadows, the Polish army committed an infamous atrocity in Pinsk.

Pinsk: Massacre by Insecure Conquerors

On April 5, a warm and sunny Saturday Sabbath-evening, twenty-nine-year-old Major Aleksander-Jerzy Łuczyński, Polish army commander in recently conquered Belarusian Pinsk, ordered thirty-five Jews, mostly young Zionists, to be shot in automobile headlights against a Catholic convent wall. News of this cruel deed worsened in Western opinion new Poland's antisemitic reputation and mocked its claim that by pushing eastward at Bolshevik expense, it was upholding Christian civilization.[38]

Pinsk was a politically significant eastern borderland town that was largely Jewish, with but a small Polish population, and many Orthodox Christians of Russian or Belarusian mentality. In 1910 it counted 36,400 souls. Wartime deportations and flights from Pinsk's war zone reduced this number in 1921 to 23,497, but the Jewish proportion of some 75

---

[37] JDC, AR 19/21 188 (Poland), fos. 47–48, 52, 59–60 (April 30, May 14–18, 1919). On Wilno-Lida, see also CZA. Z3/181 (May 13, 1919); L6/119, "cables"; L6/118 (May 9, 1919).

[38] Przemysław Różański, *Stany Zjednoczone wobec kwestii żydowskiej w Polsce 1918–1921* (Gdańsk: Wydawnictwo Uniwersytetu Gdańskiego, 2007); Carole Fink, *Defending the Rights of Others: The Great Powers, the Jews, and International Minority Protection, 1878–1938* (New York, NY: Cambridge University Press, 2004), chap. 6 (on Pinsk), and *passim*; Sam Johnson, *Pogroms, Peasants, Jews: Britain and Eastern Europe's 'Jewish Question', 1867–1925* (Houndmills: Palgrave Macmillan, 2011), chaps. 4, 6, and 7; Jerzy Tomaszewski, "Pińsk, Saturday 5 April 1919," *Polin*, vol. 1 (1986), 227–51; Józef Lewandowski, "History and Myth: Pińsk, April 1919," *Polin*, vol. 2 (1987), 50–72; Czerniakiewicz, "Ekcesy." These works aim to establish an empirically sound political narrative and do not pose these pages' interpretive challenges.

percent held steady. As elsewhere west of historic Muscovite lands, the numerous estate owners in the surrounding countryside were largely Polish aristocrats and gentry, still served by Jews. But here, unlike in the former Congress Kingdom and Galicia, there were few Polonized – let alone Polonophile – Jews.[39]

The Brest-Litovsk treaty fated Pinsk to German-satellite Ukrainian rule, but as the fallen Kaiser's army withdrew, Bolshevik forces in January 1919 captured the war-plagued town, only to lose it to east-ward-charging Poles. Yet they could not drive the Red army from Pinsk's hinterland, and as April arrived, fear of Soviet engulfment stalked Polish minds. In the shooting's aftermath, both higher military authorities and a delegation of Sejm deputies, including Jewish militants Itzhak Grünbaum and Noach Prylucki, gathered evidence in Pinsk from perpe-trators, victims, and other witnesses. Eventually the massacre figured in reports by US government emissary Henry Morgenthau, British Jewish investigator Sir Stewart Samuel, and the Socialist International.[40]

Voices testifying before the Sejm deputies and military investigators have been heard only fragmentarily in earlier historiography and then mostly as witnesses to the army's antisemitism, brutality, and alibis.[41] Here they will speak – names bureaucratically Polonized – by way of self-revelation, for they are extraordinarily evocative of the war-torn borderlands and of their inhabitants' incommensurable, often uncom-prehending, and only rarely conciliatory mentalities. Nowhere in this book's pages are opposing realities as Poles and Jews perceived them more starkly – and subjectively – displayed.[42] The interpretational chal-lenge is to draw from traumatized, self-defensive, and self-righteous testimony an explanation – above all, of murdering unarmed and unag-gressive Zionists in the midst of an anti-Bolshevik war – that rises above empirically reliable narrative truth (though such narratives are elusive) to insight into culturally embedded symbolic behavior.

---

[39] www.sztetl.org.pl/pl/article/pinsk/6,demografia.

[40] National Polish Committee of America, *The Jews in Poland: Official Reports of the American and British Investigating Missions* (Chicago, IL: American Commission to Negotiate Peace, 1920).

[41] Azriel Shohet, *The Jews of Pinsk, 1881 to 1941* (Stanford, CA: University of California Press, 2012 [Hebrew original: 1977]), 368–421.

[42] CZA, A127/75. This file contains testimony given before both an investigative commis-sion of the national parliament (Sejm) and one formed by the Polish army. Further details are provided below. Copies of the original Polish-language testimony and other proceed-ings of the Pinsk inquiries comprise some 150 pages in this CZA file. The Sejm Commission's members: Kowalczuk, Prylucki, Grünbaum, Szymczak, Mizera, Zagórski, and Wróblewski. In existing literature, Shohet alone consulted this rich source, though with legalistic questions alone in mind.

Women Witnesses

Women were drawn into the maelstrom and, unlike executed men, survived to tell of it. Thirty-eight-year-old Szejna Sliwka, "Jewess," presided over a Zionists' meeting center and cafeteria in the Jewish People's Home (*Beit Ha'am*). Here an April 5 meeting, approved by municipal authorities, convened members of the town's Jewish cooperatives. They aimed to decide how money delivered by the JDC's American agent Baruch/ Barnet Zuckerman on behalf of Pinsk Jews' American relatives should reach appointed hands. Zuckerman had brought 1,000-mark notes, which "no one in town could exchange for smaller sums." Decisions also loomed about supplying the poor with matzo flour for impending Passover – time-worn season for Easter-conscious Christian anti-Judaic aggressions. Some hundreds were present, elders in one room, youths in another.

Polish soldiers burst in. It was thought they were seizing people for compulsory labor. Sliwka said, "soldiers pried open buffet doors and took pastries." They forced those present to raise their hands and show papers, rifle butting resisters and stealing indignant Kobrynski's wallet with 1,000 rubles. "Seeing the affair could get very serious," his colleagues muffled him.

Though they found nothing incriminating, soldiers led them off. On the street, "an officer appeared who reviled the arrestees, expressing himself very filthily about the women at the rear, saying 'shoot them all.' He kicked them, including me." At the police station Sliwka learned the officer was a doctor (he was Catholic priest Bukraba's brother). Taken in the dark to a wall to be shot, she heard the order "release women and old men."

When they told me to leave the wall I grasped my neighbor's hand, I wanted to lead him away, to rescue him, but I was hit on the hand, stumbled and fell. A soldier lifted me up. My muff also fell, and the soldier picked it up and gave it to me.[43]

An automobile drew up, its lights illuminating the scene. They were told in Russian "to say your last words and pray." She thought this meant they should plead for mercy. One man stepped forward and asked to be spared, since he was crippled and cared for an old father. Another also pleaded, "but the others asked for nothing. They prayed." At the last words of the Hebrew prayer at death, "Hear, O Israel" (*Szma Israel*), the soldiers fired. "We were forbidden to scream, cry, or speak. They made us stand in fours, looking straight ahead to see what was happening to our

[43] Sliwka's testimony: CZA, A127/75, "Protokół posiedzenia z d. 28 kwietnia 1919 r. w Pińsku," fos. 33–39 (hereafter: Sejm Commission).

brothers." Miss Syma Holcman collapsed, and a soldier told her in Russian to get up or he would shoot her, except it would be a wasted bullet. The onlookers were then marched to prison, robbed on the way of wallets and watches. She said she had nothing, "though I had with me money and jewelry. The whole night we sat, clothed, waiting for them to lead us to our death."

Next day she was taken to a room, told to undress, and interrogated. What was she doing at People's Home? "I was ordered to pull down my panties, lie on a narrow bench, and received four blows from something like a knout [*nahajka*]. During the beating the presiding officer left the room." The women after her suffered worse beatings. "I could neither lie nor sit." A soldier administered the blows, "another holding a revolver threatening to shoot if the victim cried out." At midnight soldiers appeared, telling them in Russian to pray, for they would be shot at dawn. "The girls began to cry. They started to calm us, saying they were joking."

She admitted to Sejm investigators that she only understood "easy words" in Polish, but they accepted her account. She added that after Pinsk's Polish conquest, shops opened, only to close as plundering began. In the ensuing pogrom, soldiers killed Prizant, "a strong old man" who threw two soldiers from his house but was shot by a third. She closed, saying "I have no intention of leaving Pinsk."

Elka Milecka, twenty-five, was an unmarried Jewish dentist and Zionist. On April 5 she went to People's Home to see if two male relatives were to receive American money transfers. Awaiting each were 190 marks. She recalled that Germans had sanctioned the Jewish center's creation, which stayed open under Ukrainians and Bolsheviks. Polish occupiers ordered removal of all Hebrew or Russian inscriptions. Even Christian Poles frequented the library. She heard a shot fired, and then arrests began. "We walked the street with no fear, for we felt no guilt." At People's Home, soldiers released those who gave them money, but most refused, believing themselves innocent.

The soldiers beat us with rifle-butts, without regard for age or sex. Some men left the field hospital, one a doctor, priest Bukraba's brother, who asked the soldiers "what kind of gang is this?" Told they were "Bolsheviks," he said "shoot every last one." Upon these words the soldiers began beating us really terribly. They ordered us to run at a gallop.[44]

At the police station her twelve rubles were taken. "Then came a civilian gentleman, working in headquarters, who wanted to pull off one of the

---

[44] Milecka's testimony: ibid., fos. 8–13, 15.

arrestees' boots, but the officer said, 'never mind about that now.'" They were lined up against the convent wall. People tried to show legitimizing papers – a pass to Warsaw, "a testimony from apothecary shop owner Mrs. Wasanska that [the bearer] was an honorable non-partisan person." But the commanding officer didn't read it. "Seeing that my girl-friend fainted, and that they dragged her off to the side, I followed on my own initiative." A soldier tried stopping her, but another said, "you're a lady, you may pass."

As the victims recited the pre-death prayer, an officer cynically asked, "what are they singing, the Marseillaise?" Another said, "no, it's a Jewish prayer." Mr. Krasilszczyk was strolling nearby with witness's friend Miss Polak. "He was seized, joined with us, and shot without even knowing why." The victims did not weep, neither were they bound or blindfolded, but "stood facing the soldiers."

Jail officials treated survivors "very well," soldiers "very badly." Milecka recalled officers entering their cell with electric lanterns, addressing them "ironically" in Russian as "comrades," and announcing impending execution. "The women began to cry." Next day, when ordered to undress to her shirt, stockings, and shoes and lie on the bench, she told them it was "her time" and that she was ill, but yet they beat her. She screamed despite the revolver facing her. "After the punishment they ordered me to take my clothing and propelled me with a kick down the corridor to another room, where I dressed." She joined other women in listening to beaten men's screams. Her father sent an army doctor to her, enabling her jail release earlier than other prisoners.

One prison beater had visited victims' families seeking money to avert punishment. Before release, the gendarmerie chief told of an "American commission's" coming arrival. Should they be asked whether they were beaten, he commanded them to say no, but that one or another had been "hit." Meanwhile he ordered guards to treat them "humanely" (po ludzku), feeding them and getting straw into their narrow cell. Asked by investigators whether arrestees had been wearing "red cocardes," she said no. The "red and beet-colored stamps" found at the Home had been made under Bolshevik occupation for children, Zionist blue-white stamps having been confiscated as "counter-revolutionary."

Unmarried, "non-partisan" schoolteacher Mela German, twenty-six, was present at People's Home's children's nursery, where they were rehearsing a play for "Easter" (Wielkanoc). Colleague Glojberman, who "knew the poor people very well," was registering them for matzo flour distribution. When soldiers appeared, "we even joked about it, not expecting anything bad." The soldiers, finding cheesecake, "began eating and joking." But then one spied a "Shield of David," bearing multicolored cocardes. He shouted, "what's this?" but ignored their explanations. No one was wearing any such insignias, which had served at a children's fest under the Bolsheviks.

She said Dr. Bukraba asked, "are there no Christians among them? Just Jews? Shoot them all!" Only when soldiers told him they were Bolsheviks did she and other arrestees realize the danger of the their plight. One women, during her prison beating, was asked, "what were they saying at the meeting about the Poles, about the Bolsheviks?" The soon-to-be-executed men, "standing at the wall, wept and pleaded for mercy." "I still have traces of beating on my body."[45]

Polish Commanders' Explanations

Soldierly violence's flare-up at People's Home, bustling with peaceful and beneficent projects, struck the women like a diabolical thunderbolt. Each of them thought fateful choleric Dr. Bukraba's exhortation to massacre. To their voices the parliamentarians juxtaposed those of Pinsk's military masters, led by Major Łuczyński, "commander of 'Kobryń Group' and Pińsk garrison," from Skierniewice near Warsaw, married Roman Catholic.[46] He was struck from Polish occupation's start by "disturbing aspects" of Jewish behavior, especially large bands of Jewish youth on the streets (in this largely Jewish town). "Continually arriving reports of planned attacks on the Polish Army" forced him to constrain civilian behavior. The gendarmerie chief warned him of personal danger. Then, on April 5, he learned of the Poles' nearby military "misfortune suffered in anti-partisan action" – "news that traveled lightning-fast among civilians, as was evident especially in Jewish youth's arrogant behavior." He knew of a "Jewish fighting organization, whose photograph [this will figure below] we possess in which the Jews are all armed, while their banner proclaims revolutionary slogans." Some Jews were said to have fought Polish entry and refused to hand in arms.

At 8:00 PM he heard shots and noise from the main square. He found a "huge crowd of Jews." They were holding up their hands, "and despite soldiers' prohibitions carrying on a lively discussion." They were

[45] German: ibid., fos. 21–24.

[46] Aleksander Jerzy Narbut-Łuczyński (1890–1977), rose from Austrian Polish Legion captain to colonel soon after the Pinsk massacre, later attaining brigadier general rank. He served during World War II under the government-in-exile in France and Britain, later emigrating to the United States. His dense memoirs, *U kresu wędrówki. Wspomnienia* (London: Gryf, 1966), are silent on the Pinsk massacre and his responsibility for it, expressing only his conviction that the Bolshevik foe was aided by Jewish riflemen shooting from dwelling windows and that Pinsk Jews were "hostilely disposed" (191, 199).

exhibiting papers (their claims to JDC payments) pulled from their pockets. They were, he was told, meeting "under pretext of discussing cooperative matters." They had exceeded their time allowance, and soldiers fired shots to force dispersal. Jewish soldiers from the Polish technical company assigned to monitor the meetings "testified that their civilian coreligionists were cooking up a surprise for us." Told of two meetings, of elders and youths barricaded within People's Home, and commanding only a small number of troops, he decided to act to forestall the "planned attack."

Rumors coursed of village-murdered Polish soldiers, "which completed the picture of treachery lurking against us from outside." In discussions with other officers, effectively a "field tribunal," he prescribed arrests and, as for the men, "I ordered them, after collection of their identity papers, to be shot," which then occurred "by automobile light." Civilians were ordered not to watch.

Next day he learned of a Bolshevik captive's testimony claiming Poles' operational plans were known to the Reds and that "revolution in Pinsk" was brewing. "In Pinsk, revolt [powstanie], town in our hands, and in two days power will be ours." JDC representatives Zuckerman and Rykwan had wanted to hold a meeting that day to distribute money, but the town commandant had refused permission. Rykwan returned after the bloody "incident" to the commandant, "very nervous, wanting to leave to him the money's distribution and himself depart, so that he would not be taken, as he said, for a Bolshevik."

Łuczyński took leave on April 7 to travel westward. He added, as further evidence of hostility, that Pinsk Jews boycotted a fund-raiser for the town's largely Polish-manned militia. They also failed to turn street lights on at 5:00 PM but waited until 8:00 PM. Soldiers said, "every one of the participants in the [People's Home] meeting entering the room identified himself conspiratorially by showing a little red banner pinned under his lapel."[47]

Łuczyński embodied military anti-Jewish paranoia, discovering in trivia malevolent design and finding himself in a numerous throng of unfriendly foreign-speaking Jews, highly fearful of ambush. Town commandant Lieutenant Konrad Landsberg, twenty-nine, unmarried scion of Lithuanian Polish landowners, displayed similar suspicions but sought distance from "the incident." He had approved the People's Home meeting in consultation with the Christian cooperative regulator. When

---

[47] Ibid. "Sprawozdanie Komisji Śledczej wyznaczonej z rozkazem Dowódcy Grupy wojsk Podlaskich z dn. 8 kwietnia 1919 r. [consisting of Colonel Strzemieński and four other officers] dla przesłuchania świadków planowego zamachu na wojsko polskie w Pińsku 5. IV.1919 r.," fos. 3–5 (hereafter: Army Commission).

soldiers arrested the eighty suspects, some began "to violently tear up papers." Confiscated Hebrew-language membership cards were translated as "Populist-Socialist Zionist Section of Zionist Youth" or "Populist-Zionist Socialist Youth Party." Landsberg was absent from the "field tribunal" decreeing execution. When American Rykwan sought to relinquish 10,000 marks, he refused, suggesting the priest take them. On April 5 there had been "unusual stirring among Jewish youth" on hearing of the Polish antipartisan unit's "painful defeat." They gathered around city hall "on pretext of standing in line." He saw arrestees tearing up papers.[48]

Pinsk gendarme chief Kazimierz Staromiejski, twenty-seven, collected these papers. One said, in Russian, "slaughter all Poles and officials [*wyrjezatj wsiech poljakow i wsiu właśtj*]." There were proclamations signed by the "Russian Bolshevik Revolutionary Alliance" and rubber stamped in shape of a (seemingly Zionist) shield. News had arrived on massacre day afternoon that "Lieutenant Kóg's [antipartisan] unit had been defeated." Standing at the convent wall, "the arrestees made a terrible clamor." Major Łuczyński told them not to cry out. His officers had decreed "a bullet in every second head." This order was changed to exclude women and elders. When victims were told this was "'your last hour,' one Yid [*żydek*] began singing in Hebrew; others followed him." When the order to shoot was given, they quieted, "stood as if dead," and were shot at fifteen to twenty paces.

The gendarme called himself a Dowborczyk, or veteran of the Polish – formerly tsarist, subsequently anti-Bolshevik – notoriously antisemitic force commanded on civil war-tormented Russian territory by aforementioned General Józef Dowbor-Muśnicki, later army commander in Poznań. Staromiejski was coldly tough minded. Culling execution victims, he didn't exclude men aged thirty-nine to forty-two. "I consider an old man someone who is decrepit and looks like a cripple." As for jail beatings, no one was talking. Addressing Grünbaum, he said, "if I beat you, I would admit it to no one." Before April 5, the Polish-Jewish relationship wasn't "correct" (*akuratny*). If street crowds were ordered to disperse, they looked askance. Now "they run off immediately." Before, when investigations were made at night, "they didn't want to open the door and they turned out the lights. Now they open immediately." An investigator asked about prostitution. Did those women who went with the Germans later go with the Bolsheviks? Staromiejski said one did. "When prostitutes walk the streets, it happens that 4–5 Jewish men are seen with two of them." He didn't know whether Polish soldiers

---

[48] Ibid., fo. 6 (April 9, 1919); Sejm Commission, fos. 2–4 (April 17, 1919).

patronized them. Among gendarmes, there was "one Yid, local agent who reports for us."[49]

Student Josef Szawzis, nineteen, survived to testify to Polish soldiery's brutality and "cold jokes." Stood against the wall, victims were made to hold their hands over their heads for a half hour. They were rifle butted while soldiers "contended among themselves, saying 'I'll shoot this one, I'll shoot that one.'" "We began to scream," whereupon he and others spared shooting were jailed. Later, soldiers took them to the nearby cemetery and, "standing among the graves, they were told, 'we'll give you a few minutes, pray to God before death.'" (The stenographer interjected: "here witness broke down in tears.") A noncommissioned officer said, "we won't be such fools a second time; you dig your own graves." Szawzis was "very anxious." Soldiers demanded arrestees' money and all good shoes. Back in jail he was beaten with *nahajka* and rifle-barrel cleaning rods, three soldiers striking him simultaneously below the waist. As he fell from the bench, they hit his arm, severely injuring it. His doctor (unjustly suspected of pro-Bolshevism) would testify. "I screamed terribly."

Later, the Polish officer present during the beatings told victims he would seek their release at Brześć army headquarters. He it was who warned them not to report having been "pushed around" to the antici-pated "American commission" because "after all, you're better off than those who were shot." He commanded soldier guards to cease abuse and to procure them soup. "Before then we had only eaten what was brought for us from home."[50]

This last-mentioned, unheroic but not altogether inhumane officer was cavalry Commander Stefan Strzemieński, thirty-eight. He testified that unable to decide which prisoners deserved release, he consulted Rabbi Jakob Hurwicz, who, when himself called before the Sejm Commission, had said, "I stake my head on it that none of them could have belonged to a conspiracy aiming to attack the army, stage an uprising, or the like. They were people incapable of that."[51] Strzemieński insisted that the People's Home meeting entailed illegalities, judging by window jumpers and paper destroyers. He defended anti-Zionist accusations of Jewish soldier-spy Kozak, "a very simple and guileless person." Strzemieński mouthed anti-Jewish tropes, referring to a noncommissioned officer as "Pole, Christian of Semitic type." Strzemieński played no role in the "field tribunal." He asked Major Łuczyński why there was no list of the condemned men's names and was told, "considering the difficult situation at the front, the

---

[49] Army Commission (April 27, 1919).
[50] Sejm Commission (April 30 and May 1, 1919).   [51] Ibid. (April 17, 1919).

very thin army ranks in the town itself, which can't even guard the arrestees, and fearing that they will escape and cause even greater turmoil, he was forced to act very fast."[52]

Fajnstejn's Wartime Memories

Among arrestees was "ex-teacher" Abram-Oszer Fajnstejn, fifty-four. He chaired the American money-transfers meeting, where some participants "got excited." Fajnstejn tried to get "outsiders" to leave, but they hung around, some to their ruin. He observed none wearing red cocardes. When a soldier found him with a Russian-language document on exchange rates, he called him a Bolshevik. Fajnstejn said, "we hadn't yet managed to learn Polish well enough to write the document in it." For this he suffered rifle butting. When his group heard the firing squad, they thought a Bolshevik offensive against Pinsk had begun. The soldier guarding him and a young woman wanted to leave, but they took him by the hand and made him stay, fearing that if he disappeared, they would be charged with murder. Fajnstejn repeatedly expressed willingness to die with the others.

A noncommissioned officer offered to release him and five others for 50 rubles each. The arrestees asked why he called them Bolsheviks. He replied, "I was in the prayer-house yesterday. I heard how young Jews said it was necessary to oppose the Polish legions. And I can speak Yiddish well." Fajnstejn dismissed the idea that people would talk openly of armed resistance in a synagogue. "How can you, an educated man, tell me such lies?" The reply was, "hand over the money, you'll all be free." They offered 50 rubles, he wanted 100. "We're poor people." He took one man's wallet and freed them. Fajnstejn was stricken. "All those killed were either my teacher-colleagues, or Zionist-colleagues, or former students." He made a list of the dead: thirty-five plus two unknown men, evidently refugees.

Fajnstejn later testified that 2,400 rubles were paid to release jailed arrestees. At a tailor's house, a reception was held for one of the administrators of the beatings, who was promised a new suit of clothes and a silk dress for his fiancée "if beatings would stop." After Fajnstejn's release, his wife was pressured to surrender her gold ring, "but she broke into tears and would not hand it over." The "pretty daughter" of high-standing people mediated between arrestees and "this gentleman [Strzemieński], involved in the beatings." "Miss Rabinowicz" pleaded successfully that Mr. Kitelman not be shot. She had "acquaintances." It was said that,

---

[52] Ibid. (May 1, 1919).

returning from Warsaw, "she sat with a certain military personage (Strzemieński) who presided over the beatings."

Fajnstejn reported that seventeen arrestees were taken to the cemetery to exhume executed men's bodies so that they, too, after being shot, could be buried with them. But then they "were calmed," learning that the graves needed opening for medical confirmation that all were dead. The Sejm Commission asked about the American money distribution's legality. JDC's Zuckerman told Fajnstejn, "our rabbi visited priest Bukraba and permission was as good as in our pocket." Zuckerman, with the JDC's 100,000 Polish marks, consulted Zionist notables and Rabbi Hurwicz on their distribution.[53]

Fajnstejn recalled Pinsk under Bolshevik occupation. The Reds' first demand was for 250,000 rubles, mainly from Jews. The sum being undeliverable, hostages were taken. A 45,000-ruble bribe was paid to "Commissar Morawczyk, Jew, to discourage further levies or reduce them." At first, Jews' relation to Bolsheviks was "undefined."

Later we convinced ourselves that among them terrible chaos ruled. Every few days officials changed, one even arresting the other. There was no order. [No one initially greeted Bolsheviks. On the third day he watched a Jewish gathering from afar.] Bolsheviks (some 50 raggedy soldiers) marched to [the Jewish Pinskers'] music, behind them a crowd of adolescents with red banners with inscriptions . . . Then came the Bund's flag in the Jewish language and Poalej Sion's likewise. I was indignant over Jewish youth's participation. In the synagogue that day, after prayer, I complained, saying "are you crazy?" since I knew that in Russia all the Jewish socialist parties opposed Bolsheviks, and I read in the newspapers about Bolshevik terror's atrocities.[54]

The youth said they feared repression after the Bolsheviks announced that all workers' parties must participate.

Bolshevik relations with local workers worsened. Their delegates council was closed. Protests arose against "imported instructors." Hebrew teachers trying to organize learned that "he who accepts communism may belong, others not." So they all went home. Young Zionists had nothing to do with Bolsheviks. They held a meeting "where Rudenski from Minsk opposed the Bolsheviks," even charging that in Moscow communist voices called for pogroms ("*gremit jewrejew*"). A local speaker who seconded this accusation in a "fiery speech" was later shot. People were also against Bolshevism because it meant hunger.

Fajnstejn, who was away when the Poles arrived, had been a Zionist, he said, since 1882 (in 1881 pogroms' aftermath). When Poles arrested him, "I explained I was a house owner, therefore cannot be a Bolshevik." Jews'

---

[53] Army Commission (April 9, 1919).   [54] Sejm Commission (April 27, 1919), fos. 41ff.

relations to the Polish army, he said ironically (or cynically), were "normal. They only complained that soldiers fell on them at night and robbed them."

The notorious criminal Kopel, droshky-driver, who couldn't even sign his name, was the only local resident who joined the Bolsheviks, and he ran the Cheka [*czrezwyczajka*]. He terrorized everybody, ordered requisitions, robbed, etc. I categorically testify that no one in Pinsk joined or favored the Bolsheviks. At least no one I know. [They didn't even pay municipal workers' wages.]

German occupiers, he remembered, trying to reduce Pinsk's provisioning, had deported some 12,000 Jews and 700 Christians. Fajnstejn remembered how Jews raised 60,000 rubles to aid expellees, including a few thousand for Christians. Jews were against the Germans, whatever people might say. Bolshevik Commissar Lucki and all other commissars were outsiders. At People's House library, if a newspaper turned up by chance, "as many as fifty people would gather, tear it into pieces so that a few people could read each bit." Shown the photograph of the Bundist armed group, he identified one man who had been gone for twelve years, from which he concluded that the photo dated from the 1905 Revolution.

On "the day of catastrophe" two Jewish youths – both among the executed – had been seized for compulsory labor. "They were forced to gather up manure with their hands." A Jewish soldier overheard their laments and took them to an officer, saying they were Bolsheviks who told him the Red Army would soon liberate them. For this they were sentenced to death. But American Red Cross major Frączak – aiming, evidently, to raise money to bribe the Polish authorities to release the two arrestees – agreed to discuss their fate with merchant Harbuz, at whose house Frączak received 500 rubles for the young men's lives. He later returned, saying it was too little for two lives, and departed with 1,000 more rubles. To this coldly Machiavellian tale officer Frączak, evidently pressured by the investigative commission for his extortionate behavior, penned a note saying that 500 Duma rubles would be donated to "the neediest."[55]

Fajnstejn continued: Officer Bielecki, who received the additional thousand rubles, had previously been "cinematographer" at Pinsk's *kasyno*. "He squandered his money and with that which he robbed from the unfortunate youths covered the deficit."[56] These were not the first innocents whose deaths eased soldierly debt. Altogether, Fajnstejn painted a Balzacian picture (excepting massacre victims) of self-interest,

[55] Cf. JDC. AR 19/21, No. 188 (Poland). Pinsk Massacre, fo. 24.
[56] CZA. A127/75: Fajnstejn responding to Grünbaum (n.d. [May 1919]).

fear, pride, and greed animating both soldiers and civilians, Jews and Christians, as they stood in circumambient death's shadow.

Tribulations of Jewish Common Folk

Humbler witnesses testified to fate's vagaries at humanity's street level, mostly tragic but not without instances of decency. Widow Hercelman, forty-nine, lost eighteen-year-old son Josef. "He lived from giving Hebrew lessons and supported me." He aimed to go to Palestine. When he left for People's Home, he had with him 436 tsarist rubles [and] four shields of David inscribed with "Sion," as well as one on his chest. "He was my one and only caretaker, so he had the money with him." The stenographer added: "because of severe attack of hysteria, interrogation was interrupted."[57]

Mowsza Bregman's perished son Israel, twenty-three, long-standing Zionist, held a travel pass to Warsaw, which seemingly made it safer for him to possess money, so various of his comrades entrusted him with their now-vanished cash. Mordka Fryman, seventy-seven, lost two sons. Mowsza, forty-three, owned an apothecary's shop. Honorable and religious, he was invited to the People's Home meeting. Chaim, twenty-seven, had a watch store and went to People's Home to ask for matzo flour for a poor colleague. A Zionist, he carried 9,030 rubles. Mowsza's wife, Tauba, went with her husband to donate linen for the poor. He forgot that he had been invited to the Zionist cooperative meeting and went late. "My husband was an extremely peaceful man, even timorous."

Zelik Reżnik, fifty, druggist, knew seven executed men personally. "They were very honest people, having nothing to do with Bolshevism. They were Zionists." He couldn't identify Bolsheviks "because I'm non-partisan." He knew Zionists because "I'm interested in Palestine." He refused a signature because it was Sabbath. Abram Feldman, seventy-five, lost son Fyszel, forty. Abram had long farmed a Polish-owned property, while Fyszel leased *pan* Skirmunt's estate. The landowners could have vouched for Fyszel, as could have another estate owner too, living in Pinsk. "When she learned yesterday of his death, she clapped her hand on her head, saying: 'why wasn't she told he had been arrested,' she would have rescued him."[58]

Josef Burman, unemployed teacher, was going to the meeting when he and others were pressed into compulsory labor sawing wood. They asked to be released, "since it was Sabbath and they were wearing clean clothes,

---

[57] Army Commission (April 9, 1919).
[58] Sejm Commission, fo. 118 (April 27–28, 1919).

and his brother-in-law was a very religious man," but in vain. They proceeded to the People's Home, searching for rations, "for we had no more bread." As they later stood, hands up, they laughed when a soldier, discovering a shield of Davis, said it was a "Bolshevik insignia." They didn't believe they would be shot but were only being frightened. Finally, he asked to be spared because of his small children and was waved away.

They tormented me in jail. I was beaten on the naked body until I fainted. During the beating I lay on the bench, and one man held my head between his legs. My pants were down, shirt raised. I don't know what I was beaten with, I think it was iron. My buttocks were so swollen I couldn't walk for three days, I walked like a cripple, and couldn't sit. Now there are no more traces.[59]

Taken to the cemetery and told to dig a pit, they began to recite "*Szma Israel*." But a policeman calmed them, saying if they hadn't been shot on Saturday they wouldn't be on Sunday.

Gravedigger Morduch Wajnberg, fifty, told of how gendarme Chief Sell – "a German" (bilingual Pole from West Prussia) – warned him on massacre night, "stay home, on the street they'll kill you." Wajnberg later asked tailor Miller to plead with the chief that prisoners not be beaten. Miller replied, "I'm a poor man, I can't ask the chief without money." Wajnberg gave him 100 rubles. Later they collected money for poor arrestees' families, including for matzo.[60]

Judel Ajzenberg, fifty-seven, was a large-estate tenant farmer, three months' resident in Pinsk. He found himself chairing the cooperative meeting. "Previously I lived in the country and didn't take part in social life." At People's Home, many protests arose against compulsory labor. Polish soldiers caught them, saying, "give us 1–2 rubles, we'll let you go." They asked Ajzenberg for 5 rubles, although he was too old to work. He refused. They followed him home, but soldiers living there protected him. Since then, authorities forbade such practices.

Under the Bolsheviks, "as an estate-lessee and thus a *burżuj* I feared to leave my dwelling." He saw Bolshevik troops "singing in Russian as they walked, and behind them a mass of children and rabble." He and his acquaintances were glad to see Poles arrive and get rid of "those animals." They feared retreating Bolsheviks would plunder them, but it was Poles who did so, saying "give us bread." "I was afraid. I immediately took out bread and gave it to them. I said we were glad because Poles were 'our own people' [*swoi ludi*]. I always had dealings with [Polish] gentlemen. I traveled to Warsaw." Yet, for two days Polish soldiers robbed. Anti-Bolshevik Ajzenberg, a brave and resourceful old man, accustomed to

[59] Ibid. (May 2, 1919).   [60] Ibid.

interactions with well-mannered Polish gentry, was shocked and fearful of unaccustomed Polish violence.[61]

Michel Kerman, sixteen, worked with his cabinetmaker father. A policeman awakened them early Sunday morning, ordering his father to get a shovel "and go bury your comrades, or I'll shoot you." With his mother sick with typhus, Michel agreed to go instead, and with fifteen other Jews found thirty-seven bodies at the convent wall. Soldier guards took victims' boots, especially if German, as well as his own. Gravediggers saw that several victims were still alive. One struggled to his feet and cried, "for God's sake, don't shoot." He tried to run but was halted and shot. Another they counseled, "don't move. We'll save you," but his legs moved and the guards messily killed him, as they did unfortunate young Rolnik, stomach perforated, at grave's edge. Bodies were doused with carbolic acid. On Saturday evening, as he went to feed their cow, Kerman had heard from the square cries not to shoot, "weeping," and then salvos. Jankiel Kuszner, thirty-one, carter, was also forced to bury the dead. "I was sick at heart, because I saw many acquaintances among the corpses ... I don't read newspapers, don't respect them. I respect a bottle of beer." He could read Yiddish. "At the square, I wept."[62]

Polish Policemen's Views

Pinsk police Chief Józef Konarski, twenty-six, Roman Catholic, spoke knowingly of Pinsk's political minefield. Uninvolved in the massacre, he thought that long-standing antagonisms between Jews and Christians, Orthodox and Catholic, worsened under German occupation because Jews and Germans came to "understandings." German-ordered evacuations embittered especially the Orthodox, politically least influential. People knew too of "commercial abuses": misappropriation of valuable requisitioned materials – Ukrainian copper, local hemp. The Officers' Legion (*Legja oficerska*), an irregular armed force now cooperating with Poland, had headed Pinsk's pre-Bolshevik Ukrainian occupation. It consisted mainly of Russian officers, alongside some Poles.

Bolsheviks, aided by local people, stormed into Pinsk earlier than negotiations with retreating Germans had foreseen. Reds arrested Ukrainian officials, while Ukrainians and Germans fought back for a day, summarily executing Pinskers as "local Bolshevik fighters," whose bodies lay in the streets for three days. At their burial, "there were a thousand girls, the whole youth except for Christians. There was Bolshevik music." Bund and Poale Zion participated. There were eight

---

[61] Ibid. (April 28, 1919).   [62] Ibid. (April 27, 1919).

dead, including three Jewish fighters. "The blue-white banner with the star of Zion was there too – I saw it with my own eyes." This event worsened attitudes toward Jews, who thus showed pro-Bolshevik sympathies, as did the Jewish-led "barbarous Bolshevik attack on the Church." Clerics protested to the Bolsheviks, who condemned a Jew to death, though Konarski did not know if execution followed.

When Bolsheviks fled Pinsk, compromised persons went along, including Gotlib, people's militia's chief, whose mother operated a restaurant; Litwin, a blind man and well-known Jewish speaker, who ran (unsuccessfully) the employment bureau; Rubacha, a city official and Cheka functionary; and another Rubacha, "called *Palacz* [Arsonist], who apparently executed the Bolshevik court's sentences." Konarski didn't know how many members of the "Communists' Club" there were, but they were "exclusively of the local Jewish population, except for Christian students Jakubowski, non-local, and Goreglat, Russian, artists' committee president. These two [non-Jews] were Bolshevism's pillars."

Under the Germans, "entertainments, masked balls were staged, under unknown direction, at the *kasyno*, with considerable earnings." Relative freedom prevailed, allowing Jewish socialists to contest municipal power with previously entrenched conservatives. Under the Reds, "the town was inundated with Bolshevik illegal press [*bibula*]. I assume money for this came from funds gathered at aforementioned entertainments."[63]

Konarski damningly described the massacred men's banner, doubtless sewn under Bolshevik occupation, not as blue-white but "with a red background crossed by two stripes, blue and white, with Hebrew inscriptions above a star of Zion." The guilty fled with Bolsheviks. Those who merely favored them remained – Bundists, United Socialists. A hotel owner's one son had been Chekist, the other a follower of Dr. Serebrjany, "*idealista-bolszewik* – Yid, seemingly." The Bolsheviks permitted formation of a catch-all workers' and artisans' council but dissolved it when elections proved "bourgeois." They appointed their own people "and the peasants swallowed this bait." With Bolsheviks came "a fashion for fur caps."[64]

Wacław Pawliczenko, twenty, Catholic policeman, encountered an older woman crying at police headquarters. Asked why, she said "her son was killed." A soldier replied, "don't cry, there's no reason. Your son was certainly a Bolshevik. They began to speak in Yiddish." Pawliczenko told the soldier – perhaps Jewish, possibly a Yiddish-speaking Pole – to desist. Prison director Dmitri Szyngel, twenty-three, Russian, Orthodox, testified that he released twenty-six arrestees on army command to dig

[63] Ibid. (April 29, 1919).   [64] Ibid. (April 30, 1919).

victims' graves. "It's forbidden to beat people in prison," but gendarmerie orders took precedence.[65]

However tendentious these policemen's testimony, it illuminates the crevices war opened among Pinskers, consuming those who leaped to one or another momentarily wrong side.

Trofimowicz, Orthodox Christian Observer

Principal Orthodox witness before Sejm deputies was Konstanty Trofimowicz, twenty-nine, cooperative manager in Pinsk's Food Provisioning Department. He secured municipal approval of the fatal assembly, addressed it himself, and understood the Yiddish speakers' key points. He defended the twelve to fifteen young Jews in the tea and reading room. It was a well-known locale and not "some sort of secret organization." In his view, soldiers seized Jews there in forced-labor recruitment to collect bribes. He himself was menaced, "taken once for a Jew." After the executions, he "felt somewhat morally responsible," warily asking the town commandant "if he didn't wish to tell me the reason for the arrests and shooting." He later heard, inaccurately, that "soldiers passed by, noticed the meeting, [and] wanted to enter; apparently there were barricades, [and] one soldier was shoved, even wounded."

"I move in all circles, including among Poles." Civilians didn't help retreating Bolsheviks "but were in hiding like me." Asked about the Officers' Legion, now Polish allies, Trofimowicz said, "who they are I don't really know," despite former tsarist officers among them. "They don't know themselves who they are." Some said they heeded Ukrainian leader Petliura; others said White leader Denikin. They were "lovers of war." They mostly said, "we go against Bolsheviks."[66]

Privileged Miss Rabinowicz

A curiously self-absorbed view of the tragedy emerges from testimony of Sonia Rabinowicz, twenty-one, a prosperous merchant's daughter. She witnessed the shootings from afar, seeing "black silhouettes against the convent wall, illuminated by auto lamps." She assumed they were assembled for labor service, but "when we went out to synagogue we heard terrible inhuman cries and gunshots." She knew that Kitelman had pleaded not to be shot, that he was old (fifty), gray, ill, with seven children. "The officer struck him with his *nahajka* so that he would not plead and weep. But when the officer turned away, a soldier approached

---

[65] Ibid. (April 18 and 27, 1919).   [66] Ibid. (April 29, 1919).

him furtively and led him away to those who were to be spared." Fajnstejn
had credited "Miss Rabinowicz," who was the "pretty daughter" he also
mentioned, with rescuing Kitelman. But she made no such claim, saying
that all victims were innocent, being only Zionists.

She admitted her presence at a "reception" seeking prisoners' release to
which not only the senior gendarme supervising beatings was invited but
also – to her surprise – army officers involved in the shootings. "There was
fish, vodka, but no wine. And tea." There was no question, she claimed,
of "rewards" (bribes). Answering Deputy Grünbaum's criticism, she
weakly said she didn't know "people would hold it against me that,
while they were plunged in bereavement for the innocent men's shooting,
I danced at that ball." But she approved its purpose and also, "as an
amateur actress," wanted to go. The gendarme, presumably having
enjoyed his hosts' drinks, walked her home, saying,

'I may be bad [zły], but if they're innocent, I'll see they're freed.' And he said he
was very bad and beat them all. All day families came and wept, and he couldn't
listen. There was no talk at the reception of clothing for the gendarme or a dress
for his fiancée (I know he has a fiancée in Warsaw).

He told her she was similar to his fiancée and couldn't refuse her wishes.
"He said he was a very rich person."

Later she learned that an ensign gendarme had taken 10,000 marks for
prisoner release. She was surprised that the senior gendarme, regarded
"as the worst," bowed to her request to release prisoners. Polish officers
were billeted in her family home, and one accompanied her – presumably
this was cavalryman Strzemieński – on her Warsaw trip. She was allowed
to cross the border at Brześć because "he gave his officer's word that he
knew me and my family, and vouched for me." He said, "it was all the
same to him whether [I] was Jewess, Pole, or Russian."

People thought her family was "making millions" because they billeted
officers and because she and her sister made two trips to Brześć. The
Jewish population didn't like them "because we stroll with officers and
danced at the 'ball' last week" (to benefit the Polish public shelter). No
other Jews attended. She suffered denunciations to army leaders "by Jews
or Polish girls jealous of the great success enjoyed by my younger sister,
more beautiful than I, and myself." In particular, "Rubinsztajnowa is not
beautiful and is a fanatic – pious."

They were glad to offer their large house to Poles entering Pinsk. They
were five people with six rooms. The cavalry officers they hosted protected them from robbery. Bolsheviks had threatened to expel them but
then, considering their sick mother, allowed them to keep the upstairs
rooms. Polish infantrymen plundered her brother-in-law's store of

goods worth 100,000 rubles, but later guards were posted at its doors. Poles' arrival spread fear, people knowing of previous pogroms in Kobryń and elsewhere. The Polish soldiers robbed every house, including those of Russian officers, some Germans, and local Poles. Captain Miennicki told her that nothing could be done to control troops on the first day "because soldiers are hungry, ragged, dirty" and fearful of lingering Bolsheviks. Thus did common soldiers force their will to plunder on lenient masters.

Under Bolshevik occupation, all nationalities and religions were treated equally. "Workers, who under the Germans had no work and suffered terribly, were satisfied with Bolshevik entry, expecting material improvement. They were the littlest people, with nothing to lose." But Bolsheviks delivered no jobs, while prices skyrocketed. People died of hunger. "Disappointed workers were ashamed that in German days they dreamed of Bolshevik arrival, but they said nothing." No one volunteered for the Red army or regretted their retreat.[67]

It seems Sonia Rabinowicz spoke good Polish. Possibly she and her well-cushioned family were assimilationists. Though she attended synagogue, she scorned pious Jewish critics. Did she embody Polonization, lamented by so many Polonophobes worrying over prosperous Jewish families' daughters? Did she read Sienkiewicz and daydream of mustachioed noblemen?[68]

Jewish Soldiers Kozak and Kolkier

Questions of Jewish identity and loyalty arose in interrogation of two Jewish-born Polish soldiers who figured, *perhaps decisively*, in the Pinsk massacre. Daniel Kozak, whom officer Strzemieński had described as "very simple and guileless," was nineteen, born in border town Brześć. Mordka Kolkier, twenty-one, was son of Congress Kingdom Poland's Biała Siedlecka. Neither was a Zionist hero. Kozak described himself as a day laborer. Both were recently inducted volunteer members of a "technical company."

Kozak testified that though he guarded the arrestees, neither he nor other soldiers beat or abused them. On Friday, April 4, he and Kolkier attended Jewish prayers. They heard that "Jews had removed the golden eyes from the Heavenly Mother's image in Pinsk church." Later he learned that the eyes were found during soldierly inspection in a certain Jew's

---

[67] Ibid.
[68] See Yad Vashem Photo Archive, item 5723610, for what is probably a picture of Sonia Rabinowicz (1897–*ca.*1942), taken in the Nazi-established ghetto in Brest-Litovsk.

possession, "who had buried them in a box along with 10,000 Kerensky rubles and tobacco." If true, this story shows that Jews too might seek to disable a rival religion's supernatural magic. Asked in synagogue by two Jews ("bigger than him") about Polish army service, Kozak answered, "no good, rotten, in exercises they call you 'ugly Jewish mug [*żydowska morda*].'" He and Kolkier were taken to People's Home, where (they learned) Zionists would enroll them in the Bolshevik army for 350 rubles monthly. Recruiters were absent. They were given wine and pastry and asked to return next day with their guns, if they wanted to sell them. On April 5, they encountered the big crowd at People's Home, stampeded by soldiers. Asked about evidence of Bolshevism, Kozak said that he saw in a nearby house "scraps of Bolshevik paper," but being illiterate, he could not decipher them. This provoked Prylucki, seemingly, to invoke an obligation of Jewish solidarity. Kozak nervously and incoherently replied, "I know you want to trap me. I know, I already said that Yid holds with Yid [*żydek trzyma za żydek*]."

Kozak said that he and Kolkier went with the two Jews "because I wanted to catch them." They said they had rifles and machine guns, and he wanted to confirm this. The shadowy Jews asked why he wanted to join the Bolsheviks. He replied that they paid better, and "everybody says, 'comrade, comrade [*towaruszcz, towariszcz*].'"

He told the commission: "I have no father. What mother does, what she lives from, I don't know, because I haven't been home for a year ... It's nothing to me, she doesn't feed me." He earlier worked for Germans. "They treated me well. If I didn't bother them, they didn't bother me."

I studied a bit in the cheder. I fell ill with typhus when I was little. Then I went to school. I can't read Yiddish. I don't know how to pray. Now I'm no longer a Yid [*teraz już nie jestem żydkiem*]. [He displayed the cross he wears on his chest.] Three-four days ago I told a soldier I wanted to go over to the Polish religion. Nobody encouraged me. I myself don't want it – I don't want to be a Jew. To the question why I don't want to be a Jew I answer: 'because.' Our courier, to whom I said I wanted to go over to the Polish faith, gave me this cross. To the question, whether since I expressed my wish to go over to the Polish faith, people no longer say to me "You ugly Jewish mug [*żydowska mordo*]," I say: no, they don't say it.[69]

That a poor, ill-educated Jew might call Roman Catholicism the "Polish faith" points again to interchangeability in popular culture of religion and ethnonationality. Kozak's self-conversion to Christianity obviously stemmed from his separation from Judaic practice and wish to escape discriminatory abuse. Some at least of his Christian fellow soldiers welcomed him.

[69] Kozak's testimony: Sejm Commission (April 29, 1919).

Kozak defended their denigration to synagogue Jews of the Polish army, saying "maybe they would say something and I'd go straightaway to headquarters." Prylucki needled him, suggesting that it was his changed faith that got him his present job as lieutenant's orderly, but he countered by saying, "there weren't any others so small and well dressed and well booted as I am. That's why I got the *ordynans* job. It's better to be a guard." He didn't know whether "Kolkier also didn't want to be a Yid." He answered Grünbaum, saying he joined the army in Kobryń because he had nothing to eat. "The Yids in Kobryń are afraid to go to the army. I'm not and I went. If death doesn't come today, it will tomorrow, it's all the same." Jews gave Russians money not to serve and will do the same with Poles. "In Russian times they cut off their fingers."

What was a Bolshevik? "He's a troublemaker [*na grandę idzie*], or he robs." The older men they sat with over wine "looked like robbers." Prefect Wróblewski wondered why Kozak referred to "our army" (assuming only Catholic Poles would speak thus, but Jews never). It was "because I'm no longer a Yid, and if I serve in the Polish army, then it's ours." He reiterated: "I don't want to be a Yid because I don't like them." Wróblewski, addressing Kozak formally (as *pan*), asked if he thought the "Polish faith" was better. "In the army, I see that they're a little better. That's why I went over to the Polish faith." He told no one in his company, which included three other Jews, about his conversion.

Prylucki wondered whether, if Kozak had obtained work and housing from Jews, he would have "rejected Jewishness [*porzuciłby żydowstwo*]." Yes, "I'd rather be a Pole." His stubborn response to another question probing motives for conversion: "my parents loved me." Russian workers had tried to persuade him to embrace their faith. "No one ever told me about Jewish religion's principles." He wanted to accept the "Russian faith," but then the Poles came, so I went over to the Polish faith." And if the Russians returned and threatened to hang him if he did not renounce Catholicism? "Let them hang me." He felt no pity for the executed Pinskers "if they were *bolszewiki*."

Kozak's earlier testimony before the army's investigative commission had confined itself to his and Kolkier's actions on April 4–5 and harmonized with later testimony that we have just examined – except for several significant details. One was that talking over wine and pastry with the robber-like Jewish Bolsheviks on April 4, they told him *they planned to attack the Polish army on the following night.* The other was that when he and Kolkier went to People's Home on Saturday, Jews present fled, and when the two returned with a corporal and other soldiers, *a shot was fired at them.* Almost certainly Kozak was coached to make these (otherwise unmentioned) points, which might have been thought to justify the massacre.[70]

The Sejm Commission's Jewish parliamentarians, understandably, did not like Kozak. In June 1919, the Zionist Club interviewed Henoch Gingold of Kobryń. He knew of Kozak from a friend who employed Kozak's sister as servant. Kozak was a tailor/rag dealer's son. When Germans deported Jews from Brest-Litovsk, Kozak moved to Kobryń, where he worked for them while his mother subsisted on alms. When Kozak lost this job, "he began to frequent the company of thieves." Then he joined the Polish legions. "In Kobryń, Kozak's reputation is very bad."[71]

His partner, Mordka Kolkier, suffered withering appraisal in the Zionist Club by Biała Podlaska resident Chuma Kagan. She heard that after the Pinsk shootings, he "looted the murdered of gold watches, rings with precious stones etc." – and also "many long papers – '*kierenok* [Kerensky ruble notes].'"

He bragged that he lacked for nothing, for they take from Pinsk Jews everything they want and then sell it at high prices. He announced that the legions are an excellent source of enrichment. [He said to Rozenbaum] "join the legions, I vouch you'll have 100,000 marks by Green Holidays [Whitsuntide/Pentecost (*Zielonych Świąt*)]."[72]

Whether an accurate quotation or not, the sentiment – that low-ranking Polish soldiers could enrich themselves through plunder – must have seemed plausible and will have animated many a soldierly mind, along (allegedly) with Kolkier's. Here too we see again how Jewish voices in official records invoked Christian holidays as temporal signposts.

The Sejm Commission interrogated Kolkier, who could read but not write. Asked why he stared "studiously" at the stenographer's text, he was testy: "I've got eyes. Where am I going to look? Down at the floor?" He said he and Kozak went to the synagogue with four or five "Yids/soldiers." When (as they claimed, perhaps truthfully) Jews there called for two soldiers, they volunteered, going to People's Home. But they refused to join the Bolshevik army. Why, then, were they given wine and pastry? "I'm hungry; it's war." They then reported to superiors what they had learned. Returning next day to "catch the Bolsheviks," youths ran off, while the elderly, "who couldn't run," stayed. This happened after the midday meal but before coffee. Normally, food-conscious Kolkier said, his unit dined at noon and had coffee at five, six, or seven o'clock. What

[70] Army Commission (April 9, 1919).   [71] CZA. A127/75 (June 23, 1919).
[72] CZA. A127/75 (May 10, 1919).

about today? "When I came here, they had cut the meat but had still to set out the cabbage."

Among arrestees tearing up papers, there were but nine or ten, who stopped when he ordered it. "His mother had no occupation; his father previously was in trade." Disarmingly, Kolkier said that before April 5, *no one in the barracks thought Jews in Pinsk might have arms*. "The Jews were very happy to see [us] in synagogue, but they complained they were being drafted." He had joined because he knew he would have to serve. "I've heard about Zionists, but I can't explain what that means."

Yids told us in church . . . "we removed the Heavenly Mother's golden eyes and we also took the wine." [Asked whether it was not lamentable that arrestees were shot, he replied] "what's to be done? If they'd attacked us, they would have killed us. Too bad is too bad [*szkoda, to szkoda*]. I can't say if it was necessary to shoot them."[73]

Soldiers' Testimony to Their Superiors

The Army Commission interviewed Corporal Stanisław Ciebosz, of Kozak's and Kolkier's technical company. He said the two Jewish soldiers returned from synagogue saying local Jews, having machine guns and ammunition, "intend to launch an attack on the Polish armed force in Pinsk." Next morning Ciebosz, in civilian clothes, entered People's Home. "There I asked a Jew, in Russian, having first winked at him and received a wink in reply, 'where's our meeting?'" The answer was here at 7:00 PM. Looking around, Ciebosz saw Jews whispering. Street passage of nine military cyclists caused panic. People ran, shots rang out; Ciebosz couldn't shoot because he fell while running and muddied his gun. Soldiers awaiting his command began firing as they entered the building. Some sixty Jews remaining there "began ripping Russian papers." Many wore red cocardes under their lapels. Ciebosz's story seems fanciful and was uncorroborated by any other witness.

Another soldier, Piotr Mleko, twenty-one, illiterate, suffered a head injury storming People's Home. He found Jews there – some 100, mostly youths, some women – hostile and insubordinate, escaping through windows if only they could. Most sported red cocardes. Soldiers found two revolvers and "a big box with empty cartridges." (But when Mleko testified later before the Sejm Commission, he said only that he saw at the "Bolshevik meeting" a soldier confiscate a revolver from someone's pocket.) Officer Cadet Marjan Drobnik, twenty, testified that "the whole [People's Home] inspection was undertaken because of the report of

[73] Sejm Commission (May 2, 1919).

technical company soldier Kozak, whom the Jews urged to join the Bolsheviks." On Major Łuczyński's orders, "I shot thirty-four Jews aged roughly seventeen to twenty-five."[74]

A hard-boiled army defender before the Sejm Commission was Józef Baj, twenty-four, advanced on April 9 from gendarme lieutenant to commander in Pinsk. "Our rear positions are seriously endangered by Jews and peasants in revolt – more by Jews." Pinsk was a "hotbed" of Jewish Bolshevism. He was winning peasants' trust, investigating their grievances, but "I will never win Jews' confidence, even if I were here a hundred years." All of Pinsk "went about with nose in air, thinking Polish forces were too small. But receiving such a cut as on April 5 will have its effect." Challenged about peasant revolt, he explained: "because they murder the gentry [obywatele], take over estates, cut telephone wires, etc." If Bolsheviks captured Pinsk today, the "whole Jewish population, from richest bourgeois [burżuj] to beggar, would shoot at us." He admitted "there are robberies by the army: their cause is the lack of the most essential things" – that is, on the market, so seizure by force was justified.[75]

The Army Commission, whose president was cavalry commander Colonel Strzemieński, described its work as inquiry into "the planned coup [zamach] against the Polish Army." It heard briefly from other friendly witnesses. Officer Cadet Kontopf, twenty-two, learned from a war prisoner that "on April 6 [Bolsheviks] were going to strike our positions, thanks to revolution staged in Pinsk, where the population, mainly Jewish, was going to disarm the Polish army." Gendarme Chief Franciszek Sell recalled "unusual movement" on April 4. "Young Jews strolled defiantly around the [police station], looking in windows" and generally stalking police. He found no compromising documents among materials confiscated from the massacred.

Lieutenant Count Jan Tenczyński, manning an armored train, said that at night on April 5–6 he saw lights beamed toward Pinsk from outside town. On following days, there were "very bright, completely white streaks of light, rising and falling in arcs." A sergeant also witnessed mysterious strong lights, implying treacherous collusion with the Bolsheviks. Three Jewish women witnesses claimed inability to testify on grounds of having been, during the April 5 catastrophe, "very nervous." Among them was Elka Milecka, who testified at length before the Sejm Commission.[76]

---

[74] Army Commission (April 9, 1919); Sejm Commission (April 17, 1919).
[75] Sejm Commission (April 19, 1919).   [76] Army Commission (April 9, 1919).

The Army Commission concluded that "in Pinsk a widespread Jewish Bolshevik organization incontrovertibly exists," communicating with the enemy front. Further, on April 5, this organization, planning to attack the Polish army, held a series of conspiratorial meetings, one discovered through report of a soldier (Kozak) whom local Bolsheviks sought to recruit. The intended attack by "Bolshevik Jews" against numerically weak Polish forces, amid "unfortunate news from the front," failed owing to discovery of the People's Home meeting and "radical counter-action measures ordered by Major Łuczyński." The executions alone prevented uniting of separate "Bolshevik-Jewish bands," formed at several conspiratorial meetings, into a single whole capable of attacking. Finally, "the Jewish population in Pinsk clearly sympathizes with the Bolshevik-Jewish movement" and was hostile to Polish army and state.[77]

Yet no other meetings than those that allegedly took place in People's Home were identified; no arms for use in the alleged uprising were discovered; no effort was made to distinguish between Zionism and Bolshevism; only one witness (Baj) argued that executing Zionists, whether Bolsheviks or not, was necessary to thwart the feared Jewish-spearheaded assault. The Army Commission's reasoning assumed that Bundists and other Jewish leftists who, willingly or unwillingly, cooperated with Bolsheviks during their control of Pinsk – their parties in Ukraine and the eastern borderlands were on record in Red army's support – stood for the town's Jews generally; that Zionists too were revolutionary leftists; that Pinsk Jews were unequivocally anti-Polish and thus, with few exceptions, Polonophobic Bolsheviks.

It seems gendarme Commander Baj unguardedly articulated the massacre's instrumental logic: Pinsk's pro-Bolshevik Jews arrogantly assumed Poles could not hold the town – "but receiving such a cut as on April 5 will have its effect." The emotional logic was that Pinsk Jews' antiassimilationism and ethnocentrism – whether Bolshevik, Zionist, or merely Jewish – were a rejection of "Poland" amounting to a murderous threat justifying bullet hail. The thought is uncomfortable that Jewish-born soldiers' reportage of a suspected Zionist-Bolshevik revolt triggered – or helped trigger – a massacre. If so, their action was enveloped in military antisemitism, whose corrosive effects on their psyches they sought to mitigate by zealously hunting down the Polish army's imagined enemies.

The Bukraba Brothers' Mother

The Sejm Commission interrogated Polish Catholic witnesses, including Zofia Bukrabina, fifty-five, mother both of a priest and vengeful Dr.

---

[77] Ibid. (April 5, 1919), fos. 1 and 2.

Bukraba, who clamored for arrestees' execution. She had lived in Pinsk five years and thought "the Jewish population's disposition toward Christians very hostile." When Bolsheviks arrived, "Jews beamed. A speaker's platform appeared on the square. Processions marched, with a red banner displaying Jewish-language inscriptions." A shopkeeper told her, "you'll all croak." She said: "my son, the priest, can confirm that; when he crossed the street, Jewish children spat on him." Led by "local Jew Lucki," Bolsheviks entered the church, "searched the altar for arms," even "raised up the gravestones." They "wanted to pour out the Hosts, though unblessed, but I would not allow it, and they heeded me. Lucki took three bottles of wine." Soldiers took silver objects and candles. She omitted theft of the Heavenly Mother's golden eyes that Kozak and Kolkier had – credulously or misinformedly – reported.

She conceded that Polish soldiers committed excesses during their first night in Pinsk. There were rumors during the Polish conquest of "light signals, broken telephone lines." Two soldiers had been murdered, at whose burial her son presided. Local Catholics believed Jews had arms, even machine guns "and intend[ed] to slaughter the Polish army and civilians." Her experience at the priest's house persuaded her that "the Belarusian peasantry's relation to [Polish] authorities is very good." She knew executed apothecary Frydman. "It seems to me he wasn't a Bolshevik."[78]

Polish Upper-Class Views

Edward Łojko, thirty-two, had been leasing and farming one of prestigious Drucki-Lubecki family's manorial estates. Bolsheviks appeared, led by a Jewish neighbor, demanding "a contribution" of 120,000 rubles. He absconded. Rumors were flying, spread by Jewish refugees, of pogrom in Łuniniec, where "Jews had all been slaughtered, Lenin was dead, Trotsky had fled," and Kerensky again headed the Russian army and had surrounded the Reds. When Bolsheviks entered panic-stricken Pinsk, Jews greeted them at the train station "with a brass band and wild dancing [muzyką dętą i rżniętą]."

When Poles arrived, people locked doors. Jews didn't come out for three days. Two Polish soldiers were shot from windows. "Soldiers, deprived of the most indispensable things, had to go about in private dwellings, searching and taking." Pinsk Poles, "very few and poor," refrained from greeting the army. Jews were anti-Polish before April 5 and more after. Under Germans, prices were relatively low, soaring then

---

[78] Sejm Commission (April 18, 1919).

under the Bolsheviks. Only one merchant had much to sell. People called him "lords' Yid [*pański żydek*]."

April 5 was "like today, warm and sunny ... Never were more young Jews seen on the street," but no one thought this odd. In his opinion, People's Home meetings were suspect. "It's a fact there are Bolshevik partisans among the Jews. The Jews must be charged with handing them over." He himself, as estate manager, handed over to Germans, "when they came to crush Bolshevism," four peasant criminals and two Poles, all then sent by a German court to Prussia as workers. They had "plundered a certain property. They were urging that my livestock be crippled and I be killed." After 1918's German revolution, they returned, threatening and forcing him to flee.[79]

Łojko's fate was characteristic of this twilight era of eastern borderlands Polish nobility and gentry and those dependent on them. He viewed the Pinsk scene with resigned detachment and – though seeing Jews as ethnopolitical antagonists – without pronounced antisemitic accents. Franciszka Zawistowicz, widow and self-described local *bourgeoise*, radiated anti-Jewish hostility. The Jews, she said, greeted Germans "with bread and salt" and later "yearned for Bolsheviks," whom Jewish girls favored with red cocardes. She saw Jews greeting Bolsheviks: "Long live Soviet Russia! Death to the bourgeoisie! [*Da zdrawstwuje sowicskaja Rosyja, Smiert burzuazji*]." Some Polish workers were at first drawn to Bolshevism. In the ensuing price rise, "people were convinced Jews were hiding goods." Under Germans, Jewish merchants would pretend not to understand Polish. A shop girl refused to sell her humble buckwheat.

Jews met Poles' arrival "with bullets." Zawistowicz claimed to have seen how a Jew who killed a cavalryman with a stone was celebrated. She billeted Polish soldiers, who complained of the people's hostility. "I replied: 'they aren't people, they're Jews.'" Jews tore down posters announcing Polish rule, saying "damned Polacks [*verfluchte polaken*] ... They pointed at my daughter – 'damned Polack girl' [*verfluchte polaczke*] ... The Polish population's hatred toward Jews is now elemental. Jews are reaping what they sowed in the last few years."[80]

The Pinsk Massacre's Reverberations in Poland

The shooting echoed long and far, adding force to arguments for minority protection clauses the Versailles Treaty imposed on Poland in June 1919. On April 7, Jewish Sejm deputies interpellated the government on the "mass murders." They cited JDC's Zuckerman's letter, in which he

[79] Ibid. [80] Ibid.

announced that People's Home had been "razed to the ground" and that the Polish military had retracted its initial claim to have found machine guns there, while insisting on red cocardes and a single revolver. Zuckerman had earlier telegraphed that fifty to 100 had been shot and that Polish soldiers he talked with "bragged that what has so far happened is nothing and that it will get 'hotter' for the Jews." Zuckerman wrote JDC's Bogen of Pinsk's "terrible occurrences," which transpired while he was in Brest-Litovsk, saying he "was a nervous wreck" and "must talk to somebody."[81]

Zuckerman later reported that, on the train, he watched Polish soldiers robbing Pinsk Jews who had gone to Brest-Litovsk to shop. "The Jews, being already frightened from previous occasions, have had to look on silently how their food, [which] they had hoped to bring home to their families, was being taken away from them." One Jew "had courage enough" to follow a soldier, threatening to report him to army command and thereby recover stolen meat. Finkelstein, traveling with protective Christian merchants, told him the 141 Jews in Święta Wola were starving. "The relations of the Polish authorities to them are of a terrible character. The Jews are killed without any purpose whatever. There is no authority to complain to." In Pinsk, Zuckerman had distributed cash subsidies, including one for Mr. Epstein, a "learned Jew, who was one of the richest Jews in the town and is now absolutely starving."[82]

London Zionists excitedly cabled New York, reporting Pinsk deaths at fifty-six. "Three Jewish women, accompanying arrested husbands, flogged in prison on naked bodies. Miss Muletka [Milecka?], Jewish school mistress, insane through ill treatment." They reported too that "well-known Catholic Clergyman Bukrawa [Bukraba] protests against accusation [that] executed Jews were Bolsheviks." To his credit, Father Bukraba – tolerant, in contrast to his mother, not to mention his bloody-minded brother – went to Warsaw to "interpellate the government."[83] "Pinsk cmdr Lutchinski who ordered execution dismissed. All J. papers Warsaw publishing crime confiscated. Numerous proclamations

---

[81] CZA. A127/75 (April 7, 1919). JDC. AR 19/21, No. 188 (Poland), section 2: Pinsk massacre, fos 18, 22–24.

[82] Ibid., fos. 13–16 (April 25, 1919).

[83] Kazimierz Bukraba (1885–1946), educated in St. Petersburg, Innsbruck, and Kraków, served in World War I as a priest and school inspector in Pinsk, held intermittently by Germans as a hostage. In 1932, he became bishop of the Pinsk diocese, supporting Piłsudski's regime. He was hospitalized under Soviet occupation 1939–42 in Lwów for a heart ailment and nervous depression. Forbidden thereafter by German occupiers to return to his diocese, he performed priestly service in 1944's Warsaw Uprising.

distributed [in] Warsaw, announcing new great pogrom. Every hundredth Jew to be shot. Population desperate, only hope European help."

London ZO later cabled New York that Polish Army Command (General Listowski) had conceded to the press that Major Łuczyński "mistook meeting Jewish Hall for Communist assembly. That innocent people were shot due [to] war conditions." Warsaw's Yiddish-language *Haynt* correctly reported that Listowski had called Łuczyński's mistake regrettable but understandable, while Copenhagen Zionists accurately reported that Listowski defended Łuczyński for having done what any good officer would do.[84] The Londoners also relayed judgment in the *Times* of prominent Labor Party journalist and East European analyst Henry Brailsford, who after a tour of Poland "thinks Piłsudski humane and liberal, but not strong enough to prevent oppression, and even slaughter of Jews." Taking account of Endek antisemitic propaganda, "overwhelming impression left on him after talks with Polish officials and officers and with Jewish leaders that Polish intolerance in incurable."[85]

Zionists collected other Yiddish-language press reports. Deputy Grünbaum wrote in *Dos Judisze Folk*, condemning Polish excuses: "The art of washing bloodied hands has been raised in Poland to virtuosity."

The Jew is a Bolshevik, he must be ... With this argument [Polish nationalists] want to win sympathy and regard from the [Western] coalition seeking to extinguish Bolshevism. They constantly proclaim themselves bearers of civilization [*kulturtregerami*] in Lithuania and Belarus, who are bringing the culture of the west, not eastern culture resting on Bolshevism and anarchy ... But [theirs] is a culture based on lash and firing squad.[86]

The Bund's *Lebensfragen* exploded in purple prose characteristic of the demotic Yiddish press.

Elderly Jews weep ... Young Jews clench their fists at the actions of the lowest and most sinister animal – "man" ... What an abyss of hellishly red-bloodied black content!

Lawlessness, monstrousness, violence and barbarism, sadistic delectation in human blood, wild gamboling of untrammeled instincts, flogging and torture, dull and self-satisfied hatred of Jews, and crowning all ... icy, calm, calculated slaughter of dozens of unarmed and innocent people ... The torturers' cynical laughter resounds, spreading throughout the country ... Youth need no words. They long for deed, great deeds, capable of destroying at one blow the stinking

---

[84] Shohet, *The Jews of Pinsk*, 401–20.
[85] CZA. A127/75 (April 7, 1919); JDC. AR 19/21, No. 188 (Poland), section 2: Pinsk massacre, fos. 31, 34–35, 41, 43–45.
[86] CZA. A127/73: *Dos judisze Folk* (April 9, 1919).

mud of life's putrefaction. They yearn for the iron hammer, the tempest, the great revenge of history. Together with them we too hear the thunder of the coming storm.

Powering this chaos-welcoming – Bolshevik-spirited – call to revolution was immeasurable Jewish embitterment over poverty and oppression.[87]

Unrevolutionary, Zionist-leaning *Moment* rejected labeling the killings as pogrom. They were "not bandit deeds, nor a bestialized mob's. No! They took place in the name of young, organized, and liberated Poland." Antisemites are "cooking a new *kasza*" about Jewish Bolshevism. "Such deeds cannot go unpunished."

We know from experience that people for whom antisemitism is a kind of alcoholism, which they cannot foreswear, even though sober thinking demands it – such people can only rage and destroy, and not lay foundations and build solid edifices.

Here was a well-honed stab at one of the Poles' weak points but also a plea to put aside hatred's intoxication in their own national self-interest. Populist *Hajnt* found the shootings to "exceed every concept of crime and barbarism." Nothing in recent years rivaled it, not even the "dreadful pogrom" in Lwów. "It was not a pogrom, but something we cannot even describe and name in words." The best and brightest "were led like sheep to the slaughter."[88]

American Reactions

In summer 1919, Henry Morgenthau and colleagues visited Pinsk to gather evidence for a report on anti-Jewish violence that, in June, Hoover, Paderewski, and Wilson had agreed to compile to clarify the Polish government's responsibility for postwar pogroms and, if possible, pacify the Polish-Jewish battlefield. Morgenthau's coemissaries, Homer Johnson and General Edgar Jadwin, dissented from the chairman's insistence, in their report of October 1919, on reckoning antisemitism among pogroms' causes, preferring to emphasize military exigencies and Christian-Jewish commercial competition. Yet the three were united in foregrounding the role of soldiers and other armed men in the chief pogroms – Kielce, Lemberg, Pinsk, Kolbuszowa, Lida, Wilno, Częstochowa, and Minsk (where on August 8, 1919, Polish soldiers,

---

[87] Ibid., *Lebensfragen* (April 9, 1919). Similarly, Shohet, *The Jews of Pinsk*, 398–99.
[88] Ibid., *Moment* and *Hajnt* (April 9, 1919). A Zionist Hebrew-language photographic memorial to the massacre victims, highlighting their unrevolutionary respectability: https://pl.wikipedia.org/wiki/Masakra_w_Pi%C5%84sku.

having captured the town from Bolsheviks, staged a pogrom killing thirty-one Jews and plundering 377 Jewish shops).[89]

In his 1923 memoirs, Morgenthau confessed that his experience in Pinsk "has haunted me ever since, and has seemed a complete expression of the misery and injustice which is prevalent over such a large part of the world today." He described the massacre ordered by Major "Letoviski" (his garbling of Polish names was virtuosic), ending in the mass grave coldly receiving victims' corpses.

> Up to the time that our Commission came, not a single Jew had been permitted to visit that cemetery, but I was allowed to inspect the scene of this martyrdom, and, when I entered, a great crowd of Jews, who had followed me, also went in. As soon as they reached the burial place of their relatives, they all threw themselves on the ground, and set up a wailing that still rings in my ears; it expressed the misery of centuries.
>
> That same evening I attended divine service at the Pinsk synagogue. The building was crowded to its capacity, the men wedged into an almost solid mass. Those that could not enter were gathered outside. All the Jews of Pinsk were there ... This huge mass cried and screamed until it seemed the heavens would burst. I had read of such public expressions of agony in the Old Testament, but this was the first time that I ever completely realized what the collective grief of a persecuted people was like.[90]

Morgenthau's report emphasized the "chaotic and unnatural state of affairs" in postwar Poland. "The chauvinistic reaction created by the sudden acquisition of a long-coveted freedom ripened the public mind for anti-Semitic or anti-alien sentiment, which was strongly agitated by the press and by politicians. This finally encouraged physical manifestations of violent outcroppings of an unbalanced social condition." The Commission agreed to eschew the word "pogrom," finding the word applied "to everything from petty outrages to premeditated and carefully organized massacres." About Pinsk the commissioners agreed that charges of Bolshevism against victims were unfounded. They recorded that such reports "had been received by two Jewish soldiers." Morgenthau, for his part, found Major Łuczyński to have shown "reprehensible and frivolous readiness to place credence in such untested assertions," whereas "any well-known non-Jewish inhabitant" would have confirmed the victims' "loyal character." Still, "none of the offenders answerable for this summary execution have been punished."[91]

---

[89] www.sztetl.org.pl/pl/article/minsk/5,historia.

[90] Henry Morgenthau, with French Strother, *All in a Life-Time* (New York, NY: Doubleday Page, 1923), 369–70.

[91] Ibid., 409, 411.

Morgenthau distinguished between soldierly motives that were political – instilled by propaganda charging Jews with Bolshevism (and by existence of specifically Jewish political parties) – and those that were antisemitic, based on religious-ethnic antagonism toward Jews in general. (This book differs in emphasizing the former's derivation from the latter.) Violence he attributed to "undisciplined and ill-equipped Polish recruits, who, uncontrolled by their inexperienced and ofttimes timid officers, sought to profit at the expense of that portion of the population which they regarded as alien and hostile to Polish nationality and aspirations." He warned against condemning all Poles for the violence of "uncontrolled troops or local mobs."

These excesses [in the major pogroms and massacres] were apparently not premeditated for if they had been part of a preconceived plan, the number of victims would have run into the thousands, instead of amounting to about 280.[92]

The Polish government having accepted the Versailles Treaty's minority-protection paragraph, article 93, Morgenthau expressed confidence that eventually a strong and democratic Poland would protect its citizenry and educate "the masses beyond the state of mind that makes such aggression possible."

Morgenthau condemned National Democrats' antisemitism and boycott propaganda, which had created "in the minds of some of the Jews the feeling that there is an invisible rope around their necks, and they claim that this is the worst persecution that they can be forced to endure." Yet his report was suffused with benevolent optimism about Poland's future and the welfare of its Jewish population, which he reckoned at 14 percent of the whole. Of a "solution" to Polish-Jewish tensions, he wrote: "the fact that it may take one or two generations to reach that goal must not be discouraging."[93]

Morgenthau figured prominently among American Jewish anti-Zionists, whose platform announced not only that "the Jews ... ceased to be a nation 2,000 years ago" but also that pursuit of a Jewish state in Palestine "involves the limitation and possible annulment of the larger claims of Jews for full citizenship and human rights in all lands in which those rights are not yet secure." Anxiety among Western – including American – Jews radiated from the further anti-Zionist argument that "all Jews repudiate every suspicion of a double allegiance, but to our minds it is necessarily implied in and cannot by any logic be eliminated from establishment of a sovereign State for the Jews in Palestine."[94]

---

[92] Ibid., 415.   [93] Ibid., 419.
[94] Ibid., 349–50, quoting a 1919 statement by Berkowitz et al.

Anti-Jewish violence in Poland ignited mighty American protests. "In New York, 15,000 Jews packed Madison Square Garden, and many thousands more, including 3,000 in uniform, stood in the surrounding streets." Charles Evan Hughes, Wilson's Republican counterpart, was principal speaker. Such manifestations of outrage and apprehension heightened pressure on Wilson to dispatch Morgenthau's team to Poland. In Paris, the Polish delegation having bowed to article 93, Morgenthau met with Roman Dmowski, whom he misdescribed as "a heavy, domineering figure, with a thick neck and a big, close-cropped head bearing the bulldog jaw and the piercing eyes of the ward-boss." Telling him "I understand that you are an Anti-Semite," he pressed Dmowski to explain himself, which he did, "in an almost propitiating manner":

My Anti-Semitism isn't religious; it is political. And it is not political outside of Poland. It is entirely a matter of Polish party politics. It is only from that point of view that I regard it or your mission. Against a non-Polish Jew I have no prejudice, political or otherwise.

"He said that unless the Jews would abandon their exclusiveness, they had better leave the country. He wanted Poland for the Poles alone."[95]

In Poland, Morgenthau found that "the Jewish masses looked upon us as hoped-for deliverers, and upon me as a second Moses Montefiore" (British Jewish eminence visiting Russia in the 1840s, reporting influentially on their plight under tsarist knout). But neither Polish nor Jewish leaders welcomed his Commission, which nonetheless crisscrossed the land in myriad discussions, hearings, and interrogations. Morgenthau concluded that, especially among Jews, "the chief source of trouble could be traced to a comparatively few factional leaders." Rabbi Rubenstein from Wilno, flogged for defiance of Polish authorities, impressed Morgenthau with his Christ-like face. His account of anti-Jewish violence was periodically "broken by spasmodic ebullitions of resentment which he could no longer repress."

Among Zionists, Morgenthau found some "pro-Russian; all were practically non-Polish [in self-understanding, if not speech and demeanor], and the Zionism of most of them was simply advocacy of Jewish Nationalism within the Polish state." It was they, he learned, who had "complained to the world of the alleged pogroms." The assimilators "we found ... very intelligent and deeply interested in the future of Poland – distinct in no detail of dress or speech, and holding membership in political parties on purely Polish principles, just as a Jew in America

[95] Ibid., 357–58.

may be a Democrat or a Republican without reference to his religion."
Speaking to eminent historian and diplomat Szymon Askenazy, an integrationist, he heard that the minority treaty's guarantees would only
"widen the difference between [Jews] and the Poles."[96]

In Wilno, Morgenthau met Piłsudski, misperceiving him as he had
Dmowski: "he was a huge, forbidding man. His uniform, buttoned tight
to the base of his big neck, was unadorned by any orders – the uniform of a
fighter. His square jaw was thrust out below thick lips firmly set; his face
was abnormally broad, with cheekbones high and prominent." He denied
there having been pogroms in Poland – "nothing but unavoidable acci-
dents." Asked to explain the difference, he replied:

A pogrom ... is a massacre ordered by the government, or not prevented by it
when prevention is possible. Among us no wholesale killings of Jews have been
permitted. Our trouble isn't religious; it is economic. Our petty dealers are Jews.
Many of them have been war-profiteers, some have had dealings with the
Germans or the Bolsheviki, or both, and this has created a prejudice against
Jews in general.[97]

He added that while Russia would "return to autocracy," Poland would
remain a "free republic ... The Poles and the Jews can't live together on
friendly terms for years to come, but they will manage it at last. In the
meantime, the Jew will have all his legal rights." Morgenthau told
Piłsudski that as Commission chief, he was "no Jew, not even an
American, but a representative of all civilized nations and their religions.
I stood for tolerance in its broadest sense." This won the Marshal's
confidence and goodwill, and he promised release of Jewish prisoners.
As for charismatic Paderewski, Morgenthau found him "not only not an
Anti-Semite: he is infinitely the greatest of the modern Poles."[98]

At one of the dazzling political-aristocratic suppers to which
Morgenthau was invited, Piłsudski spoke of his abiding faith, throughout
his adventurous and perilous career, that "I was destined to become
dictator of Poland," for a gypsy woman had found this future in a star in
his palm. Morgenthau possessed the star, and eminent guests searched
their palms for it, but "unsuccessfully."

Morgenthau reckoned, with rough accuracy, that 80 percent of Polish
Jews, including Hasidim, subscribed to religious Orthodoxy. They were,
the powerful Gerer rebbe Alter told him, "satisfied to live side by side with
people of different religions." Their principal conflict "is with Jews," at
"every step" with the Zionists. "We are exiled," said Rabbi Levin. "We
cannot be freed from our banishment, nor do we wish to be. We cannot

---

[96] Ibid., 362–66.   [97] Ibid., 371–74.   [98] Ibid., 377.

redeem ourselves ... We will abide by our religion [in Poland] until God Almighty frees us."

Morgenthau and his colleagues finally concluded:

There was no question whatever but that the Jews had suffered; there had been shocking outrages of at least a sporadic character resulting in many deaths, and still more woundings and robberies, and there was a general disposition, not to say plot, of long standing, the purpose of which was the make the Jews uncomfortable in many ways; there was a deliberate conspiracy to boycott them economically and socially. Yet there is also no question but that some of the Jewish leaders had exaggerated these evils. There, too, were malevolent, self-seeking, mischief-makers both in the Jewish and Polish press and among the politicians of every stripe. Jews and non-Jews alike started out with the presumption that there could be no reconciliation.

Morgenthau closed his reminiscences of the Poland mission by (pejoratively) comparing "Nationalist-Zionists" to "walking delegates in the labour unions, who had to agitate" to maintain authority. "It was quite evident that one of the deep and obscure causes of the Jewish trouble in Poland was this Nationalist-Zionist leadership that exploited the Old Testament prophecies to capture converts to the Nationalist scheme."[99]

The Commission's legal counsel, Captain Arthur Goodhart, in 1920 published his diary of their Polish tour. Well-educated, polished, confident of his own authority, and also Jewish, he understood better than his chief the argument for Zionism in Poland, even as, like Morgenthau, he recognized the virtues embodied in many upper-class Poles and the charms of their refined ways. Of Paderewski, whom he found in mid-1919 "the most powerful man in Poland," he wrote that "the Jews feel that [he] is anti-Semitic; this is not unlikely, as virtually all Poles are." He recorded, condescendingly, how General Jadwin addressed a crowd in Grodno, "in true American fashion," coaxing them to repeat after him: "What is good for the Jews is good for Poland, and what is good for Poland is good for the Jews." Goodhart was content to ascribe soldierly murders during plunder riots to blood lust and accept that when soldiers threatened Jews in eastern Poland with wholesale slaughter on return from anti-Bolshevik war, reducing Jewish women to tears and anticipatory mourning, they were but "joking." He accepted too that Polish soldiers, so ill equipped, should rob Jews. A Polish officer told him, "When my men are going barefoot, I have to close one eye while they try to get boots for themselves."[100]

---

[99] Ibid., 375, 378–79, 382–84.
[100] Arthur L. Goodhart, *Poland and the Minority Races* (London: Allen & Unwin, 1920), 35, 49, 86, 88–89. Goodhart was scion of New York's Lehman banking family. He made a

In Minsk, where thirty-one Jews were killed after the city's conquest, Goodhart coolly judged deaths looting's collateral damage. He recorded the "fantastic story about Jewish girls signing [Bolshevik] death warrants," which was "one of the most frequent that is told." Such female commissars were said to authorize executions following Bolshevik rulings or even to carry them out themselves with communist revolvers. Goodhart quoted London's *Times*: "So much that is terrible is true, that much more that is simply hearsay is readily believed."

In Lemberg, he was assured that there were enough "educated Ruthenians" to govern independent Ukraine. They deplored Jewish massacres, attributing them to veneration for "Bogdan Khmelnitzki, the Ukrainian peasant leader who in 1648 swept the country, murdering Poles and Jews alike. As he was still considered a hero by the oppressed peasants, they unfortunately thought there was something heroic in murdering the Jews." Partisan of Western liberalism, Goodhart favored non-Hasidic "Lithuanian" Jews – shorn of long beards, suited rather than robed – over their "Polish" coreligionists. "With their long black kaftans and queer, ugly little caps, these Polish Jews looked like a survival of the Middle Ages. They seemed to have no energy – they just stood in groups on the street corners gaping at our car." The Jews of Wilno or Grodno, by contrast, "were modern and efficient and better able to take care of themselves than these hopeless-looking, down-trodden men in the Polish villages."[101]

In Częstochowa they encountered Haller troops, who "drilled by French officers, seem more efficient and better disciplined than the regular Polish Legionaries." Yet they had "begun the beard-cuttings." An officer explained to Goodhart that "as these soldiers came from foreign countries [France, United States, Imperial Germany] the Jewish kaftans and beards were more noticed by them than by the native Poles, who had become accustomed to them." Another officer said that his men, disgusted by Jews' appearance, "did not want to hand over the cities they had captured for Poland to people like the Jews, who talked a different language and dressed differently. Also, they believed that all the Bolsheviks were Jews." Moreover, "the soldier is not a logical animal."[102]

Goodhart accepted without defensiveness that the Polish press highlighted reports of 1919's "Negro race riots in Washington, D.C., and Chicago." Nationalist newspapers "suggested that a Polish Mission be sent to America to investigate the Negro pogroms." He thought that

distinguished career at Oxford University as professor of jurisprudence, gaining knighthood and appointment as Master of University College.
[101] Ibid., 91, 140, 107.   [102] Ibid., 117–18, 141.

Polish Jews embraced Zionist nationalism largely in reaction to Christian antisemitism. Even if wholesale emigration to Palestine were impossible, leaving in Poland a vast Jewish population, it was essential they be made to "feel that they had a great history behind them and an equally noble future before them" so that "they would recover the self-respect which they had lost during the past two thousand years." Jews told him, "The Polish government and people do not wish to consider us as Poles and in no way encourage us to feel that we have any real interest in the culture and life of the country. Our only hope is to develop a true love for Jewish ideals." Another said, "In Poland a Jew is like the title of one of your books, *A Man Without a Country*." But a Zionist doctor, asked "whether he thought the situation would be changed if Poland treated the Jews as they were treated in America," said, "it unquestionably would. Many of the men who were now so enthusiastic in building up Jewish culture would devote the same enthusiasm to Polish ideals." Like Morgenthau, Goodhart inclined to accept, as "many of the Jewish leaders have said," that "if it were not for the press there would be little real anti-Semitism."[103]

Morgenthau – seasoned, gifted, and humane statesman – took an Olympian view of Poland's "Jewish trouble." He certainly wished new Poland well, seeking to strengthen it economically. It was axiomatic to him that it must play a vital role in stabilizing Eastern Europe and holding Russia at bay. Goodhart, himself a member of the privileged and successful American Jewish intelligentsia, better understood the intense frustration and disappointment of his Polish counterparts who embraced Zionism in assertion of national pride and defiance. A wide experiential and intellectual gulf separated his viewpoint – and Morgenthau's – from the Yiddish press's rage over Polish anti-Judaism.

Viewed from Polish and Western liberal elites' perspectives, anti-Jewish violence in Poland embodied collateral damage of state building in the aftermath of ruinous nationalism-intoxicated war and in Bolshevism's terrifying, even apocalypse-summoning shadow. Viewed from below, it was heartless, evil cruelty spearheaded by armed fighters but eagerly joined in by their entourage of conscience-less scum – proletarian, bourgeois, and aristocratic. Beyond these visions lay the fantasies pogromists unthinkingly, unconsciously enacted: humbling, dispossession, physical punishment, banishment, even murder of those whose

---

[103] Ibid., 112, 149, 154. On widespread postwar American violence and political radicalism, see William M. Tuttle, *Race Riot: Chicago in the Red Summer of 1919* (New York, NY: Atheneum, 1970); and Anne Hagedorn, *Savage Peace: Hope and Fear in America, 1919* (New York, NY: Simon & Schuster, 2007).

existence, by religiously infused magic, accounted for the present moment's and a suffering-suffused society's miseries. Why, otherwise, could it not be accepted that Jews, on whom pitiless blows had also rained, were – if only peace returned – one of Poland's valuable assets, so that, in General Yadwin's rosy-lensed formulation, "what was good for the Jews was good for Poland"?

8 On Apocalypse's Edge
Army and Jews during the Polish-Soviet War, 1920

In mid-1919, as the Versailles Treaty brought resurrected Poland hope of peace on its western borders, its rulers' longings to possess the eastern borderlands and their antagonism toward Russia, whether Bolshevik or White, fated that Polish soldiers' blood would still flow. Fighting in 1919 against Ukrainians and, in Lithuania and Belarus, against pro-Soviet forces, Poles succeeded in conquering East Galicia, Wilno, Minsk, and Pinsk. Farther east, Soviet successes undermined Symon Petliura's Ukrainian People's Republic. In 1920, seeing that neither White armies nor Petliura's could crush the Red Army, Piłsudski unleashed his French-backed forces against Trotsky's divisions, whose triumphs in the Russian civil war inspired in them crusading zeal to raise Bolshevism's flag in Warsaw and after that on Berlin's Brandenburg Gate and Paris's Arc de Triomphe.

It was communist Russia's first foreign war. In April 1920, Piłsudski, having subordinated desperate Petliura to himself, drove Polish-Ukrainian armies to Kiev, but Russian counterattack repulsed them. By early July the Soviets penetrated ethnographic Poland, crossing the Vistula in mid-August and assaulting Warsaw. The Polish army counter-attacked, winning a great victory and forcing the Bolsheviks back east-ward. Both sides exhausted, negotiations began in September that yielded a formal truce in October and Riga's 1921 Peace Treaty.

The Red Army's invasion of their national heartland quickened anti-Russian, anti-Bolshevik Poles' worst fears, both of loss of independence and cultural obliteration under Christianity-crushing communism. In early July, Piłsudski's government sounded alarms of all-out war, intensifying compulsory regular army recruitment and calling on intelli-gentsia youth to join a new "volunteer army" (*armia ochotnicza*) forming, under General Haller's command, alongside the regular army. Fighters streamed also into Haller's Blue army, which in 1919 had incorporated the *Armia Wielkopolska*, earlier raised in the Prussian partition zone to spearhead breakaway from German rule.

For Poland's Jews, escalating war signaled heightened danger. While some leftists hopefully anticipated Soviet victory, the great majority – religious Jews, business owners, educated professionals – appreciated that Lenin and Stalin were their nemeses too. As the saying attributed to the Muscovite rabbi went, "Trotskys make revolution, Bronstejns [Trotsky's well-off family's name] pay for it." Yet, in independent Poland's short life, Jews had suffered unprecedented pogrom violence and continual abuse at antisemitic soldiers' and civilian rabble's hands. Now the government appealed to all citizens to wage war – as soldiers, civilian volunteers, or war-bond purchasers. Were Jews too meant to respond? Did they have the heart and will to do so? Would they be accepted as comrades in anti-Bolshevik arms, or would the stereotype of "Jewish Bolshevik" stamp and imperil them as national traitors?

There are no modern scholarly accounts of Polish Jewry during the 1920 war. In 1921, the Zionist-spirited National Jewish Club of Sejm Deputies assembled and published the two-volume *Bolshevik Invasion and the Jews: A Documentary Collection*, a weighty compilation of parliamentary inter-pellations, eyewitness protocols, and other documentation of anti-Jewish violence. Such records were supplied to the government Council of Ministers in advance of Sejm debates. This chapter relies on the archivally housed manuscript versions. In the revolutionary and violence-filled 1918–20 era's aftermath, taboo-mandated silence descended on the pogroms and other anti-Jewish assaults of those years. The lavishly produced two-volume *Jews in Reborn Poland* (Warsaw, 1932–33), authored by many prominent and respected scholars, addressed Jewish political parties and parliamentary activity but was silent on postwar violence.[1]

Jewish Patriotism in July 1920

The National Club of Jewish Sejm Deputies sounded a Zionist response to Piłsudski's call to arms. Solidarizing with it were the

---

[1] Narodowy Klub Żydowski Posłów Sejmowych przy Tymczasowej Żydowskiej Radzie Narodowej, *Inwazja Bolszewicka a Żydzi. Zbiór Dokumentów* (Warsaw: n.p., 1921); Ignacy Schiper et al., *Żydzi w Polsce odrodzonej: działalność społeczna, gospodarcza, oświatowa i kulturalna*, 2 vols. (Warsaw: Nakł. Wydawn. "Żydzi w Polsce odrodzonej," 1932–33). Similarly silent on anti-Jewish violence is Norbert Getter et al., *Żydzi bojownicy o niepodległość Polski: 1918–1939* (Lwów: Rada Ochrony Pamięci Walk i Męczeństwa, 1939),chap. 10, "Żydzi Polscy w czasie wojny światowej i w legionach"; Fuks, *Żydzi w Warszawie*. For older bibliography, see Polonsky, *Jews of Poland and Russia*, vol. 2. Above-cited Szczepański, *Społeczeństwo polskie*, is presently authoritative on Polish Christian society in 1920, but see also Knyt et al., *Rok 1920*. Zdzisław Musialik, *Wojna polsko-bolszewicka 1919–1920 a Żydzi* (Częstochowa: Włocławskie Wydawn. Diecezjalne, 1995) focuses in one-sidedly nationalist manner on Polish-Jewish political relations.

Figure 8.1 Polish prisoners of war in Soviet captivity, 1920. Many are barefooted, all are ill dressed, ragged, thin, unwashed. Their state of mind seems a mix of defiance and misery. Not a few Poles held by Russians during World War I had been drawn to revolutionary Bolshevism, but in 1920 its luster had greatly dimmed. Men such as these will have been involved in plunder riots against Jews.
Source: Provenance unknown.

Central Council of Jewish Town Councillors, Warsaw University's Jewish student organization (*Żydowska Strzecha Akademicka*), the Central Union of Jewish Artisans, and the Central Union of Small Merchants and Retailers – influential and large branches of Polish Jewry encompassing much of Zionism's social-political base but also reaching beyond it. "Jews! Poland is in danger." A "terrible enemy" approaches. "We Jews too have sprung to our feet to fulfill the responsibilities weighing on us." Yet

we have not heard a single word that might cause us to forget the abuses we have suffered, that summons us to true reconciliation, to a just arrangement of domestic relationships. On the contrary, from various sides we continue to hear words of hatred. Calumnies and slanders are still thrown at us.

Jews! Let us not forget what we owe the country we live in. [The war must be a just war of defense, not of conquest.] ...

RUSSIAN COSSACKS   3212-9

Figure 8.2 Russian Cossacks, 1914. During the 1920 war, some Cossack formations fought in alliance with the Polish army against the Soviets. Such men, typically superior soldiers, celebrated for their group cohesion, proved often to be enactors of brutal pogroms, but in some cases political considerations led their commanders to restrain them.
Source: PhotoQuest, Getty Images, 477569529.

Jews! Fulfill your citizenly obligation! Let everyone make the indispensable sacrifices, both in blood and life as in property. Let no one be absent in defense of the Polish State's freedom and independence![2]

This proclamation breathed ambivalence, avoiding embrace of Polish identity and characterizing Poland as "the country we live in" but emphatically affirming the Polish state – shield, hopefully, against antisemitism, anti-Jewish violence, and Bolshevization too. Jewish Academic Youth struck similar notes. Alluding – seemingly – to widespread physical impairments among Jewish students, its manifesto concluded: "let him who is able to bear arms join the army. He who lacks necessary strength and physical ability – let him devote in another way all his powers to the Polish State's good."[3] Conversely, the Council of Jewish Artisans – who

[2] AAN. PRM, 21431/20, fo. 431 (n.d. [early July, 1920]).
[3] Ibid., fo. 432 (July 9, 1920).

could only prosper in market-friendly setting – pledged their "overworked but hardened muscles" to Warsaw's defense against the "fierce enemy."[4]

More Polonophile tones sounded from proclamations of communal religious bodies, among whose leaders assimilationism and Jewish oligarchy had long been strong. Warsaw's "Old Testament Commune's" governors appealed to their "Brothers in Israel," conjuring the "eastern enemy" who aims once again, "as is his custom, to destroy Poland in fire and drown it in blood." Following "Supreme Leader" Piłsudski, Jews must seize arms. "So we once did in the Promised Land," and so did their forefathers in the nineteenth-century uprisings and their brothers in the lands of the "coalition" (Entente).

Away with hurts and resentments when threats hang over the land. We do not, indeed, march to defend our internal enemies, but only the land that none of us will cease to love. May God grant that we, in common effort, repel the eastern oppressor.[5]

The assimilationist Union of Poles of Mosaic Faith of All Polish Lands spoke still more fervently, with romantic nationalism's pathos, exhorting Jewish "citizens, male and female," to "stand arm in arm with our brothers, our fellow citizens, in common defense of our Mother – the FATHERLAND (*Matki – OJCZYZNY*). Let them, in whose hearts burns the holy flame of pure love toward Her, hasten to the defenders' ranks."[6]

Kraków's Judaic commune conjured "vast enemy hordes" who, like medieval Mongols and Tatars, aim to "trample and destroy our centuries-old culture and strangle the newly arisen Fatherland." Common sacrifice would "assure us in future our own way of life in a great, free and happy Poland."[7] From Kalisz came promise to aid volunteer soldiers' families: "we must remember that in defending Poland we protect the freedom of that land to which we do not wish to abandon our devotion." Chil Kestenberg, chief rabbi in Radom, cited the deeply ingrained injunction, "pray for the well-being of the State."

We are not foreigners in Poland. The bones of our forefathers from hundreds of years rest in this soil, and our great rabbis and scholars lived and taught here under the POLISH EAGLE. May you revive and breathe the spirit of the great patriot [supportive of 1863's revolt] rabbi Majzels and the Jewish hero [of Napoleonic-era Polish Legions] Berek Joselewicz.[8]

---

[4] Ibid., fo. 433: *Nasz Kurjer* (August 10, 1920).   [5] Ibid., fo. 434 (July 8, 1920).
[6] Ibid., fo. 437 (n.d. [July 1920]).   [7] Ibid., fo. 438 (n.d. [July 1920]).
[8] Ibid., fos. 439–42 (n.d. [July 1920]).

Częstochowa's commune, damning "our eternal enemy," told its followers "time has come to convince those who do not believe it that we are not worse sons of this land than they." A powerful free Poland – "that is our prosperity, our happiness." Another announcement, urging war-bond purchase, noted that this was "not sacrifice, but convenient location of capital, carrying interest and transferable in exchange for 80 percent of face-value."[9] Kutno's commune also appealed to self-interest: Jews, preserving Poland, would save themselves "because Bolshevism, for you Jews, living mainly from commerce, is the grave!" "Go do battle. The God of Abraham, Isaac, and Jacob will be with you."[10]

Rabbinate and governors of Tomaszów-Mazowiecki's commune perhaps most fulsomely apostrophized the Polish homeland:

> The Fatherland where we have lived a thousand years, which alone in Europe, during our medieval wanderings and distress, drew us to itself; Poland, under whose beneficent sun our faith and culture matured; the LAND to which thousands of memories and spiritual ties bind us; the paternal country to whose building we contributed in considerable measure and which we have defended with blood and treasure – now stands under threat of obliteration [*zagłady*] and loss of self-determination, freedom, and national existence.
>
> Jews! In this moment let us forget all dissensions, especially as they are instigated by particular elements hostile to the Polish state. For we well know the Polish people's tolerant spirit and Poland's old traditions.[11]

Signaled here are Endeks and other groups antagonistic to Piłsudski's Poland. Opposed to them was a culture understood as friendly to Polonophile Jews and protective of them.

These and the nine other Jewish communal calls to arms Zionist parliamentarians archived will have had many similar counterparts, for pro-government sentiment was widespread, despite all abuse in ethnographic Poland's Congress Kingdom heartland or violence-scarred Galicia.

The Army's Anxious View of Its Soldiers

The Central Military Archive in suburban Warsaw's Rembertów houses the *Komunikat Informacyjny* (*KI*), a secret (*tajny*) weekly report on the soldiery in their material and psychological circumstances and on the war's political setting but not its battles. Recipients included Piłsudski as Supreme Commander, central and regional army chiefs, select ministries and gendarmerie, but not prime minister and cabinet. Its spirit was

---

[9] Ibid., fos. 445–46 (n.d. [July 1920]).   [10] Ibid., fo. 453 (n.d. [July 1920]).
[11] Ibid., fo. 449 (n.d. [July 1920]).

Figure 8.3 In this famous photograph, Marshal Józef Piłsudski receives bread and salt – offerings of loyalty, friendship, and respect – from Jewish inhabitants of Dęblin, right-bank Vistula *shtetl*, after its reconquest from Soviet occupiers in the 1920 war.
Source: Centralne Archiwum Wojskowe, Warsaw-Rembertów.

Piłsudskiite, antagonism toward Endeks undisguised. Political and social-cultural historians of Polish Jewry and the Polish-Jewish relationship have left it undiscovered.

The *KI* thematized antisemitism and Poland's Jews, but surprisingly rarely. Even so, in October, in war's aftermath, it bluntly proclaimed that "antisemitism represents the soldier's most characteristic trait [*antysemi-tyzm stanowi narbardziej charakterystyczny rys żołnierza*]," adding that "the press whips it up, writing incessantly of Jewish treason." Yet, during July and August's desperate fighting, army intelligence analysts were much more concerned with antiwar attitudes among Poland's village-dwelling majority, and communist revolt's menace in the civilian heartland, than anti-Judaism and its manifestations.[12]

Six years of war and plunder, market chaos, and currency gyrations widely impoverished the Polish lands. The army exposed its soldiers to sometimes beggarly, health-destroying conditions, firing their aggrieved sense of deprivation and readiness to express it in anti-Jewish abuse. Of the Warsaw/Mazovian Command District, the July 2 *KI* reported that at the big Jabłonna-Legionowo base near the capital, "troops must often perform exercises barefoot," while "recruits go about mostly in their own clothes, torn and dirty, often shoeless." Diet was "monotonous – "soup from dried rutabagas was served almost uninterruptedly for three weeks." Another kitchen served salted herring six days in ten; there was little fat; potatoes were often spoiled. Soldiers' "morale level" was "very low." Officers alone played soccer. Nor did officers and enlisted men interact off-duty. Vodka was sold illegally, venereal disease lurked, "suspicious women circulate around the base." Among one group of 997 men, 304 were classed as illiterate, 365 as "half-illiterate."

Women volunteers (*Legionistki*) were exhausted by duties and exercises:

A big percentage of [women's] illnesses are sunburns and leg injuries from daily marches. A considerable number succumb to illnesses requiring operations, negatively affecting future motherhood. There are daily faintings on duty – six on June 20 ... [Literate women alone were recruited.] Morale and intellectual level is high.

Kraków/Galicia District reported that 150 venereally diseased soldiers had returned from the eastern front to Rzeszów. They had been "causing trouble, robbing even," and so were denied disembarkment. Armed confrontation followed, other soldiers facing them down with machine guns while railroad workers took their side. In general, "educated and reliable non-commissioned officers are lacking." Many were surly and dishonest. Desertions were frequent: over 400 in April and May.

Łódź District reported that "the soldierly masses generally are uninterested in political life. There can be no talk of any specific influences on them." Jewish soldiers alone sometimes attended Zionist meetings. For the rest, recruited mainly from villages, material well-being – food and equipment – alone mattered. Kielce District complained of unworthy behavior among officers, given to "flaunting themselves." Pińczów

---

[12] The *Komunikat Informacyjny* is housed in the Centralne Archiwum Wojskowe (CAW) in section VII: Oddział II Sztabu Ministerstwa Spraw Wojskowych za lata 1918–1921. Sygn. I.300.76. It will be cited below as *KI*, with issue number and date. Its reports were organized by regional command districts (*Dowództwa Okręgu Generalnego*).

garrison officers were "too familiar with Jewesses." It was said that "officers' [sexual] dealings with Jewesses greatly undermine their authority in troops' eyes." Officers drank and played cards daily. Alcoholism was on display. Former Austrian officers "ride out daily from town, trampling ploughed fields and returning noisily."[13]

This dispiriting picture grew darker when July 2's *KI* turned to national politics. Endeks' relentless opposition "undermined Chief of State Piłsudski's prestige," already suffering heavy criticism for retreating from Kiev. Gnawing uncertainty about Poland's susceptibility to Bolshevism filled intelligence agents' minds. Strikes in Warsaw showed that "revolutionary forces" were alive but limited by the "masses' passive resistance, who want no revolution." Facing threat of internal revolts, "the Polish intelligentsia, unlike the Russian, will not agree to be a passive element of social self-vivisection."

More worrisome than proletarian rebelliousness was rural radicalism. Peasant parties' demand for land reform at big landlords' expense grew more insistent as village lads marched to war. In industrial Dąbrowa Basin, communists led strikes against the army's drafting of workers that the war-backing PPS was hard pressed to counteract. In Ukrainian districts, despite little overt engagement in nationalist-irredentist politics, villages were loath to hand over recruits. In Pomerania, German-speaking youth were threatening, should they be drafted, to desert and fight for Russia.[14]

Much idealism, determination, and stoicism were demanded of young Jews thrust into an army beset with such deficiencies and anxieties. July 9's *KI* noted a populist millenarian religious movement active in Kraków calling itself "Body of Christ" and preaching that "all will be destroyed, church will fall as well as state, for Bolshevism is overthrowing everything." Army recruitment in Galicia (Little Poland [*Małopolska*]) "produces very meager results. Many draftees fail to report at all, or desert after induction." "Powerful agitation" in town and village exhorted draft evasion. Kielce police, "fearful of the crowd," released three arrested communists. The PPS explained the war's unpopularity among worker masses by governmental failure to convince them that the war was self-defensive only, not one of eastern conquest (as it partly was).[15]

Contemplating the "powerful Bolshevik offensive" pouring into the country, July 20's *KI* warned of possible "psychological and moral demobilization." Yet Piłsudski's exhortations were producing "strong

---

[13] *KI*, no. 37 (104), July 2, 1920 (*Sprawy Wojskowe*).
[14] *KI*, no. 38 (105), July 2, 1920 (*Sprawy Polityczne*).
[15] *KI*, no. 39 (106), July 9, 1920 (*Sprawy Polityczne*).

enlistment of good human material" into Haller's army; for example, 5,000 in one Warsaw day. Communist propaganda predicting imminent social upheaval and soldierly mutiny was having no effect in the army, even though communists were voluntarily joining so as to bore from within. But it fell on fertile ground in Little Poland and Congress Kingdom villages, where "strong aversion to reporting for service" persisted. Whole villages boycotted the call, and "punitive expeditions" were of little use.

Antiwar propaganda "disseminates most fantastic rumors, which spread among the dark masses," for example, "those in Piotrków and Kielce districts that doggedly claim about Piłsudski that 'he murdered Archbishop Kakowski' or that 'he took state monies and fled before the Bolsheviks.'" In the villages,

suspicious wanderers were turning up in beggars' guise, artfully suggesting to peasants that they had no representatives in government, calling the current ministry "a gentlemen's government of magnates and priests," and planting belief in listeners' minds that there already exists a "secret worker-peasant government" that will take power at any moment.[16]

July 20's *KI* also addressed Jewish reactions to Bolshevik invasion. Among workers and artisans supportive of Bund and Poale Zion, "attitudes prevail that emphatically sympathize with Bolshevik successes and are hostile to army recruitment." Opposed to them were Orthodox Jews and "partly assimilated bourgeoisie," devoted to Zionism. "Among these latter is observable an effort to break the ice separating Polish society from Jews." There were many Jewish calls to sacrifice for the war. Although they "constantly underscore the hostile attitude – in their view – of Polish society toward Jewish nationality," they also "feel moved to solidarity facing the external foe." The wealthier were loyally buying war bonds. "These groups of Jews fear any sort of upheaval, any change of government; in view of the [bloody] experiences in Hungary and Ukraine the idea terrifies them of social movements and civil war." Jewish politicians, including internationally prominent Zionist Alfred Nossig, were seeking "Polish-Jewish reconciliation" in the Sejm. To this end, then-Prime Minister Grabski, Endek luminary, had called an inter-party conference.

Such was Piłsudskiite army intelligence's view of Poland's Jews: mildly benevolent but lofty and distant, assuming it was Jews' responsibility to improve Polish-Jewish relations by drawing closer to the state, underplaying the gravity of demotic and Endek-style antisemitism.

---

[16] *KI*, no. 40 (107), July 20, 1920 (*Sprawy Polityczne*).

Facing Bolshevik onslaught, Piłsudski, with all Sejm parties' backing, recalled moderate peasant leader Wincenty Witos as prime minister. A national-unity Council for Defense of the Republic (ROP) emerged. Appeals to Poland's sorely abused villagers, gripped by millenialist yearnings for land reform, were of burning importance. July 24's *KI* reported that all the country's military districts "complain continually of the *peasant masses' almost total holding back* from army enlistment." They perhaps realized the battlefield's critical state but still thought wider age cohorts should be called up. "Each waits on the other." "No one wants to fight for those who stay home." In Lublin District many villages say "they will hand over the soldier [*dadzą żołnierza*] if land reform is carried out."

"The sense of general national interest is weakly developed in the peasant mass." PPS workers were shouldering guns while "villagers often put up resistance that must be fought with force." The Bund, having joined Lenin's Third International and seemingly yielding power internally to communists, had been disbanded by state decree. In Polish-controlled eastern borderlands, Ukrainians, Jews, and Germans appeared anti-Warsaw and pro-Bolshevik, and even Catholic villagers were tempted by communist land reform. When recruiters pressed Ukrainians to shoulder arms, they made a show of agreeing, saying, "we'll show you how we'll serve you."[17]

A week later, voluntary enlistment of peasants was yielding "inexpressibly weak results." It was intelligentsia, students, and artisans who supplied the main contingents, so that new soldiers' "intellectual and ideological level was comparatively high." Villagers would only yield, and then not everywhere, to compulsory recruitment. In Lublin District, near the front, "deserter bands are disturbing law-abiding people." Polish officers' behavior, especially bribe taking, aided enemy propaganda. NCOs evaded service; draftees had to be forcibly mustered.[18]

August 5's *KI* nervously noted Moscow radio's proclamation on July 31 of the formation on Polish soil, under Russian bayonets, of the Provisional Polish Revolutionary Committee (*Rewkom*) – a communist government, headed by Julian Marchlewski and including Felix Dzerzhinsky (Polish-born Dzierżyński), dreaded Cheka chief. It promised, apart from big landlords' expropriation, imminent nationalization of factories and

---

[17] *KI*, no. 41 (108), July 24, 1920 (*Sprawy Polityczne*) (author's emphasis).

[18] *KI*, no. 42 (109), July 31, 1920 (*Sprawy Wojskowe*). A poster exhorting the reluctant peasant farmer to enlist in the army warned that if he did not, "tomorrow you'll hand your property over under Bolshevik lash." It was an unvarnished appeal to peasants' material interests, silent about patriotism. Knyt et al., *Rok 1920*, 117.

workshops.[19] A week later, as the Poles' "Miracle of the Vistula" repulsed Soviet assault on Warsaw, army intelligence breathed relief.

Communist influences proved totally superficial. The terrible danger from the East, a danger stripped of the mendacious and deceitful lies about brotherhood and peace, achieved more than the best organized counter-propaganda ... Poland's working masses were never more distant from communist slogans than today.[20]

The Soviet advance, paradoxically, cut whatever communist roots were growing in Poland, also damaged by rumors of dissension among Polish communists – some relying on Soviet arms, others hoping to ignite Polish civil war leading to unaided communist victory.

In Poland's villages, "decisive changes for the better" had finally occurred. Previously, August 15's *KI* observed that deserters

found support among farmers, expressing itself as sympathy for desertion as such and for hunted runaways' fate and aiding them in hiding ... Peasants, sometimes even peasant elite [*elita chłopska*], delegates to Agricultural Circles, did not hide their indifference to the State's fate, divorcing their interests from the Nation's.[21]

Yet events moved with such elementary force that "villages too lurched into movement." Recruitment picked up, announcement of the death penalty for deserters, and amnesty for those who returned to their units before August 3 had their effect, although enlistment among peasants remained weaker than in towns. This derived – in a formulation again recalling Thomas and Znaniecki's portrait – from "the peasant's particular psyche."

Necessities of state appear to the peasant only in the form of compulsion from above, enforced by stern punishment. To appeal to his good-will in fulfilling the hardest of citizenly duties is for the peasant of all three partition areas an incomprehensible novelty, incompatible with a tradition inculcated in him through many generations.

Village life's microscale meant that "everybody fears they might alone go while the others remain behind." Nor did they want to be absent during

---

[19] *KI*, no. 44 (111), August 5, 1920 (*Sprawy Polityczne*).

[20] *KI*, no. 45 (112), August 15, 1920 (*Sprawy Polityczne*).

[21] Here and below: *KI*, no. 45 (112), August 15, 1920 (*Sprawy Polityczne*). From war-roiled East Galicia the *KI* reported "an enormous influx of refugees from the East [Dnieper Ukraine]. Fantastic stories sown among them by soldiers spread panic. Retreating army units, pulling huge cart-trains loaded with bags and suitcases [including plunder's booty] are totally disorganized." Many soldiers enforce requisitions "in form incompatible with soldierly dignity." The "withdrawal of our army and arrival of Ukrainian forces, often barefoot and famished, engaging in excesses [pogroms and assaults on local Poles], elicit not only panic" but also a feeling that state breakdown as in November 1918 is imminent.

harvest. But when enlistment was imposed, they accepted it, as now, "with much good will, even enthusiasm, and above all toughness and endurance."

One of the Central Front army's "weekly advisories" reported on regions where the Red Army had earlier broken through. In Lublin, the leftist parties – communists, Bund, Poale Zion – "follow the idea of Soviet Poland and alliance with Soviet Russia." But after the Poles' successes, they were backtracking "to regain lost popularity in worker circles." Jews "are generally not friendly." Bełz burned, and Poles departed. "Only Jews remained, who say they are indifferent to who rules, but in their soul's depth they're Bolshevik partisans." The Ukrainian population "impatiently await Bolsheviks, so as to rid themselves of hated '*lachiw*' (Poles) ... In the villages, agitators are rural schoolteachers and Ruthenian priests." From the Ukrainian front, censors reported that soldiers' letters reflected confidence in looming victory. "They write of agitation in the army, spread mainly by Jews."[22]

In late August, the *KI*, which valued Polish Socialists' backing of Piłsudski and the war, complained that in various places, as in Kielce District, "clergy and large landowners paralyze PPS's recruitment efforts and generally those of people of leftist conviction." Here too "the Jews' behavior is negative, except for the Jewish bourgeoisie, whose war contributions are large. This undoubtedly flows from fear of Bolshevism and pogroms." Jewish draft evasion was considerable. In Kielce, 300 failed to report, "mostly Jews." Authorities here and in Łódź District were staging "nightly roundups." Introduction of the death penalty for deserters was causing many to turn them themselves in, including a "considerable percentage of Jews." Villages were starting to hand over deserters and "Bolshevik agitators."

In Little Poland, communist propaganda "defamed *Naczelnik* [Piłsudski] and government," calling for "settling account 'with the *szlachta*.'" In Warsaw, "the best spirit prevails among working-class soldiers." The rigors of training or disappointment on learning that education didn't determine rank tempted the intelligentsia to quit. The women's section of the antisemitic organization *Rozwój* mobilized many volunteers for auxiliary services and nursing, but also for firing guns.

August 24's *KI* declared Warsaw out of danger. Reflecting on preceding perilous weeks, it was gratified that none of the parties, from Endeks to PPS, entertained the thought of capitulation to the "invading hordes."

---

[22] CAW. I.311.4.224. Dowództwo Frontu Środkowego. Oddział II. Sekjca Defensywna. No. 1454, "Tygodniowy Meldunek Sytuacyjny Defensywny No 5," August 17, 1920.

PPS had formed a Workers Committee for Defense of Warsaw that aimed to recruit communist-inclined proletarians. It argued that

the Bolshevik "*czrezwyczajki*" [Chekists], if they succeeded in ruling Poland, will murder workers along with "bourgeois." Together with Bolshevism, hunger and oppression will descend on us, for the Polish government the invader installs will be but tool in Soviet Russian government's hands.[23]

If in German-settled parts of the new Poland the Red Army was greeted as harbinger of their return to the Reich, in the Congress Kingdom the Soviets encountered "an unconditionally hostile attitude among Poles of both town and village."

The *KI* suffered a singular lapse into rhetoric of "Jewish Bolshevism" in discussing pro-Russian collaboration. Some Soviet-type authorities – *rewkoms* – were, admittedly, set up with cooperation of local communists. Agitation was intensive, led by "'forces' imported from Russia, mainly Polish-speaking Jews, but results were nil" (even though Trotsky broadcast to Poles that Soviet victory would entail no violence such as tsarism had unleashed but that the Red Army "was bringing 'on its bayonets the beams of world revolution's red sun'"). In a few localities, there was

pronounced participation of Jewish youth in communist government and Jews' friendly attitude toward the Red Army. General Staff reports even confirmed in two places volunteer units, comprised of Jewish communists, fighting on Bolshevik side.

Unfortunately, gendarmes did not always soon arrive in Soviet-vacated towns, so "valuable material" was lost that could have illumined local collaboration. While some Russian units paid for requisitions in Soviet rubles (one equaling 2 to 3 Polish marks), robbery and violence were common, largely explaining "peasants' zeal cooperating with the army in capturing isolated Bolshevik bands hiding in the forests."[24]

At August's end, *KI* found that following the army's regaining of the Polish eastern ethnographic border, society was succumbing to war weariness and desire for recruitment's end and demobilization. Yet morale was good. "The *Naczelnik*'s cult grows in the ranks," even among Endek-minded Poznanian and Pomeranian units. Soldiers' treatment of civilians in the east, "often stripped of everything by Bolsheviks," was commonly rapacious. "It frequently comes to anti-Jewish excesses committed by units passing through, especially from Poznania." Soldierly complaints were rife about "Jews buying themselves free of the army, especially in Kielce District."

[23] *KI*, no. 47 (114), August 24, 1920 (*Sprawy Wojskowe*).
[24] *KI*, no. 48 (115), August 24, 1920 (*Sprawy Polityczne*).

Kraków Military District reported that "among soldiers, especially of Tarnów and Rzeszów garrisons, a powerful feeling spreads of Jew-hatred. This hatred manifests itself plainly in general attitudes and sporadic attacks on individual Jews – even, as happened in Tarnów, by whole army detachments." More than 800 deserters were captured in Upper Silesia (thought by many draft evaders to be a safe haven). "Most were Jews." A court-martial ordered four shot, alongside a Bolshevik propagandizer.[25]

In early September, KI declared that "for the first time since state independence, the government really does have the whole nation behind it." But the army's plundering of eastern civilians was massive, despite introduction of "flying courts-martial." "Soldiers burn with special hate for gendarmes and police" – seen as agents of governmental law and order – "and make trouble with them at every step."

Poznania reported that "ragged and dirty soldiers have become objects of derision among Germans, who don't hide their poisonous reactions to conditions prevailing in Poland." The Polish soldiers there "display a certain local pride, deriving from a feeling of scorn for conditions elsewhere in Poland." Wanting to distance themselves, they demanded that their officers' posts be reserved for (often previously German-trained) Poznanians alone. These, in turn (like many previously Russian army officers), "stand with the National Democrats and unconditional anti-semitism." Army officers otherwise leaned toward populist and progressive parties.[26]

September 27's KI claimed of "Jews in the army" that in some units there is a high percentage of Jews (e.g., 800 of one battalion's 4,000). Jews exert a harmful effect on soldiers' mood, since they use every means to free themselves. Families visiting Jewish soldiers often bring food with ingredients inducing illness. One battalion forbade such meetings, especially since "visitors spread groundless rumors." In the east, "anti-Jewish excesses repeat themselves continually, led by Poznanian formations."[27]

In early October, army intelligence found the soldier politically "colorless" and disinterested. But here followed the statement opening this section: "antisemitism represents the soldier's most characteristic trait." It was a prominent feature too of Lublin-area women legionnaires.[28] In late October, KI observed an uptick in soldierly political interest. Opinion was spreading that "after the war the state will proceed on

[25] KI, no. 50 (117), September 3, 1920 (Sprawy Wojskowe).
[26] KI, no. 54 (121), September 19, 1920 (Sprawy Wojskowe).
[27] KI, no. 56 (123), September 27, 1920 (Sprawy Wojskowe).
[28] KI, no. 60 (127), October 10, 1920 (Sprawy Wojskowe).

grand scale to land-distribution in the eastern borderlands." Many hoped to settle there. Such would be their imperialist-style war spoils (though some had begun collecting preliminary prizes through plunder).[29]

Among other confidential governmental sources, it was not only the *KI* that showed few traces of paranoid antisemitism. As the July war intensified, government intelligence took stock of Poland's Jews – a population much discussed but little studied – in a survey of their religious and political life by unnamed authors in the Interior Ministry's Press Division. They divided religious observance into 80 percent Orthodox (reckoning 50 percent of all Jews Hasidim) and 10 to 20 percent "progressive." The latter, wearing "European dress," allegedly rejected Talmud but honored Torah, savored edifying sermons, and observed religious holidays. They were growing in number and splitting off into their own religious communes.

"Assimilators" – students, intelligentsia, upper bourgeoisie – were religiously largely indifferent or were progressives. "This group has now become more foreign to Jewry than German or Russian assimilators," a drastic judgment seemingly meant to highlight their discomfort with stringent Orthodoxy and Hasidism, both far stronger in Poland than to west or east. They advocated "complete self-dissolution in Polish culture as a condition of authentic citizenly equality." Younger "neo-assimilators" showed more tolerance for religious tradition.

Agudas-Haortodoxim now called itself "Szlome Emune Izrael" ("Peacefully Faithful Israelites"). "In principle apolitical," it was anchored among merchants, real estate owners, artisans, petty traders, and workers who spoke Yiddish "jargon," though women in these circles, attending Polish schools, "readily speak Polish." The "nationalists" (Folkists), who arose at the turn of the century with the Yiddish press, took no religious stand.

Zionists too recruited from all classes, but especially lawyers, doctors, students, merchants, and the bourgeois, including many "Litvaks." Religious Mizrachi Zionists skirted theology, defending the faith for national reasons. The shift of international leadership from Berlin to London and the Entente's embrace of a Jewish Palestinian homeland fortified Polish Zionists' demand for national autonomy. As for Jewish socialists, the Bund "towers among Jewish workers," with a "strictly social-democratic program (Marxist) with nationalist emphasis" and membership, together with Poale Zion, in Lenin's III. International, putting them "in communication with communists."

---

[29] *KI*, no. 63 (130), October 25, 1920 (*Sprawy Wojskowe*).

This assessment was broadly accurate and demonization free. Had it shaped ruling elites' minds, they would have known that blanket suspicion of Poland's Jews, as "Judeo-Bolsheviks" or fellow travelers, was absurd.[30] Yet army intelligence filed a report on the American Jewish Joint ("*Joined*") Distribution Committee depicting it as "Jewish plutocrats'" creation. "Every Jew must compulsorily make an appropriate contribution under threat of boycott." The JDC's emissaries in Eastern Europe, whose work was actually highly beneficial, were said to practice furtive black marketeering. "Many are Bolshevik sympathizers," widely seen as German or Russian spies. During the Bolshevik invasion, they concentrated their aid near the front lines "so as to give the Bolsheviks, in the event of sudden Polish evacuations, the chance to capture their warehouses." Another report accused the JDC of working with "Jewish banks in Warsaw" against Poland. "Every dollar in private hands, especially Jewish, is used to depress the Polish mark." Here were main elements of world-conspiracy theory.[31]

General Wróczyński, attached to the Interior Ministry, wrote army Supreme Command about numerous press reports on Jewish pro-Bolshevism. He requested evidence showing "that Jews relate to our army in unfriendly manner or even act hostilely toward it." Seemingly in response, a file was assembled of field reports on the number of Jewish youth who had volunteered for the Red Army, both in eastern Poland and in the Polish-occupied borderlands beyond. From eighteen localities the total number accepted for service by Russian recruiting offices was 1,193, including 142 from Chełm (who "crossed lines and reported to the Bolshevik army"). In one unspecified region, "apart from evidence of sympathy, there has been no noticeable cooperation of the Jewish population with enemy actions." Whether these data were inflated or underestimated is presently unclear, but they do not seem improbable. While Polish authorities may have thought they had a claim on borderland Jewish loyalties, many Jewish youths living there believed they were free to choose in the brutal war for survival raging about them.[32]

The Internment Camp at Jabłonna

Despite government intelligence agencies' distance from paranoid anti-semitism, leaders both of the regular army and of Haller's volunteers were

---

[30] AAN. PRM. No. 21431/20, fo. 286 (July 1920), "Żydowskie Grupy Religijne i Polityczne w Polsce."

[31] CAW. I.301.8.771. Oddział II. Protokoły spraw sądowych. 1920–21. Doc. A (n.d. [late 1920]).

[32] Ibid., docs. I and H (August 30 and September 16, 1920).

complicit in branding Jewish recruits as potentially traitorous collaborators with Russian "Jewish Bolshevism." No less a personage than General
Władysław Sikorski, commander of the regular army's central front and
thus defender of Warsaw and hero of the "Vistula miracle" – later iconic
embodiment during World War II of pro-Western Poland – signed an
announcement, undated but formulated as the Russians retreated
in August and September. Here is the full text:

Polish People [*Ludu Polski*]!
   Bolshevik Muscovite bands under Jewish commissars' command dared to
cross the glorious Polish Republic's border. Worse still – they stood before
beloved Warsaw's walls and threatened our capital. Polish People! The Polish
soldier's patience ran out. Under my command the army, in a fury, attacked the
accursed Bolshevik hordes and routed their hostile bands. The enemy retreated in
panic. Some of them were cut off and now roam the forests. Villagers, a new
harvest awaits you. Sharpen your scythes, your pitchforks, your axes and pursue
the enemy. Let the accursed Bolshevik bands and their Jewish commissars feel the
strength of your arm on their necks, the sharpness of your scythes, pitchforks, and
axes. Spare only those who willingly lay down their arms and deliver them to
military command.[33]

Origin and impact of this exhortation to the peasantry to commit far-
ranging murder with farm tools remain to be explicated, but that it
illustrates the highest army leadership's embrace of the "Jewish
Bolshevik" obsession is indubitable.
   Haller's volunteer army's General Inspectorate proclaimed to the country the Bolshevik Government's Program in Poland: Lenin and Trotsky
envisioned communist government under veteran socialist radical Julian
Marchlewski, "married to a Jewess." Foreign minister was to be Karl
"Radek-Sobelson from Tarnów," once expelled from the PPS "for
theft." Minister of interior was to be Dzierżyński, "well-know Cheka
operative and chief, murderer of thousands of Polish women and children." Jewish-born Alexander Parwus-Helfand's name alone served to
affright. Their program would terrorize Polish farmers: to confiscating

---

[33] AAN. PRM 21431/20, fo. 357a (n.d.): Sikorski, Generał i Dowódca: "Ludu Polski!" –
Bolszewickie bandy moskiewskie pod dowództwem żydowskich komisarzy ośmieliły się
wkróczyć w granice Najjasniejszej Rzeczypospolitej polskiej. Mało tego – stanęły pod
murami ukochanej Warszawy i zagrażały naszej stolicy.
   Ludu polski! Cierpliwość żolnierza polskiego wyczerpała się. Wojska stające pod moim
dowództwem z wściekliwością uderzyły na przeklęte hordy bolszewików i rozbiły wraże
bandy. Wróg rozpoczął paniczny odwrót. Część tych band została odcięta i obecnie
włóczy się po lasach. Ludu włościanski, nowe żniwa czeka na cię. Naostrz kosy, naostrz
widły i siekiery i dalej na wroga. Niech poczują przeklęte bandy bolszewickie i żydowscy
komisarze na swoich karkach moc twego ramienia, ostrze twych kos, wideł i siekier.
Oszczędzaj tylko tych, którzy dobrowolnie złożą oręż i odstawiaj ich do komend
wojskowych.

grain for shipment to Russia; organize emigration of Russian paupers for settlement on Polish land; and disarm Poland, occupying it with Red Army and Cheka, the latter (bizarrely) disposing of *"Chinese death battalions."* Finally, it reformulated the immigration threat as settlement of "Russian and Jewish poor, emptying for them the bourgeoisie's dwellings in the towns and billeting them on the rural population. To arms! To arms!" Here was the antisemitic nightmare of Poland's "Judaization," worsened through swamping by Russia's impoverished dregs.[34]

Were such Judeophobic bugle calls the military's cold-bloodedly Machiavellian effort to mobilize a war-weary population unused to willing self-sacrifice for the sake of a state of their own? Seemingly so, but doubtless some regular army commanders also shared, as did their officers, the "unconditional antisemitism" that army intelligence attributed to Endek soldiers and tsarist army veterans. It was this disposition that led the regular army to intern in a virtual concentration camp thousands of Jewish soldiers, educated volunteers and proletarian draftees alike – and this at a time, starting in early July and stretching into October, when their contribution to the war effort was desperately needed.

The camp was Jabłonna (Figure 8.4), part of an army base complex near Warsaw, downstream on the Vistula.[35] Endek agitation in early July against alleged Jewish traitors in army service helped inspire Minister of Military Affairs General Kazimierz Sosnkowski to order arrest of some 1,000 men, predominantly Jews, some seasoned veterans, staffing the army's various regional headquarters. Zionist parliamentarians archived an undated summary of Sosnkowski's order: "expel all Jews from [army] offices, form labor detachment [for earthworks] and incorporate Jews in it."[36]

Internal ethnic-cleansing impulses were not new to the army, as evidenced by General Symon's December 1919 command that fell into Zionist hands. He had been inspecting regional headquarters and wrote that "despite relevant prohibitions I still constantly encountered volunteers and soldiers of Mosaic faith employed in staff-work. Dismiss immediately." In November 1917, General Rzędkowski, divisional Lithuanian-Belarusian front commander, confidentially sent subordinates a text giving eloquent voice to resentment of talented minorities, condescension toward Christian commoners, and Polish self-doubt.

---

[34] Ibid., fos. 335–36 (*ca.* July 20, 1920) (author's emphasis).

[35] The subject remains largely unresearched. It does not figure in Tomaszewski et al., *Najnowsze dzieje Żydów*. Heller, *Edge of Destruction*, cites older literature, 50–51, 303. www.jhi.pl/psj/oboz_dla_internowanych_w_Jablonnie sparely reports received opinion.

[36] AAN. PRM 21431/20, fo. 504 (n.d.).

Figure 8.4 Jewish soldiers interned July–September 1920 at the Jabłonna army camp near Warsaw. Thousands of such men, some volunteers, others enlistees, some World War I veterans, many ardent patriots, were confined in the midst of hysteria over "Judeo-Bolshevik" sabotage of the anti-Soviet war. Here they appear well dressed and fit, but conditions for most were perilous: inadequate food and medical care, disease, antisemitic abuse.
Source: Provenance unknown.

It was a point of honor, he declaimed, to build the Fatherland "with our own strength" and to educate Polish soldiers, drawn from peasantry or artisanry, by employing them in officers' presence and "not Jew or German, who will always be hostile to our feelings and aims, and even harmful, sowing insurrectionary ideas in our ranks." Jews or Germans, "who might seem on the surface more intelligent than our average soldier," could betray sensitive information. "The Jew takes advantage of his cleverness and so-called intelligence," hurting the army. "Meanwhile, given good-will and patience on superiors' part, our soldier, seemingly less intelligent," would serve well without exploiting his position for his own interests. Germans and Jews were to be dismissed.[37]

When army recruits, volunteers included, chose in bureaucratic procedures to specify their nationality as Jewish rather than Polish, they were

---

[37] Ibid., fo. 39 (December 17, 1919); fo. 40 (November 7, 1919).

likely to suffer exclusion from preferred duties, even from gun issuance. But the same result might follow from their identification by other criteria as Jewish, even when they insisted on their Polishness.

In August 1920, Zionist parliamentarians pressured the government to release Jabłonna's inmates. Antoni Hartglas described his visit. Relatives bringing food met with "impossibly brutal treatment" by camp guards. One thousand internees had been removed the day before to unknown parts. "This party was loaded into railroad transport cars, locked under guard, and held for several hours like cattle, until the train left." The camp had served no food for two days so that men unable to buy it at the canteen faced starvation. In the "barracks for intelligentsia" he found plank beds but no mattresses. "Engineer B.," who had volunteered, was assigned to earthworks digging before landing in Jabłonna. He suffered "impossibly" from hunger. Hartglas heard shots fired, indicating the fifteen-minute visiting period's end. Relatives were "pitilessly beaten with clubs" to move them out.

Hartglas saw a group of "non-intelligentsia Jewish soldiers" in civilian rags and barefoot. They were marched in groups of eight, each with two Christian armed guards, who "prodded and cuffed those who were walking slowly from hunger and exhaustion." Jewish charities maintained meager canteens, while Christian sergeants ran shops. Poznanian guards were most brutal, wounding inmates in their sexual parts.[38]

Zionist parliamentarians protested to the Minister of Military Affairs, saying they had spoken with his precursor, who had assured them he was not an antisemite, disapproved of "Jew-baiting" (*szczucie przeciwko żydom*), and advocated Jewish civil equality. But now "*pan* Minister issues an order [for internment] having no precedent in any contemporary European army's history." They demanded immediate retraction, along with all moves toward other segregated soldierly units.[39] Another protest letter exclaimed that interned and segregated soldiers were "mostly *inteligentni*, youthful students," now held as "criminals":

The Jew is always guilty, just for being a Jew. If he didn't volunteer, the complaint would arise: "Jews are neutralists!" "Jews resist fulfilling their citizenly obligation, they're indifferent to the country's fate," etc.; if he volunteers, he is persecuted, ground down another way.[40]

A Jewish soldier's anonymous letter to the Sejm Club from camp Jabłonna II spoke for a multitude. The front but a few versts distant, they were suddenly mustered. "Our bitterness and sadness was endless,

[38] Ibid., fos. 519–20 (n.d.).   [39] Ibid., fo. 819 (August 16, 1920).
[40] Ibid., fos. 824–25 (August 17, 1920).

for they separated Christians from Jews," sending the former on a mission while returning Jews to barracks.

Here we sit, doing nothing, having no exercises. Rumors circulate that we will eventually be given uniforms and rifles and sent to the front. Not only do we not defend the natal soil, but our lives are doubtless lost. No relatives who could bring us food are admitted, nor can we go to them (nor, obviously, go home). How to explain this we don't know. We can't decide whether we're soldiers, prisoners or slaves. But they don't allow us to wear the soldier's caps, and remove it from anybody who tries.

New inmates were stripped of their uniforms. "Finding ourselves in this hellishly hellish hell," ignorant of their fate, he begged for immediate aid.[41]

Another anonymous plea claimed Jabłonna housed 3,000 Jews, sharing one cooking cauldron. "Non-student Jews" were surrounded by barbed wire; parents could not visit sons. They had no beds, only "bare boards." Vermin were profuse, toilets filthy. There was no doctor, no medicine. "Many are sick with dysentery, many with fevers, seemingly from typhus. All without aid, there is no infirmary." Their mood was terrible. Three additional kettles and medical aid were essential.[42]

Jakób Sawicz wrote that his son Borys, "trained mechanic and registered chauffeur," was receiving further army training when he was suddenly expelled from his mobile corps. His commander told him "he had nothing against Jews assigned to him, and recognizes their qualifications, but is bound by all authorities' orders." Kalman Arbeitman told of how his interned son gave him, on camp visit, "a torn Torah roll, which he received from Christian soldier colleagues, saying 'Jew, take your law [zakon].' It obviously had been robbed." Hersz Dąb told of how his son, responding to Piłsudski's call for volunteers, fell into Bolshevik hands while going for induction. They robbed him, destroyed his papers, and put him to forced labor. But when the Polish army liberated him, they sent him to Jabłonna.[43]

Hartglas wrote the War Ministry documenting soldiers' ill treatment, which he denounced as senseless. Many Jews were well suited to office work. By imprisoning them, the government gives hostage to the right-wing press, which later will claim it made a secret deal with Jews, "helping them take cover while sending Christians to the front, to slaughter." To suggest that Jews evade the battlefield will embolden "marauders and various scum unintentionally to be found in the army to commit barbarous murders and raping of women," as many such cases prove.

---

[41] Ibid., fos. 507–8 (August 14, 1920).   [42] Ibid., fo. 512 (n.d.).
[43] Ibid., fo. 511 (August 17, 1920); fo. 570 (August 13, 1920); fo. 850 (August 28, 1920).

"Humiliating treatment of soldiers and Jewish volunteers – the latter almost exclusively university students and intelligentsia – might lead them to revolt and unnecessary bloodshed."[44] Zionist chief Thon described his visit to a friend's son at Jabłonna. "Student-volunteers" slept on a bare stone floor or wooden pallets, without bed-covers. Daily food rations were one half-loaf of half-baked bread, dangerous to eat. "For soup and coffee soldiers must go to the camp gate," waiting an hour because of a kettle shortage.[45]

Poznanian soldiers in a train halting at Jabłonna fired on the camp and plundered Jewish shops in nearby towns. "When a representative of the authorities, apparently a higher officer, ordered them to disperse, they beat him."

A patrol was dispatched, which exchanged fire with them. In the camp all were ordered to lie on the floor, extinguish lights and cigarettes, to give no sign that anyone was there. Among internees terrible panic arose, because they didn't know what was happening and had no weapons.[46]

A volunteer engineer found himself stranded with 240 "other intelligentsia." They had no bread. Medical doctors among them were sent to workers' barracks, former accountants to workers' battalions' offices. The rest did nothing but exercises without arms. "There's a guard company that received rifles, because Poznanians lurk about … They attack our barracks … The workers' battalions are behind bars, in rags, misery."[47]

Majer Sadowski reported that his son, earlier inducted, learned from his major that, as a Jew, he would have to be interned either in Jabłonna or a Poznanian camp. "In view of [the major's] sympathy for him, he would do him the favor of sending him to the front instead. My son replied that he preferred, as a Jew, to share the fate of all soldier-Jews as internee." The major offered the "friendly advice" that he should reconsider, "for he knew that all the interned Jewish soldiers would be sent into the first line of fire at the front." But his son persisted and departed for the Poznanian camp.

Toward war's end, an internee wrote that he and others, released for front duty, were "treated inhumanly, brutally." They were given horse-drawn wagons, half full of horse manure. Denied cleaning tools, they had to find other means to dispel the "dreadful stench." Eventually they reached a train station where canteens run by Prylucki's Folkist Party fed them. As their train approached the front near Lublin, it derailed,

---

[44] Ibid., fo. 500 (August 19, 1920).   [45] Ibid., fo. 515 (August 30, 1920).
[46] Ibid., fo. 474 (August 24. 1920).   [47] Ibid., fo. 509 (August 25, 1920).

killing some soldiers. "These boys," before the accident, "were singing, full of strength, hope and courage."[48]

A timid Jewish assimilationist or Christian liberal view appeared in the press. Its author, Feliks Kuchowski, visited the camp and found not starvation but "great indigence." The chief problem was psychological: how to explain confinement of 3,000 sorely needed soldiers. "It's easy to imagine the moral wounds these young people suffer." Nor will "soldier-Christians" be indifferent, for they feel that Jabłonna "violates the [Christian] Polish soldier's honor."[49] On September 5, Zionists protested to army authorities that promises to disband Jabłonna remained unfulfilled. Internees now numbered 5,300. But by mid-September the camp was empty.

Hartglas wrote General Staff, saying the Military Ministry had earlier tried to justify Jabłonna's existence by appeal to "various rumors" and the "fact of [Jews'] hidden treachery," or to prevent treachery of which they were suspected. Now, though, the ministry was claiming that Jabłonna proved (praiseworthily) that "there was a disproportionately large representation among Jews of rank-and-file soldiers," saying, "no treason had been committed by Jews, nor any acts inconsistent with soldierly honor." The ministry was seeking to deny its antisemitic deeds and whitewash itself.[50] An example of the "rumors" appeared in testimony of a member of the volunteer army's Invalids' Battalion, one-quarter of whose 600 members were Jews (their patriotic feelings "not respected"). Explaining to Christian soldiers why Jews were being interned, their commander said: "some ten thousand soldier-Jews in the Polish army rebelled and were disarmed and confined to Jabłonna. They'll have to be guarded there, and maybe even shot."[51]

The camp's existence – evidence of unheroic paranoia and war hysteria – like so much else in these years was repressed both in Polish Christian and Jewish public memory and remains so.

Forced Labor and Imprisonment

Bolshevik shadows over Warsaw elicited furious army-directed earthwork building. Civilians volunteered for this work but were also dragooned. Jewish experience was predictably debilitating and humiliating. Bernard Cynamon told the Sejm Club that "I sent my wife Jadwiga to the PPS's labor office to enroll me as earthwork volunteer." She was informed he

---

[48] Ibid., fos. 523–24 (n.d.).   [49] Ibid., fos. 521–22 (September 1, 1920), from *Naród*.
[50] Ibid., fos. 903–4 (September 5, 1920); fos. 498–99 (September 16, 1920).
[51] Ibid., fo. 839 (August 24, 1920).

should report next day, but when he arrived, even after "expressing the wish to work with a shovel," the engineer "asked me, am I a Pole, to which I replied, I'm a Jew. He explained: 'I can't take you. I'm just afraid of you Jews. Clear out, don't hang around here, or the army will take you away' [as had happened already to two other Jews]. Thus were crushed our good intentions."[52]

Izaak Rechte said, "I was seized while standing at our building's entrance by a uniform-wearing youth" and forced to join a work party. They were driven on foot "like cattle without food or water."

We carried out no work and exhausted ourselves pointlessly and uselessly ... When, on the road, a woman asked for water, a corporal struck her with full strength. She fainted. He acted like a beast ... It's obvious that this has only to do with harassing Jews, for there were more voluntary Christian workers and Russian prisoners than work for them to do ... It's only tormenting of Jews, for they put sick and weak people to work who are completely unfit for it.[53]

Here was symbolic violence – conjuring enslavement – that Rechte, its victim, only dimly perceived. Two men spoke for some 2,000 Jews arrested on the streets and sent to the Jabłonna-Serock-Zegrze defense complex, where they worked nonstop for fifteen days. "Their treatment was barbarous." They lived on watery potato soup and daily half-pound of bread. Four hundred sickened but were not released.

They talked antisemitic rubbish [dudu antysemickim], that we're Bolsheviks, spies, saying they wouldn't release us but would murder us. We weren't sure of our lives. We worked with shells flying above, bullets whizzing past our heads ... Some of us died – those who fell sick – and were buried under Polish crosses. For three days we ate only raw fruit.

Now they wanted pay, compensation for ruined clothing, and proof of their labor.[54]

Hersz Zakheim told of being pulled from a tram and working with 8,000 Jews, without sleeping quarters, eating potato soup, with long marches, documents confiscated. Marja Iger testified to her husband's similar suffering, although "supervising soldiers treat workers properly and take pity on them. The engineer bears the main blame for their ill-treatment." Other wives intervened for husbands, saying, "they all have bloody and wounded hands from the barbed wire and can't work fast, so they are beaten."[55]

---

[52] Ibid., fo. 527 (August 18, 1920).   [53] Ibid., fo. 466 (August 15, 1920).

[54] Ibid., fo. 475 (n.d.); fo. 473 (August 20, 1920).

[55] Ibid., fo. 474 (August 20, 1920); fos. 462–53 (August 16, 1920); fo. 464 (August 16, 1920); fo. 472 (August 10, 1920).

Rojza Krone, speaking for five women, testified that soldiers "make them call out various provocative things, for example, 'long live the German army,' pitilessly beating non-compliers ... It's not work, but mockery of them." Overseers were Poznanian soldiers, one of whom seriously wounded a man as he shouted that Jews were "Bolsheviks" to be exterminated. "We add that the Polish engineer in charge advised us to seek counsel in Warsaw, because he couldn't stand to look at Poznanians' beatings." Pesse Rzetelna, having visited her brother, said he and other labor-captive Jews "have changed completely and lost their human aspect."[56]

Unsurprisingly, none of these plaintiffs, excepting Cynamon, expressed what civilian Jews' proper role in Warsaw's defense should be. By virtually enslaving and brutally mishandling Jewish emergency workers, the army forfeited whatever loyalty – doubtless variable – they were inclined to feel.

Panic over suspected Jewish pro-Bolshevism inspired arrests and incarceration. Zionist parliamentarians protested to Piłsudski.

Masses of people are being brought to various Warsaw prisons accused of anti-state activity. Most were suddenly removed from their homes, they are barefoot and naked, dying of hunger. Their families go from office to office seeking their whereabouts. No one knows. The condemned are bereft of the human right to take leave of their families before death. Some families discover their vanished ones in official lists of the executed. The accused Jews only weakly command the Polish language and, without defenders and because of misunderstandings, fall into wartime errors' net.

The Military Ministry stonewalled, refusing on principle to publicize arrests, saying that information on individuals could be obtained from public prosecutors. Nor did the army review death sentences imposed by frontline court martial. "Reproaches for maltreatment of Jews in particular ... are not supported in a single instance." The army "views them as groundless."[57]

Abuse of On-Duty Jewish Soldiers and Volunteers

Fulfillment of soldierly duty was no defense against antisemitic assaults within the ranks. Szloma Radom told the Sejm Club that as new draftees, he and colleague Panusz were summoned for work.

---

[56] Ibid., fo. 465 (August 16, 1920).
[57] CAW. Oddział II Sztabu Min. Spraw Wojsk. za lata 1918–1921. Sygn. I.300.76, file 103: doc. B (August 6, 1920); ibid., doc. C (August 25, 1920).

They led us to the toilets, ordered us to disrobe and with our own clothing and overcoats wipe the floor. Because we didn't want to do this, so as not the ruin our clothing, they clubbed us.

Pleas unavailing, they offered money – 5 to 10 marks, buying them free. Taken to bathe, a sergeant withheld 16 to 20 marks from their wallets. A corporal asked Radom about his work. "When I said I was an Artisans Union secretary, he struck me twice in the face." Jews were given the dirtiest work, often pointless. Bribery to avoid beatings was rife. He pleaded for Sejm Club intervention for all those who "endure inexpressible suffering."[58]

Hersz Freider was sweeping an office when a soldier hammered his head, only ceasing on receiving 3 marks. Relaxing with Jewish colleagues, the canteen manager and cook "beat them pitilessly on the head with their keys," relenting for 4 marks. Later a barracks commandant told him to wash the floor, although usually four women servants did the job. "He ordered me to jump and perform other stupidities, to amuse the women. Fearing a beating, I did all he commanded." A soldier tormentor took their money to buy bread but refused delivery. While they were sleeping, the same soldier smothered one of them, until he was given money.[59]

An anonymous victim reported a company commander who formed a "punitive unit" of Jewish soldiers, subjecting them to "inhuman thrashing" on pretext that ten Jewish soldiers had deserted. But absconding was higher among Christians, including officers. He and his mates were called "'Awrum Josef,' dishonoring the name of Abram Józef Trumpeldor," celebrated Russian-Jewish soldier recently martyred in Palestine. Treated "worse than dogs," they were forced while marching "to sing songs defaming us."[60]

The draft commission allowed a student to serve "without arms." Lieutenant Fröhlich told him, "you'll understand, as adherent of Mosaic religion, that we can't give you [a gun]. Change your confession, it'll be another thing."[61] Baumritter, former Warsaw Citizens Committee member, attempted to join the new armed Citizens Guard but was rebuffed. Seeking an explanation, "I heard one of the female office workers (wearing eyeglasses) say, 'a real Jew [żyd z żydów]' – obviously there was talk of rejecting Jews." His unit commander was an antisemitic Rozwój member. Judka Szyber submitted the requisite application with three citizens' recommendations. "They refused, promptly destroying it."[62]

---

[58] AAN. PRM, no. 21431/20, fo. 50 (April 20, 1920).   [59] Ibid., fo. 53 (n.d.).
[60] Ibid., fo. 51 (n.d.).   [61] Ibid., fo. 546 (n.d.).
[62] Ibid., fos. 528, 530–31 (August 10–13, 1920).

PPS's *Robotnik* published a reader's letter saying that "as a Pole tied with entire soul to the land of my birth," he had volunteered for the artillery but was rejected because of "my Mosaic confession." "Wounded by such treatment, and – unfortunately – with great sadness, I gave up on the army."

Is not the wish of Poles of Mosaic confession to fulfill patriotic obligations hindered by the Polish Christians themselves – although not a few Jews love their country more than Christian patriots?[63]

Conversely, the Zionist parliamentary bureau supplied several supplicants who believed they had been wrongly drafted with a text including the phrase: "I do not aim to evade military duties, but will do so when summoned as law prescribes."[64]

The parliamentarians protested to the army judiciary the execution for desertion of soldier Szmul Dynia. The draft board ignored that "he was beset with tuberculosis in both lungs." In unhealthy barracks, Dynia sensed he was dying and went home to continue his cure. He couldn't inform his superiors because of waiting lines and weakness. In the court martial, the prosecutor acted, as now alleged (perhaps rightly), from anti-Jewish bias.[65]

In October, Sejm Club bureau employee Miss Zyberdykówna visited Strzyżów, where she found 102 Jewish soldiers, recently released from Jabłonna, serving as infantrymen. She spoke with their commander, pointing out that, as volunteers, they were entitled to choose their army branch, yet all were now foot soldiers. He replied that he only knew they had been in a "concentration camp," for which they must have committed punishable actions. Despite her "lively" rebuttal, he insisted "emphatically that no one sits in a camp without guilt."

Proceeding to Lwów, she spoke with Colonel Marjański, who accepted her argument and empowered the soldiers to choose fitting units. Hearing about Jabłonna, "he was deeply offended," not understanding how such divisiveness could grip an army requiring unity. He assured her nothing similar could happen in Lwów. Charges of Jewish treason outraged him, "for he receives daily reports" that, in previously Russian-occupied East Galicia, "it was only Jews who hid generals, officers, and Polish POWs from Bolsheviks." After a two-hour conversation, during which Marjański arranged by telephone the Jewish soldiers' transfers, "I thanked him for this prompt and humane solution, to which in Jewish affairs we in the former Congress Kingdom are not accustomed."[66] Resolute Miss

---

[63] Ibid., fo. 535: *Robotnik* (July 28, 1920).   [64] Ibid., fos. 873–74 (September 2, 1920).
[65] Ibid., fos. 910–13 (August 20, 1920).   [66] Ibid., fos. 758–60 (October 10, 1920).

Zyberdykówna communicated comfortably with highly placed, liberal-minded Poles and was seemingly well disposed toward them. This was an instance of Polish-Jewish cooperation, of which there doubtless were many more, if not enough.

Jewish Women's Grievances

The war disappointed Jewish women, whose acculturation and family orientation inclined them toward Polish patriotism but whose efforts to join the struggle met antisemitism-inspired rejection. Students, both Polish and Jewish, were under pressure to volunteer for war work, for officialdom had made clear that admission to future higher education would depend on it. Roza Dobrecka wrote the Zionist bureau that when she and others volunteered for the Piłsudski-summoned Academic League for Defense of the State, their confession and nationality were recorded. "With this segregation went a certain partisanship," for individual qualifications were ignored. "All Jewish girls were placed in sewing circles or asked to solicit money." Protests were answered with citation of military orders, including that names of those declaring Jewish nationality should be erased. This would have "fatal consequences for some dozens of students."[67]

Zionists in Pabianice wrote the Sejm Club on behalf of gymnasium graduate Beila Rozenfeld, who, "inspired by the girl students' resolution," wanted to take nursing courses but was refused by the female director because of Jewishness.[68] Lea Fiszerówna, Chełm gymnasium graduate, lamented, "seeing the Fatherland in danger, I wanted to find some way of working for it, rendering urgently needed aid in a decisive moment." She was accepted as a nurse in Dr. Fiszel's field hospital, yet in Warsaw, when asked whether she was Catholic or Jewish, "I replied I was a Jewess, and was told that for this reason admission to the hospital was rejected."[69] Such incidents exemplified both Zionists' advocacy of fulfillment of Polish citizenly duties and their argument that Polish culture would reject Jewish assimilation.

Maria Pinczowska, Warsaw University student, testified that "student-Jewesses, registered for auxiliary service in accord with university regulations, are not being assigned jobs." Reporting to Polish Red Cross with her Christian colleagues, she was told only Polish girls were accepted. "This did not discourage me, since in registering I gave my nationality as Polish." The woman registrar asked, "but you're a Catholic?" Hearing

---

[67] Ibid., fo. 542 (August 2, 1920).   [68] Ibid., fo. 28 (July 28, 1920).
[69] Ibid., fos. 56, 541 (July 19 [or August 18] 1920).

she was Jewish, "she crossed my name off the list, saying, 'such people they don't take.'" Following "this affront," she protested the "unpleasantry" to the university coordinator. She was told to go to the Society for Equal Rights for Polish Women. "There they'll take you," but she found they had no internships.

> Colleague Dorabialska [university coordinator], assuming I was Christian, wanted to send me to do office work for General Haller's army, but when I corrected her, she desisted. She began to think about what to do with me, for because of my Polish-sounding name I was on the eligible list. Finally she decided to send me to Brest train station to sell anti-Bolshevik handbills. When I remarked that my Jewish confession would again be involved, she said 'that's not supervisorial work' and "'it' [her Jewishness] won't be relevant."[70]

Evident here are ambiguities and blurred borderlines accompanying Jewish acculturation.

A letter from "a former legionnaire of the Women's Legion" displays more antisemitism-inflicted psychic wounds. She was admitted to the pro-Piłsudski legion on recommendation of her uncle, Dr. Leon Goldsobel, veteran both of the 1863 rising and the 1905 revolution, one of whose pro-Polish brothers suffered execution in 1906. "Dr. Goldsobel's grandfather, Kępiński, died fighting in Napoleonic times in the Polish Legion at the battle of Saragosa." For this distinguished political genealogy, the Legion admitted her, "as sole Jewess." But then "I was expelled – evidently by special order. Earlier they had expelled baptized Jews." She held female commanders responsible. "I don't ask for intervention. If they expel me, I wish to serve no more."[71]

Berta Cukiert reported that she, as "assistant surgeon [felczerka] and operation-room nurse," requested Warsaw Red Cross appointment without pay to a hospital – work she had performed already in 1918. Interviewer Baroness Lesser, asking about religion and learning she was Jewish "told me she had received a military order not to admit Jewesses ... this pained her, but she must follow government regulations." Cukiert earlier visited another Red Cross office where its administrator, Zdzichowska, said, "it's good that Jews aren't accepted, because Jewish felczerki and nurses were already on trial, accused of deliberately administering poisoned injections to Polish soldiers." Such were rumors of diabolical deeds circulating in Warsaw's fashionable Nowy Świat District.

Yet the Zionist bureau obtained a letter text from Red Cross's national directorate, signed by vice president Helena Bisping, addressed to the

---

[70] Ibid., fo. 58 (July 22, 1920).   [71] Ibid., fo. 72 (August 25, 1920).

Government Commissioner for Polish Red Cross Affairs. She denied the
Red Cross ordered exclusion of Jews from volunteer work. If this had
occurred, it was without directorate knowledge, for it was their policy that
Jews with appropriate skills were admissible.[72]

Stefania Hornblas and Helena Brodt protested their firing on Red
Cross orders as nurses in Lublin's Military Epidemic Hospital, where
they worked from March 1919 to August 30, 1920. Hornblas spoke on
her last workday with Baroness Lesser, who said Jews "could not work in
military hospitals." Miss Hornblas "assured the baroness that she was
a good Pole, and religion should not concern anyone," but Lesser
invoked army orders. Brodt had worked in Lublin hospital since 1915,
earning an invitation from Austrian authorities to transfer to Vienna.
But her commandant demurred, "saying that as a Pole she ought to work
in the homeland. She complied, and now she encounters such
ingratitude."[73]

Railroad Violence

Jewish train riders remained targets of soldierly violence in ways this book
has chronicled, but also in some others. Revealing of assimilated Jews'
reactions was Sejm Club testimony of Dr. Isachar Ber Frey, journeyman
lawyer traveling to Przemyśl to join the state judiciary. At a provincial
station, 100 volunteer soldiers arrived. "They amused themselves by
beating and thrashing Jewish passers-by." Police were absent, and
NCOs found the "pranks" amusing. As Frey approached the station, he
heard shouts: "our faith is coming [nasza wiara idzie]!" – a crusading
Christian anti-Jewish battle cry we have not previously encountered.
Hiding behind the third-class buffet, Frey witnessed "bestial attacks on
Jews and wild scenes staged by a few volunteer-soldiers," who with rods
and bullwhips bloodied their victims, one a hunchback returning from
medical treatment. While railroad officials declined to intervene, saying
courts dismissed such cases, it finally sufficed for two policemen to take
one soldier's papers to pacify the scene.

In his second-class unlighted train seat, Frey suffered "punches
[kulaki] from every side." A trainman said nothing could be done
"because they're going to the front." After his failure to identify his
attackers to the conductor, they returned, saying "where is he, that fat-
head [fafral]?" They threatened to throw him from the moving train, but
"his pleas softened them." They left after taking his cane, worth 100

---

[72] Ibid., fos. 537ff. (September 1, 1920).
[73] Ibid., fos. 1054–55 (September 1, 1920). Cf. ibid., fo. 540.

marks, and cigarettes, as well as another passenger's wallet containing 16,000 marks. This victim, "in quiet despair, wringing his hands, kept repeating, 'what do I do now, how can I return to my wife and children?'" Frey appealed to an NCO, saying, "such events compromise the Fatherland even more now, when it's in danger."

Going to the soldiers' section, the robbery victim identified the thief, but the money had vanished. The NCO, facing soldiers' "hostile stance," gave up. He said that "he would vouch for [Frey's] life, but advised me to leave the train at the next stop." Yet Frey braved the ride to Przemyśl, where a colleague, *starosta*'s son, met him. At every station he heard embattled Jews' cries. A railroad official refused help, saying he had already been punitively transferred "for intervention in Jews' defense." The young and seemingly sheltered Frey's indignation at cruel violence, like his faith in the law, were perhaps a Habsburg legacy. Some Polish officials shared these feelings but were battle scarred and wary for their own survival. If Frey was right, soldiers sometimes attacked their enemies – with priestly blessing? – in name of their "faith."[74]

In late July the Sejm Club bureau registered numerous train riders' complaints. Zelcer, attempting to telephone ahead for arrest of thieves, heard from stationmaster Lępicki: "For Jews there are no gendarmes, there are no laws for them, you all need to be slaughtered [*wyrżnąć*]." Henryk Niemczyk reported that Poznanians "beat all recognizable Jews painfully with their [metal] mess-bowls." Other abuses he witnessed not by Haller troops but by "our soldiers."

Balcia Rosenberg saw soldiers call out in her train car, "where are those Jews? We have to butcher them [*zarżnąć*]." The Christian travelers "nodded assent, one saying, 'cut them into four pieces,'" as formerly befell those whom executioners quartered. Rosenberg and husband, like other passengers, gave soldiers "little gifts." One Christian, "whom I asked for help, restrained the soldiers, pointing out the disgrace and embarrassment caused by such behavior, for which other passengers heartily shouted him down." Dziubalowski scuffled with attackers, who "stabbed me with pins and bayonet, cut off my beard with knife and scissors, ordering me, as is usual, to shout 'long live Wielkopolska! May the rabbi croak!'" One then tried "to force on me a piece of pork sausage and tore up my mouth."

Soldiers pulled Silberstein's beard. "At my outcry, the [Warsaw] station police chief told them: 'stop this! It's forbidden at the station.'" In the train he was again pummeled, losing his silver watch. "I pleaded with the soldiers, telling them that my two sons are also in the army, one

[74] Ibid., fo. 136–37 (n.d. [July–August 1920]).

a volunteer, but it did no good." Only when his train approached Łódź "did a corporal of my acquaintance offer protection, leading me to the tram."[75]

Zionists against Antisemitism

Zionist parliamentarians – seven in 1920 – formed the Sejm Club of Deputies of the Jewish People's Party, whose bureau collected the aforementioned grievances. These were evidence for charges deputies raised in parliamentary interpellations. The Club office also assembled its own trove of anti-Jewish propaganda and actions. Deputies' protests were the politically most influential articulation among Poland's Jews of the wartime dangers they faced.

In May they wrote Prime Minister Leopold Skulski, saying Polish Jews had lived for a year and a half "in constant unrest and uncertainty of life and property." Pogroms, "commonly known among us as 'excesses,' have indeed ceased for quite a while," but lower-level assaults, especially by soldiers and in the railway system, continued, despite orders against them and some punishments. Gendarmes and railroad police were generally passive, while military officers, with few exceptions, "looked with indifference or indulgently smiled on 'hunting' for Jews."

Such abuse, they wrote, occurred in waves, as at Easter, but often together with events unrelated to the "Jewish question," such as the Upper Silesian German-Polish nationality conflict or Warsaw strikes. Close inspection showed that anti-Jewish excesses were preceded by intensified distribution of antisemitic handbills by the *Rozwój* Society, "various social self-help organizations," and other anonymous parties. *Rozwój* also published its libelous "lists of [Christian] sellers" – of land or other property to Jewish buyers – before Christmas and Easter, when crowds formed "and it's easy then to stage scuffles, stir up people's minds, and commit excesses." The deputies concluded that "this all shows that we have clearly to do here with planned action by certain social groups." On the southeastern front in the eastern borderlands, there were no posters or propaganda inciting to pogroms, and none had (as they thought) occurred, while in the northeast, around Pinsk and Lida, such agitation had led to violence. The propaganda was in Ukrainian or Belarusian, but style and content revealed its Polish provenance.

The government waffled, the deputies wrote, sometime claiming Jews only imagined abuses, sometimes forbidding removal of antisemitic

---

[75] Ibid., fos. 396–404 (July 21–26, 1920); also fos. 407–9. Cf. CAW.Oddział II, no. I.300.76.166, doc.1 (December 3, 1920).

posters. It tolerated press articles inciting to violence. The official *Monitor Polski* charged that illegal distilling was the work not of individuals but of "the Jews." If worse outbreaks hadn't occurred, it was because antisemitic organizations didn't judge time ripe. Here again was the theory of behind-the-scenes antisemitic wire pulling, serving highly deliberate, intentionalist objectives, as antisemitic world conspiracy theory also did.

Among evidence submitted with this protest was a *Rozwój* Society handbill reproducing an allegedly authentic (but invented) document found in a dead German Bolshevik's pocket and written "IN YIDDISH." Signed by the "Central Committee of the Petersburg Section of the International Jewish Union," it appealed to all Jews to persevere in their campaign for "world-domination." Great progress had been made in subjugation of Russia and the Russian people (although "they will ever remain [Bolshevism's] mortal enemy"). Against enemies: "UTTER BRUTALITY, without mercy."

The handbill's readers learned "who in Poland sows anarchy, who leads workers by the nose, exhorting them to continual strikes, fatal for our Fatherland, and to class struggle, who wants to starve Poland and weaken it so as to rule it as in Russia ... We must overpower this most vile enemy of our national solidarity, unity, and labor." This forgery's contrived and naive character may have escaped many gullible readers of Judeophobic persuasion. Its denigration of Polish worker radicalism pointed to linkage of much political antisemitism to the right-wing struggle against the left. If it did not incite directly to violence, it authorized it, although it required flare-up on Polish soil of anti-Soviet war to trigger new pogroms.[76]

Similar in character and thrust was an antistrike manifesto of the Central Polish Trade Union, which claimed to represent 60,000 workers' families in Warsaw alone. Addressed to "Brother Worker of Poland," it interpreted Bolsheviks' message as saying, "If the Polish intelligentsia try to stop you [from joining their red revolution], murder them." "Thus does the evil spirit tempt – leftist Satan in Jew's shape." And from the other side, "the right-wing Satan – the Prussian Junker, who seeks with boot and fist to enforce his will and make of us blind tool of Prusso-Jewish capital."

The poorest and weakest among us say they will not hold out until harvest. But do we want to share what bread we have with the insatiable German and the depraved Bolshevik-servant Jew? [Strikes will ruin Poland's industry and currency.] The Russian workers couldn't stand the test and gave in to the Judases, murdered tsarist generals, and began murdering each other. [The magnates' gold

[76] AAN. PRM, no. 21431/20, fos. 16–19, 36–37 (May 5, 1920).

disappeared, factories closed.] And today – O horror! Out of poverty and hunger they submit to Jewish command in eternal enslavement to Judas-capital, to death and perdition ... Should we not instead shake the hand offered us by the healthy Polish intelligentsia and create proper national well-being?

Interesting in this veiled confession of working-class weakness – Christian commoners anxiously awaiting next harvest – is a blanket description of educated and propertied (and authority wielding) Christians as "the intelligentsia" (and the abiding ascription to Poland's Jews of pro-Germanism). Hellish depiction of Bolshevized Russia will have been as much heartfelt horror as calculated propaganda.[77]

The antisemitic Polish newspaper *Iskra* reported in August that Jewish deserters – allegedly 20,000 strong – had gathered in internationally neutral Upper Silesia. From there German authorities would take them to Berlin for training as anti-Polish agitators and, eventually, as cadres in Bolshevized Poland.[78]

The Club received a letter from youthful Zionists in Lublin District's Bełżyce. A meeting to sell war bonds had turned into "blatant Jew-devouring agitation." A speaker conceded that Jews "very readily sub-scribed" but only – their iron rule – "from personal interest," not patri-otism. A priest railed against "Jewish reports" about difficulties at the front, seeding ground for "Jewish-Bolshevik rule." School director Kurczewski (labeled "Christian") challenged these views, calling for social solidarity, "especially since Jews show good will by lending money to the state." The meeting's chairman was indignant that "one of our people should speak in Jewish interests' defense, for Jews have sufficiently blackened both us and you in homeland and foreign press. They shout about every little thing to all corners of the earth. They're well enough off and can defend themselves." Despite this, local Jews sub-scribed, but others, as a protest signal, did so only later in Lublin.[79]

Something similar occurred in Słupno village, where Pinkus Warszau, from the capital, was spending the summer with his wife "because of their illness." Płock schoolteacher Dorobek arrived to sell war bonds. Warszau and family, fearing "the crowd would attack us," listened behind closed doors to the speaker's insults against Jews, "who [he said] should be wiped out [*wytępić*]," and

that Jews fully deserved pogroms, but we won't do that, but instead will arrange things so they flee from here ... He said further: we won't take loans from Moshkys and Yoshkys [*od Mośków i Jośków*]; we don't need their money.

---

[77] Ibid., fo. 334 (n.d. [*ca.* July 20, 1920]).   [78] Ibid., fo. 343 (August 7, 1920).
[79] Ibid., fos. 323–24 (July 7, 1920).

Warszau thought this a "true pogrom speech," replete with anti-Talmudic invective.[80]

The Club archived a *Rozwój* article entitled, "The Jews' Collective Responsibility." Taking "Judeo-Bolshevism" for granted, it concluded that Poland's Jews "must be held collectively responsible for treason and injuries it inflicts." The army may rightly charge whole Jewish communities for acts of sabotage or enemy aid. There must be "punishment by death and confiscation of property."[81] This was unapologetic incitement to localized ethnic cleansing and massacre. When, *Rozwój* indignantly asked, would Piłsudski comply? Expressing Christian anti-Jewish paranoia, *Rozwój* urged battlefield-fit (and pious) readers "to utterly smash the rule of the bloody Jew Trotskys, Sobelsohns, Nachamkes, Joffes, etc., whose goal is to murder Christ's followers."[82]

Deputy Hartglas wrote the Ministry for the Former Prussian Region, protesting *Rozwój*'s screeds and their posting in public buildings. One raised alarums against an alleged wave of Jews engulfing Poznania. "They want to judaize it like Warsaw, Kraków, and Lwów." They were buying up food and selling it elsewhere in Poland and hoarding silver and gold to take to Germany. What could the Poznanian Pole do? Refuse all commerce, including real estate rental. "FOR THE CURSE OF FUTURE GENERATIONS WILL FALL ON YOU! Away from our region, Jew! All society pours contempt on you and spits in your face!"

Poles! Know that no state on earth wants to have these Jewish parasites, and that's why the poorest state of all, our unhappy Poland, must suffer them and nourish them in their millions. "*Swój do swego po swoje.*" May God help us to this end.[83]

Here was exceptionally frank admission that Poznanian antisemites feared incursion of central and eastern Polish Jews, voicing the harshest possible deterrent rhetoric, spiced with boycott battle cry and feelings of self-pity and national inferiority.

Częstochowa's Israelite commune reported, over rabbinical signature, on a crowd estimated at 20,000, assembled to hear Polish-born, ironically named American priest Salomon's anti-Jewish tirade, interrupted by frequent chants of "Away with the Jews [*Precz z Żydami*]." Judging from American reports on anti-Jewish violence, he said, one would think there wasn't a single Jew left alive in Poland. It suffices "to touch a Jew's beard and they trumpet pogrom." While Poles fight and die, Jews "flee to the Bolsheviks and shoot at our army." In hospitals, only Poles. "And who cut off their ears and gouged out their eyes?" Father Salomon,

---

[80] Ibid., fo. 358 (n.d.).   [81] Ibid., fo. 326 (July 17, 1920).
[82] Ibid., fo. 327: *Rozwój* (August 20, 1920).
[83] Ibid., fos. 345–47 (n.d. [from *Rozwój*, July 31, 1920]).

knowing that Jewish agitators urged villagers not to enlist, self-sacrificingly tours the countryside to fight back, "and that's why he can't join the army." He lamented, "they live in palaces, while our children rot in basements." After the war, "we will settle things with them, as our greatest internal and external enemy."[84]

Złoczew's Communal Council echoed Salomon's thoughts. "Our enemies, Jews, go about villages on pretext of trading and agitate among benighted people not to subscribe to war-bonds, not to give the army volunteer soldiers and aid, because Bolsheviks will rule over us anyway." It was hard to refute this, for the "rural population lacks consciousness and enlightenment." The council resolved, "guided by patriotism toward the Beloved Fatherland, to prohibit Jews from any kind of commerce in our commune's villages." Landlords, villagers, and *starosty* were all exhorted to cooperate. Here was a revealing case of blaming the rural population's distance from the national cause on Jewish machinations (while benefiting Christian tradesmen).[85]

The Sejm Club found noteworthy a Rzeszów newspaper's article, "Jewish Worldwide Kingdom." News was, allegedly, surfacing of clandestine Bolshevik committees in Poland's big cities, prepared for Red Army arrival with their own banners and rubber stamps, their members nearly all Jewish. Living among foreign peoples, Jews always feel "foreign, and their dream is SUBJUGATION OF THE ARYAN RACE AND BENDING THE GOYS BENEATH THE CHOSEN PEOPLE'S YOKE." Bolshevism is but a means to this end. They have always felt "contempt and hatred for foreign tribes," believing God had chosen them to rule. "Through the centuries, secretly and in solidarity, making use of dishonesty, feigned humility, and subservience, Jews work steadily toward this end."

Proof could be found in the *Protocols of the Elders of Zion*, set down (as falsely alleged) at Basel in 1897 (Zionism's First Congress). Jewish "RAGE AND HATRED TOWARD POLAND" resulted from Poland's resistance to Bolshevism. Diligent search would turn up Rzeszów's underground Judeo-Bolsheviks. Those Jews who perhaps were friendly to Poland's cause were few. Danger posed by the Jewish majority justified Poles' abandonment of "our inborn tact [*delikatność*] and courtesy" so as to "decisively exclude Jews from all civic activities." Let them buy war bonds and – here ambivalence feebly flickered – otherwise prove themselves worthy of citizenly rights. Unsurprisingly, it was in Rzeszów, the flashpoint of Polish antisemitism, that the only recently

---

[84] Ibid., fo. 328 (July 20, 1920).
[85] Ibid., fo. 333 (July 24, 1920, from *Ziemia Sieradska*).

translated but by 1920 widely noticed *Protocols* should figure (although the idea that Polish Jews might qualify for active citizenship contradicted them).[86]

Zionist parliamentarians focused protest over antisemitic propaganda on *Rozwój* and the publishing house Polish Soldier (ZP), the latter allegedly heavily influenced by the armed forces. Hartglas wrote the Military Ministry, denouncing display of ZP material, saying this contradicted its "anti-excess proclamation."[87] These flyers and city wall posters were incendiary. One, released during the Soviet advance, announced that now that Bolsheviks controlled all Ukraine, the Cheka there spread torture and mass shootings, murder of hospital patients, and "putting to death [*uśmiercenie*] above all of Poles." Imploring "workers, farmers and you, gray-clad and manly soldier," to resist "Judas-like promises of red Russian whip-bearers," it asked, "why do [Soviet cavalry leader] Budienny's mounted hordes burn, murder, torture the Ukraine?" It was wild Cossack behavior, familiar from tsarist days. The worker could take heart that the Sejm was legislating new freedoms and social reforms. If Bolsheviks triumph, "Poland's beautiful land will be covered in a blackened shroud of clotted blood," as were Russia and Ukraine. Governing in Warsaw will be not "sovereign parliament but Lenin's and Trotsky's numerous band of Jews and Muscovites." "Let the whip-lashing Hundreds return to their Mongol steppe!" An alternate version of this handbill screamed out: "COUNTRYMEN! YOU AND THE WHOLE WORLD ALL KNOW THAT RUSSIANS DO NOT WAGE THIS WAR AGAINST YOU, BUT ONLY JEWS, CALLING THEMSELVES BOLSHEVIKS."[88]

Another ZP publication accused Bolsheviks of spending millions in gold rubles "to weaken Polish soldiers' devotion and love for Granddad [*Dziadek*] Piłsudski." Poland's army might be momentarily retreating, but the soldiery with greater discipline would prevail. The "red Muscovite army" was staffed, ZP claimed, by former German officers and NCOs. "At the Soviet Muscovite army's head stands Prince Tuchaszewski, leading it in the field is tsarist general Brusilov, and managing it is Jewish capitalist Bronstein-Trotsky."[89] A Russian-language handbill urging Soviet soldiers to surrender denied rumors that the Polish army was shooting captives. The fight was not against ordinary Russians. "Turn your bayonets against your deceivers, the Jewish commissars!" "Long live freedom." "This [handbill] serves as free safe passage to us."[90]

---

[86] Ibid., fos. 329–31 (July 23, 1920, from *Ziemia Rzeszowska*).
[87] AAN. PRM, No. 21431/20, fos. 814–15 (August 10, 1920).
[88] ibid., fos. 327–28, 340 (n.d. [July 1920]).   [89] Ibid., fo. 339 (July 1920).
[90] Ibid., fo. 341 (August 5, 1920).

On July 26, the Club sent more evidence of anti-Jewish actions to then–Prime Minister Grabski, including aforementioned internal circulars against army employment of Jewish office workers by Generals Symon and Rzędkowski. A manifesto of the self-styled "Liberation Army" (*Armja Wyzwolenia*), paper creation of fevered Judeophobes, denounced Piłsudski's government as a German tool and unvarnishedly threatened Poland's Jews with violence: "God is our witness that we don't want to spill blood, but let us be aware of the defeats that await our country if limits are not placed on Jewish arrogance."

From Galicia, the Christian-National Self-Defense authored a text stereotypically blaming poverty and backwardness on Jews and ending with antisemitic doggerel entitled "Ten Counsels." These included

> "Thou shalt not enter into trade and collusion with the Jew, for he will eat the cottage as he swallowed many a manor."
>
> "The Jew is thine worst enemy – because a homeland enemy."
>
> "Escape Jewish captivity in time, so you won't have in future to honor *szabas*."
>
> "Don't believe in the Jew's word . . . for profit, he'll break it."
>
> "Three things are the worst . . . Jew-landlord, Jew-friend, Jewish vodka."
>
> "Don't let the Jewish livestock dealer into your barn, for he won't milk your cows, but you instead."
>
> "When you sell the Jew a horse, calf, grain, don't you feel you're selling yourself?"
>
> "Always remember: 'to each his own.'"
>
> "The farmer must pray in the morning – 'guard me, Lord God, from the Jew!' – and at noon – 'that I may not fall into poverty, Lord God, protect me from the Jew' – and in the evening – 'prevent, O God, that the bearded Jew enters my cottage' – and at night – 'Help me fulfill my intention: to live through the day without the Jew.'"

Here, ultraobsessively, was derivation of all social-economic ills (plus threat of religious extinction) from the omnipresent, uncanny ("bearded") Jew. A more alarming message to the uneducated land-poor peasant, all too aware of his weakness and insignificance, was hardly imaginable. It also made many a villager doubt his own senses, for he knew the Jew as neighbor, with usual human virtues and frailties. But who were humble peasants to reject such intelligentsia-prescribed commandments, especially when familiar Jewish social roles embodied so plausibly the treacheries of impersonal markets?[91]

[91] Ibid., fos. 38–48 (July 26, 1920).

The Sejm Club interpellated the government on August 24, again charging the publishing house Polish Soldier with saturating the country with its "Judeo-Bolshevik" posters, often presented as if officially sanctioned. Yet the Jewish population had backed the war effort in every possible way, including creating the Jewish Committee for Defense of the State (whose proposal to create a separate hospital for Jewish wounded the government vetoed). The army had decreed reduction of Jewish office personnel to 5 percent and internment of all Jewish field soldiers in Jabłonna pending formation of separate Jewish "worker cadres."

The Club charged that while, after a month of Jewish protest, the government had finally "liquidated" Jabłonna camp, Jewish soldiers continued to be segregated, discriminated against, and suspected. As Bolsheviks retreated, rumors spread, including by army proclamation, of Jewish collaboration, though unproven. Apart from peasant farmers, Jews suffered most under the Bolsheviks through forced sales in rubles, hostage taking, and plundering by Christian scum. Many more Christians, even rightists, held office under Bolsheviks than Jews. Prime Minister Witos had approved a proclamation by the Polish-Jewish Commission affirming the Jewish community's posture during the war as "completely citizenly," but present Prime Minister Christian Democrat Antoni Ponikowski, citing charges of Judeo-Bolshevism in Płock and Siedlce, refused signature. It was no surprise the army's post-independence anti-Jewish violence persisted in a spirit of "*complete innocence*," its soldiers gulled by "fairy tales of Jewish treason." Nor could the Jewish press, "muzzled by censorship," reveal these legends' groundlessness. Falsehood overshadowed truth, "and hatred of Jews deepens in the Polish popular masses." The deputies called for an investigative commission, including Jews, and punishment of perpetrators of specified anti-Jewish crimes.[92]

The Club later warned of anti-Jewish excesses occurring in the Polish counteroffensive. It recalled to the Military Ministry its own earlier circulars declaring officers responsible for soldiers' criminal acts and the Interior Ministry's warning to police against passivity toward soldierly excesses. "Unfortunately all these circulars remain merely Platonic evidence of the relevant Ministry's good will." Meanwhile, the Vistula's eastern bank witnessed disastrous pogroms. "Not one sentence has so far been pronounced against plunderers or their officers."[93]

---

[92] Ibid., fos. 307–13 (August 24, 1920). Reprinted in *Inwazja Bolszewicka a Żydzi*, vol. I: 1–9 (author's emphasis).

[93] AAN. PRM, No. 21431/20, fos. 861–63 (August 28, 1920); fos. 963–64 (September 7, 1920).

The Club compiled an undated list, doubtless incomplete, of 143 Jews murdered by soldiers, mainly in the eastern borderlands. Among victims, thirty-four fell to Petliura's gunmen, four to Bałachowicz's, and the remaining 109 to the Polish army.[94] The Club protested summary execution of civilians by military field courts, including many innocents such as Płock Rabbi Szapiro. It protested the army's inability to control its allies in Petliura's and Pawlenko's units, guilty of bestial murders of Jews in East Galicia, even though "local Christians with pity and charity hid Jews from pogroms," including also those inflicted by "Black Cossacks" under Ukrainian peasant anarchist Nestor Makhno's command.[95]

Courts Martial

To what degree did the army punish Jewish desertion and anti-Jewish violence among the soldiery? Documentation of a handful of cases and statistics compiled on 1920 death sentences are suggestive, if not definitive. In January 1920, four soldiers in Galician Tarnów fell on Chaim Aberdam and his mother Süssel as they shuttered their money-exchange office, robbing them of 120,000 korony. Judging by names, one soldier – Warsaw droshky driver Ehrlich – was of Jewish parentage. The court martial, finding the crime – to which the accused confessed – premeditated, stringently sentenced Ehrlich and an accomplice to death and the third, under age twenty, to fifteen years in prison, "sharpened by 12 days monthly of fasting with hard cot and 24 hours confinement to dark cell." A firing squad executed the sentences immediately.[96]

Soldier Szpis deserted in March 1919, after serving two weeks. He returned home, where "he purchased an identification document under another name." Arrested in July, he sat in prison for six months. In his favor was a "previously unblemished life." He was sentenced to six more months in prison, to be served after demobilization so that he could be sent immediately to the front, where he was needed.[97] A Kraków court martial tried thirty-year-old Corporal Hoffmann, lawyer, for desertion. He had been earlier sentenced, as a civilian, to eight months' imprisonment for "swindling, theft, black-marketeering, and charging usurious prices." Corporal Rauscher testified that Hoffmann "was in civilian dress, and asked him not to arrest him, for Jew should not arrest Jew." Hoffmann had written his Viennese uncle, seeking help in proving he was not a Polish citizen. Found guilty, he was shot two hours later.[98]

---

[94] Ibid., fos. 744–47 (n.d.).
[95] Ibid., fos. 304–6 (September 28, 1920). On Makhno, see Schnell, *Räume des Schreckens*.
[96] CAW. Oddział VI: I.300.12. No. 29 (January 29, 1920).
[97] Ibid., No. 29 (February 5, 1920).   [98] Ibid., No. 29 (August 17, 1920).

Soldier Biegeleisen, merchant, faced charges of having "intentionally injected himself in the leg with kerosene or alcohol to induce illness and render himself unfit for front-transfer, thus through self-crippling" betraying his duties. The charge was found to derive from hospital rumors, with no medical proof. Biegeleisen explained that his leg abscess resulted from "scuffling with a madman in a convoy he was leading." This explanation proving irrefutable, he was acquitted. The case typifies suspicions plaguing Jewish soldiers.[99]

Artillery soldier Gelb, employed in his father's fabrics shop, deserted in September 1919, returning home and then moving from place to place, dealing in dairy products. In July 1920, after a foot chase of 1.5 kilometers, a gendarme arrested him, "from whom he tried to escape, even hurling himself into the water while fleeing so as conceal himself." But "with help of people working in the field he was pulled from the water." He had told acquaintances, "if it came to arrest he would drown himself." Geld said he left the army because he was responsible for his siblings, including young children. The court martial found the grandfather performing this service. Gelb frequented places where official warnings against desertion were posted. As "habitual deserter" who had earlier absconded, he was immediately shot.[100]

Christian soldier and civilian farmer Jakób Król, twenty-one, was sentenced to eight months' imprisonment. Guilty of three short desertions, he pleaded illness from dysentery, as well as need to help parents in harvesting. But his brother-in-law provided this service. He benefited from the amnesty decree of February 1919 "reducing punishability." Yet his bad example required sanctions as warning to others in an army "exposed to harm through soldierly flight." Here, plainly, the court showed bias favoring peasant runaways, though the sentence was stiff enough.[101]

Król's mother, Apolonia, petitioned the court, signing the document, seemingly composed by a local scribe, with X. Jakób, she claimed, was her only help on their small farm. Her plea vividly conjures villagers' wartime travails.

I myself am busy with spinning and kitchen and caring for remaining cow and calf, for I had to sell the pair of work-horses for lack of ploughman ... I also care for my husband, Wojciech Krzywy, unfit for any farm work, for he is a deaf old man of 95 years, worn out from excess of industriousness expended on his land, whose every hope is lodged in his Kuba [Jakób], and now with his having been taken away to the Army, nay! to the garrison-jail in Kraków, he knows not what to do with

---

[99] Ibid., No. 29 (August 19, 1920).   [100] Ibid., No. 29 (August 24, 1920).
[101] Ibid., No. (December 9, 1920).

himself. He doesn't eat, can't sleep, feels hopeless, inconsolable – he goes to his grave. [In 1918 Jakób returned from the Austrian army and worked for his parents.] He is very industrious, obedient to me and necessary. [His parents called him back from the Polish army] for the love of God because not many days remained to his father ... who has no one else for consolation [*nikogusienko pociechy*] and won't have any other in his decrepit old age. So Jakób obeyed his father and me, his mother. He hid for a while ... moving about furtively, cutting wood, grinding oats for horses ... Now all I have, O Almighty God, is wretchedness – our meager property falls apart, if there is harvest, the army takes it. – The authorities are hard as stone. – [The gendarmes take others' children, while their own are spared.] Already for a month the court holds Kubuś in some sort of dungeon full of suffering, for he writes: "Mama, I beg of you on Christ's wounds to get me home, for I am hardly alive, and if not, you'll be coming to my funeral" ... Sell the fields! Sell the fields! I would let my heart's blood run from my fingers ... In the name of the Highest Principles, in the name of the Republic of the folk, in the name of the Nation – Father *Naczelnik*! Ruler of the Army! I beg on my knees and beseech with my last breathe, so long as I live – give me back my child, give me my son ... and give his [father] this final satisfaction on earth, which is the return of soldier-agricultural laborer Kuba, before he dies, may God forbid! With tears in my eyes, and convinced of the Justice of the Government of the Nation and the Peoples [*Narodu i Lodow*]! – Apolonia Królowa.[102]

Kuba's fate remains unknown, but these few cases show that military justice struck Jews and Christians both hard and soft blows, with some leniency shown toward young soldiers. To them we add one further prosecution, in 1921, of highway robbery of Jewish textile merchants by two Christian soldiers, yielding a verdict of "expulsion from army and death by firing-squad, sentences to be executed simultaneously," as followed immediately.

In 1922, the army compiled statistics on "crimes by military personnel with intent of material profit." In 1920, 771 such cases were tried, one-quarter against officers, three-quarters against rank-and-file soldiers. Found guilty were, respectively, (only) eleven and ninety-three; of these, death sentences numbered ten and forty-nine; executions actually carried out numbered seven and fifteen. The 1921 data were more numerous (1,259 indictments), with but thirty-three guilty verdicts against officers and 240 against soldiers. Only seven officers' executions took place and two of soldiers. Thus, in these two years, thirty-one death sentences for robbery were carried out, including fourteen against officers.

A different army tally, encompassing a broader and more serious range of offenses and entitled, "Specification of Death Sentences Delivered and Carried Out," numbered for 1920 thirty-two cases in the regular courts,

---

[102] Ibid., No. 29 (April 7, 1921).

317 in courts martial. Twelve officers were among the executed. Altogether, 125 sentences were for desertion, 107 for treasonable acts, forty-eight were for robbery and plunder (doubtless mainly at Jewish expense), fourteen for murder, ten for spying (a seemingly small number in light of frequent propaganda against "Judeo-Bolshevik" spies), and seven for cowardice. The corresponding total number of death sentences in 1921 was, at thirty-two, far lower.[103]

Official posters announcing execution of death sentences, posted publicly to warn against indiscipline, were haphazardly archived. Among names on eight of them, all from 1920, sixty-one were seemingly borne by Polish Catholics, executed for various offenses. Forty-seven seemingly Jewish names appeared, executed largely for desertion, most of the others – mainly civilians – for treason, including office holding under the Bolsheviks.[104]

If punishment of antisemitic plunderers and murderers occurred in small measure, it seems too that court-imposed death of Jewish defendants was not massive. The army attempted self-interestedly to uphold soldierly discipline and obedience. Its firing squads were reminders to those tempted to rebel. The great Jewish tragedy of 1920 played out not before the courts but in the war zone east of Warsaw, amid temporary loss of military and state power, efforts to install Bolshevism, and – still farther eastward – the shifting, murderous tides of revolutionary civil war and barbarous antisemitic freebooting.

[103] Ibid., No. 31 (n.d.), *Wykaz zapadłych i wykonanych wyroków śmierci.*
[104] Ibid., No. 31, *passim.*

9   In Armageddon's Shadow
Anti-Jewish Violence in the Polish-Soviet War Zone, July–October 1920

In late September, the Bolshevik tide having ebbed, Endek Sejm deputies interpellated the government over Jewish collaboration with the invaders.

Again the whole world resonates with the echo of pogroms to which Jews among us here in Poland allegedly fell victim during our nation's deathly struggle with Bolshevism's exterminating power. But reality looks entirely different: there are no pogroms in Poland, nor were there any, but rather the Jews, commonly and with rare cynicism, stepped forth openly in armed opposition to our army as it was being withdrawn, and thus in its most critical moment . . . Jews' antagonism was so great that they abandoned their homes [following Bolsheviks eastward].

The deputies demanded governmental publication of documents "on the Jewish population's collective treason and active cooperation, arms in hand, with the enemy when he, partly thanks to this cooperation, managed to reach the Republic's capital's walls and when our Fatherland's independence was in mortal danger."[1]

Thus did Endeks, largest Sejm-seated party and voice of one-third of Poland's voters, translate anti-Jewish violence inflicted by Polish hands, soldierly and civilian, into justifiable self-defense and righteous punishment of the traitorous. Zionist deputies had energetically and vividly publicized abuses Jews suffered so that no one in Poland's political class could pretend ignorance of them. The challenge was to explain the violence or transmute it into a self-preservation narrative.

These final two chapters assess the 1920 war's culminatory violence. It raged in three half-circle zones radiating east from embattled Warsaw. The first encompassed the capital's environs, beyond its nearest protective defenses. Here the Red Army briefly penetrated, sometimes erecting local collaborationist "revolutionary committees" (*Rewkoms*). In withdrawal as in reconquest, the Polish military both perpetrated and

---

[1] AAN. PRM, no. 21431/20: "Materjały przedłożone przez Club Sejmowy Posłów Żydowskiego Stronnictwa Ludowego w sprawie położenia żydów, wywołanego inwazją bolszewicką," fo. 301 (September 24, 1920), signed by some thirty deputies of the Związek Ludowo-Narodowy (ZLN).

tolerated scattered orgies of uniformed and civilian pogromists. The second zone fanned out into northern, northeastern, and eastern Poland, where longer-lasting pro-Bolshevik bridgeheads sometimes arose. The third extended beyond ethnographic Poland's frontiers into Belarusian, Volhynian, and Ukrainian borderlands, where Poland's army, joined by Ukrainian Petliurites and Bałachowicz's volunteers, pursued retreating Bolsheviks. Here the new Polish state implicated itself, as in 1919 Pinsk, in the Russian civil war's bloodshed. After "Vistula miracle" came nightmares of eastern front and *Kresy*.

The Polish-Soviet war witnessed atrocious killings such as this book's documentation has so far not depicted, and they grew worse as battle fronts moved east. Yet already beneath Warsaw's walls they were ominously brutal. If it were known a priori why perpetrators committed such acts, it might suffice to enumerate victims and condemn killers. But the violence itself was expressive of motives undiscoverable through the fact of killing alone. This justifies repicturing the murders, which otherwise would be better left in history's darkened vault. Each locality visited here exemplifies a different configuration, a different potentiality realized. It is, unfortunately, a kaleidoscope of cruelty.[2] We shall see that the symbolism it embodied cast distinct anxiety-ridden shadows, its scenarios new collective imaginings. Yet Christian Poles, authorities and commoners, sometimes also confronted and blocked the metastasizing violence, and not only from self-interest.

Warsaw Besieged

As in Poland's other big cities and towns – once November 1918's anarchic tremors subsided – anti-Jewish violence in Warsaw simmered on low flame, stoked by soldiers and plunder-hungry civilians or thieves. Under Bolshevik onslaught, Warsaw authorities displayed imperfect resolve to block attacks on Jews, which mushroomed as soldiers flooded the city. And in some suburban settlements – beyond city trenches, exposed to Soviet incursions and Polish army's counterattacks – Judeophobic violence grew more brutal, often transmuting into ethnic cleansing.

In Bolshevik onslaught's midst, Zionist leader Antoni Hartglas heeded August morning summons to the main Jewish district's Sienna Street. There he found Poznanian volunteer soldiers, around whom "bustled little groups of Christian agitators, exhorting them to rob

---

[2] Władysław Broniewski, prominent interwar leftist poet, took an intellectual army officer's hardboiled view of the 1920 war, betraying little interest in Jewish fate, in *Pamiętnik 1918–1922* (Warsaw, 1984).

Jewish shops." They were "*mostly older people, tenants in nearby houses*," together with adolescents, "some with Citizens Guard arm-bands." A gendarme stopped soldiers attempting a break-in. Hartglas wrote:

[City] police do what they can, patrolling and dispersing throngs, but they can arrest neither soldiers nor agitators for fear of provoking a soldierly reaction, which could lead to tumults, whereas the incidents are petty and usually end peacefully. The deputy commissioner thinks . . . there's no reason for fear.[3]

But, as Chaim Finkelstein of right-bank Warsaw's proletarian Praga District reported, Jews lived under "constant military terror." Troops arriving there by rail "very quickly snatched all bread and fruit, giving it away mostly to boys and women who eagerly pointed out where Jews lived and had their stores." Soldiers entered apartments, "provoking indescribable panic." Gendarmes arrived, "ordering all Jews to their dwellings, advising them not to mill about in the street." Depredations then declined, but merchants now hesitated to market their wares.[4]

Not only "boys and women" led soldiers to Jewish shops and homes. Sara Kocowicz testified that Poznanians stormed into her apartment at 11:00 PM, having seen her husband through their window, whereupon they shouted, "there's a bearded Jew." They robbed them of good-quality clothing and footwear worth nearly 17,000 marks. "Let me add that a gymnasium student led the Poznanians, showing them where to rob."[5]

Protection remained unpredictable. Symcha Gutbrot, curbside cigarette seller, complained that Poznanians robbed him. A policeman refused intervention, advising "me to cut off my beard myself." Poznanians beat Dr. Mieses, a "state official." When he sought aid from nearby guard soldiers, "one shoved me brutally, saying 'get to work,' pulling on my cravat." Here an assimilationist Jew engaged in the state-building project suffered humiliation.[6] A tavern keeper reported how soldiers beat Jews, shouting, "now everything is allowed [*teraz wszystko można*]," while boys exhorted them, crying, "he must be beaten; he's a Jew!"[7] Police told Chaja Rosenblum, complaining of soldierly violence, that "it's not possible to seize these people and cut off their heads." The murderous image was not out of place.[8]

---

[3] AAN. PRM. No. 21431/20, fo. 412 (August 10, 1920) (author's emphasis).
[4] Ibid., fo. 408 (n.d. [July 1920]).   [5] Ibid., fo. 393 (July 27, 1920).
[6] Ibid., fo. 404 (July 7, 1920); fo. 410 (August 8, 1920); fo. 392 (July 29, 1920).
[7] Ibid., fo. 392 (July 29, 1920).
[8] Ibid, fo. 410 (August 10, 1920); fo. 411 (August 5, 1920); fo. 407 (n.d.). See also, on Warsaw, fos. 244, 409, 411, 416, 418, 999, and 1000.

Otwock: Smashing Christian-Jewish Modernity

Near Warsaw on the Vistula's right bank lay Otwock (Yiddish: Otvosk), with bourgeois villas, pension hotels, and tuberculosis sanatoria in a sandy, pine-forested terrain whose air was thought curative by the metropolis's respiratorially oft-plagued inhabitants. Otwock mushroomed from the 1890s, especially its Jewish population, first Litvaks, then Polish Jews – partly assimilated, partly Orthodox (Góra Kalwaria ["Mt. Calvary"], Hasidic Rome, lay across the river). In 1918, population stood at 8,630 – 64 percent Jewish. Otwock represented Jews' hopes for healthy, comfortable, safe suburban life beyond old inner-city confines.[9]

Bolshevik troops poured in on August 14, but the Poles expelled them three days later. "Christians say Jews received the Bolsheviks with bread and salt. A list was made of fifty Jews accused of spying."[10] But Jews "were at [Shabbat] services in the prayer-houses, so there could be no talk of their greeting them." Russian behavior was disputed. "Bolsheviks at the market bought wares, paying good prices" but also took a Catholic priest hostage and committed sporadic robberies before retreating.[11]

Jakób Muszkatenblitt, sanatorium Zofjówka's director, distinguished himself rendering moral and material aid. He transferred war-wounded Jews to Warsaw, while harboring during fighting the "greater part" of Otwock's population, including the Góra Kalwaria rabbi, Christians, and other refugees. The "richest citizens escaped in time." Now twenty Polish military trains stopped daily, soldiers disembarking and plundering Jews, "beating them pitilessly." Soon Jews would be reduced to "the condition of Adam." Rabbi Aceman's daughter-in-law, robbed, appealed to a passing officer. "In reply, he asked where he could get vodka." The Civil Guard stood passive and anyhow were powerless. If influential people in Warsaw couldn't protect Otwock, "we're condemned to extermination [*zagłada*]."

When Soviets withdrew, "adolescents came out and threatened Jews, saying now they would be slaughtered." They exhorted army patrols "to attack Jews, telling incredible stories." A man robbed of 30,000 marks said, "they didn't beat me, nor any of my household, because we gave them everything they wanted." The soldiers went to tsadik Rabinowicz to cut his beard, but he paid 1,500 marks, and again, "they only beat him."

---

[9] www.sztetl.org.pl/pl/article/otwock/6,demografia/ (accessed July 28, 2015). On interwar Otwock, see Theodore Hamerow, *Remembering a Vanished World: A Jewish Childhood in Interwar Poland* (New York, NY: Berghahn, 2001).

[10] Here and below: AAN. PRM. No. 21431/20, fo. 74 (August 20, 1920); fo. 83 (August 28, 1920).

[11] Ibid., fo. 92 (August 20, 1920).

"Whoever can, escapes, and that's obviously what the agitators intend, so they can rob the villas left unprotected."[12] Grocer Sokolnicki told soldiers "he would gladly share his wares, sugar, dried peas, salt, etc." When they began robbing, "I asked them to take what they needed personally, but not to ruin me." When he refused to give money, "a soldier hit me in the eye and pointed his gun at me ... My shop was cleaned out; my loss tallies 30,000 marks."

Soldierly violence persisted long after Bolshevik exit. After a servant girl's rape:

> Some women went to the [Christian] mayor for help. He told the soldiers to halt their actions or he would have them arrested. They threw themselves on him and beat him, crying, "boys, give it to this bourgeois." He ran to the station and appealed to officers and railway guards, who restored order.[13]

Taube Goldfarb reported that returning to Otwock, where soldiers had earlier killed her father, she found them leading tailor Zysman "to his death." She screamed, pleading for his release. "Soldiers, influenced by my tears and thinking he was my father, freed him." When she did not cease her laments, they learned her real father's fate and rearrested Zysman, "but an older soldier arrived, asking them, 'why did you seize this tailor?' They replied: 'we received an order to rob, to kill all the Jews. We met him, so we take him away.' But he managed to free the tailor." Of such "orders" we have often heard before, but no direct evidence of them has surfaced, unlike commands from on high to officers and troops not to abuse Jewish citizens.[14]

"A soldier decided to shoot me," said Rachmiel Mokotowski, robbed and beaten, "but after consulting with another soldier reversed his decision and spared my life." They raped three Jewish women before his sister's eyes, "threatening her with a revolver." He added bitterly, "I signed for a 10,000 mark war-bond, which is now my only property, and I also collected money among Jews for the Haller army" (if true, an ill-considered gesture).

> After soldiers beat the mayor, he called a meeting where he spoke to assembled Christians, pointing out that Jews were fulfilling all obligations, paying taxes, making donations, and called for peace. It was agreed to send a memorial to the government detailing injuries the state suffered through incessant anti-Jewish excesses. He delivered it to the appropriate authorities, threatening to close the mayoral office if peace were not imposed in Otwock and if soldiers' dreadful

---

[12] Ibid., fo. 92 (August 20, 1920).
[13] *Chłopi, weźcie się do tego burżuja.* Ibid., fo. 85 (August 30, 1920).
[14] Ibid., fo. 86 (September 2, 1920).

excesses against Jews continued. Generally, the mayor is trying as much as he can to restore order and protect the Jews against soldiers' depredations.[15]

Otwock's war wounds healed. Before 1939, it witnessed flourishing Jewish private, religious, and educational life. Yet these few weeks of 1920 violence showed, despite the Christian mayor's goodwill, on what shifting sands it perched.[16]

Garwolin: Patriotic Rabbi's Humiliation, Christian Elimination of Jewish Rivalry

Garwolin was a typical Vistula right-bank *shtetl* (1912: 7,300 souls, 57 percent Mosaic, mostly provincial merchants, artisans, and men of religion). In 1919's city council, nine Jews sat alongside fifteen Christians. Bolshevik occupation lasted four days. Rabbi Moszek Romer testified that parish priest Bloch – "baptized Jew" – and Christian town officials consulted with him about the invaders. Romer advised everyone to stay, saying panic-inducing "rumors were false. I announced this under *cherem.*"

"No one met [the Bolsheviks], nor greeted them," said Romer, adding that "as a Polish citizen he could not receive the Fatherland's enemies." Two unfamiliar Christian merchants, "one a hunchback," came to him asking "whether it would not be better if he welcomed them with bread and salt," but "I replied that the priest was not going out, so neither would I." "Our soldiers" (*nasi*) would return. They said, "'rabbi is right,'" and left. Were they unfriendly provocateurs?

The Bolsheviks dissolved town council and synagogue commune and canceled Romer's salary. Their *Rewkom* included a Warsaw worker communist, two local peasant organizers, and "a newly arrived commissar who spoke Polish." The invaders paid at ruble-mark equivalency. Bundists occupied no offices, "confining themselves to singing the 'Internationale' at Bolshevik meetings." The communists called a Shabbat meeting that both Christians and Jews attended, "mainly youth." A Sunday assembly drew local peasants, who learned of impending land redistribution and "prosecution and crushing of black marketeers and smugglers."

The Polish army recaptured and plundered the town. "From me," said Romer, "they took everything; they left me literally without clothing, shoes, or underwear." They summoned him, "commanding I pronounce

---

[15] Ibid., fos. 195–96 (September 25, 1920).
[16] See Jack Jacobs. *Bundist Counterculture in Interwar Poland* (Syracuse, NY: Syracuse University Press, 2009).

cherem on those harboring Bolsheviks. I did, and one communist was handed over." Army intelligence imprisoned Romer in Warsaw, where he was held until parliamentarian Halpern vouched for his release. "The major who investigated my case was very surprised that they arrested me and ordered twenty-four-hour confinement of those who held me under lock and key. I asked that their guilt be forgiven."[17]

On Polish reconquest, tavern keeper Rotberg was shot, alongside Warsaw communist and Soviet-subordinate Civic Guard's PPS commander. Two days of post-Bolshevik plunder struck 300 families at 7 million marks' cost. Army imposition of compulsory labor was initially brutal, but a new commander "accepts that Jews remained loyal under the Bolsheviks and promises he will combat all abuses."[18]

The murdered tavern keeper's embittered wife, Chaja, testified that Christians too had hosted Bolsheviks with food and cigarettes, while Jews "at first didn't show themselves." After Soviet retreat, rival Christian tavern keeper Zając arrived with two Poznanians, saying of Rotberg, "take him, he's a communist." They "beat him pitilessly, despite assurances he was not a communist and was house owner." The Christian Maszkiewicz agreed to vouch for him, but soldiers "took Rotberg outside town and, without investigation or trial, shot him." A Poznanian (seconded by local Christians) said it was tavern keeper Zając who killed him, for soldiers had no revolvers. The widow said Zając invited Bolsheviks to his tavern, "personally leading a Bolshevik on his horse. Everyone saw this."[19]

Such Christian neighborly treachery inflicted painful psychological wounds. Jankiel and Hersz Rozenberg, Garwolin textile manufacturers, confronted Polish soldiers, led by locally born Winiarek, before the Bolshevik attack. They took goods worth a million marks, plus 100,000 marks in cash, and movables worth as much. Protesting to the army commandant, "he shouted at us, wanted even to beat us, saying it was army requisition." A Christian told of seeing Winiarek in Warsaw with a horse covered with a Rozenberg-manufactured cloth. The Rozenbergs wondered in their Zionist Club protocol if, assuming the requisition was lawful, "it might not be worthwhile to address the relevant authorities about receiving recompense." "We just might die of hunger. Our whole fortune was stolen. Our firm is known on [Warsaw's] Gęsia St. and in Łódź." Such testimony from once-prosperous Jews is rare. In their bitterness, they omitted patriotic accents.[20]

[17] AAN. PRM 21431/20, fos. 96, 661 (August 24, 1920); fo. 660 (n.d.).
[18] Ibid., fos. 656–59 (September 9. 1920).
[19] Ibid., fos. 222–23 (September 1, 1920). Cf. fos. 394–426.
[20] Ibid., fo. 426 (September 6, 1920).

The Sejm Club protested Rabbi Romer's arrest.

It is curious that civil and military authorities announce on every possible occasion that they harbor greatest confidence in the Jewish Orthodox population, having no reproaches against them. Yet it is precisely the Orthodox who suffer most from every sort of excess and other persecution: their beards are shorn, they are beaten on the street, in the railway stations and train cars.[21]

They offered no explanation, but this book has shown that it was the Orthodox Jews' very difference – or, in hostile eyes, their strangeness or uncanniness – that triggered aggression.

Meanwhile, readiness of such Jews as Rabbi Romer and the textile-manufacturing Rozenbergs to support the new Polish state – regardless whether patriotism ran hot or cold in their veins – suffered rebuffs not easily forgotten, the more so for being unjustifiable by the values Poles applied to themselves.[22]

Glinianka: Dejudaizing through Massacre

Bolsheviks captured Glinianka village (1908: 274 souls, 66 Mosaic). Four days later, Polish soldiers arrived. Eight Jewish refugees had appeared from nearby *shtetl* Wiązówna. They found shelter in Chana Majnemer's house, with shop and bakery. Polish soldiers seized her husband and eleven other men. Later, soldiers told her he was dead because he "had pulled down the cross near the church (though the cross stands undamaged to the present day)." Seven others had been shot, including her

---

[21] Ibid., fo. 835 (August 25, 1920).

[22] The website of Warsaw's POLIN – Museum of the History of Polish Jews, in its Polish-language entry on Garwolin, offers notes jarring with those here sounded. "The Polish population was unfriendly to the invaders, but the Jewish population was friendly, gladly sharing information, helping with provisioning – robbing Polish shops."

Yet, once the *Rewkom* was established, "the Jewish population – both Orthodox and intelligentsia – maintained a mostly loyal posture toward the Polish state, the Bundists succumbing to propaganda." As Bolsheviks withdrew, "the would-be creators and foot-soldiers of the projected revolutionary Bundist army fled with them." Once they were gone, "the Polish population helped provision the army," i.e., aided in plundering Jews.

The source of these dubious and contradictory claims was a 2008 publication sponsored, though seemingly not actually written, by Warsaw's venerable and – especially in postcommunist form – eminently reputable Jewish Historical Institute. In 1920, Sejm deputies and other nonrevolutionary Jews found evidence of Jewish collaboration with Bolsheviks highly unwelcome, though they could not deny individual Bundists' and other leftists' temptation in that direction. But, in my sources' light, the website's blanket generalizations breathe tendentiousness, whether of Stalinist provenance – pro-Bolshevism was once praiseworthy – or perpetuation among Polish writers of the Judeo-Bolshevik legend, with its accompanying translation of anti-Jewish violence into virtuous patriotism. Such myths die hard. See www.sztetl.org.pl/pl/article/garwolin/5,historia /?action=view&page=3 (Accessed December 16, 2016).

brother. She met Tyszler, who survived. He said soldiers asked Majnemer if he harbored Bolsheviks in his house, which he denied. "Before the shooting, they were beaten. I saw my husband's corpse. One eye had been plucked out, the whole body was covered with wounds ... My brother's teeth had been knocked out." She was pregnant, widowed with three children. Her grocery store loss was 40,000 marks.

She said Tyszler showed soldiers "where my husband had hidden money and valuables (under the floor). At the cost of this denunciation, he stayed alive." Earlier, Bolsheviks demanded with threats that she bake bread from flour they delivered. "Obviously I had to fulfill this order. Everyone in town knows I have a bakery. I must add that Christians without exception baked bread for Bolsheviks, even on Sunday." Her sister-in-law testified that her husband too – Chana's brother – was taken for labor and then shot near the church. "Peasants told me that, before shooting, they made him cry out 'long live Poland.'" Toba Goldfarb's father, killed by eleven bullets, had a broken hand and his throat pierced by bayonets.

Wolf Zysman was meant to be shot. "I had already dug my grave. I was saved thanks to the priest's intervention, after peasant friends of mine requested it. The soldiers had told us we were to bury fallen 'Bolsheviks.' They robbed my whole house, leaving nothing. They smashed the sewing-machine to pieces," as happened also to two others.[23]

From among Wiązówna refugees, ten men were shot, including Raca Goldfarb's husband. As they approached Glinianka, they encountered a Bolshevik camp, breaking up as Poles attacked. "I begged my husband not to go to Glinianka, because there was a battle there. But he did not heed my advice and we went, staying at Majnemer's, since our acquaintances from Wiązówna were there." The battle that night was so fierce that a peasant jumped through the explosion-shattered window and hid with them until dawn. Soldiers then seized the Wiązówna men, dragging her husband by his beard. Another Jew, disabled, saved himself with 200 marks. A girl of sixteen, "who didn't wear a kerchief over her hair like all the women," was raped. The women were threatened with shooting, but "one of the girls pleaded with a soldier to take pity on them. He assented and led us from the house. As we ran off, we heard two shots. Tyszler said they were shooting [her husband] and Goldstein." These same soldiers were now in Otwock. "They're Poznanians."

Another widowed Wiązównian, Pessa Upfal, said that "Bolsheviks held a party, played harmonica and danced. None of the girls, neither Christian nor Jewish, danced with them." When Polish soldiers arrived,

[23] Ibid., fos. 87–88 (September 1–2, 1920); fo. 692 (n.d.).

"they told us we were theirs to do with what they liked."[24] Another witness said, "before shooting, [the soldiers] vented their rage ['avenged themselves'] pitilessly, clubbing them, knocking out teeth and inflicting bloody wounds."

Soldiers told us they were doing this because someone tore off the wreath from the roadside cross, no one knew who ... They wouldn't let us approach the corpses, threatening to kill us. [They stole] cows, clothing, linen, money, just everything.

Two other nearby-resident Jews were also to be shot, "but the local Christian population asked they be spared."[25]

A delegation of Jews from "Last Aid" (*Ostatna Pomoc*) found the bodies "in a ditch, from which a hand and part of a trunk protruded, and under a thin layer of earth twelve executed Jews: two tailors, two furniture-makers, one *malemed*, one dyer, five merchants, one unidentified." Most had smashed skulls. One wore ritual garments. Srul Siedlecki, an executed man's son, "bought himself free by letting soldiers take anything from his house that pleased them."[26]

Such was some two dozen Jewish men's bloody fate and the widowing and orphaning of their wives and children amid destruction of homes and workplaces. Pretexts were cynically flimsy: Jewish refugees were "Bolsheviks," Glinianka Jews had baked bread for Reds and desecrated roadside cross. It was by now a ubiquitous fusion of religious and anti-Bolshevik rationales. Violence was arbitrary: Christian pleas for individual Jewish lives, from peasants or priest, were efficacious. Killers could be bought off for 200 marks or household valuables.

The executions' brutality reflects a practice of unknown geographic breadth, probably (but not certainly) deep rooted, cruelly dehumanizing. It cannot be dismissed as "peasant barbarism," for the perpetrators were, in whole or part, Poznanians, while educated Polish officers were present and in command. At bottom, it was murderous ethnic cleansing, or "de-Judaization," as Polish antisemites said. The soldiery's intent – as can be read from their actions – was to destroy the Jewish presence, uproot it, and cast it to the wind. Yet, because escape was hard, scattered survivors often – to frequent doom – came back.

De-Judaizing through Battlefront Politics: Kałuszyn

Counting 6,100 souls, 82 percent Jewish, this town was Hasidic strong-hold, known for prayer-shawl manufacture. When Christians confined

[24] Ibid., fos. 589–91 (August 24, 2015).
[25] Ibid., fo. 74 (August 20, 1920); fo. 89 (n.d.).   [26] Ibid., fos. 90–91 (n.d.).

their Jewish neighbors to but ten of twenty-four town council seats, Jews refused them. "There remained a 'de-Judaized' council." As Bolsheviks approached, Polish police demanded of chief rabbi 60,000 marks for ostensible defense, settling finally for 10,000. But in vain, for Bolsheviks seized control for a week, confiscating Jewish wares in exchange for inflated rubles. "Very many Poles clamored for Bolshevik jobs." The Russians took mayor, priest, two aldermen, and three Jewish notables hostage, holding them in Siedlce's Hotel Angielski.

When Polish soldiers returned, they meant to kill Jewish hostages returning by foot, but the Christian mayor intervened to save them. In nearby Bojmie, twelve peaceful Jews were shot as communists on a Polish commandant's orders. Some said that local villagers assisted, but "these same peasants would not allow shooting of one Bojmie Jew, a mason." A Kałuszyn military court ordered three Jews shot, including Popowski. "He had an application showing he wanted a Bolshevik job." The three Jews were shot "stripped naked." Many others were missing and feared drowned in river Bug.[27]

Three Christian Sejm deputies arrived to probe Jewish collaboration with the *Rewkom*, "Jewish councillors disinvited." They found that "the Jewish population favored Bolsheviks and (as a group) tore down the Polish eagle and trampled it underfoot." A Jewish witness retorted:

It's true that a certain irresponsible individual, Opfal, did this. He was a communist and long had no connection to the Jewish community. It's enough to say about him that he caused arrests of Jews by Bolsheviks ... The Christians now settle personal scores with Jews.[28]

In reconquered Kałuszyn, "gardener Tenterenta wrote on every closed Jewish shop: 'communist here,'" ensuring plunder. Maria Święcicka, "Catholic," sought police intervention, saying "she could no longer look at how they were robbing old Jews of their shoes." Released hostage Pięknawies said,

Outside Bojmie, Christian acquaintances warned me not to enter, because they were murdering Jews there. Chrościcki told me they were shooting Jews who didn't get along well with Christians even if they weren't communists.[29]

The Sejm Club protested the shooting of Jewish Soviet collaborators, while Christian offenders escaped punishment. But they did not demand retribution, "for we are in principle opponents of the death penalty and of convening military courts to adjudicate political matters."[30]

[27] Ibid., fos. 127–29 (September 5, 1920).   [28] Ibid., fo. 130 (September 6, 1920).
[29] Ibid., fo. 610 (August 23, 1920); cf. fo. 1074 (September 15, 1920).
[30] CAW. I.300.76.103, Doc. J (September 7, 1920).

Army Intelligence charged that Kałuszyn Jews greeted Bolsheviks "with ovations." Two Poles and two Jews, including executed Popowski, spoke publicly for them. "Following the meeting a parade commenced, led by Jews carrying red banners, singing communist songs, cheering Trotsky and Lenin." At City Hall, "one tore down the white eagle." Paraders numbered 2,000 to 3,000, mainly Jewish youth. In the Red Workers Militia nineteen Jews and two Christians served. Its secretary "even applied to the 'Rewkom' for employment, composed calls to meetings in his own hand, etc., and yet has not been called to responsibility." Two Christian collaborators, for whom Kałuszyn citizens vouched, were freed. "The main Rewkom leaders," Poles and Jews, "fled with Bolsheviks."[31]

Though reconquering Poles plundered, Kałuszyn evaded bloody violence. It was in pastoral Bojmie that Jews were murdered, though peasants there did not "permit" a Jewish mason's execution. While uniformed firing squads killed most Jews, victims' Christian neighbors sometimes –perhaps often – possessed veto right over their fate. In Kałuszyn, strife was ethnic and ideological. Jews' predominance provoked Christian rivals to unseat and eclipse them politically. Jewish youth's susceptibility to Bolshevism's promises emboldened Christian nationalist foes of their Hasidic elders. Jewish Kałuszyn survived and grew, but in 1944–46 three leftist Holocaust survivors were murdered there.[32]

"White Negroes": The Army's Mock Enslavement of Kołbiel's Jews

This *shtetl* (Yiddish: Kolobeel) of some 1,100 souls, two-thirds Jewish, bordered on one of mighty Zamoyski family's palace-centered estates. The Sejm Club reported that when Polish troops expelled the Bolsheviks, Kołbiel's Jews met them "happily, giving them fruit, cigarettes and other gifts. Soldiers took them gladly, then proceeded to rob Jewish property," while the commanding officer looked on "in Olympian calm." The army requisitioned some 200 Jews for compulsory labor, while "peasant onlookers enjoyed the cost-free spectacle, splitting their sides with laughter." Jews were made especially to clean up the Zamoyski palace as fitting residence for the mounted company billeted there, grandly named "Cavalry of Polish Knighthood in honor of Head of State Józef Piłsudski."[33]

---

[31] Ibid., Doc. I (October 24, 1920).

[32] www.sztetl.org.pl/pl/article/kaluszyn/5,historikoa/ (Accessed September 30, 2015).

[33] On Kołbiel, see AAN. PRM, No. 21431/20, fo. 163 (September 9, 1920), fo. 688 (August 22, 1920), fos. 1033–36 (September 12, 1920); CAW, Sygn. I.301.8.771, file 10 (September 12, 1920).

"The knights were so bold as to burst into the prayer-house on horseback and disperse the people at prayer." Jewish workers thus rounded up, or by peasant-aided soldiers, performed typical household servants' tasks. Notables among them were humiliated by having to clean latrines by hand, or – like one merchant and communal leader – "forced to wash a soldier's feet" – an act with unmistakable Christian overtones.

The Club invoked Interior Ministry regulations on compulsory labor, which was not meant for Jews alone, "as if Jews were Christians' slaves." Hearing of such abuse, one thought of medieval romances "recounting pirate assault on a peaceful hamlet to seize its residents and enslave them." Kołbiel troops' behavior was "one chain of abuses, characterized by zoological antisemitism, inhuman torment, and trampling of human dignity, spreading Jew-hatred among local Christians."

Communal official Mojzeson urged the commanding officer to halt worker raids. "If Jews are white Negroes, obliged to be at knightly lords' beck and call," let there be summons for specified numbers, whom Mojzeson would then supply. Another notable complained that no Christians were taken for compulsory labor, "for the Christians, as some say, are 'blessed' [święci], or as others say, 'they're so busy, they have no time; the Jews are idlers.'" Jewish women and children were not spared. "Soldiers, when they have to transport the tiniest object, call Jews and order them to do the work for them."

Jewish protests may have availed nothing, but the army folded the abusive cavalry into another formation. Kołbiel's experience is significant for its enactment and theatricalization of Jewish subjection to Christian pseudoaristocratic will – for the "blessed" Christian common folk's delectation. It was one of many cases of Rabelaisian reversal that resentful Christians imposed on the "idle" Jews, who had historically deep reason to bridle at thoughts of slavery.

De-Judaizing through Official Expulsion: Nowy Dwór, Zakroczym, Pomiechówek

Nowy Dwór – with 7,800 souls, half Jewish – figured earlier in Haller soldiers' "pranks." Polish soldiers arrived again in August, emptying Jewish shops and imposing compulsory labor, including forcing a city councillor to carry five-*pud* (200-pound) loads, "under which he twice fainted." On Sunday morning, bells rang at 5:30. Jews feared fire, but it was soldiers bursting into their dwellings to march them to town square. Eight hundred were led off to potato digging, the rest held under guard as Christians attended church and then strolled about, showing that Jews alone were put to forced labor. This instilled in them a feeling of "constant fear, panic, and depression."[34]

An anonymous complaint against the commandant, a lieutenant, said "he creates the impression of an abnormal person – he is practically always drunk." In rare sober moments one could deal with him, but when drunk he committed atrocities. "He publicly hanged one and the same Jewish soldier four times in different places; no one knows for what crime." Jews arrested for any reason "he beats horribly, smashing their heads against the wall."[35]

As Bolsheviks approached, the army evacuated all Jews. The Sejm Club bitterly protested, saying it revived tsarist practices the whole world condemned. "Expulsion of Jews alone only proves they are suspected of hostile relationship to the State, which is groundless."[36] When Nowy Dwór's Jew were allowed to return, they found that

of everything left behind nothing remains, except for traces of ashes where those movables that couldn't be carried off were burned ... Books seized from former beautiful libraries can be found in all the better-off houses. [At the Jewish communal center] torn-up documents lie about, meeting room transformed into latrine, bathhouse destroyed, its tubs hauled off, heater disassembled.[37]

Here, too, as in Kołbiel, forced labor was theatricalized to contrast Christian ease and freedom with Jewish captivity and exploitation. To some Christians, at least, such spectacles were deeply satisfying, reversing paranoid master-servant imaginings. As for ethnic cleansing, could Nowy Dwór's antisemites have spoken more plainly?

Nearby was Zakroczym (1921: 1,865 souls, 38 percent Jewish). Its rabbi testified that when Jews (alone) were evacuated, they brought Torah rolls to him. He locked them, along with his books, in the prayer house's attic, "since we were confident no one would dare enter and dishonor a holy place." But on return they found "Torahs torn up on the ground and covered with horse excrement, the books pierced by pitchforks, pages flying about the floor." Prayer-house servants had hidden Jews' personal possessions in the building's foundations, secured with iron plates. But, again, nothing remained, except "feathers flying in the air. They say that Christian shopkeepers are wrapping food in Jewish book-pages."[38]

---

[34] Ibid., fo. 406 (August 5, 1920). Population figures here and below: from 1921.
[35] Ibid.   [36] AAN. PRM, 21431/20, fo. 489 (August 13, 1920).
[37] Ibid., fo. 494 (September 7, 1920).
[38] Ibid., fo. 242 (September 7, 1920); cf. fos. 78, 243 (August 19 and September 5, 1920). On nearby rural Jews' material losses, see ibid., fos. 417, 427 (August 14 and 18, 1920).

Christian Protection of Jews in the Mazovian Hinterland

Beyond Warsaw's suburban towns, Bolshevik occupation usually lasted longer. Before turning the Red tide, Polish military sway was shakier, civilian anxieties more unnerving, anarchy's temptations greater. Yet many communities escaped violence. These were the majority, about which our sources are silent. It would be rosy lensed to suppose that anti-Jewish violence did not wound and scar them but without military bloodshed and plunder, not so deeply as in pogrom-stricken settlements. Towns in the war zone might also evade Christian-perpetrated mayhem if cooperative Polish-Jewish relations prevailed, as they did in the following instances.

Lipno (1921: 8,600 souls, one-third Jewish) was a textile and leather-working town. Itzhak Grünbaum wrote of its week-long Bolshevik occupation. The *Rewkom* counted two Christians and a "Jew-Bundist," backed by "laborers and railway workers." A militia counting fifteen to twenty Christians and eight Jews arose, under a new Citizens' Committee, including priest, rabbi, and Protestant pastor. It filled the vacuum left by the *starosta*, who fled. "The priest gave a sermon commanding that no one be denounced, that no one disturb the unity and friendly attitude prevailing among citizens." When Bolsheviks arrested the priest for antisocialist agitation, threatening to shoot him, rabbi and pastor gathered signatures for his release, attesting that he was unpolitical. The priest, freed, "went to the synagogue to thank the Jews."

Outside town, Bolsheviks shot some landowners, including three Jews. When Poles returned, they began plundering, but "the priest restrained them." The Citizens Committee resigned in protest against Poznanians' later robberies, whereupon the army arrested two Hallerites. Their mates then readied two cannons, threatening to bombard the town. An army colonel negotiated the Poznanians' release in return for their unit's withdrawal. He assured them that Jews had behaved "completely correctly" under occupation. Poznanians were charging Lipno Jews with greeting Soviets with "two thousand flowers while firing on Polish officers." Some young people fled with the Bolsheviks, but eight returned to be arrested. Despite their militia service under Russian occupation, they were freed "because the town vouched for them." In other nearby towns, "Bolshevik retreat was peaceful."

Civilian elite solidarity and risk-taking assertiveness and army commanders' determination to maintain discipline both among subordinate soldiers and unruly Hallerites blocked explosions of anti-Jewish violence. Crucial, evidently, was the "friendly attitude" among ethnoreligious groups (including Protestants), which the antisemitic Right had failed to disrupt.[39]

Nearby Włocławek (Yiddish: Vlatzlavek) was relatively large and important, counting 40,200 souls, one-quarter Jewish. Influences of German Reform Judaism were strong, as was assimilationism among educated and propertied Jews. Jewish patriots joined in a four-day battle successfully repelling Bolsheviks. Paweł Golde supplied soldiers with food and cigarettes, for which Lieutenant Gromczyński praised him in the press. Lieutenants Szymek and Katz distinguished themselves on the battlefield. "In the hospital, so long as it was unknown that [Szymek] was a Jew, he was pampered, visited by local aristocracy, but when they learned of his Jewishness, all visits stopped, and he was sent to Ciechocinek. It's said he was promoted to captain." As for Lieutenant Gromczyński, an anonymous plaintiff charged him with forcing Jewish compulsory laborers to sing out, "long live Poland, may the Jews croak!"

The town's Committee of National Defense "stood in Jews' favor." So did town councillors, "for which they received an army command letter condemning them as Jewish flunkies." A Committee for Soldiers' Aid "cared for Jewish soldiers, since the Ambulance Service announced that it would render aid only to our soldiers [naszym] and not Jews."[40] Here conciliatory and liberal-minded city government confronted antisemitic opposition, seemingly anchored in army and countryside. But no ethnic violence erupted.

Grünbaum's colleague, historian and Poale Zion leader Ignacy Schiper, reported on Ciechanów (11,000 souls, 37 percent Jewish), where Bolsheviks encamped for eight days, returning later for several more. Their soldiers raped two Christian women. The czerezwyczajka/Cheka "threatened investigation, but no one was punished." When Poles retook the town, "Jankiel Misier (Zionist) greeted them with cigarettes, but a certain officer thrashed him with a knout. Later, Christians apologized for this incident. The Polish army [excepting offending officer] behaved the whole time very correctly," most of the soldiers being volunteers. "When Poles took Ciechanów the second time, nothing happened to Jews, thanks mostly to the local Poles' attitude. They were friendly and protected them."

Nonetheless, the army roughly requisitioned Jewish laborers, seizing them from synagogue, "many worked in prayer-shawls they hadn't been able to leave behind." Finally, city government regulated Jewish labor

[39] Ibid., fos. 269–70 (n.d. [after August 19]).
[40] Ibid., fos. 267–68 (n.d. [after September 2, 1920]).

provisioning. Fifty Jews joined the new Citizens Militia, "now energetically carrying out inspections that yield rich finds [requisitionable items] in Christian dwellings, but among Jews they find nothing."[41]

In Ciechanów, as in Lipno, Christians did not attack Jewish neighbors, and soldiers – as volunteers, mainly educated youth – refrained from plunder. But it required more than individual officers determined to maintain discipline to restrain pogrom-minded soldiers, as Zambrów's experience shows. This town of 6,200 (52 percent Jewish) lay on Warsaw-Bia łystok road. Bolsheviks occupied it for eighteen days. Before they arrived, the commandant "invited Jewish representatives and let them know that if they gave him 25,000 marks he would maintain order and no anti-Jewish excesses would occur." After a "certain bargaining, he accepted 18,000 marks." No robbery ensued. Did the commandant share his winnings?

When Poles returned, violence flared. Finally, commandant Burhart arrived, "whose actions deserve special acknowledgment, for on the town square he categorically forbade soldiers to rob, and often intervened to prevent excesses and plunder." He also freed from arrest parents of youths who cooperated and then fled with the Soviets. (A woman thought "all young men of draftable age withdrew with the Bolsheviks.") Unfortunately, Burhart's stay was short, and violence resumed. A woman tried to prevent soldiers from beard cutting. Shot in the leg, she later died. Apothecary Szklowin, who served on the Bolsheviks' "Prodkom," obtaining food supplies for the town, was murdered on the road with bayonets. In the town,

soldiers rousted from homes and synagogue all men, some 150, and ordered them to race an automobile, which drove very fast. Whoever could not run so fast was beaten. Poles stood around, watching this spectacle and laughing.

This theatricalization with modern stage setting followed on similar torment Polish soldiery imposed at first withdrawal.

They dragged Jews regardless of age from [Saturday] synagogue and harnessed them to an automobile. When they couldn't move it, they were beaten with thick cudgels. A major driving through put a stop to this spectacle. Panic broke out. Jews denounced soldiers to him. In the uproar the crowd dispersed.[42]

Here again is the tendency of anti-Jewish crowd violence, having broken free of political authorities' top-down control, to crystallize into stylized, metaphorical dramas – in this case, demonstrations of Jews' weakness in confrontation with modern technology. Perhaps their tormentors were unreflectively gratified to see that, armed with it, they could break Jews' strength and become their masters.

---

[41] Ibid., fos. 200–1 (n.d.).
[42] Ibid., fo. 145 (September 8, 1920); fo. 271 (September 23, 1920).

Łomża was an important administrative and light-industrial town of 22,000 souls, 41 percent Jewish, northeast of Warsaw. It lay not far from Jedwabne village, where Poles under a Nazi umbrella staged a terrible 1941 massacre, influenced to some degree by political and religious figures in Łomża.[43] Sejm Club investigator Kahanowicz reported that before Bolshevik arrival, Jews comprised half the town militia and firemen. He thought these high proportions minimized Bolsheviks' plundering, if not their shooting of a young Jew before his sister's eyes on charges of firing on them (showing that it was not Poles alone who imagined such improbable aggression).

Local intelligentsia, mainly Christians, decided to remain at their posts "with intent to block inappropriate elements' access." The *Rewkom* counted but one Bundist, who later fled. The Bund had a hand in the new Bolshevik militia, admitting only working-class Jews. "In the various Bolshevik offices *starostwo* officials kept their jobs, including – noteworthily – Endeks." Teachers stayed on post. The gymnasium director entered the *Rewkom*, hoping to protect schools from requisitions.

Christians and Jews alike welcomed returning Polish troops, but on the first night soldiers killed three fighting-age Jews, cutting off ears and gouging out eyes. On the road soldiers seized some dozen Jews arrested by gendarmes for an alleged flight with Bolsheviks and shot them, "including three brothers Segalowicz from Grajewo." Limited plunder occurred, but "not on the scale of organized pogroms." Local Endeks pushed for purge of allegedly "Judaized" city hall and council, but with the former mayor's return, pre-Bolshevik staffing prevailed.

Prominent, vociferously antisemitic Endek parliamentarian and writer Father Kazimierz Lutosławski spoke in Łomża (where other Lutosławskis were notables), saying "there exists a Jewish organization [Zionism] pursuing anti-state activities with Jewish Sejm deputies at its head. The Jews must be fought – not with terror and murder but by civilized means." Such agitation doubtless fired the post-Bolshevik burning of local Zionist offices and institutions.

Russians interned Łomża's bishop, local Anti-Bolshevik League chief. Kahanowicz reported that local Jews petitioned massively for his subsequent release, as did Jewish school youth, even though "his relation to Jewish students left much to be desired." When Piłsudski later visited Łomża, "the bishop on his own initiative mentioned Jews' loyal behavior, and innocent victims, under the Bolsheviks. Thanks to this the Head of State pronounced his well-known [positive] judgment on Łomża's Jews."[44]

---

[43] See Gross, *Neighbors*; Bikont, *The Crime and the Silence*, and Introduction, above.
[44] Ibid., fos. 263–64 (September 23, 1920).

It appears that resolve among Łomża's Christian officialdom to stay at their posts under the invaders stabilized the town. That Bundists collaborated with Bolsheviks is plausible, and they may have faced firing squads for it. Yet, in town, it was Zionist headquarters that Polish anti-semites burned. The bishop's gratitude for Jewish support must have been crucial in reining in would-be "revenge-takers." Piłsudski's praise was not the first or only such official acknowledgment of Jewish loyalty. He certainly wished for their patriotism.

Collective Christian resistance to anti-Jewish abuse was more efficacious than individual efforts, unless someone very influential was involved. Chawa Kuperberg, resident in Brok near Łomża, wrote the Sejm Club bureau, saying her sister Róża, twenty-two-year-old teacher, had been arrested on false pro-Bolshevism charges. This followed "deliberately mendacious testimony of one defendant, Kacpura, whose guilt was proven and who identified my sister as communist." Kacpura later recanted. Bolsheviks compelled Róża against her will and under threat of violence to perform office work for a few days. Ten Christians and seventeen Jews petitioned for her release, yet she was scheduled to face a Lublin field court if Club intervention failed. Her fate is unknown, but she was at high risk despite twenty-seven signatures.[45]

A lone Christian's pro-Jewish testimony was weaker still. Watermill owner Joel Lewin informed the Club that four days before Bolsheviks appeared, his millpond dam burst. "The local Christians calumniated my manager, 68-year-old Szmul Lewin, and 54-year-old miller Joel Rotbart, saying they deliberately broke the dam to prevent the Polish army from using the bridge, so they were arrested."

A witness – Christian – Jan Glinka, member of Kalinowiec Citizens' Militia, went to Polish officers in Wólka, where the arrested men were taken, and testified that they were completely innocent, since on the night the dam broke they were overnighting with the Christian Mikołaj Czarnecki in Kalinowiec.

Nevertheless, the two men were shot without trial. "Local Christians still believe the executed Jews were rightly punished, creating an unjustifiable attitude toward Jews."[46] "Judeo-Bolshevik" phobia doomed two Jews despite seemingly authoritative Christian intervention.

Soldierly Brutality

Corporal disfigurement of murdered Jews was reported near Chorzele (2,500 souls, 38 percent Jewish). "Bolsheviks murdered Polish soldiers

---

[45] Ibid., fos. 1039–40 (September 11, 1920). [46] Ibid., fo. 764 (October 13, 1920).

captured in Chorzele. This outraged the Polish army, which resolved to avenge its colleagues on Jews. I note [said Rachela Hercek] that among the horribly murdered Polish soldiers were twelve Jews." Poles showed the corpses to a visiting "English commission." Polish soldiers, "terribly agitated by the sight, immediately murdered two Jews, first gouging out their eyes, then cutting out their tongues, cutting their bodies in pieces, and finally, taking pity on them, shooting them." The Polish-Soviet war – and probably earlier Eastern European clashes – generated such atrocities out of inner military dynamic, sustained, seemingly, in Cossack tradition and practice. But we have also encountered charges of cruel blinding in connection with pogroms outside the war zone, while blood-libel legendry was replete with tales of Jewish butchery.

Polish reconquest terrified Chorzele's Jews. "Christians immediately began exhorting soldiers to wipe out [*tępić*] the Jews. They said there was a list of Jews to be slaughtered." Jews fled to nearby German-ruled East Prussia, "even women and old people. Decent [*porządni*] Christians warned Jews they would certainly be beaten." Seven Jewish refugees turned up and were about to be executed when "Jewish women lamented, so that the lieutenant relented, since they had personal identification papers." He ordered his soldiers to escort them to their homes in nearby Mława, but in a village "the soldiers shot them, together with a soldier-Jew." A policeman came with three Jews to bury the victims. The seven murdered refugees "looked terrible, their eyes had been cut out and bodies hacked. Every day they bring murdered Jews' bodies to town from the surrounding country" – twenty so far, names known. "Sala Zylberberg was raped by Polish soldiers. She was terribly beaten and bruised. Obviously she defended herself. She wanted to give them money to ward off disgrace, but the soldiers wouldn't agree."[47]

In Sierpc – 6,700 souls, 43 percent Jewish – similar atrocities occurred. Eyewitness Berta Garfinkel reported that, after taking the town, Bolshevik soldiers robbed until commanders arrived. Chekists shot landowners, including three Jews, one "whose day-laborers testified he mistreated them." Another's body was "greatly disfigured, ears and nose cut off, eyes burned out." Seemingly this was two Cossacks' work, whom Chekists also shot "on people's complaints." The Bolshevik commissar reportedly called Cossacks "a wild element, hard to cope with. But they had to be counted in, as an outstanding force necessary to the army." The *Rewkom* tried to recruit Atlas (Jewish), "but he simulated sickness, barricaded his door and did not go to work." When Poles returned, local Christians' "relations with Jews were completely tolerable, probably

---

[47] Ibid., fos. 197–98 (September 9, 1920).

because Jewish shopkeepers suffered most during Bolshevik invasion." Nevertheless, triumphant Polish soldiers "according to their custom" beat and abused them, including a city councillor and a war-bond promoter.[48]

In Różan, Bolsheviks arrested some sixteen Christians. Bluma Segal said their wives pleaded with her husband – former city councillor – to intervene. He went with the priest, pledging especially for apothecary Strupczewski, but the Bolsheviks arrested Segal instead, holding him six hours and warning against further interference. Nevertheless, "Christians spread the rumor that my husband could free them all, but didn't want to." The Segals fled before the conquering Poles, who then arrested their two draft-age sons. "I was told the priest went to the military authorities to vouch for my sons, but they told him to go to his church." Her sons were "not communists, but Zionists."[49]

The outcome was tragic. An anonymous unlettered female witness reported that many Jews fled because seventeen coreligionists died during the fight for the town, seemingly as suspected communists. The Polish army ordered Jews' return, and when they did so, soldiers and armed civilians abused them "mercilessly."

They beat Aron Przysuski, smearing him then with gasoline and throwing him into the ice-cellar. [Another, similarly treated, died.] They toss others daily into the ice-cellar, beating them for 2–3 days. The Jews hide in basements and don't walk the streets ... Beards are cut or torn out daily ... Polish youth pelt Jews in compulsory labor-service with mud and stones. [She saw murdered Safersztein.] As he lay dead, the soldiers ordered remaining Jews to stone his body. The Jews, fearing beatings, were compelled to do so, to bestialized soldiers' amusement. The commandant told arrested Jews he had already murdered 16 Jews. The Segal children were horribly beaten and wounded, so one wouldn't recognize them, continually lashed with the knout.[50]

Here vengeful Poles, including the army commandant, brusquely rebuffed Christian and Jewish notables' efforts to mitigate abuse and violence. Segal's intervention endangered himself and his family while fueling paranoid antisemitic suspicions that he wielded powers he would not exert on Christians' behalf.

In Śniadowo, military gendarmes, heeding Christian denunciations, arrested six "outstanding Jewish citizens." In Łomża, they were each given "30–40 powerful lashes," followed by rifle butting. Rabbi Klepfisz went with Dr. Goldlust and Sejm Deputy Kirszhorn to army headquarters, attesting the arrestees were "orderly, religious and non-partisan

---

[48] Ibid., fo. 266 (September 12, 1920).   [49] Ibid., fo. 104 (September 1, 1920).
[50] Ibid., fo. 102 (September 2, 1920).

people," also delivering "Jewish and Christian inhabitants' signed testimony to their loyal behavior under the Bolsheviks," so three (only) were immediately released.[51]

In Nasielsk (5,300 souls, half Jewish), Christian plunder followed Bolshevik retreat, even if, by Jewish reports, it was Poles alone who joined *Rewkom* and the Red militia. Berek Tchorek sought police aid, "but the robbers, insulting the gendarmes," carried on. "They wanted to beat the gendarmes for intervening, but limited themselves to thrashing Tchorek before their eyes." A Jewish blacksmith was arrested for Bolshevism after having allegedly said that under the invaders "he could now be sure of his beard." The study house was now a prison holding "prostitutes the Bolsheviks escorted." Here tepid efforts by the gendarmerie to protect Jews met with scorn.[52]

Near Sochaczew, west of Warsaw, soldiers plundered a cucumber field on Samuel Gitejn's leasehold farm. "Then some women who harbored malice toward him because their daughters had been refused work began agitation among the soldiers." They arrested him and plundered his house, pocketing 60,000 marks in cash. "One woman assured Mrs. Gitejn she had rescued her bed-clothes." Farm manager Dominiak retrieved her "leather bag with passport." Here spurned workers took revenge, while servants proved loyal.[53]

Ritualized Mass Retribution: Wyszków and Pułtusk

In Counter-Reformation Poland, Catholic clergy organized court sessions in which sinners, self-announced or unmasked by righteous neighbors, were indicted and punished before communal eyes. Reminiscent of them, and of hoary military practices, were events in these northeastern Mazovian towns. Pułtusk was larger and more important (13,500 souls, 44 percent Jewish), while half-Jewish Wyszków numbered 9,100 souls. Wyszków was Polish Bolshevism's last headquarters, housing after August 11 the Provisional Revolutionary Committee under Marchlewski and comrades (Figure 9.1). Their forces' expulsion a week later sank Bolshevik hopes in ethnographic Poland.

Wyszków witnessed extraordinary theatricalized retribution against alleged Judeo-Bolsheviks. The Zionist bureau recorded two eyewitness accounts. The first told of hearing "despairing cries" from afar.

[51] Ibid., fo. 261 (n.d. [after August 30, 1920]); cf. fo. 234 (September 19, 1920).
[52] Ibid., fo. 146 (September 7, 1920); fos. 965–69 (September 9, 1920).
[53] Ibid., fo. 834 (August 18, 1920).

Figure 9.1 Communists. The Provisional Polish Revolutionary Committee (TKRP), photographed in Białystok in August 1920. Seated at center is Chairman Julian Marchlewski (1866–1925), flanked by veteran Polish socialist Feliks Kon and widely feared Polish-born Bolshevik Cheka leader Feliks Dzierżyński/Dzerzhinsky. Marchlewski, born of a Polish-German family, distinguished himself in cooperation with Rosa Luxemburg/Róża Luksemburg, both in Russian Polish socialist politics and in the German Social Democratic Party. He authored many knowledgeable studies, including one unveiling the reactionary nature of working-class antisemitism. The men pictured here display various communist self-images, from Western bourgeois intellectual, to nineteenth-century revolutionist, to Bolshevik fighter. *Source:* Laski Collection. Getty Images, 109400109.

As I entered town, I saw how Jews were being led, entirely disrobed. There were 400–500. They took them to a shed, where soldiers placed them individually on a table and asked local Christians if they had any reproaches against the Jew in question. (The table was covered in blood.) If any Christian raised a charge – and someone always did – they beat the Jews horribly, soldiers and civilians. They beat the unfortunates until they fainted. Jews with beards were separated out and their beards were burnt. Jews without beards were whipped with knouts. Among these were many Zionists, alongside others who took no part in politics. They're all locked in the shed, denied food. If wives try bringing it, they are pitilessly beaten.

Jews are not allowed to leave town, so that they won't report the atrocities. Dozens of Jews are to be shot. They parade the disrobed Jews through town from time to time, beating them all.

When a local Pole, an electrician, wanted to vouch for an arrested Jew, "the provincial scribe refused permission, shouting he had been bribed." The town rabbi had fled to Warsaw. Arrestees begged to be shot. Poles were threatening to burn all Jewish houses.[54]

The second eyewitness account spoke for three Jewish men in their twenties who, returning home, were taken to the firemen's shed and told they would be shot. They waited with others in a city park, where "a few hundred Polish civilian residents were already gathered. Arranging us in a row, we were beaten." The police ordered male youths to identify communists, while civilian onlookers were asked to present charges. "Among us were old men. Those the youths identified were removed from the row and beaten with clubs, knouts, and wires with stones attached." Tables were set up, at which the provincial official and two older soldiers sat. "Polish civilians and soldiers formed two rows," channeling Jews as they were called to the table, "and each of us moving through was horribly beaten."

They were interrogated, stripped to undershirts, possessions confiscated, and made to lie on the table and shout, "long live Poland and may the rabbi croak." They were then told to ask the crowd "whether anyone has a complaint or grievance against me." Someone always spoke out. "Then they threw us on the table, tipping it so we fell off. Not allowed to rise, we were beaten lying down with knouts and rods." They were made to run the gauntlet once again. Many lost consciousness. This lasted from 8:00 AM to 3:00 PM. They were then made to sit until 7:00 PM "like Tatars," legs tucked underneath – a clue, conceivably, to this drama's roots in pitiless premodern borderland wars. Present during "execution" were Mayor Pawlowski, town doctor Rybka and his military colleague, priest, and "so-called town intelligentsia." Those administering punishment harkened to town police Chief Starzyński.[55]

The Club's investigator accepted these accounts, adding that Bolsheviks had behaved "relatively peacefully," though plundering in retreat. Cries went up that Jews were firing on advancing Poles, sparking threats to shoot all inhabitants of the suspected apartment house, some twenty-five to thirty people. "Because of Polish neighbors' testimony that accusations of shooting from windows were unfounded, they were freed." Wyszków's punishment inflicters were "several hundred from among the worst elements, mainly boys and young men." Jewish victims numbered

[54] Ibid., fo. 97 (August 26, 1920).   [55] Ibid., fo. 188 (n.d.).

some 200. "I was told that before the torture began policemen and soldiers went about summoning people to the garden 'for entertainment [*na zabawę*].'" Many town notables attended, including two priests. The present town commandant ordered imprisoned Jews' abuse to cease.[56]

Two Wyszków women reported arrest of Town Clerk Stare Rynek, who worked under German occupation and "is known in town as assimilator." Bolsheviks forced her to serve them.

They summoned her three times, as a neighbor woman will testify ... Miss Rynek was remanded to court-martial. She's an orphan, having no parents whatever.[57]

Zionist Sejm deputies protested the army judiciary's imprisonment in Warsaw Citadel of forty-eight Wyszków Jews charged with fighting alongside Bolsheviks. Court martial was inappropriate. The war was ending. "The excitement it sparked will fade. Wounds should not remain," the Zionists warned (not without strategic hopefulness), "that will not quickly heal, but rather will poison the political and social atmosphere for generations, excluding possibility of conciliation among nationalities."

It suffices to look at these people, as they are led down the street, to know that the very idea they could have committed the deeds charged against them is baseless. For they are mostly Orthodox and Hasidic Jews, in their typical long caftans – representatives of that sphere standing far from politics who could not possibly collaborate with Bolsheviks.[58]

The Club learned that Wyszków's *starosta* had held an inquest, in which mayor and police chief, two Jewish representatives, and "two injured" participated. "Pogrom director [*kierownik pogromu*]" had been the (unnamed) "provincial judicial official." "The prefect addressed the [tumultuous] audience, exhorting them to order, to calm, after what had happened." Now "complete peace" reigns. "They arrested a certain Karp, because, so they say, after Bolshevik departure he unjustly denounced Jews."[59]

If we assume the court martial did not shoot Miss Rynek and that Citadel gate opened to the caftaned prisoners, Wyszków's story, which took so bloody a turn, found resolution affording victims some minimal satisfaction and eliciting from perpetrators some remorse, if miniscule. The gauntlet running and beatings, delivered following denunciations from the cruel spectacle's city-park audience, reanimated premodern

---

[56] Ibid., fos. 190–92 (August 29, 1920).   [57] Ibid., fo. 619 (August 26, 1920).
[58] Ibid., doc. A (August 30, 1920).
[59] AAN. PRM 21431/20, fo. 618 (September 22, 1920).

practices of smiting sinners and rebels at the hands of local authorities and neighbors. Such theatricalized punishments –the Last Judgment may have glimmered in devout observers' minds– were torture of accused and potent warning to onlookers. The state saw fit to countenance them.

Something similar occurred in Pułtusk. A woman saw several hundred Jews "under age forty" assembled in rows on the main square.

Soldiers surrounded them on both sides, beating them with knouts so that blood ran in streams. Soldiers along with Christian civilians watching the spectacle shouted out in chorus "hurra." Their voices mixed with the victims' terrified, heart-rending cries.[60]

One man's face was so disfigured that an officer stayed the soldier's hand beating him. The witness, asking why this torture, heard: "they ran off with Bolsheviks; they shoot at our army; they eat our bread, etc." She observed Christian communists standing about undisturbed. "People didn't tear their clothes, as they did the Jews.'" Why did the rabbi not intervene? "There's such mad antisemitic mood here," it would be futile.

"A certain known antisemite," Town Councillor Igielski, confirmed that Bolshevism charges against two Jews were "inventions and so saved these innocents from death." Jews were denied travel passes. "I myself, because I don't look Jewish, was able to get out." Another woman told of how "they stripped a certain Jankiel Bom naked on the street and prodded a dog to savage him." "The assistant rabbi was made to sweep the square. They tried to put the rabbi to the same task, but he hid." "Christians of lowest spheres" had dealings with Bolsheviks, but when the Polish army retook Pułtusk, they – basking in soldierly "trust" – identified Jewish shops. During looting, "braver Jews managed to defend themselves against robbery, demanding assistance" – and, seemingly, getting it from unidentified quarter.

Ewa Brzezińska's husband Szaja was arrested following Pułtusk starosta's branding him Bundist. The Bund once ran him for city council, but he was "a man of democratic convictions," not a party member. Yet he now sat in Galician prison while Bundist leaders had been freed. Another woman sought release of son-in-law Zajdenart, charged with signaling Bolsheviks as they attacked. This was "base calumny." His "loyalty [prawomyślność] to the Polish State" was beyond reproach: "he is director of Pułtusk's steel smelter and agricultural machinery factory, working exclusively on Ministry of Industry and Commerce contracts." Previously he was a state official. "His servant, Catholic Marja Mikołajczuk, being always present at

---

[60] Here and below: ibid., fos. 122–25 (August 29, 1920).

his home, will testify that my son-in-law gave no sign to Bolsheviks from his attic or anywhere else."[61]

So high in socioeconomic scale did anti-Jewish panic rise and so low – as Pułtusk's main square's bloodletting showed – did violence's threshold fall, exposing any male Jew to death-threatening abuse. In Serock, the "hunt" (*heca*) had started a day earlier. Soldiers assaulted Lejb Tykulski, robbing him and cutting his beard as he was forced with other Jews to cry out – a phrase new to our documentation – "may the Jews rot [*niech zgniją żydzi*]!" He tried to seat himself in a "Christian omnibus," but the driver "didn't want to let me, and only after several hours of agony did he allow it. The Jewish autobus had instantly departed, fearing soldiers." How widely public transport's segregation was practiced remains unknown.[62]

Bolshevism and Jewish Magic in Płock

Judeo-Bolshevik obsession stamped this tragedy, which swirled around an enigmatic tsadik – sole such visitor to these pages. Its stage was Płock, important lower Vistula town (29,000 souls, one-third Jewish). The archival record is unusually full, yielding the following picture, drawn on a larger canvas than most of this book's evidentiary vignettes.

"What a brave rabbi that is, standing in the balcony's open doors, unafraid of bullets." So said Christian washerwoman Dramińska to Jewish housewife Plucer about the Hasidic spiritual leader Chaim Szapiro, fellow occupant of their apartment house.[63] It was August 18 and Bolsheviks were shooting their way into the picturesque town. As Rebbe Szapiro defied whistling bullets, his wife Hudel was pleading at city hall for his exemption from forced labor. Russian advance inspired panic, spurring local army command to order all men aged seventeen to forty to report for military duty at Ciechowice, across the river.

Natan Graubard, banker, and other Jews departed "in a crowd," finding the army at a country estate. They were commandeered into a garden, under villagers' and young estate laborers' eyes. Soldiers emptied Graubard's knapsack and pockets "while cudgeling us." He was ordered "to take off my boots, but I said I wouldn't do it willingly, so they threw me down and took the boots by force, beating all the while." When a Polish major appeared, Graubard demanded his tormentors' arrest.

---

[61] Ibid., fos. 1006–7 (September 11, 1920); fos. 877–78 (September 2, 1920).
[62] Ibid., fos. 624–27 (August 26–28, 1920).   [63] Ibid., fos. 648–9 (September 8, 1920).

"Muscovites didn't beat me, and neither did Germans. Now I report for conscription and my own army pummels and plunders me."

The major shot back self-righteously: "Silence! Do you know what the Jews did in Płock? They fired on our troops!" More conciliatorily, he asked Graubard if he could identify the soldiers who stole his boots, but they had vanished. The major then took Graubard to headquarters, where he witnessed Colonel Zapaśnik telling the commanding general how, when "he was driving along Cathedral Street, Jews shot at him from Lewenstein's house." Graubard protested, saying all Jews had been summoned for conscription. He was heatedly told: "You, sir, may thank God that you're alive, that you didn't meet the same fate as the four previous Jews." These were communal leaders who had gone before the others to recruitment camp and who were shot under seemingly disorderly circumstances, Elbaum "wrapp[ing] himself before death in his prayer shawl."

Graubard saw how, next day, a dozen Jewish recruits arrived at headquarters "with battered heads." "They had all been injured by soldiers and peasants." He ran into Cygański, commander of Płock's Citizens' Guard, who introduced him to Lieutenant Ostrowski, who replaced his stolen boots. He told two Polish judges, a notary, and an estate owner of his tribulations. One asked if he knew that "our army was fired on from Goldkind's apartment in Lewenstein's house" and that Goldkind had been interned. "I denied this with indignation." Graubard recalled that the major "who had rescued me" was "troubled" and said there would be an investigation. An acquaintance told him Bolsheviks had held Płock for not quite a day. They robbed the city, mainly its Jews, beating them as they went. "Street battles raged."[64]

Denouncing anti-Jewish calumnies, a witness said, when Bolsheviks attacked, "Polish soldiers fled, but Jewish soldiers fought in the trenches to the last minute and didn't want to surrender." Jewish townspeople "disguised Polish soldiers in civilian dress and hid them in their homes." It was an "absurd lie that Jews poured boiling water and sulphuric acid[!] on the troops." Everyone was hiding from bullets, and every family had someone under arms, so that in tormenting soldiers they might have hurt "their own kinfolk."[65]

In Warsaw, hard-line Endeks framed a tale through their widely read press of Jewish betrayal. The capital's *Monday Gazette* (*Gazeta poniedziałkowa*) published a news release in connection with Prime Minister Wincenty Witos's postbattle visit to Płock. The National Wire Service (PAT) widely distributed this story, with its allegations of Jewish

---

[64] Ibid., fos. 75–76 (August 20, 1920).   [65] Ibid., fo. 118 (September 2, 1920).

disloyalty. Two days later, the Płock city council, caught in national publicity's glare, rejected the charges.

In Warsaw, Zionist eminence Hartglas wrote to PAT's director, observing that his agency, while it had recently conceded that Płock authorities viewed hostile charges against Jews as false or unproven "old wives' tales," still claimed Jewish traitors had poured boiling water on troops and maintained an underground telephone. Hartglas demanded a total retraction.[66]

City councillors understood PAT's indictment to hold also that "four Jews had been caught communicating with the Bolsheviks by telephone," that local Jews in general "openly sympathized with Bolsheviks," and that "sub-rabbi Szpiro was caught red-handed giving a sign from his balcony to Bolsheviks, guiding their movements against Polish soldiers." To the Investigative Branch of the Military Police, these were "established facts, though there are so far no culprits." The councillors, however, eventually resolved that "the Jewish population in general comported themselves loyally toward our soldiers and did not show sympathy to Bolsheviks, who robbed their property and persecuted them as they did the Christian population." Alleged crimes against the military had not yet been proven.[67]

Two weeks later, *Kuryer Płocki* offered "rectification" of further anti-Jewish allegations in the national press, especially the Warsaw National Democrats' popular *Two-Penny Morning News* (*Gazeta poranna dwa groszy*). "Not a single person injured by scalding, military or civilian, passed through the one and only treatment station authorized to hospitalize the wounded." To this assertion both female commandant of the National Service and Red Cross chairman legalistically assented. The newspaper added, with the equivocation and subliminal aggressiveness characteristic of many statements ostensibly exonerating Jews from hostile charges, that "the investigation and punishment of actual anti-state agitation and criminal acts during the invasion can only be carried out with full stringency" – words implying that dark deeds might still be brought to light – "if vague and frivolous rumors do not befog sound judgment and divert the public's vigilance onto false tracks."[68]

Events in Płock seemed ominous enough to bring Zionist chief Grünbaum there. He penned a lengthy report, eloquent revelation of his thoughts on antisemitism.[69] He reported that after the nationwide Association for State Defense (*Związek Obrony Państwa*) hardheartedly

[66] Ibid., fos. 152, 154 (September 17, 1920).
[67] Ibid., fos. 156–59 (September 15, 1920).
[68] Ibid., fo. 645, from *Kurjer Płocki* (September 19, 1920).
[69] Ibid., fos. 628–31 (n.d. [after August 31, 1920]).

excluded Jews from its ranks (as did its women's auxiliary), Płock Jews proceeded undeterred to "enlist volunteers, aid soldiers, and set up a hospital." But then three of their leaders, seemingly Zionists, were jailed for four weeks: banker, engineer, and physician, about whom "monstrous tales were circulated." The hand was detectable in this "ignominious business" of liberal-turned-antisemite Andrzej Niemojowski, who had denounced the medic in his widely read nationwide journal, *Independent Thought* (*Myśl Niepodległa*). Though their colleagues' arrest "depressed" the local Jewish committee, it nevertheless set up a sewing circle and collected linen for troops, while "students and Jewish white-collar workers reported as army volunteers."[70]

After Soviet troops captured nearby Mława, local Poles began, Grünbaum wrote, to change their demeanor toward Jews.

The *generality of Christians* [*ogół chrześcijański*] here – as everywhere else, by the way – *think that Bolsheviks actually are Jews* [*że bolszewicy to właśnie Żydzi*]. So people began taking their stocks of various provisions and supplies to their *Jewish acquaintances* for safe-keeping, and asked them for help and protection, should the Bolsheviks enter the town, etc.[71]

Once having captured Płock, Bolsheviks robbed Jews, Grünbaum reported, with abandon. One Jew died seeking to shield his daughter from rape. "As usually happens, Bolsheviks attracted street rabble, prostitutes and pimps, watchmen and gutter urchins, who led the Bolsheviks about, showing them where to rob." After plundering Jewish manufacturer Sarna's apartment, they chased him into his factory. "But workers[!] got him to disguise himself by changing clothes and wouldn't surrender him." Russians called a meeting, telling the workers that advancing in the rear was "*Germaniec*" [an armored and weaponized train], and that they would pass through Germany and invade imperialist France. They handed over the factory to the workers. Bolsheviks stole city hall's cash strongbox and a supply train, which hadn't been evacuated because of earlier reassuring, though false, military news. "This was the basis for the rumor that the town government, which is leftist, greeted the Bolsheviks with pastry and gave them money."[72]

Bolshevik soldiers occupied Lewenstein's house and fired from its windows. "Lewenstein himself (baptized Jew) rescued injured and helped throughout the battle." Płock Jews entered the fray en masse. A Jewish officer defended barricades in one town corner. "He even wished to attack, but soldiers, sitting in the basements, didn't want to, even though women pressed them to go fight." Jewish children, under fire, gathered up

---

[70] Ibid., fo. 628.   [71] Ibid., fo. 629 (author's emphasis).   [72] Ibid., fos. 629–30.

unspent ammunition. Jews could do no more, since Bolsheviks held their district and were terrorizing them with violence and robbery, "not even overlooking the paralytics' home, nor the Jewish cooperative, nor the shelter for the aged."

A dozen or so Jews, soldiers and civilians, died in night-long battle. Finally the Polish army, shelling the town from the Vistula's opposite bank, drove the Russians out. Polish soldiers then poured into the Jewish district, Grünbaum wrote, searching "in people's cupboards and drawers" for Bolsheviks. In one house, Jaruchemson, though he wasn't landlord, was severely beaten and arrested when cartridge shells were found in a Russian officer's wife's third-floor apartment, although the officer had been gone in Russia since 1914. Soldiers led Jaruchemson and other Jews to a Polish major, who freed them all.

Soldiers accosted attorney Oberfeld, "well-known assimilator, crying that he had doused them with boiling water." This rumor spread among troops and commoners. Pogrom fear arose. Jewish leaders requested protection from the newly arrived Warsaw Province governor, who "received their report very seriously, stressing that all measures would be taken to prevent pogrom." Next morning, authorities issued an announcement that forbore charging Jews with wrongdoing and threatened severe punishment for robbery. Troops patrolled streets, military gendarmes arrested plunderers, Jews closed shops and stayed at home. Polish soldier Bielski, condemned for plundering, died before a firing squad. After only two days, violence had ceased. "In this way a pogrom was not allowed to happen." Here was more proof that pogroms were stoppable through firm intervention of civil and military authorities.[73]

Just as Płock was calming, anti-Jewish aggressions flared in cross-Vistula villages, where many had fled. Rumors buzzed, and ominously, some among Polish officialdom – prefect, notary public, judge – embraced them, even alleging, among other "concocted fairy tales," that Jewish Alderman Bley had "stood on his roof and fired at soldiers." Violence erupted. Many Jews were beaten and some killed. "A kind of madness [obłęd] seized crowds of peasants and soldiers. The most monstrous rumors were repeated from mouth to mouth." A girl accused a Jew, already beaten bloody, of trying to knife a corporal. The army officer to whom she made this charge "kept a cool head and did not have the Jew shot." In Płock, Alderman Bley demanded a prefect and judge withdraw their libelous charges. Chastened, they admitted to repeating "in excitement what they heard," promising retraction in local press. Bley's wife filed court charges against Mrs. Tołpycho, director of women's health

---

[73] Ibid., fos. 632, 636.

programs, for "accusing her in a public place of pouring boiling water on soldiers."[74]

Grünbaum left Płock engulfed in anti-Jewish shadows. Many authorities were unshakably prejudiced. Local army commander, Captain Przyłuski, "expatiated on the hostile attitude of immigrant Jews from Russia. But of these there are only a few, settled for decades." The prefect, guilty already of dangerous outbursts, "repeated all the rumors and legends, even such as I heard from no one else, such as 'that four Jews were caught with an underground telephone and cut to pieces on the spot,' about which literally no one in Płock knows anything."

Płock's council president, while assuring Grünbaum of his confidence in Jews' loyalty, and in Rebbe Szapiro's innocence, "suspects nonetheless that there could be individuals – fanatics, Bolsheviks – who, overcome by frenzy, or wanting to get rid of a soldier standing under their windows and shooting at the Bolsheviks, poured down boiling water." But he rejected the story Grünbaum heard from the prefect that "two Jews were apprehended, one giving signals to the Bolsheviks with a mirror, while the other stood guard in front of the Gymnasium." The council president had spent the night in the school and witnessed nothing of the kind.[75]

Grünbaum also pondered the fate of Chaim Szapiro, whom he dignified as "tsadik." Self-declared hostile witnesses were cabinet maker, locksmith, and female house manager living across from the rebbe. Efforts were made on the Jewish side to persuade attorney Oberfeld to serve as defense lawyer, but he declined owing to "nervousness and illness."

An interesting figure was Szapiro's next-door neighbor, schoolteacher and part-time grocer Daczyński. Grünbaum learned that "between the two families there were best of relations." During fighting, Daczyński gave refuge to tsadik and family. The schoolteacher saved Szapiro's life, assuring hostile soldiers that the rebbe had not been out of his sight. Szapiro, in turn, hid the grocer's sugar from marauding troops. Yet, at the trial, Daczyński did not contradict the prosecutor's charge that Szapiro was briefly alone with Bolshevik soldiers. "This sufficed," Grünbaum lamented, "for the [military] court to condemn the rebbe to death for treason – a man divorced from politics, foreign to this world. Nor did any exertions on his behalf avail, even by Catholic clergy." City council's and antisemitic prefect's requests to delay execution for four hours while inquiries were made in Warsaw met with refusal. Instead, General Lasocki ratified the verdict, and the rebbe was immediately shot.

---

[74] Ibid., fos. 632–33.   [75] Ibid., fo. 637.

Szapiro died, Grünbaum wrote, convinced (rightly enough) that he was "a sacrifice for the whole Jewish community." Grünbaum's reference to rumors that "rich Jews" had tried to ransom the rebbe's life for half a million marks were later overwritten in the typescript. The execution made "the worst possible impression" in Płock.

When things calmed down, and it was discovered who the rebbe really was, conviction prevailed that judicial error had occurred. The rebbe died, wrapped in prayer shawl, with his back to the firing squad, so as – following Talmud's commandment – not to look upon his relatives as the "divine countenance [oblicze boskie]" was lost to them.

Two-faced Daczyński "agitated at the marketplace for boycotting Jews, urging peasants not to sell food to Jews." This happened on Szapiro's trial day. "When they asked him why he didn't identify the people who poured the boiling water, he picked up a cudgel and started a row."[76] The schoolteacher, distancing himself from his erstwhile friend and now-doomed neighbor, was reacting with self-protective fury to mocking neighbors' accusations that he might have been a "Jewish uncle."

The other witnesses to Szapiro's behavior were women. His neighbor, Dwojra Plucer, testified to the Club's investigator that as fighting raged, "the rabbi stood," as was his daily ritual, "on the balcony threshold, between the open doors." It was then that her washer women praised his courage. The women took cover. When they returned, he was still "standing there like a pillar." Military investigators later summoned Plucer to Hotel Warszawski, housing the court martial. Asked whether her testimony was true "on risk of excommunication [pod chajrem]" she replied, "may I drop dead if it isn't."[77]

Two other Jewish neighbors, Cybulska and Morowiczówna, were also present. They recalled that washer-woman Dramińska was "thunder-struck" at the rebbe's defiance of bullets. They heard how military inter-rogators asked "whether the rabbi was waving his hands or a red handkerchief." Dramińska said she saw nothing more than that he stood there. "They then said to her: 'why don't you tell the truth like the others?'" She replied that she couldn't testify to what she hadn't seen, nor could she take it "on her conscience" to lie. "They threatened her then with jail, saying she had certainly been bribed into silence." She protested that she did not know the rebbe personally. Though summoned to the trial, neither she nor Plucer were called to speak. Now "she is terrified, talking constantly of other witnesses' [damning] testimony. In her fright she was asking that suppers be sent to her in prison now

---

[76] Ibid., fos. 634–35.   [77] Ibid., fo. 648.

and then, should she be arrested." Cybulska added that "people are still constantly threatening [her]; neighbors call her a 'Bolshevik.'"[78]

The rebbe's wife, Hudel, told of how, returning on the day of Soviet attack, she cooled herself on the balcony with him. When shots rang out, she hurried to neighbor Daczyński, "who invited me with the children, giving me a separate room and receiving me very politely." Later her husband joined them. Around six o'clock in the evening six Russians knocked on the door. "I don't know whether they were Cossacks; I don't know about such things." They said someone had been shooting from the direction of their house. "Daczyński took fright and said nothing." Looking at Szapiro, the Russians said "*ty rawin*" ("you're a rabbi"), and he assented. They searched Szapiro's room but, finding nothing, left.

Another six Russian arrived, demanding sweets, for which they paid. Others ambled in, sitting at tables in Daczyński's store. Though the grocer's maidservant was present, they asked the rebbe for vodka, but he said there was none – it was forbidden now to manufacture it. After overnighting in Daczyński's lodgings, he went next morning to his apartment "to make tea for the children." Polish troops appeared, saying there had been shooting from the direction of Szapiro's house, but the schoolteacher defended Szapiro and denied the charge. The soldiers left, telling the rebbe: "you are lucky, sir, that this gentleman testifies on your behalf."

But five days later soldiers arrested him, taking him to Hotel Warszawski. Hudel spoke with him there. He told her that two officers and the prefect had interrogated him. She reported her husband's words:

The officers asked, are you rich? He answered no. Then they asked, why aren't your Jews trying to do something for you? He replied, maybe they're trying. Then the officers said: Jews are rich; they could give a half million for you. At this the prefect said: a whole million even.[79]

The rebbe said, "the prefect came out very much against him." She continued: "right away I flew to Alderman Bley and begged for intervention." Bley reassured her that the army chaplain had asked the bishop to intervene for the rebbe.

Thursday morning she brought her husband tea. The guard let her talk with him. My husband said

---

[78] Ibid., fos. 648–49.

[79] Here and below: ibid., fos. 646–47, Hudel Szapiro's testimony in Warsaw, September 5–8, 1920.

that his ordeal is a new Beilis trial. I replied: important people [*wielcy ludzie*] exerted themselves for Beilis. You're facing a court martial. They could shoot you. Then he said, if God wills that they shoot me, then it's too bad. If that pleases him, then it pleases me too. In tears I asked, what will happen to me and our little children? He said that God, who has fed them so far, won't forget about them.

She flew again to Bley, saying that her husband (not a foreigner, but wholly absorbed in Judaism) "doesn't know Polish" and needed an interpreter. With seeming coldness, Bley advised her to tell her husband to demand one. She went also to the "Płock rabbi" – the commune's religious leader – to tell him of the officials' talk of money.

I asked him to try to give them such a sum in bail, but the rabbi didn't believe me, saying that obviously they were joking around with my husband. But I pleaded with the rabbi not to take it lightly, and to exert himself, saying that I myself would sell everything I have. But the rabbi kept saying, they're only jokes.

She persuaded the rabbi to return with her to Alderman Bley. They agreed her husband should have legal defense. She went to lawyer Oberfeld, who had earlier refused requests to represent the rebbe. "He didn't want to agree, since he was terribly nervous and unwell." Next day she learned that Oberfeld had arranged that lawyer Forbert would defend Szapiro. During the trial, she was barred from the courtroom, though her daughter was present. When the judge pronounced the verdict, Rebbe Szapiro, with firing squad evidently in mind, posed the question, "Already [*już*]?" and then began reciting, in anticipation of death, "*szma isroel*." Grotesquely, people thought he was cursing the government. But then a [Jewish] soldier explained his action.

The rebbe asked for twenty-four hours. The judge replied, speaking patronizingly in the familiar mode of address, "you're obviously trying to evade the sentence." He said he only wanted to write his will "because he has a wife and eight children." The judge refused. "When they led him out I approached him in tears, but they pushed me away. I never saw him again."

That Hudel's husband's Hebrew prayer had the unnerving effect on the courtroom audience of a curse on the government indicates the depth, among most Poles, of suspicion toward such an intensely Jewish, distant, and mysterious figure as Rebbe Szapiro. Was he impervious to bullets? Could he somehow communicate vital military intelligence to Bolsheviks from his balcony by furtive gestures, perhaps with red handkerchief? Were his curses to be feared? These apprehensions cohabitated in the minds of such figures as the prefect, a man of substance and standing, with stealthier and earthier notions of enrichment through massive bribery to spare the rebbe's life. In a land with millions of Jews, they might have thought they could be forgiven for selling, for a million (or half), one dangerous tsadik his liberty: a Machiavellian bargain, open perhaps to rupture through treachery on both sides, though in reality Rebbe Szapiro threatened no one.

The rebbe's Polish interrogators were puzzled that influential Jewish protectors did not succeed in rescuing him, but it seems the Jewish establishment – figures such as banker Graubard, Alderman Bley, the Orthodox Rabbi, Zionist nationalists, and Bundist socialists, not to mention assimilators such as attorney Oberfeld or Catholic converts Lewenstein and Goldkind – felt little sympathy or responsibility for the enigmatic and self-contained Szapiro. He appears to have boasted – unlike successful Hasidic tsadiks – of no enthusiastic following crowding his rabbinical court, whether of the propertied or the poverty-stricken. And, as may be read between the lines, fear pulsing in many Jewish hearts of falling victim to soldierly violence or judicial murder doubtless immobilized more notables than lawyer Oberfeld.

Bolshevism's Polish Antechamber?

We move now into the Polish-Soviet war's outer zone, on ethnographic Poland's northeastern shelf. Here Bolshevik occupation lasted longest. Belarus, into which the Polish army had moved in 1919, lay just eastward. As the Pinsk massacre showed, military intelligence viewed the region with intense suspicion, with eyes especially on Jews. Any Red Army move westward would advance communist-inflected anti-Polonism into Poland's eastern marches, where urban populations were heavily Jewish, where Jews and Christians alike had been long accustomed to the Russian language, and where – among Jews – Lithuanian Talmudism rivaled the Hasidim, with their strong ties to Congress Poland's tsadik courts.

Military intelligence reports from early 1920 were preoccupied with countering Bolshevik agitation among front troops. Polish agents traced pro-communist handbills and placards to Belarusian and Jewish labor unionists and cooperative-society activists working through "the so-called 'Secret Organization.'" Among thirty-two arrestees, they pinned their hopes on Woroniecki, seemingly Pole, whom they sent to military headquarters in Wilno, hoping he could be induced – by rough handling? – to divulge secrets.

"The enemy's espionage right now is massive and aggressive." Among numerous refugees pouring from Russian-held to Polish-occupied territories, many spies infiltrated, finding support "among the local population, mainly Jewish." People "do not greet the Polish army gladly."

Bolsheviks had raised the "ticklish question of manor against cottage," unresolved as villagers had previously hesitated to act, "fearful of 'lords' return to estates" guarded by Polish bayonets. Intelligence officers reckoned the Western powers would demand a plebiscite before drawing Poland's eastern border. Where this was likely, "the most numerous enemy is the Jewish element." Bolsheviks had "very skillfully" penetrated "the local population's minds with the communist idea," as witnessed by masses of "graphic posters of deep communist content, sheaves of proclamations on wide-ranging subjects, extensive communist libraries."[80]

Bolsheviks used their own soldiers as spies who, if captured, posed as deserters. Everywhere "Jews serve as Bolshevik espionage's backbone." This they practiced "while plying their trade at the front in salt and medicines [to heal wounds] through bribery of our soldiers and gendarmes." A list of 235 known communist activists included very many non-Jewish names but also such descriptions as these:

> Buchsztajn – secretary of the 'Cz. K.' [Cheka] in Mozyr and recently secretary of the Communist Union of Jews in Rzeczyca. Description: average height, age around twenty-five, black clipped moustache, Semitic nose, shaven hair and beard; in Mozyr he wore a black coat and hunting boots.
>
> Pawlowa, Marta – 'Cz. K.' agent, left for agitational work in Poland, real name Fiszman or Szyfman, had forged documents in the name of Zofia Słucka.
>
> Fel – organizer of partisan units. Description: Jew, tall, stooped, round face, long moustache, shaven beard.

Along the whole front and its rear zone "there is much strengthened and feverish agitation undertaken by secret local organizations cooperating with the enemy." Prime practitioners were Jews, secondarily "local Russian elements." Payment for communist agitation was thought to be – stereotypically (improbably?) – in diamonds. Twenty-seven arrestees had been handed over to courts martial. Among them, fourteen were sentenced to be shot (including three soldiers), nine received ten-year prison sentences at hard labor, three met lesser sentences. Such was army intelligence's deeply suspicious attitude toward eastern borderland Jews.[81]

---

[80] CAW. I.311.4.207. A. Dow. IV Armji, Oddz. II, Sekcja Defensywy, *Raport Tygodniowy*, No. 1 (March 20–31, 1920).

[81] Ibid., *Raport Tygodniowy* (April 1–7 and 8–22, 1920).

Dodging Disaster in Białystok

Białystok, lying northeast of Warsaw, was Congress Poland's third industrial city, a major textile manufacturing center, and Bundist stronghold. It was battered in the 1905–6 revolution by lethal Russian soldierly and Orthodox Christian civilian-abetted anti-Jewish violence, notably the June 1906 pogrom claiming some seventy-five Jewish lives.[82] Racked during the war by death and economic dislocation, its (imperfectly countable) population gyrated, peaking in 1913 at 90,000 (69 percent Jewish) and declining to 78,000 in 1921 (51 percent Jewish).

Bolsheviks occupied Białystok for twenty-three days. Soon thereafter its Sejm deputy Farbstein, now leader of the religious Zionist party (Mizrachi), visited the city and reported back to the Sejm Club bureau. He traveled there "full of worry and agitation, for my voters stood charged with treason, and I felt co-responsible." As Russians approached, Jews fell into "panicked fear," for they knew of "social revolution's terrible consequences." As Polish officialdom withdrew, soldierly looting began, along with seizure of Jews for compulsory labor, even such "laughable tasks" as "shooing flies from horses." Military command posted warnings against theft. "Four soldiers then caught in the act were shot, temporarily halting robbery." But on evacuation's last day, major thefts occurred, and a Jewish elder was murdered "with stiletto." Jewish losses totaled 30 million marks, inscribed in 300 plaintiffs' protocols.

Rewkom of Poles and Jews arose. Establishment here of Marchlewski's and Dzierżyński's communist government followed. PPS affixed posters announcing its dissolution and merger with the communists. The Bund added "communist" to its name. Bolsheviks showed themselves characteristically hostile to specifically Jewish institutions, whether religious or secular. They banned Yiddish signs. They confiscated all shop keys and stripped factories of inventory. "The Jewish bourgeoisie was terrorized in most horrible fashion." Hunger grew desperate. Jewish socialists suffered remorse but abstained from opposition. Farbstein thought noncommunist Jews' posture toward Poland was "highly loyal," even though Christian workers in the textile branch had aggressively sought to exclude Jewish coworkers.

When the Bolsheviks withdrew, youthful Polish and Jewish collaborators accompanied them, along with unwilling hostages – sixteen shot on retreat, including four Jews. On Polish reentry, commanders denounced alleged Jewish hostility in *Gazeta Warszawska*, which Jewish spokesmen

---

[82] Staliūnas, *Enemies for a Day*, 217ff.

quoted as charging that "for twenty hours [after army return] heated street battle raged against the 53rd Soviet Division and its local Jewish allies, who considerably strengthened Bolshevik ranks." Among soldiery, plundering engulfed three days, killing one Jew and seriously injuring another. The pro-Endek National Workers' Party-Labor demanded removal again of all Yiddish-language signs, along with Jews' exclusion from public office.[83]

The Christian-dominated Białystok Citizens' Committee, joined by two army officers, an American journalist, and Jewish witnesses, debated the anti-Jewish allegations. "All speakers," the transcript declared, "agree the army communiqué did not reflect reality, since the Jewish population did not take part in battles." It was possible that individual Jews – and Christians – did so, but evidence was lacking. Zeligman declared it generally known that the "communistically inclined element among local Jewish youth, alongside active communists of other nationalities, left the city [before the Polish army arrival] in full view with departing Bolsheviks." A subcommittee, including Jewish-named delegate, Catholic priest, and Orthodox priest, was asked to draft a resolution. The town's Endek security official later said, "I must concede the Jewish population was wronged," but he opposed publicly tarnishing army leadership. He asked the Catholic priest "to calm agitated minds." The cleric agreed, on grudging condition that the Jewish Commune "exhorted Israelites to maintain complete peacefulness." Finally, mediators were unheroically summoned from Warsaw. The Citizens' Committee delicately informed the Jewish commune that controversy "was producing an irregular relationship with Jews among soldiers arriving in Białystok."[84]

Army intelligence issued late-October findings. It cited press stories that Białystok Jews greeted Bolsheviks "with ovations," while Bolshevik militia, 75 percent Jewish, fired on the reconquering Poles and, in retreat, murdered seventeen hostages. Bodies were exhumed, pictures of corpses attached to the report. Twenty-six Białystok Jews were investigated for collaboration. Intelligence officer Wosik said he entered the city before the main army, learning "that from many home windows in the Jewish-inhabited districts rifles were fired, and even maybe a machine-gun." Since advancing Poles faced gunshots in areas Bolshevik forces had abandoned, "it must be concluded that shots were fired by civilian hands."[85]

---

[83] AAN. PRM, 21431/20, fos. 709–15 (n.d.).
[84] Ibid., fos. 715–20 (August 31–September 3, 1920).
[85] CAW. I.301.8.771: Protokoły spraw sądowych. 1920–21.: K. (October 26, 1920).

Evident here is mutually self-interested effort among Białystok's Christians and Jews to swim toward peaceful shores, even as cross-currents – of pro-Bolshevism, of antisemitism – pulled them toward deadly cataracts. Jews could not deny youthful red star enthusiasts, though bourgeois voices such as Farbstein's played them down. Christians well knew of pogromists in their own ranks. The army, though it shot soldiers as looters (or for worse crimes), was unwilling to acknowledge its complicity in military pogroms – from which it benefited greatly, through soldiers' self-provisioning at Jewish expense and through its own plunder ("requisitioning") of Jewish-owned stocks. The myth of Jews' firing on soldiers from their dwellings was an essential alibi not only for soldierly pillaging but also for the army's inability to prevent it. As pogrom justification, warranting indiscriminate reprisal against any and all Jews, it was cynically – but also fanatically – antisemitic.

Siedlce: Political Hurricane, Grassroots Murder

This half-Jewish commercial-artisanal and military-administrative-ecclesiastical town (31,000 souls) had escaped war's worst ravages. Hartglas was hard pressed to deny Bolshevik backing there. More striking still was ordinary Jews' indifference, also observable in Anna Kahan's circle, to Poland's cause. Polish nationalism had long and painfully grasped the thorny problem of winning Catholic workers and villagers. So too among Jews, the weaker the bourgeois elements acculturated into Polish life and receptive to Polish nationalism's message, the greater the probability that ordinary workaday Jews' ears would be deaf to Polish patriotism and even to Polish-Jewish mainstream Zionism. They harkened instead to socialist or Bolshevik utopianism, if anything outside religiously soaked Jewish life struck a response.

After Bolshevik conquest, did draft-age Siedlce men defy Polish army instructions to evacuate the city? Did crowds attend Soviet entry? Hartglas wrote, exoneratingly:

Many men in this age [seventeen to forty], not wishing to be torn from their families, hid in attics and basements. On Bolshevik arrival, they were emboldened to go out on the streets, along with considerable numbers of gapers among youth, especially Jewish workers, suggesting that the Jewish population flooded out. But there was no Jewish delegation – despite [journalists'] insinuations – greeting Bolsheviks.[86]

Hartglas conceded that "workers' circles, both Polish and Jewish, adopted Bolshevik-friendly standpoints." He cited the local PPS's

---

[86] Here and below: AAN. PRM. No. 21431/20, fos. 107–17 (n.d. [*ca.* August 27, 1920]).

proclamation: "Revolutionary Russia's Red Army has helped us break the fetters chaining Polish workers' hands."[87]

The invaders, Hartglas credulously believed, "behaved decently, robbing no one and paying cash for everything," if in overvalued rubles. The *Rewkom* counted Alperowicz – "a Russian Jew, it seems, baptized as Orthodox" – alongside local Jews and Russian Poles. Prefect was former Siedlce official who "spoke Russian, even while emphasizing his Polishness." Town commandant was also a Russian Pole, as was provisioning chief. A "red militia" counted some 100 communist-minded members, mostly Christians, as Hartglas thought, "especially railroad workers and apartment-building supervisors." A Polish Bolshevik collaborator had previously advocated anti-Jewish boycott.

All these fled with the Reds, as did "those few Jews who, unofficially but in fact, held sway in Bolshevik circles" – seemingly pro-Bolshevik Jews' local chieftains. As for "Russian Poles," they scorned Polish nationalism in communism's favor. They were Poles but not national Poles. Remaining behind were a non-Jewish militia commander, sentenced to seven months' imprisonment, and a "land commissioner," who signed many proclamations "but is now free and nobody touches him."

Hartglas delicately noted that "social communication with Bolsheviks took place in working-class spheres and among semi-intelligentsia." But some Jews hid endangered Poles in their houses, such as Grynszpan, who shielded an army officer. "Jewish communists [*żydzi-komuniści*] and Jews in general behaved correctly," refraining from denunciations of Christians.

But working-class Poles incited Bolsheviks against Jews, accusing Jewish merchants of usury, calling red militia and Bolshevik authorities against them. Those are the same individuals who now most heatedly preach Jewish boycott and exhort Polish soldiers to robbery. The Polish working-class has recently begun to act defiantly, especially lower, less enlightened spheres: they insult lady passers-by (without regard to nationality) as "boozhies [*burżuje*]." Cases are known of women's hats knocked off.

As Polish soldiers advanced on Siedlce, refugees reported their murdering of Jews. "The panic was even greater because, already earlier, priest Halberstadt let the rabbi know there would be pogrom and churches would be open to give Jews refuge." Many men under age forty fled, "fearing to be held responsible for not evacuating themselves." Many other Jews were roaming the countryside in search of food.

When Polish soldiery entered Siedlce, "beating of Jews, robbery and violence began immediately." Forewarned, Jews avoided the streets,

---

[87] Ibid., fo. 119 (August 14, 1920).

except for those like "Dr. Stein (a Pole *w.m.* [by his own reckoning]) and dentist Goldberg, city councillors," denounced by street youth as Jews who should be pressed into compulsory labor. "Only the assaulted men's energetic self-defense saved them." Soldiers blackmailed Jews, as when they planted cartridges in rabbinical dwellings and then extracted money on threat of reportage to the court martial, "which readily believes Jews' accusers." The mother of grown daughters "ran into the street, calling for help, but neither police nor anyone else responded, and the girls were dishonored." As for compulsory labor, also blackmail pretext, "old Chil Rychter, merchant of nearly seventy years, was compelled to herd cattle and as he returned, exhausted, peasants beat him on the road, so that he dropped dead."

Siedlce Jews' "armed unit," denounced in military communiqués, was, Hartglas wrote, at most a group of some eighteen, thought to be absconded Red militiamen within a 300-strong communist force fighting Poles at nearby Drohiczyn. If so, the Jewish proportion was low, while some twenty-four local Jews were murdered in villages and forests (another reporter witnessed soldiers shooting fifteen Jews attempting to save themselves among a group forced into the Bug river).[88] Soldiers tried to hang an elderly *melamed* "who taught children, but local peasants saved him." One thousand Jews were miserably jailed in Siedlce. When led out to work, "the Christians throw rocks and beat them, calling them Jewish Bolsheviks" when they only sold goods to the invaders or yielded to demands to house them. Christians who did the same walked free.

The court martial ordered five Jewish deserters shot, along with Abram Grynszpan, who worked briefly for the *Rewkom* until dismissed as Zionist and *burżuj*. He was son of aforementioned Gryszpan, who hid the Polish officer. Piłsudski's presidential palace rejected appeal on young Grynszpan's behalf. Hartglas detected no poetical injustice in this story. He met Polish commandant Lieutenant Józwa, who "impresses as a very energetic man of best will. He showed me a whole array of a single day's protocols recording soldiers' abuses during draft labor, a whole mass of objects extorted or robbed on such occasions by the soldiers and con-fiscated from them." All this would be given the field court, while Jewish commune and city hall had struck agreement over compulsory labor. He had also created "stringent officers' patrols" to suppress robbery and violence.

If excesses were ending, Zionists needed to defend prisoners arrested on trumped-up pro-Bolshevism charges and to remember "those thou-sands of wandering Jews, hiding in forests," fearful of army repression or

---

[88] Ibid., fo. 170 (September 17, 1920).

roadside murder. In town, Jews needed food provisions, not money, "because the boycott movement has reached such a peak that soldiers throw Jews out of bread-lines, and the police can do nothing about it. No one wants to sell anything to Jews."

Mayor Roman Koślacz, alongside local bishop, school-board president, and Citizens Militia chief, issued a proclamation on the violence-marred Bolshevik withdrawal.

We should honor this day in dignity and celebration, as befits the Polish Nation. Yet its first moments were troubled by transgressions against Jews. The Polish Nation, which once brought liberation to other peoples, may not so act. True, there are among Jews elements hostile to us, but we testify with complete certainty that Jewish society stands honestly and honorably for Polish statehood.

There followed warnings not to "soil" the holiday and calls to rein in "more heated elements." Punishment for trespasses would be inflicted "here on our earth by appropriate instances, and in heaven by God! // POLES! be faithful sons of your knightly fathers and grandfathers, who upheld freedom and justice."[89]

Hartglas found mayor Koślacz, while "no philosemite," a "very judicious and tactful man." Yet political pressures led him to revise the proclamation. The new text, entitled, "Clarification," announced that the earlier admonition against "anti-Jewish excesses" had, in its wording, been "by publisher's fault, falsely printed." The authors intended to say that "part of Jewish society" stood for Polish statehood, but the printer attributed loyalty to the entire Jewish community, "which does not accord with truth and in some copies has been corrected by pen." Those responsible for misprinting would answer to a court martial. While the outcome is unknown, the Polish notables' knightly words must have paled in many Jewish minds.[90]

Siedlce's Jewish commune protested the Military Ministry's dogged claim, officialized in *Monitor Polski*, that "the Jewish population joined in battle, weapons in hand, on Bolshevik side." Not one armed and fighting Jew had been apprehended. Jewish prisoners whom Władysław Grabski had suspiciously observed while touring the front were subsequently exonerated, except for five army deserters.[91]

The Club collected victims' accounts of great brutality and ritualized humiliation. Soldiers ordered Symcha Jabkowicz, twenty-seven, to drive cattle. On his return, other soldiers seized and robbed him, marching him then with other Jews along the road. "Not only did soldiers beat us, but also villagers passing by," some with their own belts. Civilians brought

---

[89] Ibid., fo. 120 (August 18, 1920).   [90] Ibid., fo. 121 (August 21, 1920).
[91] Ibid., fo. 768 (November 10, 1920).

"torn and dirty Torah rolls, [which soldiers] ordered me and my comrade-sufferers to tear up and then read the text on the little pieces." This was mocking parody of Jewish religious study, incomprehensible to Christian outsiders. A woman wanted to give him and a boy they had beaten water, "but soldiers [like Jesus's Roman tormentors] forbade it." "One of the boy spectators said I looked like Trotsky, so they tore hair from my head." They were forced "to spit in each other's faces, and slug each other," acting as their own scourgers. This and similar acts made mockery of Jewish solidarity, feared by Judeophobes. Jailed in Siedlce, the prosecutor's inquest found him innocent, "but they only released me much later."[92]

Rachmil Jerzymowski, twenty-eight, was stripped, together with thirty-seven other captives, to his undershirt or, as he said, "naked." Beaten, they lay on the ground. "The soldiers ordered us to lick the blood off one another, forbidding us to spit it out." One soldier "took pity, saying it would be better to kill us than to torment us so. But no one noticed him." They were commanded "to kiss the dead bodies of [beaten-to-death] Jews." These humiliations, if they did not also conjure with blood-libel tradition, battered self-respect and social cohesion. One lieutenant ordered them shot. Another, saying there was no such command, "had a Russian prisoner beat us in the face, and if the officer thought he hit too weakly, then he beat the Russian." They then endured jail with thrashings for two weeks.

Szyja Celnik, twenty-seven, former Citizens Guard member, protested his shop's looting to the town commandant, "who slammed the door in my face, promising to send soldiers, which he failed to do." His former militia colleagues also refused, as did then–Town President Koślacz (now *starosta*). Here was another disappointed believer in the Polish state's readiness to protect its Jewish citizens. Unlettered Zelda Epelbaum, eighteen, unable to buy soldiers off, was raped (and whipped) by twenty of them. They meant to shoot her. "I long lay in a faint. They carted me to Sokołów. There I had to drive cattle five versts, where I managed with great difficulty to escape. I am sick to the present day."

Melamed Hersz Bercweig, thirty-one, was captured while buying food in villages. Robbed of 20,000 marks, he and other prisoners were saved from shooting "by one soldier." Shouting usual antirabbinical insults, "we were forced [as if clowns] now to laugh, now to cry." "We had to hit and kiss one another." Chaim Golgman, forty-seven, was robbed by "men wearing Polish army uniforms." They seized Golgman's son and

---

[92] Ibid., fo. 210 (*ca.* September 8–9, 1920). On the following victims' protocols, see ibid., fos. 203–18, *passim* (September 8–9, 1920).

two other youths. Later "local villagers fishing in the Bug" found the corpses. One's eyes were gouged out, one's throat was slit, the others were stabbed with bayonets and shot. One of the armed men who had led the boys away later came to Golgman, ruefully saying, "he had killed enough Jews," confessing also that he had stolen a Jew's boots. Here was evidence, unique in these pages, of pogromist remorse.[93]

Siedlce's Bloody Hinterland: Demotic Ethnic Cleansing

In nearby Łuków, soldiery spread similar death and ruination. In this Hasidic stronghold (13,000 souls, 57 percent Jewish), as four Jewish witnesses said, pre-Bolshevik "relations between Poles and Jews were good." The retreating Polish army commanded all service-age adults to enlist, "but there were volunteers neither among Jews nor Christians." To the *Rewkom*, Russians appointed three Poles and two "extreme leftist" Jews. The "red militia" counted eight Jews but more Christians. When Polish soldiery returned, "dread gripped Jews" so that, "in panicky fear" men and boys ran off, while the Christian rabble guided soldiers through two-day plunder. During looting, Piłsudski passed through Łuków, but a Jewish delegation was not allowed to reach him.

Among Jewish casualties was baker Lichter, shot for not having bread for Polish soldiers. By another account, he was beheaded with a bayonet. "Woe to him" who can't buy himself free of herding cattle to other towns, for "on return villagers beat them or kill them as alleged Bolsheviks." Soldiers threw three such Jews in a river, first taking their shoes and hats, then throwing rocks at them in the water. "Only when their wives appeared with militia-men were they rescued, barely alive."

Jews begged the Club "to forbid the army from singing antisemitic songs as they march through town." Seamstress Nute Lerner lost her whole textile inventory to plunderers, along with a "gold watch, gold bracelet, two gold rings, diamond earrings worth 3,000 marks, a crystal gooseneck decanter," and household furniture – more evidence of everyday *shtetl* assets.[94]

Soldiers burst into the rabbi's house, although "Dr. Chiczyński and one other Christian" tried to prevent it. They desisted from killing the rabbi and his children when he surrendered "much money and all valuables." Other testimony placed a wealthy man in the rabbi's household, who had brought his valuables there for protection – "worth millions." The rabbi was wounded "and now lies sick, his life reportedly in danger."[95]

---

[93] Ibid., fo. 170 (n.d.).   [94] Ibid., fo. 175 (August 23, 1920); fo. 241 (n.d.).
[95] Ibid., fo. 101 (September 1, 1920).

Three or four hundred Jews languished in jail, routinely beaten "mercilessly," stripped of caftans and shoes. These were seemingly the men who had fled Siedlce but were then arrested. "The army commands that one Jew beat the other." A Christian carted in a Jewish acquaintance who had suffered twelve wounds to his head, a broken hand, and was "terribly mutilated." "He lived into the night [and] then died amid horrible suffering." A woman said, "I saw a hand on the road." Another report had victims set to compulsory work, then to digging their own graves "before being shot by a machine-gun." Most were in their thirties, two were Jewish butchers, all Orthodox and unpolitical. It was said that Łuków police learned of their plight "and wanted to save them, but didn't manage."[96] Many Jews from Łuków and surroundings were thrown in the Bug. "Those who swam out were killed with hand grenades." "No one sells Jews bread – they are starving."[97]

These and preceding grim stories reveal the depth of rage and anxiety over frontline "Judeo-Bolshevism," tempting or driving violence-prone antisemites into orgies of physical abuse and ritual humiliation. Was it a measure of their own fears of social-cultural extinction, should the dreaded eastern foe engulf them? Or should we conclude instead that it was war's anarchy that gave them welcome opportunity to assault Jews, humble them, expel or destroy them? Were these not compatible impulses, one unconscious, one not?

From Węgrów *shtetl* some fifty to sixty Jews retreated with the Bolsheviks, among them many of draft age, mostly Bundists who during Red occupation "had held sway in the town as militiamen, giving speeches, etc."[98] The Club protested to the government that five Węgrow Christians arrested for collaboration had been freed but not two of five Jews also suspected. One was Laufman, "sixty year-old elder, one of the most prosperous citizens, owner of the town's largest apartment building, Orthodox" and thus member of that Jewish element the government praised. Yet, because a Bolshevik radio apparatus was positioned on his roof (without his consent), he was arrested, "for that was the wish of two competitors, also accusers."

While Christian collaboration was "hushed up, the Jewish element's alleged participation was fanned into flames. Needles were made into pitchforks."[99] Court-martial verdicts against Jews "are publicized in writings and placards across the whole country, while corresponding

---

[96] Ibid., fo. 173 (n.d.).
[97] Ibid., fo. 101 (September 1, 1920). On Łuków, see fos. 169–78 (September 17, 1920).
[98] Here and below: ibid., fo. 126 (August 27, 1920), fo. 140 (n.d.), fos. 900–2 (September 6, 1920).
[99] *"Robi się z igły widły."*

sentences against Poles are omitted." Even rich Jews were starving, for they had sold to Russians for now-worthless rubles and held no marks to buy food. Soldiers forbade Christians to sell to Jews at weekly market. "The cemetery fence was dismantled and dogs are pulling corpses from graves." Węgrów's Jews were "completely shattered [*rozgromieni*]."

In Suchożebry village, Christian neighbors wrote on shoemaker Jagodziński's house wall: "Jewish commandant, Bolshevik headman." Seeing this, Polish soldiers entered "and, first, pulled off my boots." He lost everything, including a sewing machine, two pairs of silver candlesticks, two golden beakers. "They dug up my potatoes." Having fled to Siedlce, he was arrested. The town commandant checked his passport and ordered it returned to him, "but the army investigators led me to an adjoining room and began beating me [and] cut off my beard, and only then returned the passport." He could not reoccupy his house because gendarmes were living there. His wife "recognized their household cookpots at the house of neighbor Mazurek, swine dealer."[100]

In Zbuczyn village, shoemaker Jagodziński's kinsman Moszko reported that "my Catholic neighbor" led plundering soldiers to his house. "They didn't even leave me my '*Twilim*' [*tefellin* or phylacteries] although I begged them, saying they were of no use, that they are holy objects, necessary to prayer" – good reason for Judeophobes to confiscate them. Tailor Feldman reported similar *Twilim* loss. Soldiers smashed his sewing machine.[101] In Mrozowa Wola, as Rabbi Blusztein testified, "Christian landlords and house owners began expelling Jewish tenants." Jewish passers-by were compelled to throw their possessions out the windows, while Jewish girls were made to clean the apartments amid "horrible blows." "All Jews' beards were cut off." Finding no more bearded victims, "they wounded Herc Guński's clean cheeks so that the doctor had to operate to stitch up his skin, saving him from dying." Here antisemitic soldiers' tonsorial zeal led them to remove imagined beards, as if to insist that shaven Jews still wore one.[102]

Club investigator Kahanowicz reported that in Małkinia, returning Polish forces immediately shot five Jews (others said more). "Only those who could hide among Christians were saved ... The militia doesn't want to intervene. There is agitation to expel the Jews completely and take their housing." Elsewhere, "only those were saved for whom local Christians vouched, and their number is not large." A village headman intervened on Jews' behalf. Rubensztein's brother-in-law, a watchmaker, was beaten unconscious and thrown in a watery ditch. "A passing soldier took pity on

---

[100] Ibid., fos. 150, 238 (September 5 and 23, 1920).
[101] Ibid., fos. 209, 211 (*ca.* August 19, 1920).   [102] Ibid., fo. 187 (August 29, 1920).

him and, wanting to distract the soldiers, cried out, 'oh, there go three Jews running down the street.'" Soldiers ran off, allowing the watchmaker to be pulled alive from the ditch "and hidden in the potato field." Soldiers forced another man "onto the street naked, beating him with a well-pole. Indescribable panic broke out."

In Ostrów Łomżyński, when Bolsheviks arrested the Christian mayor, "the Jewish population, including leftist parties, sought his release." Kahan's family "concealed a hunted priest who hadn't got out in time." Returning Polish soldiery behaved "correctly" until shooting a Jewish Red militiaman accused of "tearing up Polish money." As often happened, Jews were made to clean barracks' latrines with their hands. "Material damages were nothing compared with moral suffering."[103]

Biała Podlaska: Small-Town Revolutionaries' Ethnic Rivalries

Hartglas stopped also in this Bolshevik-exited half-Jewish town of 13,000 souls. "Local communists – Christians – behaved correctly, Jews – worse: they denounced Bolshevik opponents. At concerts staged by Bolsheviks, Jewish youth predominated." In the *Rewkom* sat Russian, Pole, and local Jew. The militia recruited unemployed men, especially Jews. In public jobs, Christians took officials' posts; "Jews were mainly police and bureau clerks." Many, fearing reprisals, fled with retreating Russians.

Reconquering Polish soldiers lined up Jewish notables for shooting, "but because of local Christians' intercession, they were freed." The City Council "voted confidence in those who worked for Bolsheviks," averting worse things. The new town commandant promised to suppress anti-Jewish excesses, eliciting Hartglas's customary – perhaps gullible or naive – praise for seemingly fair-minded and protective Polish authorities.

Army intelligence investigated Biała Podlaska's *Rewkom*, listing eight names of activists "hostile to Polish Government and all things Polish," such as "Nuchim Nuchowicz [who] worked in the town commandant's office as a very devoted Bolshevik servant; with him worked three Jews similarly hostile to Poles." Intelligence agents also noted five Christians who "*tried to start a Jewish pogrom.*"

As I heard, the pogrom was projected, not against Jews and agitators, communists and other anti-state activists, but exclusively against the rich. The battle-cry was robbery of Goldfeld, which wasn't fully achieved due to intervention of someone who accidentally learned of it, if unfortunately too late.

---

[103] Ibid., fos. 98–100 (September 3 and 5, 1920); fo. 273 (September 23, 1920); fo. 395 (July 20, 1920).

In this uncommon account of premeditated anti-Jewish violence, anti-semitic rhetoric veiled cold-blooded theft.[104]

The nine residents who occupied public posts under the Bolsheviks, as eight of them had done before under Polish rule, told of the army's visit before its retreat, during which "General Sikorski said that any positions Bolsheviks offer should be accepted, *to not allow government takeover by Jews* and keep Bolsheviks' stay very short." This alibi was tailor-made for antisemitic Poles, justifying their collaboration while excluding Jews from protection. If Sikorski actually so decreed, it conformed with his previously cited deadly manifesto against "Judeo-Bolshevik commissars."[105]

City official Błaciszewski vividly though doubtless biasedly limned Biała's Bolshevization. He and fellow notables, learning the town would fall without battle, resolved to remain in office. At city hall he found a crowd "mostly of poor Jews, with very few Christians." Soviet soldiers orated, and then local Jewish tailor Grochowski who, "speaking in Polish and communist spirit, propagated the Bolshevik idea" (another witness heard Grochowski greet the Red Army in Russian, saying "we have long awaited you").

At town hall, Soviets formed the *Rewkom*, including Grochowski and other Bundists, together with Błaciszewski and other noncommunist Poles. *Rewkom* member Kuperszmit displayed "terrible hatred of all things Polish." (Another witness told of Kuperszmit's priding himself, in closed meeting, on having "been a communist in Poland and carried out clandestine assignments ['arson work,' *robotę podpalną*]"). His colleague, furniture maker Frydman, "was a completely uneducated person hating all culture and progress." (He, too, a 1905 revolution veteran, reportedly claimed to have "recently done 'arson work' in Biała, distributing communist brochures.") Another, hospital director Kliger, was a "simple uneducated Jew." Here are flashes of conservative-nationalist Polish disdain for unassimilated Jewish mentalities.

Zenobjan Borkowski, Biała's pre- and postcommunist mayor, said of Grochowski that "when priest M. faced charges of anti-Bolshevik activities, and was to be tried before a court-martial under threat of shooting, Grochowski went to *Rewkom* President Jurjew and gained dismissal of charges and the priest's freedom." Lawyer Mosiński quoted Grochowski, "who always went about with a red cocarde pinned to his lapel," as declaiming publicly that "religion and priests are unnecessary." Kuperszmit "usually spoke Russian, saying he didn't understand Polish. During requisitions, he generally took everything of value." Polish official

[104] CAW. I.311.4.207, fos. 42–43 (n.d.), (author's emphasis).
[105] Ibid., fos. 30–33, 34–35 (August 30, 1920).

Rybnicki, seemingly a narrow-minded nationalist, reported that Mayor Borkowski spoke Russian, having emigrated from the east in 1918. "We called him a Bolshevik because he maintained constant contact with Jews and artisans. Some thought he had been a commissar in Russia." Advocate Mosiński "spoke no Polish in the Russian days." *Rewkom* official Zając, "who spoke privately only in Russian," had changed his named to (more Jewish-sounding) Zajcer and was heard to say, as Bolsheviks entered, the hostile slogan of the eighteenth-century Polish partitions: "Finis Polonji." He later fled with the Reds, along with Grochowski, Kuperszmit, Frydman, and Kliger.[106]

From such self-interested testimony it emerges that, alongside political stigmatization, credit was given, even to seemingly hard-bitten Jewish communists, for intercession on Christian Poles' behalf. Hartglas's account projected a similar picture of grudging accommodation and avoidance of murder. Perhaps this reflected small-town life, in which political and ethnic rivals or enemies were acquaintances, if not friends. Crucial too was Biała's escape from pitched battle and the bloody violence it spawned. But when it came to facing reconquering Polish authorities, absconding Rewkom activists took no chances.

Hrubieszów: Ethnic Clash Averted

This venerable town (Yiddish: Rubishov), which had endured Bohdan Khmelnytsky's 1648 slaughter of its Jews, lay athwart the Polish-Ukrainian ethnographic frontier. Tsarist evacuation of its Orthodox Christians after 1914 dropped its population from 16,000 (1913) to 9,600 souls (1921: 55 percent Jewish, the rest mainly Polish). In 1920, Hrubieszów changed hands twice before Poles finally secured it alongside Bałachowicz's auxiliaries.

Poale Zion leader Ignacy Schiper later investigated charges of Jewish treason. Soon thereafter, Zionist deputies interpellated the government, refuting the Military Ministry's public allegations that Hrubieszów Jews had volunteered in significant numbers for the Red Army, thereby ostensibly justifying army suspicion of Jewish loyalty. Schiper's research proved that Bolsheviks comprehensively looted Hrubieszów's Jews, at a loss of 40 million marks. Jews assisted Poles in repelling the Russians. "Despite many injuries, Hrubieszów Jews suffered at hands of returning Polish units (such as synagogue's bombardment, footwear-removal, demands for money), Jews greeted Polish soldiers with bread, meat, and fruit." When Poles retook the town, their commander demanded hostages and

---

[106] Here and preceding: ibid., fos. 3–11, 14–20, 23–24, 30–35.

contributions until he realized that Bolsheviks had fully plundered the Jews. The legend of Jewish pro-Bolshevism arose because "a few Jewish volunteers from the social dregs" fled with the Russians.[107]

Such defensiveness hid messier reality, yet it seems that, as in Biała Podlaska, Polish-Jewish coexistence, especially at higher social levels, withstood war's dangers. Schiper interviewed Jewish merchant Mizes Sper, to whom departing Christian Mayor Krauze, perhaps unheroically, entrusted negotiations with invading Bolsheviks (who behaved peacefully). The *Rewkom* counted two Christians (peasant's son and prison administrator) and one Jewish woman (heading the Enlightenment Commissariat). "A few young Jews belonged to the militia, having joined for bread."

When Poles returned with the Bałachowcy, the latter, numbering about 400, stayed but a few hours, busily robbing Jews. The Poles fired on the synagogue "without any reason," wounding several. They prepared to shoot two Christians who had "hidden some dozen Jews in their basements" but were deterred by other Poles' assurances the Jews were not Bolsheviks. Earlier, Jews had vouched for a Catholic priest, "who showed his thanks by speaking up for Jews with the Polish soldiery." Retreating Bolsheviks fired the town bridge. Seeing it burn, said Sper, "we ran with other Jews under gunfire from the Bolshevik side to extinguish the blaze." Aron Rejter added that after he helped in this risky task, "Polish soldiers on lieutenant's order pulled off my shoes."[108]

Interviewing the Hrubieszów county prefect, Schiper heard that "coexistence here is generally good. The Jews understand their obligations to the State. They subscribed proportionally more heavily to State loans than the Poles."

I rule out Jewish cooperation with Bolsheviks. There were indeed a few Jewish whipper-snappers [*chłystków*] who worked during the invasion in the militia, but those were all individuals from the social dregs, and it would even be hard to say what they had in common ideologically with the Bolsheviks. They wanted instead to fish in murky waters. They ran off with the Bolsheviks, but a few later returned, because they didn't find what they expected. They were arrested, then freed for lack of proof of guilt.[109]

Restored Polish Mayor Krausze concurred but conceded that there was "no lack of clashes" between religious confessions, while "the bourgeoisie" have their "suspicions" of Jews. A wall poster saying, "Women, sisters, and wives [of Bundists] demand immediate release of men from the army; otherwise 'they will not spare blood' to force it." The poster

---

[107] CAW. I.301.8.771: *interpelacja* (n.d.).   [108] Ibid. (October 27, 1920).
[109] Ibid. (October 29, 1920).

appeared after Bundists had been released from "preventive detention." The mayor said Bundists would not have affixed it, "if only out of self-preservation instinct." He surmised it was "probably a provocation by those elements [obscure pogrom triggerers] who aim to draw hate on the Bund and through the Bund on Jews generally."[110]

Army investigators could not find witnesses to Jewish treachery apart from a Pole who accused Munia Szuchman, "owner of a soda-water shop," of greeting Bolsheviks displaying a red cocarde and saying "welcome dear guests – we have waited already two years for you." She allegedly signaled to Bolsheviks by waving a white handkerchief, indicating that the Poles were retreating. Her brother deserted the Polish army and joined the Reds. But Munia denied all, saying she had only visited the Bolsheviks to "recover a gramophone they had taken in my absence from my shop." Her brother had rejoined the Polish army.[111]

A rare document detailed army interrogation of machinist Mieczysław Krasuski, thirty. He testified, possibly under duress, that he had served in the Russian army (1911–17). Working near Hrubieszów, he lived with brother-in-law Wytrzeszcz, large-estate mechanic, "revolutionist by conviction," member of PPS Left, and activist in the Union of Rural Laborers (ZRR), for which he suffered imprisonment. Krasuski described himself as more moderate, but also ZRR member. When Bolsheviks arrived, he attended their meeting with some 180 others, mainly workers and mostly Jews. Speeches were held in Russian, Polish, and Yiddish. Horowicz spoke "heatedly" about forming a committee to regulate the local economy and set prices, reserving its leadership for himself "as experienced manager." Krasuski played a minor role in the *Rewkom*. Clearly, he minimized his involvement but could not avoid revealing six other activists' names, both Jewish and Polish. His testimony took for granted the region's ethnoconfessional mixture, speaking without prejudicial accents of Jewish colleagues. This too was daily reality in the eastern borderlands.[112]

The army listed seventy-three pro-Bolshevik runaways, nearly all with seemingly Jewish names. Among militia members, twenty-eight, also evidently Jewish – whether runaways or not – appeared, including two female commissars.[113] At most, then, some 100 Hrubieszów Jews, allegedly from proletarian depths, yielded to Bolshevik temptation.

---

[110] Ibid. (October 31, 1920).   [111] Ibid. (September 14, 1920).

[112] Ibid. (September 22, 1920).

[113] Ibid. (August 27, 1920). In Lublin District, army intelligence compiled a list of fifty-five alleged Jewish collaborators, mostly militiamen, office workers, and *Rewkom* members, plus a few "secret agents" and "female agitators," but otherwise nearly all men aged eighteen to thirty. None were under arrest; all were thought to be within Polish borders. Ibid. (December 2, 1920).

The majority, and especially those with property or other stake in Polish-ruled society (including practice of religion), closed their ears. Despite the town's fought-over character, no civilian deaths were reported, no grim atrocities or (with one exception) religious desecration. Polish authorities' further reprisals, if any, are unknown, but Hrubieszów's Poles, even amid Bałachowicz soldiers' depredations, showed little zeal for anti-Jewish violence.

Armed Anti-Bolshevik Jewish Patriots for Poland

Half-Jewish Wysokie Mazowieckie, east of Białystok, counting 3,200 souls, attracted unusual attention when its civilian inhabitants, as an anonymous Jewish witness reported, "expelled the Bolsheviks before Polish army arrival." In revenge, the Bolsheviks dragged with them in retreat 250 townspeople, 90 percent Jews. They murdered five Poles and six Jews. Polish soldiers rescued the others. They also plundered the town, mindless that Jews had helped defend it. Although no Jews sat in the *Rewkom*, Polish soldiers abused the Jewish ex-hostages, stripping them naked and tearing out beards.

Yet pro-government *Kuryer Warszawski* extolled this *shtetl* as an exemplary site of Jewish loyalty.

While from many towns one continually hears the stereotypical unhappy story of local Jews – at least in part – cooperating with Soviet authorities and fighting against the Polish army, in Wysokie Mazowieckie we have unanimous and firm assurance that Jews here solidarized wholly with the Polish population. Nor was it a passive, Platonic solidarity. [After Polish army retreat] a fighting band was formed against Bolsheviks. Many Jews joined. [This force of 300 fought alongside the returning Polish army in a six-hour victorious battle in which eighteen Jewish partisans died.]

Honor to them, who did not hesitate to shed their blood in common with Poles in defense of the land where they live!

Amid gloomy reports from so many towns of Jews' sad, hostile role, the deeds of Wysokie Mazowieckie's Jewish partisans are a bright page that Polish society will not forget.[114]

Here was Polish ambivalence toward Jewish presence expressed to perfection: an exceptional case of inspiring, heart-uplifting Jewish commitment to the Polish state and citizenship juxtaposed with "stereotypical," unforgettable and unforgivable – "sad and unhappy" – Jewish passivity and hostility.

This chapter's sketches of Polish-Jewish relations on the 1920 war's eastern front exhibit much horrific violence inflicted on a Jewish

---

[114] Ibid., fos. 94–95 (September 1 and 3, 1920).

population deeply suspected among Christians of anti-Polonism. Yet the evidence shows that Jewish pro-Bolshevism was limited, especially to hard-bitten veteran leftists and risk takers among discontented and socially disembedded youth, while a majority of settled and pious Jews strove to avoid compromising themselves and hoped for protection from Polish authorities of Christian or Piłsudskiite visage. But Poles of such temperament were frequently too weak to protect their Jewish neighbors. Instead, Polish *soldateska* and civilian antisemites plunged these *shtetl*-dotted lands into bloody misery from which the collectivity of Christian Poles gained nothing substantial but lost much not only of political but also of emotional-spiritual nature. What Jews said of themselves would in time prove true also of Poles: "material damages were nothing compared with moral suffering."

The grimmer the battlefield fighting, the greater was Polish army commanders' inability to restrain soldierly violence toward Jews, the greater perhaps their disinterest in doing so. In Łosice, near Siedlce, Hersz Karcz reported that as Polish soldiers looted a municipal official's home, "a major addressed them: 'what are you doing here? The twenty-four hours, when you were permitted to rob, have passed.'"[115] Here, from an eyewitness with little motive to prevaricate, is evidence of battlefront-level military sanction for soldierly plunder and accompanying violence.

In its *symbolic* character, the anti-Jewish violence manifested in this chapter differed along civilian-military lines. Catholic townspeople, as in Wyszków, Pułtusk, and Płock, expressed their collective violence, breaking Jewish magical strength, in theatricalized ceremonies replicating judicial procedures, whether anachronistic or modern: mass exorcism amid bloody corporal punishment or kangaroo-court and execution by bullet – or, perhaps, Last Judgment and consignment to Hell. We have also encountered various "cold jokes" played on Jews – mock enslavement or tests of strength with automobiles – which also symbolically stripped them of collective powers, real and imaginary.

Among soldiers, anti-Jewish aggression, while it served similarly to expunge imagined Jewish malevolence, was far bloodier. This suggests ominous linkage between threat of atrocious soldierly death by machine gun, sword, and shrapnel and infliction on Jews of death by mutilation, eye gouging, beheading, and other cruel murder. Itzhak Grünbaum's words come to mind: "the generality of Christians think that Bolsheviks actually are Jews." By murdering civilian Jews, soldiers imposed on them their own dreaded ill fortune.

---

[115] AAN. PRM. No. 21431/20, fo. 217 (September 6, 1920).

Evident too was gathering intensity as battle front neared of ethnic-cleansing impulse. Here villagers often displayed heartless zeal, once soldiery's plunder signaled their freedom to assault Jewish neighbors. As Catholic soldiers and civilians stood face to face with Bolsheviks, in a landscape dotted with thick Jewish settlements, a dream, perhaps millenialist, of Jews' removal entered many minds.

10   In Eastern Anarchy's Orbit
Polish Soldiery among Cossacks and Anti-Bolshevik Warlords

These pages have traversed Galicia and former Russian Poland during cataclysmic war and revolution. Myriad scenes of anti-Jewish aggression and violence have blazed. Still farther east, in the Russian Revolution's enormous and deadly arena, the scale of Jewish loss and suffering was much greater. If, reduced to human deaths alone, it was measurable in the Polish lands in multiple hundreds, in Russia – and, above all, Ukraine, with its dense Jewish population and prolonged anarchy – murders soared toward 50,000 and perhaps many more.[1] Macrostatistics are uncertain, nor is death disaster's only yardstick.

The terrain of Polish anti-Jewish violence had its jagged peaks, while farther east it soared to Himalayan heights. Does this empirical disparity entail a qualitative difference? Polish and Polish-Jewish observers found it natural to speak of "eastern barbarism," frighteningly embodied in rampaging Cossack cavalrymen. Many intelligentsia-stamped Russians, and liberal-minded Westerners following in their footsteps, have imagined Russian peasant culture as soaked in brutality – of adult male householders toward their families and among themselves, of the well-off against the poor and weak, and of insiders against outsiders, whether Slavic-speaking and Christian or not. Centuries of serfdom, actualized in overseer's fists or whips, only quickened peasants' resort to violence toward rivals and those beneath them, especially when inflamed by drink. And at those not infrequent moments in Russian – and East European – history when villagers revolted against masters, was not bloody revenge exacted in sometimes fiendish punishments? And when war raged on Christendom's and Islam's borders, fought by commoners on both sides, was not enslavement of captives or their sadistic torture and slaughter all too often heartless rule?

These familiar images served enlightened liberals who summoned them as dark mirrors against which their own civilization shone more brightly, fortifying their claims to lead modernization's march. They also

---

[1] Wiese, *Pogrome*, position 6416.

accustom those who face modernity's own hard violence, as epitomized in all-consuming ultratechnologized war with often enormous civilian costs, to concentrate on its supposed premodern sources.

But recent scholarship on peasant societies and regimes of aristocratic domination, such as long prevailed in Central Europe and Russia, has discovered in them many violence-inhibiting structures. One study of Prussian villagers within a system of noble landlordism dependent on their unpaid labor services found that, in a half-dozen villages over the course of a thickly documented eighteenth century, not a single murder found its way into the court or seigneurial records, though many a head was bruised in domestic and tavern quarrels. Nor did landlordly power hound villagers to death, confining itself instead to field overseers' thrashing – not reprisal-proof – of insubordinate laborers or court-ordered lashing or imprisonment (usually brief, if strenuous) of law-breaking villagers. Intransigent youthful troublemakers might be surrendered to army recruiters. Though far from idyllic, this was also no breeding ground for violence worse than the Western world's average of its day.[2]

And yet, the ferocity of war-inflicted and religiously hued violence in imperial Russia and Southeastern European Christian-Muslim borderlands remains a fact, as does the equally or even more atrocious bloodshed of the tsardom's collapse in revolution and civil war. But without satisfactory explanation, facts remain enigmas.[3]

In this chapter, an unavoidable question is whether a downward gradient is detectable from the anti-Jewish violence we have previously addressed to a more destructive and ominous level, not as measured quantitatively – for such disparities are clear – but as manifested physically and symbolically. These pages' evidence derives principally from reports of military violence, most of it inflicted by Cossacks or Cossack-like cavalry formations, whether on Ukrainian, Bolshevik, Polish, or the Cossacks' own side. While Jewish survivors' testimony is fundamental, our understanding is deepened by Polish army intelligence's confidential (and until now neglected) investigations not only of its own troops' transgressions but especially those of allied eastern freebooter units.

The symbolical messages emanating from these pages' violent acts – always cruel, usually bloody – will be seen to recapitulate some by now familiar scenarios. But, as the scale of murder and atrocity magnified, apocalyptic shadows grew darker and longer. Aggressors on all sides closed their ears to the dissonances of historical life and cultural clash.

---

[2] William W. Hagen, *Ordinary Prussians: Brandenburg Junkers and Villagers, 1500–1840* (Cambridge: Cambridge University Press, 2002).

[3] On the interpretive opacity of the historical literature on Cossack violence, see Chapter 1, notes 27 and 28.

Many yearned, through exaction of illusory vengeance, for the harmony of final resolution.

Theorizing Pogroms

Plundering in Sejny, a largely Jewish-settled *shtetl* in the Polish-Lithuanian borderlands, triggered an army intelligence inquiry sparking rare conceptual discussion of pogroms. The anonymous author was charged to determine whether Polish soldiery's September pillaging had constituted a pogrom, "that is," he stiffly wrote, "public excesses, massively perpetrated, against one part of the population without regard for age, material possessions, or class membership, joined with acts of violence against individuals and robbery." Absent here was any suggestion that pogroms were soldierly undertakings, commonly unsanctioned – if often tolerated – by superiors, or that Jewishness was relevant. Yet, as prime characteristic of "one part of the population," religious identity fit easily into the definition, while civilians staged pogroms too. When amplified to cast soldiers or other armed men in leading roles, and making room for rape and murder, the army's formula not inaccurately encompassed the anti-Jewish violence and plunder we have considered, although it was silent on why pogroms occurred and on their justificatory rationales.[4]

The author concluded that no pogrom had occurred in Sejny.

It happened instead that army units passing through permitted themselves massive robbery of wealthier dwellings and shops. Moreover, these thefts did not strike Jews in particular, since Christian homes were also robbed. [Civilians joined in.] Household furniture and retail goods were stolen. No one was wounded or killed. One rape of a women occurred.

Nor could this have been a "Jewish pogrom" because "the population, inclined in such situations to panicked flight, remained entirely in place." Yet – damaging admission – people subsequently "fled town en masse." The army conceded that only six houses escaped plunder. The report ended complacently: "these regrettable events did not display the character of a pogrom based on racial hatred [*nienawiść rasowa*], but were ordinary robbery, expressing loosening of morality and discipline that, as one of long-lasting war's consequences, sporadically surfaces in soldierly life." Invocation of "racial hatred," if only to banish it, summoned antisemitism's ghost, but not its human embodiment.

Investigators asked Markus Dusznicki, defense lawyer and chairman of Sejny's Israelite Commune, "what, in your view, is a pogrom?" He

---

[4] Here and below: CAW. I.301.8.771 (October 27, 1920).

(clearly not an assimilator) pithily answered: "I call a pogrom excesses in relation to one nation [*naród*], joined with murder [*zabójstwo*]." Asked whether Christians were robbed, he mentioned the "former local governor's" home, adding vaguely, "later I heard many complaints from local women." The raped girl had died. "I know there were more such events, but there was no murder."

Here the army screened from its pogrom concept explicit reference to Jewishness – and to its own role as potent pogrom progenitor. The Jewish tendency was to highlight ethnicity and bloodshed while downplaying generalized, pan-ethnic robbery (of which these pages have conveyed little evidence). Nor did behind-the-scenes, faceless political wire pullers make their shadowy appearance. Both sides acknowledged rape, without according it high significance, even when fatal. Unanswered questions and mysteries loomed.

A Cossack Pogrom in Southwestern Ukraine: Wojniłów/Voynyliv

How much deadlier were Cossack pogroms than the anti-Jewish violence this book has contemplated? Let us first consider a rare report of *Polish* soldiers' anticivilian violence in the borderlands east of ethnographic Poland. The Zionist Club filed a June 1920 letter from war-torn Dąbrowiec in northwestern Ukraine's Volhynian land. On Polish army arrival, officers ordered all Jews from their houses, "and [the soldiers] began immediately to seek out food and ate everything they found," later plundering other goods. Civil authorities and gendarmes disappeared.

At noon they gathered on the square Jews and peasants, whoever they found on the road, and began flogging them. It was forbidden to cry out, or more blows were given. You can imagine the panic that arose in our town . . . During the punishment, while they beat one man, the others had to kneel and watch the spectacle.[5]

They seized a boy, took his watch, and thrashed him three times, "and when they wanted to hit him a fourth time the *starosta* stepped out, and the soldiers took fright and released him. But the town government kept silent!"

That evening soldiers ordered supper for 200. Instead, they were persuaded with difficulty to come in small numbers to individual Jews' dwellings. "They commanded that various dishes be brought to them, like roasted chicken, etc., and when that was declined, they beat the Jews, saying there must be everything [*wszystko musi być*]."

---

[5] Here and below: AAN. PRM. No. 21431/20, fo. 236 (June 28, 1920).

This was eloquent staging of Polish soldierly fantasies about Jews: that they should be flogged *en masse* (in archaic penitential fashion of such public spectacles as we encountered earlier) but that they should also be a source of unlimited material gratifications, endlessly rich in roasted chickens, free for Christians' taking.

Polish soldiers very explicitly staged symbolic anti-Judaism in Lithuania-bordering Suchowola. Rabbi Lewandersztein testified, perhaps formulaically, that prewar "relations between the Jews and Poland were completely tolerable." Officialdom's actions were "based on justice without prejudice." Under Bolsheviks, the *Rewkom* counted two Poles – one from the local Tatar-descended minority – and two Jews. Christian youth guided Bolsheviks to rob homes of Jewish "*burżuje*." Bolsheviks "led five Poles outside town and shot them." This happened suddenly and without Jewish knowledge, a point deputy Farbstein underscored in an addendum to confute antisemitic press charges that twenty Suchowola Jews signed the Bolsheviks' complaint against the executed Poles.

This charge probably served to justify returning Poles' brutalities. Rabbi Lewandersztein was summoned to the town square, where cavalrymen waited. "An officer ordered a soldier in presence of his unit and local crowd to cut off my beard. The officer then ordered that a mirror be given to me and that I view myself, and he asked me if without a beard I could still be a rabbi." Here beard cutting explicitly desacralized, demystified, and emasculated Judaism as a religion. Later, because of "constant assaults on my house," he fled, disguising himself as a cattle driver "to get out of that hell."[6]

More brutal, and symbolism free, was the army's sojourn in Wysoko-Litewsk, on the Polish-Ukrainian ethnic frontier. In response to its arson threat, Jewish merchants set up cooperatives, giving soldiers bread, milk, and cigarettes. This was, one wrote, proof of their Polish loyalty, as was their warning to the commander, waking him from sleep, that Bolsheviks were approaching. Yet, when Poles recaptured the town, "screams resounded from every house, as they robbed, beat, and dishonored women." They fought with a woman, trying to extract her gold teeth, until she gave them 600 marks. Another bribed soldiers not to cut off her finger with a ring they could not budge. In nearby Wołczyny, soldiers raped three daughters before their parents' eyes and killed five other Jews, including a temple servant (*szames*) who tried to prevent his daughter's violation. In Kutere village they threatened, if not paid 50,000 marks, to tie miller Melnik to a horse's tail and drag him to death. Apothecary Grynwald managed to buy Melnik free. It was "typical" that the next-

[6] Ibid., fos. 274–75 (September 9, 1920).

arrived Polish unit "officially praised our town's loyal relationship to the Polish government." Here was unmitigated brutality (not unknown farther west): rape, beatings, murder, alleviated only by evident readiness to accept bribes to desist.[7]

We will observe still more violent actions by Polish soldiers. But let us first consider a local Jewish Relief Committee's unpublished report on Cossack depredations – "true hell" – of August 1920 in Wojniłów. This formerly magnatially owned town south of Lwów counted 3,000 souls, its postpogrom Jewish population reduced to 30 percent. The first Petliura Cossacks to arrive numbered some 150. The Polish army had withdrawn the day before. Locally posted Polish gendarmes initially inhibited them, but false alarm – deliberately rung? – lured them away. The Cossacks assembled the "most important merchants," demanding 150 pairs of shoes, plus clothing, wine, and cigarettes. A compromise ensued, on Jewish side by "two men playing parliamentarians." The officers urged haste, "for their troops were accustomed to Jewish pogroms."[8]

Yet "it was a delusion that through voluntary sacrifices we could escape robbery and murder," for plundering erupted. Jews fled their houses, overnighting in fields or peasant neighbors' barns. Early next morning "the officer" ordered delivery within one hour of 300 pairs of shoes, "or he would destroy the town, letting his Cossacks run wild [*pohulać*]." Witnesses observed of officers and soldiers alike: "desire to rob and murder gripped each one." Where house owners had fled and so could not be tortured,

with cunning and experience of seasoned pogromists, Cossacks sought out hiding places for money, whether walled-in, buried or anywhere else. With refined instincts they searched basements where goods of many a Jew lay concealed. They tore up floors, smashed ovens, and sometimes dug a meter deep in houses and around them seeking money and hidden objects.[9]

Four basements were dismantled, "where great stores of the local merchants' wares were concealed, inflicting damages in the millions." Here was Cossack plunderers' sweaty, blistered, routinized daily toil.

Soon other Petliurites occupied Wojniłów – a Hundred (*sotnia*) of Black Zaporozhians. A Cossack began to kill notary-lawyer Hahn, "who begged to be spared, because he was a poor scribe who never hurt anyone." His neighbor, Ivan Kusyń, vouched that he was "a good Jew [*dobryj żydok*]." The Cossack replied: "there's no help for it; I have to kill you [*nic*

---

[7] Ibid., fos. 762–63 (n.d.).
[8] Ibid., fo. 755: *Chwila* (September 7, 1920); on the Wojniłów pogrom, see fos. 777–83 (September 28, 1920).
[9] Ibid., fo. 780.

nie pomoże, muszu tebe zabete]." Hahn jumped from his window, but the Cossack ran him down and sabered him.

Marauders discovered a dozen Jews' rural hiding place and raped the women. They severely burned a forest official with candles, forcing him to identify "rich people." Having recounted these and other crimes, the committee concluded: "this pogrom destroyed the existences that have been built up over decades, subjecting hundreds of people to fortune's whim. There's not a kernel of grain to be had in the whole neighborhood."[10]

Mircia Strassman was mother of Wiktoria, twenty-one, who during the pogrom "fell into madness." Twenty Cossacks broke into their house. As Mircia gave them money, Wiktoria fled to neighbors, where she hid between two wardrobes. Cossacks hunted her, intent on rape. She found refuge in an empty house. The family had fled to nearby towns, Wiktoria growing ever more "restless and nervous." "Finally the illness seized her with full force so that she had to be taken under escort to Lwów psychological clinic," then to an insane asylum, whence she was not expected to return. Her treatment cost her middle-class family 20,000 marks. Testimony to their need for aid was offered by Prof. dr. psych. Halban.

A similar fate befell ill-named Gołda Jupiter, twenty. She "lost her mind from fear of Cossacks, who chased her as she fled her house to hide among peasants." Her widowed mother, sole relative, hospitalized her in Lwów. Klara Gold, sixteen, hid with her mother and others at a creek, "but peasant-neighbors sent four Cossacks after them." The victims fled, but Cossacks ran them down, stabbing them with spears and pikes. Klara, seeking to climb a fence, suffered a skull wound that left her unconscious. Thinking her dead, the Cossacks moved on.

Josel Reinharc, seventy-three, testified that "peasants here sent two Cossacks to seize the 1,000 dollars he supposedly had received from America." Having no such money, they tore out his beard and threw him to the ground, stabbing him with sabers. His wife saved him by surrendering their 9,000 marks. A peasant neighbor bandaged him. Herszberg suffered a similar fate, Cossacks slashing off his ear, despite his having offered them his livestock. Onufry Durkało took him to his house and saved his life.

Deaths in Wojniłów went untallied, but they were, to judge from survivors' accounts, incidental to plunder rather than Cossacks' prime purpose. Sometimes their terrorizing death threats were hollow. Yet that

---

[10] Here and below, Wojniłow victims' testimony: ibid., fos. 784–810 (October 16–20, 1920).

one could insist he "must kill a Jew" – a phrase we've heard before – suggests that bloodshed was, in Cossacks' own understanding, necessary entailment of pogroms – perhaps even Cossack (or bandit) norm that every pogromist kill a Jew or suffer comradely obloquy. Certainly Cossacks flaunted bravado-charged cruelty: proudly embraced defining characteristic. But so too was finely honed skill as canny, hardworking, basement-digging plunderers.

Evident here is the hunted Jews' Christian neighbors' accustomed ambivalence, some directing Cossacks to Jews' hiding places, others vouching for them and healing wounds. No suggestion surfaces of generalized Ukrainian Judeophobia. Priests of any description were absent – so too civil officials. Military hierarchy counted for little. Compared to most or perhaps all Polish pogroms, symbolic assault on Judaism was perhaps less pronounced among Cossacks. In this, as in the salience of Cossacks' ostentatious, saber-heavy brutality, their pogroms differed from Polish-inflicted ones. But in their fixation on plunder joined to random bloodshed and sexual violence, the Cossacks had comrades in arms – if generally less robust – among Polish soldiers, armed bandits, and thuggish civilians.

Other locally authored Jewish reports on the same pogrom wave in southwestern Ukraine (East Galicia) deepen these impressions. In Bolszówka, Jews reacted to the arrival of Black Cossacks (*czarnoszlegowcy*) by taking refuge among Christians. "But under threat of burning the whole town [Cossacks] forced Christians to release Jews from their hiding places." A beheading, stabbings, drownings, burning of feet, and thirtyfold rape followed. In Tyśmienica, "a Cossack, holding saber to his neck, threatened Dr. Lieberman with beheading if he would not, before count of three, surrender all jewels and money." They raped a woman of fifty-four and then hacked her head; "the unfortunate lived another three days, then died."

Estate manager Menzelpolt told of how two Jews traveled with estate owner Popowicz. Seeing Cossacks, they fled the wagon. Popowicz later reported, without evident remorse, that when asked, he told the Cossacks, "those are two Jews who probably fled from fear of them. Doubtless the Jews have money." Later their butchered bodies were found in a thicket. Estate lessee and building contractor Diemandstein was robbed on the road of 300,000 marks, his colleague surrendering 25,000 marks and two watches. They survived to protest their loss, escorted by two Polish gendarmes and two Cossacks, to a Ukrainian general in Kamienny, who promised inquiry, "though he added that Poles did the same thing in Ukraine, justifying the Cossacks' actions."

Halicz's Polish mayor encountered at city hall "some ten naked women," who threw themselves on their knees, pleading that their husbands, facing Cossack murder, be saved. Seemingly but four survived. Cossacks, in anti-Judaic fury, entered the synagogue and "dishonored Torah rolls." In Dumicz, a young woman was (not uniquely) "bestially" killed, stabbed in her pregnant body "so that the fetus fell out." Her husband was beheaded. Two droshky drivers, forced to transport Cossack goods, "were beheaded near the iron bridge, their bodies thrown from the wagons."

Lwów's Zionist *Chwila* reported that in Bukaczowiec rabbi and rebbetzin were butchered for refusing to reveal their daughter's hideaway. The newspaper scorned efforts to whitewash such grassroots barbarism: "The Ukrainian intelligentsia helplessly contemplate these orgies of 'insurrectionary instincts.'"[11] Yet Eastern Europe's intelligentsias not only recoiled from common folk's cruelties, but they also unleashed them, themselves sharing the inchoate, subconscious aggressions, frequently leading the charge, whether on horseback, from field marshals' tents, or from political or editorial podiums.

Adrift in Ukrainian Chaos

From 1917 to 1920, ten governments claimed power in Ukraine, from conservative-aristocratic German-backed Hetman Skoropadsky's, across a middle spectrum, in which Petliura's would-be social-democratic, peasant-friendly Ukrainian nationalist Directory loomed large, to Russocentric, urban-biased, peasant-unfriendly Bolsheviks. Agrarian-anarchist armies swept about, notably Nestor Makhno's ruthless horsemen. None of the contending parties, whatever their leaders proclaimed, created conditions in daily life favoring and protecting the broad land's big Jewish population.

Instead, Ukrainian Jews were exposed for four years to depredations of whichever army approached them, their deadliness dependent on its – generally bad – state of provisioning.[12] Plundering of Jewish merchants and traders, alongside ruthless requisitioning of peasants, was such armies' only thought to repair their misfortunes. The banknotes they

---

[11] Ibid., fo. 756: *Chwila* (September 7 and 19, 1920); fos. 751–55 (August 22 and September 2, 1920); fos. 786–87 (October 18, 1920).

[12] On Ukrainian pogroms, see, in addition to above-cited works, notably Budnitskii, *Russian Jews Between the Reds and the Whites*, also Elias Heifetz's documentary collection, *The Slaughter of the Jews in the Ukraine in 1919* (New York, NY: Seltzer, 1921); Volodymyr Serhiichuk, *Pohromy v Ukraïni, 1914–1920: vid shtuchnykh stereotypiv do hirkoï pravdy, prykhovuvanoï v radiãns'kykh arkhivakh* (Kyiv: Vyd-vo im. O. Telihy, 1998), whose argument was abstracted by Andrei Ivanov.

sometimes paid in forced sales meant little when next occupiers scorned their value. If antisemitism was absent in some party programs, "racial hatred" was livid in many – probably most – soldierly minds on all sides. Even antisemitic leaders appreciated that bloody pogroms earned them no credit, yet neither they nor their professedly anti-antisemitic rivals could reliably control line officers or troops. Only peace, however repressive and funereal, promised Jews physical security.

Even when, as under 1918 German occupation, army discipline limited Ukrainian Jews' exposure to soldierly pogroms, volcanic struggle between landlords and peasantry placed Jews in both sides' crosshairs, for commercial dealings with either could justify violence in the other's mind. Kiev's Jewish Commune in August 1918 protested recent pogroms to the pro-German Ukrainian Interior Ministry. Landlordly efforts to reclaim manorial fields seized by revolutionary peasants menaced Jews who marketed the villagers' harvests. Armed pro-landlord bands – "Cossacks and/ or haidamaks" – had murdered such Jews, even burying them alive. "The most terrible case was lawyer Ehrlichmann, whom they cut into pieces." Insurrectionist posters urged villagers "to drive out Germans and kill estate owners and Jews." In favored metaphor, the Kievans warned that "pogrom atmosphere grows more feverish; new disastrous storms threaten."[13]

Petliura's and Vynnychenko's Directory publicly condemned pogroms in a January 12, 1919, announcement, blaming them on Skorpadkyites and Bolsheviks, allegedly aiming to discredit independent Ukraine "and sow hate toward Cossacks." The once-free horsemen's iconic status as embodiments of Ukrainian identity was central to intelligentsia nationalism, whose apostles averted their eyes from cruel Cossack violence. The Directory – like Poland's government – could not forebear blaming victims, calling on

democratic Jewry to energetically fight those anarcho-Bolshevist elements in their nation who act against Ukraine's working people and their government. For these elements give provocateurs pretexts for demagogic and destructive agitation against all Jewry, who have nothing to do with Bolshevism, and confuse honest and honorable Ukrainians, pledged to defend every laboring people, including non-anarcho-Bolshevist democratic Jews loyal to the Ukrainian state.[14]

Space yawned here for punishment of such Jews as did not fit this narrow ideological jacket (even those who did not seem to "work").

This ambivalent pronouncement inspired Ukrainian Zionists to condemn it to Berlin headquarters as "effectively antisemitic." They wanted

[13] CZA. Z3/188 (August 27, 1918).   [14] CZA. Z3/189 (January 12, 1919).

their western brethren to know of the more than forty pogroms accompanying Skoropadsky's fall, "especially horrible in the great Jewish centers of Berdychev and Zhitomir." These events needed publicity, "but do not do it in our name." In fall 1919, Meyer Grossmann defined Ukrainian Zionists' position in the power struggle within the Directory-sanctioned Jewish National Assembly. He declared that, to June 1919, 175 pogroms leaving 35,000 dead had swept Ukrainian towns. "Prominent Jews and especially Mr. Morgenthau need not be afraid I am exaggerating."

He called for Western observers to be dispatched to Ukraine, as had occurred in Poland. He condemned as "thoughtless and dangerous" proposals for armed Jewish legions. "In a country where pogroms are carried out by whole armies, where villages possess cannon and machine-guns, such militia would only stoke flames and supply pretext for general massacre of Jews." Grossmann had visited Western Europe, where he encountered "an atmosphere of cold indifference which suffocates all my warmer feelings." Exemplary of the land's mutual incomprehensions was Directory spokesman Andriy Livitskyi's letter of response to Grossmann, self-defensively praising his government as first in history to recognize "national-personal autonomy for Jews" and extolling its readiness to accept Jewish armed help in separate units.[15]

The Polish Fight for Volhynia

This historic region of present-day Ukraine – *Wołyn* in Polish, *Volin* in transliterated Yiddish – lay east of ethnographic Poland in the watersheds of the Bug and Prypet rivers, fanning out from Brest-Litovsk toward the 1772 border between Polish Commonwealth and Muscovy. It was, on north-south axis, borderland between Ukraine and Belarus. Its population was predominantly Ukrainian, but with many Jews and, among Poles, estate owners, urban intelligentsia, and islands of peasantry. There were German- and Czech-speaking farmer-colonists and scattered Belarusians and Russians. Interwar Poland ended up ruling most of it, to Ukrainian nationalists' rage.

Conquest of predominantly non-Polish Volhynia, alongside East Galicia and, to the north, western Belarus and Lithuania (or its southern parts), was Pilsudskiiism's postulate so as to incorporate into reborn Poland regions historically dominated by Polish nobility and their culture and to confine Russia to the narrowest of borders, weakening its westward-aimed menace. It was a measure of Polish success in the 1920 war that 1921's Riga Treaty awarded to their rule these wide,

---

[15] CZA. L6/122, "The Demands of the Ukrainian Jews" (September 6, 1919).

ethnographically foreign borderlands. But fighting was fierce; its outcome in summer–fall 1920 unknowable.

Poles viewed Volhynia as a minefield of ethnic treachery. A brilliant evocation of the dangers lurking there, especially for their upper classes, flowed from Zofia Kossak-Szczucka's pen in her passionately nationalistic, Judeophobic, anti-Ukrainian, anti-Bolshevik 1923 memoir *Blaze* (*Pożoga*), widely read and celebrated. It recounted her estate manager husband's and her own bold and strenuous armed struggle to survive in the whirlwind of violence Russia's revolution swept into Volhynia.[16]

Polish authorities, too, descried danger and duplicity. In February 1921, the Interior Ministry informed its prefects there and nearby of dangers posed by wandering beggars. Uprooted and ruined by war, wandering back and forth across a shifting front, bereft of identification papers, they harbored Bolshevik spies in their midst, whether recruited among them or in beggarly disguise. Gathered before churches, especially during previous winter holidays, beggars and invalid veteran soldiers had been found, "singing or rhythmically chanting verses of anti-state content dramatizing war's most horrible consequences and scars." The crippled and limbless soldiers themselves were embodiments of "despair and sadness." The verses depicted the demobilized soldier, "left by government in rags and without employment, while someone else had taken his prewar workshop place," or they sang of "many other negative factors frightening men away from the army." Furthermore, the suspect beggars rhythmically proclaimed that

when the Fatherland again needs him, the soldier will scornfully whistle // for why fight against those who want to be free? // and we all, without differences of class – comrade and not master [*druhu a nie panu*], joined in one brotherly circle, will be well, warm, and happy.[17]

At holiday fairs such wanderers drew crowds, distributing to them printed messages, including "an impoverished front-soldier's letter to mother and family." To Polish officialdom, it was clear that "here we have cleverly organized Bolshevik handiwork," whose standardized and scripted message "may have harmful effects among the unenlightened masses, or the half-educated." That war-ruined men might be making morally worthy appeals for peace and justice escaped the Interior Ministry's imagination.

In Lublin, the army's Borderland Guard Main Office conducted intelligence operations at and near the battle front. In September 1920 it

---

[16] Zofia Kossak-Szczucka, *The Blaze: Reminiscences of Volhynia, 1917–1919* (New York, NY:Polish Book Importing, 1927).
[17] CAW. I.311.4.207 (February 14, 1920).

received a report from undercover agent Wojtowicz in Volhynian Kovel on civilian attitudes. Jews, "as one knows," greeted invading Bolsheviks "with orchestra and flowers." Yet, in Kovel, Jews' relation to resident Poles "was very correct." They refrained from denunciations. "When Bolsheviks arrested Father Szuhajski, the richest Jews and rabbi went to the commissar to vouch for him." Municipal officials from earlier Polish occupation had been mainly friendly Jews, now all dismissed. "For young Jews," Bolsheviks opened a "communist school." Ukrainians near Kovel were divided, poor villagers favoring Bolsheviks, richer farmers – whose livestock the Red Army seized – wanting Poles back, "for then there will be order." No one read communist newspapers. "People tear them up to roll cigarettes." Red soldiers were badly clothed and armed. In one case, "they asked Polish farmers – what do Poles do with captives? For they wanted to surrender, but heard that the Polish army slaughtered them."[18]

Antoni Zaleski, intrepid Borderland Guard director, crossed surreptitiously into Soviet-held Volhynia. He judged the Red Army "well enough organized" but underequipped. He saw cavalrymen seated on pillows. Among Ural Cossacks, it was naively said that "Bolshevism is a good thing, but communism [komuna] is bad, and they will soon declare war on it." Their conduct toward civilians was "exemplary: they neither rob nor beat" (showing, if true, that Cossack violence could be situational and strategic). Bolsheviks were secretive, sensing spies everywhere. Soldiers' flimsy clothing "melted away in rain," provoking desertion. The Red Army had a psychology of defeat. Russians warned Ruthenians not to break with Poles, "for no one knows what's coming." They thought it hard to fight Poland when "other [Western] countries" backed it, while Russia had no allies.

Yet the Red Army's relation to civilians was "very correct," even if it favored Ukrainians and treated Poles worse. "Generally, there's no robbery," but requisitions were heavy. Bolshevik soldiers roamed villages begging for food, "especially in Polish villages where they feed them better from fear." Russians "consider the land around the Bug river to be Russian and the people there Russians. 'Whether they're Germans, Poles, it's all Russian [ony czy to nimci, czy to polaki, a wse taki ruskije].'" But they saw lands beyond the Bug as Polish "and their inhabitants as burżuje." They said, "well, there we'll cut loose," promising themselves "rich booty, and sparing no girl." Yet, "order, like I said, is almost exemplary in comparison with ours."

Bolsheviks arrested all strangers. "One can feel the hard and sharp Bolshevik 'regime.'" They combed suspiciously through Rewkom

---

[18] Zarząd Główny Straży Kresowej, CAW. I.311.3.52 (September 18, 1920).

applicants' curricula vitae. In towns, these were, "naturally," Jews. Jewish-staffed militias were unpracticed in weaponry, "but they show great zeal, arresting very heavily. But, besides this, they willingly take bribes." Public security was "altogether decent." Prisoners in jail got no unpaid-for food. "But the relationship to those arrested is very familiar, even friendly."

At first, "Ruthenians hastened to the '*komuna*,' along with Poles, Czechs, and Germans." Polish "marauders" – anti-Bolsheviks – were robbed and killed. But with the Reds' battlefield reverses, the "richer people thirsted for Polish return," while among the poor there was lingering satisfaction with Bolsheviks "and fear of Polish revenge." Ruthenians were withdrawing into self-contained neutrality. "It's symptomatic that estates were plundered but not divided." Indigenous Germans and Czechs were "badly maltreated. At Red Army's sight they literally tremble in fear."

On Poles, Bolshevik invasion had a salutary effect. In words supportive of this book's arguments, Zaleski wrote: "true, they were robbed, and they live in fear of total extermination [*zupełnej zagłady*], but this inspired in them great national feeling." If the Polish army appeared, they would join en masse. "In forests, deserters and marauders from the Polish army are hiding – concealed and fed by the people." They were numerous – in one forest, some 500. Poles were confident of coming victory. "The reception I received here heartened me greatly."

"The element really susceptible to Bolshevism" was Jews. Four hundred volunteered for the Red Army in Kovel and similar numbers in other towns. "Nevertheless Bolsheviks don't spare them, driving them to labor like Poles before, and even harder. So they remember the Germans with longing. The richer elements are discontent but, under militia cover, business [*gieszeft*] carries on." Peasants were farming at night to avoid horse requisition. Commerce had shriveled; towns starved. Soviet rubles were worthless. "For 100 rubles I bought eleven apples the size of pigeon eggs." People reckoned five Soviet rubles to one Polish mark but one tsarist ruble at two marks.

Zaleski was confident. He wanted more cross-border spies. "In future have people dress as if poor, but decently, like Chełm peasants, in brown garments. They can wear shoes, if well-worn, and have money – Polish and Soviet – but not too much. As for documents, best are Bolshevik civilians', without seals. I forward a sample." New agents would need to know some local villages and stay calm if arrested. They should "escape (very easy) at first opportunity, and can try to buy themselves free – this works very well. They must command the passwords, proceed confidently, boldly, crossing is very easy." Zaleski's courier would "show the best road."[19]

Zaleski epitomized the militant, fearless Polish nationalist, counterpart to Kossak-Szczucka's heroine. His colleague, Corporal Stanisław Tymiński, skirted doom to file a Volhynian report. He too stressed soldiers' dissatisfaction in the Red Army, but chiefly "Jewish rule [rządy żydów] enrages them. They torment Jewish intelligentsia," refusing orders to attack, although it was treasonous. Tymiński was arrested for spying and sentenced to death but unexplainedly escaped.[20]

These borderland voices tell not only of ethnic polarization but of class divisions, for and against Bolshevism or Polish conservative-nationalist rule. The power struggle's prize was not nationalist hegemony (alone) but class aggrandizement, while losers faced ruination, if not extermination. A group – Ukrainian villagers, for example – could (temporarily) gain economically from Bolshevism and simultaneously lose nationally or religiously. Jews, especially, could adjust to rule of any nationality prepared to defend – if not favor – them. Zaleski showed no surprise that Volhynian Poles initially showed interest in Bolshevism. In East Galicia, once the Polish army had defeated Ukrainian and Bolshevik efforts to conquer it, Jewish economic and religious elites welcomed Pilsudskiite protection.

A Spectrum of Volhynian Pogroms

In 1921, New York's Joint Distribution Committee's Warsaw office recorded (in English) several dozen pogrom survivors' stories (never subsequently published or studied). Authors were Volhynian refugees, victims of 1920's violence inflicted by Ukrainian government (Directory) soldiers (Petliurites, or *petlurowcy*), or their Bolshevik enemies, or warlord-commanded mini-armies (*balachowcy, sokolowcy,* "Machnovtzi," "Litchiviki," "Stojanovskyites"), or by "peasant bands," "bandits," "hooligans," or various Cossack groups. Some Jewish settlements endured successive attacks by several or all of these predators. Like Polish soldiers, the *petlurowcy* and Bolsheviks stood under command of governments that formally condemned pogroms and denied unleashing or condoning them. Cossacks, when subordinated to one or another of these governments, acted against them in staging pogroms. But, like the Bałachowicz army (whose fuller documentation justifies separate discussion below) and

---

[19] Ibid., "Raport Kierownika Okręgu Wołyńskiego Straży Kresowej za czas 27/8 do 9/9 1920 roku)."
[20] CAW. I.311.3.52 (September 16, 1920).

various "peasant bands," Cossacks also acted independently, intent not to spare Jewish civilians but to ruin them.

Here we look at some exemplary cases, noting variations in pogrom violence among its several inflictors, distinguishing its worst forms, how it related to the political movements contending for Ukrainian power, and how it contrasted with Polish soldiery's behavior.

Schoolteacher Abraham Ringel, twenty-nine, told of harrowing events, claiming his parents' lives, in the once Polish magnatial townlet of *Polonne*, near Berdychev. As these eyewitness reports frequently averred, in prewar times Christians and Jews "lived peacefully together." When in 1918 government authority crumbled, "a plain, but liberal-minded peasant" commanded the militia. An emissary of the Ukrainian Directory appeared. He, self-described "extreme radical," told Jewish elders of "Ukrainian Jews' present sad condition and their even more gloomy prospects," demanding 200,000 Ukrainian rubles as counterpart to requisitions of peasant grain, threatening Cossack enforcement when protests arose. Elders yielded up a list of "rich Jews," who were pressured to pay the money into city coffers.

To Purim (March) 1919, Petliura's authority held, "and thus far it may be said, it was quiet in Ukrainia." But then Galician "Litchiviki" arrived on horseback – obscure autonomous fighter-plunderers – who pillaged and pummeled. "The Jews were depressed." Petlurowcy took nine rich Jews hostage, to counter Bolsheviks' having arrested their people in Berdychev. Held in a railroad car, they "were undressed naked and beaten with swords over bodies and heads." Local Jews ransomed them. Released, they were all "sick and broken in body and mind."

A man appeared claiming to be Batka ("father-commander") Petliura. He assembled several thousand Jews.

Petlura himself, a man of 70 with a gray beard [in fact, Petliura was then forty] ascended the platform and spoke Ukrainian with here and there a Yiddish or Hebrew sentence. His speech was a sort of reproach to the Jewish people for its conduct. He deplores the terrible fate of the children of Israel and the fact that so much Jewish blood is being shed. He gave details of the pogrom in Proskurov, where 5,000 Jews were slaughtered in the course of 3 days. It is as the Jews deserved. The same fate awaits you and all other Jews of Ukrainia, he said. The only salvation is "Zdoko Tatzil Memoveth" – give money.[21]

This imposter, possibly of Jewish heritage, then negotiated with a delegation, which gave him 100,000 rubles. He departed, saying he would dissuade his troops from coming to Polonne.

---

[21] Ringel's testimony: JDC: AR 19/21, 233, fos. 67–71 (n.d.).

The Litchiviki returned, taking hostages whom they "severely tortured" before their ransoming for 200,000 rubles and "many gifts." Petlurowcy arrested Jews suspected of forming a Bolshevik Revolutionary Committee. "They were taken to a railway station, put to a wall, subjected to terrible tortures and then shot." Bolsheviks swept in, demanding mobilization. "Then the young men hid, because they did not wish to join the Red Army." Fifty-two were arrested and marched to Zhivil, where they were later caught and killed as Bolsheviks by the "Sokolovtzi" – seemingly another Galician mounted band. In Polonne, "Gillintch, a hoologan [sic] and the son of a priest joined them. He was director of the local gymnasium which was maintained by Jewish money."

Eventually Poles arrived. "They too robbed, although on a smaller scale, and cut beards" – the latter being, as we have seen, of special symbolic significance to them. Budyonny's Cossacks, oft-celebrated Red Army cavalry, appeared, raping and robbing. Petlurowcy returned and violated 200 women in "most barbaric manner."

Many Jews ran to Christian neighbors with the intention of hiding in their homes. But not all Christians had the courage to let Jews in. The bandits entered the synagogue, tore up the Torahs and other holy books and rode through the streets with fragments of them on their bayonets.

The Polish army returned, plundering. Ringel "hid in the synagogue garret, and was not found. His mother and father were killed. Now in Warsaw. Wants to go to America."

Polonne suffered pogrom violence – robbery, rape, murder – from every political compass point. Petlurowcy, despite protection money, proved ferocious, not a governmental power but a freebooting army at daggers drawn, especially with Bolsheviks, but also with other Cossack-like armies – the Litchiviki and Sokolovtzi. Poles came late to the plunder and rapine, but plunged in, possibly killing Riegel's parents.

No such tragedy as Polonne's was unsurpassable, as emerges from Basya Reidman's report on *Tutyev (Tetiiv)*, southwest of Kiev. Here there were sugar-beet factories, where many Jews labored. Before the war, "we had no pogroms." At a January 1918 fair a peasant "stood up in a wagon and delivered a speech saying, 'As I am an invalid and have suffered much in the war, the Jews wanted to kill me'" – seemingly he ascribed the war to Jewish machinations. "'So now the peasants must take their revenge on the Jews.'" A minor pogrom ensued. Under the German-backed Hetmanate, all was quiet. Then came Petlurowcy, forcing Jews into patrol duty. When they suspected armed Jews of favoring Bolsheviks, they shot them.

Under the Bolsheviks, 100 Jews were trained as self-defense force. But they could not repel bandit onslaught: "about 4,000 men under the leadership of Tutyunyuk … They killed the entire self-defense." After two pogrom days, Bolsheviks drove them out, only to yield to White Guards who violated and killed forty-five women street vendors. The Bolsheviks returned, but withdrew before some 3,000 "Machnovtzi," who "took apart all ovens in search of concealed money." Bolsheviks again arrived but fled from Denikin's Whites – 5,000 men, all Don Cossacks. They beheaded and slashed off ears. "They hanged all those who begged them to let them live." In an eight-day rampage, 140 died, with forty houses burned.

Bolsheviks again took the town. "They had then a good Commissary, and he treated the Jews well. Whenever they brought a bandit to him, he would shoot him at once." Six or seven died daily. Jews asked him to desist, fearing bandit revenge. At Passover 1920, as Jews baked matzoth, a band of Sokolovtzi with peasant accomplices engulfed Tutyev. Local Christians led them to Jews' hiding places in the two synagogues and Beth Hamadrash, where they gathered in groups of 300, 300, and 400. They were torched. "Jews began to jump out the windows and throw out the children. These the bandits threw back into the fire, sending bullets after them. The screaming of the burning people [was] terrible."

"They said they had been sent [by whom?] to kill all the Jewish inhabitants of Ukrainia." No ransom or money was accepted. "Some Jews ran to Christian houses, hoping to hide there, [but] the Christians themselves killed them." Returning Bolsheviks found 4,000 dead and 700 survivors. "On the streets there was literally a stream of blood … When the survived [sic] Jews saw what became of their nearest, they threw themselves into the river or the fire."

Again, pogromists expelled Bolsheviks, followed by Jewish remnants. Bandits found hiding Jews in the bath house. "They wanted to kill them, but a Gentile horseman came to the scene and said: 'Why kill the Jews? They are mere women and children. They will die of hunger just the same.'"

The peasants [i.e., latest conquerors] drove the survivors to a stall on a farm. There were 24 men and 300 children there. Four men were beheaded at the gate. An elderly woman was tied to a horse and was dragged along until she died. [The rest were locked in the stall.] At night a Christian woman brought a pitcher of water and three loaves of bread and gave each child some bread and water.

In the morning there came 10 mounted men with long hair and nahaikas in their hands and said: "you have lived long enough; come out and *we shall do to you what we have done to yours before.*"

The people began to cry and scream. They were all driven out of the stall and put against a wall to be killed. Then an elderly peasant came running to the scene and appealed to the murderers. "I say to you, do not kill them. *Their blood will cry unto us.* Let them live. Let them go into the world. They will die of hunger just the same." The bandits said, however: "These Jews will tell on us. Why should we let them live?"

[The peasant then proposed a meeting of all Christians to decide.] They resolved to ask the Jews themselves, what fate they would prefer: be killed or driven away without food.

The Jews replied: "We want to live." Then the bandits took their nahaikas and began to chase everybody out of the village. Whoever had strength ran away. The small children and the women were killed by the bandits. In the villages which the Jews passed through on their flight, the peasants killed them.[22]

Witness Basya Reidman, thirty-eight, was present. "Thus we ran on until we arrived in Pliskov." Jews there received them with food and drink. When quiet returned, they sent a delegation to Tutiev, learning that 4,500 had died there, including eleven families of oft-targeted ritual slaughterers. Parentless children were sent to a Kievan orphanage. Reidman aimed "to go to America."

Here was enacted cruel mass murder complete with explicit pursuit of Ukraine-wide genocide and invocations of long-past but obviously still well-remembered massacres of the seventeenth and eighteenth centuries. It seems that such bloodshed erupted not so much from the ranks of politically defined forces – Petlurowcy, Whites (White Guards, Denikinites), Bolsheviks – murderous though they could be. Rather it was among politically uncontrolled irregular peasant/bandit forces – and perhaps also the anarchistic "Makhnovtzi" – that genocidal knives were consciously and righteously drawn. Such Christian protection as occurred framed itself, as could be expected in a nominally pious peasant society, in biblical terms – as merciful provision of bread and water – but also with dishonor and fear of vengeance in mind. Yet even those who pleaded against murder found Jewish death by starvation acceptable. The Jews' theatrical mass interrogation seems to have unconsciously reenacted, in a dark, inverted way, the trial and execution of Jesus.

Aaron Barn, thirty-seven, photographer in Volhynian *Emeltchin*, witnessed degeneration of Petlurowcy into murderous marauders. Here, too, before the war, "Jews and Christians lived in peace." In January 1919 a group of peasants murdered six people in Yossel Leibman's house with an axe. "Also a maid servant, a German woman, was killed while sitting in a chair." In 1920 violence erupted before Passover. Postmaster Petrovitch, "a good Christian," telegraphed to Zhivil for help. Forty

---

[22] Reidman's testimony: ibid., fos. 84–92 (n.d.) (author's emphasis).

Petliurite horsemen arrived but immediately joined the pogromists. "They said: you sent for us to save your Jews, so now we shall take revenge," plundering and burning fifteen shops. A month later an "uprising of the peasants" occurred, headed by "the bureaucracy," under former-colonel Modestov. They arrived in a force of 300, with ramshackle cannon. "The prominent men of the town then turned to the Bolshevist intellectuals, offering them money and asking them to take steps against the new menace." NCO Sagan drove them out with his Red troops.

Bolsheviks later having retreated, the Whites' Tarashtchansk regiment plundered and burned the town. Bolsheviks, suspicious that Jews aided the White advance, forced an "apology" from the "most prominent Jews" but expelled the Whites. When they mobilized all men under forty, youths fled to Polish army–occupied Gorodintse/Horodyni. They asked the Poles to come to Emeltchin, revealing the vicinity's secrets and that only seventy Bolsheviks were holding it. The Poles then took the town "after great battles."

"While retreating, the Bolsheviki shot a great man, David Sklovsky, aged thirty-five, and pillaged the town." On Poles' departure, 5,000 of Budyonny's horsemen descended, picking Emeltchin's bones clean. Witness Aaron Barn was fortunate. He "somehow managed to pass the frontier. He nearly drowned in the river Slutsch," arriving in Poland in January 1921.[23] In this case, Petlurowcy stood with Jews' worst enemies. "Bolshevik intellectuals" – doubtless including many Jews, including the doughty Sagan – shielded them, but without earning their gratitude. Instead, Jewish draft evaders betrayed them to the Poles.

Murderous "peasant bands" – doubtless mainly young men – spilled far more blood than Petlurowcy or Bolsheviks. In *Kamenny Brod* (*Kamyanyi Brid*), as eyewitness Miss Esther Garfinkel, twenty, a merchant, reported, "Sokolovtzi" broke the pogrom-free peace that prevailed to mid-1919. Their pretext was search for assistant surgeon Kisselhoff. "The Jews asked the rabbi whether they should surrender [him]. The rabbi replied [enigmatically, resignedly, unheroically?] that he was not answering any inquiries. And the assistant surgeon was not surrendered." In subsequent bandit-perpetrated forest-sited executions, 140 men died, including the rabbi, his son, and local ritual slaughterers.

"The insurgents were peasants of the surrounding villages. They were seen carrying clothes and shoes and going home with songs." The Sokolovtzi released two girls, including Garfinkel, who went with "two Christians, Petrov and Yushko, honest men," to visit the crime scene. "We took a lantern with us and went into the woods. There we

---

[23] Ibid., fos. 32–34 (n.d.).

saw the dead lying, all naked, mutilated, cut into pieces, some without ears, some without arms, others without heads. It was a horrible sight. We began to weep and shout: 'Whoever is still alive, let him respond!' Some did respond." They fetched a wagon and removed the wounded. Kisselhoff was chased out and killed. Courageous Garfinkel aimed to join her brother in America.[24] She and the honest Ukrainians had witnessed microgenocide, whose staging inspired happy whistling in its perpetrators. Its symbolic character can only be guessed at. For some, Jews' destruction seemingly signified hoped-for entry into a land of plenty. Perhaps, too, their murder was righteous Christian revenge or prelude to Millenium.

Petlurowcy and followers committed an orgy of violence – mix of ethnic cleansing and mass murder – in *Dibova* (*Dubovo*), a *shtetl* counting some 1,000 Jews near Uman (site of the grim "Haidamak" mass slaughter of Poles and Jews in 1768, apostrophized by Ukrainian national poet Shevchenko). Esther Berditchevsky, seventy-five, rebbetzin, called it "a great town. That Christians should fight with Jews was a thing unheard of." Petlurowcy arrived mid-1919 with Poles, plundering, house searching, and shooting twenty Jews. There followed "a great company of Cossacks with Hetman Kazakov" alongside Petlurowcy and many armed peasants and village and town boys. "Some [Jews] ran to good Christians."

Two Petlurowcy entered the elderly rabbi's house. They were "dressed in gold, gold was on their sleeves, their clothing was very rich" – befitting proper bandits. Demanding money and jewels, they beat rabbi and rebbetzin with bayonets until their feet bled. "Someone told then of a place near the wood prepared for the winter, where a fiddle was hidden containing 4,000 Czarist rubles, a gold bracelet, 3 silk handkerchiefs and other jewelry and other valuable objects." This they found but continuing beating. "The rabbi was very weak." In their garret many lay concealed under straw, including women and children. Though Cossacks went to the garret, they at first didn't find the people.

They broke up everything in the house, turned over the closets and the beds, tore up the bedclothes, let the feathers out and took away the new pillows. Later they killed her husband by beating, as they aimed to do to her too. Eventually someone among the hidden Jews sneezed. "Now we know where the Jews are hidden," shouted one of the hooligans. [They dragged them all out, taking their valuables.] Then they undressed everybody and stabbed and shot them all dead [twenty men].

---

[24] Ibid., fos. 35–37 (August 3, 1921).

They drove women away, later killing some. The rebbetzin found cover in the privy. Later she hid with a daughter from her first marriage, also wounded. "A small lad with an axe stood near me. He said, 'If you won't give any money, I will kill you with this axe.'"

When they had killed all the Jews, 400 men, and taken everything away, they drank and became intoxicated and danced in the middle of the street. [Her daughter hired a wagon to take her to hospital.] There was in the town a good Gentile and he gathered all the orphans in his house and fed them and gave them night lodgings until they were taken to Uman.

"The good Gentile Dmitry was a shoemaker." The Petlurowcy ordered all Jews to leave town or also be killed. She sold her house for 5,000 Soviet and other rubles. Dmitry helped get them to Uman, whence she made her way to Odessa before arriving in Warsaw. "I want to go to Palestine."[25] Such were the words, and terrible experiences, of the only rebbetzin to offer testimony in these pages. The carnage fulfilled to grim perfection the stereotype of Cossack pogrom – greed and sadistic murder.

The JDC heard two accounts of disastrous violence in *Zhivil* (*Novohrad Volynskyi*), pitting Bolsheviks against peasant bands under intelligentsia leadership. One report was Rabbi Jacob Korf's, the other Menahe Segal's, city councilman and former zemstvo member. The mostly Jewish town counted some 30,000 souls. Jews, Segal thought, lived in "comparatively favorable circumstances," holding twenty-three of forty city council seats. After 1917's February Revolution, a Menshevik Social Democrat organized a militia. "Being a tender hearted man he was unable to manage properly and resigned," replaced by tsarist officer Bakov.

Soldiers arrived. "The reactionary, nationalistic elements of the town" – especially city officials – "at once began a Ukrainizing and anti-Jewish agitation in the army." The first pogrom occurred in January 1918, as demobilizing and deserting soldiers with civilian followers plundered stores. It was "not of an openly anti-Jewish character, but an act of revenge on the part of the soldiers upon the peaceful town population for their experiences at the front. While robbing, the soldiers would say: '*We are taking everything back.* The city people had been robbing enough.'"

Bakov's militia pretended to oppose the looting but fired in the air. A revolutionary workers' council summoned soldiers to halt the riot. "A certain very sympathetic officer from St. Petersburg, who agitated against the pogrom, was lynched by the mob." In January 1919, "great struggles" began between Petliurites and Bolsheviks.

---

[25] Ibid., fos. 46–51 (August 2, 1922 [1921]).

The "terrible pogroms" in Zhitomir, Berdychev, and Proskurov followed. Zhivil only escaped because Petliurite Commandant Fedalko took big bribes from Jews and distributed money and goods "among the enraged bands of Petlurovtzi, whenever there was danger of a pogrom."

In April 1919, Bolsheviks captured Zhivil, unveiling a *Rewkom* including Jews. They were weak and, fearing counterrevolution, suicidally fired into a church during Sunday service (Rabbi Korf had them bombarding nearby villages, where anti-Bolshevik war was preached in church). Three hundred nearby peasants, "armed with sticks," overpowered the *Rewkom*, taking its money and killing fifteen members. Some seventy "Jewish lads" aided the town's eighty Bolsheviks, but their foes – Sokolovtzi – overwhelmed them, killing forty-five Bolsheviks and twelve Jewish boys but losing 200 on their side.

Hunt was on for "Jewish Bolsheviki." Some 500 Jews were taken to the Sluck river bank, forced to dig a mass grave, stripped of clothes, and then brutally murdered – some having their arms chopped off, others being forced to do the same to each other. "The author of this account, Menashe Segal, stood all night naked waiting for his turn to be killed." Finally, an order called off the murder, keeping survivors under arrest. "A very sad episode" involved Kababial, "an outcast who served in the Chiezvitchnika (Cheka)." Petlurovtzi ordered Jews to capture and kill him. They found him in a garret "and had to kill him with their own hands in the court of the synagogue."

Jews, fearing Bolsheviks could not hold the town, "formed a common secret committee together with the Christian population to see that no more bloodshed occurred." They urged against killing "pogrom makers." But Judeophobic agitation was strong, aiming to exclude Jews from office. "Later they advocated the extermination of all the Jews under 30 years of age." This cost some 100 victims.

The local Stojanovsky band appeared. Jews sent a delegation to its leader, pleading against violence. Stojanovsky replied "that he will not leave a single Jew alive." Yet nearby Directory forces seemingly restrained him, and when his fighters entered Zhivil, "the Jews greeted them with music." On hearing this, the Bolsheviks, across the river, "threw down from aeroplanes [doubtful detail] several explosive gas bombs, which caused a great fire." Three thousand Jewish houses, 1,000 businesses, and twenty-six synagogues burned. A Jewish delegation, including witness Segal, informed the Bolsheviks of what they had done and were given – seemingly as compensation – 900,000 rubles, salt, sugar, cloth, "and 300 boxes of glass."

The Stojanovskyites and Petliurites departed, whereupon vengeful peasants, led by former exciseman Kotchergin, attacked, killing seventy Jews. "According to the story of a half insane women, named Etele, the hooligans choked with an 'Etz-Chayim' [Torah roll handle] an old Jew who sat over a Gemora. While killing a Jew, the hooligans would shout, '*Here you have a commune* [communism].'" Surviving Jews fled to Yara, where 8,000 to 9,000 refugees were stricken with spotted typhus. "Many of the native population also contracted the disease." Segal was robbed on the road, arriving naked in a village where "a native Jew gave him an overcoat." A JDC representative, Mr. Shien, brought 25,000 marks for Zhivil and promised clothing.[26]

Rabbi Korf hid in a cellar. A "Jewish sister of the Red Cross" said to him, "Rabbi, why don't you do something? They are slaughtering the Jews!" He asked her to fetch the priest.

The rabbi and priest had always been good friends. In bad times when the Reds would persecute the Priests, the priest of Zhivil would hide in the Rabbi's house; and when the Whites would come, the Rabbi would find refuge in the priest's house.

But the priest was gone. Korf went to "the rich man of the city, David Mererichsky," but he "was hidden in his garret and did not want to go." So the rabbi took the synagogue's Torah and, with two old rabbis and other religious figures,

and with bread and salt upon a tray he went to the [insurgent] staff to ask for mercy and greet and congratulate them on taking the city. While they were on their way many Jews were being killed and thrown into the river. On their way they were stopped and beaten, even mocked by the passing bandits. [They passed Christian bank director Stankovsky, whom the rabbi knew and asked to join them.] But the Christian gave him an evasive reply and passed on.[27]

They made their way through a crowd of 10,000 to 12,000 and begged with tears for their people. "Their leader was Pagoriloff, an intellectual." In a scene (again) recalling Jesus' trial, he "then went on the balcony and addressed the peasants, asking them if they would make peace with the Jews. The rabble then began to shout, 'Shoot them together with their Tora. Imprison them, let them give up their weapons.'" The rabbi and "a young Jewish intellectual" spoke, saying they had no weapons.

In their joint presence "several young men were stabbed by bayonets. The murderers lifted them in the air shouting, 'hurrah.'" The insurgents vehemently insisted on surrender of weapons. After conferring with "Reb Lipa, a Jew prominent in the town," they decided to buy some revolvers

---

[26] Ibid., fos. 93–101 (n.d.). (author's italics).
[27] On Zhivil: ibid., fos. 51–56 (August 3, 1921).

and hand them over as "the Jewish weapons." Korf collected money and "went to a Jew dealing in weapons, bought 5 revolvers," and turned them in to "the staff."

The priest turned up, helping end the violence by arresting communists and releasing others. In the end, 480 Jews died, along with some women, raped and murdered. The Sokolovtzi left the town to reel in anarchy for two weeks before another band – the "Sotchviki" (Segal's "Stojanovskyites") – arrived, killing more Jews. The rabbi went with the [pro-Directory] mayor and with musicians and bread and salt to meet the invaders, provoking outlying Bolsheviks to shell the town – Korf said nothing of airplanes – killing thousands and burning it and its synagogues. The rebbetzin died along with other elders, including nursing-home residents. "The Bolsheviki did this, taking revenge for the city's receiving the insurgents with music." "*Ataman* [warlord] Pogorielov" tried escaping with booty but was seized at the train station and shot. Thereafter spotted typhus and other diseases struck, killing 7,000. Only 4,000 Zhivil Jews remained. "The Rabbi intends to go to America."

Here again, where no political overlordship held sway and the town's occupiers changed kaleidoscopically, regional peasant bands – headed (apart from shadowy Stojanovsky) by demobilized tsarist officers, municipal bureaucrats, and white-collar workers – inflicted the worst violence. For Bolshevik mistakes Jews paid with lives and ruination. As Korf's experience shows, rabbis tried, in league with Catholic priests, wealthy Jewish businessmen, and young intellectuals, to represent their communities before conquering peasant army leaders and halt the atrocious violence in whose midst they bravely walked. Joining local Bolsheviks was another strategy Jewish young men followed, though in Zhivil's case it only led to disaster.

In nearby *Shepetivka*, a town with some 4,000 Jews, a Jewish militia proved of some value. Teacher Chayim Atlas – averring that until 1917 "Jews and Christians were in the friendliest relations" – reported that in response to anarchy in departing Germans' wake, "the more intelligent Jews organized a Jewish self-defense with the Kehila." Nevertheless, Petliurites, "Red bands," "Tatarki," and "Red Bazunti" forces descended, plundering Jews. "Workers and intellectuals had no hand in them."

"Money could save life and the Kehila was on the watch and always had prepared money and clothing collected [from] the rich Jews." Before pogroms, there was always agitation "among the masses," especially charges of Jewish armed aggression. "The Jewish self-defense would come out at each pogrom or robbery, organized and armed, and more than one pogrom [was] thus stopped," even though "only part of the

Christians would respond warmly to the appeals and help chase the bandits out." Atlas, in Warsaw, stressed the postpogrom rise of economic antisemitism, straining Christian-Jewish relations badly. Half the Jews had fled. Death's toll was "very great."[28]

Jews found protection in unlikely quarters – for example, on a German farm. Young Jehiel Katz, eighth-grade high-schooler from *Kianka*, Zhitomir province, witnessed the death of his prosperous parents, owners of pottery factories with 200 workers "in the best relations with their employer." Until August 1919, their town escaped plunder, but then four bandits arrived, sporting red ribbons and demanding 59,000 rubles. His parents, on offering but 39,000 rubles and jewelry, were brutally disemboweled. Jehiel found them dying on their house floor. His father enjoined him, "you must be father for the remaining children." As he tried to aid his dying mother, "I saw that Christian neighbors had come in and were robbing ... Just then an old Christian woman came in, and I asked her assistance. She said, 'A Jew is also to be pitied.'"

She warned that bandits were returning, to drive him and his sisters away and continue pillaging. A peasant seized a honey jar from the father's hand, saying "give me the honey. You are dying. What do you need it for?" The three children hid in a field. A Christian teacher found them, saying "go away, *you are communists*. All yours were already slain. They might yet kill me too, on account of you." They fled to a nearby German colony. "The German hid us in a stall and told us to keep quiet, so that he might keep us all night, but in the morning we must leave him." He "gave us a glass of milk and told us to go, lest they kill him too on account of us." They managed to return temporarily to bury their parents. Their pet dog would not leave the bodies. A peasant said (mysteriously), "'a live being must not be buried together with Jews,' so they killed it and then buried it."

"For seven days we were in the German's stall, and he gave us food. We did not want to leave. The German proved to be an excellent man." They arranged their parents' proper burial. The German gave them a wagon, and a Jew gave them horses. They transported the naked bodies to a nearby Jewish cemetery. The German gave them bread. In Zhivil, they found relatives there dead, the town ruined. They lost three houses and two factories. Six orphans survived. "My elder sister also died of aggravation."

Young Katz wanted to go to America. "He has lived through many great misfortunes." When Bolsheviks returned, one of the bandits was imprisoned, while the Katzes sought to reclaim their property. But Poles

[28] Ibid., fos. 21–22 (n.d.).

later invaded, and the bandit was released. Katz, fearing revenge, fled to Poland. His younger brother stayed to fight with the Red Army. A sister worked in a Zhivil drugstore. They were owed much money,

but the notes had also been robbed away. The debtors are Christians and pretend not to know anything. Mr. Katz is now in Warsaw, alone and tortured by the recollections of his sad experiences. He frequently has nervous fits.

The above was submitted by Mr. Katz in a state of the greatest irritation. During the story he once fainted. Signed – L. B. Warsaw, August 2, 1921.[29]

The Katz family tragedy was a small, red-beribboned criminal band's handiwork, heightened by pervasive fearful belief, such as Grünbaum found in Poland, that all Jews were communists. Nevertheless, some Christians aided Jechiel and his siblings.

In *Slovetchko shtetl*, north of Zhitomir, anti-Bolshevism-inflamed peasant bands turned on their Jewish neighbors, with whom, as teacher Melamed recalled, they had recently lived "on very good terms," In July 1919, as gentiles returned from church on "the great Christian holiday, the day of St. Peter and St. Paul," they told Jews, "Now expect the worst." A Jewish delegation heard from the priest "that as the Jews took part in severing the church from the state, *they are communists*, and this is why the peasants are angry with them." Melamed was then given a statement from "the Revolutionary Committee" saying "that the *Jews were counter-revolutionists, all of them being Zionists*."

Slovetchko's Jews hired six guards to strengthen the six-man Christian militia, but local peasant bands entered town, "headed by a stranger, a hooligan, just arrived in town, 'Maxim the Lame.'" Pillaging followed, killing four people.

The director of the post-office, Neustoff Oleyevitch, a tartar, was a good friend of Mr. Malemed ... and permitted him to hide in his, Neustoff's cellar. [Looting recommenced.] Many Jews of the town were hiding with the peasants in the villages ... In an adjacent room, many women were hidden. In the post director's house there would often be held conferences of the bandits. They would drink all night, and Mr. Melamed could hear all they were saying. And through a little window he could see what was going on in the street.[30]

Jews asked the priest to help end the violence, authorizing him to offer much money. Rabbi and priest went to the bandits, rabbi saying, "Jews were no communists ... they wished to live in peace with their neighbors." But he was shouted down: "Beat the Jews! Beat the communists!"

---

[29] Ibid., fos. 22–27 (August 2, 1921) (author's emphasis).
[30] On Slovetchko: ibid., fos. 41–45 (n.d.) (author's emphasis).

The priest then said that the Jews themselves were to blame for sympathizing with the communists. *He told the peasants that the Gospel also forbids to kill Jews.* The priest advocated boycotting them, but if they disagreed with him, "let them do whatever they pleased."

The rabbi and colleagues collected 40,000 rubles, offering it to the bandits if they would leave, which they did, but only to plunder nearby Valednick. There they encountered a Jewish self-defense group that shot four bandits, driving them away. They returned to Slovetchko, plundering and killing, stabbing the rabbi. "People screamed frightfully." Among the twenty-five murdered was "well-known student Neiditch of Kiev."

Melamed overheard how the postman sought to persuade bandits not to kill Jews "but only take their money, for they are rich enough." On Friday, Melamed's father came to him in his cellar to say "the peasants now decided to go from house to house and find and kill every Jew. *Now they are driving out the cattle into the field. They call it a sin to kill in the presence of cattle. They are growing wild.*" Here again, microgenocide, framed in archaic magical belief, such as Thomas and Znaniecki had evoked, and Judeophobia pervaded with anticommunism, perpetrated by a peasantry with whom Jews had until recently lived "on good terms."

The postman urged Melamed to flee. "It appeared as if the Jews were running away from Goluth." Most escaped through a four-hour flight to Ovruch town. In some villages, peasants blocked their way until they were paid off. Finally, Jewish wagons fetched them. Ovruch's Bolshevik *Rewkom* "reproached us. 'You always go hand in hand with the peasants and now you come to us for help.'" But next day they sent Red soldiers to Slovetchko, who shot the "ring leaders of the bloody affair."[31]

Red Cossacks were sometimes perpetrators-in-chief, though pogrom scripts varied. Zalman Girzhel, twenty-eight, student in *Lyubar*, west of Berdychev, told of the three-cornered struggle between Poles, Bolsheviks, and Budyonny's Red Cossacks for primacy in plundering this leather-working town. The horsemen – not shrinking from killing *Rewkom* members – finally won out, in May 1920 taking the town. Its refugee-swollen Jewish population, some 10,000 Jews, panicked. "Not all Christians wanted to take [them] in, for they feared that the Cossacks would kill them, too." A Cossack meeting resolved to stage the pogrom "with cold weapons only" – without gunfire. Here, revealingly, we see how rules of mayhem could be set by (nominally communist) Cossack deliberation and acclamation.

---

[31] Ibid., fos. 41–45 (n.d.) (author's emphasis).

Massive pillage and rape followed, with thirty Jews killed, 200 injured. When Bolsheviks returned, Jews were "overjoyed." The Red leader promised "his soldiers were no pogrom makers." But they withdrew, leaving Lyubar to other (unspecified) military units until Poles' arrival. These newcomers stripped a thousand Jewish houses, walls and ceilings destroyed "when the bandits looked for places where money might have been hidden." In the end, amid rampaging typhus, 6,000 Jews were ruined. Many trekked to Poland, with America in mind.[32]

Ostropol (*Ostropil*), near Lyubar, housing some 3,000 Jews, fell under Bolshevik occupation. Zabarko, gymnasium student, reported that neighboring anti-Red villages formed bands of "Shepals, Sakalovtzi and others, named after the agents of Petlura's bands." A Jewish self-defense force assembled, numbering 300 with fifty rifles and a machine gun. "When the peasants found out that a self-defense was active, they stopped their assaults." But Petlurovtzi, learning of armed Jews, descended, plundering until a Jewish delegation agreed to surrender the guns to them.

At 1919's end, as Directory forces crumbled, 100 Polish cavalrymen rode into town. Their commander forced all Jews to assemble before the Catholic church, threatening to kill those who didn't disarm. In accustomed Polish style, "those who denied having weapons were thrown upon the snow, undressed naked and beaten very severely." A thousand peasants drove the Poles out, but they returned and pillaged until Budyonny's Cossacks conquered the town. Here the double-edged sword of Jewish self-defense again gleams, for while it repelled relatively weak peasant bands, it provoked better-armed forces to brutally disarm and abuse Jews who had dared unsheathe it.[33]

From Belarus the JDC recorded a single testimony – Shleime Kommissar's, sole unscathed survivor of a three-day rampage in *Koitritz*, near Bobruisk (Babruysk), that killed 105 and wounded seventy. The unidentified perpetrators' victims "were killed not by firearms but by knives, axes, spades, etc. and also by spears. Mercilessly the murderers turned out legs, arms, pricked eyes out, crushed skulls, pulled out hair even of small babies in cradles." Kommissar was profoundly embittered, mocking the meager aid his townsfolk could expect from the Soviets but also indignant that those who had earlier emigrated to America were now enjoying prosperity. He himself had brothers there, "and I hope they will not leave me." The pogrom survivors needed money to buy off robbers. "I appeal especially to the men who left their wives years ago." He supplied a list of victims, including seven murdered women, among them "one slaughterer's daughter, throat cut," and Gussie Feibels,

---

[32] Ibid., fos. 72–76 (n.d.).   [33] Ibid., 77–79 (n.d.).

nineteen, "her hair pulled out, she died." Rocha Hamam, "a Froebelist [progressive liberal children's educator], twenty-two, was violated in the [train]car before everybody."[34]

If Poland in these years witnessed Jewish tragedy, in Volhynia and across revolution-beset Ukraine it was the grimmest of catastrophes, recalling Khmelnytsky's deluge (as one marauding bandleader reminded his victims), perhaps exceeding it. In these JDC testimonies, in contrast with our Polish documentation, symbolic violence looms lower amid the torrent of genocidal murder the Russian civil war released against Jews. Yet magically grounded Judeophobia reveals itself in the Volhynian violence, while pitiless reflections are perceptible of Christian motifs – judgments against deicidal unbelievers, suffering along the *via dolorosa*, evocations of hell – that also appeared in Polish lands.

Striking too, again by comparison, is atrocious murder's salience in Volhynia's violence, though it occurred also, sporadically, in Poland. It is another inquiry's challenge to plumb this disparity, but its existence seems to heighten the significance in the Polish lands of the theatricalized and metaphor-rich, brutally humbling, desacralizing and delegitimizing, but mostly nonlethal violence this book has repeatedly brought to light. Still, in their anti-Bolshevik and borderlands-conquering zeal, Piłsudski's state and its armed forces implicated themselves in the hellish bloodshed raging in the east.

Batka Bałachowicz, the Jews, and the Polish Army

Stanisław Bałachowicz (1883–1940), Belarus-born Pole and "forgotten hero" of present-day nationalist writings, rose to prominence after 1914 as Russian cavalry commander (Figure 10.1). In 1917–19, he formed a small force fighting alongside various White armies. Fleeing collapse of Yudenich's White front in northwestern Russia, he and his polyglot followers found Piłsudski's favor, forming in the Polish-Soviet war an "allied volunteer army," though Bałachowicz, appealing to his mostly East Slavic soldiers, sometimes called it the "Russian National Volunteer Army." Its numbers, though variable, approximated 800 horsemen and 1,800 infantry. Bałachowicz strove to profile himself as dashing populist captain of death-defying horsemen, paying well and sharing booty with them. He called himself, seemingly in Belarusian wind metaphor, "Bułak-Bałachowicz," attaching as well the title "batka," paternalism customary among Cossacks and their *ataman*s.

---

[34] Ibid., 102–7 (n.d.).

Figure 10.1 Bałachowicz (left foreground, in fur hat) among Russian officers, presumably those in his own freebooter force. They do not seem to wish to be photographed. A picture eloquent in its evocation of the 1920 war's atmosphere, its brutalities hinted at but left offstage. The automobiles' modernity did not clash with this force's extremely bloody deeds, committed Cossack-style by mounted officers and common soldiers alike.
Source: Provenance unknown.

In the Polish-Soviet war, his forces conquered border town Włodawa, then Soviet stronghold, before moving into Belarus, where they took Pinsk amid pogrom violence. Bałachowicz proclaimed an independent anti-Bolshevik Belarusian republic, but it melted away. He found refuge in interwar Poland, but – Soviets having branded him traitor and war criminal – the Polish army did not embrace him. He played a minor role in nationalist politics before falling to Gestapo bullets in 1940.[35]

---

[35] *Ochotnicza Sprzymierzona Armia.* For laudation of Balachowicz and dismissal of his war crimes, see
   http://jpilsudski.org/artykuly-personalia-biogramy/generalicja-oficerowie-zolnierze/item/1810-general-bulak-balachowicz; https://pl.wikipedia.org/wiki/Stanis%C5%82aw_Bu%C5%82ak-Ba%C5%82achowicz;
   http://historia.wp.pl/title,Stanislaw-Bulak-Balachowicz-dowodca-bialoruskiej-armii-sprzymierzonej-i-bat-na-bolszewikow,wid,16453950,wiadomosc.html?ticaid=118284.
   Similarly, Marek Cabanowski, *Generał Stanisław Bułak-Bałachowicz: zapomniany bohater* (Warsaw: Mikromax,1993).

During the Polish-Soviet war, Bałachowicz's forces were nominally subordinate to the Polish Third Army, commanded by post-1935 Piłsudski successor Edward Rydz-Śmigły. Army intelligence and gendarmerie observed the troublesome but militarily useful force, filing monitory reports with their superiors. These records open the curtain on brutal dramas enacted by a little-remembered anti-Soviet warlord. They illumine pogromist-soldiers' character and mentality in harsh light, revealing an apocalyptic dance of death amid feverish accumulation of bloodstained booty.

Keenest observer was intelligence officer Stanisław Błoński (1890–1939). His dispatches, intersecting other witnesses', form a multiframed text in which the borderlands auxiliaries' disastrous actions gradually emerged in consciousness of men inclined not to condemn but excuse or heroize Bałachowicz.[36] On August 30, Błoński reported to superiors in Third Army intelligence on Bałachowicz forces' battling with Reds near Włodawa. Though Soviet losses were tenfold those of Bałachowicz, they grittily managed to advance. Here, where ethnographic Poland, Belarus, and Ukraine intermingled, amid a large Jewish population, "local people aided Bolsheviks with all their power: all the youth from the surrounding villages ... and the healthier peasants made their way through the forests to the Bolsheviks."[37]

Błoński may have been traveling in disguise.

Going through villages, I encountered in each one bands of Jews who greeted us with ovations, thinking we were Bolsheviks, and informed us about the Polish army and offered their services. As a result, *whoever did not run off was hanged.*

Similarly, "spies are captured at every turn, carrying documents and stamps of local organizations, and are hanged without trial."

He sketched Bałachowicz, "called 'Batka' by everybody."

Loftily proud, he wants to be famous, shouts much, is close to soldiers, often talking or reading a newspaper with them, sometimes telling stories. Soldiers are very attached to him. I have the impression, though, that he would gladly serve Chinese or Gypsies if he could only be much written about in the papers. [He was restless,] making constant sallies. His relation to officers is collegial, they mostly say "*ty*" to him and he to them. When he falls in a rage he reviles them on the town square or in their housing. He'll often draw his lash and lay it on, 25 blows for first offense and so on, depending on his mood and the crime's severity. He likes to

---

[36] Błoński, also known as Lis-Błoński, later wove his wartime reports into an unpublished memoir of Bałachowicz: Lis-Blonski, Stanisław. *"Balachowcy" Stanislawa Lisa-Blonskiego jako przestreń refleksji i historyczny dokument*, ed. Grzegorz Jacek Pelica (Lublin: Best Print, 2011). The pages below follow the original reports, archived in Warsaw-Rembertów's Centralne Archiwum Wojskowe.

[37] Here and below: CAW. I.311.3.52 (August 8, 1920 et seq.). (All subsequent italics are the author's.)

attend executions and corporal punishments. After any kind of victory he plies the soldiers with spirits and drinks himself too, telling the triumphal story a few or a dozen times, and going to sleep in his clothes.[38]

His colonel brother Józef (reputed follower of Russian Orthodoxy) was taciturn but proud, aloof from soldiers but always leading them into battle. After a sortie, he changed into a fresh uniform and paraded about. He slept only at night. "He knows no other punishment for soldier or officer than 'shoot him,' for peasant or Jew 'hang him.' Usually it's one word – 'shoot/hang [*powiesić-rostrzelać*],' the sentence immediately carried out." Of the brothers, Błoński wrote "they have middling education, no military schooling, they write poorly in Polish, also speak it badly."

Ninety percent of their officers were tsarist army "Muscovites." They behaved accordingly, "accustomed to hit soldiers in the face, or slap their heads. At the most dangerous moments they're all capable of getting drunk. They like to say 'I shit on everything [*plewat na wsio*].'" All wanted tsar's return. Older officers, if they could no longer do the job, moved down into the ranks. None had higher education, while those with middle schooling "are cocaine-addicts, drunks, thieves, and even by outward appearance give the impression of bandits." Altogether, there were some 160 cavalry officers, 540 line officers.

Common soldiers were from the former tsarist army, or captured and turncoat Bolsheviks. They had "no political orientation" but were a "nomadic band" interested only in drunkenness, robbery, and self-enrichment. In fighting they followed orders. They didn't care whom they shot. *"They especially don't like Bolsheviks, declaring all are Jews. A Jew is never taken prisoner but murdered.* Capturing a Bolshevik, the Muscovite feeds and clothes him, urging him to join the *bałachowcy*." The soldiers shared their loot, giving one-third to their superior. Bałachowicz army's relationship to Poles was one of political convenience, but when it could do so, it appealed in its own name to Russians and Ruthenians, never presenting itself as Ukrainian. That is, they flaunted their Russophile, non-Polish, non-Ukrainian character.

"I was witness to their searches of Jews' cellars," everything torn to pieces, all valuables stolen. The officers flaunted watches and festooned their fingers with gold rings. He confronted Captain Aksakov, Włodawa commandant, saying that filling his house with stolen goods was improper. "He was embarrassed, especially his wife, a born Pole, and gave the things to the mayor for return to owners."

The *bałachowcy* stripped villages of cattle for food and sale, embittering peasants against Poland. "Sooner or later the whole world will learn about

[38] Ibid. (August 30, 1920).

their violence [which Błoński had largely tiptoed around] and will raise a great cry. Among other things [there were many of these] in Dratów they murdered the old Jewess Goldberg, whose relationship to the Polish cause was very good." Błoński recommended attaching Polish soldiers to the *bałachowcy*. Otherwise, he warned, the whole army would end up being interned.

Traveling parallel to Błoński's letter was commander Lieutenant Brusznicki's (gingerly) damning report on Bałachowicz, posted to Third Army intelligence. The Włodawa-stationed "auxiliary army's" actions were "beneath criticism." They had comprehensively destroyed all Jewish homes, as well as those of Poles who had fled before the "Bolshevik hordes," abandoning government offices. It was typical that a Włodawa Jew who criticized *bałachowcy* found himself arrested, his wife charged with paying a 100,000-mark fine. When she could muster but 50,000, she was ordered to collect the remainder from her coreligionists. "I immediately took steps to block such excesses," of which this was but "a drop in the ocean."

No less troublesome was Bałachowicz's harboring of Polish army deserters and other fugitives from justice, "even female legionnaires." There were many Polish officers among them, while the numerous Bolshevik turncoats were of "uncertain character." Brusznicki also encountered "various journalists whose identity is puzzling. I couldn't penetrate their political affairs, which might be possible with the help of agents, especially female agents, who could frequent evening social events staged almost daily." He recommended crackdown on Bałachowicz criminality, because it demoralized nearby Polish troops who viewed the irregular army "as shelter from deserved punishment."[39]

Gendarmerie Sergeant Królak viewed the *bałachowcy* less as an army than "partisan unit." Soldiers received nothing but rations (*fasunek*). "Under fire there is iron discipline, but in the rear officers have no real authority" because of "their participation in robberies or indulgent attitude toward them."

Antisemitism is taken to highest level, manifested in thorough-going and systematic robbery of Jewish dwellings. The various unit commands do nothing to limit such abuses. One gets the impression they live from robbery, which simply substitutes for pay. (The soldiers possess on average some 10,000–20,000 marks in cash.) Antisemitism is exploited to divert robbery away from the Christian population.

This was a theoretically minded gendarme, with interesting hypotheses, albeit little appreciation for antisemitism's rich meaning in its apostles'

---

[39] Ibid. (August 31, 1920).

minds, far transcending mere calculation. Nor did he properly consider that potential Christian victims of plunder had means of resistance and revenge denied to Jews.

"Gendarmerie interventions are seen [among *bałachowcy*] as a special defense of Jews and provoke opposition even among highest officers"? General Bałachowicz possessed "enormous personal authority," and his presence would suffice to diminish abuses. Królak complained of many Polish deserters among Batka's soldiers – "the worst sort of disintegrative element," urging violence against gendarmes seeking their arrest. There was even a separate armed band, loosely tied to Bałachowicz, consisting largely of Poles under the command of "*ataman* Iskar (probably a pseudonym)." Here were self-orientalizing Polish freebooters.[40]

Intelligence officers chronicled anti-Jewish violence accompanying the army's and Bałachowicz's push eastward into Volhynia. Gendarmerie Sergeant Zgiett reported on "pogrom in Shatsk village." He found that, of eighty families living there, but ten people remained. Locals told him that fifteen had died, but "judging by the atrocities the soldiers [*bałachowcy*] permitted themselves, the number of those killed was larger."

They were killed in horrible [*okrutny*] manner, some tortured for several hours. Young women or girls were immediately raped by some dozen soldiers; others were dragged off who knows where. [Some were taken back to Włodawa.] Many ran off into the fields and forest. I myself saw five dead, corpses quartered.

The soldiers threatened that wherever they go they will beat the Jews. During the pogrom officers stood passive. A few tried to prevent it, but they were just driven away.[41]

Gendarme Zgiett reported from another village on further atrocious murders: a mother and her two sons shot in their cottage, "in another a young Jew hung from the rafters, having been so badly beaten that his body flamed, and a Jewess of eighteen, after having been raped, killed with three revolver shots in the head, two of which I myself witnessed."[42]

An anonymous reporter from the fifteen-man "field gendarmerie platoon" attached to the *bałachowcy* informed his Third Army superiors:

I confirmed that in every conquered village General Bałachowicz's units stage formal Jewish pogroms: they murder all men without regard for age, they rape women and even young girls and comprehensively rob all goods and livestock. Local peasants participate, whether robbing whatever the *bałachowcy* ignore or buying their booty for trifling sums.

---

[40] Ibid. (September 3, 1920).   [41] Ibid. (September 12, 1920).
[42] Ibid. (September 19, 1920).

[Sixty were killed in Shatsk.] Killing is usually done in this manner: money is demanded (especially gold); after receiving it – two or three shots in the head.

[Some 100 were killed in Krymno village.] The victims were tormented (a dozen were drowned in the lake). *The bodies at the lake were propped up in standing position with rods in their hands as if they were fishing.*

The prayer-houses are comprehensively destroyed, the parchment pages of the Hebrew books scattered in the street. [All Jews– some 100 – were killed in three additional villages.][43]

Amid such genocidal murder *bałachowcy* took time to stage a macabre display of corpses outfitted with fishing rods – cruel mockery of a favorite pastime but perhaps also suggesting that, in Christian soldiers' murky subconscious, Jewishness was not really a living state.

Farther east, in Kamień Koszyrski/Kamin' Kashirs'kyi, the *bałachowcy*'s pogrom killed 600 Jews, though counting victims was difficult because "many people took refuge beforehand in the swamps and forests, whom the Cossacks tried to hunt down – there were many drowned corpses. Those attempting to defend themselves were horribly wounded by bayonets. *In eleven acts of violence specific officers participated.*"

Any intervention by the Group's more humanitarian [*humanitarnych*] officers, as well as by Military Ministry's liaison officer, Lieutenant Skarbowski, and Third Army gendarmes [such as the writer], encounter[s] hostility from bestialized soldiers, who laconically say: "Batka permitted it [*Batka pozwolił*]."[44]

They also killed Warsaw-based Polish-Jewish politician Leon Schönbrot, who had traveled to Kamień Koszyrski before the invasion to visit his brother and had then been arrested by Bolsheviks as a spy. "Collection of bodies in the town, their removal from houses and burial is undertaken by surviving Jews, whose security is provided by local Command, which assigned gendarmes to them." Peasants were pouring into town in "whole bands," intent on postpogrom plunder. Some had been involved from the start, "stealing mainly grain and clothing."

"Remaining women and children – there are very many orphans – are housed in the Orthodox priest's house. They face starvation. State aid necessary. Many wounded people lie in hiding."

Only General Bałachowicz can halt the murder and robbery, who up to now has been riding through villages and, seeing murdered victims, even expressing satisfaction. The general reportedly distributes cattle stolen from Jews to poor peasants and to reward village haulers [pressed into service by his troops]. In this way winning popularity for himself, *he usually takes his leave with the words "beat the Jews."*

---

[43] Ibid. (September 17, 1920).   [44] Here and below: ibid. (September 17, 1920).

The reporter lamented, in words supportive of moral-economy interpretation, that Christians viewed gendarmerie interventions "as special protection of Jews against meting out of *righteous justice* [*przed wymiarem jakoby sprawiedliwości*]." Various individuals threatened shooting the gendarmes. "The Jewish population sees in every Polish soldier a savior [*wybawiciel*] and bombard them with questions whether the Polish army will soon arrive."[45]

Liaison officer Zadora Skarbowski's report to Third Army Command on the Kamień Kaszyrski pogrom was, in comparison with his gendarme colleague's, cool and self-justificatory. He stressed that Bolsheviks' local communist allies, led by Klenberg, had fired on *bałachowcy* who, when they retook the town, arrested thirty-five, condemning some dozen before a field court. He blamed soldiers liberated from Bolshevik captivity for launching excesses which Bałachowicz's officer "were unable to restrain."

The fact, known to all soldiers, of Jews' firing on the Group during their [earlier] retreat sparked desire for revenge and punishment. The soldiers literally threw themselves on Jews' homes, shooting at them and sparing no one. The local Orthodox priest and officers tried all means to influence the bestialized soldiers, but nothing helped. [Eighty people of both sexes were killed] and practically the whole population (Jewish) has been hacked to pieces.[46]

After the plundering peasantry were dispersed, "soldier Markov was today seized committing theft and was shot. A few others received beatings." With the Orthodox priest's help, "I managed to organize immediate aid for the injured." When Bałachowicz arrived, Skarbowski informed him that two Russian officers had done little to halt the pogrom, whereupon the general summoned them before a field court, "now deliberating." Skarbowski stressed local peasants' involvement in anti-Jewish "soldiers' pranks," even though "village Rewkoms arose everywhere, and the population was exceptionally friendly to Bolsheviks." Kamień Kaszyrski's Rewkom ordained parcellation of Catholic and Orthodox priests' arable fields. Elsewhere a Rewkom shot an Orthodox priest, while villagers plundered his possessions. In general, local people were, despite their collusion in plundering Jews, completely hostile to *bałachowcy*, "and they speak even worse of Poles." They awaited the Red Army's return.

Officer Cadet Mielczarek analyzed Bolsheviks' taxation from records they abandoned during retreat. He found that they "exposed communist slogans' mendacity about fighting for the proletariat, since they levied

---

[45] Ibid. (September 17, 1920).   [46] Ibid., Adora Skabowski [*sic*] (September 17, 1920).

a sum on Christians – mostly artisans and small farmers – considerably higher than on Jewish merchants. This shows clearly that the Soviet government always favors Jewish welfare and interests above all." Here was a young Pole empirically demonstrating the "Jewish-Bolshevik nexus."[47]

Błoński reported that, when Bałachowicz's force left Włodawa for the front, "I heard the general, taking leave of departing lieutenant Darski, commander of a mounted squadron, casually say: 'I give you three days freedom to have some fun [Daju wam tri dnia swobodno pogulać].'"[48]

As Błoński followed the bałachowcy, he encountered their handiwork in the villages. "In Shatsk I saw with horror corpses of young and old Jews and Jewesses lying about. Some sixty slaughtered." He noted, in Krymno, that corpses of some dozen elderly Jews "for humor had been propped up as if they were fishing." In Kamień Kaszyrski, "officers and soldiers violated a ten-year-old girl and then smothered her and threw her in the water." The soldiers say: "give money [dawaj dziengi]," and even if they get it, they shoot and kill on the spot. They murdered a Jewess of seventy-five years, walking with a cane. "Another young Jewess, an artist, when asked for money, said she had none. They shot and killed her and then checked to see."

When we left Kamień Kaszyrski I saw crimes such as in my life I never witnessed (and hope I never will again). A group of children and young Jewesses that liaison officer Lieutenant Skarbowski had led to the Orthodox priest's house, to protect them against final destruction, wailed and tore their hair at the loss of their mothers and fathers. At the sight of such misery, tears flowed from my eyes. Lieutenant Skarbowski's efforts and protests accomplished nothing. The soldiers beat their victims in his presence ... Terrifying screams are heard in the town and no one reacts. Fear rules the whole region. The local Orthodox priest fell on his knees before the soldiers, begging that lives and meager goods be spared of those who had been led to him.[49]

The soldiers had set up "regular markets," selling pants, overcoats, carpets, pillows. "Officers can afford to pay a half-million rubles or marks, soldiers too." They had stolen 1,500 cattle, plus carts and horses. Some livestock they ate; the rest they sold

or give to refugees fleeing Russia, former border guards and so on, who hanged Poles, and then ran off with the tsarist army. Then they were self-declared Bolsheviks and came with the Red army as practiced communists to make order in Poland. Their army defeated, they wander about at others' mercy ... They go to "Batka" for a handout, and depending on how he likes them, on how they speak of

[47] Ibid. (September 20, 1920).   [48] Ibid. (September 20, 1920).
[49] Błoński, here and below: ibid. (September 20, 1920).

the general's valiant army, each gets a cow or a horse. Here peasants know no other authority, only "Batka."

In Krymno, Bałachowicz's officers handed out twenty rifles to local youth, urging them to slaughter (*wyrżnąć*) Jews – reckoning they would later join the *bałachowcy*. But none had turned up, and when Batka moved out, Błoński bitterly predicted they would use the weapons against Poles.

Gendarmerie Lieutenant Fedyszyn reported on Kamień Kaszyrski's pogrom to superiors in Kovel. He too emphasized that armed Jews had earlier helped drive Bałachowicz and Polish forces from town. When they returned, they demanded 71,000 marks, eighty loaves of bread, and 100 quarts of milk, along with surrender of those who had resisted with weapons. "The town fulfilled not one of these conditions, and therefore it was totally plundered." Seventy-one died; twenty-one were seriously wounded. *Bałachowcy* killed forty other people in neighboring villages, where they saw that no Polish soldiers were present. Some 100 women were raped, including a "sixty-year-old woman, and because she was cold for them they poured kerosene on her sexual parts and set them aflame, to warm her up." Such acts were "chronic" among them and "are starting to be shared by Polish soldiers in contact with them." "All Polish dregs whose aim is to enrich themselves through plunder gravitate to the *bałachowcy*."

Military intelligence collected Bałachowicz victims' protocols. Pinchos Wejsman, thirty-four, knew of five local Bolsheviks, including two Jews. He and his wife took refuge with the Orthodox priest, who refused admission to soldiers, saying, "in his house he wouldn't allow a hair on anyone's head to be touched." Merchant Alexander Rose, twenty-four, had come from America to fetch his parents and distribute 20,000 dollars in the "Jewish quarters." He kept 500 dollars for himself. As the Poles and *bałachowcy* retreated, they behaved "correctly enough, apart from isolated breaches." When they returned, he bribed a soldier with 200 dollars not to kill him. "I hid at a peasant's house for six days until the Polish units arrived, after whose entry all theft and murder stopped." He had earlier seen "two Jews and a few peasants" join Bolshevik fighters.

Perla Zawidowicz, thirty, gave soldiers 500 marks that "I had in the open." Her husband "fled and hid" until the next day, when, "concealing himself in the swamp, he froze and came to the cottage to warm up." Soldiers found him and other Jews, demanded money but got none, ordered them to remove their boots, and shot them. The day before, a soldier raped her, "and then I fled, dug up 12,000 Polish marks, 5,000 rubles, 10,000 rubles belonging to the cooperative, a gold watch, a chain, a half-dozen silver spoons, twenty silver cups and other valuables worth about 15,000 rubles." That was treasure pogromists dreamed of. The next day another soldier came, "and when I said I had nothing he ordered me to lie down and raped me."

Chaja Czartoryska, eighteen, resident with her parents in Lutsk, was vacationing in Kamień Kaszyrski "with grandma." As the town fell, she escaped with others to the forest, where "local peasants saw us in hiding and showed the *balachowcy*, who started shooting." Fleeing, she was captured by an officer.

He gagged me, wanting to rape. I begged him to release me, or better kill me than rape, but he said killing would be a shame, since I was still young, and ignoring my plea committed violence on me. Then an officer colleague of his raped me, then a third, I don't know whether officer or soldier.[50]

The men departed. A soldier, threatening to kill her, took her two gold rings. Making her way out of the forest, other soldiers robbed her of some 1,200 tsarist rubles, taking her shoes too. "I myself am student in Lutsk gymnasium's fifth form."

Icek Ajzenberg, fifty-five, and wife bribed soldiers with 20,000 marks, repairing then to his brother's house, where they paid 10,000 marks "and ransomed Szymbred" – his brother's penniless tenant – "from death." Szymbred "fled and hid near the Orthodox priest's house, but was seized and murdered." They killed Ajzenberg's second brother and his son, raping his daughter and then "slashing her with their sword above the knee and later cutting out her tongue. While still alive, another *balachowiec* came and killed her with bayonet to the breast."

Later they fired that house, where the corpses lay, and all the bodies burned, and at the fire there was some Polish officer [Błoński, seemingly] who saw these atrocities and wept with me over it all.[51]

The Zionist Club filed an undated letter from Kovel:

With tears and bleeding heart I inform you, honored Sir, that the Ajzenbergs were all killed in Kamień a few days ago. General Bałachowicz's army killed 350 Jews there, among them were killed and burned the whole Ajzenberg family, and also my granny [*babunia*], counting ninety years. You may imagine how it is, if there were in Kamień 500–600 people and 350 were killed. There remained only children and a small handful of old folks. The whole road from Włodawa to Kamień and beyond is awash in blood. We have the good fortune that Poles got to Kovel, for we too would not be alive if the Bałachowicz army were in Kovel. We thank Lord God that there is Polish rule here.[52]

[50] Ibid. (September 27, 1920).
[51] Ibid., (r) (September 25, 1920); (t) (September 27, 1920).
[52] AAN. PRM. No. 21431/20, fo. 253 (n.d.); cf. fos. 774–75 (November 18, 1920). Cf. fo. 227 (n.d. [Lublin]).

On September 27, Błoński's superior, Lieutenant Brusznicki, summed up his investigation of the Kamień Kaszyrski pogrom. He listed eighty-six murder victims, nearly all young or mature men, including one "unknown rabbi" and middle-aged or older women. Twenty men were wounded, including three teenagers. He described the pogrom as *bałachowcy*'s "retaliation (*odwet*)" for having been fired on. Brusznicki had determined that one Jew (*żydek*) and a few Ruthenians were guilty. "The Jew stayed alive during the plunder" and had been "delivered into justice's hands."

But, Brusznicki exclaimed, "can this really be called retaliation?" – as if, were it so, it would be justified. "Never," for plunder served material gain. It was more proof of Bałachowicz's army's "animal instincts," seeking self-enrichment. "Practically every soldier possesses 50,000–100,000 marks or rubles, minimum. Money's excess is evident in its squandering in card games." Such behavior is rubbing off on Poles. "For the moment such cases are infrequent," but they could mushroom, "since I don't see anyone being punished for crime."

Brusznicki submitted his own victims' protocols. At his house, Lej Goldsztajn, fifty-two, surrendered 20,000 tsarist rubles. "The soldiers were greatly delighted and, shaking my hand, took their leave." But then other soldiers came, demanding money from Goldsztajn's three sons while holding revolvers to their heads. They led the soldiers to where were buried 100 silver rubles, twelve silver mugs, and two gold rings. From son Jankel they took 100 rubles both in gold and silver and a gold watch. These losses saved their lives. Goldsztajn declined to identify the perpetrators. In Sławatycze, gendarme Górski asked his subordinates, "were marauders there really *bałachowcy*?" "Yes, they wore American-style caps with white feathers and death's heads on their peaks."

In late September reports appeared on the *bałachowcy*'s ravaging of Włodawa after having driven out Soviet occupiers. The Warsaw Club received a letter whose unnamed author, describing the reconquest, wrote that "Jews in groups of one hundred hide in single rooms, passing days in fear and despair." Some 200 Jewish families had been murdered in the area, "under most terrible inquisitions."

Can you imagine that, during New Year's holy days, there was not one prayer group [*minjen*] in all Włodawa. [All Torahs were desecrated and destroyed.] All basements in people's houses were dug up and emptied of everything. [Two hundred Jews sat in jail, including the letter recipient's son.] Your daughter too goes barefoot, for they stole her shoes.

A Włodawa man wrote his wife: "we are an unhappy nation, when will our sufferings cease? When will we breathe a little more freely? Man is stronger than iron if he manages to bear all this." A woman wrote: "imagine, for a month we were not sure of our lives. We, the women, lay in the basements or wherever we could hide ... And our fear was indescribable. On the streets in all directions there were screams ... Thirty women raped, and that in Włodawa alone. What happened outside town, terror forbids to say." Another Włodawa resident wrote of how the *bałachowcy* plundered everything – "they even dug up goods buried in privy-pits" and "desecrated all things holy to Jews."[53]

Army intelligence listed nineteen Włodawa Jews arrested in late September as "spies" or "for communism," all men except a merchant with wife and daughter. Half were farmers, the others typical townspeople. Their average age was thirty-four. Gendarmes arrested 222 Jews, charged with fleeing with Bolsheviks. An investigation of ten such men found their parents' relation to the Polish state in past and present "correct." These were youths of fifteen to eighteen years who ran off to a village. "They did this thoughtlessly, seeing masses of other fleeing Jews." One such youth testified that *bałachowcy*, who killed his uncle, told him they would murder all Jews. He was freed. Another said that "being in Jewish school when Bolsheviks fled, some Jews came and ordered us also to flee. Our teachers ran, and I with them." He signed in Hebrew. These boys and many others were released.[54]

Following the truce ending the Polish-Soviet war, Błoński, near Pinsk, reformulated his views on Bałachowicz's army. He estimated that 15 percent were old fighters who had made their way through the Baltic lands with the Batka. Fifty-five percent were Bolshevik turncoats, of whom some 1,000 had joined on the march from Włodawa to Kamień Kaszyrski (another report told of 900 escaped Don Cossacks volunteering to join Bałachowicz).[55] Thirty percent of the officers and foot soldiers were, damningly, Polish army deserters, "who came here with aim of robbery and banditism." How to describe their present mood? Conflating "bandit" and "fantastic" (in psychological sense), Błoński answered, "*bantystyczny*." On their marches around the borderlands, "they left behind everywhere thousands of corpses." While they targeted Jews, "where there was no Jewish property or riches they took what was at hand." Such was their "mental disposition – worthy of highest indignation and punishment."

Błoński was disgusted. He had requested "his recall from here." The idea that the Polish army would disarm the *bałachowcy* put them in a panic. Among them, the

---

[53] Ibid., fos. 228, 254–55 (n.d.).   [54] CAW. I.311.4.212 (October 16, 1920).
[55] Ibid., I.311.3.58 (September 13, 1920).

Polish officers began to flee, disguised even in civilian dress. They were resolved to throw away their gold: necklaces, watches, brooches, diamonds, also millions of rubles and marks. The Muscovites decided to defend themselves and not be disarmed. [Błoński spent hours persuading them Poles would not seize their weapons.] There are so many guilty that the whole Group, with few exceptions, would have to be shot.[56]

Now that the Polish army was advancing, the *bałachowcy* rejoiced, thinking they were going to Russia. "They are keeping whole wagon-trains of booty to take home." Here in Pinsk "they commit scandals unheard-of and never before permitted in the Polish army: they drink vodka day and night and gamble at cards."

The greater number of officers are cocaine addicts [*kokiniarze*], often to the point of idiotism. [Toward Poles they were] continually hostile. This is explicable by *their inborn hatred of us, their desire to tower above us.*

When Poles among them got "fed up, unable to look any more at their bestialities," their shoes and clothes were confiscated, and they suffered twenty-fives lashes before release.

Błoński viewed the *bałachowcy*'s fighting prowess dimly. They managed against Bolsheviks "because Jews spread panic," fleeing from *bałachowcy* to the Bolsheviks and "telling them of terrible things" so that Red soldiers fearfully retreated. He closed with the perhaps obligatory observation that Bałachowicz leaders "reckon with the strength, or at least the patriotism, of Poland and respect her."

In a missive to his Intelligence Department superiors, Jasiński and Boerner, marked "strictly secret," Błoński commented on the pogrom investigation following Bałachowicz's recent entry into Pinsk. He rephrased what he overheard Bałachowicz saying to subordinates about the Kamień Kaszyrski pogrom: "I give you three days to have some fun. Slaughter the Jews, but be smart about it" [*riezcie żydów, tolko umno*].

I won't go on about cruel tormenting of the defenseless, but only emphasize that there is a great difference between punishing guilty Jews and impulsive [*odru-chowo*] slaughter [on one hand] and brutal mistreatment [on the other] of women, children, violation of infants, the infection of an eight-month-old with venereal disease as happened in Pinsk (there are proofs).

Here Błoński apparently thought that "impulsive slaughter" was instinc-tual and ungovernable. Polish General Krajowski was supposed to have confronted Bałachowicz's officers over their army's plundering, but "they made *mir* [peace] and started to drink and play cards. Under such cir-cumstances 'one crow does not pluck out the other's eye.' All Pinsk talks

---

[56] Błoński, here and below: CAW. I.311.3, no. 7 (October 16, 1920).

of how General Krajowski's intelligence department chief won [i.e., was allowed to win] some 100,000–300,000 Polish marks at cards."[57]

Third Army intelligence chief, Major Boerner, later reported to superiors. Having reviewed subordinates' assessment of the Bałachowicz group, as well as Jakowlew's and Salnikow's irregulars (Polish-associated remnants of the Russian Whites), he concluded that while efforts had been made to halt their excesses, "these are committed ever more often, disgracefully, and horribly." He corroborated Błoński's and colleagues' *bałachowcy* reports. He noted that two of his own intelligence agents, sent behind the lines, had "arrested a rabbi, placed his head in a noose, and demanded ransom by local Jews. The agents gained 50,000 marks, 100 loaves of bread, four pair of boots, and 100 ells of silk." For this excess they were "merely" punished by dismissal from intelligence and front transfer. Boerner seemed to accept that association with *bałachowcy* corrupted his subordinates.

Boerner recounted how a Russian officer ordered "two Tatars" to bloodily knout a peasant who had offended him and how Russian auxiliaries lost a battle because nearly all officers were drunk. All this and more had the ill consequences for Poland of driving "part of the Jewish population to seek protection in Bolshevism." It "incites civil war, since the slogan 'beat the Jews' becomes popular among peasants and various social dregs," as evidenced by civilians' rush to join military pogroms. It increased "poverty and price-rises," burdening the state with new costs. It attracted Polish army units to plundering and provoked desertion. It created "excellent material for enemy agitation" and "disgraces in the world's eye the Polish army, under whose aegis such scandalous barbarism occurs."[58]

Third Army intelligence assembled files on *Soviet* atrocities, a few of which found their way into the archive. Chaplain Milik reported that it was hard to identify bodies of Polish soldiers killed in battle because they were stripped of clothing and buried in mass graves. "The inhabitants of Monjatycz village told of the pitiless murder of our wounded by Bolshevik Cossacks," none hospitalized, "but all killed without exception." Chaplain Ślizowski reported from Zamość how Polish captives were stripped of uniforms and shoes and, led by horsemen "riding ear-to-ear [*kłosem*]," were forced to run among the horses. "At Sitno village, in view of civilians and Budyonny's Bolshevik cavalry, they were ordered to escape into fields. Cavalry chased them, cutting them down [*zarąbując*] with sabers despite pleas to spare them and protestations of their innocence." Villagers later buried them in coffins.

[57] CAW. I.311.3.52.no. (K) (October 16, 1920).
[58] CAW. I.311.3.52, no. (L) (September 25, 1920).

Chaplain Wierzejski testified that Bolshevik soldiers stripped captives to undershirts "and amused themselves beating them with knouts and clubs." They forced them to reveal military information, urging them to join Bolshevik ranks. Wounded or exhausted captives were brutally killed, "for example, they cut off hands and head, or stabbed out eyes with sabers. In general, they committed great atrocities." From Bolshevik-occupied Grodno it was reported that from July to September 1920 the Cheka deported some 1,000 civilians in ten transports. Locals said Chekists shot some 200 to 300 people. "The enclosed photographs of victims confirm by eye how bestially people are tormented." Bolsheviks attacked the Red Cross clinic, where Cossacks raped two merciful sisters. People talk of prison tortures: "pushing pins under fingernails and burning of heels are the least of it." Gold teeth of the dead were cut out.[59]

All armies tormented borderland Jews, but with varying frequency and murderousness, and with more or less symbolic display. *Bałachowcy* practiced antisemitic violence as a primary raison d'être, to feed, clothe, and enrich themselves. Jews were, for this reason, prime enemies but also and no less because in "slaughtering" them – their preferred rhetoric – they believed they were destroying Bolshevism and so opening the gate homeward to Russia under restored Romanovs or White stand-ins. Bałachowicz's army bowed most deeply before the Judeo-Bolshevik fetish. Willingly beholden to no state power, espousing no ideology, representing no social constituency, there were no conflicting interests or cross-cutting considerations mitigating anti-Jewish violence. In consequence, their practice, left unhindered, led directly to mass murder on which they brazenly prided themselves. Unalloyed antisemitism, like other paranoid obsessions about demonized out groups, called for – dreams seem, after all, to be free – elimination, extirpation, extermination.

Some Polish observers found it natural to call *bałachowcy* Cossacks. With Batka's men, Cossacks – and various Cossack-like peasant bands crisscrossing Ukraine – shared unquestioning preparedness for murder of Jews while showing comparable zeal for methodical robbery, piling booty on their long wagon trains. Cossacks as military formations had been meant to serve the Russian state, just as Polish soldiery served, not themselves, but "Poland," as its idea glowed in Piłsudskiite and Dmowskian minds. Anti-Jewish aggression required repression for higher ends' sake. But because Polish nationalists too swallowed the Judeo-Bolshevik potion, there was continual bloody return of the repressed, reenactment of revenge for imagined traumas.

[59] CAW. I.311.3.58 (n.d. [after September 1920]).

Conclusion
Lords of Commerce and Lords of Communism, Print-Antisemitism and Popular Anti-Judaism

---

This book's strongest claim is that the anti-Jewish violence it has summoned from history's shadows commonly took form as symbolic acts expressive of deep-rooted popular beliefs about how relations between Christians and Jews should be governed. The violence served, at one level, to put right a *moral economy* of ethnocultural relations that, in aggressors' view, war and revolution had upended. At deeper level, it veered toward exacting vengeance for Jews' very existence as Christians' mythical antagonists.

Pogrom violence's meaning lies more in observers' than in perpetrators' eyes, for rioters rarely thought to justify or explain their actions but rather compliantly – or under communal pressure – assumed their roles in time-honored dramas of punishment, humiliation, desecration, physical injury, expulsion, even murder, both individual and collective. Their actions – though not their *intent to plunder and injure* – welled up largely unconsciously out of social-cultural depths, leaving it to us to interpret them. Only rarely, if ever, did Judeophobic violence follow upon rational calculation of its imagined advantages. As Zionist paladin Itzhak Grünbaum wrote of anti-Jewish rioting in Płock: "A kind of madness [*obłęd*] seized crowds of peasants and soldiers. The most monstrous rumors were repeated from mouth to mouth." Yet the madness assumed historically structured, culturally coded forms.

Let us recall some of these. Christian grievances over what was thought to be Jewish merchants' economic abuse – seemingly unfair purchasing practices, usurious money lending, price gouging, withholding of essential foodstuffs and clothing from sale – sometimes led to anachronistic open-air trials on town or village square, ending in long-practiced public whippings on bare buttocks of individuals or groups of alleged offenders. *Penitence* was exacted. The same torture was later inflicted by soldiers in the fighting of 1919–20 on Jewish men thought to be Bolsheviks or draft dodgers. Such bloody thrashings sometimes occurred as victims ran the gauntlet, organized formally or chaotically by soldiers or civilians, in town or on the road.

In these and other such proceedings, there appeared inverted evocations of the trial, scourging, and martyrdom of Jesus, memory of which pulsed in Christian hearts. Dwelling houses and religious buildings were sometimes set afire, their inhabitants, blocked from escape, burned to death, passers-by sometimes forced into the flames. These acts, accompanied by jeers, were martyrdoms by fire, reminiscent of earlier, oft-enacted religious immolations. Jews might be compelled to wash Polish officers' feet. They were rounded up in symbolical enslavement. They were, especially in the eastern borderlands, murdered as if in the bowels of hell – another familiar Christian landscape.

We have seen also that journalists and other educated observers, in both ethnoreligious camps, commonly employed theatrical and carnival metaphors to describe anti-Jewish rioting. Carnavalesque behavior conjured medieval and early-modern European worlds-turned-upside-down. Looters reveled in stolen finery, ate and drank copiously of plundered stocks, sang and danced amid flames and carnage. Burghers, intelligentsia, respectably hatted ladies, gentlemen with ivory-headed canes might promenade before such scenes, smiling at the common folk's crude enjoyments, occasionally pocketing a memento striking their fancy or whetting their appetite. Soldiers, believing hidden Jewish treasure chests bottomless, might assemble a war-stricken, impoverished town's Jews and demands fairy-tale banquets of them. Women of all ages were avidly raped, individually or en masse. Christians whistled and sang in midst or aftermath of mayhem and murder.

Imposing, in theatricalized manner, humiliating forced labor on dragooned Jews, especially civic and religious notables, deeply gratified many Christians, reversing their paranoid master-servant imaginings and reaffirming in themselves pride in their own "blessedness," "ease," and "freedom." It was yet another Rabelaisian reversal that resentful Christians imposed on the "idle" Jews, who had historically deep reason to bridle at thoughts of enslavement.

These pages have repeatedly shown how the Jewish presence, especially in its most insular religious forms – as in the figure of Rebbe Szapiro, Hasidic victim of judicial murder – induced apprehension, anxiety, and fear in antisemitic hearts and minds. Blended with the self-doubt of a politically fragile and materially poor Christian people, such uncomfortable feelings about Poland's massive Jewish population powered the drive toward aggression, punishment, subjugation, and ethnic cleansing.

Mosaic faith and practices were desecrated and mocked, perhaps most commonly by brutal beard cutting, whose effect was sometimes plainly understood to rob religious men of their charismatic authority. Emasculatory symbolism is detectable and – especially when beards were half-removed – cruel creation of, for Christian eyes, butts of laughter. In another light, beard cutting simulated mock conversion of pious Jews into disempowered, banal figures blending into everyday Polish Christian life or their elimination as a disquieting mass of outsiders to it.

Groups of Jews were made to cry out for their rabbi's death. Torah rolls were comprehensively stabbed, trampled on, obscenely defiled – in one case, cut into bits that captive Jews were then required, absurdly, to read aloud. Soldiers, and women too, danced about with Torah covers and other sacred paraphernalia on their heads. Synagogues were made into stables, or worse. Jews in Shabbat dress were put to work soiling or ruining it, as in cleaning latrines, sometimes with bare hands. They were, on occasion and in the war-zone, made to defile, humiliate, and bloody – even kill – one another. Jews, especially Orthodox and Hasidic Jews, but those too in "European" dress and even Polish army uniforms, might be made to dance, sing out self-insulting or self-damning phrases, leap over benches and tables, pull carts in place of draught animals, race automobiles, shoo flies from horses. Jewish speech was reviled, Hebrew signage and inscriptions destroyed. Pork was forced into kosher mouths. Graves were exhumed, corpses violated. These and other aggressions served to demystify Judaism; rob it of its charisma, gravitas, social solidarity, and magic; humiliate and make it impracticable.

Some or all of these acts occurred in the plunderous pogroms, wholly or largely civilian, that exploded in Polish-majority West Galicia in early 1918 and again, amplified by armed bands' presence, during tumultuous post-Habsburg November 1918. They were staged in the hugely destructive, soldier-spearheaded November 1918 pogrom in Lwów and in the increasingly militarized anti-Jewish violence of 1919 and 1920, including the insurrectionary, armed-band assaults on Galician *shtetls* and cities in May 1919. As the new Polish state's police and gendarmerie slowly and imperfectly imposed law and order, pogrom making and other attacks on Jews became increasingly soldiery's province.

Army intelligence's secret-classified *Komunikat Informacyjny* in 1920 bluntly said, "antisemitism represents the soldier's most characteristic trait." It was typical of newly drafted soldiers, on their way to induction, to inebriate themselves with liquor extorted or robbed from Jewish merchants and to "beat Jews" along the way with saber-surrogate wooden rods. Recruitment pogroms broke out. Soldiers commonly believed their status shielded them from legal reprisals for abuse of Jews and that they were entitled to take freely what they needed from Jewish shops. They imagined that having been chosen to face death while Israelites allegedly evaded conscription, "everything was allowed," especially plunder and commission of often bloody anti-Jewish "pranks."

They often proclaimed, in pogroms' course, that their superior officers had given them legal permission, for two or three days, to "run wild," "have some fun," and "raise hell." But our mountainous evidence has yielded no such authorization by Polish army commanders and but rare and ambiguous allegations against line officers. Still, these pages have frequently shown that army officers sympathized with soldierly anti-Jewish violence and often joined it. As a certain cavalry captain was reported in a fellow officer's 1919 diary to have said: "even my departed mother, who was a saintly woman, taught me that crushing the Jew [gnębienie Żyda] is no sin."[1]

In 1918–19 the focus of pogroms broadened from victimization of Jews on grounds of economic or commercial exploitation to encompass punishment for lack of Polish patriotism and for pro-Bolshevism. Economic grievances never lost force, for soldiers, too, like war-immiserated civilians, were often woefully lacking in essential provisions. But where pre-war Galician peasants expressed determination to end "the rule of Jews [żydowszczyzna]," as they had earlier overthrown aristocratic-landlordly domination [pańszczyzna], soldiers – most of them of peasant birth – now also aimed their blows against "Judeo-Bolsheviks" [żydokomuna]. As Itzhak Grünberg averred, they viewed Jews and Bolsheviks interchangeably, just as, during the apocalyptic moment in summer 1920 of Soviet invasion of the Polish heartland, many civilians did.

Now soldierly violence often took the form of brutal, even atrocious executions of Jews suspected of pro-Bolshevism, caught behind the lines, or without protective papers or Christian defenders. The more exposed Polish armed forces felt themselves to be to Russian attack, the greater was the likelihood of massacres such as that in Pinsk in April 1919. Here violence's expressiveness told a story of demystification of Jewish power, merged now with Bolshevism, through murders that symbolized a larger victory, even if panicked shooting of innocent Jews or their thousandfold internment at the height of the Red Army's onslaught injured Polish state interest. Anti-Jewish violence retained its function of breaking what Christians understood – or felt – to be Jews' magical power and of toppling them from hidden or not so hidden seats of power over "poor Christians" and "martyred Poland." But it shifted away from wartime civilians' concerns to those of the 1919–20 armed forces, seeing Jews less as "lords of commerce" and more as "lords of communism."

---

[1] Czerniakiewicz, loc. cit., 582.

Anxiety over supposed Jewish power has towered over these pages. Rooted in archaic agrarian and religious conceptions brought to intellectual light by ethnographer-historians and anthropologists, and confirmed in judgments by Polish writers and officials documented in these pages, pervasive popular-cultural attitudes invested Jews with strong magical powers – traditionally understood as partly beneficent but increasingly viewed as malevolent – over Christian Polish well-being. These they exerted, with hidden intent to harm, on the country's agricultural and commercial-monetary economy, with resulting Christian misery and frustration, and on its political fortunes, with resulting impotence and defeat. There was among ordinary Christian Poles acknowledgment, despite often eye-shocking poverty among lesser Jews, of Jewish civilizational and ethical strength, even superiority: greater wealth and luxury, greater learning and social discipline (including abstemiousness), deeper piety and surrender to God's will. Partly real, partly imagined, these attributes, paranoically or even self-abasingly perceived, only heightened Christians' sense of vulnerability. This sometimes yielded projection-laden fears that Jews threatened Poles' very survival, such as when a Christian woman in the Lwów pogrom labeled them "Hamans" (after the Jews' mortal enemy in the biblical Book of Esther).

Recovery of independent statehood went together with determination among many Christians to break Jewish power not only through the now-democratic ballot box but also through pogrom looting and destruction, and even violence driving Jews away from village, town, or whole land. Stalking this mentality were fantasies of mass "slaughter" – a word unnervingly often on pogromists' lips, if never actualized (except sporadically and locally by Cossacks and other armed bands in the eastern borderlands). The more that Jews were seen to refuse Polish nationality and patriotism – and this was how Zionism was understood – and the more the Judeo-Bolshevik concept entered Polish consciousness, the greater the zeal for showdown with "*żydowszczyzna*" and the weaker the belief that Polish Jews sought acculturation, assimilation, solidarity with Polishness, and full citizenship.

These pages have dealt with *Jewish* history in Poland principally in its reactive relationship to wartime and postwar pogroms and the complex accompanying psychology among Poles of self-righteousness, aggression, denial, and shame. The pogroms' traumatic impact may have revealed itself in subsequent Jewish forgetfulness or repression of their memory. In any event, Jewish attention in post-1920 Poland was ineluctably fixed on self-defense against new onslaughts of hostile politics and legislation. Jewish assimilationism as a worldview and life-strategy suffered post-1918 bruising and on occasion bloody rebuff.

Thanks to militant and talented journalists, parliamentarians, and social activists, Zionism rocketed forward as vehicle of Jewish self-defense and national pride, while Jewish leftists, if unwilling to march under Zionist or Soviet colors, fell into social-cultural isolation (though not impotence). Religious conservatives, wary of Wilsonian (or Zionist) modernity, cleaved to their trust in protective Christian state power, whose collapse and arduous reconstruction after the war could be thought to explain the eruption from below of Judeophobic magma. Yet these same postwar years drove home to the Jewish consciousness that Poland, if inescapable through emigration, was their fate, and subsequent interwar years witnessed rapid linguistic-cultural Polonization among them. It was integration, if also negative integration.

Popular aggression's death toll – whether inflicted by civilians, bandits, or soldiers – eludes precise knowledge. Different sources reported varying losses in the same incident. This book's documentation yields a maximum number of 279 anti-Jewish riots or pogroms staged in historically Polish lands outside the orbit of the Russian civil war, about half in Galicia. The lowest number of deaths inflicted in these incidents, as documented in these pages, is 400; the highest number is 532 (the October 1919 Morgenthau report reckoned deaths at 280). But because murders committed during the Polish-Soviet war are certainly imperfectly quantified in our sources, despite the Zionist Club's scrupulous efforts, maximum deaths will have climbed higher, probably by some hundreds.

The great majority of deaths here documented occurred at armed men's hands. These were "Green" or "Red" brigades of demobilized soldiers and motley irregulars in Galician winter–spring 1918–19, sometimes fighting against but sometimes joined in anti-Jewish violence by soldiers of Piłsudski's or Haller's armies, who in the course of 1919 and 1920 gradually became principal perpetrators of pogrom violence. As for documented arrests of suspected pogromists, this book yields an imperfect total of some 1,300, but guilty verdicts, imprisonments, or executions numbered far fewer, though punishment by civil and military justiciars was not, as we have seen, insignificant.

Absent from calculation here are the multitudinous victims of Bałachowicz's and other eastern warlords' forces tactically allied with Poland in the anti-Soviet borderlands war. The Judeophobic violence underpinning their rapacious economy of antisemitic plunder towered high, unrestrained by cultural norms and nationalist state-building priorities, above that inflicted by Poles. Scholars commonly reckon Jewish deaths in pogrom violence committed by the Russian civil war's contending forces in the tens of thousands, with 50,000 (or many more) for

Ukraine alone oft-mentioned totals. But even at half that number, the disparity with losses in Poland's ethnographic heartland, with its 2 million Jews, is clear. As for Jewish property owners' material losses, they were immense, while restitution through the state was miserly at best.

This book has questioned the power of rational-actor analysis alone to account for the violence it depicts. Yet it has not been my aim to deny its utility in its own (psychologically and emotionally subordinate) sphere. We have witnessed, as I earlier wrote,

Polish Christian rage and anxiety over frontline "Judeo-Bolshevism," tempting or driving violence-prone antisemites into orgies of physical abuse and ritual humiliation. Was it a measure of their own fears of social-cultural extinction, should the dreaded eastern foe engulf them? Or should we conclude instead that it was war's anarchy that gave them welcome opportunity to assault Jews, humble them, expel or destroy them? Were these not compatible impulses, one unconscious, one not?

Obviously, no culturally or historically derived expressivity – no beard cutting, for example – was required to plunder Jews. Yet for robbery there were myriad irrational justifications, rooted in Jewish fault and defect – and in the widespread assumption that Jewish possessions had been unjustly extracted from Christian society and so could be righteously reclaimed. While seizure of Jewish-owned food stocks relieved some Christians' misery, pogromists' gains from looting and robbery were mostly exiguous, in part because wealthier Jewish businessmen, as Jewish sources testify, sometimes succeeded in escaping plunder, whether through flight, payment of bribes, or dwelling in cities where police protection was effective, if grudgingly so.

When large-scale plunder did occur, it was at the hands of powerful groups in possession of guns and trucks – armed forces or professional thieves. It was mostly *shtetl* Jews who suffered expropriation by mobs. The booty, skimmed by soldiers, shared around among plunderers and their hangers-on, was usually more paltry than rich. At a macro level, nothing of lasting economic value was gained and much lost, and the same was true at the micro level of the smallholding villager and poor townsman.

These pages have said much about antisemitic ideology, which in historiographical and scholarly tradition has towered over explanations of anti-Jewish violence. It may be hazarded, by way of creative simplification, that a kind of standard model has long existed, persisting strongly today. It holds that the theologically infused aggressiveness of premodern Christian anti-Judaism underwent, in the post-Enlightenment era of rationalism, nationalism, and capitalism, transformation into ideological antisemitism, often defended as scientifically ("racially") grounded. Embraced most influentially by nominally Christian nationalist-conservative middle and lower middle classes, it served to combat and undermine Jewish positions in the commercial-industrial economy and block Jewish entry into educated professions and institutions of state power.

Pogroms, as we have seen Jewish leaders of all persuasions insisting, and as much authoritative historical literature still holds, could be traced to ideologically driven antisemitic instigators in elite-steered politics and government. This was a theory of *intentionalist* Christian antisemitism, manifested especially in journalism and oratorical propaganda widely thought irresistible to targeted audiences, from whose midst ideologically fanaticized crowbar- and truncheon-wielding pogromists sprang forth. In this view, pogromists and pogroms were the stuff of anti-antisemitic conspiracy theories mirroring those of the Judeophobes who posited and pilloried imagined Jewish world conspiracies. They who imbibed the ideological poison, responding with pogrom violence – "benighted" peasants, "*lumpenproletaryat*," criminals, bandits, "rabble," "scum" – were dupes of antisemitic politicians.

In this book's voluminous documentation, no evidence surfaced of pogroms planned and unleashed from on high, whether by Christian Polish political parties or state, church, or army. Nor do the extensive state papers on which much of this book rests show that judicial authorities attempted to prosecute anyone for masterminding pogroms, though many were charged with participation in them. Numerous were official civilian, military, and clerical exhortations against anti-Jewish rioting and mob violence, and not infrequent the judicial prosecution and punishment of their perpetrators, who suffered in dozens of cases the death penalty, while far more endured prisons' darkened cells and "hard cots." These were not punishments of antisemitism but of crimes against life and property.

Pogrom violence was emphatically unwelcome to the new Polish state's architects, as it was to higher Catholic authorities and to politicians and journalists speaking for the nationalist and agrarian-populist parties. Many rightly perceived in anti-Jewish upheavals revolts against the social order. The educated and propertied classes were also uncomfortably aware of the reputational losses Poland suffered in these years because of a Judeophobic violence that, deny it though they might, raged – sometimes uncontrollably – in their lands. That "Jewish power" succeeded in heartrendingly publicizing it abroad, "blackening" Poland's image, was further embarrassment and humiliation.

We have heard some advocacy, from beneath power's highest echelons, of anti-Jewish plunder and attendant physical abuse, whether from middle-range or lower officials and politicians, local intelligentsia, or artisans and tradesmen. There were low-ranking priests who exhorted to assault on Jewish wealth and influence. Ill-educated common folk, especially villagers, were deeply conditioned to harken to such notables' voices as authoritative and righteous. But we have also glimpsed many obscure activists in villages and *shtetls* who, composing their plebeian manifestos, preaching pogrom on horseback, pounding their drums, passing their anti-Jewish fetishes from house to house, fomented pogroms, often in league with forested bandits. These shadowy folk figures were the essential and most influential *civilian* "triggerers" of anti-Jewish violence.

Women were pogromists alongside men, sometimes dying of bullet wounds in consequence. They raised ritual-murder cries, risking authorities' occasional dismissal as superstitious hysterics. They exhorted to plunder and murder and – most commonly – gathered up the stolen goods in their ever-handy baskets, bags, and aprons. For their transgressions, more than a few served half-starved prison terms. Far more grievous were the sufferings of Jewish women, robbed, battered, and – especially when bandits or soldiers assaulted them – raped and often cruelly or even atrociously murdered, sometimes along with their infants. The despoliation of women and children is a metaphor for pollution, desecration, and genocide. The taboo-breaking it entails initiates perpetrators into brotherhoods of murderous misogyny, freeing them for worse things. Sexuality transmutes into sadism in service of ethnic exorcism.

Among soldiers, we have seen that officers commonly lost control over enlisted men plunging into anti-Jewish "pranks," nor could army gendarmes or civilian police effectively halt them. They stood, rather, in physical danger themselves, exposed to derisive charges as "Jewish uncles," allegedly bribed to defend the Jewish community (as was likewise formulaically claimed of any and all opponents of anti-Jewish violence). Doubtless army officers, like their underlings, embraced the Judeo-Bolshevik myth, sometimes participating in Jews' torment, sometimes suffering resultant court martial and even, if rarely, execution. But this they did against higher army policy, even if General Sikorski recklessly commanded villagers to slaughter with their farm tools renitent "Jewish-Bolshevik commissars" fleeing Soviet battlefield defeat.

The standard model of pogrom explanation does not describe the Polish landscape we have traversed. Much of the controversy that simmers in the literature and in present-day political life derives, if unrecognizedly, from this circumstance. For Christian Poles, too, accepted the pogrom concept as it figured in Jewish discourse, usually under the heading of "pogrom on the Russian model": furtive instigation by state actors, whether at high or lower level, for reasons of ideological antisemitism and to advance conservative-nationalist-Christian interests at the expense of liberal-democratic or socialist strivings (which, if once triumphant, would self-professedly usher antisemitism out of the world). If anti-Jewish violence in Poland did not stem from such deliberate pogrom launching, it did not deserve the opprobrious label but should be understood instead as work of the "dark masses," criminals, and "scum," whose disciplining the new Polish state aimed to achieve as soon as its police powers allowed. Such was Piłsudski's and many another upright and honorable Pole's view.

If, however, pogroms are understood as grassroots eruptions of Judeophobic aggressions, fueled by the manifold obsessions, envy of real or imagined Jewish riches, and fear of (worldly or magical) Jewish power that these pages have uncovered, the term rightly applies to anti-Jewish violence, both civilian and soldierly, in Poland in these years. Should evidence surface for pogroms intentionally plotted and instigated from above, in which street-level perpetrators were but manipulated dupes of political schemers, the concept as it figured in the now largely discredited standard model will fit handily. But in the 1914–20 years, when perhaps the most widespread and possibly deadliest anti-Jewish violence in modern Polish history exploded, such evidence has not come to light. A crippling defect of the top-down model will, however, remain, in that it eclipses the motives and impulses of the ordinary people comprising the mass of participants, active and passive, in ethnic violence.

This study proposes that in tracking the sources of popular anti-Jewish violence, antisemitic ideology, as formulated by political intellectuals, be set aside in favor of concentration on folk-cultural wellsprings of grassroots aggression. Though Christianity flowed through those channels too, alongside other earlier-discussed currents of magical thinking, the reader will have observed that, in these pages, priests more often opposed than instigated anti-Jewish violence and sometimes risked their lives trying to halt it. In the hundreds of cases this book has contemplated, but two efforts at justification of violence by charges of ritual child murder occurred, in both cases collapsing as the would-be avengers concluded that no bloody deed had transpired. The Catholic clergy did propagate anti-Jewish resentments, but rarely violence, nor did pogromists, summoned before courts, offer religious justification for their mayhem.

Instead, it was complaints of popular suffering, misery, and existential fear brought forth by imagined Jewish power and magic – in causing ruinous war and introducing into the world the apocalyptic Bolshevik threat to Polish-Catholic identity – that fired the violence these pages witness. And for these reasons the violence was *righteous* in its inflictors' minds and hearts. If there was remorse in its aftermath, it has left vanishingly few traces. In this book's pages, one man alone, participant in Jewish boys' murder, repented to a bereaved father, ruefully saying that "he had killed enough Jews" and confessing also that he had stolen a Jew's boots. Otherwise the silence that descended on these years' vast brutality, physical and psychological, and until now on the very memory of it, was deafening. To Judeophobes, the punishment and retribution were wholly deserved. To nationalists, they were the price of national resurrection and salvation from Bolshevism.

The subterranean power of Judeophobic anxiety in Polish popular culture manifests itself in the tendency among those gripped by it to summon "*żydowszczyzna*" as explanation for *newly arisen* threats to Christian society or *newly perceived* weaknesses within it. This tendency survives today, although the Jewish presence has shrunk enormously in Poland.

It is imaginable that the violence we have contemplated would have raged even in the absence of nationalist-purveyed, stridently ideological print-antisemitism. It is better to think of formalized antisemitic politics as intellectuals' characteristically word-rich rationalization of *their own anxieties* about Jewish power and magic, anchored in widely shared, deep-rooted popular culture within Christianity, than as launch pad of common folk's anti-Jewish violence. For many people of aggressive disposition, and others communally pressured into it, this violence – with its many-faceted, seemingly "natural," unself-conscious ritualiza-tions – possessed a compelling, even irresistible, culturally justified, emotionally driven call to return the world to order and righteousness.

Bibliography

I. Archival Sources

A. Poland

1. Warsaw.
   a. Archiwum Akt Nowych.
   Prezydium Rady Ministrów.
   Sygn. No. 5990/21: Rozruchy antyżydowskie w Średniej Galicji (1919).
   Fos. 1–213.
   Sygn. No. 21431/20: Materjały przedłożone przez Klub Sejmowy Posłów
   Żydowskiego Stronnictwa Ludowego w sprawie położenia żydow,
   wywołanego inwazją bolszewicką (1920). Fos. 1–1072.
   b. Centralne Archiwum Wojskowe, Warsaw-Rembertów.
   Oddzial II Sztabu Ministerstwa Spraw Wojskowych za lata 1918–21.
   Sygn. I.300.76: *Komunikat Informacyjny*.
   Sygns. I.123.1.324; I.311.4.205; I.311.4.207; I.311.4.212; I.311.4.224;
   I.311.3.52.
2. Kraków: Archiwum Państwowy w Krakowie.
   Oddział IIh. Sąd Okręgowy. S8/II (trial records).
   Sygns. J 819/20; J 2210/20; J 708/20; S8/II. J 2491/20; Vr 986/23.

B. Israel

1. Central Archive for the History of the Jewish People, Jerusalem.
   a. Microfilm from the Ukrainian State Archive, L'viv: Soviet-era signature,
   GALO/g.Lvov/FOND 271/Opis.1/Od. 3B.446): HM2/8299: 1–19; HM2/
   8300.1–10; HM2/8856.7; HM2/8860.10.
   b. Microfilm from Archiwum Akt Nowych, Warsaw: CAHJP. PL 578(4).
2. Central Zionist Archives, Jerusalem.
   A15 Papers of Max Bodenheimer.
   A127 Papers of Itzhak Grűnbaum.
   L6/109–110, 114 Ostjudenfrage 1918.
   L6/119 Ostjudenfrage 1919.
   Z3/174 CZO Berlin: Diaspora Politik – Polen 1918–19.

Z3/178 Judenverfolgungen in Polen und Galizien in der Revolutionszeit nach dem Ersten Weltkrieg 1918–20.

Z3/179–183 Judenverfolgungen in Polen und Galizien in der Revolutionszeit 1918–20.

Z3/184 Hilfsaktion für die Opfer der Pogrome in Galizien, Polen, und Russland während der Revolutionszeit 1918–19.

C.   *Austria*

Österreichisches Staatsarchiv, Vienna.
 a. Allgemeines Verwaltungsarchiv (AVA). Staatsarchiv des Innern und der Justiz. Ministerium des Innern.
  Präsidiale 1848–1918: Galizien.
  Sign. 20. Fsz. No. 1877 (1900–18).
  Sign. 22. Fsz. No. 867 (1877–98).
  Fsz. No. 2116 (1914–15).
  Fsz. No. 2117 (1916–17).
  Fsz. No. 2118 (1918) [Zahl 1–16,000].
  Fsz. No. 2119 (1918) [Zahl 16,001–].
 b. Kriegsarchiv. Kriegsministerium, Präsidium (KMP): Galizien: Materien A–K, L–Z 1918–19.

D.   *New York*

1. American Jewish Joint Distribution Committee New York
  AR 14/18, file 136: Poland.
  AR 19/21, file 188: Poland.

II.   Published Primary Sources

Ansky, S. [Shloyme Rappoport]. *The Enemy at His Pleasure: A Journey through the Jewish Pale of Settlement during World War I*, trans. Joachim Neugroschel (New York, NY: Metropolitan, 2002 [Yiddish original: 1920]).

Assaf, David, ed. *Journey to a Nineteenth-Century Shtetl: The Memoirs of Yekhetzkel Kotik* (Detroit, MI: Wayne State University Press, 2002).

Babel, Isaac. "1920 Diary," in *The Complete Works of Isaac Babel* (New York, NY: Norton, 2002), 377–472.

Bendow, Josef (pseudonym for Joseph Tenenbaum). *Der Lemberger Judenpogrom, November 1918–Jänner 1919* (Vienna: Hickl, 1919).

Book of Kielce, trans. Sefer Kielce, ed. Pinchas Cytron (Tel Aviv, 1957), available at www.jewishgen.org/Yizkor/kielce/Kie047.html (accessed February 7, 2015).

Bujak, Franciszek. *Galicya*, 2 vols. (Lwów: Altenberg, 1908).

The Jewish Question in Poland (Paris: Levé, 1919).

Chasanowitsch, Leon. *Die polnischen Judenpogrome im November und Dezember 1918: Tatsachen und Dokumente* (Stockholm: Verlag Judaea, 1919).

Cohen, Israel. *A Report on the Pogroms in Poland* (London: Central Office of the Zionist Organisation, 1919).

"The Pogroms in Poland," in *A Jewish Pilgrimage* (London: Vallentine Mitchell, 1956 [typescript version: CZA. L6/119]).

Dobroszycki, Lucjan, et al. *Image before My Eyes: A Photographic History of Jewish Life in Poland, 1864–1939* (New York, NY: Schocken, 1977).

Döblin, Alfred. *Journey to Poland* (New York, NY: Paragon House, 1991 [German original: 1924]).

Feldman, Wilhelm. *Geschichte der politischen Ideen in Polen seit dessen Teilungen (1772–1914)* (Munich: Oldenbourg, 1917).

Getter, Norbert et al., *Żydzi bojownicy o niepodległość Polski : 1918–1939* (Lwów: Rada Ochrony Pamięci Walk i Męczeństwa, 1939).

Goodhart, Arthur L. *Poland and the Minority Races* (London: Allen & Unwin, 1920).

Grünbaum, Izaak, ed., *Materjały w sprawie żydowskiej w Polsce* (Warsaw: Biuro Prasowe Organizacji Sjonistycznej w Polsce, 1919).

Hamerow, Theodore. *Remembering a Vanished World: A Jewish Childhood in Interwar Poland* (New York, NY: Berghahn, 2001).

Heifetz, Elias. *The Slaughter of the Jews in the Ukraine in 1919* (New York, NY: Seltzer, 1921).

Jackowski, Aleksander, and Jadwiga Jarnuszkiewicz. *Folk Art of Poland* (Warsaw: Arkady, 1968).

Kacyzne, Alter *Poyln: Jewish Life in the Old Country* (New York, NY: Metropolitan, 1999).

Kahan, Anna. "The Diary of Anna Kahan, Siedlce, Poland, 1914–1916." *YIVO Annual of Jewish Social Science*, Vol. XVIII (1983), 141–371.

Komisya dla Sprawy, Żydowskiej. *W sprawie polsko-żydowskiej. Przebieg ankiety odbytej w dniach 2, 3, 4, 9 i 16 lutego 1919 we Lwowie, tudzież wnioski Komisyi wydelegowanej przez Tymczasowy Komitet Rządzący uchwałą a 1. stycznia 1919* (Lwów: Nakładem Komisyi rządzącej we Lwowie, 1919).

Kossak-Szczucka, Zofia. *The Blaze: Reminiscences of Volhynia, 1917–1919* (New York, NY: Polish Book Importing, 1927).

Kułakowska-Lis, Joanna, et al. *Poland in Old Photographs* (Olszanica: Bosz, 2005).

Levine, Louis, ed. *Lives Remembered: A Shtetl through a Photographer's Eye* (New York, NY: Museum of Jewish Heritage, 2002).

Lis-Blonski, Stanisław. *"Balachowcy" Stanisława Lisa-Blonskiego jako przestrzen refleksji i historyczny dokument*, ed. Grzegorz Jacek Pelica (Lublin: Best Print, 2011).

Morgenthau, Henry, with French Strother. *All in a Life-Time* (New York, NY: Doubleday Page, 1923).

Narbut-Łuczyński, Aleksander Jerzy. *U kresu wędrówki: Wspomnienia* (London: Gryf, 1966).

Narodowy Klub Żydowski Posłów Sejmowych przy Tymczasowej Żydowskiej Radzie Narodowej. *Inwazja Bolszewicka a Żydzi. Zbiór Dokumentów* (Warsaw: n.p., 1921).

National Polish Committee of America. *The Jews in Poland: Official Reports of the American and British Investigating Missions* (Chicago, IL: American Commission to Negotiate Peace, 1920).

Ringel, Michał. *Antysemityzm w Polsce* (Warsaw: Wende, 1924).

Salsitz, Norman (Saleschütz). *A Jewish Boyhood in Poland: Remembering Kolbuszowa* (Syracuse, NY: Syracuse University Press, 1992).

Schoenfeld, Joachim. *Shtetl Memoirs: Jewish Life in Galicia under the Austro-Hungarian Empire and in the Reborn Poland 1898–1939* (Hoboken, NJ: KTAV, 1985).

Serhiichuk, Volodymyr. *Pohromy v Ukraïni, 1914–1920: vid shtuchnykh stereotypiv do hirkoï pravdy, prykhovuvanoï v radiäns'kykh arkhivakh* (Kyiv: Vyd-vo im. O. Telihy, 1998).

Singer, Isaac B. *In My Father's Court* (New York, NY: Farrear, Straus and Giroux, 1966).

Singer, Israel Joshua. *Of a World That Is No More* (New York, NY: Vanguard, 1971).

Słomka, Jan. *Pamiętniki włościanina od pańszczyzny do dni dzisiejszych* (Kraków: Towarzystwo Szkoły Ludowej 1929) available at www.linux.net.pl/~wkotwica /slomka/slomka.html.

From Serfdom to Self-Government. Memoirs of a Polish Village Mayor 1842–1927 (London: Minerva, 1941).

Szczepanowski, Stanisław. *Nędza Galicyi w cyfrach* (Lwów: Gubrynowicz i Schmidt, 1888).

Tenenbaum, Józef. *Żydowskie problemy gospodarcze w Galicyi* (Vienna: Nakł. Dr. W. Berkelhammera, 1918).

Tomaszewski, Jerzy. "Raport delegacji Ministerstwa Spraw Zagranicznych R.P. w sprawie wystąpień antyżydowskich we Lwowie," *Przegląd Historyczny*, vol. 35, no. 2 (1984), 281–85.

Żydowski Instytut Historyczny et al. *Żydzi Warszawy/The Jews of Warsaw 1861–1943* (Warsaw: Żydowski Instytut Historyczny, 2003).

III. Newspapers

1. Biblioteka Narodowa, Warsaw *Czas* 1919–20 *Gazeta Warszawska* 1918.
2. Biblioteka Uniwersytetu Warszawskiego *Piast* 1918, *Robotnik* 1918, *Kuryer Warszawski* 1918, *Kuryer Polski* 1918.
3. Biblioteka Jagiellońskich MF 575: *Nowy Dziennik* 1918–20.
4. Leo Baeck Institute, New York *Im Deutschen Reich* 1918–19, *Jüdische Rundschau* 1918–19.
5. New York Public Library, Jewish Division *Allgemeine Zeitung des Judenthums* Jg. 82–83 (1918–19).

IV. Internet Sources

Wirtualny Sztetl: www.sztetl.org.pl/.

JewishGen: www.jewishgen.org/.

YIVO Encyclopedia of Jews in Eastern Europe: www.yivoencyclopedia.org/default .aspx.

V.   Secondary Literature

A.   On Polish-Jewish Relations and Jewish History in Poland and Eastern Europe

Aschheim, Steven. *Brothers and Strangers: The East European Jew in German and German Jewish Consciousness, 1800–1923* (Madison, WI: University of Wisconsin Press, 1982).

Bacon, Gershon. *The Politics of Tradition: Agudat Yisrael in Poland, 1916–1939* (Jerusalem: Magnes, 1996).

Barkan, Elazar et al., eds. *Shared History, Divided Memory: Jews and Others in Soviet-Occupied Poland, 1939–1941* (Leipzig: Leipziger Universitätsverlag, 2007).

Bartal, Israel. *The Jews of Eastern Europe, 1772–1881* (Philadelphia, PA: University of Pennsylvania Press, 2005).

Bartal, Israel, and Anthony Polonsky, eds. *Focusing on Galicia: Jews, Poles, Ukrainians, 1772–1918 (Polin*, vol. 12) (Portland, OR, Littman, 1999).

Bikont, Anna. *The Crime and the Silence: Confronting the Massacre of Jews in Wartime Jedwabne* (New York, NY: Farrar, Straus and Giroux, 2015).

Blobaum, Robert. *Rewolucja: Russian Poland, 1904–1907* (Ithaca, NY: Cornell University Press, 1995).

A Minor Apocalypse: Warsaw during the First World War (Ithaca, NY: Cornell University Press, 2017).

Blobaum, Robert, ed. *Antisemitism and Its Opponents in Modern Poland* (Ithaca, NY: Cornell University Press, 2005).

Buchen, Tim. *Antisemitismus in Galizien: Agitation, Gewalt und Politik gegen Juden in der Habsburgermonarchie um 1900* (Berlin: Metropol, 2012).

Cała, Alina. *Asymilacja Żydów w Królestwie Polskim, 1864–1897: postawy, konflikty, stereotypy* (Warsaw: Państwowy Instytut Wydawniczy, 1989).

The Image of the Jew in Polish folk culture (Jerusalem: Magnes Press, 1995 [Polish original: 1992]).

Żyd – wróg odwieczny? Antysemityzm w Polsce i jego źródła (Warsaw: Wydawnictwo Nisza, 2012).

Cichopek, Anna. *Pogrom Żydów w Krakowie 11. Sierpnia 1945 r.* (Warsaw: Żydowski Instytut Historyczny, 2000).

Czerniakiewicz, Andriej. "Ekcesy antyżydowskie wojsk polskich na Kresach Północno-Wschodnich RP (IV–VIII 1919 roku)," in Krzysztof Jasiewicz, ed., *Świat niepożegnany: Żydzi na dawnych ziemiach wschodnich Rzeczypospolitej w XVIII-XX wieku* (Warsaw: Instytut Studiów Politycznych PAN, 2004), 581–89.

Dynner, Glenn. *Men of Silk: The Hasidic Conquest of Polish Jewish Society* (New York, NY: Oxford University Press, 2006).

Dynner, Glenn, et al. *Jews in the Kingdom of Poland, 1815–1918. Polin*, vol. 27 (Portland, OR: Littman, 2015).

Engel, David. "Lwów, 1918: The Transmutation of a Symbol and Its Legacy in the Holocaust," in Joshua D. Zimmerman, ed., *Contested Memories: Poles and Jews during the Holocaust and Its Aftermath* (New Brunswick, NJ: Rutgers University Press, 2003), 32–46.

Fink, Carole. *Defending the Rights of Others: The Great Powers, the Jews, and International Minority Protection, 1878–1938* (New York, NY: Cambridge University Press, 2004).

Fuks, Marian. *Żydzi w Warszawie* (Poznań: Sorus, 1992).

Gierowska-Kałłaur, Joanna. "Żydzi i Polacy na Wileńszczyźie I Grodzieńszczyźnie w latach 1919–1920," in Krzysztof Jasiewicz, ed., *Świat niepożegnany: Żydzi na dawnych ziemiach wschodnich Rzeczypospolitej w XVIII-XX wieku* (Warsaw: Instytut Studiów Politycznych PAN, 2004), 354–63.

Gitelman, Zvi, et al. *The Emergence of Modern Jewish Politics: Bundism and Zionism in Eastern Europe* (Pittsburgh, PA: University of Pennsylvania Press, 2003).

Głowacka, Dorota, and Joanna Zylinska, eds. *Imaginary Neighbors: Mediating Polish-Jewish Relations after the Holocaust* (Lincoln, NE: University of Nebraska Press, 2010).

Golczewski, Frank. *Polnisch-Jüdische Beziehungen 1881–1922. Eine Studie zur Geschichte des Antisemitismus in Osteuropa* (Wiesbaden: Steiner, 1981).

Gontarczyk, Piotr. *Pogrom? Zajścia polsko-żydowskie w Przytyku 9 marca 1936 r.* (Biała Podlaska: Oficyna Wydawnicza Rekonkwista, 2000).

Grabowski, Jan. *Hunt for the Jews: Betrayal and Murder in German-Occupied Poland* (Bloomington, IN: University of Indiana Press, 2013 [Polish original: 2011]).

Gross, Jan. *Neighbors: The Destruction of the Jewish Community in Jedwabne, Poland* (Princeton, NJ: Princeton University Press, 2001).

Fear: Anti-semitism in Poland after Auschwitz: An Essay in Historical Interpretation (New York, NY: Random House, 2006).

Golden Harvest: Events at the Periphery of the Holocaust (New York, NY: Oxford University Press, 2012).

Gross, Jan, ed. *The Holocaust in Occupied Poland: New Findings and New Interpretations* (Frankfurt/M: Peter Lang, 2012).

Guldon, Zenon, and Jacek Wijaczka. "The Accusation of Ritual Murder in Poland, 1500–1800." *Polin*, vol. X (1997), 99–140.

Gutman, Israel, et al. *The Jews of Poland between Two World Wars* (Hanover, NH: University Press of New England, 1989).

Hagen, William W. "Before the 'Final Solution:' Toward a Comparative Analysis of Political Antisemitism in Interwar Germany and Poland." *Journal of Modern History*, vol. 68 no. 2 (June 1996), 351–81.

"Murder in the East: German-Jewish Liberal Reactions to Anti-Jewish Violence in Poland and Other East European Lands, 1918–1920." *Central European History*, vol. 34 no. 1 (2001), 1–30.

"A 'Potent, Devilish Mixture' of Motives: Explanatory Strategy and Assignment of Meaning in Jan Gross's *Neighbors*." *Slavic Review*, vol. 61, no. 3 (2002), 466–75.

"The Moral Economy of Popular Violence: The Pogrom in Lwów, November 1918," in Robert Blobaum, ed., *Antisemitism and Its Opponents in Modern Poland* (Ithaca, NY: Cornell University Press, 2005), 124–47; also in *Geschichte und Gesellschaft*, vol. 31, no. 2 (2005), 203–26.

Haumann, Heiko. *Geschichte der Ostjuden* (Munich: Deutscher Taschenbuch Verlag, 1990).

Heller, Celia. *On the Edge of Destruction: Jews of Poland between the Two World Wars* (New York, NY: Columbia University Press, 1977).

Hertz, Aleksander. *The Jews in Polish Culture* (Evanston, IL: Northwestern University Press, 1988 [Polish original: 1961]).

Hundert, Gershon David. *Jews in Poland-Lithuania in the Eighteenth Century: A Genealogy of Modernity* (Berkeley, CA: University of California Press, 2004).

Jacobs, Jack. *Bundist Counterculture in Interwar Poland* (Syracuse, NY: Syracuse University Press, 2009).

Jagodzińska, Agnieszka. *Pomiędzy: Akulturacja Żydów Warszawy w drugiej połowie XIX wieku* (Wrocław: Wydawn. Uniwersytetu Wrocławskiego, 2008).

Janion, Maria. *Do Europy tak, ale razem z naszymi umarłymi* (Warsaw: Wydawn. Uniwersytetu Wrocławskiego, 2000).

Hero, Conspiracy, and Death: The Jewish Lectures (Frankfurt/M: Peter Lang, 2014).

Jasiewicz, Krzysztof, ed. *Świat niepożegnany: Żydzi na dawnych ziemiach wschodnich Rzeczypospolitej w XVIII-XX wieku* (Warsaw: Instytut Studiów Politycznych PAN, 2004).

Jedlicki, Jerzy. "The End of the Dialogue: Warsaw, 1907–1912," in Sławomir Kapralski, ed., *The Jews in Poland* (Cracow: Judaica Foundation, 1999), vol. II, 111–23.

Johnpoll, Bernard. *The Politics of Futility: The General Jewish Workers Bund of Poland, 1917–1943* (Ithaca, NY: Cornell University Press, 1967).

Johnson, Sam. *Pogroms, Peasants, Jews: Britain and Eastern Europe's 'Jewish Question', 1867–1925* (Houndmills: Palgrave Macmillan, 2011).

Kołakowski, Leszek. "Antysemityzm: pięć tez nienowych i przestroga," in Kołakowski, ed., *Światopogląd i życie codzienne* (Warsaw, 1957), 156–73.

Kopówka, Edward. *The Jews in Siedlce, 1850–1945* (New York, NY: JewishGen, 2014).

Landau-Czajka, Anna. *Syn będzie Lech ... Asymilacja Żydów w Polsce międzywojennej* (Warsaw: Instytut Historii PAN, 2006).

Leon, Abram. *The Jewish Question: A Marxist Interpretation* (New York, NY: Pathfinder, 1970 [French original: 1946]).

Lewandowski, Józef. "History and Myth: Pińsk, April 1919." *Polin*, vol. 2 (1987), 50–72.

Lewin, Isaac and Nahum Michael Gelber. *A History of Polish Jewry during the Revival of Poland* (New York, NY: Shengold, 1990).

Liekis, Sarunas, et al. "Three Documents on Anti-Jewish Violence in the Eastern Kresy during the Polish-Soviet Conflict." *Polin*, vol.14 (2001), 116–49.

Małecki, Jan. "Zamieszki w Krakowie w kwietniu 1918 r. Pogrom czy rozruchy głodowe?," in Andrzej Paluch, ed., *Jews in Poland* (Cracow: Jagiellonian University, 1992, 1999), vol. 2: 245–57.

Marcus, Joseph. *Social and Political History of the Jews in Poland, 1919–1939* (Berlin: Mouton, 1983).

Markowski, Artur. "Anti-Jewish Pogroms in the Kingdom of Poland." *Polin*, vol. 27 (2015), 219–56.

McCagg, William. *A History of Habsburg Jews, 1670–1918* (Bloomington, IN: University of Indiana Press, 1989).

Mendelsohn, Ezra. *Zionism in Poland: The Formative Years, 1915–1926* (New Haven, CT: Yale University Press, 1981).

The Jews of East Central Europe between the World Wars (Bloomington, IN: University of Indiana Press, 1983).

Mędykowski, Witold. *W cieniu gigantów: pogromy 1941 r. w byłej sowieckiej strefie okupacyjnej. Kontekst historyczny, społeczny i kulturowy* (Warsaw: Instytut Studiów Politycznych Polskiej Akademii Nauk, 2012).

Michlic, Joanna. *Poland's Threatening Other: The Image of the Jew from 1880 to the Present* (Lincoln, NE: University of Nebraska Press, 2006).

Musialik, Zdzisław. *Wojna polsko-bolszewicka 1919–1920 a Żydzi* (Częstochowa: Włocławskie Wydawnictwo Diecezjalne, 1995).

Pacholkiv, Svyatoslav. "Zwischen Einbeziehung und Ausgrenzung. Die Juden in Lemberg 1918–1919," in Alexandra Binnenkade et al., eds., *Vertraut und fremd zugleich: Jüdisch-christliche Nachbarschaften in Warschau–Lengnau–Lemberg* (Köln: Böhlau, 2009), 155–216.

Paluch, Andrzej, ed. *The Jews in Poland*, 2 vols. (Cracow: Jagiellonian University, 1992, 1999).

Polonsky, Anthony. *The Jews in Poland and Russia*, 3 vols. (Portland, OR: Littman Library of Jewish Civilization, 2010–12).

Rosman, Murray. *The Lords' Jews: Magnate-Jewish Relations in the Polish Lithuanian Commonwealth in the Eighteenth Century* (Cambridge, MA: Harvard University Press, 1990).

Rozenblit, Marsha. *Reconstructing a National Identity: The Jews of Habsburg Austria during World War I* (New York, NY: Oxford University Press, 2001).

Różański, Przemysław. *Stany Zjednoczone wobec kwestii żydowskiej w Polsce 1918–1921* (Gdańsk: Wydawnictwo Uniwersytetu Gdańskiego, 2007).

Schiper, Ignacy, et al. *Żydzi w Polsce odrodzonej: działalność społeczna, gospodarcza, oświatowa i kulturalna*, 2 vols. (Warsaw: Nakł. Wydawnictwo "Żydzi w Polsce odrodzonej," 1932–33).

Schuster, Frank. *Zwischen allen Fronten: Osteuropäische Juden während des Ersten Weltkrieges (1914–1919)* (Köln: Böhlau, 2004).

Shanes, Joshua. *Diaspora Nationalism and Jewish Identity in Habsburg Galicia* (New York, NY: Cambridge University Press, 2012).

Shohet, Azriel. *The Jews of Pinsk, 1881 to 1941* (Stanford, CA: Stanford University Press, 2012 [Hebrew original: 1977]).

Shore, Marci. "Conversing with Ghosts: Jedwabne, Żydokomuna, and Totalitarianism," in Michael David-Fox et al., eds., *The Holocaust in the East. Local Perpetrators and Soviet Responses* (Pittsburgh, PA: University of Pittsburgh Press, 2014), 5–28.

Sierakowski, Katarzyna. *Śmierć – Wygnanie – Głód w dokumentach osobistych: ziemie polskie w latach Wielkiej Wojny, 1914–1918* (Warsaw: Instytut Historii PAN, 2015).

Sinkoff, Nancy. *Out of the Shtetl: Making the Jews Modern in the Polish Borderlands* (Providence, RI: Brown Judaic Studies, 2004).

Smolar, Aleksander. "Jews as a Polish Problem." *Daedalus* (Spring 1987), 31–73.

Staliūnas, Darius. *Enemies for a Day: Antisemitism and Anti-Jewish Violence in Lithuania under the Tsars* (Budapest: Central European University Press, 2015).

Steffen, Katrin. *Jüdische Polonität. Ethnizität und Nation im Spiegel der polnisch-sprachigen jüdischen Presse 1918–1939* (Göttingen: Vandenhoeck & Ruprecht, 2004).

Steinlauf, Michael. "Mr. Geldhab and Sambo in *Peyes*: Images of the Jew on the Polish Stage, 1863–1905." *Polin*, vol. 4 (1989), 98–128.

"Whose Poland? Returning to Aleksander Hertz." *Gal-Ed*, vol. XII (1991), 131–42.

Bondage to the Dead: Poland and the Memory of the Holocaust (Syracuse, NY: Syracuse University Press, 1997).

Szarota, Tomasz. *On the Threshold of the Holocaust* (Frankfurt/M: Peter Lang, 2015).

Tazbir, Janusz. "Obraz Żyda w opinii polskiej XVI-XVIII w," in Tazbir, ed., *Mity i stereotypy w dziejach Polski* (Warsaw: Interpress, 1991), 64–98.

Teter, Magda. *Jews and Heretics in Catholic Poland: A Beleaguered Church in the Post-Sacrilege after the Reformation* (New York, NY: Cambridge University Press, 2006).

Sinners on *Trial*: Jews and Sacrilege after the Reformation (Cambridge, MA: Harvard University Press, 2011).

Ther, Philipp. "Chancen und Untergang einer multinationalen Stadt: Die Beziehungen zwischen den Nationalitäten in Lemberg in den ersten Hälften des 20. Jahrhunderts," in Philipp Ther and Holm Sundhausen, eds., *Nationalitätenkonflikte im 20. Jahrhundert: Ursachen von inter-ethnischen Gewalt im Vergleich* (Wiesbaden: Harrassowitz, 2001), 123–46.

Tokarska-Bakir, Joanna. *Legendy o krwi. Antropologia przesądu (z cyklu: Obraz osobliwy)* (Warsaw: Wydawnictwo WAB, 2008).

"Cries of the Mob in the Pogroms in Rzeszów (June 1945), Cracow (August 1945) and Kielce (July 1946) as a Source for the State of Mind of the Participants," in Jan Gross, ed., *The Holocaust in Occupied Poland: New Findings and New Interpretations* (Frankfurt/M: Peter Lang, 2012), 205–30.

Tomaszewski, Jerzy. "Pińsk, Saturday 5 April 1919." *Polin*, vol. 1 (1986), 227–51.

"Zaburzenia antyżydowskie na Rzeszowszczyźnie wiosną 1919 roku." *Kieleckie Studia Historyczne*, vol. 15 (1999), 108. English version: "Spring 1919 in Rzeszóv: Pogrom or Revolution?," in Tamás Csató et al., eds., *Challenges of Economic History: Essays in Honor of Iván T. Berend* (Budapest: Budapest University of Economic Sciences, 1996), 183–91.

"Lwów–Listopad 1918. Niezwykłe losy pewnego dokumentu." *Dzieje Najnowsze*, vol. 25, no. 4 (1993), 164–73.

Tomaszewski, Jerzy, et al. *Najnowsze dzieje Żydów w Polsce w zarysie (do 1950 roku)* (Warsaw: Wydawn. Nauk. PWN, 1993).

Weeks, Theodore R. *From Assimilation to Antisemitism: The "Jewish Question" in Poland, 1850–1914* (DeKalb, IL: Northern Illinois University Press, 2006).

Weinryb, Bernard. *The Jews of Poland: A Social and Economic History of the Jewish Community in Poland from 1100 to 1800* (Philadelphia, PA: Jewish Publication Society of America, 1973).

Weiser, Keith. *Jewish People, Yiddish Nation: Noah Prylucki and the Folkists in Poland* (Toronto: University of Toronto Press, 2011).

Wierzbieniec, Wacław. "Zajścia antyżydowskie w Przemyślu pod koniec 1918 r," in Krzysztof Jasiewicz, ed., *Świat niepożegnany: Żydzi na dawnych ziemiach wschodnich Rzeczypospolitej w XVIII-XX wieku* (Warsaw: Instytut Studiów Politycznych PAN, 2004), 573–80.

Wodziński, Marcin. *Haskalah and Hasidism in the Kingdom of Poland: A History of Conflict* (Portland, OR: Littman, 2005 [Polish original: 2003]).

Hasidism and Politics: The Kingdom of Poland, 1815–1864 (Portland, OR: Littman, 2013).

Wróbel, Piotr. "Foreshadowing the Holocaust: The Wars of 1914–1921 and Anti-Jewish Violence in Central and Eastern Europe," in Jochen Böhler et al., eds., *Legacies of Violence. Eastern Europe's First World War* (Munich: Oldenbourg, 2014), 167–208.

Zaremba, Marcin. "Mit mordu rytualnego w powojennej Polsce. Archeologia i hipotezy." *Kultura i Społeczeństwo*, vol. 51, no. 2 (2007), 91–135.

"Trauma wielkiej wojny. Psychospołeczne konsekwencje drugiej wojny światowej." *Kultura i Społeczeństwo*, vol. 52, no. 2 (2008), 3–42.

Wielka Trwoga. Polska 1944–1947. Ludowa reakcja na kryzys (Kraków: Znak, 2012).

Zechlin, Egmont. *Die deutsche Politik und die Juden im Ersten Weltkrieg* (Göttingen: Vandenhoeck & Ruprecht, 1969).

Zieliński, Konrad. *Stosunki polsko-żydowskie na ziemiach Królestwa Polskiego w czasie pierwszej wojny światowej* (Lublin: Wydawnictwo Uniwersytetu Marii Curie-Skłodowskiej, 2005).

Żbikowski, Andrzej. *Dzieje Żydów w Polsce. Ideologia antysemicka 1848–1914* (Warsaw: Instytut, 1994).

Żydzi (Wrocław: Wydawnictwo Dolnośląskie, 1997).

U genezy Jedwabnego: Żydzi na kresach północno-wschodnuch II. Rzeczypospolitej wrzesień 1939 – lipiec 1941 (Warsaw: Żydowski Instytut Historyczny, 2006).

Żyndul, Jolanta. *Zajścia antyżydowskie w Polsce w latach 1935–37* (Warsaw: Fundacja im. K. Kelles-Krauza, 1994).

Kłamstwo krwi. Legenda mordu rytualnego na ziemiach polskich w XIX i XX wieku (Warsaw: Wydawnictwo Cyklady, 2011).

B. On Polish (and Ukrainian and Eastern Borderland) History Generally

Bailly, Rosa. *A City Fights for Freedom: The Rising of Lwów in 1918–1919* (London: Publishing Committee Leopolis, 1956).

Baranowski, Bohdan. *Życie codzienne wsi między Wartą i Pilicą w XIX wieku* (Warsaw: Państwowy Instytut Wydawniczy, 1969).

Kultura ludowa XVII I XVIII w. na ziemiach Polski Środkowej (Łódź: Wydawnictwo Łódzkie, 1971).

Beauvois, Daniel. *Trójkąt Ukraiński: szlachta, carat i lud na Wołyniu, Podolu i Kijowszczyźnie 1793–1914* (Lublin: Wydawnictwo Uniwersytetu Marii Curie-Skłodowskiej, 2011).

Binder, Harald. "Making and Defending a Polish Town: 'Lwów' (Lemberg), 1848–1914." *Austrian History Yearbook*, vol. 34 (2003), 57–82.

Böhler, Jochen, et al., eds. *Legacies of Violence: Eastern Europe's First World War* (Munich: Oldenbourg, 2014).

Bonusiak, Włodzimierz, et al. *Galicja i jej dziedzictwo*, 2 vols. (Rzeszów: Wydawnictwo Wyższej Szkoły Pedagogicznej w Rzeszowie, 1994–95).

Bystroń, Jan. *Megalomania narodowa* (Warsaw: Rój, 1935).

Cabanowski, Marek. *Generał Stanisław Bułak-Bałachowicz: zapomniany bohater* (Warsaw: Mikromax, 1993).

Conze, Werner. *Polnische Nation und deutsche Politik im Ersten Weltkrieg* (Köln: Böhlau, 1958).

Crago, Laura. "The 'Polishness' of Production: Factory Politics and the Reinvention of Working-Class National and Political Identities in Russian Poland's Textile Industry, 1880–1910." *Slavic Review*, vol. 59, no. 1 (2000), 16–41.

Davies, Norman. *White Eagle, Red Star: The Polish-Soviet War, 1919–20* (London: Macdonald, 1972).

God's Playground: A History of Poland 2 vols. (New York, NY: Columbia University Press, 1984).

Fäßler, Peter, et al. *Lemberg-Lwów-Lviv: Eine Stadt im Schnittpunkt europäischer Kulturen* (Köln: Böhlau, 1995).

Figes, Orlando. *A People's Tragedy: The Russian Revolution, 1917–1924* (New York, NY: Viking Press, 1997).

Frank, Alison. *Oil Empire: Visions of Prosperity in Austrian Galicia* (Cambridge, MA: Harvard University Press, 2005).

Fras, Zbigniew. *Galicja* (Wrocław: Wydawnictwo Dolnośląskie, 1999).

Gerwarth, Robert. *The Vanquished: Why the First World War Failed to End* (New York, NY: Farrar, Straus and Giroux, 2016).

Gerwarth, Robert, ed. *Empires at War, 1911–1923* (New York, NY: Oxford University Press, 2014).

Gerwarth, Robert, and John Horne, eds. *War in Peace: Paramilitary Violence after the Great War* (Oxford: Oxford University Press, 2012).

Hagen, Mark von. *War in a European Borderland: Occupations and Occupation Plans in Galicia and Ukraine, 1914–1918* (Seattle, WA: University of Washington Press, 2007).

Himka, John-Paul. "Ukrainian-Jewish Antagonism in the Galician Countryside during the Late Nineteenth Century," in Peter Potichnyj et al., eds., *Ukrainian-Jewish Relations in Historical Perspective* (Edmonton: University of Alberta Press, 1988), 111–58.

Religion and Nationality in Western Ukraine: The Greek Catholic Church and Ruthenian National Movement in Galicia, 1867–1900 (Montreal: University of Montreal Press, 1999).

Hryniuk, Stella. *Peasants with Promise: Ukrainians in Southeastern Galicia 1880–1900* (Edmonton: University of Alberta Press, 1991).

Ihnatowicz, Ireneusz, et al. *Społeczeństwo polskie od X. do XX. wieku* (Warsaw: Książka i Wiedza, 1996).

Jedlicki, Jerzy. *A Suburb of Europe: Nineteenth-Century Polish Approaches to Western Civilization* (Budapest: Central European University Press, 1999 [Polish original: 1988]).

Judson, Pieter *The Habsburg Empire: A New History* (Cambridge, MA: Harvard University Press, 2016).

Knyt, Agnieszka, et al. *Rok 1920. Wojna Polski z Rosją Bolszewicką* (Warsaw: Karta, 2005).

Kolbuszewski, Jacek. *Kresy* (Wrocław: Wydawnictwo Dolnośląskie, 1998).

Kozłowski, Maciej. *Zapomniana Wojna. Walka o Lwów i Galicję Wschodnią 1918–1919* (Bydgoszcz: Instytut Wydawniczy "Świadectwo," 1999).

Krzywiec, Grzegorz. *Szowinizm po polsku. Przypadek Romana Dmowskiego (1886–1905)* (Warsaw: Wydawnictwo "Neriton," 2009).

Kuzmany, Börries. *Brody: Eine galizische Grenzstadt im langen 19. Jahrhundert* (Vienna: Böhlau, 2011).

Latawski, Paul, ed. *The Reconstruction of Poland, 1914–23* (New York, NY: St. Martin's Press, 1992).

Lis-Błoński, Stanisław. *Bałachowcy* ([n.p.], 2013).

Liulevicius, Vejas. *War Land on the Eastern Front: Culture, National Identity and German Occupation in World War I* (New York, NY: Cambridge University Press, 2000).

The German Myth of the East: 1800 to the Present (New York, NY: Oxford University Press, 2009).

Magocsi, Paul Robert. *A History of Ukraine: The Land and Its Peoples* (Toronto: University of Toronto Press, 2010).

Mick, Christoph. "Nationalisierung in einer multiethnischen Stadt. Interethnische Konflikte in Lemberg, 1890–1920." *Archiv für Sozialgeschichte*, vol. 40 (2000).

Lemberg, Lwów, L'viv, 1914–1947: Violence and Ethnicity in a Contested City (West Lafayette, IN: Purdue University Press, 2016 [German original: 2010]).

Molenda, Jan. *Chłopi, Naród, Niepodległość* (Warsaw: Instytut Historii PAN, 1999).

O'Rourke, Shane. *The Cossacks* (Manchester: University of Manchester Press, 2007).

Pease, Neal. *Rome's Most Faithful Daughter: The Catholic Church and Independent Poland, 1914–1939* (Athens, OH: Ohio State University Press, 2009).

Podhorodecki, Leszek. *Dzieje Lwowa* (Warsaw: Oficyna Wydwanicza Volumen, 1993).

Porter, Brian. *When Nationalism Began to Hate: Imagining Modern Politics in Nineteenth-Century Poland* (New York, NY: Oxford University Press, 2000).

Faith and Fatherland: Catholicism, Modernity, and Poland (New York, NY: Oxford University Press, 2011).

Poland in the Modern World: Beyond Martyrdom (Chichester: Wiley-Blackwell, 2014).

530   Bibliography

Prusin, Alexander. *Nationalizing a Borderland: War, Ethnicity, and Anti-Jewish Violence in East Galicia, 1914–1920* (Tuscaloosa, AL: University of Alabama Press, 2005).

Rudnytsky, Ivan. "The Ukrainians in Galicia Under Austrian Rule," in Andrei Markovits et al., eds., *Nationbuilding and the Politics of Nationalism: Essays on Austrian Galicia* (Cambridge, MA: Harvard University Press, 1982), 23–67.

Rumpler, Helmut. *Eine Chance für Mitteleuropa: bürgerliche Emanzipation und Staatsverfall in der Habsburgermonarchie* (Vienna: Ueberreuter, 1997).

Sadkowski, Konrad. *Catholic Power and Catholicism as a Component of Modern Polish National Identity, 1863–1919* (Seattle, WA: University of Washington Press, 2001).

Sanborn, Joshua. *Imperial Apocalypse: The Great War and the Destruction of the Russian Empire* (Oxford: Oxford University Press, 2014).

Schöpflin, George. *Politics in Eastern Europe, 1945–1992* (Oxford: Blackwell, 1993).

Simons, Thomas. *Eastern Europe in the Postwar World* (New York, NY: St. Martin's Press, 1993).

Stankiewicz, Witold. *Konflikty społeczne na wsi polskiej 1918–1920* (Warsaw: Państwowe Wydawnictwo Naukowe, 1963).

Stauter-Halsted, Keely. *The Nation in the Village: The Genesis of Peasant National Identity in Austrian Poland, 1848–1914* (Ithaca, NY: Cornell University Press, 2001).

Stomma, Ludwik. *Antropologia kultury wsi polskiej XIX wieku oraz wybrane eseje* (Łódź: Piotr Dopierała, 2002).

Struve, Kai. "Die Juden in der Sicht der polnischen Bauernparteien vom Ende des 19. Jahrhunderts bis 1939." *Zeitschrift für Ostmitteleuropa-Forschung*, vol. 48, no. 2 (1999), 184–225.

"Gentry, Jews, and Peasants: Jews as Others in the Formation of the Modern Polish Nation in Rural Galicia during the Second Half of the Nineteenth Century," in Nancy Wingfield and Pieter Judson, eds., *Creating the Other: Ethnic Conflict and Nationalism in Habsburg Central Europe* (New York, NY: Berghahn, 2003), 103–26.

Bauern und Nation in Galizien: Über Zugehörigkeit und soziale Emanzipation im 19. Jahrhundert (Göttingen: Vandenhoeck & Ruprecht, 2005).

Szczepański, Janusz. *Społeczeństwo Polski w walce z najazdem bolszewickim 1920 roku* (Warsaw: Naczelna Dyreckja Archiwów Państwowych, 2000).

Thomas, William I., and Florian Znaniecki. *The Polish Peasant in Europe and America*, vol. 1 (New York, NY: Dover, 1958).

Tomicka, Joanna and Ryszard Tomicki. *Drzewo życia: ludowa wizja świata i człowieka* (Warsaw: Ludowa Spółdzielnia Wydawnicza, 1975).

Watson, Alexander. *Ring of Steel. Germany and Austria-Hungary in World War I* (New York, NY: Basic Books, 2014).

Wolff, Larry. *The Idea of Galicia: History and Fantasy in Habsburg Political Culture* (Stanford, CA: Stamford University Press, 2010).

Wrzesiński, Wojciech, ed. *Polskie mity polityczne XIX I XX wieku* (Wrocław: Wydawnictwo Uniwersytetu Wrocławskiego, 1994).

C.   *On the Interpretation of Christian-Jewish Relations and Antisemitism in General*

Anderson, Benedict. *Imagined Communities: Reflections on the Origin and Spread of Nationalism* (New York, NY: Verso, 1983).

Bauman, Zygmunt. *Modernity and the Holocaust* (Ithaca, NY: Cornell University Press, 1989).

Bergmann, Werner. "Ethnic Riots in Situations of Loss of Control: Revolution, Civil War, and Regime Change as Opportunity Structures for Anti-Jewish Violence in Nineteenth- and Twentieth-Century Europe," in Wilhelm Heitmeyer et al., eds., *Control of Violence: Historical and International Perspectives on Violence in Modern Societies* (Berlin: Springer, 2011), 487–516.

Biale, David. *Blood and Belief: The Circulation of a Symbol between Jews and Christians* (Berkeley, CA: University of California Press, 2007).

Biale, David, et al. *Cultures of the Jews: A New History* (New York, NY: Schocken, 2002).

Brede, Karola. "On Social and Psychological Foundations of Anti- Semitism," in Jürgen Straub and Jörn Rüsen, eds., *Dark Traces of the Past: Psychoanalysis and Historical Thinking* (New York, NY: Berghahn, 2010), 139–58.

Budnitskii, Oleg. *Russian Jews between the Reds and the Whites, 1917–1920* (Philadelphia, PA: University of Pennsylvania Press, 2012).

Connelly, John. *From Enemy to Brother: The Revolution in Catholic Teaching on the Jews, 1933–1965* (Cambridge, MA: Harvard University Press, 2012).

Engel, David. "What's in a Pogrom? European Jews in the Age of Violence," in Jonathan Dekel-Chen et al., eds., *Anti-Jewish Violence: Rethinking the Pogrom in East European History* (Bloomington, IN: University of Indiana Press, 2011), 19–38.

Frosh, Stephen. *Hate and the "Jewish Science": Anti-Semitism, Nazism and Psychoanalysis* (Basingstoke: Palgrave Macmillan, 2005).

Glover, Jonathan. *Humanity: A Moral History of the Twentieth Century* (London: Cape, 1999).

Hagen, William W. "The Three Horsemen of the Holocaust: Antisemitism, East European Empire, Aryan Folk Community," in Helmut Walser Smith, ed., *The Oxford Handbook of Modern German History* (New York, NY: Oxford University Press, 2011), 548–72.

Hoffman, Eva. *After Such Knowledge: Memory, History, and the Legacy of the Holocaust* (London: Public Affairs Press, 2005).

Hoffmann, Christhard et al. *Exclusionary Violence: Antisemitic Riots in Modern German History* (Ann Arbor, MI: University of Michigan Press, 2002).

Judge, Edward. *Easter in Kishinev. Anatomy of a Pogrom* (New York, NY: New York University Press, 1992).

Klier, John. *Russians, Jews, and the Pogroms of 1881–1882* (Cambridge: Cambridge University Press, 2014).

Klier, John, Shlomo Lambroza et al. *Pogroms: Anti-Jewish Violence in Modern Russian History* (Cambridge: Cambridge University Press, 1992).

LaCapra, Dominick. *Representing the Holocaust: History, Theory, Trauma* (Ithaca, NY: Cornell University Press, 1996).

Laqueur, Walter. *The Changing Face of Antisemitism: From Ancient Times to the Present Day* (New York, NY: Oxford University Press, 2006).

Nirenberg, David. *Communities of Violence: Persecution of Minorities in the Middle Ages* (Princeton, NJ: Princeton University Press, 1996).

Anti-Judaism: The Western Tradition (New York, NY: Norton, 2013).

Poliakov, Leon. *History of Anti-Semitism*, 4 vols. (New York, NY: Vanguard, 1965–85 [French original: 1956–77]).

Simmel, Ernst et al. *Anti-Semitism: A Social Disease* (New York, NY: International Universities Press, 1946).

Weinberg, Robert. *Blood Libel in Late Imperial Russia: The Ritual Murder Trial of Mendel Beilis* (Bloomington, IN: University of Indiana Press, 2014).

Wiese, Stefan. *Pogrome im Zarenreich. Dynamiken kollektiver Gewalt* (Hamburg: HIS, 2016).

D.   On Interpretation and Theory in History and the Social Sciences, Including Exemplary Historical Works

Aijmer, Göran, and Jon Abbink. *Meanings of Violence: A Cross-Cultural Perspective* (Oxford: Berg, 2000).

Baberowski, Jörg, et al. "Gewalt: Räume und Kulturen." *Zeithistorische Forschungen*, vol. 5, no. 1 (2008).

Bell, Catherine. *Ritual: Perspectives and Dimensions* (New York, NY: Oxford University Press, 1997).

Jakub Beneš, *Workers and Nationalism: Czech and German Social Democracy in Habsburg Austria, 1890–1918* (Oxford: Oxford University Press, 2017).

Bergholz, Max. *Violence as a Generative Force: Identity, Nationalism, and Memory in a Balkan Community* (Ithaca, NY: Cornell University Press, 2016).

Berman, Bruce et al., eds. *The Moral Economies of Ethnic and Nationalist Claims* (Vancouver: University of British Columbia Press, 2016).

Bocock, Robert. *Sigmund Freud* (London: Tavistock, 2002).

Brass, Paul R. et al. *Riots and Pogroms* (New York, NY: Columbia University Press, 1996).

Brubaker, Rogers. *Ethnicity without Groups* (Cambridge, MA: Harvard University Press, 2004).

Brubaker, Rogers and Frederick Cooper. "Beyond 'identity.'" *Theory and Society*, vol. 29 (2000), 1–47.

Brubaker, Rogers and David Laitin. "Ethnic and Nationalist Violence." *American Review of Sociology*, vol. 24 (1998), 423–52.

Brubaker, Rogers et al. "Ethnicity as Cognition." *Theory and Society*, vol. 33 (2004), 31–64.

Brubaker, Rogers et al. *Nationalist Politics and Everyday Ethnicity in a Transylvanian Town* (Princeton, NJ: Princeton University Press, 2008).

Cash, W. J. *The Mind of the South* (New York, NY: Knopf, 1941).

Cancik, Hubert et al., eds. *Handbuch religionswissenschaftlicher Grundbegriffe*, 5 vols. (Stuttgart: Kohlhammer, 1988–2001): Hanna Gekle, "Aggression," vol. I, 394–406; Jürgen Ebach, "Antisemitismus," vol. I, 495–504; Hans Krippenberg, "Magie," vol. IV, 85–97; Aleida and Jan Assmann,

"Mythos," vol. IV, 179–200; Hubert Seiwert, "Opfer," vol. IV, 268–84; Renate Schlesier, "Strukturalismus," vol. V, 106–23; Gerhard Bauty, "Tod," vol. V, 207–26.

Cassirer, Ernst. *An Essay on Man: An Introduction to a Philosophy of Human Culture* (New Haven, CT: Yale University Press, 1944).

Chancer, Lynn et al. *The Unhappy Divorce of Sociology and Psychoanalysis. Diverse Perspectives on the Psychosocial* (New York, NY: Palgrave Macmillan, 2014).

Collins, Randall. *Violence: A Micro-Sociological Theory* (Princeton, NJ: Princeton University Press, 2008).

Connerton, Paul. *How Societies Remember* (Cambridge: Cambridge University Press, 1989).

Conteh-Morgan, Earl. *Collective Political Violence: An Introduction to the Theories and Cases of Violent Conflicts* (New York, NY: Routledge, 2004).

Darnton, Robert. *The Great Cat Massacre* (New York, NY: Basic Books, 1984).
"Reading a Riot." *New York Review of Books* October 22, 1992.

Davis, Natalie Z. *Society and Culture in Early Modern France* (Stanford, CA: Stanford University Press, 1975).

Dray, Philip. *At the Hands of Persons Unknown: The Lynching of Black America* (New York, NY: Random House, 2002).

Duckitt, John. "Prejudice and Intergroup Hostility," in David O. Sears et al., eds., *Oxford Handbook of Political Psychology* (Oxford: Oxford University Press, 2003), 559–600.

Eley, Geoff. *Nazism as Fascism: Violence, Ideology, and the Ground of Consent in Germany 1930–1945* (London: Routledge, 2013).

Elliott, Anthony. *Psychoanalytic Theory. An Introduction* (Durham, NC: Duke University Press, 2002).
Social Theory since Freud: Traversing Social Imaginaries (London: Routledge, 2004).

Fiske, Alan and Tage Rai. *Virtuous Violence: Hurting and Killing to Create, Sustain, End, and Honor Social Relationships* (Cambridge: Cambridge University Press, 2015).

Geertz, Clifford *The Interpretation of Cultures: Selected Essays* (New York, NY: Basic Books, 1973).

Geschiere, Peter. *The Modernity of Witchcraft: Politics and the Occult in Post-Colonial Africa* (Charlottesville, VA: University of Virginia Press, 1997).

Girard, René. *Violence and the Sacred* (London: Continuum, 2005 [French original: 1972]).

Group for the Advancement of Psychiatry. *Us and Them: The Psychology of Ethnonationalism* (New York, NY: Brunner/Mazel, 1987).

Hagedorn, Anne. *Savage Peace: Hope and Fear in America, 1919* (New York, NY: Simon & Schuster, 2007).

Hagen, William W. *Ordinary Prussians: Brandenburg Junkers and Villagers, 1500–1840* (Cambridge: Cambridge University Press, 2002).
"Master Narratives beyond Postmodernity: Germany's 'Separate Path' in Historiographical-Philosophical Light." *German Studies Review*, vol. 30, no. 1 (February 2007), 1–32.

Hall, John R. *Apocalypse: From Antiquity to the Empire of Modernity* (Cambridge: Polity Press, 2009).

Hobsbawm, E. J. *Primitive Rebels: Studies in Archaic Forms of Social Movement in the 19th and 20th Centuries* (Manchester: Manchester University Press, 1959).

    Bandits (London: Weidenfeld & Nicolson, 2000).

Hobsbawm, E. J., with George Rudé. *Captain Swing* (New York, NY: Pantheon, 1968).

Horkheimer, Max and Theodor Adorno. *Dialectic of Enlightenment* (New York, NY: Herder, 1972 [German original: 1944]).

Horowitz, Donald L. *The Deadly Ethnic Riot* (Berkeley, CA: University of California Press, 2001).

Kakar, Sudhir. *The Colors of Violence: Cultural Identities, Religion, and Conflict* (Chicago, IL: University of Chicago Press, 1996).

Kalyvas, Stathis N. *The Logic of Violence in Civil War* (New York, NY: Cambridge University Press, 2008).

Katz, Jack. "Criminals' Passions and the Progressives' Dilemma," in Alan Wolfe, ed., *America at Century's End* (Berkeley, CA: University of California Press, 1991), 396–420.

Kołakowski, Leszek. *The Presence of Myth* (Chicago, IL: University of Chicago Press, 1989 [Polish original: 1972]).

Kuper, Adam. *Culture: The Anthropologists' Account* (Cambridge, MA: Harvard University Press, 1999).

Le Roy Ladurie, Emmanuel. *Carnival in Romans* (New York, NY: Braziller, 1979).

Mann, Michael. *The Dark Side of Democracy: Explaining Ethnic Cleansing* (Cambridge: Cambridge University Press, 2005).

Muir, Edward. *Ritual in Early Modern Europe* (New York, NY: Cambridge University Press, 1997).

Patterson, Orlando. *Rituals of Blood: Consequences of Slavery in Two American Centuries* (New York, NY: Basic Civitas, 1999).

Petersen, Roger D. *Understanding Ethnic Violence: Fear, Hatred, and Resentment in Twentieth-Century Eastern Europe* (Cambridge: Cambridge University Press, 2002).

Pinker, Steven. *The Better Angels of Our Nature: Why Violence Has Declined* (New York, NY: Viking Press, 2011).

Rogin, Michael. *Ronald Reagan, the Movie, and Other Episodes in Political Demonology* (Berkeley, CA: University of California Press, 1987).

Rudé, George *The Crowd in History: A Study of Popular Disturbances in France and England, 1730–1848* (London: Lawrence & Wishart, 1964).

Ruff, Julius R. *Violence in Early Modern Europe 1500–1800* (Cambridge: Cambridge University Press, 2001).

Schnell, Felix. *Räume des Schreckens: Gewalt und Gruppenmilitanz in der Ukraine (1905–1933)* (Hamburg: Hamburger Edition, 2012).

Scott, James. *Weapons of the Weak. Everyday Forms of Peasant Resistance* (New Haven, CT: Yale University Press, 1985).

Domination and the Arts of Resistance: Hidden Transcripts (New Haven, CT: Yale University Press, 1990).

Searle-White, Joshua. *The Psychology of Nationalism* (New York, NY: Palgrave, 2001).

Semelin, Jacques. *Purify and Destroy: The Political Uses of Massacre and Genocide* (New York, NY: Columbia University Press, 2007).

Sewell, William H. "Geertz and History: From Synchrony to Transformation." *Representations*, vol. 59 (Summer 1997), 35–55.

"The Concept(s) of Culture," in Victoria Bonnell and Lynn Hunt, eds., *Beyond the Cultural Turn: New Directions in the Study of Society and Culture* (Berkeley, CA: University of California Press, 1999), 35–61.

Slotkin, Richard. *Gunfighter Nation: The Myth of the Frontier in Twentieth-Century America* (New York, NY: Atheneum, 1992).

Sofsky, Wolfgang. *The Order of Terror: The Concentration Camp* (Princeton, NJ: Princeton University Press, 1997 [German original: 1993]).

Staub, Ervin and Daniel Bar-Tal, "Genocide, Mass Killing, and Intractable Conflict," in David O. Sears et al., eds., *Oxford Handbook of Political Psychology* (Oxford: Oxford University Press, 2003), 710–40.

Thompson, Edward P. "The Moral Economy of the English Crowd in the Eighteenth Century," and "The Moral Economy Revisited," in Thompson, ed., *Customs in Common* (London: Merlin, 1991), 185–351.

Turner, Victor. *The Ritual Process: Structure and Anti-Structure* (Chicago, IL: University of Chicago Press, 1969).

Tuttle, William M. *Race Riot: Chicago in the Red Summer of 1919* (New York, NY: Atheneum, 1970).

Wagner, Peter. *A Sociology of Modernity: Liberty and Discipline* (New York, NY: Routledge, 1994).

Waugh, Patricia, ed. *Literary Theory and Criticism* (Oxford: Oxford University Press, 2006).

Weber, Max. *Economy and Society*, vol. I (Berkeley, CA: University of California Press, 2013).

Zahra, Tara. "Imagined Noncommunities: National Indifference as a Category of Analysis." *Slavic Review*, vol. 69, no. 1 (2010), 93–119.

Index